SUPERVISION
WORKING WITH PEOPLE

SECOND EDITION

SUPERVISION
WORKING WITH PEOPLE

Stephen E. Catt
Professor of Communication

Donald S. Miller
Professor of Management

Both of Emporia State University

Homewood, IL 60430
Boston, MA 02116

The previous edition of this book was published under
the title of *Supervisory Management and Communication.*

© Richard D. Irwin, Inc., 1985 and 1991

Sponsoring editor: Karen Johnson
Developmental editor: Kama Brockmann
Project editor: Rita McMullen
Production manager: Diane Palmer
Cover illustration: John Nelson
Designer: Jeanne Regan
Artist: Jill Smith
Compositor: Graphic World Incorporated
Typeface: 10/12 Garamond Light
Printer: R.R. Donnelley & Sons Company

Library of Congress Cataloging-in-Publication Data

Catt, Stephen E.
    Supervision : working with people / Stephen E. Catt, Donald S.
Miller. — 2nd ed.
        p.   cm.
    Rev. ed. of: Supervisory management and communication. 1985.
    Includes bibliographical references and index.
    ISBN 0-256-06904-2
    1. Supervision of employees.   2.   Business communication.
I. Miller, Donald S. (Donald Stanley).   II.   Catt, Stephen E.
Supervisory management and communication.   III.   Title.
HF5549.12.C38   1991
    658.3′02 — dc20   90–37491
                                                                              CIP

Printed in the United States of America
1 2 3 4 5 6 7 8 9 0 DOC 7 6 5 4 3 2 1 0

To my mother, Virginia Mae Catt — SEC

To Linda, for her patience,
encouragement, and assistance — DSM

Preface

The job of a supervisor places much emphasis on accomplishing organizational goals by working with others. Consequently, this second edition has been titled *Supervision: Working with People.* The importance of effective communication to successful supervision is a priority concern; therefore, coverage of relevant communication skills is retained in this edition. The topics discussed are appropriate to a broad range of organizational settings, including service-oriented firms, nonprofit organizations, and manufacturing companies.

Thousands of students studied supervision from the first edition of this text. We have received many positive comments from students who indicated that the text provided them with essential knowledge necessary for success in their personal careers. Also, they have often commented about the clear, easy-to-read writing style. One professor noted that some students who had full-time jobs as supervisors had received frequent requests from co-workers to borrow the text. These co-workers claimed that the concepts presented helped them deal with many problems experienced on their jobs.

In this second edition, we continue to provide a practical, "real world" approach to supervision. The focus of explanations is straightforward with emphasis on readability. The content has been updated and expanded to provide comprehensive coverage of relevant supervisory topics. For example, new topics include job satisfaction and morale, interpersonal relations, management information systems, written communications, employee compensation, reinforcement theory, smoking, AIDS, employee counseling, and prejudice/discrimination issues. In addition, expanded coverage is given to problem solving, management by objectives, interviewing, EEO issues, motivation, leadership, ethics, and creativity. Also, more detailed explanations and a greater number of examples are included in this edition.

Several special features are included in each chapter. These features are designed to aid students in studying and understanding the subject matter.

Each chapter begins with learning objectives, which state the goals of the chapter and focus attention on major topics. Important points are identified by headings and symbols to aid learning and review. To encourage discussion, practical thought-provoking questions, identified by the title "Consider This," have been interspersed throughout the chapters. Marginal notes signal key concepts presented to the reader. After the last key concept is discussed in each chapter, the learning objectives are restated as summaries to refocus attention on the major topics covered. Review and discussion questions give students an opportunity to reflect on the important concepts and evaluate pertinent implications for supervision. Realistic, "action-incident" cases enable students to apply their knowledge and skills to resolve practical, "real world" problems. In this new edition, the number of these cases has been increased from two to three per chapter. A glossary at the end of the book provides a ready reference for the highlighted terms used in the text.

The book contains five parts: The Role of Supervision, Applying Supervision Skills, Applying Supervisory Communication Skills, Developing an Effective Work Environment, and Understanding Workplace Concerns. Part I describes the supervisor's role as a first-line manager. Emphasis is placed on examining the work environment, supervisory functions, and leadership skills.

Supervisors must plan and manage the activities of their work units in order to accomplish important work goals. In doing so, the consequences of job satisfaction and dissatisfaction must be considered. As a result, Part II discusses the topics of setting objectives and making decisions, time management, training and development, and job satisfaction.

Understanding how to be a good communicator, along with developing interpersonal skills and mastering the ability to interact with work groups, is also an important part of supervision. Therefore, Part III discusses the topics of communication, interpersonal relations, and work groups.

Part IV examines a wide variety of topics that supervisors must understand to develop an effective work environment. The topics are motivation, interviewing and selecting employees, appraising and compensating employees, handling conflict, and dealing with grievances and discipline.

Finally, Part V examines important issues and concerns the modern supervisor must deal with in today's workplace. The topics discussed in this last part include maintaining a safe and healthy work environment and special concerns for supervisors.

The Student Study Guide contains chapter reviews and provides outlines, lists of concepts and definitions, exercises, and a variety of review questions for each chapter. This learning companion is designed to complement the text and reinforce the concepts of supervision.

In writing *Supervision: Working with People*, we received valuable input from many individuals, including managers and employees from a variety of organizations. We are especially indebted to those who provided the many fine suggestions and examples that we were able to incorporate into the manuscript. Unfortunately, space prevents us from acknowledging all of the people who contributed to the development of this book. However, we wish to give special thanks to the following reviewers who offered many valuable suggestions during the preparation of this revised edition:

James R. Carlson
Manetee Community College

Ronald B. Johnson
Floyd College

William J. R. Almeraz
Southwestern College

James Stewart
Prestonburg Community College

M. E. Hilton
Brookhaven College

Kirby L. Everette
Greenville Technical College

C. S. Everett
Des Moines Area Community College

Carl F. Jenks
Purdue University—Calumet

Ronald Herrick
Mesa Community College

Their pertinent comments and useful recommendations strengthened our manuscript. Whatever shortcomings remain are ours alone. Linda Miller deserves special recognition for her excellent work in typing drafts of the textbook and the instructor's manual.

Stephen E. Catt

Donald S. Miller

Contents

Part III   Applying Supervisory Communication Skills   189

Chapter 8   Supervisors as Communicators   190

Chapter 9   Practicing Effective Communication   210

Chapter 16   Dealing with Grievances and Discipline   425

Part V   Understanding Workplace Concerns 447

Part I

The Role of Supervision

▼

Chapter 1

The Supervisory Environment

Chapter 2

Supervisory Functions

Chapter 3

Supervisors as Leaders

The Supervisory Environment

Chapter

1

Learning Objectives

To assist your study of concepts, each chapter includes learning objectives. This chapter presents a foundation for the study of supervisory management and is designed to:

1. Explain the nature of management.
2. Describe the importance of communication to supervisors.
3. Discuss how to prepare for supervision.
4. Emphasize the importance of productivity.
5. Examine characteristics of the workplace.
6. Specify formal and informal supervisory expectations.
7. Provide an overview of supervisory skills.
8. Describe common difficulties supervisors encounter.

Management, Supervision, and Communication

Management involves using human and equipment resources to attain certain results, called **objectives.** Companies try to expand marketshare, meet customer needs, and earn a profit. Employees want satisfying jobs, recognition, and opportunities to express their views. Management must strive to reach both company and employee objectives, which at times may be in conflict. For example, the need to remain competitive can force a firm to pay lower wages. Nobody ever claimed management's task is easy, yet challenges must be met in an environment characterized by advancing technology, changing customer demands, and uncertain economic conditions.

    All organizations need managers. A firm's growth increases the number of management levels and the necessity for specialized job skills. In a "ma and pa" grocery store, owners generally perform all duties — from waiting on customers to bookkeeping. However, firms such as Exxon, General Motors, and General Electric have thousands of employees who do only certain job specialties — production, marketing, accounting, or human resources. The typical arrangement is top- and middle-level management and supervisors. Supervisors and the roles they play are the topics of this text.

    Supervisors, often called first-line managers, are the only managers required to have direct contact with employees. They have been called the people in the middle because they must represent management's position to workers as well as relate workers' concerns to management. Supervisors and other managers spend much time and energy carrying out their duties, but supervisors' responsibilities are different from those of other managers. To illustrate, Figure 1.1 compares selected activities of top managers and supervisors. It shows that supervisors are involved in short-range planning, close contact with workers, and hiring workers at the operative level. They control a more restricted work area, usually a department or a certain work shift.

    Effective supervision is vital to a firm's success. Supervisors must be skilled at understanding human behavior and applying management principles. They are leaders who must demonstrate initiative, be flexible, and serve as role models to subordinates. Perceptions of others cannot be overlooked. Judgments about factors such as appearance, temperament, sensitivity to concerns, credibility, and knowledge are made on a daily basis. Many supervisors do not really recognize the influential nature of their behaviors.

    Communication — the sharing of meaning between senders and receivers of messages — is very important to you as a supervisor. You must interpret data, give directions, explain work procedures, and listen carefully. Miscommunication causes inaccuracies, wasted time, ineffective job performance, and poor human relations. Incorrect information might necessitate recalculating an entire set of numbers, and interpersonal relations can

Managers seek results

Supervisors are managers

Perceptions are important

Communication skills are critical

Figure 1.1   **Comparison of Managerial Activities between Top Management and Supervisors**

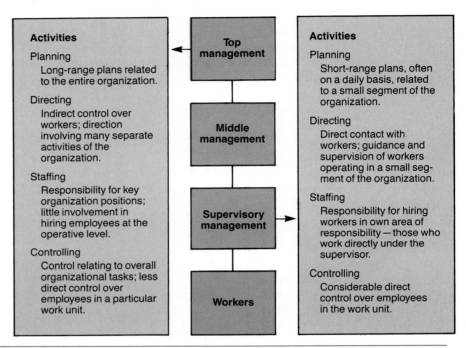

Activities

Planning
Long-range plans related to the entire organization.

Directing
Indirect control over workers; direction involving many separate activities of the organization.

Staffing
Responsibility for key organization positions; little involvement in hiring employees at the operative level.

Controlling
Control relating to overall organizational tasks; less direct control over employees in a particular work unit.

Top management

Middle management

Supervisory management

Workers

Activities

Planning
Short-range plans, often on a daily basis, related to a small segment of the organization.

Directing
Direct contact with workers; guidance and supervision of workers operating in a small segment of the organization.

Staffing
Responsibility for hiring workers in own area of responsibility — those who work directly under the supervisor.

Controlling
Considerable direct control over employees in the work unit.

become strained because of vague or incorrect instructions. The need to redo work creates frustration and contributes to deterioration of morale.

Managers and workers commonly voice complaints about lack of or poor communication, yet we can conclude that the need for excellence in communication is discussed to a greater extent than actually practiced. Successful supervision depends on integrating a knowledge of both management fundamentals and communication skills. If you do not master both of these essentials, you will likely be ineffective as a supervisor. For instance, a talent for planning and organizing work duties does not necessarily imply an ability to get along with people and respond appropriately to their concerns or problems.

Supervisors: Who Are They?

Supervision is unique

Supervisors are known by a variety of job titles. Nevertheless, a key point to remember is the unique nature of the position, which includes obligations to both managers and workers. As you will learn, supervisors must be perceptive, demonstrate job competence, and respond to unanticipated events. Supervisors can be found in practically every kind of firm. In your everyday business transactions, be observant; notice how supervisors interact with their subordinates. You will likely discover many different patterns of behavior and ways of doing things. Figure 1.2 shows representative job titles for supervisors in different types of firms.

How does one get to be a supervisor? Most supervisors are selected from the ranks of workers on the basis of their work record and experience. However, some are chosen because of specialized job knowledge or educational attainments. For example, a college graduate with a major in computer science might be appointed to manage a group of initial-entry data operators. Employers establish criteria to help predict success as a supervisor. Several personal characteristics are viewed favorably by decision makers who select supervisors, including:

Individual backgrounds do vary

- ☐ Positive attitude toward job performance.
- ☐ Willingness to work hard.
- ☐ Ability to get along with others.
- ☐ Loyalty to the firm and bosses.
- ☐ Acceptance of increasingly greater job responsibilities.
- ☐ Even temperament and disposition.
- ☐ Reputation for treating others with dignity and respect.

The transition from worker to leader does create anxiety for new supervisors. This is especially true for those who must manage former co-workers. A new supervisor's behavior must evidence a concern for the entire work unit, and her actions will be carefully observed by followers. She must seek involvement, resolve problems of others, and respond to many

New supervisors experience anxieties

Examples of Supervisory Job Titles   **Figure 1.2**

Job Title	Type of Business
Crew chief	Fast-food restaurant
Head nurse	Pediatrics, surgery, or other sections in hospitals
Produce manager	Grocery store
Department head	College or university
Leadperson	Construction job
Head teller	Bank
Office manager	Real estate agency
Department manager	Large retail clothing outlet
Director	Direct-marketing cosmetics firm
Foreman	Processing/manufacturing plant
Head cashier	Large grocery store
Night manager	Auto service facility

unanticipated events. Differences of opinion will arise, and she will discover that everyone's desires cannot be satisfied. Some people are difficult to manage and resent authority, but the supervisor must maintain a positive, respectful attitude. Capable supervisors understand workplace realities and realize that criticism cannot be escaped. They learn from their mistakes and retain realistic perspectives. While some people supervise only a few employees, others may be responsible for many. The nature of company operations has a bearing on the number of supervisors employed. A small manufacturing firm might employ 11 supervisors for 185 production workers, while a computer-service company uses 24 service representatives and 2 service managers. On the other hand, the director for a direct-sale cosmetics firm might supervise more than 100 beauty consultants.

In summary, successful supervisors combine technical knowledge with an understanding of human behavior. They strive to attain company objectives and satisfy employees' job-related concerns.

Supervision requires many skills

In the process, many hats are worn—facilitator, diplomat, decision maker, communicator, motivator, negotiator, and instructor. Supervision is not for everyone. Some choose to concentrate on their own job duties without being responsible for the work of others. There is nothing inappropriate about such personal decisions, but supervisors have opportunities to serve as catalysts and blend together the talents of many individuals to attain personal and professional goals.

The Importance of Productivity

Productivity measures output per labor hour worked. Businesses seek to increase productivity through better utilization of workers and equipment. Advanced computer technology has radically altered our methods of processing data. Packages can be mailed with guaranteed next-day delivery to any location in the United States. Hand-held calculators can perform a myriad of calculations without delay. Maybe you have taken a reading-improvement course and no longer read documents several times to glean relevant information. With conscientious effort, efficiency at many types of tasks can be improved.

Business must use resources wisely

A declining rate of productivity is of much concern to a nation. In 1987, the United States spent approximately $123 billion on research and development and continues to lead the world as a producer of basic research. Compared to Japan, West Germany, Britain, and France, however, the percentage of expenses for research and development continues to decline.[1] Based upon productivity measures, including quality defects/rework, average age of equipment, and annual investment per worker, the United States lags behind Japan in terms of competitiveness.[2]

What has caused this productivity problem? There is no single cause; the answer can be attributed to a number of factors—government policies, union agreements, management/worker policies, and attitudes. Tax policies that do not stimulate investment have some bearing, as do regulations calling for mounds of paperwork. When negotiations with workers add benefits without corresponding increases in output, productivity will be affected. Management tolerance of inefficiency and disregard for job excellence are also contributing factors.

Many causes of declining productivity exist

Supervisors and Productivity

As a supervisor, you demonstrate a concern for productivity through words and actions. Unless you set an example, it does little good to stress quality, solicit suggestions for improvement, and emphasize avoidance of unnecessary waste. How is productivity to be encouraged? These recommendations help promote a productive work environment:

Supervisors must seek improved productivity

☐ Examine performance and do not accept shoddy work from employees. Quality is important and redoing the work is costly and nonproductive.

☐ Ask for ideas and suggestions from employees who do the job. Frequently, people who actually do the work are not asked about how it can be done.

☐ Promote an efficient work environment. Training practices should be adequate, and recommendations for job restructuring can be an alternative to wasted time.

☐ Select personnel on the basis of job competency. Keep up-to-date descriptions of requirements to perform jobs properly.

☐ Recognize employee contributions and reward outstanding performance. Excellent work is often taken for granted—until capable employees leave or assume duties with other departments of the firm.

☐ Understand objectives so that work efforts can be properly directed toward attaining them.

☐ Examine communication practices. Ineffective communication creates confusion and wastes time.

☐ Provide meaningful, challenging work opportunities for employees.

To achieve gains in productivity, all members of a business must try to improve all aspects of operations. It is important to grasp the *need* to cut costs and improve efficiency. Many firms have systems that reward ideas for improved practices or cost-saving suggestions. Supervisors must make the concern for better ways to perform tasks an integral part of their daily work lives. Fragmented efforts are not likely to yield desired outcomes. Remember, inefficiencies consume greater time and expense than is often realized.

Results depend on people

> Today, in most American industrial companies, making sure things are done right and fixing things that are done wrong consumes 15 to 30 cents of every sales dollar. The figure is about 35 cents of every dollar in the typical service organization.[3]

Table 1.1   **Employed Persons Classified by Age**

		Percentage of Employees by Age Classification			
Year	20–24	25–44	45–64	65–Over	
1960	9	49	37	5	
1970	11	46	38	5	
1980	14	51	31	4	
1988	12	57	28	3	

Source: *Handbook of Labor Statistics*, U.S. Department of Labor, Bureau of Labor Statistics, August 1989, p. 64.

Characteristics of the Workplace

The workplace is changing

Workplace demographics have not remained constant. Employees are better educated. Greater numbers of females are working. America's labor force is aging. From 1954 to 1982, the proportion of minority employment increased by 2.1 percent; it is projected to grow another 1.7 percent by 1995.[4] During the 1970s, the labor force grew by slightly over 25 percent; it increased an additional 1.5 percent between 1980 and 1983.

More women are working

For the past 30 years, the number of working females has increased consistently and is rapidly approaching half of all employed workers. Women are making a wide range of career choices outside of the traditional female fields of teaching, nursing, and secretarial work. From 1978 to 1984, the percentage of women in management positions rose 20 percent.[5] During the 1990s, dual-income households will be even more commonplace, as families strive to maintain and improve their standards of living.

The labor force is aging

During the 1970s, the median age of the population increased from 28 to 30, and by the year 2000, it is estimated that it will reach 35.[6] Table 1.1 presents a breakdown of the labor force according to age. In the 1980s, a slight decrease occurred in two age groups (20–24 and 45–64). The percentage of workers between the ages of 25–44 increased considerably; within a few years, these workers will create an increase in the 45–64 age category.

Technology has changed the workplace

Technological developments have revolutionized the workplace. Processing of information has emerged as a major source of employment. Messages are communicated in seconds, and much repetitive work is performed mechanically. For instance, computerized painting machines, called robots, are used by automobile manufacturers to paint cars. Advanced word processing equipment enables secretaries to correct spelling errors, insert missing words, and rearrange paragraphs without retyping letters or documents. At Georgia-Pacific, use of a stronger metal alloy for saw blades permits reclaiming enough sawdust to be made into 800 railcars full of products each year.[7]

Educational Attainment of Employed Persons   Table 1.2

	1968	1978	1988
High school	37.5%	39.5%	39.9%
4 or more years of college	12.4%	16.9%	25.7%

Source: *Handbook of Labor Statistics,* U.S. Department of Labor, Bureau of Labor Statistics, June 1985, p. 164, and August 1989, p. 280.

Today's labor force is better educated. As Table 1.2 illustrates, the percentages of high school and college graduates has continued to increase in the past 30 years. In 1988, four out of ten employed persons possessed a high school diploma, and 25.7 percent held a college degree. These statistics should not imply a sense of complacency, as there is a continual need to become more knowledgeable and upgrade job skills. John Naisbitt, a noted social forecaster, observes that "the most formidable challenge will be to train people to work in the information society," which he describes as a society where more people work with information than produce goods.[8]

More workers are educated

Understanding Employees

As a supervisor, you must understand the work environment. You should also be aware of your employees' attitudes and values. Each individual has different experiences, perceptions, and aspirations. Workers are the key to an organization's survival and growth. Without them, nothing will be accomplished. We probably can conclude that human resources are management's most undervalued asset. When their views are recognized, employees are more likely to exert more effort, develop loyalty, and have greater job satisfaction.

Workers are an undervalued asset

The late 1960s saw the start of activism and pressure for social change. During the 1980s, a greater concern for job security emerged. Many people view work life not as just employment but as an opportunity for personal fulfillment and contribution. Since you must work closely with your employees, knowing their expectations is important. Figure 1.3 compares the viewpoints of today's workers with those of the past. As you review them, consider the numerous changes that have occurred in our society. Today, for example, workers expect to be involved in decisions affecting them and are more likely to overtly challenge supervisory authority. Consider the paperwork revolution. Between 1960 and 1985, the number of copies produced by dry copiers each year increased from 70 million to 500 billion.[9]

Viewpoints change

It is said that we are products of our experiences. Therefore, it is wise to recognize that younger employees may have perspectives that are different

Perspectives differ

Figure 1.3   **A Comparison of Viewpoints**

Today's Viewpoint	Yesterday's Viewpoint
1. Women should have equal opportunities to pursue careers—many dual-income families.	1. Men are the primary breadwinners—commonly single-income familes.
2. Education is a "right" that should be available to all people—numerous financial programs to aid college students.	2. Education is a "privilege"—few financial-aid programs available for persons to continue their education beyond high school.
3. Actions should not be carried out just because of a supervisory directive—individual inputs and perspectives are relevant.	3. If the boss says "do it," it should be done without challenge to supervisory authority.
4. A job should contribute to individual objectives—fewer hours worked; expectations of personal satisfaction from the job.	4. Work is a necessary part of life—longer hours and separateness between work requirements and individual satisfaction.
5. First marriages at later ages—divorce more commonly accepted; many single parents in the work force.	5. Family stability as a unit—divorce regarded as a social stigma.
6. As well as provision of a place to work, organizations have many obligations toward employees—various programs that recognize the importance of employees' programs and welfare.	6. Organizations have little responsibility for factors that are not job related—few company-sponsored programs to provide day care for children, help with employee drug/alcohol problems, or offer personal financial assistance.
7. Considerable governmental legislation and paperwork requirements—equal employment guidelines, mandated safety regulations, and numerous compliance rules.	7. Relatively few governmental regulations—main emphasis upon task objectives without formal regulatory controls.

from those of older workers. These differences may frustrate supervisors. To a youthful supervisor, the views and habits of older employees may be equally frustrating and baffling. You will likely have a mix of ages as well as a variety of outlooks among your subordinates, and you will need to know which approaches work best. For example, senior personnel possess the experience to provide valuable ideas and suggestions, and you might find that a recent technical school graduate is excited about doing a special assignment involving application of skills learned at school.

Consider This

1. What is the most important action a supervisor can take to increase worker productivity?
2. Why should supervisors strive to be excellent communicators?

An Overview of Supervision

Supervisors play various roles when performing job duties. You need to help employees understand job essentials as well as company policies and procedures. Also, you are a learner who needs to keep up-to-date on changes and developments related to your area of responsibility. In addition, you are a communicator who responds to questions and provides information. Supervision involves being perceptive and relating to people. After listening to an employee complaint, for example, you have to decide whether it has merit or if the subordinate is just "letting off steam."

> Supervisors do many things

Formal roles refer to the expectations stated in the description of job duties. These include evaluating workers, developing plans for the work unit, and handling information. Supervisors schedule work activities, send reports to higher-level bosses, prepare budgets, and monitor work performance. Such duties are usually specified in a formal written statement of job duties, known as a **job description.**

> Formal roles are specified

What other roles do supervisors play? They also have **informal roles,** which are unwritten expectations that arise as a result of a leadership position. As a supervisor, you may be expected to clarify rumors, be a sounding board for ideas, and make suggestions on employee career possibilities. You might need to listen to workers' personal problems and be an expert on everything from politics to sports. Successful fulfillment of informal expectations can contribute to your self-confidence and help you gain the respect of employees.

> Informal roles accompany leadership positions

In performing formal and informal roles, communication factors must not be ignored. Reactions of others depend on how responses are interpreted. For example, assume an employee makes an unsolicited suggestion, and you respond, "It just won't work. Think about it and come up with something useful." This is a good way to stifle further ideas. Why not reply, "That's a possibility. Is there anything else that we need to consider?" With encouragement and additional thought, a feasible recommendation might ultimately evolve.

Potential conflicts between formal and informal roles require you to be realistic and to recognize appropriate boundaries. Involvement in workers' personal problems may lead to a loss of proper perspective toward your company's objectives. Your personal opinions on controversial issues may be interpreted as representing management's viewpoint. Figure 1.4 presents guidelines for responding to requests. Review them carefully to avoid creating unnecessary difficulties for yourself.

> Role conflicts do occur

Preparation for Supervision

Earlier in the chapter, several personal characteristics that indicate potential for supervisory success were cited. Now, let's examine how you can prepare to assume a supervisory position. Both on- and off-the-job experiences

> Experiences provide insights

Figure 1.4   **Guidelines for Responding to Requests**

---

1. Remember your position.

   Before responding, think about implications that may result from requests.

2. If in doubt, gather facts.

   Judgments made on opinions may not coincide with facts.

3. Treat employees with fairness and equity.

   Favors given to one employee can be the basis for allegations of bias and unfairness that can cause innumerable difficulties.

4. Be certain of commitments.

   Don't make promises that you cannot keep or do not have the authority to make.

5. Be careful about involvement in workers' personal problems.

   This is a difficult view; however, you need to draw the line about the extent of involvement that is reasonable.

6. Be careful of personal, social relationships with employees.

   As a guideline, most supervisors prefer not to have close, intimate personal relationships with subordinates; such friendships do not make your job any easier.

7. Think about precedents and making exceptions to policies and rules.

   You can be sure that one exception will lead to other similar requests.

8. There may be a "hidden agenda" in requests.

   At times, workers may not reveal the real reasons or all of the particulars; you need to ask questions and read between the lines.

---

provide insights to develop valuable knowledge and skills. Consider an example. You are serving as treasurer of a community service organization. Because of your carelessness, the checking account is overdrawn. When do you tell the group? What explanation should be given? If a member becomes angry, how will you respond? This situation is not unlike dealing with an employee whose performance is unsatisfactory. Assume you dislike a co-worker but must work closely with the person. Do you act indifferently, fake friendliness, or say, "I may have to work with you, but I certainly don't like you." How you choose to react contributes to your accumulation of learning experiences.

Take advantage of opportunities to learn

Reading texts and periodicals about supervision builds your knowledge of the subject. Taking part in professional groups helps you understand how organizations function. College courses and attendance at seminars or workshops that examine supervisory concepts develop your ability. Listening and learning through daily contacts with people promote an understanding of how people express themselves and justify their viewpoints on issues.

If you are already working, there may be company training programs to teach management skills. Continuing education courses provide opportunities to learn about supervision. You may be involved with community groups in which you have the opportunity to observe how leaders set goals, encourage involvement, and handle differences of opinion within the group. Note how people react to others' views and to decisions that have major consequences.

Supervisory Skills

Supervisors are frequently expected to be everything to everybody—their bosses, employees, and even customers. To meet this challenge, a variety of skills are required—communication, people, job, and administrative. Let's discuss these skills and illustrate how they are applied to first-line management.

As a leader, **communication skills** are an intrinsic aspect of every action taken. Information must be transferred to and from bosses and employees as well as accurately interpreted. Good communication skills require clarity and understanding of messages transmitted in written and oral forms. You must listen carefully to comprehend meanings others express. Try to understand gestures and facial expressions. Ask questions to clarify meanings and gain additional information.

Information is an essential concern

Good supervisors recognize that employees are people who have wants, needs, and desires. **People skills** are your abilities to lead, direct, motivate, and understand others. Consideration of workers' views on various issues enables you to rate high on these human relations skills. Think about how your remarks will be perceived by others. If a subordinate requests to be reimbursed for unauthorized expenses, you can say, "No way; forget it," or you can reply, "I'm sorry; all expenses must be approved in advance." Either way, the answer is no, but the latter response promotes a more positive work relationship. Lastly, develop the habit of treating all people with dignity and respect to avoid disruptive personal antagonisms.

Tasks are accomplished through people

Supervisors must develop their knowledge of the jobs they oversee. **Job skills** are abilities to understand technical aspects of jobs. Some jobs are more complex and difficult to master than others. For example, a receptionist who routes telephone calls has a less demanding job than a secretary who types letters, files documents, provides product information, and processes orders. You will need to keep up with trends and new developments in job specialties. To illustrate, repairing today's automobiles necessitates a more sophisticated level of knowledge than that required for vehicles built in the 1950s. In understanding jobs, it is necessary to handle unusual and emergency situations, which can arise without warning. You will need to learn to spot ways to improve procedures and get more accomplished.

Technical knowledge is necessary

Supervisors must have or develop **administrative skills,** which include knowing how to prepare and send reports, forms, and other types of paperwork. Administrative skills are the skills necessary for operation of a department or unit. They include recordkeeping, guiding and overseeing operations, budget preparation, and employee appraisal. They entail sending information to upper-level managers and providing feedback data to workers. Administration also requires organizing job activities without creating obstacles, making timely responses to requests, and seeing that supplies and work materials are available when needed. Failure to meet deadlines and scheduling errors hinder efficiency. Sometimes, your boss will unexpectedly

Supervisors are administrators

request information. If you are disorganized, excessive time will be spent just trying to locate the needed data.

Supervisors and Their Difficulties

Supervision provides an opportunity to handle problems, thereby giving you many rewarding experiences and much professional development. It is usually easier to assume your supervisory role after a poor or inept supervisor leaves, but you may follow a capable, well-liked, and respected person. Some supervisors create many of their own troubles. A look at some possible sources of difficulty is valuable.

Know the job capabilities of employees

Aloofness and Closeness. Many supervisors watch employees closely and are always looking over their shoulders. On the other hand, some supervisors are not available when needed. They seldom make inquiries and show little desire to be personable with employees.

It is necessary to maintain a balance between being too aloof and too close. Workers like concern and approachability, but they also want breathing room. Supervisors who set themselves apart and don't "come around" lose opportunities to interact with employees. At the opposite end, some supervisors don't permit adequate freedom to perform. They oversupervise. Either extreme can result in discontent. How much supervision is appropriate? A key factor is knowledge of employee abilities. With some, directions need to be very detailed and repeated frequently. Others can be depended on to complete tasks with minimal supervision.

Consider the views of others

Lack of Empathy. In supervising, you will be quite busy and have many things on your mind: handling unexpected crises, monitoring productivity, and responding to questions or complaints. It's easy to lose perspective on employees' concerns. From their view, you might exert too much pressure to meet deadlines or fail to consider their day-to-day problems and needs. Such difficulties arise when you focus on your own responsibilities and fail to recognize how subordinates envision your actions.

Empathy means that you see situations from another's viewpoint. Lack of empathy does not itself trigger problems, but it may cause hard feelings to surface when other difficulties emerge. For instance, a failure to communicate informally with an employee (stop by to say hello, ask how things are going, or inquire about the family) generally may be overlooked. However, if the individual believes he or she has received a less than adequate raise in salary, the supervisor is likely to be blamed, possibly on the basis of personal dislike. Perceptions may be inaccurate but do influence behaviors.

Be a self-starter

Lack of Initiative. Firms need consistent work output directed toward goal achievement. Both employees and managers share this responsibility and must always put forth their best efforts. Supervisors should not lose sight of goals or be satisfied with "just getting by." When initiative is not demonstrated, an improper message is conveyed to subordinates. Remember, work does not get done by itself. If you do not set a good example, it is unreasonable to expect high levels of sustained efforts from those you manage.

Small problems evolve into larger ones because nothing is done to resolve them. Ignoring a problem does not mean it will go away. Do not assume that a problem of minor importance to you is viewed similarly by somebody else. As a supervisor, you must exert initiative to enforce compliance with policies. For instance, a worker may develop the habit of arriving just a few minutes late. If this situation is not corrected, others may get the message that this is acceptable, or the offender may start arriving later and later.

Supervisory Indecisiveness.   Nobody knows the answers to everything, but it is important to respond to workers' requests. Do not communicate inaccurate information. When necessary, check with superiors for answers and try to reply within a reasonable time. Granted, people do not like uncertainty, but some choices are difficult and cannot be made instantly. Perhaps such decisions can be delayed for awhile, but they cannot be postponed indefinitely. A complaint workers often voice is, "I can live with yes or no answers, but I cannot tolerate 'maybe' or 'we'll see' responses."

Make choices

Forgetting the Supervisory Role.   Supervisors hold highly visible positions and are important components of the management team. As such, they need to recognize the delicate relationship between managers and employees. Subordinates tend to look at issues from their own self-interests, and most consider their supervisor to be "the management." As noted earlier, many first-line managers are promoted from the ranks. When this happens to you, you are no longer part of your old work group. Problems can occur because of friendships and close ties with former colleagues. You must not forget the demands of your new role or underestimate the relevance of your newly acquired responsibility.

Remember your role

Doing Things Better.   It is likely that you possess much knowledge about jobs that are managed and see how they can be done better or faster. It is tempting to do many things yourself and avoid taking the time to give explanations and correct inefficiencies. However, the workday is not long enough to supervise and also do the work of others. It is necessary to be realistic and recognize that, while most employees will not attain perfection at completing assigned responsibilities, they must produce acceptable work. A key is to clarify job duties, train properly, and expect compliance with performance standards. When working with others, the following pointers are valuable.

You can't do everything

It's Worth the Effort

1. To be certain employees know how to do their jobs.
2. To communicate clearly—who, what, when, where, and why.
3. To solicit employee viewpoints.
4. To give workers credit for their ideas and suggestions.
5. To recognize job-performance excellence.
6. To respect subordinates and treat them fairly.
7. To be honest in dealing with workers.
8. To demonstrate a caring attitude.

Remember: Your success as a supervisor depends on how well your subordinates do their jobs.

Figure 1.5 summarizes potential sources of supervisory difficulties. Not every source will create problems. However, you need to be aware that problems *might* occur. On the job, it is easier to avoid complications than to correct them. Before acting, think ahead and try to anticipate implications. Such a strategy will eliminate many obstacles to your efficiency.

Consider This

1. Successful supervisors focus most of their attention on informal role expectations. Do you agree or disagree with this statement? Why?
2. How can supervisors avoid creating difficulties for themselves?

Picture Yourself as a Supervisor

Take a look at yourself

Is supervision for you? It is exciting, offers many challenges, and can bring considerable personal satisfaction. Even so, look at yourself and try to determine your interest in first-line management. The checklist in Figure 1.6 covers several aspects of supervision. As you review the questions, notice the variety of factors involved—conflict, problem solving, criticism, decision making, and so on. Capable managers strive to know themselves, comprehend workplace challenges, and understand human behavior. Mastery comes with experience, and you will make many mistakes along the way. Try to learn from them. Be receptive to ideas and suggestions from others. Whenever possible, observe interactions between supervisors and subordinates. Then picture how you would react in similar circumstances.

To aid learning, this text is divided according to topic concepts. On the job, however, you often have to apply many skills simultaneously. Assume you are face-to-face with an employee who has violated a company rule and is a

Potential Sources of Supervisory Difficulties   **Figure 1.5**

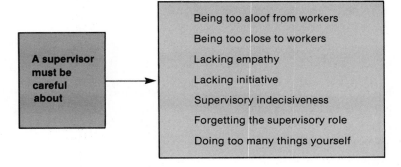

A supervisor must be careful about →

Being too aloof from workers

Being too close to workers

Lacking empathy

Lacking initiative

Supervisory indecisiveness

Forgetting the supervisory role

Doing too many things yourself

How Well Do You Understand Supervision?   **Figure 1.6**

1. Do you enjoy getting work done even though there are problems to overcome in the process? _____ Yes _____ No
2. While working, can you think about a number of unrelated concerns that occur at the same time? _____ Yes _____ No
3. Can you handle interruptions without losing track of the job? _____ Yes _____ No
4. Would you be comfortable in circumstances that involve responsibilities to both employees and bosses? _____ Yes _____ No
5. Even though you feel it is unjustified, can you accept criticism without becoming upset? _____ Yes _____ No
6. Do you like to work with other people and help them achieve both company and personal goals? _____ Yes _____ No
7. At the end of a workday, do you continue to think about your job and, if necessary, willingly put in extra time to get tasks finished? _____ Yes _____ No
8. Even when they make you look bad, are you able to accept workers' mistakes? _____ Yes _____ No
9. Can you discipline workers, fire them, or tell them their performance is unsatisfactory? _____ Yes _____ No
10. Can you implement, explain, and support company policies with which you do not agree? _____ Yes _____ No

Number of times Answered Yes	Interpretation of Your Answers
10–8	You have an excellent grasp of supervision.
7–5	You have a good foundation for building an understanding of supervision.
4–0	You have recognized a need for becoming more familiar with the concepts of supervision.

marginal performer. You must administer discipline, offer suggestions, encourage improved performance, and retain respect for the person as a member of your work group—all at the same time. Remember, your ability to communicate is involved in each of these actions. Now you are ready to study the many facets of supervision.

Looking Back

After each chapter, you will find a restatement of chapter objectives, including a brief summary of the content covered. Develop the habit of reviewing this material to help you understand major concepts. Now that you have read Chapter 1, let's review some of the highlights.

☐ **Explain the nature of management.** Management involves using human and equipment resources to attain objectives. It is normally separated into three levels: top, middle, and lower. Supervisors, often called first-line managers, represent the lowest level of management having direct contact with employees.

☐ **Describe the importance of communication to supervisors.** Communication refers to the sharing of meaning between senders and receivers of messages. Supervisors must interpret data, give directions, explain work procedures, prepare reports, and listen carefully. Miscommunication causes inaccuracies, wasted time, ineffective job performance, and poor human relations.

☐ **Discuss how to prepare for supervision.** Many supervisors are promoted from the company work force. People hired for their particular technical expertise and those with formal training are also sources of supervisory talent. Reading, attending seminars and training programs, taking courses, and participating in community organizations are among ways to prepare for supervision. Job experience and an ability to learn from daily life are also valuable.

☐ **Emphasize the importance of productivity.** Poor productivity increases expenses and negatively affects competitiveness. Therefore, supervisors need to be concerned about quality work, improved performance, and employee competence. Tolerance of inefficiency and disregard for job excellence are major obstacles to productivity.

☐ **Examine characteristics of the workplace.** Females are entering the labor force in increasing numbers. More minorities are employed than in the past. Employees are better educated today. More workers are high school graduates, and many have four or more years of college. America's labor force is aging. Technological developments have accelerated the pace for completion of many work activities.

☐ **Specify formal and informal supervisory role expectations.** Formal roles are the result of the supervisor's stated job duties. These include evaluating workers, developing plans, scheduling work activities, preparing budgets, and sending reports to middle managers. Informal roles are unwritten expectations that arise from the supervisor's position as a leader. Supervisors may be asked to clarify rumors, be a sounding board for ideas, or listen to workers' personal problems.

☐ **Provide an overview of supervisory skills.** First-line management involves four types of skills: communication, people, job, and administrative. Communication is an intrinsic aspect of every action taken. In addition to technical knowledge, supervisors must relate well to people. Administrative skills include preparation of reports, forms, and other types of paperwork necessary to maintain the ongoing operation of a work unit.

☐ **Describe common difficulties supervisors encounter.** Job-related difficulties arise from a variety of factors. There must be a balance between aloofness and the type of supervision that permits little employee discretion in job performance. Employee discontent can arise from the supervisor's lack of empathy and initiative, indecisiveness, forgetting the supervisory role, and an "I can do things better" attitude.

Key Terms

administrative skills	job skills
communication	management
communication skills	objectives
empathy	people skills
formal roles	productivity
informal roles	supervisors
job description	

Review and Discussion Questions

1. Why are supervisors often characterized as people in the middle?
2. What objectives must supervisors consider in performing their duties?
3. Why is productivity so important to supervisors as well as to the entire organization?
4. What changes do you think will take place in the labor force during the next 10 years?
5. Why should supervisors strive to understand employees and their attitudes?

6. How should supervisors handle situations where informal expectations conflict with formally stated job duties?
7. Which type of skill is most important to success in supervision: people, job, administrative, or communication?
8. What are several actions supervisors can take to avoid difficulties arising from employee perceptions of lack of empathy and indecisiveness?
9. How can people determine whether they have interests in becoming supervisors?

Action Incident 1.1

The Ponderer

Gloria Haines has been offered a promotion to supervisor. Following her graduation from high school, she began working as a press operator for Uniform Printing Company. She has been employed at Uniform for three years and has made many suggestions for improved operations that the firm has adopted.

Even though she is prone to minor mistakes that create extra work for the department, her work is generally regarded as satisfactory. She doesn't like being criticized for these mistakes and wonders how she might handle situations involving employee discipline. Gloria is also concerned about being accepted by workers who are predominately male and white, since she is a female and black.

In addition, Gloria ponders the aspect of supervising persons who are considerably older and more experienced at their jobs. To complicate matters, she feels that she may have been offered this opportunity partially because of her race and sex.

Gloria had planned to take some courses in management at the local college. Somehow, though, she never got around to enrolling in them. Therefore, she believes that her understanding of management principles may be somewhat weak. However, this is her one chance to jump in with both feet and become a manager. Such an opportunity doesn't come along every day, and it might never be offered again, at least not at Uniform Printing Company.

Discussion Questions

1. In making her decision, what should Gloria consider?
2. If she accepts the promotion, what types of problems might she expect?
3. If she does not accept, how might she feel about herself one year later?
4. Is Gloria qualified to be a supervisor?
5. Should she accept the offer?

Action Incident 1.2

The Promotion Decision

Manuel Rodriquez has worked for six years in the custom fabrication department at Harrington Manufacturing. He is well organized, shows initiative, and has received excellent ratings on his work. In fact, Manuel appears to have idle time because of his ability to get assignments done ahead of schedule. While others are struggling to get tasks finished, he seems occupied with other than job-related activities.

Fellow employees seem to resent his abilities, the ease with which he handles the job, and his self-confident attitude. Manuel gets along well with Helen Scott, his immediate superior. However, he doesn't seem to go out of his way to develop close relationships with peer-group members and in fact is somewhat indifferent toward many of them. Still, Manuel cooperates with them on tasks when required.

After many years of service, Helen has decided to retire, and a new supervisor will be chosen. Manuel has said that he wants to be considered for her job. Sally Robinson, the processing manager who makes hiring recommendations, has had two employees stop by her office and give support for Manuel because of his intelligence and concern for getting things done. Two other workers have called Sally to make sure that she knew of his potential for disrupting harmony and being too demanding.

Sally contemplates the promotion decision. She is concerned about productivity, as well as reaching objectives. She notes that Helen didn't emphasize output or push performance as much as she might have. But Helen was congenial, and the workers were used to her friendliness and good nature.

Discussion Questions

1. As to supervisory potential, what positive as well as negative characteristics does Manuel possess?
2. What value should Sally place on the comments that were made to her?
3. If Manuel is promoted, what changes in supervisory style might take place?
4. If he is not promoted, what changes might occur in Manuel's work behavior?
5. Should Manuel be promoted? Explain your response.

Action Incident 1.3

They've Got It Made

Better pay, greater prestige, and more authority, thought Betty Jones. "Gee, I'd like to be a supervisor," she exclaimed to Tom Hollerin, her co-worker. "They really have it made." Tom responded, "Sure do. And, what's more, they don't have to do the actual work like we do." At this moment, Jan Sparks, their colleague, joins them.

Jan: How are you two people today?

Betty: Just fine. We've been talking about supervisors and what a good deal they have.

Jan: I'm glad you think so. I wouldn't want their problems. Supervisors earn every penny they get and are caught in the middle between people like us and other managers.

Tom: But remember, we do the work that makes this place run.

Jan: Tom, just a minute. Who gets the problems? Think of all the skills needed to keep everything running.

Betty: Jan, you've missed the point. Not one of us has ever created a problem. So, don't give me that problem-solving story.

Jan: True, but we're not typical employees. Think about some other people. Trying to manage them would be a real nightmare.

Tom: Not really. You just have to give instructions, and if they don't do the job, fire them.

Jan: Folks, it's not all that easy.

Discussion Questions

1. Who has the most accurate perspective of the supervisor's job? Why?
2. What factors might influence Betty's and Tom's attitudes about supervision?
3. Do most employees share Tom's view about supervisors? Explain your response.

Notes

1. Stuart Gannes, "The Good News About U.S. R&D," *Fortune* 117 (February 1, 1988), p. 49.
2. Karen Pennar, "The Productivity Paradox," *Business Week* No. 3055 (June 6, 1988), p. 102.
3. Robert W. Goddard, "In Quest of Quality," *Management World* 17 (May–June 1988), p. 19.
4. Fred Best, "The Nature of Work in a Changing Society," *Personnel Journal* 64 (January 1985), p. 40.
5. Fairlee E. Winfield, "The Changing Face of Corporate Relocation," *Personnel* 63 (January 1986), p. 33.
6. Douglas T. Hall and James G. Goodale, *Human Resource Management Strategy, Design, and Implementation* (Glenview, Ill.: Scott, Foresman, 1986), p. 80.
7. G. David Wallace and others. "America's Leanest and Meanest," *Business Week* No. 3019 (October 5, 1987), p. 78.
8. John Naisbitt, *Megatrends* (New York: Warner Books, 1982), p. 250.
9. Lawrence Kilman, "Paperwork Explosion Started 25 Years Ago," *Kansas City Star* (September 29, 1985), p. 1H.

Suggested Readings

Bell, Chip R. "Productivity Improvement Begins Today." *Management Solutions* 33, June 1988, pp. 11–13.

Brower, Barbara A. "Transition to a New Supervisor." *Supervision* 46, February 1984, pp. 3–4, 10.

Cook, Mary F. "What's Ahead in Human Relations?" *Management Review* 77, April 1988, pp. 41–44.

Hinkin, Timothy, and Chester A. Schriesheim. "Power and Influence: The View from Below." *Personnel* 65, May 1988, pp. 47–50.

Josefowitz, Natasha. "What That New Supervisor or Manager Should Know." *Management Solutions* 31, October 1986, pp. 5–13.

Nelson, Andre. "An Often Neglected Supervisory Tool . . . Talking." *Supervision* 49, August 1988, pp. 10–12.

Rogow, Robert B., and Charles P. Edmonds. "Tallying Employees as Assets." *Personnel Administrator* 33, June 1988, pp. 168–170.

Tracey, William R. "Deft Delegation: Multiplying Your Effectiveness." *Personnel* 65, February 1988, pp. 36–39, 42.

Weiss, Donald H. "How to Handle Difficult People." *Management Solutions* 33, February 1988, pp. 33–38.

Wilkinson, Roderick. "Do You Have What It Takes." *Supervision* 49, January 1988, pp. 6–8.

Supervisory Functions

Chapter 2

Learning Objectives

These objectives will give you insight into the functions performed by supervisors. This chapter provides fundamental information to develop a perspective of what supervisors do. It will prepare you to study how supervisors perform their leadership duties.

1. Understand the role of supervisory planning.
2. Explain the concept of organizing.
3. Differentiate among types of organizational structures.
4. Know how to give effective directions.
5. Apply the control function to attain desired performance expectations.

An Overview of Supervisory Functions

Supervisors perform various functions

Every organization has a purpose, and all try to reach goals. **Functions,** which are activities involved in attaining goals, are carried out by all managers. Supervisors must plan, organize, direct, and control. Knowledge and skillful practice of these functions are critical to the success of an organization. **Planning** means setting goals and forming policies and procedures. **Organizing** is grouping tasks and assigning authority. **Directing** is the process of instructing and guiding work activities of subordinates. **Controlling** provides the basis for knowing whether actions conform to plans. It includes setting standards, checking performance, and correcting errors.

Communication skills are important

Communication plays a vital role in determining how well functions are performed. Employees must know what they are to do, and resources must be used productively. Desired outcomes cannot be left to chance. Frequently, sufficient explanations are not provided, and needless confusion occurs. Having standards is not enough; workers need to be aware of them and know how to correct any deficiencies. Inadequate feedback is an invitation to confusion and likely deterioration of quality. Communication provides a key link to ensure that operations run smoothly and to minimize nonproductive use of time and energy.

At every level, managerial functions must be administered. However, top management considers functions from a broad perspective, including long-term plans, organizing numerous divisions or departments, and directing an entire organization. As a supervisor, you are involved in more limited tasks and day-to-day duties. For example, you schedule work hours, ensure that equipment functions properly, prepare daily or weekly reports, and discipline employees who violate company rules. Much time is spent controlling employee performance. This does not imply less emphasis on other functions. It means that giving instructions and seeing that work duties are done right consumes a lot of your time. Figure 2.1 shows a comparison of time spent in performing functions by upper management and supervisors.

Wise supervisors value employee perspectives

Participative management, which solicits employee involvement in decisions affecting them, is an emerging trend in many firms. With this approach, employees are given opportunities to express opinions, make suggestions, and react to management's views. The intent is to recognize human resources as valuable assets capable of making meaningful contributions to further an organization's interests. Also, personnel benefit in terms of higher morale, greater job satisfaction, and an increased sense of personal importance. Successful application of the participative philosophy requires supervisors to be facilitators, not just order givers. Consequently, the importance of communication, especially listening skills, cannot be overlooked.

Some supervisors incorrectly assume that participation necessitates sacrificing their authority. Clear explanations and setting of boundaries can overcome this hesitancy. For example, assume higher-level management asks for your view about a possible change in work hours. According to the

**Comparison of Time Spent in Performing Functions by Upper Management   Figure 2.1
and Supervisors**

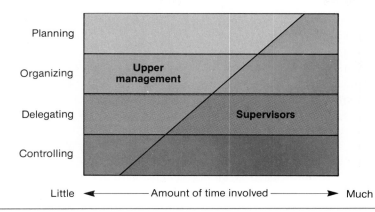

proposal, employees are to report for work 30 minutes earlier but will also leave a half hour sooner. While some employees will welcome such a change, others are likely to oppose it. After explaining the proposal, you might say, "I've been asked for my view on the schedule change, but since it affects all of you, I'd like your advice. Please remember that my final recommendation will be based on a concern for the entire work unit, but I do want to consider your individual viewpoints."

To participate effectively, subordinates must have access to relevant information so they can understand the pros and cons of choices and make informed judgments. Often, you will have attended management meetings where formal discussion of issues takes place. Therefore, it is easy to assume that subordinates possess greater insights into various considerations than they actually do. Assume management is considering whether to replace typewriters with a modern computer system. This change, which has the potential to improve productivity, likely will be welcomed. However, employees may not realize that purchase of the computers will create restrictions on budget allocations. Funds may no longer be available for them to attend out-of-state training programs or professional meetings.

"They ask everyone but me, and I do the job." "If they would just have asked me, I could have told them it wouldn't work." "It's another instance of managers who think they have all the answers." These are common complaints of workers who are not consulted about decisions. Participation helps to develop commitment and gain the cooperation necessary to attain desired results. When workers do not support decisions, their actions can create difficulties. They might put forth only minimal effort, find plausible

Is my opinion important?

excuses for not getting tasks completed on schedule, or, unfortunately, even fail to properly maintain equipment.

The Role of Planning

Planning is an essential function

Planning is the starting point for achieving goals. It involves thinking ahead, anticipating events, and preparing a course of action. It is important to seek information and advice, but the responsibility for planning cannot be delegated to subordinates. Supervisors must recognize how plans for their work units correlate with those of their bosses. Frequently, circumstances necessitate revising plans. For example, you might plan to purchase new equipment only to learn that upper management has initiated a cost-cutting strategy. Instead of adding new machines, you must plan to get by with existing equipment.

Planning includes three components

Besides naming goals, planning includes setting policies, procedures, and rules. **Policies** are general guidelines, **procedures** are steps to follow to reach a goal, and **rules** set limits on performing a job. All supervisors must know about these aspects of planning and help employees to understand them. Failure to recognize their importance hinders effectiveness and contributes to disarray.

A company policy might state that products should be of high quality. Top management sets this kind of policy. Middle management is concerned with the broad details of quality. Finally, the policy becomes specific at the job and supervisory level. Here, it could indicate that defects are not acceptable.

Procedures are developed to attain policy goals. They spell out details of how tasks are to be completed and specify responsibilities. At each stage of a manufacturing process, procedures indicate the steps necessary to ensure compliance with quality standards. These steps include job titles of persons who must approve the work and identify paperwork to be completed. Other examples of procedures include steps to follow in emergency situations and forms to complete for initiating budget requests.

Rules provide detailed guidelines for workers. Supervisors must know company rules and communicate them to subordinates. An employee might not realize that a shovel cannot be removed from the premises to use overnight. Rules are designed to cover a wide variety of situations, such as the following causes for dismissal.

☐ Missing work for two consecutive days without notifying the supervisor.
☐ Coming to work under the influence of alcohol.
☐ Stealing company or other workers' property.
☐ Distributing illegal drugs on company property.

Notice that these rules set limits on employee behavior and, if broken, promise a penalty. Not all rules cover such major concerns or carry such a severe penalty for violation. Differences among circumstances should not be overlooked. Smoking in dangerous areas of an oil refinery is different from accidentally smoking in the no-smoking section of the cafeteria.

Advantages of Planning

Planning is an essential aspect of successful first-line management. It promotes awareness of job expectations, consideration of possible future events, and formulation of insights into alternative courses of action. Knowledge gained from plans enables you to communicate more effectively with your boss, other supervisors, and workers. Plans help you understand the relationship between departmental goals and those of the organization. They also enable you to recognize needed changes and see opportunities to improve job performance through efficient use of human and equipment resources.

Why plan?

Over time, machinery wears out, becomes outdated, and needs to be replaced. Rather than incur costly expenses all at once, a plan can be developed to purchase machines at periodic intervals. Depending on market conditions, demand for a company's products may fluctuate, especially if seasonal items are manufactured. In this case, it is necessary to look ahead, forecast personnel needs, and plan accordingly. Well-developed plans demonstrate that supervisors have thought about issues and concerns related to their work units. Consequently, such plans are more likely to be approved. Whenever possible, subordinates should be involved in formulating plans because suggestions may emerge that you might never have considered.

Obstacles to Planning

Planning does present problems. Commitment to a plan means you may have to exert much energy in order to attain results. Frequently, you find yourself in the middle between the demands of your boss and the expectations of your subordinates. Plans often have to be altered because the operating environment changes. If you are not flexible in adjusting to changing circumstances, plans can fail. Success is not guaranteed just because plans have been developed; you must constantly monitor progress to ensure results. Besides inflexibility, another obstacle to good planning is overlooking available information or not trying to gather data before forming plans. If you introduce plans without checking with your boss, you may become frustrated because he or she might not approve needed resources. Plans must always be approved.

Plans do not guarantee results

Overcoming obstacles is a constant, yet realistic, challenge. When things do not work out as planned, objections arise. Sickness, absenteeism, or budget cutting can create a need to revise plans. A plan to rearrange equipment and improve operations may be unworkable because relocation of equipment proves to be far more expensive than anticipated. The role of assumptions is a key obstacle. For example, a company decided to install energy-efficient windows and proceeded to take measurements from the first floor of a large building. The new window frames and glass were ordered; only later was it discovered that window dimensions on each floor were different.

Uncertainty complicates planning

It is human nature to resist uncertainty, and sometimes workers are hesitant to support proposed plans, especially if they are not fully understood. To overcome anxiety and gain support, provide clear explanations and solicit input. Such a strategy can alleviate concerns and encourage cooperation. For instance, an hourly salary plan may be recommended to improve compensation for workers being paid on a straight weekly basis. Without knowing specifics about how the plan will affect them, employees are quite likely to react negatively toward it. Points recognized by good planners are listed at the bottom of the page.

The Planning Process

You cannot depend on chance and good fortune to attain desired goals. While few plans guarantee results, careful attention to planning increases the likelihood that pertinent factors are recognized and considered before a course of action is selected. Figure 2.2 illustrates the planning process and gives an example of how it can be applied by a restaurant supervisor. Review it and note how each step relates to the goal, which is to serve customers promptly. Planning consists of six steps; let's examine each of them.

Planning involves six steps

What is to be accomplished?

Determine Goals. Without knowledge of goals, it is impossible to plan. Goals must be specified so that time, effort, and energy can be channeled toward attaining them. Goals of the organization must be considered in determining those of departments or other subunits. When formulating goals, do not overlook the future need to measure whether they are attained. Refer to Figure 2.2; the goal lends itself to evaluation because the supervisor can observe how many customers are waiting to be served and count the number of complaints received.

An Effective Planner

1. Values advice and suggestions made by experienced persons.
2. Strives to obtain as much relevant information as possible in developing a plan.
3. Seeks to involve subordinates and others who will be affected by a plan.
4. Is prepared to justify the rationale for a plan and answer questions about the plan itself.
5. Is realistic and realizes that some aspects of a plan will ultimately need revision.
6. Considers the importance of clarity in communication with workers and upper-level managers.
7. Understands that failing to plan means planning to fail.

Illustration of the Planning Process   **Figure 2.2**

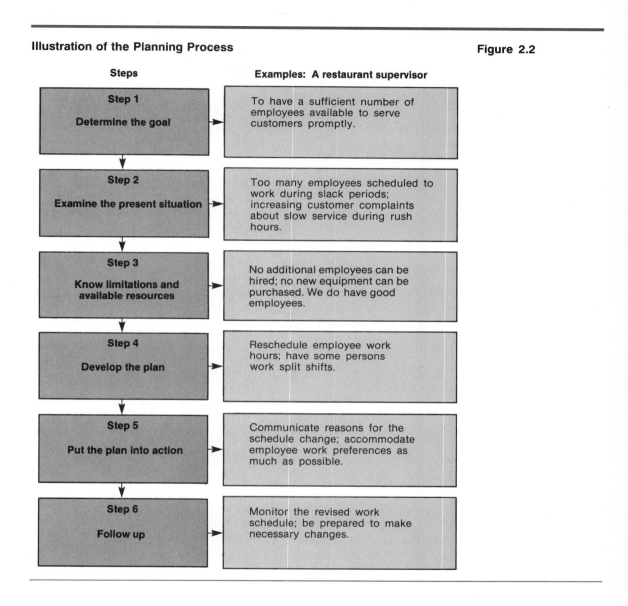

Steps	Examples: A restaurant supervisor
Step 1 **Determine the goal**	To have a sufficient number of employees available to serve customers promptly.
Step 2 **Examine the present situation**	Too many employees scheduled to work during slack periods; increasing customer complaints about slow service during rush hours.
Step 3 **Know limitations and available resources**	No additional employees can be hired; no new equipment can be purchased. We do have good employees.
Step 4 **Develop the plan**	Reschedule employee work hours; have some persons work split shifts.
Step 5 **Put the plan into action**	Communicate reasons for the schedule change; accommodate employee work preferences as much as possible.
Step 6 **Follow up**	Monitor the revised work schedule; be prepared to make necessary changes.

Examine the Present Situation.   Be aware of the current situation in relation to the desired status. If you know where you are and where you want to be, you can set a course of action and give your planning a sense of direction. This insight enables you to recognize unattainable or unrealistic goals and determine when goals need to be revised.

Where do we stand?

Know Limitations and Available Resources. Seldom, if ever, do supervisors have access to unlimited human, equipment, and financial resources. The amount of money available, space limits, and employee abilities all affect plans. In practice, unexpected events can restrict plans. For example, an unrealized budget deficit might require the return of previously allocated funds. You must be aware of limitations and think of resources you do not have as well as those at your disposal.

What obstacles might be encountered?

Develop the Plan. In this step, the plan itself is formulated. Do not overlook its purpose and think carefully about what you are trying to accomplish. The development process includes specifying tasks, assigning responsibilities, and recognizing benefits as well as potential problems. Before the plan is finalized, review it to see if all relevant factors have been considered. In Figure 2.2, for instance, it is essential for the supervisor to check if employees are available to work split shifts.

What factors must be considered?

Put the Plan into Action. At this point, the plan becomes reality and is implemented. Communication is vital because all people affected must understand their responsibilities. Provide information, give clarifications, and respond to inquiries. Make arrangements for necessary materials, equipment, and personnel.

The plan becomes an actuality

Follow Up. In practice, events do not always conform to plans. Machines break down, humans make mistakes, and the unexpected happens. Follow-up involves monitoring to ensure your outcomes conform with expectations. Continual feedback is important. It may be necessary to revise initial plans and adjust to changing circumstances.

Don't just assume things will get done

Organizing for Results

Organizing involves grouping tasks and assigning authority relationships. Work loads need to be divided up and decisions made about who will do the work. The failure to organize is a certain invitation to chaos. For a moment, assume you are in charge of the company picnic, and the date, time, and location have been selected. What about the food? If each person is told to bring a food dish, it's possible that nobody will bring the main meat dish, and an overabundance of salads and desserts is likely. To overcome this possibility, you must be an organizer. Perhaps a food committee could be appointed, or certain persons might be told to bring specific kinds of food dishes.

Organization is a key to accomplishments

Most activities show the need for organizing skills. Even though employees do not know for sure how a work activity should be done, they frequently make assumptions and proceed anyway. Several consequences emerge from disorganized attempts to perform work duties: wasted time, costly mistakes, and missed deadlines. Workers may be ready to do their jobs, only to discover that needed materials and equipment are not at hand. They may not understand who has the authority to ensure that tasks are accomplished. If you fail to consider relationships among jobs and do not assign authority, organization is lacking and productivity declines.

The principles of unity of command and span of control are closely associated with effective organization. Imagine that you receive conflicting directions from two bosses. What action will you take? Maybe you will choose not to do anything. **Unity of command** stresses that every worker reports to a single boss. This can reduce the nonproductive results of confusion, wasted efforts, and inconsistency.

How do you handle conflicting instructions?

Span of control refers to the number of people that one person can manage effectively. Its size depends on the complexity of job duties and extent of expertise possessed by subordinates. If workers are well trained and do similar tasks, a wide span of control is possible. For example, a supervisor can manage 25 persons on an assembly line. But if workers have a variety of dissimilar job responsibilities or job skills have not been mastered, close supervision is necessary, and the span of control must be narrower. Depending on the size of an organization, top executives have from three or four to ten managers who report to them. The number of workers reporting to any one manager increases at lower levels of the managerial hierarchy.

How many people can effectively be managed?

Supervisors assign personnel, arrange for equipment and materials, and schedule work. Many do not organize these resources or communicate clearly. In organizing, why do supervisors experience difficulties? Problems arise because supervisors fail to recognize the importance of the concept of organization or lack the skill to organize effectively. Sometimes they simply get in too much of a hurry.

Organization Charts

An **organization chart** portrays a firm's structure and chain of command. Several arrangements exist. However, charts have the common purpose of showing relationships among units. In cases where too many or too few employees report to each supervisor, a chart can show the need to alter reporting procedures. It may indicate a need to eliminate positions because job responsibilities are unnecessarily duplicated. Also, changes may be necessary because some employees are accountable to more than one boss.

Charts show reporting relationships

Line Organization.   In a firm, a direct chain of command from top to bottom is a **line organization,** which is often called a military approach. With this form of organization, each job position reports directly to the next higher level in a straight line pattern. For example, Figure 2.3 shows that employees report to the zone manager who reports to the vice president of sales and

The line organization clearly specifies reporting relationships

Figure 2.3   **Line Organization Chart**

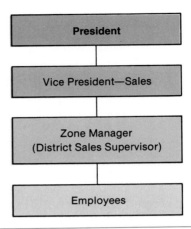

so on up the line. Such a structure clearly specifies authority relationships, facilitates the speed of decision making, and holds managers accountable for their actions. However, it places a considerable burden on managers to be capable of performing an extensive number of job duties.

Line and Staff Organization. Another structure, called **line and staff,** includes staff departments, which provide special services to help line departments perform duties. Generally, staff functions include such things as personnel/human resources, accounting/finance, legal concerns, research and development, and purchasing. These departments help the firm take advantage of special services and are a source of information for supervisors. For example, a personnel/human relations department tests and screens job applicants so that supervisors need to interview only a few of them. Accounting/finance departments maintain records of budget allocations and expenditures. Figure 2.4 illustrates a typical line and staff structure. Notice that the personnel and purchasing departments do not have direct involvement in the production process but are accessible to the departmental supervisors.

Staff departments provide special services

Functional Organization. A firm can be organized according to functions performed by various work units. Such an arrangement is called **functional organization.** A key feature is specialization by jobs. In a large retail outlet, departments might be set up with separate supervisors for houseware, hardware, shoes, and clothing. Each supervisor knows his or her department well but most likely knows much less about the others. In Figure 2.5, each

Functional organization features specialized activities

Line and Staff Organization Chart   **Figure 2.4**

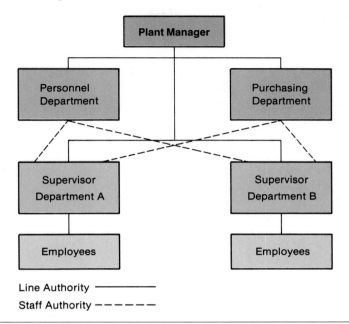

Line Authority ─────────
Staff Authority ─ ─ ─ ─ ─

Functional Organization Chart   **Figure 2.5**

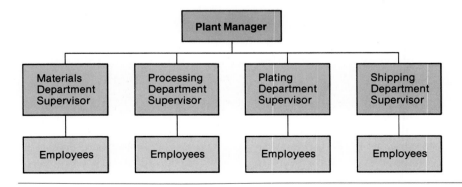

department is responsible for a specific aspect of production—materials, processing, plating, and shipping. Sometimes, supervisors view their own departments as independent entities and lose sight of relationships among departments and the firm itself.

Geographic Organization.   A method of organization used by firms having physically separated facilities or operations is called **geographic organization.** Such an arrangement is appropriate for a direct marketing firm with salespeople and customers who reside in widely dispersed geographic areas. Figure 2.6 illustrates an example of the geographic structure. The United States is divided into four regions, and the midwestern region shows how regions are further divided into groups of states managed by a district supervisor. In practice, additional subdivisions by cities, towns, or counties are possible.

Steps in Getting Organized

Effective organization means finding the most productive way to use resources. You must know what is to be achieved and also how people and equipment can be combined to get results. The importance of clear communication cannot be ignored. Otherwise, needless mistakes will occur, and subordinates will not understand their roles. The first task is to recognize

Figure 2.6   **Geographic Organization Chart**

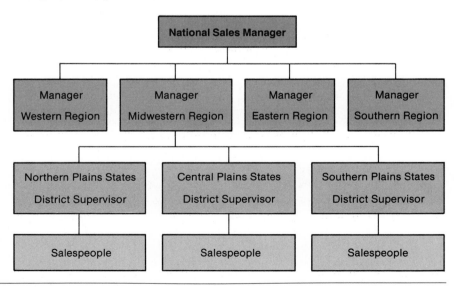

the goal. It should be carefully set, realistic, and observable. Progress toward a goal has to be measurable because you cannot judge effort if it is not measured.

Next, you must consider resources, including people, machines, and money. Questions need to be asked. Are there enough skilled workers? Do we have the right tools and materials? Is there enough money in the budget? If you have the resources, take the next step. If not, either ask for more or alert management to potential problems.

Are sufficient resources available?

The third step is to group activities and make assignments. This is the heart of organizing and requires careful thought. You should consider workers' abilities. Be sure groupings are realistic, for what looks good on paper may not be feasible. Clearly define responsibilities to maintain accountability. Logically arrange work tasks so that work duties can be performed successfully. Then, review your goals before taking any action.

How can activities be grouped?

Assigning responsibility to perform tasks and the authority to accomplish them is called **delegation.** This is an important concept because supervisors cannot do everything themselves. To get desired results and minimize complications, carefully choose activities that are assigned to others. Several guidelines are useful.[1] You can delegate tasks needing job skills the worker is expected to have or assign work an employee can handle well. You should not delegate your duty to plan, improve morale, or resolve conflicts. Also, it is not appropriate to assign any responsibility you are expected to perform personally or jobs no one is qualified to do.

Let's consider how to apply the principle of delegation. You have an unexpectedly heavy work load because several workers are absent, and your boss has directed you to complete a lengthy project. Appraisal forms for three people must be completed today, and a valued customer just called to complain that Jane Conrad, a new employee, was rude and discourteous. Also, next week's work schedule and the weekly summary report are due tomorrow. You might ask John Holloway, your most experienced and knowledgeable subordinate, to assist with preparation of the schedule and report. However, you should not delegate responsibility to do appraisals or investigate the complaint about Jane's performance. As supervisor, it is your responsibility to perform these tasks.

The final step involves following up to be sure that things are working as anticipated. You may want to alter groupings and assignments. Unexpected employment terminations, absenteeism, or revised scheduling might necessitate a reallocation of personnel. You may have to reorganize because of unanticipated developments. Perhaps, as a cost-cutting measure, management reduces the number of employees in your department. Should this occur, it is likely that work loads will have to be shifted, with at least some employees assuming new or different duties. Figure 2.7 illustrates the steps in organization.

Why is follow-up necessary?

Figure 2.7   **Steps in Organization**

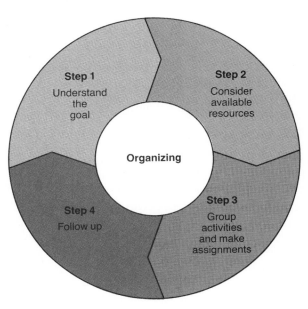

Step 1
Understand
the
goal

Step 2
Consider
available
resources

Organizing

Step 4
Follow up

Step 3
Group
activities
and make
assignments

Consider This

1. Well-developed plans are essential to successful first-line management. In planning for their work units, what is the major problem encountered by supervisors?

2. In practice, why do many supervisors fail to follow up and determine if plans are being implemented as expected?

3. What can be done to encourage supervisors to better organize their own work duties and those of subordinates?

Giving Directions

What is directing?

Directing is the process of instructing and guiding work activities of subordinates. It involves communicating and motivating to encourage desired employee performance. While leadership focuses on the way or style of doing things, directing concentrates on activities or the substance of what must be done.[2] In later chapters, we will examine the topics of motivation and leadership. For now, recognize that directing is a major supervisory function necessary to assure satisfactory completion of work activities.

Directives include requests, commands, suggestions, and invitations for volunteers.[3] While requests express a desire for something to be done, commands are more authoritative. Suggestions, which are least forceful, indicate a feeling or preference for a particular course of action. Finally, an invitation for volunteers solicits offers to participate. As supervisor, you need to be perceptive and select a directive that is appropriate for given individuals and situations. For example, some subordinates will not take hints, comply with suggestions, or volunteer their efforts unless a specific directive is issued. Others may respond eagerly and begin work at the mere mention of tasks needing to be completed. Emergency situations may arise where there is no alternative but to give commands and expect compliance.

Giving instructions is a primary supervisory responsibility. Workers must know what they are to do, how it must be done, and when to have assignments completed. They need to understand how to handle the complications and problems that inevitably arise. Before issuing orders, know what *you* want done and clearly word instructions to convey intentions. Sometimes managers issue conflicting directions or expect subordinates to read their minds. When this happens, confusion and mistakes are more likely to occur. After giving instructions, observe worker performance, ask questions to ascertain understanding, and encourage feedback. Frequently, misunderstandings can be corrected before they evolve into major problems.

All supervisors give directions

As noted previously, communication plays a significant role in the process of directing. To illustrate how a simple assignment can create an enormous problem, assume you are a supervisor on an assembly line producing window shutters. You tell a subordinate, "Pack the shutters in the boxes." To you, these instructions are perfectly clear. The worker is to place shutters of the same size into boxes and prepare them for shipment. However, the individual proceeds to pack whatever size shutters fit into available boxes and disregards their dimensions. Consequently, boxes contain shutters of various sizes. Unless you catch the mistake, when will the error be discovered? It likely will go undetected until a customer purchases the shutters in a retail store. What will happen? Without doubt, the customer will become upset and return the shutters, and in the future, the retailer may be unwilling to carry your firm's brand of shutters.

Strive to promote understanding

Do not force workers to guess at what they should do. They need clear, understandable directions. While helping them understand their duties, good directions reduce the risk of having to redo jobs. Clear directions also build confidence and promote feelings of security. They provide reasons why tasks must be performed in certain ways. Giving proper directions helps develop an atmosphere in which employees realize the importance of good work habits.

In addition to the wide range of organizations with different managerial philosophies, supervisors have varying background experiences and attitudes toward supervision. In giving directions, they practice various approaches. At the extreme, some supervisors are autocratic; they tell subordinates exactly what to do and expect unquestioned obedience. Others are democratic, allow workers to be involved, and give flexibility to perform assignments.

Think before issuing directions

Between these extremes, any variety of democratic-autocratic behaviors are possible. A specific approach depends on numerous factors, including pressure to meet deadlines, assessment of employee capabilities, and personal perspectives toward supervising. It is a myth to conclude that a democratic approach is always superior or that "democratic supervisors are nice and autocrats are obnoxious."[4] A review of the following guidelines is useful and can help determine the best method for giving directives.

☐ *The situation.* Strive to understand each situation, and you will better understand how much direction people are willing to take. Generally, they are more responsive to requests and suggestions than blunt commands. If you are respected and have earned their confidence, subordinates are more likely to cooperate and respond without hesitation. Whenever possible, remember to explain why a particular directive is necessary.

☐ *Types of job expertise.* Giving directions to a department of specialists with many years of experience is much different from giving them to a group of untrained, temporary workers. Persons who do not possess a high level of job competence, especially new workers, require more specific, detailed directives.

☐ *Individual differences.* People accept directions differently. While some workers are willing followers, others may resist and be frustrating to handle. Know your subordinates, be aware of personality differences, and anticipate likely reactions. With some, a direct, straightforward approach is essential. Others may respond better if their views are solicited as part of the direction-giving process.

☐ *Past practices.* People become accustomed to doing things in certain ways, and changes in routines can be disruptive. Therefore, think of past practices. Employees may be accustomed to receiving directions in a low-key, informal manner. If so, a new supervisor should recognize this.

The Control Function

The process of knowing how well actions conform to plans is **controlling.** It includes forming standards, measuring performance, and correcting deviations. No business can function without controls. They are essential to ensure that financial, equipment, and human resources are used to further an organization's best interests. Sometimes, controls are resisted because they are not understood. Therefore, the rationale for having controls needs to be communicated. For instance, some grocery store customers become rather rude when asked to produce two pieces of identification before paying by check. Therefore, it is important for checkers, who must deal directly with customers, to realize why such a control is absolutely essential.

There are many examples of controls. Among them are performance expectations, budgets, employee evaluations, absenteeism policies, required reports, and quality-control checks. Controls should be set and used wisely for providing feedback to supervisors. Assume you are a supervisor who has been given a budget of $1,200 to purchase this year's supplies. Four months have passed, and your budget shows a $400 balance. You know that spending will have to be reduced or else higher management must be persuaded to provide more money.

Standards

Standards are guidelines used to establish expectations for managers and workers to meet. In a manufacturing firm, the standard level of production for a machine operator might be six units per hour. A salesperson could have a quota of $30,000 sales per month. A college professor might be expected to attain an average of 2.5 on a five-point student evaluation rating scale. For some jobs, standards are set according to a minimum allowable number of errors or customer complaints. Standards are bases for comparisons, and to be of maximum value, they must be developed logically.

What are standards?

Standards can be set to recognize various levels of employee capabilities. For example, a novice data-entry worker is not expected to be as rapid or accurate as a veteran with five years of experience. Also, standards should not be established arbitrarily without awareness of relevant concerns that influence performance results. In setting sales quotas, several questions merit consideration. How much training and experience does the salesperson possess? To what extent are competitors entrenched in the sales territory? Do current economic conditions exert a positive or negative impact on potential sales? In general, standards are based on the following factors.

How are standards established?

☐ *Management expectations.* Management formulates standards to indicate acceptable levels of performance. Each supervisor administers standards related to his or her work unit. Ideally, higher management provides opportunities for feedback from first-line managers.

☐ *Past performance.* Records reveal whether standards are appropriate. Prior results show if standards need revision, and they serve to justify formal quota expectations.

☐ *Technological capabilities.* Recognition of machine and plant resource availability is necessary. Advances in computer and equipment technology increase a firm's productive capability. Accordingly, standards need to be adjusted.

☐ *Personnel capabilities.* Abilities the firm's employees possess are important. Performance potential is influenced by their level of experience, training, and job skills.

☐ *Market absorption.* Through their purchase decisions, consumers determine if products and services meet their criteria of acceptance. Therefore, the level of demand is a consideration.

☐ *Funds availability.* This factor recognizes present financial resources or the amount that can be borrowed. It is relevant because availability of financial resources affects every aspect of an organization's operations.

Measurement

The process to determine if standards are being met is **measurement.** Dollar volumes of sales, number of units produced in a given time, or amounts of funds spent are examples of measurements. The process makes it possible to compare performance outcomes with standards. Reporting procedures are needed to communicate what has actually happened. Take care to complete sales, production, expense, or other types of reports.

Good measurement has three characteristics

Good measurement requires accuracy, proper interpretation, and completeness. Do not be haphazard or hasty. Maintaining good records is a necessary part of your job. Relevant data are sometimes omitted simply because they are overlooked. Some firms require weekly or monthly departmental reports; others request them on a quarterly, semiannual, or annual basis. When preparing a report in December, it is very easy for you to forget an event that happened in August. Good records are great memory aids.

Taking Corrective Action

Why is monitoring necessary?

Work activities require constant monitoring to ensure that anticipated results occur. Resources (equipment, materials, and supplies), paperwork (memos and reports), product quality, job performance, and expenses must be controlled. If actual performance falls below standards, it cannot be ignored. Problems do not correct themselves and can cause further burdensome complications. If machines are programmed inaccurately, defective parts will be produced. Should the mistake go undetected, the difficulty will only get worse. Frequently, much time and effort are wasted because controls are not applied. To initiate corrections, effective communication is essential. It may be necessary to meet with employees and discuss performance. Perhaps additional training is needed to understand how equipment operates and to clarify work expectations.

Take corrective actions

How are corrective measures implemented? Upon learning of a problem, size up the situation and determine what has happened. Recognize why things have gotten out of control and whether the difficulty involves equipment malfunction or human error. Think before acting and recognize the complexity of the circumstance. Only then should you give instructions regarding your recommended course of action. Remember to practice positive human relations and avoid accusations you may regret later. When emotions run high, it becomes more difficult to apply remedies. Frequently, resentments evolve, cause frustrations, and further complicate opportunities for improvement. Whatever the circumstances, failure to take corrective actions shows poor supervision.

At times, controls seem quite negative because they are restrictive. It is human nature to resist compliance with many rules and regulations, especially if they are not understood. Time taken to communicate why controls exist is seldom wasted and increases the likelihood that employees will accept them. For example, as supervisor, you may well understand the rationale for setting budgets, production standards, and quotas. Without clearly formulated explanations, however, subordinates may consider them to be arbitrary. You must be consistent; apply controls uniformly without exceptions. Strive to avoid vagueness. Confusion and failure to accept standards are major obstacles to overcome in maintaining control over operations.

Consider This

1. How can supervisors become more proficient at giving directions to subordinates?
2. Why does the control function consume so much of a supervisor's time?
3. What is the relationship between standards and controls?

Looking Back

Knowledge of supervisory functions is a prelude to understanding the supervisor's role in the workplace. You have studied the nature of these functions and how they apply to your job. A review of chapter objectives will refresh what you have learned.

☐ **Understand the role of supervisory planning.** Planning is the starting point in building a foundation to achieve objectives. Besides determining goals, planning includes forming policies, procedures, and rules. It promotes awareness of job expectations, consideration of possible future events, and formulation of insights into alternative courses of action. The planning process consists of six steps: determine goals, examine the present situation, know limitations and available resources, develop the plan, put the plan into action, and follow up.

☐ **Explain the concept of organizing.** Organizing involves grouping tasks and assigning authority relationships. It involves having appropriate human and equipment resources available when needed and helps ensure that these resources are properly used to accomplish objectives. The principles of unity of command and span of control are closely associated with effective organization. Unity of command stresses that every worker report to a single boss. Span of control refers to the number of people that one person can manage effectively.

☐ **Differentiate among types of organizational structures.** An organization chart shows the structure for managing and chain of command. Different groupings are possible, including line, line and staff, functional, and geographic arrangements. While the line structure represents a direct chain of command from top to bottom, the line and staff configuration has staff departments to offer special services. In functional organizations, job activities are grouped according to the kind of duties performed. Geographic organization, as in direct marketing firms selling nationally, is used by firms having buildings or operations physically separated from one another.

☐ **Know how to give effective directions.** Directing is the process of instructing and guiding the work activities of subordinates. It involves communicating and motivating to encourage desired employee performance. Requests, commands, suggestions, and invitations for volunteers are examples of directives. When giving directions, it is necessary to consider these factors: the situation, types of job expertise, individual differences, and past practices.

☐ **Apply the control function to attain desired performance expectations.** Controlling is the process of knowing how well actions conform to plans. It includes forming standards, measuring performance, and correcting deviations. Standards are based on management expectations, past performance, technological capabilities, personnel capabilities, market absorption, and funds availability. Through measurement, it is possible to determine if standards are being met. Corrective actions enable supervisors to change deviations not conforming to desired performance expectations.

Key Terms

controlling	organizing
delegation	participative management
directing	planning
functional organization	policy
functions	procedure
geographic organization	rules
line and staff organization	span of control
line organization	standards
measurement	unity of command
organization chart	

Review and Discussion Questions

1. Which management function is most important? Why?
2. What steps are involved in planning? For each of these steps, give examples of concerns supervisors should recognize.
3. To organize effectively, what actions must supervisors consider?
4. Why should supervisors carefully consider the types of tasks they delegate?
5. How do supervisors benefit from giving their workers clear, understandable directions?
6. What factors can be used to set standards for operations?
7. Since controls are restrictive, how can supervisors increase the likelihood that workers will accept them?
8. Differentiate between the concepts *unity of command* and *span of control.*
9. What role does communication play in the process of giving directions?
10. How can supervisors determine the best method for giving directions?

Action Incident 2.1

The Supervisor's Lament

It is 8 A.M. You, a supervisor, have just arrived for work at the Hargrave Company, a downtown department store serving a regional clientele. The store opens at 8:30 A.M., and there are 15 employees in your department.

Upon arriving, you are confronted with the following events.

1. The elevator is not working.
2. One of your employees has fallen. The extent of injuries is not known.
3. Two employees just called and said they cannot come to work. One person was in an automobile wreck; the other is sick.
4. The electronic cash registers are not operating properly.
5. You thought that the monthly summary report was due next week and just noticed that it should be submitted tomorrow. It takes about two hours to complete.
6. The supervisors' weekly meeting has been scheduled for 11 A.M. It lasts 30 minutes.
7. Personnel informs you that interviews with three applicants for a job in your department are scheduled for 9, 9:30, and 10 A.M.
8. There was a robbery last night. You are requested to prepare a listing of any missing inventory by 1 P.M.
9. One of your employees arrived for work obviously drunk.
10. Your boss wants to see you at 1:30. You have no idea what's on his mind.

Discussion Questions

1. List your priorities for handling these events.
2. What is the justification/explanation for each of your rankings? To achieve realism, arrange the priorities over an eight-hour workday.

Action Incident 2.2

I'm a New Supervisor

John Collins, newly appointed office supervisor at Midland Specialty Company, has been thinking about the problems of the past few months. Many records seem to get misplaced. Customer statements are not sent promptly. Invoice payments are late. Employees are confused about who is responsible for what. John tries to help out and does as many things as possible himself.

Clara Smith, John's boss, recently asked him to make a list of immediate goals for the office unit. She also wants his opinion about a major change in company structure. John worries about meeting Clara's expectations. She is demanding, doesn't tolerate mistakes, and probably will reduce office personnel to save money. This bothers John because the unit is already understaffed, and he shudders to think about laying off subordinates.

John says to Carol Westfield, his secretary, "I guess I've been concentrating on the wrong things and haven't given enough thought to supervision." Carol responds, "What do you mean? The employees like and respect you." John replies, "I'm glad, but I'm uncomfortable with the way some things are going."

Discussion Questions

1. How well does John practice the functions of supervisory management?
2. What can he do to overcome the apparent problems in the office unit?
3. How can John alleviate his worries about meeting Clara's expectations?
4. Since subordinates like and respect him, will John succeed as a supervisor? Explain your response.

Action Incident 2.3

The Informed Newcomer

You supervise the milling department. Joe Granger, a new hire, has just arrived for his first day of work. The conversation is as follows:

You: Good morning, Joe. Welcome to our group. We're glad to have you join us.

Joe: I'm glad to be here and ready to get started.

You: Let me show you around.

Joe: Don't bother. I have no trouble meeting people, and I've had eight years of job experience. You don't have to do a thing.

You: Well, let me go over the company policies with you.

Joe: I've saved you the trouble. I have a copy of the policy manual. Besides, I have friends who work here, and they've told me everything I need to know.

Discussion Questions

1. What should you do in this situation?
2. If your response to Joe is "OK, you have really saved me some time; go ahead and get started," what might happen?

3. Is Joe's attitude and behavior typical of new employees?
4. What supervisory functions should you perform in this circumstance?

Notes

1. Lawrence L. Steinmetz and H. Ralph Todd, Jr., *First-Line Management: Approaching Supervision Effectively,* 3d ed. (Plano, Tex.: Business Publications, 1983), pp. 66–67.
2. Thomas O. Kirkpatrick, *Supervision: A Situational Approach* (Boston, Ma.: Kent Publishing, 1987), p. 185.
3. Joseph T. Straub, *Managing: An Introduction* (Boston, Ma.: Kent Publishing, 1984), pp. 367–369.
4. Jerry L. Gray, *Supervision: An Applied Behavioral Science Approach to Managing People* (Boston, Ma.: Kent Publishing, 1984), p. 87.

Suggested Readings

Drucker, Peter F. "The Coming of the New Organization." *Harvard Business Review* 66, January–February 1988, pp. 45–53.

Farrant, Alan. "Keep Your Subordinates." *Supervision* 49, April 1988, pp. 3–5.

Mamis, Robert A. "Details, Details." *Inc.* 10, March 1988, pp. 96–98.

McConkey, Dale D. "Planning in a Changing Environment." *Business Horizons* 31, September–October 1988, pp. 64–72.

Nelson, Andre, "A Supervisory Principle—Chain of Command." *Supervision* 49, May 1988, pp. 14–17.

Odiorne, George S. "Measuring the Unmeasurable: Setting Standards for Management Performance." *Business Horizons* 30, July–August 1987, pp. 69–75.

Phillips, Jack J. "Authority: It Doesn't Just Come With Your Job." *Management Solutions* 31, August 1986, pp. 35–37.

Reynolds, Helen, and Mary E. Tramel. "Organizing That Major Assignment." *Management Solutions* 33, September 1988, pp. 29–30.

Roman, Mark B. "Span of Control: The Manager's Zone of Power." *Success* 35, January–February 1988, pp. 50–51.

Tracey, William R. "Deft Delegation: Multiplying Your Effectiveness." *Personnel* 65, February 1988, pp. 36–38, 40–41.

Supervisors as Leaders

Learning Objectives

After reading and studying the material contained in this chapter, you should be able to:

1. Define leadership.
2. Explain the trait approach to leadership.
3. Explain the style of leadership approach to leadership.
4. Explain Fiedler's Contingency Model of Leadership Effectiveness.
5. Explain Situational Leadership Theory.
6. Identify factors to consider in choosing your own leadership style.
7. Identify communication skills needed for effective leadership.
8. Provide suggestions for effective leadership.

Leadership Defined

Specifically, **leadership** is the ability to influence the activities of others, through the process of communication, toward the attainment of a goal. As a supervisor, you are expected to influence the efforts of your workers to achieve goals, and it is through communication that you direct your workers. For example, you may have a great plan for achieving a goal, but if you can't communicate the plan to employees, they won't be able to implement it. Your ability to communicate with workers is crucial to your success as a leader.

The concept of leadership has been analyzed from many different viewpoints. As a result, three major leadership approaches have evolved: trait, style of leadership, and situational.

The Trait Approach

The **trait approach** to leadership tries to identify characteristics found in all successful leaders. During the early 1900s and into the 1950s, the personal characteristics of successful leaders were studied closely by researchers.[1] They thought that once they found the common traits of successful leaders, they could use those traits to identify individuals who would be good leaders. In essence, the trait approach grouped all successful leaders together without looking at the specific situation each faced.

Three problems, however, have continuously plagued this approach. First, just being in a leadership position often requires a person to behave differently in certain respects compared to subordinates. However, successful leadership is more complex than simply playing the role of a leader. Second, the trait approach fails to consider the nature of the leadership situation itself. In short, all such situations are considered alike, which is not the case in reality. A successful religious leader, for instance, clearly does not need exactly the same traits as a successful military officer. The situations and the measures of success are different from field to field. Third, not all successful leaders are alike. Some are tall, well educated, extroverted, patient, and people oriented. Others are short, poorly educated, introverted, impatient, and task oriented. Many successful leaders have such traits as self-confidence, enthusiasm, and courage. However, having these qualities does not guarantee that a person will necessarily be successful. Analyzing traits of successful leaders is interesting. However, no single personality trait or set of traits has been found that consistently differentiates leaders from nonleaders. Therefore, research-

ers began to look at leadership styles.

The Style of Leadership Approach

The **style of leadership approach** tries to identify the styles of successful leaders. Researchers focused on this approach in the 1950s and 1960s and identified three leadership styles: authoritarian, democratic, and laissez-faire.

Authoritarian

Leaders who are **authoritarian** keep power to themselves and insist on making most or all decisions. They decide what is to be done and how. Then they direct workers to implement their orders. Authoritarian leaders tend to remain aloof from their workers. They discourage upward communication and try to motivate workers through threats and punishment, while reserving praise for those workers they like.

Sometimes an authoritarian leadership style can get the job done. For example, a quality-control supervisor may have to insist on specific inspections and a standardized procedure. Certain levels of production or performance may be maintained by an authoritarian leadership style. Still, there are drawbacks to relying heavily on this approach. For example, over the long run, the authoritarian style often fosters a work force that shuns responsibility. Workers lack creativity and depend on the leader. A leader who uses the authoritarian approach can make and implement decisions quickly. However, that leader will usually have to engage in constant supervision to make sure the work is done according to instructions.

Authoritarian leaders often have to engage in constant supervision

Democratic

Under a **democratic** leadership style, the leader involves followers in the decision-making process. Specifically, the democratic leader informs subordinates of the organization's goals and the problems and constraints confronting them. Being open-minded, the leader respects the ability of the workers and, therefore, solicits their ideas for accomplishing goals. Help is offered when needed and, as a result, authority is decentralized and upward communication is encouraged. However, although authority and responsibility are shared, the democratic leader never gives up the right to manage and make the final decision.

Democratic leaders do not give up their right to make final decisions

In many settings, the democratic approach has proven very effective. For example, it works well in overseeing skilled engineers in high-technology companies. Highly educated, experienced, and motivated, these individuals do not require close supervision. They can make important contributions to the decision-making process, and as a result, they are likely to develop a commitment to the plans and strategies they have helped formulate. In turn, the subordinates develop increased capacity for accepting responsibility and demonstrating creativity. In such a situation, the leader, the followers, and the organization all benefit. In some cases, however, this style of leadership may impede progress. Some employees, for example, lack the interest, training, and experience needed to make a meaningful contribution to important decision-making discussions. They may view their jobs as uninteresting and prefer to be told what to do rather than seek decision-making responsibilities. The democratic style can also be very time-consuming for a manager and, therefore, may not always be useful.

Laissez-faire

Laissez-faire leaders do not get very involved

Under a **laissez-faire** style, the leader basically abdicates responsibility to lead. The laissez-faire leader does not know or care much about what goes on in the work unit. That leader will provide help when asked, but workers are expected to be self-sufficient. They must motivate themselves and acquire the training and information needed to make decisions. Unlike the authoritarian or democratic styles, under a laissez-faire style workers are expected to set and achieve goals without the leader's direction or help.

It has been suggested that a laissez-faire style is a good way for a leader to conduct brainstorming sessions with workers.[2] However, such a leader generally is not involved in the work unit's activities. As a result, serious problems can arise when a decline in performance or missed deadlines go unnoticed. Therefore, the laissez-faire style does not work in most leadership situations. There are, of course, blends of leadership behavior beyond the three leadership approaches just discussed. For example, Figure 3.1 shows

Figure 3.1　　　　**Continuum of Leadership Behavior**

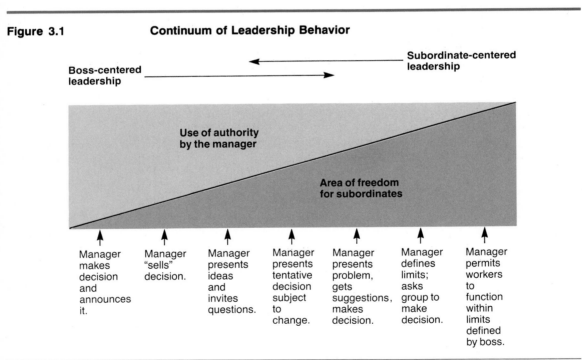

a continuum of leadership behavior. The boss-centered leadership behavior on the far left is typical of an authoritarian leader who maintains a high degree of control. Position power is used by the leader to dictate decisions that satisfy his or her own interests, opinions, and feelings. The main emphasis is on "getting the job done." In moving right, toward the subordinate-centered end of the continuum, that control is gradually released. As a result, increased attention is given to the interests, opinions, and feelings of the workers. The subordinate-centered behavior on the right side of the continuum is representative of a democratic leader.

Authoritarian leaders rely much on their position power

To include laissez-faire leader behavior, the continuum would have to go beyond subordinate-centered leader behavior. This was not done because a laissez-faire atmosphere really represents the absence of formal leadership.[3] Any leadership that does take place here can be classified as informal or emergent.[4] As an observant supervisor, you will naturally be aware of the characteristics and leadership styles of other supervisors. However, it is risky for you to simply hope that what works for others will work for you. You should carefully analyze the situation to identify a proper leadership style. Note the following characteristics of authoritarian, democratic, and laissez-faire leadership styles.

What works for one leader may not work for you

Characteristics of Leadership Styles

Authoritarian leaders

1. Keep power to themselves.
2. Insist on making most or all decisions.
3. Direct workers to implement their decisions through downward communication but discourage upward communication.
4. Attempt to motivate through threats and punishment.

Democratic leaders

1. Decentralize authority.
2. Involve workers in the decision-making process.
3. Encourage upward communication.
4. Allow workers freedom to work within constraints set for tasks.

Laissez-faire leaders

1. Abdicate their right to lead.
2. Provide little if any guidance or direction for workers.
3. Expect workers to set goals, motivate themselves, and acquire the training or information necessary to make decisions.
4. Do not know or care much about what goes on in the work unit.

Consider This

1. What do you think is your natural style of leadership? That is, do you tend to feel more comfortable using a democratic or an authoritarian style?
2. What trait or characteristic do you have that you think would help you lead others as a supervisor?

The Situational Approach

The **situational approach** to leadership requires a leader to analyze the situation to determine the right leadership style. Since the late 1960s, researchers have focused on ways to do this. They have looked into such things as leader-follower relations, the leader's position power, the nature of the workers, and the type of work being done.

Fred Fiedler was one of the first leadership researchers to develop a situational theory of leadership. The leadership model Fiedler and his associates created is known as the **Contingency Model of Leadership Effectiveness.** It presupposes that leaders face different situations when attempting to influence others. Therefore, a major assumption of the model is that the most effective leadership strategy varies depending on the situation. As a result, Fiedler's leadership model is viewed as a contingency approach. Specifically, the model states that a leader's success in leading a group is contingent upon the degree of task or relationship motivation of the leader and the extent to which the leader has situational control and influence.[5]

Motivational Structure of the Leader

Fiedler's model asks leaders to think of their least preferred co-worker

The leader's motivational structure is measured by asking the individual to think of all the co-workers he or she has ever known and to then identify the one person with whom it has been most difficult to work. Fiedler refers to this person as the least preferred co-worker (LPC). Next, the leader is asked to describe the LPC according to 18 bipolar items using a semantic differential format. For example, two of the 18 bipolar items are shown below.[6]

Pleasant	$:\_:\_:\_:\_:\_:\_:\_:$	**Unpleasant**
	1 2 3 4 5 6 7 8	
Friendly	$:\_:\_:\_:\_:\_:\_:\_:$	**Unfriendly**
	1 2 3 4 5 6 7 8	

A leader whose ratings of the LPC are low (less than 57) is considered to be task motivated. That is, the leader is viewed as being primarily production oriented. In contrast, a leader whose ratings of the LPC are high (above 62)

is considered to be a relationship-motivated individual. In other words, he or she is primarily people oriented and generally interested in establishing good relations with employees.[7] It is important to note that LPC scores by themselves do not generally predict leader behavior. Apparently, they are more a reflection of the leader's attitude toward work relationships.[8]

LPC scores tend to reflect a leader's attitude toward work relationships

Situational Control

Beyond identifying the motivational structure of the leader, the Contingency Model also examines the degree to which the work situation provides the leader with control and influence. The three factors affecting situational control, in order of importance, are:

1. *Leader-member relations.* In general, **leader-member relations** refers to the degree to which the leader has the support and loyalty of group members. To measure this dimension, a leader is asked to estimate leader-member relations with his or her own group as well as between subordinate managers and their groups. Two items from a scale to measure leader-member relations are shown below.[9] When a leader has a good relationship with group members, he or she likely has the support and loyalty of the members and can depend on them. On the other hand, poor leader-member relations hinder a leader's ability to influence subordinates.

2. *Task structure.* Interestingly, the task itself can be a factor in determining how much control and influence a leader has. For example, suppose a leader instructs a work group to devise a company slogan. Such a task is considered to be unstructured. That is, the leader cannot tell the group members exactly how to create a slogan, and it would be difficult to dictate the group's decision or predict the acceptability of their decision. However, structured tasks which operate according to a blueprint of detailed operating instructions allow the leader to exert more control and influence. With a structured task, subordinates realize that, whether they like it or not, a set procedure is required to complete the task. The

Structured tasks usually allow leaders to exert much control

	Strongly Agree	Agree	Neither Agree nor Disagree	Disagree	Strongly Disagree
The people I supervise have trouble getting along with each other.	1	2	3	4	5
There is friction between my subordinates and myself.	1	2	3	4	5

step-by-step procedures associated with structured tasks make it easier for the leader to dictate what is to be done and to predict the outcome of the group's work.

3. *Position power.* Specifically, **position power** is the formal authority an organization gives a leader to make decisions and to give orders to subordinates. Supervisors with a lot of position power are given much responsibility and are allowed to make important decisions. They also can assign work to subordinates and reward or punish individuals based on their performance. Leaders in volunteer organizations generally have weak position power, whereas supervisors and military officers usually have strong position power.[10]

Being promoted to supervisor gives you more position power

When leaders have good relations with subordinates, a structured task, and strong position power, their situational control is considered to be high. An example would be a popular supervisor who is placed in charge of an assembly line by the plant manager of a manufacturing company. On the other hand, when leaders have poor relations with subordinates, an unstructured task, and weak position power, their situational control is viewed as being low. A likely candidate is a disliked president of a volunteer, church-related, adult singles' group who is trying to get agreement on activities the group should sponsor and finance.

Conditions for Effective Leadership

As mentioned earlier, leaders can be characterized as being either task motivated or relationship motivated. Both types of leaders face situations in which leader-member relations, task structure, and leader position power vary. The natural question that arises at this point is, "Which leadership orientation is the best?" The answer, according to Fiedler's Contingency Model is, "It depends." Fiedler's research shows that both task and relationship-motivated leaders perform well under some conditions and poorly under others. Specifically, as shown in Figure 3.2, task-motivated leaders (low LPC) generally perform best when their situational control is either high or relatively low, whereas the relationship-motivated leaders (high LPC) perform best when they experience moderate situational control.

Different leaders perform well under different conditions

In short, the above findings can be explained as follows. When conditions of situational control are favorable to leaders, they can get away with a task orientation because their subordinates are ready to be influenced. Conversely, when conditions of situational control are unfavorable to leaders, a task orientation may be the only way to get anything accomplished. However, under conditions of moderate situational control, a relationship orientation seems to help make the best of a situation that is difficult for the leader but not impossibly bad.[11] The fact that leaders of different orientation perform well under some conditions and poorly under others implies, according to Fiedler, that it is inappropriate to think that there is one best leadership style.

How the Effectiveness of Two Leadership Styles Varies with the Situation   **Figure 3.2**

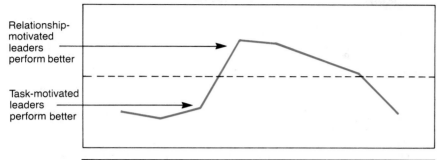

Leader-member relations	Good	Good	Good	Good	Poor	Poor	Poor	Poor
Task structure	Structured		Unstructured		Structured		Unstructured	
Leader position power	Strong	Weak	Strong	Weak	Strong	Weak	Strong	Weak

Source: Fred E. Fiedler and Martin M. Chemers, *Leadership and Effective Management.* Glenview, Ill.: Scott, Foresman, 1974, p. 80. Adaptation of an exhibit from "Engineer the Job to Fit the Manager" by Fred E. Fiedler, *Harvard Business Review,* September–October 1965. Copyright © 1965 by the President and Fellows of Harvard College.

Instead, a leader who always uses the same leadership approach may be effective in one situation but not in another. Leader effectiveness, according to the Contingency Model, depends on the proper match between leader motivational structure and situational control.

Although useful, Fiedler's model has been criticized because it suggests that there are only two basic leadership styles—task oriented and relationship oriented. Critics argue that, especially in terms of behavior, a leader who demonstrates high task behavior is not necessarily high or low on relationship behavior. Some claim that a combination of the two dimensions may occur.[12]

Another situational approach to leadership is **Situational Leadership Theory** developed by Paul Hersey and Kenneth Blanchard.[13] This theory requires a leader to analyze the **task-relevant maturity** of workers to find the right leadership style. The workers' level of maturity is found by evaluating them on the following:

The nature of your followers can influence what leadership style you select

☐ What is the workers' level of *achievement-motivation?* This refers to their willingness to set high but attainable goals and their concern for doing a good job regardless of rewards.
☐ How *willing* are workers to accept responsibility on the job?
☐ How much *ability* do workers have to accept responsibility?
☐ How much task-relevant *education* and/or *experience* do workers have?[14]

Once the workers' level of maturity has been determined, you must
consider the different leadership styles available. According to Situational
Leadership Theory, your leadership style includes both "task behavior" and
"relationship behavior."

Task Behavior. The leader's efforts to set well-defined patterns of organization, channels of communication, and work procedures constitutes **task
behavior.**[15] In other words, you tell the workers what task to do and when,
where, and how to do it.[16]

Relationship Behavior.   The other aspect, **relationship behavior,** refers to
the leader's efforts to develop rapport, trust, friendship, and open communication with workers.[17] When you tell your workers they are doing a good
job, show confidence in them, and offer them more responsibility, you
practice relationship behavior.

Four Leadership Styles of Situational Leadership Theory

According to Situational Leadership Theory, leaders engage in either high or
low levels of task and relationship behavior. Therefore, four different
leadership styles are possible.[18]

High Task and Low Relationship Behavior. This style is referred to as
telling because the leader defines roles and tells workers how to do
everything. Here, one-way, downward communication dominates. This
leadership style is different from an authoritarian one because it displays
more relationship behavior than an authoritarian style does.

High Task and High Relationship Behavior. This form of leadership is
called the *selling* style and involves much two-way communication between
leader and workers. The leader still provides most of the direction. However,
the maturity of the workers is such that the leader feels they will perform best
if they understand the reasons for certain decisions. To gain cooperation, the
leader sells the workers on what has to be done.

Low Task and High Relationship Behavior. In this style, called *participating,* leader and followers share in decision making. Here, workers have the
ability to help the leader make task-related decisions. This encourages
two-way communication.

Low Task and Low Relationship Behavior. This style is called *delegating*
because the leader delegates much decision-making responsibility to
workers. Although similar to the democratic, the delegating style shows
slightly more concern for the task and less for relationship behavior. The
delegating leader does not have to devote much time to supervising the

workers because they can run their own show. This style is different from laissez-faire because it displays more task and relationship behavior.

After determining the workers' maturity level, you simply draw a straight line up from the appropriate point on the continuum. The point at which that line crosses the curved line on the Situational Leadership Model shows the proper leadership style. For example, as the dotted line in Figure 3.3 shows, the model suggests that you engage in both high task and low relationship behavior in leading low-maturity workers. For workers who are below average in maturity, a high task and high relationship leadership style would be best. With those of above-average maturity, a low task and high relationship style would suit. Last, in dealing with followers who have a high level of maturity, you should use a low task and low relationship leadership style, according to the model.

Workers' maturity level helps determine the appropriate leadership style

The following example illustrates how Situational Leadership Theory can be applied to a leadership situation. Suppose you must supervise the work of a group of apprentice carpenters. The apprentice carpenters in this example are individuals who do not know how to do skilled car-

Situational Leadership Model for Determining Appropriate Leadership Style

Figure 3.3

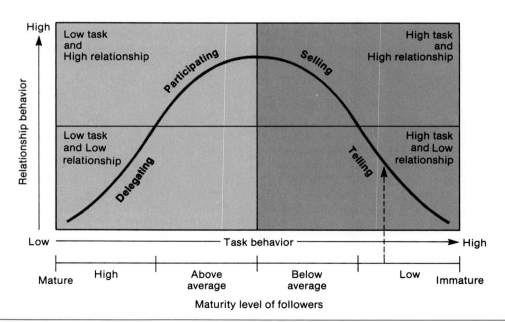

Source: Paul Hersey and Kenneth H. Blanchard, *Management of Organizational Behavior: Utilizing Human Resources,* 4th ed., © 1982, p. 200. Adapted by permission of Prentice-Hall, Inc. Englewood Cliffs, N.J.

pentry work but want to learn the carpentry trade. The nature of the apprentice carpenters' situation is such that it is probably appropriate for you to evaluate or classify them as having an above-average degree of *achievement motivation.* That is, the apprentice carpenters probably set generally high but obtainable goals on the job. Also, they likely are more interested in how well they do their work as apprentice carpenters than in how much they are being paid while serving as apprentices. The reason it would be inappropriate to classify them as being high in achievement motivation is that there are areas of a carpenter's job about which they are naive. Some of them will not be so excited about a career in the carpentry trade as they learn more about it. This phenomenon is common to most career areas.

Next, you must evaluate the apprentice carpenters' *willingness* to accept the responsibility for doing carpentry work. Since they are just starting their apprenticeship, there are many carpentry tasks that they realize they do not yet know how to perform. Therefore, their willingness to accept responsibility for performing many of these tasks is currently below average. The apprentice carpenters' *ability* to accept responsibility for performing carpentry tasks must be analyzed next. Even if these individuals were very willing to attempt many carpentry tasks, their ability to do so is probably below average. That is, they may be able to do some nailing and sawing, but they certainly are not skilled carpenters at this point. Last, what level of *education* and/or *experience* do the apprentice carpenters have concerning carpentry in general? In this case, the level is low.

Having made the above evaluations, it is necessary to average or collapse the evaluations so that one overall level of worker maturity can be determined. For the apprentice carpenters, the evaluations made earlier indicate that it is probably appropriate to classify them as being below average in task-relevant maturity. As a result, according to Situational Leadership Theory, it would be best for you to use a high task and high relationship behavior style of leadership.

Needless to say, Situational Leadership Theory and leadership theories in general are not scientifically precise in nature. For example, some may argue that people going into an apprentice carpentry program have a somewhat higher level of task-relevant education and/or experience in carpentry than indicated in the earlier analysis. However, this change in the analysis would probably still produce an overall indication that the apprentice carpenters have a below-average level of task-relevant maturity. As a result, the leadership style recommended by the theory would remain the same.

Factors to Consider in Choosing a Leadership Style

The task of leading others on the job has never been easy. However, you will enhance your success as a leader if you consider the following factors when choosing a leadership style.

Look at the Job Itself

Jobs vary in organizations, and the leadership style that seems appropriate for one may be inappropriate for another. Look, for example, at whether a particular job is routine or nonroutine. Routine jobs generally require that the work be performed in a specific way. Employees on an assembly line, for instance, have little choice about how their work is to be done. Therefore, you must tell the workers exactly what to do and then make sure the directions are followed. Workers can make suggestions for improving the process, but modifications in procedure must be approved before routine jobs can be changed.

Different types of jobs may require different types of leadership styles

Nonroutine jobs, on the other hand, cannot be easily structured. By their very nature, they require workers to adapt to changing situations. Imagine you must supervise counselors at a mental health center. Patients who come to the health center will have problems that vary as to type and severity. You would not want to structure the counselors' jobs so that every patient received the same treatment. Instead, you should delegate responsibility and authority to the counselors to deal properly with different situations.

Adjust to Special Circumstances

Things do not always go as expected on the job, especially for supervisors. Sometimes, special circumstances develop and temporarily take priority over other aspects of a leadership situation. A crisis on the job, for example, will require your full attention. As another example, you may learn unexpectedly that the deadline for completing a project has been moved up considerably. In this new situation, you lack the time for engaging in much relationship behavior or for discussing what needs to be done. As a result, you must quickly make the necessary decisions and direct their implementation.

You need to adjust your leadership style to special circumstances

Consider the Workers

Workers are not all alike. As explained in the discussion of Situational Leadership Theory, workers vary in their levels of task-relevant maturity. Therefore, unless the nature of the job or special circumstances prevent it, you should adopt a leadership style that fits your workers' maturity level. If their maturity level is high, you will not have to supervise closely. Instead, it is appropriate to delegate a great deal of responsibility to such workers and include them in decision-making discussions. After all, they know how to do their jobs well without much direction from you. However, more caution must be exercised in leading workers of low task-relevant maturity. These employees may lack the motivation, knowledge, and skills necessary to perform all aspects of their job without guidance. Therefore, they may need to be supervised closely; you will need to tell them what to do and monitor their performance to make sure the work gets done.

Consider Your Natural Leadership Style

Not everyone prefers to use the same leadership style

What kind of leadership style are you most comfortable with? Your answer to this question represents your natural leadership style. If your natural style is proper for a particular situation, everything is fine. However, when it is clearly wrong for a situation, you will run into problems if you insist on using it anyway. If possible, choose jobs or leadership situations that fit your natural leadership style. When your natural leadership style is not appropriate, accept this fact and select a style that does fit the situation.

Respond to Orders from Your Boss

Orders from your boss can influence the type of leadership style you select. In a large company, the president ordered participative decision making at all levels. This required supervisors to consider their workers' comments in making decisions. The president's order forced some supervisors to change their leadership styles. In a different company, a supervisor was ordered to make a recommendation concerning a problem facing her department without discussing the situation with her subordinates. Although this was not her natural style, her boss feared that the confidentiality of some information would be jeopardized in an open discussion.

Examine Organizational Norms

Supervisors must consider the norms of their organizations

Organizations have both written and unwritten policies that govern the behavior of members. Over time these expectations come to be recognized as the norms of acceptable behavior for all employees. Even the reward structure encourages and discourages the manner in which employees use their time on the job. It is a fact of life that supervisors must take these organizational norms of behavior into account when attempting to lead subordinates. For example, the manner in which duties are assigned and the pace and size of work loads may be governed by such norms. Of course, changes can be made in expectations despite existing norms. However, supervisors must realize that there may be barriers to overcome in making such changes.

▼

Consider This

1. Think of an occasion in which your supervisor had to adjust to a special circumstance that developed on the job. How would you have handled the situation and why?
2. Leaders often believe that it is inappropriate to give important responsibilities to inexperienced workers, yet these workers have to get the experience of handling important responsibilities somehow. How would you handle this situation as a supervisor?

Communication Skills for Effective Leadership

Good communication skills and effective leadership are closely intertwined. As a result, supervisors find that their ability to be good leaders is enhanced by practicing the following communication skills.

State Instructions Clearly. To act on your instructions, workers must correctly understand what you want. If they misunderstand because your instructions are vague or confusing, problems will naturally arise. As an example, suppose you instruct your workers to tell you when their supplies run low. They may wait until they are almost out before informing you. "Low" may mean a gross to you and a dozen to workers who do not understand how much time is necessary to restock. *If miscommunication of a key word or concept in your message could cause major problems, make a special effort to clarify your meaning.*

Anticipate what parts of your messages may cause communication problems

Avoid Confusing Jargon. Supervisors in most companies are familiar with and often use jargon that is unique to their specialized work. Your vocabulary and use of jargon as a supervisor may impress new workers. However, they may not understand what you are saying, and communication problems increase when confused workers fail to ask questions for fear of appearing ignorant. If you must use jargon when discussing work procedures, make sure workers are familiar with your terms. This caution is especially important with new employees.

Jargon can cause confusion on the job

Be Careful in Making Assumptions. An **assumption** is a thought or statement accepted or considered true without proof. When dealing with workers, assumptions you make can cause communication problems. *Assumptions critical to a discussion should be identified and clarified.* You can do this by simply pointing out assumptions: "I assume you will use the paint sprayer." If your assumption is incorrect, the worker will tell you at that point. "No, this has to be done by hand because . . ."

Be Aware of Your Paralanguage. Paralanguage, which will be discussed further in Chapter 9, refers to the fact that the way something is said can influence how it is interpreted. Workers are sensitive not only to what you say but to how you say it. For example, you might say to a worker, "I need to talk to you about the work you just finished." If you use a normally pitched, pleasant tone of voice, the worker will not feel anxious. However, if you make the same statement in a loud, tense voice, the worker may think you disapprove of the finished work.

Watch what you say and how you say it

Encourage Questions from Workers. New workers can become confused by certain procedures or things you say, but they may be reluctant to ask questions. You must encourage workers to speak up whenever they feel they do not understand you. If your attitude convinces workers that you are sincere in wanting them to ask questions, they will be more likely to do so. Such feedback helps avoid communication problems that would otherwise go unchecked. Being approachable as a supervisor is not a sign of weakness. Being arrogant or aloof is not a sign of strength.

Explain Reasons for Rules and Policies. As a supervisor, you will be called on to set rules and policies. It is easy to inform workers of rules, but gaining complete compliance is another matter. For example, if you instruct grinding-wheel operators to wear safety goggles, all operators might not follow your instructions. Some might find the goggles to be uncomfortable, and they may decide that it would be all right not to wear them. However, if you explain that the rule is an OSHA requirement, established because a grinding wheel can fly apart and *blind* an unprotected operator, compliance will be much greater.

Don't expect workers to automatically understand the importance of all rules

Practice the Tentative Approach. When important issues are being discussed on the job, different points of view typically exist. The productivity of these discussions often depends on whether a cooperative or confrontational stance is taken by the discussants. To avoid unproductive clashes, the tentative approach calls for you to begin suggestions with tentative words or phrases.[19] Typical examples of these are *could it be, possibly,* and *perhaps.* It is especially appropriate to use this approach when you are discussing with motivated, capable workers how a certain problem might be solved. In the discussion, rather than saying, "I think we should make these changes," you should say, "*Perhaps* we should make these changes." The tentative approach creates a climate especially good for the free exchange of potentially beneficial ideas.

The tentative approach promotes open discussion

Encourage Workers to Notify You if a Problem Develops. In ancient times, messengers bringing bad news were often killed, simply because the news was bad. Your workers will hesitate to bring you bad news if they fear you will take your displeasure out on them. To counteract this possibility, encourage workers to inform you if a problem arises. Explain that problems only get worse if they are ignored and that you need to know when they develop. You must also practice what you preach. When a worker does notify you of a problem, do not take your displeasure about the problem out on the worker.

Keep Workers Informed. Studies consistently show that supervisors are considered by their subordinates to be the preferred source of work-related information. Do not let your workers down by withholding important information from them. Doing so can affect their job performance, and it can cause the rumor mill to speed up. Also, be quick in disseminating news to workers; information arriving too late may be worthless.

Let workers know how they are doing

Suggestions for Effective Leadership

You have seen that different leadership styles fit different situations. However, to be effective, an appropriate style must be backed up by sound leadership principles. The following suggestions will help you with this.

Be a Good Communicator. Your workers cannot read your mind. They must rely on your verbal and nonverbal messages to determine what you mean. Use familiar words, be specific, and give examples when appropriate. Also, be a good listener when employees bring information or ask questions.

Set a Good Example. Whether supervisors realize it or not, they often lead by example. You can't escape this fact by saying, "Do as I say, not as I do." Supervisors' actions are observed by their subordinates. Similarly, your behavior will set standards for your followers. For example, if you take pride in your work, they will feel an obligation to take pride in theirs.

> Supervisors need to set good examples on the job

Provide Workers with Feedback. Workers desire feedback on how they are doing, and it is your responsibility to provide it. Acknowledge good performance. Identify unsatisfactory performance early and correct it.

Be Fair and Consistent. Subordinates respect supervisors who insist that rules be followed by everyone and enforce the rules without showing favoritism. Also, the morale and commitment of employees are enhanced when they sense that work assignments are distributed in an equitable manner. Employees realize that when special circumstances or problems arise, a manager may have to make difficult decisions that will not please everyone. However, as a supervisor, it is important for you to appear reasonable and show understanding when making such decisions.

> Workers will likely support decisions that seem fair and consistent

Show Consideration for Your Workers. If you treat your workers with respect and loyalty, you enhance their morale and productivity. Remember, you are the link between your workers and higher-level management; make sure that workers' concerns and ideas are made known to your boss.

Set Realistic But Challenging Goals. You are expected to set goals. Be realistic about what your workers are capable of doing. Goals that are too difficult bring failure. Goals that are too easy fail to stimulate workers. You must set realistic but challenging goals for them.

> Give careful thought to the goals you set as supervisor

Motivate Your Workers. Whether you call it persuasion, contagious enthusiasm, or offering incentives, your workers will perform best when they are motivated to achieve a goal. You must understand workers' needs and interests and choose forms of motivation that will have a positive influence on them.

Follow Up.   Once you give an order or make an assignment, you have a responsibility to check periodically on how the work is progressing. You do not have to peer constantly over workers' shoulders, but you do need to make sure deadlines are met and everything goes smoothly.

Take Time to Make Sound Decisions.   Rushed decisions often turn out to be poor decisions. Take the time to analyze the facts before committing your work group to a goal that requires great effort. You are responsible for making sound decisions based on careful analysis.

Looking Back

You have studied the concepts of leadership and communication skills that will enhance your ability to lead effectively. Now briefly review the chapter objectives, restated below.

- ☐ **Define leadership.** Leadership is the ability to influence the activities of others, through the process of communication, toward the attainment of a goal.
- ☐ **Explain the trait approach to leadership.** The trait approach to leadership tries to identify characteristics found in all successful leaders. Three problems plague this approach. First, just being in a leadership position often requires a person to behave differently in certain respects than subordinates. However, successful leadership is more complex than simply playing the role of a leader. Second, not all leadership situations are alike. Third, not all successful leaders are alike. As a result, no single personality trait or set of traits has been identified that consistently distinguishes leaders from nonleaders.
- ☐ **Explain the style of leadership approach to leadership.** The style of leadership approach tries to identify the styles of successful leaders. Researchers have identified three leadership styles: authoritarian, democratic, and laissez-faire. Authoritarian leaders keep power to themselves and insist on making most or all of the decisions. Democratic leaders involve followers in the decision-making process. Laissez-faire leaders basically abdicate their responsibility to lead.
- ☐ **Explain Fiedler's Contingency Model of Leadership Effectiveness.** Fiedler's leadership model assumes that the most effective leadership strategy varies, depending on the situation. Specifically, the model states that a leader's success in leading a group is contingent upon the degree of task or relationship motivation of the leader and the extent to which the leader has situational control and influence.
- ☐ **Explain Situational Leadership Theory.** This theory requires a leader to analyze the maturity of workers to find the right leadership style. After doing so, the leader selects the appropriate leadership style from four options.

☐ **Identify factors to consider in choosing your own leadership style.** Look at the job itself and adjust to special circumstances. You should also consider the workers you will lead and your natural leadership style. In addition, you need to respond to orders from your boss and examine organizational norms.

☐ **Identify communication skills needed for effective leadership.** You should provide clearly stated instructions, avoid confusing jargon, be careful in making assumptions, and watch your paralanguage. In addition, encourage workers to ask questions if they are confused, explain the reasons for rules, and practice the tentative approach when appropriate. Finally, encourage workers to tell you if a problem develops and make a special effort to keep them informed.

☐ **Provide suggestions for effective leadership.** As a supervisor and leader, you have a responsibility to be a good communicator and to set a good example for your workers. In addition, the workers need feedback from you as to how they are doing. Be fair and consistent, show consideration for your workers, and set realistic but challenging goals. Motivate your workers, follow up on work to be completed, and take time to make sound decisions.

Key Terms

assumption

authoritarian

contingency model of leadership effectiveness

democratic

laissez-faire

leader-member relations

leadership

position power

relationship behavior

situational approach

situational leadership theory

style of leadership approach

task behavior

task-relevant maturity

trait approach

Review and Discussion Questions

1. What are three major problems with the trait approach to leadership?
2. What are the differences between authoritarian and democratic leaders?
3. Why might a laissez-faire leadership style be a good way for a supervisor to conduct a brainstorming session with subordinates?

4. How can you explain the fact that Fiedler found that task-motivated leaders generally perform best when their situational control is either high or relatively low?

5. How, according to Situational Leadership Theory, is a worker's task-relevant maturity determined?

6. What do you think is your natural leadership style? What difficulties might you face if you accepted a job that required you to adopt a different style?

7. Think of an instance in which you observed a communication problem on the job between a supervisor and an employee. Which of the communication skills discussed in the chapter were violated in this instance?

8. When giving instructions to others on the job, what general rule is appropriate for you to use in deciding whether you should clarify any part of your message?

9. As a supervisor, why is it important for you to set a good example for your subordinates to follow?

Action Incident 3.1

The Transferred Supervisor

Jim Hunt started the Precision Plastics Manufacturing Company 25 years ago to produce small, precision, plastic items. These include plastic parts for such products as medical instruments, airplanes, and photography equipment. Few companies compete in this market because of the difficulties in designing molds to produce small, intricate plastic parts. However, Precision's tool-and-die makers have developed an excellent reputation for designing plastic molds and producing high-quality plastic items.

All projects originate in Jim's office. A client contacts him regarding the production of a plastic part. He designs and draws the blueprints for the mold. Next, the blueprints go to Joe Casey, the supervisor in charge of the tool-and-die workers. Joe then supervises the making of the mold.

The tool-and-die workers are highly trained and experienced in making high-quality molds. They take a great deal of pride in their work, for which they are well paid. Since no two molds are ever alike, the tool-and-die workers feel they are custom craftsmen. The emphasis is on quality, and Joe gives workers the time and responsibility to do a good job. They enjoy their work and often comment that it is sad that young people are not taking up the trade the way they used to.

Once a mold is completed, it is transferred to Bill Smith for installation in a molding machine. Bill supervises the molding machine workers. It is his job to make sure they operate the machines safely and efficiently. Operating them is a routine job, requires little skill, and does not pay well.

The turnover rate among molding-machine workers is high, and Bill always has trouble getting workers to follow safety procedures. He feels he can't trust them with much responsibility, so he spends much time overseeing their work and making sure they follow orders. According to Bill, the workers show little interest in their job or loyalty to the company. This displeases him, so he spends little time trying to develop rapport with his workers.

Bill believes most workers need close supervision, which is fine with him because he enjoys being that type of supervisor. Due to his close supervision, production stays high, problems are dealt with quickly, and production usually remains on schedule. As a result, Jim regards Bill as an excellent supervisor.

One day, Joe was seriously injured in an automobile accident, and it appeared unlikely that he would ever return to work. As a result, Jim assigned Bill to supervise the tool-and-die workers. Bill moved quickly to establish new rules and policies for them to follow.

As was his custom, Bill began to closely supervise these workers and look for ways to speed up the production of molds. He noticed that each worker had a slightly different approach to making molds. Therefore, he sought to identify strengths in the different approaches in hopes of standardizing the process.

Soon after Bill assumed Joe's job, the following conversation took place between Jeff Wood, a senior tool-and-die worker, and Jim.

Jeff: Something has to be done about Bill Smith.

Jim: What's wrong with Bill?

Jeff: We can't get any work done because he's always trying to tell us how to do our job.

Jim: Well, he's the supervisor, and I must say, he had a very good record in the production department.

Jeff: Jim, I speak for all the tool-and-die workers when I say he's not a good supervisor.

Discussion Questions

1. At what level of maturity did Bill Smith apparently rate the molding-machine workers? Explain whether you agree or disagree with his assessment.

2. With what type of leadership style does Bill Smith seem to feel most comfortable? Does he seem to have the flexibility to change leadership styles?

3. What leadership style should Bill Smith use in supervising the tool and die workers? Why?
4. Jim Hunt says Bill Smith is a good supervisor. Explain why you either agree or disagree with Jim Hunt's assessment of Bill.

Action Incident 3.2

Drop the Fries

At a fast-food restaurant, frozen french fries are placed in a metal strainer basket directly above a basin of hot grease. When the supply of french fries at the serving counter runs low, the supervisor yells, "Drop the fries!" The employee nearest the french-fry machine then lowers the basket of frozen fries into the hot grease. Soon a new order of french fries will be ready. One morning a new employee standing next to the french-fry machine heard the supervisor yell, "Drop the fries!"

Discussion Questions

1. When the new employee heard the supervisor yell, "Drop the fries!" he did the wrong thing. What do you think the new employee did?
2. Which communication skills did the supervisor fail to use in this incident?
3. What should the supervisor have done to reduce the chances that the new employee would experience communication problems on the job?

Action Incident 3.3

Commander or Supervisor?

About a year ago, Greg Ryan retired from the military. For the last few months, he has held the position of supervisor for an electronic manufacturer, where he supervises employees in a data processing department. Although Greg is sufficiently knowledgeable about computers and data processing duties to perform the technical aspects of the job, he has very little supervisory experience in private industry. However, he thinks he knows what good leadership is all about. "It's very simple," he says. "Leaders give orders and workers follow them." Greg is good at giving orders, but he can't figure out why his work unit has the worst performance record in the company. The employees are well qualified to do their work, and they earn salaries that are equal to or higher than employees doing similar work at other companies in the area. As a result, Greg believes the reason the employees' performance is so poor is that they have a bad attitude. He also thinks they are lazy. Greg doesn't see any other explanation for the situation.

A good leader, according to Greg, is aggressive, domineering, task oriented, and independent. Having served in the military, Greg's idea of leadership is built on the characteristics of certain commanders he admires and respects. In essence, he admires their traits and wants to model his leadership style after their approach. However, what bothers Greg is that the leadership style that worked for them doesn't seem to work for him.

Greg has noticed that other supervisors have improved the productivity of their work units by adopting suggestions made by their subordinates. However, Greg is dismayed by the fact that employees in his department never make any suggestions to him. Even when problems develop on the job, he is not informed until they become serious. Greg just doesn't understand why his leadership style isn't working!

Discussion Questions

1. How good is Greg's understanding of what good leadership involves? Explain.
2. How effective is Greg going to be as a supervisor if he continues to follow the trait approach to leadership?
3. Why is it necessary for Greg to receive more leadership training?

Notes

1. For an excellent review of trait research in leadership, see Ralph M. Stogdill, *Handbook of Leadership: A Survey of Theory and Research* (New York: Free Press, 1974), pp. 35–91.
2. Jerry W. Koehler, Karl W. E. Anatol, and Robert L. Applebaum, *Organizational Communication: Behavioral Perspectives,* 2d ed. (New York: Rinehart & Winston, 1981), p. 229.
3. Paul Hersey and Kenneth H. Blanchard, *Management of Organizational Behavior: Utilizing Human Resources,* 4th ed., © 1982, p. 87. Adapted by permission of Prentice-Hall, Inc., Englewood Cliffs, N.J.
4. Hersey and Blanchard, *Management of Organizational Behavior,* p. 87.
5. Fred E. Fiedler, "The Contingency Model and the Dynamics of the Leadership

Process," in *Advances in Experimental Social Psychology,* ed. Leonard Berkowitz (New York: Academic Press, 1978), pp. 59–66.

6. Fred E. Fiedler, Martin M. Chemers, and Linda Mahar, *Improving Leadership Effectiveness: The Leader Match Concept* (New York: John Wiley & Sons, 1976), p. 8.

7. Robert A. Baron, *Understanding Human Relations: A Practical Guide to People at Work* (Boston, Mass.: Allyn and Bacon, 1985), p. 225.

8. Gary Johns, *Organizational Behavior: Understanding Life at Work,* 3d ed. (Glenview, Ill.: Scott, Foresman, 1988), p. 319.

9. Fiedler, "The Contingency Model," p. 63.

10. Johns, *Organizational Behavior,* p. 320.

11. Johns, *Organizational Behavior,* p. 320.

12. Hersey and Blanchard, *Management of Organizational Behavior,* p. 95.

13. Hersey and Blanchard, *Management of Organizational Behavior,* pp. 149–75.

14. Hersey and Blanchard, *Management of Organizational Behavior,* p. 157.

15. Ralph M. Stogdill and Alvin E. Coons, eds., *Leader Behavior: Its Description and Measurement,* Research Monograph No. 88 (Columbus, Ohio: Bureau of Business Research, Ohio State University, 1957), p. 42.

16. Hersey and Blanchard, *Management of Organizational Behavior,* p. 162.

17. Stogdill and Coons, *Leader Behavior,* p. 42.

18. Hersey and Blanchard, *Management of Organizational Behavior,* p. 153.

19. James W. Davis, at the University of Arizona, introduced this author to the concept of the tentative approach.

Suggested Readings

Austin, T. W. "What Can Managers Learn from Leadership Theories?" *Supervisory Management* 26, July 1981, pp. 22–31.

Bassin, Marc S. "Developing Executive Leadership: A General Foods Approach." *Personnel* 65, September 1988, pp. 38–42.

Byars, L. L.; R. Dillon; and L. E. Wilson. "The Servant Approach to Leadership." *Supervisory Management* 27, March 1982, pp. 18–20.

Donnelly, John F. "Participative Management at Work." *Harvard Business Review* 55, January–February 1977, pp. 117–127.

Drake, Rodman L. "Leadership: It's a Rare Blend of Traits." *Management Review* 74, August 1985, pp. 24–26.

Fiedler, Fred E.; Martin M. Chemers; and Linda Mahar. *Improving Leadership Effectiveness: The Leader Match Concept.* New York: John Wiley & Sons, 1976.

Glassman, Edward. "Creative Problem Solving: Your Role as Leader." *Supervisory Management* 34, April 1989, pp. 38–42.

————. "Leadership Style's Effect on the Creativity of Employees." *Management Solutions* 31, November 1986, pp. 18–25.

McAfee, R. Bruce, and Betty J. Rickie. "Leadership by Example: 'Do as I Do!' *Management Solutions* 31, August 1986, pp. 10–17.

McMaster, I. "A New Look at Leadership." *Supervision* 43, July 1981, pp. 10–11.

Robinson, Dana Gaines. "The 1990's: From Managing to Leading." *Supervisory Management* 34, June 1989, pp. 5–10.

Rodrigues, Carl A. "Identifying the Right Leader for the Right Situation." *Personnel* 65, September 1988, pp. 38–42.

Schoonover, Stephen C., and Murray M. Dalziel. "Developing Leadership for Change." *Management Review* 75, July 1986, pp. 55–60.

Part II

Applying Supervision Skills

▼

Setting Objectives and Making Decisions

Chapter
4

Learning Objectives

Objectives are standards of achievement by which you can measure progress. As a supervisor, you must constantly make decisions. Some will be easy, but many will require considerable skill. Understanding the objectives listed below will help you grasp how supervisors set objectives and master the art of decision making.

1. Understand the importance of objectives.
2. Describe the various kinds of objectives.
3. Explain the technique of management by objectives.
4. Discuss the role of decision making.
5. Explain the decision-making process.
6. Examine the concept of management information systems.

The Role of Objectives

Statements of desired outcomes or expectations are **objectives.** A clear-cut objective might be "achieve at least 90 percent accuracy in filling orders for goods during July." An admirable but vague goal might be "receive few complaints about orders throughout the next month." To be useful, objectives must be measurable. How do you know what "few complaints" means? Each supervisor can interpret the phrase differently. Efforts to set objectives should not be wasted. Figure 4.1 lists objectives, plans, and measurement techniques for a supervisor of cosmetics salespeople. The worksheet approach encourages use of written objectives. Also, it is a handy way to check on progress and make necessary revisions.

What are objectives?

Peter Drucker, a management expert, observes that objectives are necessary wherever performance results influence company survival and growth.[1] Objectives help you understand what actions should be taken. They also focus attention on human, equipment, and financial resources needed to attain goals. Objectives justify reasons for orders you give to subordinates. They provide a basis for developing both *standing plans,* such as policies and procedures, and *single-use plans* for specific programs and projects.

Why are objectives needed?

Worksheet of Objectives for a Supervisor of Cosmetics Sales Representatives   **Figure 4.1**

Name _____ **Date** _____

Objectives	Plans	Measurements	Comments
1. Introduce new products to sales staff.	1. Recommend that each representative order 10 units of each item to show customers.	1. Ask sales staff about customer receptivity to these new products; note extent to which these products are being ordered.	
2. Increase sales by 15 percent in the next quarter.	2. Sponsor a sales contest with bonus prizes; provide recognition for sales performance in the monthly newsletter; schedule motivational/ informational seminars.	2. Sales data reported by sales staff.	
3. Increase the number of new sales representatives by 8 percent in the next quarter.	3. Interview 5 prospects each week; provide recruiting bonus to salespeople.	3. Number of new sales representatives hired.	
4. Reduce turnover of sales staff by 10 percent in the next quarter.	4. Schedule training seminars; provide necessary information and sales materials to sales staff; establish a time for assisting sales staff.	4. Turnover statistics reflected on roster of active sales staff.	

Objectives are used to give direction, provide data on results, and indicate potential problems. Failure to develop objectives is like taking a trip without knowing the destination. Any route will do, and you won't know when you have arrived because you never knew where you were going. As a supervisor, you are responsible for achieving objectives set for your department, shift, or work unit. These may include:

- ☐ Developing your own job targets for certain periods.
- ☐ Selecting employees who are capable of doing the job.
- ☐ Scheduling workers so that enough are present at any given time.
- ☐ Performing jobs with a minimum of defective products, accidents, or absenteeism.
- ☐ Justifying and recommending the purchase of new equipment or the hiring of additional employees.
- ☐ Preparing budget requests.
- ☐ Keeping accurate records.

Merely having objectives does not imply that desired outcomes will occur. Objectives are guidelines, not ends in themselves. Continued emphasis on them is necessary to ensure they are implemented successfully.

Communication is a relevant concern. Supervisors must set priorities and clearly convey to employees their role in attaining objectives. Without knowing what they are to do, it is unrealistic to assume that workers will necessarily direct efforts toward critical tasks. Provide explanations, answer all questions, and give encouragement. Recognize objective-oriented job performance; such a practice helps to keep attention focused on objectives and reinforces the likelihood of getting continued results.

Classification of Objectives

A company's success depends on cost controls, profitability, and maximization of market opportunities, which are **strategic objectives.** Top management formulates such objectives for an organization to survive, prosper, and attain long-term success.

> Successful top managers take the time to think about their business, where they are with the business, and what they want to be as an organization, and then implement action programs and policies to get from where they are to where they want to be at the end of a reasonable time horizon.[2]

Short-range objectives relating to performance of routine job tasks are **tactical objectives.** These characterize much of the supervisor's world; they usually include planning and scheduling and occur on a regular basis. Checking to see whether doctors' orders have been carried out in a hospital or ordering supplies for an office illustrate the supervisor's work with tactical objectives. Consider these examples that require supervisory action.

Examples of Qualitative and Quantitative Objectives   **Figure 4.2**

Qualitative Objectives	**Quantitative Objectives**
1. To motivate workers so that they will perform at their highest levels of capability.	1. To increase production by 100 units per month.
2. To encourage employee suggestions for improvement of work practices and department policies.	2. To reduce the operating expense budget by $1,000 per month for the next six months.
3. To provide a high degree of organizational loyalty.	3. To reduce the number of employees in department X by five persons before January 1.
4. To ensure that employees have respect for their supervisors.	4. To achieve a score of at least 90 percent on the proficiency exam.

On the morning of a special sales promotion, you discover that all five of your department staff will not be at work. What are your tactical objectives?

You have just learned that a large order must be ready for shipment by a certain date or the order will be given to another company. What is your immediate reaction?

Objectives can also be grouped on the basis of two criteria: quality and quantity. **Qualitative objectives** are related to the presence or absence of an acceptable level of excellence. Measuring quality is not necessarily easy because of subjectivity and the lack of precise standards. You can list attributes to describe a "quality" employee—enthusiastic, motivated, and capable—yet it is difficult to measure these traits precisely. Nevertheless, you must recognize the importance of quality in setting objectives.

Qualitative objectives tend to be somewhat subjective

Quantitative objectives are determined and measured on the basis of production. An objective might be to produce 40 units per day or to make sales totaling $4,000 per week. It is easy to know whether these objectives are reached. You can measure an exact number of units or count the money. Recognize the importance of both quality and quantity in forming objectives. Figure 4.2 gives examples of both types.

Quantitative objectives are easily measured

Kinds of Objectives

There are various ways to classify objectives, but, as a supervisor, you are most concerned with decision-oriented, routine, creative, and personal objectives. It is important to consider the end result you want because many variables are involved—personalities, employee and organizational needs, and job priorities. Figure 4.3 illustrates these objectives and provides a brief description of each.

There are four types of objectives

Figure 4.3   **Kinds of Objectives**

Objective	Description
Decision-oriented objectives	A decision must be made to remedy a problem or issue, and that decision determines the objective.
Routine objectives	Relate to everyday work operations; concerned with repetitive jobs.
Creative objectives	Involve new ideas that can be applied in imaginative, flexible ways to enhance productivity, profitability, or both.
Personal objectives	Specific goals that people seek to accomplish for themselves in their work.

Decision-Oriented Objectives

It is necessary to make decisions

When solutions to existing or potential problems require decisions, you form **decision-oriented objectives.** Without warning, you are told to reduce the departmental budget by 15 percent. Such an unanticipated event necessitates contemplation; you will need answers to these questions:

☐ What budget items can be sacrificed with the least negative impact on normal operations?
☐ What are the tradeoffs between long- and short-run implications of the ultimate decision?
☐ Has management imposed limitations to recognize in forming your objectives?
☐ How will you justify the objective to those persons most affected by the budget reduction?

In forming decision-oriented objectives, you benefit from weighing alternatives instead of making snap judgments. Be realistic about a problem or issue and form strategies to reach desired targets.

Routine Objectives

Routine objectives are important

Objectives related to performance of repetitive tasks are **routine objectives.** You have to make a weekly summary of sales, units produced, absenteeism, accidents, and so on. Employees may do the same task over and over. These duties are essential and must be done correctly. At a fast-food counter, for example, many customers are served during a work shift. Key objectives are to greet them courteously, fill orders promptly, and make change correctly. Sometimes these job activities are taken for granted because of their repetitive nature, yet routine objectives are needed to assure satisfactory levels of performance.

Creative Objectives

Imaginative ideas that can be applied to improve profitability, productivity, or both are **creative objectives.** These come from all ranks of the company, not just top management. An employee who actually does a job often has outstanding cost-cutting ideas. One order packer's suggestion for reusing costly corrugated cartons saved a company thousands of dollars. Encourage your employees to think of new and different ways to get jobs done. Many companies have suggestion systems that encourage creative thinking. They recognize and reward suggestions that can be implemented.

Do not underestimate the value of creativity

Personal Objectives

Employees come to jobs with various expectations. For most people, a job is necessary because they need income. For some, though, the workplace may also be a major source of enjoyment. What people seek to achieve for themselves are called **personal objectives.**

Personal objectives vary among individuals

For both supervisors and workers, personal objectives influence the ways they accept job assignments and the amount of effort exerted to fulfill them. You must recognize the role of these objectives and try to achieve a balance between them and others. An individual's goals may conflict with one another. The prestige and income of a management position can be appealing, but people differ in their desires to work with the issues and frustrations such jobs bring. Also, there may be disagreement between personal and company objectives. If strongly opposed to use of nuclear resources, a person employed by a firm involved with nuclear energy could experience much frustration.

Setting Objectives

Peter Drucker notes that any business has only two basic objectives: marketing and innovation. He believes objectives must be specified for areas such as innovation, job performance and attitude, financial and physical resources, profits, employee development, market standing, and public responsibility.[3] As a supervisor, you are directly affected by:

- ☐ Output expectations for a department, unit, or shift.
- ☐ Number of defective units produced.
- ☐ Absenteeism rate of your workers.
- ☐ Turnover rate for workers in the department or operating unit.
- ☐ Sufficient training of your employees so they perform effectively.

The Process of Setting Objectives

To set objectives, supervisors must have a practical understanding of circumstances and people. Every supervisor wants more money, people, and equipment. If you do not judge situations realistically, you will be frustrated when your boss does not support you. Imagine you supervise an office and

Be realistic; consider alternatives

believe your staff can do the job more effectively with updated word processing equipment. Your feeling is especially strong because the firm has installed new processors for some other units. When you ask for the equipment, you are told that no more money can be allocated. You know others got the equipment, and it is easy to get upset. However, money simply is not there for you at this time.

Subordinates desire involvement in decisions that affect them. They may establish higher objectives for themselves than bosses would set for them.[4] Supervisors should be especially careful to get feedback on objectives they think are necessary and logical. If openness of communication prevails, employees may provide valuable ideas, suggestions, and comments. A consensus is not necessary, but opportunities to express views and sentiments generate employee satisfaction. Workers are more likely to support objectives they helped set.

Objectives are not equally important

All objectives are not of equal importance. Concentrate on those that are most pressing. For instance, you might have three primary objectives: a budget request to add another employee; approval to replace several worn, heavily used pieces of equipment; and approval for a three-year reorganization plan. Which of these has your highest priority? You will probably agree that the equipment does. If it fails to function, no production is possible; without production, there will be no products. The request for personnel is next important. An additional person is needed soon, and a proposal takes only a short time to draw up. Finally, your reorganization plan requires several meetings and much thought and planning. It suffers least from being last.

Ask relevant questions

Setting objectives requires knowing exactly what is to be accomplished. It includes assigning responsibilities, specifying a time period, and determining a method of evaluation. Figure 4.4 shows the relationship among these factors. Let's examine each of them from the perspective of a nursing supervisor who desires additional training for subordinates.

Be results oriented

What Is to Be Accomplished?   The best response to this question is a statement of the objective. Too frequently, objectives are not clearly specified. As a nursing supervisor, for example, you seek to increase training. What does this mean? Are you trying to improve knowledge of technical skills, patient care, or nursing as a profession? It is better to restate the objective and say, "Floor nurses must enroll in at least three approved continuing education courses."

Assigning responsibility minimizes complications

Who Is Responsible?   If you do not fix responsibility, there is little chance for accountability and a great possibility that miscommunication and frustration will occur. Your objective might be to encourage enrollment in workshops. Therefore, you inform the nurses that enrollment forms are needed but do not give any further instructions. Do you think each nurse knows that he or she must be responsible for enrolling? Specific assignment of responsibility is necessary to obtain the best results. If you keep this principle in mind, you are likely to have fewer employee mistakes and less morale problems.

The Process of Setting Objectives   **Figure 4.4**

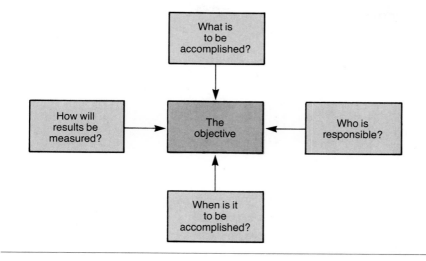

When Is It To Be Accomplished? Your original objective for floor nurses did not include a time dimension. As stated, the training could take place anytime. To make the objective functional, state a time period. You might say, "Floor nurses must enroll in at least three approved continuing education courses in each 12-month period." This approach enables priorities to be adjusted and provides nurses with structure and time to achieve results.

Deadlines provide targets for allocating efforts

How Will Results Be Measured? In setting objectives, evaluation is important. Contrary to what you might think, some supervisors do not recognize this concern. As a result, they often find themselves searching for explanations, especially when actual results differ from expectations. In our nursing example, progress might be measured by whether a specified grade is earned in each course. For many objectives, observing and questioning are ways to assess results. Often, job performance can be observed directly. At other times, you must ask about progress. Whenever corrections are needed, make them before things get out of control.

Assessment cannot be overlooked

Features of Good Objectives

Good objectives are a starting point on the path toward productive results. To give a sense of direction, they should be well thought out and clearly explained. Existence of objectives increases the possibility that effective feedback and attainment of specific job tasks will occur.[5] However, even the

What are good objectives?

Figure 4.5   **Features of a Good Objective**

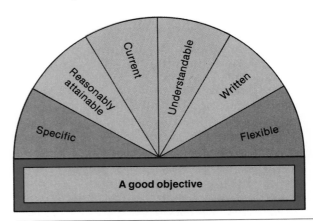

best-developed objectives do not assure preferred outcomes, which usually happen because of dedicated work efforts. Figure 4.5 illustrates how features combine to make a good objective.

Specific Objectives. As previously noted, objectives relate to the accomplishment of specific tasks. Such goals as "improving output," "meeting expectations," and "cutting expenses" are noble, but they are achieved only if sufficient thought is given to *how* to attain them. If top management establishes an objective of implementing cost controls, you have to set specific goals for your department, such as "increase output by six units per day" or "reduce rejects from the current eight per week to four per week by month end." These steps are exact, measurable, and conform to company criteria.

Clearly specify expectations

Reasonably Attainable Objectives. Individuals and groups will work to reach challenging objectives, but perception is important; they must consider the objectives to be reasonable and attainable. A supervisor for a firm engaged in the direct sale of household products might state that a new distributor must recruit 48 others and have them selling at the close of next year. This is a major accomplishment for a seasoned veteran. How do you suppose a new person might react? Unrealistic goals create so much pressure and frustration that workers become demoralized and give up. You can also give people too many objectives at once. Rather than overwhelming workers with too many objectives, introduce them on a periodic basis.

The impossible cannot be accomplished

Current Objectives. Change characterizes our world. Rapid advances in technology have a direct impact on the workplace. Objectives need to be kept current to reflect changes in budgeting, personnel allocations, and daily

Concerns of yesterday and tomorrow may differ

operations. A review of objectives keeps you abreast of work loads and provides a basis for measurement. When you know what needs to be done, you are in a better position to take action.

Understandable Objectives. You must be sure that workers understand objectives. Do not just ask. Few subordinates like to admit they do not understand. Provide background information and then invite employees to state their perceptions. Of course, to the best of your ability, you will already have involved workers in setting objectives.

People must know what to do

Communication is a key factor. Perhaps you have tried to assemble a piece of equipment only to discover that directions were hard to follow. The workplace is full of objectives that are hard to interpret because they are not clear. Assume a subordinate is to "improve job performance." You and the employee can have vastly different views of what it means, but both of you can agree on the meaning of "50 percent fewer rejects by the end of next month."

Written Objectives. Objectives are more useful if written. The act of writing forces you to think about intentions and desired results. When written, objectives are usually better developed and serve to document expectations. You might have a goal of reducing the accident injury rate by 20 percent during the next six months. This provides a well-defined course of action, and your boss may be reluctant to impose a higher, unreasonable objective.

Writing aids recall and review

Writing brings benefits that help supervisors and employees do the job. A written record will help minimize differences of opinion or discrepancies. It provides a means for review and examination. Written records reinforce the recall of specifics that may become vague with the passage of time. This is especially true if reference points or figures are needed for comparisons. Written objectives convey a sense of importance.

Flexible Objectives. The work environment features both expected and unanticipated change. Thus, objectives need to be flexible so they can be adjusted to realities. You might need to reduce employees by 10. This will have an impact on work output. Reassignment of work responsibilities likely will be necessary, and production goals will need revision.

Circumstances do change

Consider This

1. What is the most important factor to consider in setting objectives?
2. Why do many supervisors neglect to update objectives for their work units?
3. To what extent should supervisors be involved in formulating strategic organizational objectives?

Management by Objectives

What is MBO?

In the 1950s, Peter F. Drucker introduced the term **management by objectives (MBO),** which involves joint manager participation to establish job objectives and includes progress reviews of those objectives. In addition to better two-way communication, MBO stresses future priorities and recognizes that objectives should be "specific, measurable, time bounded, and joined to an action plan."[6] MBO, which is probably today's most discussed method of setting goals, emphasizes the importance of employee commitment in gaining improved performance.[7]

MBO programs are most effective in an environment where managers are supportive and willing to be accountable. Favorable attitudes of managers and supervisors at other levels are also vital.

> Perhaps the most critical prerequisite to successful MBO programs is commitment by top management . . . They must communicate their commitment through both words and actions — through policy statements, through the implementation of decisions, and through personal involvement.[8]

Participants must demonstrate a receptive attitude toward shared involvement, recognize the importance of establishing goals, and accept the possibility of change to get desired results. Where MBO has been successful, managers were aware of the importance of their relationships with people. On the next page, the list shows considerations needed to implement MBO. Review all 12 of the items. Each is important, strengthens the program's acceptance, and contributes to its effectiveness.

The MBO Process

The essence of MBO is to have personnel concentrate on definite, known objectives rather than just routinely doing daily jobs. This technique gives them discretion over how to attain objectives.[9] The MBO process involves determining objectives, comparing performance to them, making revisions, and forming goals for the next period of accountability. Each step requires careful thought and planning.

Know what you are trying to accomplish

Determining Objectives. Top management sets objectives for the entire firm. Then, goals are formed for divisions, departments, and other sublevel units. As you develop goals, consider the features of good objectives discussed earlier in this chapter. Focus attention on what is to be done and remember that individuals must have enough authority to achieve stated objectives. For example, a subordinate responsible for maintaining a predetermined level of office supplies needs the authority to replenish them.

Is the work progressing as anticipated?

Comparing Performance. At this stage, actual results are compared to objectives. Note that uncontrollable events can always occur, and remember to focus evaluation on job factors, not personal whims. Bosses and workers

Considerations for MBO Programs

1. Start MBO at the top of the organization; be sure to have the full support and cooperation of top management.
2. Before starting the program, make sure that participants understand the system and know how they can benefit from it.
3. Tailor the program to the organization. Avoid the canned programs of self-styled MBO experts.
4. Avoid excessive paperwork. Keep it simple.
5. Be extremely cautious when evaluating performance solely on results. MBO can easily be viewed as just another gimmick used by task-oriented managers to get something for nothing.
6. Where the firm's overall leadership style permits, allow individuals to set their own goals. Avoid authoritatively assigning goals to persons who value personal autonomy and responsibility.
7. Make sure that a person who is held responsible for results has access to the resources needed to achieve them (e.g., authority, money, materials, personnel, technology).
8. Provide for team effort where the success of one individual is dependent on the productivity of others over whom he or she has no authority.
9. Do not place too heavy an emphasis on results. Otherwise, people may be considered only as a means to an end.
10. Insofar as possible, allow participants the freedom to determine the means for achieving their goals.
11. Establish good controls and feedback systems to track the progress of subordinates, but avoid excessively close supervision.
12. Provide for changing goals as conditions change. Be adaptable enough to change any aspect of the MBO program that proves to be unworkable.

Source: Henry L. Sisk and J. Clifton Williams, *Management & Organization,* 4th ed. (Cincinnati: South-Western Publishing, 1981), p. 76. Reprinted with permission of the publisher.

can discuss obstacles to overcome, or they may find that objectives were achieved. This two-way communication provides an opportunity to explain actions, clarify concerns, and reduce misunderstanding. Workers should feel free to initiate this two-way conversation.

Making Revisions. MBO stresses what has or has not happened in a straightforward manner. Therefore, changes are more obvious and less personal to all involved. Those involved may not always agree on most appropriate courses of action. If disagreements arise, employees are entitled to differing ideas about the best strategies to reach goals. Through discussion, most differences of opinion can generally be resolved.

Initiate needed changes

Developing Future Objectives. In addition to possible revision of existing goals, periodic reviews should include development of future objectives. These will vary among groups, so managers should carefully assess the relationship between current activities and future priorities. MBO programs

Plan for the future

provide a structure to organize courses of action for continuity and consistency. They force participants to think about the future and plan accordingly.

An Illustration: The MBO Worksheet

Now that you have surveyed features of the MBO process, you are ready to look at a typical worksheet. This approach can be adapted to any kind of firm or job. The purpose here is to see what is involved.

Figure 4.6, a worksheet of five columns, includes tasks to be accomplished and measurement standards, priority indicators, results, review dates, and actions to be taken. As you apply MBO, there are some essential concerns.

☐ *Tasks and measurement standards.* This step is the essence of MBO. For those not accustomed to writing objectives, a key point is to focus on three things: what is to be done, when it must be finished, and how results will be measured. For example, the first goal illustrated in Figure 4.6 is "to reduce absenteeism by 20 percent in the next three months." It includes the task (to reduce absenteeism), the time (three months), and the evaluation standard (20 percent).

☐ *Priorities.* One view holds that every objective is critical or it should not be included. In practice, even essential goals vary in terms of priority. For example, Figure 4.6 notes major concerns for increasing production and reducing absenteeism as well as product defects. These goals are more

Figure 4.6   **Example of an MBO Worksheet**

Tasks and Measurements	Priority	Results	Date Reviewed	Comments/ Actions
To reduce absenteeism by 20 percent in the next three months.	1			
To increase production by 10 units per week.	1			
To reduce product defects by 10 percent each week.	1			
To computerize recordkeeping during the next quarter.	2			
To attend one professional development seminar before the next review.	3			

urgent than computerization of recordkeeping. While attending a seminar is relevant, failure to do so is not likely to have a detrimental impact on operations.

☐ *Results.* Here you indicate whether objectives have been met, surpassed, or not achieved. Carefully compare expectations against evaluation criteria. Focus on demonstrated accomplishments, not personalities or unreasonable excuses. Be realistic; goals may not be met because of factors beyond the subordinate's control. Because of equipment break-downs and lengthy repairs, for example, it may be impossible to increase production by 10 units per week.

☐ *Comments and actions.* Record pertinent comments and recommended courses of action. Recognize factors contributing to actual performance results. Observation can be shared with your subordinates and used to plan ahead for the next review period. Your recorded comments do not have to be lengthy but should emphasize key points to remember.

Advantages and Disadvantages of MBO

MBO has been widely adopted and has gained acceptance as a manage-ment technique. The concept is easily understood and can be applied in all types of businesses. Nevertheless, research on its effectiveness is rather limited.

MBO is widely practiced

> On-the-job research is lacking because in complex organizational settings it is very difficult to prove causation between a multidimensional management technique and job performance . . . Additudinal studies are often deficient because they merely infer rather than improve MBO's effect on actual performance. Laboratory studies of MBO generally are oversimplified and unrealistic.[10]

MBO provides specific knowledge of job expectancies and helps coordinate objectives among a company's units. It encourages employee participation and promotes job satisfaction. However, MBO requires a sincere commitment from management and, in practice, is time consuming. Some objectives, such as trying to measure if employees exert maximum effort, are hard to quantify. Results are likely to be greater when workers consider objectives to be reasonable, and feedback is given promptly.

Success with MBO depends on a number of factors. One key is to gain worker acceptance of demanding objectives.[11] This is more likely if trust and open communication prevail. It is important for supervisors to demonstrate positive attitudes. Should they evidence a dislike for the amount of time and paperwork required or MBO itself, a negative message is conveyed. Existence of an MBO program does not ensure that a company will function smoothly. It should be viewed as a blueprint to provide guidance and understanding.

▼

Consider This

1. How can supervisors ensure that MBO provides desired feedback from subordinates?
2. What circumstances necessitate revision of previously established objectives?
3. Which level of management (top, middle, or first line) is most likely to resist MBO? Why?

The Role of Decision Making

Choosing one among several courses of action in order to reach desired goals is **decision making.** It occurs throughout the workplace and is a vital part of the supervisor's job. Decisions do not always work out as expected. Poor results can happen even if decisions are logical and rational. Consequences of decisions affect productivity, morale, profits, and operations. There are levels of importance in decisions. Good supervisors recognize that even routine decisions affect employees. You take part in a number of appraisal interviews, yet each worker has only one. You face immediate decisions or may ignore the need for them. Circumstances govern how events are viewed and handled.

What influences decisions?

Facts, expectations, experiences, and opinions influence decisions. Employee views, unanticipated events, and availability of financial, equipment, and human resources affect decision alternatives. Even though all desired information is unavailable, you must make recommendations and resolve issues. Review the examples in Figure 4.7. Notice how the time framework, level of perceived importance, and extent of emotional involvement varies among types of decision situations. Emergencies have highest priorities and require immediate remedies. Decisions concerning the future can be made over a longer period of time. Possible layoffs and negative performance appraisals can trigger immediate emotional responses.

Individuals or members of groups make decisions, and people can approach the same objective with widely divergent recommendations. Their views are based on experiences, backgrounds, and prior training. Figure 4.8 shows several behavioral elements that influence perspectives on decision making. You will recognize some of them, for they are interrelated in thought and action patterns. You must learn to deal with each element to make effective decisions.

When is a "good enough" decision appropriate?

Acceptance of "good enough" results is termed **bounded rationality.** Because of a desire not to exert more effort, shortage of time, or lack of money, you may settle on a less-than-best decision. Be cautious in making any decisions that, in effect, are limiting. Such a decision might be one that sets a single minimum standard for rewarding performance. This may result in

Examples of Decision Situations **Figure 4.7**

Examples	Characteristics	Type
Departmental reorganization. Possible layoffs. Potential relocation. Performance appraisal.	Strong pro/con sentiments present.	Intense/emotional
Approaches for complying with safety regulations. Deciding when to reorder materials/supplies. Determining which applicant to hire for a position.	Typical, customary operational decisions.	Routine
Long-term developmental plans. Planned projections for equipment change. Commitment of resources to potentially emerging market opportunities.	Emphasis on the future: involves determining direction and possible setting of priorities.	Future
Evacuation of persons from elevators when electricity goes off. How to continue operations when several employees are unexpectedly absent at the same time.	Immediate decisions, little time for evaluation.	Emergency

little or no effort being exerted beyond that level. For example, you set a standard whereby each worker is to produce 25 items per day but intend it to be a minimum expectation. Without additional incentives, production is unlikely to exceed 25 items per worker. In effect, attaining the standard is perceived as a "good enough" maximum by subordinates.

Lesser attainment of some worthy goals to maximize a meaningful objective is **suboptimization.** You must concentrate on what is pertinent and not get sidetracked by a "go-ahead-anyway" decision, which ignores longer-term factors. For example, you may have to terminate the most productive order processor on your staff because he or she fails to abide by rules, is belligerent, and intimidates less competent employees, but in the absence of this worker, the rest of the group works well together and increases their productivity. When faced with a need to reduce costs, you decide to reduce advertising expenses. Ultimately, though, this means many lost opportunities for sales.

All objectives cannot be fully achieved

Figure 4.8   **Behavioral Elements Influencing Decisions**

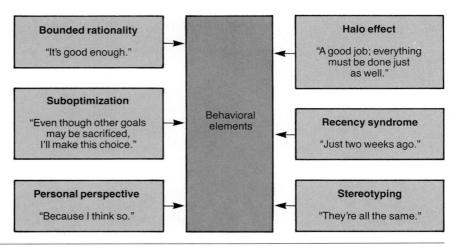

One's own view of things, resulting from experiences, attitudes, and aspirations, is that individual's **personal perspective.** In your decisions, don't think that your views are the only things to be valued. If you overemphasize personal views, excluding other information, you will overlook data, and misinterpretations are sure to occur. Practice weighing all available facts and balancing viewpoints so you learn to make the best decision. As a restaurant supervisor, for instance, you may oppose installing salad bars because of a personal dislike for them. If the competitive trend is to have salad bars, your personal preference will cause much lost business.

When one factor dominates all other aspects of a person or a job, the **halo effect** exists. For example, a worker may be extremely capable at getting new customers, yet do poorly in servicing accounts and maintaining records. In judging, you might assume that the entire performance was outstanding because of the one factor—obtaining new accounts. You need to look at the whole picture in forming decisions. Otherwise, the halo effect will distort your view of what actually happens.

The **recency syndrome** is a natural tendency for people to be more aware of most recent events. In decision making, the main problem is that results from earlier events are obscured and not properly considered. If your work load suddenly increases, it is easy to overlook the possibility that this is only temporary. In personnel evaluation, supervisors may base decisions on most-recent performance, neglecting results happening earlier in the appraisal period.

In **stereotyping,** judgments based on limited contacts with individuals or groups are generalized to all persons or groups having similar character-

Personal views can differ

Be aware of the halo effect

Memories can fade over time

Stereotyping is inappropriate

istics. Perhaps you have heard people say such things as "Women (or men) are temperamental;" "Teenagers (or some other group) are lazy;" or "Hourly workers lack initiative." You should avoid making decisions on the basis of stereotypes because they are inaccurate and distort reality. It is important to judge each person on his or her own merits, not on unsubstantiated rumors or opinions.

Making Decisions

Decision making requires you to assess a variety of data, weigh alternatives, and make recommendations. Theoretically, the process is logical, sequential, and comprehensive. In practice, decision making can sometimes be anything but calm and orderly. Self-interests, emotions, and attitudes are reflected in decisions. Effective communication is a key to successful decision making. If a decision is not understood by those who implement it, confusion and needless mistakes will occur. Should you make a decision to discipline a subordinate, shouting or screaming create unnecessary hostilities and can negatively affect future relationships.

Decision making involves communication

The Decision-Making Process

Decision making includes a sequence of steps aimed at a solution that has the best chance of success. Too often, supervisors get hasty and do not do necessary homework. In the end, it pays to take time to form a good decision rather than being forced to make time to handle the problems a poor decision brings. Figure 4.9 shows these steps: recognize the problem, consider alternatives, collect data, evaluate alternatives, make and implement the decision, and follow up. Now let's review each of these steps.

There are six steps to effective decisions

Recognize the Problem.   The problem must be clearly recognized; only then is an appropriate solution possible. Peter F. Drucker notes that an important consideration is to find the critical factor — "the element in the situation that has to be changed before anything else can be changed, moved, or acted upon."[12] Whenever a difference exists between actual and expected results, there is a potential problem. For example, analysis of output reveals that a work unit formerly producing 20 widgets daily is now making only 12. Obviously, something is wrong. It is necessary to determine the reason for this decline in productivity.

Focus on the problem, not symptoms

Learn to search for the real difficulty and do not get sidetracked on symptoms. Failure to determine the actual problem only makes matters worse. Assume that your records show a significant increase in defective products. Are performance standards too demanding? Is the equipment too old to function properly? Or is a lack of training for new employees the real problem? Problem identification can be complex and involve a multitude of factors, yet all other steps in decision making depend on knowing what is to be accomplished.

Figure 4.9   **The Decision Process**

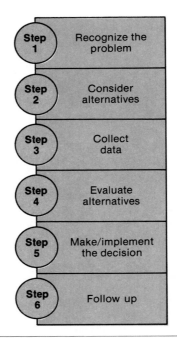

Consider Alternatives. Once the problem is clearly specified, consider
various ways to reach a solution. Take enough time to generate as many
alternatives as possible. Gather suggestions from employees and any others
who may be involved in the decision. It is tempting to reject ideas because
of perceived restraints. If they ultimately prove to be meritorious, needed
funds or personnel can possibly be obtained. Do not confine yourself to easily
identified alternatives. Explore as many alternatives as time permits.

Recognize possible
courses of action

Collect Data. Next you have the challenge of gathering information. Collection of all pertinent data is impossible, yet every reasonable effort should be
made to collect as much data as feasible. Objectivity is a major concern; avoid
personal biases. Consult secondary sources (such as libraries, trade publications, government documents, and materials already compiled by other departments and organizations) before you conduct surveys or begin studies.

Gather relevant data

Evaluate Alternatives. Evaluate the information you have and formulate
possible choices. Although time, cost, and other resource requirements may
differ, several options generally exist. Assessment involves foresight and
sometimes a concern about setting precedents. An outline is often useful to

Weigh the options

Evaluating Decision Alternatives   **Figure 4.10**

Possible Decision Strategy / Consequences of Each Decision	What is the Impact on Expenses?	What Are the Positive Effects?	What Are the Negative Effects?
Ask present employees to work overtime.	Increased wages for overtime worked.	Employees earn more money; no training is necessary.	Fatigue; provides less time for family and off-the-job activities.
Temporarily transfer employees from another work unit.	Expenses are increased.	A stop-gap measure; useful for a short-term duration.	May create a strain on capability for performing job duties in other work units.
Employ additional workers.	Expenses are increased.	Increases the number of available workers.	New employees may have to be trained; more supervisors may be needed.

help you grasp details and weigh various factors. For example, Figure 4.10 shows how you might evaluate alternatives to meet personnel needs. Each alternative will accomplish the objective, but costs as well as positive and negative effects must be weighed.

Make and Implement the Decision. Careful thought and attention to previous steps make this step easier. A choice still can be difficult, especially when it is critical and alternatives are not clear even after much thought. At such times, rely on your previous experience, intuition, and judgment. Once made, communicate the decision to people it will affect. Be sure all persons understand their responsibilities, and explain reasons for decisions. Employees who understand "whys" will more readily accept them.

Decide and put the decision into action

Follow Up. Desired outcomes do not just happen. You must monitor implementation of your decisions. Unless unexpected problems arise, follow-up activities often do not receive enough attention. Recognize when changes are necessary or errors are likely. For example, assume that a new method to pack products for shipment has been introduced, and you observe an employee packing boxes incorrectly. By being alert, the mistake can be corrected immediately to reduce the likelihood of customers receiving damaged merchandise. Through follow-up, possible difficulties are discovered *before* they evolve into major problems.

Things do not necessarily happen as intended

Decision-Making Guidelines

Supervisors are accountable for decisions, a fact that is sometimes not fully grasped by subordinates. Reacting to decisions made by others is different from making them yourself. Some uncertainties and complexities prevail in all but the most routine decision-making situations. By now, you probably recognize that careful analysis of relevant factors does not guarantee positive results. There are, however, several guidelines to assist you.

Decisions can be challenged

Justification. This implies that decisions adhere to a firm's policies or directives. If uncertain of your authority, check procedures and regulations before making a decision. Take time to consider possible consequences of your actions. "If the supervisor is not prepared to make a decision but is being pressured for one, he or she should always say no."[13] This response provides an opportunity to weigh relevant concerns before making a commitment.

Sooner or later a crisis will occur

Crisis Circumstances. Crisis situations require immediate decisions. When emergencies arise, you must respond quickly. Remain calm, rapidly assess strategies and possible outcomes, and then act. In other words, thought must precede action. Crisis decisions should not make situations worse. For example, rapid evacuation is essential in case of fire, but a hasty directive to escape on the elevators can be a death sentence. When the electricity goes off, people are quickly trapped with little chance of escape. Crises range from emotional outbursts to death threats, but common sense and forethought work with your experience to bring about the best decisions.

Your boss should know what is going on

Informing the Boss. In weighing alternatives, you studied the importance of gathering ideas and suggestions. Remember that it is essential for your boss to be well informed about the activities of your work unit. When contemplating a major decision, know how the boss views it. His or her support cannot always be obtained, and changes may be recommended. If ultimately supportive, however, this person can play a crucial role in securing additional resources and making suggestions to overcome obstacles.

Decisiveness. This implies an ability to be conclusive in your decisions. You should respond to decision situations within reasonable periods of time. Too often, inept supervisors tell employees, "I'll get back to you," but they rarely do. The passage of time generally does not change the final decision or make an unpleasant one easier.

Don't be wishy-washy

Supervisors who constantly change their minds create a difficult working atmosphere for employees. If you have worked for supervisors who gave directions but then often changed their minds, you know that constant changes cause lower productivity and morale. So what should supervisors do? As a rule, they should alter a decision only when it becomes obvious that it is not working. Complications can be minimized by carefully following the decision-making process before giving directions.

Group Decision Making

When members of a group make recommendations or decisions, the process is called *group decision making*. It encourages involvement, sharing of perspectives, and exemplifies the trend toward participatory management. A better-educated labor force, more complex decisions, and evolving technological innovation have accelerated the growth of group decision making. In today's environment, decisions must comply with an enormous number of government regulations and utilize specialized knowledge, which often is not possessed by any one individual. Managers incur increasingly greater demands for job-performance excellence and, if objectives are not met, are susceptible to much criticism. Therefore, they must be receptive to others' insights. Circumstances favoring a group approach to decisions are noted at the bottom of the page. Since you will work with groups, it is important to review them.

Advantages and Disadvantages of Group Decision Making

Through the group approach, many opinions, beliefs, and viewpoints can be gathered, and more potential alternatives can be generated. While groups are more likely to accept solutions they have helped formulate, participation promotes better understanding of problems or issues. Nevertheless, much time is consumed in group deliberations. Dominant personalities can unduly influence a group, and group members may tend to avoid individual responsibilities for decisions. Because of a desire for conformity, some members may not express their true beliefs or feelings.

Two or more heads may be better than one

Circumstances Favoring Group Decisions

1. The problem has a definite and identifiable solution.
2. A range of possible solutions is initially available for consideration.
3. Rewards and punishments are given to the group as a whole rather than to individuals within the group.
4. The task can be subdivided and includes "traps" that single individuals might miss.
5. There is little need for expression of personal, self-oriented needs.
6. There is a generally pleasant atmosphere; the participants recognize the need for unified action, and feel warm and friendly toward one another.
7. The group's problem-solving activity is understandable, orderly, and focused on one issue at a time.
8. The chairman aids the group in penetrating its agenda problems.

Source: Gene E. Burton, "The Group Process Key to More Productive Management," *Management World* 10 (May 1981), p. 15. Reprinted with permission of the publisher.

Improved communication is a major advantage of group involvement. Shared information promotes greater understanding of organizational functions. People gain firsthand awareness about how others view issues and have opportunities to explain perspectives, seek clarifications, and answer questions. At General Motors' Lake Orion plant, workers and engineers meet to exchange views before production of automobiles actually begins. As a result, six months of product-planning time has been eliminated.[14] Cooperation is enhanced, and the company is in a better position to succeed in a highly competitive industry.

Groups must know their roles

In practice, the extent of group involvement varies according to guidelines and expectations. Is the group to make recommendations only, or is it to select courses of action? Before discussions begin, clearly explain the group's role. This helps overcome possible dissatisfaction over decisions or recommendations that ultimately may not be approved or implemented. For example, management may be considering alternatives to reduce labor costs and ask supervisors to solicit *recommendations* from subordinates. In other cases, group members themselves have the power to make *decisions*. A cemetery maintenance crew could decide beginning and ending work hours. So long as the normal workday is completed, the group might decide to begin work early during summer months and avoid later afternoon heat.

Approaches to Group Decision Making

Group formats differ

Groups may consist of colleagues who work closely together or include persons who have few, if any, on-the-job interactions. For example, your department could have a committee that meets periodically to discuss methods of reducing the number of product defects, or a special company-wide task force might be appointed to recommend procedures to follow in the event that reductions of personnel are necessary. Frequently, groups meet together personally; at other times, it is impractical for group members to meet in person because of geographic limitations. In such situations, each person might indicate his or her response on a survey questionnaire, which is then summarized and reported. Let's examine several approaches to group decisions.

Ordinary Group Technique.   An approach that is not highly structured and consists of exchanging viewpoints among participants is termed the **ordinary group technique.** When discussion does not digress from designated topics, it results in a stimulating in-depth examination of issues. If the group strays from its task, time is not being used productively. An agenda provides structure and helps maintain control. You can always say, "Let's stay with our agenda; perhaps we can move along and get finished earlier." You must be fair and serve as manager of an open discussion of pros and cons.

Keep the group on track

Does group participation influence members' perspectives? Yes, but there is a potential danger. A group might be closely knit and composed of persons with considerable respect for each other. In this case, suppressing dissenting viewpoints because of a desire for group cohesiveness, or **groupthink,** may result. When like-mindedness becomes the main concern, groupthink thrives. It prevailed in the group decision processes the Kennedy administration used to plan the Bay of Pigs action in 1963. The decision makers tended toward "concurrence seeking." A fiasco resulted from faulty intelligence, failure to question Central Intelligence Agency assumptions, and a vast underestimation of Fidel Castro's ability to respond.[15]

What is groupthink?

Before stating your views on issues, encourage others to express their opinions. Recognize that especially vocal individuals can intimidate some persons. Try to get all members involved, and remember that silence does not necessarily mean agreement. Have you ever failed to state your viewpoint because it seemed different from that of respected group members? If so, you have an idea of how groupthink works.

Brainstorming.   Having group members express viewpoints about a topic or indicate possible solutions to a problem, regardless of whether they appear logical or sensible, is **brainstorming.** The purpose is to generate as many ideas as possible. For example, a group might be asked for suggestions to reduce expenses within a work unit or to recommend changes that will help increase productivity. Later, merits of these suggestions can be critically discussed and evaluated.

Keep the ideas and suggestions rolling

The physical layout for brainstorming groups should encourage communication, and the best results are attained when sessions are not unduly lengthy. For example, members face each other around a table and generate ideas for 30 to 45 minutes. People should be seated so that eye contact is possible and they can easily hear each other. As ideas are presented, no one comments on their worthiness. One person is chosen to record suggestions. Participants are encouraged to keep ideas coming and to keep them brief. They are urged to take cues from each other as a basis for expressing more thoughts. Frequently, many ideas are generated during the first few minutes of brainstorming. The group sifts out those with the greatest potential and spends the rest of a session refining the better ideas.

Statistical Analysis. The procedure of **statistical analysis** consists of gathering numerical data and computing results based on averages. Two such averages are the arithmetic mean and median. The arithmetic *mean* is the sum of a group of figures divided by the number of items in the group. Suppose you want to compute the mean hourly wage for employees in your department. The records show that the five workers earn hourly wages of $4.30, $4.10, $3.90, $4.50, and $4.80. The mean is $4.32 ($21.60 divided by 5). A second average is the *median,* the middle score in a distribution of numbers. The median salary for the five employees is $4.30.

Statistical analysis uses averages

Statistical analysis is nonpersonal and does not encourage group members to discuss various viewpoints. Analysis is restricted to classifying and interpreting numbers. Many decisions involve use of averages. If a salary issue arises, a decision to revise the wage scale might be based on how present salaries compare to averages of those paid by other companies. To gather opinions about the effectiveness of sales training, a regional sales supervisor could develop a questionnaire and solicit the views of the sales staff. Each salesperson could be asked to use a numerical scale and evaluate a series of statements. When the questionnaires are returned, the manager can compute averages to use in making decisions or recommendations.

▼

Consider This

1. People tend to categorize decisions as either "good" or "bad." What are the characteristics of a "good" decision?
2. How is communication related to effective decision making?
3. Under what circumstances should decisions be changed or revised?

Supervisors and MIS

What is an MIS?

Management information systems (MIS) provide managers with the information they need to perform their managerial responsibilities.

> Information affects almost everything we do—especially the way we do business. Among the important problems that must be resolved in handling information are (1) determining what information is required, by whom, and in what form; and (2) providing the necessary information where and when it is needed and at an acceptable cost.[16]

Even though computers are often a major component of MIS, they are not an absolute requirement. For example, well-organized, current data stored in file folders can serve as a source of information in the process of preparing reports or making decisions. Nevertheless, the term "MIS" has become associated with computer technology.

How do computers work?

The basic principle of how computers work is simple; they are machines programmed to perform specific operations, such as keeping a record of merchandise available for sale or processing payroll data. Computers accomplish tasks by using **hardware,** the equipment itself, to perform a series of instructions provided by **software,** often called programs. **Database,** another component of MIS, consists of data items stored within the system. A database might include records of absenteeism, days lost due to injuries, and turnover statistics. The computerized system can convert these data into meaningful information by computing absenteeism rates, comparing injury statistics over different periods of time, or calculating employee turnover ratios among various departments. Computers perform a phenomenal number of calculations in a short period of time.

Computer Technology is Amazing

Today, computers are abundant and impact every facet of the workplace from recordkeeping to strategic planning. The computer revolution began in the 1940s with development of the ENIAC, which weighed 30 tons, at the University of Pennsylvania. While it performed calculations over 1,000 times faster than electromechanical devices of its day, today's portable computers can do calculations many times faster than the ENIAC. In one minute, the Cray-2 supercomputer can do the work accomplished by a personal computer in three weeks, and the Cray-3 can do 10 billion calculations each second. Performance capabilities of computers will continue to increase with tomorrow's computers processing data at unimaginable speeds.

Business applications of computer technology include word processing, electronic spreadsheets, graphic displays, and database management.[17] **Word processing** is a system linking electronic hardware and software to produce and process written communication. Word processors combine features of an ordinary typewriter with software capability to do tasks such as generate repetitive letters, meaningfully combine separate paragraphs into documents, and replicate formats for office forms. Since data can be entered, stored, and retrieved on disks, tasks of revising and editing can easily be accomplished. Most word processors incorporate display screens to give operators a visual image of input entered into or contained within the system.

Word processing improves communication

Electronic spreadsheets consist of worksheets divided into columns and rows of numerical data. Through spreadsheets, users can alter one or more of the figures with the computer calculating the resulting change on all remaining rows and columns. Consequently, the need to do many manual calculations is eliminated. In forecasting sales, for example, it is possible to enter projected sales revenue and simulate outcomes under various economic conditions.

Spreadsheets eliminate hand calculations

Graphics programs enable numerical data to be converted into line graphs, bar charts, or pie charts. This technique is useful to show pictorial displays and indicate relationships among variables. Rather than looking at a series of numbers representing sales percentages for various geographic areas, it might be more useful to illustrate them through an easily interpreted pie chart.

Charts and graphs promote understanding

Database management systems let any number of users share a common database without duplication of available data. For instance, a record of employee social security numbers, hourly salaries, or mailing addresses can be accessed by users in payroll, personnel, and other departments. Whenever information needs to be updated, it need only be changed in the one database.

Why keep data stored in many files?

As users require greater access to companywide information, organizations are turning to databases to integrate their information and provide access to end users throughout the company. DBMS allow different application programs to easily access the same database and simplify the process of retrieving information from databases in the form of displays and reports.[18]

Using MIS Concepts

Supervisors play a key role in the flow of information

Supervisors are sources of information for employees, customers, and upper management, and they make information requests of others. As a supervisor, you are constantly involved with receipt or generation of information. For example, you ask for policy interpretations, approval of necessary equipment purchases, and authorization to hire employees. Generally, it is necessary to report operating statistics, submit payroll data, ensure adequate inventory levels, and administer departmental budgets. Through MIS, you have access to pertinent records, avoid the need to do burdensome manual calculations, and can readily generate repetitive report formats.

Overcome resistance to MIS

To gain maximum benefit from MIS, understand its role. A system should serve user needs, not complicate operations. Some supervisors hesitate to accept MIS primarily because they do not understand how it operates. These considerations can help overcome resistance to use of information systems.

☐ *Determine specific information needs.* Know what information is desired and share these views with MIS personnel. Too frequently, these people make inaccurate assumptions leading to generation of too much or too little data, often in a format that does not meet the needs of users.

☐ *Overcome anxieties about computers.* Learning to use computers is not something to fear. As is the case with operating any item of equipment, effectiveness requires familiarity and practice. Rather than stressing intricate complexities of how computers function, focus attention on practical workplace applications.

☐ *Emphasize the importance of computer literacy.* In the future, computers will become more commonplace and even easier to operate. Managers and employees who do not possess basic computer skills will be at a severe disadvantage in terms of needed workplace skills.

☐ *Recognize opportunities for improvement.* MIS must be flexible to accommodate changing circumstances. Systems should not be designed, installed, and then neglected. Information needs change; accordingly, a system must be revised and updated to serve persons who depend on it as a decision-making tool.

Supervisors and MIS specialists must work together

Successful supervision depends on effective performance of managerial functions, and communication represents a key factor in determining how well each function is performed. MIS provides ready access to data within a short amount of time, yet complications can arise between specialists who design MIS and the managers who use them. Some managers consider MIS personnel to be too technical and impractical. On the other hand, system specialists argue that managers are too vague and do not clearly specify their information needs. Communication can be improved by having both parties meet together, exchange views, and gain insight into each other's perspectives. Briefly, let's examine how MIS can assist supervisors to plan, organize, and monitor activities.

☐ *Planning.* Even though the pace of daily activities is hectic, supervisors cannot overlook the need to plan. MIS enables them to conserve time, reduce much repetitive paperwork, and keep updated records. Available data can be used to project expenses, estimate material needs, and determine personnel requirements. Maintaining adequate inventory is an important application of MIS. Supervisors quickly know current levels of inventory and can decide whether restocking is necessary to avoid shortages.

MIS aids planning

☐ *Organizing.* Increasing competitiveness, pressures to maintain quality, and reduction in the number of middle managers necessitate an emphasis on organizing human and equipment resources. MIS helps supervisors assign tasks, delegate work duties, and administer a broader span of management. Information and instructions can quickly be transmitted to employees and customers who are widely separated in terms of geographic location. A supervisor for a firm marketing merchandise over nationwide cable television can use MIS to structure program presentations, organize telephone sales representatives, and process orders from customers. Failure to organize can cause lost sales, mixed-up orders, and delayed shipments.

Use MIS to organize activities

☐ *Monitoring.* Through MIS, supervisors monitor budgets, quality, and production to compare actual results against standards. In addition, they have access to relevant facts and figures for an analysis of alternative courses of action necessary to maintain control of operations. Let's illustrate a practical example. You think that the number of product defects is too large. If data have been recorded consistently, MIS enables you to obtain desired statistics categorized by type of product, workshift, and equipment operator. Therefore, you are better able to resolve any apparent problems.

MIS helps supervisors monitor performance

▼

1. In the workplace, what obstacles must be overcome before MIS can be successfully implemented?
2. How can supervisors most effectively use MIS?
3. In the future, what impact will management information systems have on supervisors?

Consider This

Looking Back

You have studied the fundamentals of how to set objectives and make decisions. Now let's examine the objectives restated from the beginning of the chapter. As you review them, remember the importance of these concepts to the practice of effective supervision.

☐ **Understand the importance of objectives.** Objectives represent desired outcomes or accomplishments. They reflect company purposes, provide guidelines to implement functions, and identify resources needed for a firm's survival and growth. Supervisors use objectives to provide direction to their units, measure results, and create awareness of concerns requiring increased attention. Typical objectives involve scheduling of work, employee developmental activities, budget or staff recommendations, and performance of work duties with a minimum of defects.

☐ **Describe the various kinds of objectives.** Objectives can be categorized according to their purposes: decision oriented, routine, creative, and personal. Decision-oriented objectives involve making decisions to resolve existing or potential problems. Objectives related to performance of repetitive tasks are routine objectives. Creative objectives involve imaginative ideas that can be applied to improve profitability, productivity, or both. Finally, personal objectives represent what people seek to achieve for themselves.

☐ **Explain the technique of management by objectives.** MBO emphasizes employee involvement to determine objectives, compare performance against expectations, make necessary adjustments, and develop future objectives. Primary advantages of MBO are knowledge of work responsibilities, participation of employees in goal setting, coordination of work effort, and emphasis on productivity and job satisfaction. Problems involve getting management commitment, time-consuming paperwork activities, and inflexible responses to uncontrollable factors.

☐ **Discuss the role of decision making.** Decision making involves all parts of a firm and has a great impact on productivity, morale, and profits. The goal is to choose from various alternatives in a realistic manner. Supervisors must make timely decisions and clearly distinguish between major and minor concerns. The workplace includes decision makers with different attitudes, experiences, and expectations. Decision situations vary in the nature of emotional involvement, degree of emergency or routineness, extent of emphasis on the future, and the time available.

☐ **Explain the decision-making process.** Before making a decision, people should consider objectivity and foresight, recognize precedents, examine available resources, and understand the issues. The decision process consists of problem recognition, consideration of alternatives, collection of data, evaluation of alternatives, making/implementing the decision, and following up.

☐ **Examine the concept of management information systems.** MIS provide supervisors with information needed to perform their managerial responsibilities. In practice, most systems combine use of the computer, software, and a database. To be of maximum benefit, information from MIS must be timely, accurate, concise, relevant, and complete. Availability of desired facts and figures helps supervisors respond to inquiries, prepare reports, and make decisions.

Key Terms

bounded rationality	objectives
brainstorming	ordinary group technique
creative objectives	personal objectives
database	qualitative objectives
database management systems	quantitative objectives
decision making	recency syndrome
decision-oriented objectives	routine objectives
electronic spreadsheets	software
graphics programs	statistical analysis
groupthink	stereotyping
halo effect	strategic objectives
hardware	suboptimization
management by objectives (MBO)	tactical objectives
management information systems (MIS)	word processing

Review and Discussion Questions

1. What is the difference between quantitative and qualitative objectives?
2. A supervisor has been asked to improve the productivity of a unit. Explain the process of setting objectives to fulfill this responsibility.
3. Identify and discuss the most important features of good objectives.
4. To increase output per worker by 5 percent in the next six months, how might a supervisor implement the MBO process?

5. Because of a consultant's recommendation, your firm instituted the MBO approach within the last six months. The program is not working. What might be wrong?
6. Describe factors to recognize in distinguishing between major and minor decisions.
7. When making decisions, why must supervisors consider objectivity, past precedents, and resource availability?
8. Why is brainstorming a useful technique?
9. What is the difference between the arithmetic mean and the median?
10. How can MIS improve a supervisor's capability to make decisions?

Action Incident 4.1

The Goal-Oriented Supervisor

Jerry Marsh supervises 20 employees who work somewhat independently at their respective job assignments. Recently, he has become aware of the merits of having specific work objectives.

The firm has never used a formal approach to set objectives. Jerry is not sure how a suggestion to consider such a program might be received by either higher management or his workers. Yet he feels that something should be done to improve organization, reduce duplication of effort, and provide more cooperation and communication.

In addition, Jerry doesn't know whether to discuss these ideas with employees before sharing them with his boss. Traditionally, upper-level managers have been hesitant to accept any major change. If his suggestions should be received favorably, Jerry has mixed feelings regarding how objectives should actually be developed.

Discussion Questions

1. Is it necessary for a firm to use a formal approach to determine objectives?
2. Should Jerry Marsh discuss his concerns with employees and/or management? If so, which group should he contact first?
3. What impacts might specific work objectives have on Jerry's concerns about better organization, reduced duplication of effort, and improved communication?
4. How are specific objectives actually formed?

Action Incident 4.2

Doing It Over

Like most firms, Amze Company wants accurate records submitted to supervisors who in turn forward the data to middle managers. Several years ago, a procedure was begun whereby forms were given to employees to use when submitting information. Guidelines accompanied the forms. No one ever checked to see if employees followed the guidelines in filling out forms.

Middle management decided to find out whether the forms were being completed properly. In numerous cases, it was discovered that desired data were omitted, incomplete, or too general and vague. It was decided to require supervisors to have employees resubmit the most recent set of data in a form that followed the original guidelines. To help employees do this, an analysis sheet showing the needed revisions was returned with the forms employees were expected to correct.

Before the decision was implemented, it was presented as a routine item at the weekly supervisors' meeting. Middle management believed the procedure would improve future compliance and thought that many employees did not realize just what was required of them. Each supervisor was directed to implement the revision/correction process.

You were one of the supervisors at that meeting. It was your opinion that employees would respond negatively to the decision. You thought they would express their sentiments directly to you, and you anticipated that a considerable amount of time would be necessary to answer their questions.

Upon receiving the directions, the majority of employees indeed reacted unfavorably. They considered the request impractical, time consuming, and a waste of effort. Employees also complained about the amount of secretarial time necessary for typing the information correctly and believed that the revised form would only be checked and placed in files.

Discussion Questions

1. Was the decision to require revision and correction of the forms a good decision? Why or why not?
2. To what extent was the decision-making process recognized in forming the decision?
3. Assuming your superior disagrees with your opinion, should you have strongly expressed your viewpoints at the meeting?
4. What factors should you recognize in implementing the decision in your area of responsibility?
5. In responding to employees' objections, what types of considerations should you recognize?

Action Incident 4.3

The Wrong Decision

Upon her promotion to supervisor, Ann Rogers was determined to maintain close relationships with as many employees as possible. Ann wanted to be considered one of the group, and she made it a point to become involved in many off-the-job social functions. She was successful in forming, as well as maintaining, numerous personal friendships among her workers.

As time passed, Ann realized that this decision caused considerable difficulty in performing her duties. Employees took advantage of the personal friendships and failed to develop respect for her as a supervisor. Many workers ignored her requests, did not work any harder than they wanted to, and became undisciplined in performing work assignments. As a result, productivity declined and the work unit became disorganized.

George Mullen, Ann's boss, had not given her any indication that he was aware of the situation. However, Ann believed that he must know something about what was happening. She was reluctant to approach him on the matter, but she knew something had to be done to avoid further complications.

Discussion Questions

1. Explain whether Ann's original decision to become one of the group was appropriate.
2. Under the circumstances, what alternatives should Ann consider before making a decision on how to handle the situation?
3. Ann has the option of not taking any action. How can she justify a decision to do nothing?
4. Assuming that George is aware of the situation, what type of decision should he make?

Notes

1. Peter F. Drucker, *The Practice of Management* (New York: Harper & Row, 1954), p. 63.
2. Fred R. David, *Fundamentals of Strategic Management* (Columbus, Ohio: Charles E. Merrill Publishing, 1986), p. 28.
3. Drucker, *The Practice of Management,* pp. 37, 63.
4. Heinz Weihrich, "How to Set Goals that Work for Your Company—and Improve the Bottom Line!" *Management Review* 71 (February 1982), p. 65.
5. "Feedback: Informing People, a Management Tool," *Supervision* 49 (July 1988), p. 10.
6. R. Henry Migliore, "MBO Redefined," *Management World* 11 (May 1982), p. 19.
7. Arthur G. Bedeian, *Management* (Hinsdale, Ill.: Dryden Press, 1986), pp. 146–47.
8. Edmund R. Gray and Larry R. Smeltzer, *Management: The Competitive Edge* (New York: Macmillan, 1989), pp. 172–73.
9. Richard L. Daft, *Management* (Hinsdale, Ill.: Dryden Press, 1988), pp. 112–13.
10. Robert Kreitner, *Management,* 4th ed. (Boston: Houghton Mifflin, 1989), p. 160.
11. Kreitner, *Management,* p. 160.
12. Drucker, *The Practice of Management,* p. 354.
13. J. T. Burton, Jr., "The Subjective Factor in Decision Making," *Supervisory Management* 27 (July 1982), p. 11.
14. Jacob M. Schlesinger and Paul Ingrassia, "GM Woos Employees by Listening to Them, Talking of Its 'Team'," *The Wall Street Journal* (January 12, 1989), p. A1.

15. Irving L. Janis, "Groupthink," *Psychology Today* 5 (November 1971), p. 46.

16. John J. Stallard and George R. Terry, *Office Systems Management,* 9th ed. (Homewood, Ill.: Richard D. Irwin, 1984), p. 9.

17. Ricky E. Griffin and Ronald J. Ebert, *Business* (Englewood Cliffs, N.J.: Prentice-Hall, 1989), pp. 310–13.

18. Paul L. Tom, *Computer Information Systems* (Glenview, Ill.: Scott, Foresman, 1989), p. 158.

Suggested Readings

Carr, Clay. "Expert Support Environments." *Personnel Journal* 68, April 1989, pp. 117–18, 120–26.

Doitzer, Bernard A., and Alan G. Krigline. "When Making That Decision." *Management Solutions* 33, November 1988, pp. 3–8.

Drange, Kenneth. "Decision-Making in an Era of Changing Technologies." *The Office* 107, June 1988, pp. 79, 159.

Finney, Martha I. "Fair Game." *Personnel Administrator* 34, February 1989, pp. 45–48.

Harper, Stephen C. "Becoming an Objective-Minded Manager." *Management World* 17, June 1988, pp. 25–27.

Kaufman, Steve. "Going for the Goals." *Success* 35, January–February 1988, pp. 39–41.

Logan, George H. "Solve Problems Easier." *Supervision* 50, March 1989, pp. 14–16.

Post, Tom. "Managing the Unknown." *Success* 35, July–August 1988, p. 20.

Rowe, Alan J., and Richard O. Mason. "A Case of Alignment: Tying Decision Styles to Job Demands." *Management Solutions* 33, April 1988, pp. 15–22.

Sitterly, Connie, and Beth Whitley Duke. "How to Make the Right Decision." *Working Woman* 13, August 1988, pp. 25–26.

Managing Time

Learning Objectives

Where does it go? How can you use it better? These are basic questions about time. Many people fail to grasp the critical importance of using time wisely—until it is gone. These objectives have been developed to help you become a better time manager.

1. Emphasize the importance of time as a valuable resource.
2. Recognize common time wasters.
3. Understand the purpose of time logs.
4. Identify strategies to improve time management.
5. Explain how effective communication skills save time.

Time: A Valuable Resource

Time is a limited resource

"Time is the scarcest resource, and unless it is managed, nothing else can be managed," notes Peter Drucker, a leading management expert.[1] We can do nothing to create more time. We cannot bring back time that has passed. We can, however, develop strategies for using time better to achieve objectives. Some aspects of time usage can be measured precisely. Others defy direct calculation. It is easy to measure the number of units a production worker turns out per hour. It is much more difficult to determine exactly the time salespeople, office employees, or nurses spend on specific work duties.

Are you efficient as well as effective?

There is an important difference between efficiency and effectiveness. **Efficiency** implies doing a task properly. **Effectiveness** is the proper selection of the task in the first place. Assume that you have an important test in a couple of days. If time is set aside for study, you are effective. However, poor study habits and failure to concentrate on the material demonstrate a lack of efficiency. A clear determination of objectives and understanding of needed actions leads to efficient and effective use of time. Oral and written communication can be ineptly conveyed, which causes time to be lost clarifying misunderstandings and inaccuracies.

We all have different approaches to getting things done and a variety of personal peak working periods. Our life experiences, habits, abilities, and job expectations are dissimilar, and we have separate sets of personal problems and concerns. All of these factors influence how we use time available for the job. How do people rate as time managers? One observer says, "Only about 5 percent of the world's population practices 'superior' time management."[2]

Time theft is a major problem

Besides unintentional or careless misuse of time, some workers engage in **time theft.** This is deliberate waste or abuse of time that should be spent on job-related duties. They attend to their own affairs on company time, often using the firm's equipment or facilities for personal business. It is estimated that during 1988 time theft cost employers a whopping $200 billion.[3] Supervisors must be aware of the close relationship between time and cost. Time truly is money.

Recognizing Time Theft

1. Excessive socializing with colleagues and customers.
2. A consistent pattern of arriving late for work and leaving early.
3. Deliberately lying about illness to take advantage of sick-leave days.
4. Conducting another business on an employer's time or property.
5. Intentionally slowing the pace of productivity during regular work hours.

Source: Adapted from Anita Miller, "Time Thieves Erode Office Productivity," *Topeka Capital Journal* (August 21, 1988), p. 1D. Based on information from Robert Half International.

Supervisors and Time Management

Since supervisors are "middle persons," others make many demands on their time. Consequently, self-discipline and skillful time management are keys to meeting deadlines and getting work done. Unforeseen problems arise. Often, the amount of time necessary to complete tasks is uncertain. Picture yourself in this situation. The phone is ringing. Two workers are waiting to see you. A report has to be completed within the next two hours, and there is a meeting with the boss in a half hour. Within this environment, supervisors must function and keep things running smoothly. You will study techniques to help you in such situations.

Your time is not your own

Focus on Job Performance

Alas, supervisors do not have control over all of their time. Bosses require responses to requests. Employees need questions answered or information so they can do their work. Many supervisors do not think about how time is spent, nor have they learned where to concentrate their efforts. Performance expectations based on clear-cut knowledge of what needs to be done can conserve time. Supervisors often hesitate to start assignments because they are anxious about outcomes or they feel uncertain about something new and different. Instead of drawing up justifications for needed equipment, a new nursing supervisor might spend time examining facilities for cleanliness or checking the completeness of patient records. Let's examine several techniques to improve job performance.

The job must be done

Establish Priorities. Tasks are not equally important. A key strategy is to concentrate on those that are most urgent and have the highest potential payoffs. Top-priority tasks (A level) are essential and must be completed. Some tasks (B level) are of lesser importance and do not have pressing deadlines. Others (C level) are relatively unimportant and can be set aside, perhaps indefinitely. You've noticed that the filing system needs to be cleaned out and updated, and the annual report is due in three days. Also, two periodicals, which include several interesting articles, have just arrived. What are your priorities? The report (A level) must be completed. It has an immediate deadline and will not get done by itself. Revision of the filing system (B level) probably can be delayed for awhile. Finally, reading the periodical articles (C level) is the lowest priority and certainly is not mandatory.

You cannot do everything at once

To-do Lists. Given the hectic pace of the workplace, it is easy to overlook appointments, meetings, and deadlines. How can this be avoided? The answer is **to-do lists,** which consist of things to do, names, places, and dates. Regardless of where the information is recorded (on a notepad, calendar, professionally prepared time organizer, or even a piece of paper), write things down as soon as possible and keep the list in a handy place, such as by your telephone. Some people have been known to lose or misplace their to-do lists.

Don't forget; write it down

Some tasks are not fun
to do

Difficult or Disliked Tasks.   You may dislike doing a task or consider it to be difficult, yet another supervisor may have an entirely different view toward it. Nevertheless, we all must do things that are not our favorite activities. It is advantageous to tackle these tasks while you are fresh and have a high level of energy. This approach provides mental relief when the tasks are completed and helps avoid the additional frustration caused by procrastination. The key is to get started. In practice, many tasks turn out to be less problematic than anticipated, and time is not needlessly consumed worrying about the necessity to do them.

Learn to say no

Saying No.   It is customary for bosses, employees, and customers to make demands on time. You must recognize that you can do only so much and hesitate to obligate yourself to do more than can reasonably be accomplished.

> If you don't learn to say no, some people will let you do their jobs for them. Often, there is a discretionary choice. It's important to be selective and, if necessary, learn to say no tactfully. Otherwise, insufficient time will be available for essential work, and productivity is likely to suffer.[4]

By accepting additional responsibilities, self-imposed time pressures are created. Some supervisors overcommit themselves and then discover they simply cannot give their best efforts. People can use many rationales to justify why you should do whatever they want done. Usually, they do not consider your work load or other commitments you have undertaken.

Do you get results?

Results-Oriented Strategies.   "Organizing a day's work has never been known as the easiest job the manager faces," observes R. Alec Mackenzie, a noted expert on time management. "Still few of us recognize how hard it really is or how poorly we execute it."[5] How many situations have you encountered where improved planning and organization could have saved time? Several strategies are useful. Set reasonable priorities for each work period and stick with them. Try to think in terms of intended results and ask "what if" questions. Divide work into parts with subgoals for accomplishing portions of tasks. If necessary, ask questions and seek clarifications before proceeding with tasks. Figure 5.1 lists some practical observations on using time.

Applying Time-Management Techniques

Recognizing time wasters

Are you distracted by the usual time wasters—drop-in visitors, phone calls, socializing, indecision, procrastination, and meetings? Many supervisors simply do not realize how much nonproductive time is consumed by these activities, largely because they have not developed the habit of thinking about time. Let's look at several common time wasters and learn to recognize them.

Practical Observations about Time   **Figure 5.1**

---

1. Most tasks take more time than originally anticipated.
2. Time spent thinking things through usually is not wasted.
3. Unless new information is received or situations change, the length of time spent making a decision does not necessarily reflect the decision's quality.
4. Most persons make the best use of time by concentrating on the job at hand rather than attempting to accomplish several tasks at once.
5. Effective time usage generally decreases as the number of persons on the scene increases.
6. Short breaks can increase productivity; however, they should not replace periods of work.
7. Work on inappropriate tasks does not provide time-saving results.

Common Time Wasters

Time wasters, a term that refers to nonproductive uses of time, are categorized as either internal or external. *Internal* time wasters involve your ineffectiveness as a time manager. The *external* category consists of unnecessary time consumption initiated or controlled by others. For example, you decide whether to work or procrastinate and are responsible for your own self-discipline. However, you do not control the length of meetings called by your boss or whether another person decides to drop in for a visit. Figure 5.2 illustrates several common time wasters. Let's discuss each of them and help you become a master manager of your time.

You and others are the cause of wasted time

Drop-in Visitors. Unannounced visitors are commonplace in many firms. Even if business is discussed, conversations often digress from reasons for the visit. You may inadvertently encourage drop-ins because of your expressed desire to be infomed about everything. Nevertheless, such visitors interrupt your schedule, especially if you are working to meet an important deadline.

Unexpected visitors interrupt your schedule

Several techniques can be used to handle drop-ins. Should you not have time to visit, politely explain why. Perhaps a more convenient time can be arranged. Or tell the visitor you have only so many minutes to talk. The person is then aware your time is short. If you have one, your secretary can perform a valuable screening function by arranging an appointment for the visitor.

Stand while you talk. Be alert for an appropriate point to end the discussion. Express gratitude, and say what action will or will not be taken. If all else fails, say you have to end the visit and leave — go check on something, go to the restroom, or go down the hall for a drink of water.

Socializing. Drucker observes: "There is little doubt that the more people have to work together, the more time will be spent on interacting rather

Avoid excessive socializing

Figure 5.2   **Common Time Wasters**

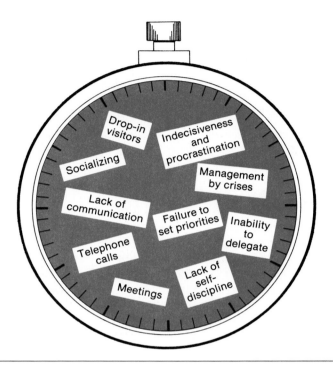

than on work and accomplishment."[6] Such interactions with others have meaning to most of us and certainly add enjoyment to our workdays. Yet excessive **socializing**—engaging in visiting, usually about things unrelated to the job—wastes time. There are ways you can control this. Don't hesitate to say that you have to finish a task. "I've got to get this work done. Could we chat later—at lunch or on a coffee break?"

Set time limits for conversations not related to the job. For example, since time is lost gossiping, discussing family activities, and talking about sports, decide the amount of time to spend on these activities and occasionally glance at your watch to check on how much time has slipped away. Do not prolong socializing. If you act busy, most people will catch the clue. Think about your unfinished work. Remember, it will not get done by itself. As a reminder, ask yourself, "If I don't complete my work, how will I feel about facing it again tomorrow?"

Communicating Effectively. Misinterpretation, vagueness, and omission are great sources of lost time. In oral communication, two people can think they agree on a topic when they really do not. You might instruct a worker to "get the work done and papers filed before leaving," but each of you has different work tasks and papers in mind. Written communication is also problematic. "Be sure to attend the meeting at 2 o'clock." What meeting? Which day? Where?

Emphasize why, who, what, where, and when in your communication. This reduces the likelihood of confusion and misunderstanding. Ask questions and seek clarifications before working on tasks. As might be imagined, your enthusiasm will decrease as the likelihood of doing them over again increases.

Get right to the point you want to make in memos, reports, and letters. Cordiality is important; don't ignore it, but also don't prolong the message. It is good practice to make and file copies of letters and other documents. Things not only get lost in transit, but copies of memos or reports can aid greatly as models for future reference.

Miscommunication causes lost time

Keep good records

Phone calls. The telephone is an essential method of communication, but it is also a source of much wasted time. Be brief and do not let conversations stray from pertinent topics. If one begins to lengthen, say you have an appointment, another caller waiting, or a meeting to attend. On calls you make or plan to receive, write down key points and have necessary information ready. You will save time and make fewer errors.

If possible, ask receptionists or secretaries to take calls when you do not want interruptions. You can group calls and return them at a convenient time. Telephone equipment with call forwarding is an aid. Don't waste time playing "telephone tag." If a person is unavailable, try leaving a message indicating when and where you can be reached.

Make your telephone time count

Meetings. Much of a supervisor's time is spent at meetings. They are a valuable method of communication to keep people informed, provide explanations, and give answers to questions. However, many meetings are nonproductive. Almost two decades ago, R. Alec Mackenzie commented that 90 percent of business people considered half the time spent in meetings to be wasted.[7] This observation is still valid; so how can time be saved at meetings?

Hold meetings only if necessary and set the time with care. Meetings scheduled before lunch breaks or near quitting time usually end promptly. Notify participants well in advance and indicate needed information or preparation. Start and finish promptly, and do not let the discussion stray from relevant topics. Stop any interruptive "subdiscussions" by saying, "One at a time, please. We all need to hear you." Discourage strong personalities from dominating discussions. See that everyone has an

Plan effective meetings

Is the meeting really necessary?

opportunity to speak. Do not let your meetings become one- or two-person productions.

The meeting place is important. Select one that minimizes chances for interruptions. Members can use coffee breaks to respond to calls or messages. Include only those who need to be present. Distribute proceedings to others who need to know what transpired. Before each meeting, check to be sure that buildings and rooms are unlocked. Too often, meetings are delayed because facilities are not accessible. If using handout materials, duplicate enough copies for all participants.

Figure 5.3 shows the format to use in preparing an agenda and developing a meeting plan. The **agenda** provides a guide to help you conduct meetings. It lets participants know what topics will be discussed so that they can be prepared. The **meeting plan** is a method for recording decisions made on each agenda item. It helps you keep notes, know who is responsible for assignments, and remember deadlines. Written minutes avoid later

Figure 5.3   **Formats for an Agenda and Meeting Plan**

Agenda Format

Meeting Announcement

Date: Time:
Place:
Names of Participants:

Tentative Agenda Items

1.
2.
3.

Additional Agenda Requests from Participants

1.
2.
3.

Meeting Plan Format

Agenda Item	For Action	For Discussion Only	Follow-Up
	Notes	Notes	Who is responsible? What are they to do? What is the deadline?

disputes over what occurred at meetings. Time is saved because you will have a record you can refer to later without having to contact others or search your memory to remember what happened.

Indecisiveness or Procrastination. Fear of mistakes and lack of certainty about outcomes of decisions are major causes of indecisiveness and procrastination. Most decisions cannot be postponed forever; sooner or later they must be made. For instance, it is easier for employees to accept yes or no responses than to be frustrated with maybe or we'll see replies.

Time lost through indecisiveness and procrastination can be reduced. Set deadlines and stick with them. Establish reasonable periods for thinking and gathering needed information. Then, *take action.* Get started and work on a task. Progress toward getting it finished will motivate you and develop incentive to do the remaining work. Mistakes will occur, but the fear of being wrong can lead to inaction. Everybody makes mistakes — the secret is to learn from them. Perfection is difficult to attain, and "good enough" results may be acceptable. Develop a sense for an appropriate degree of excellence. A clerk who handles many transactions will not always make correct change. Therefore, a reasonable amount of inaccuracy should be anticipated.

Putting things off is not the answer

Crisis Management. Reacting to situations and making decisions without an opportunity to plan is **crisis management.** Upon arriving at work, you find that two of your three order-processing machines are down. One of three order clerks and the person who can repair the machines have called in sick. A report on last week's production, needed for a 10 A.M. meeting with the regional manager, will not be ready because of computer problems, and you have a message that the company vice president wants to see you at 9.

Crises occur unexpectedly

You can handle such crises and reduce wasted time if you avoid hasty reactions. Think before acting. Learn to anticipate outcomes. Plan for contingencies and leave some time — 10 percent — for unforeseen situations. Don't wait until the last minute to finish a task essential to meet a deadline and then get sidetracked. Concentrate on necessary tasks. Consider available alternatives.

Set Priorities. You cannot do everything at once. If you spread yourself too thin, you will work on many assignments but complete few of them. Anxieties increase, frustrations build, and time is wasted. Make to-do lists. Break daily lists out of weekly lists. Assign work a first, second, or third priority and allocate efforts accordingly. Tackle the most necessary, difficult tasks before others. They should be the ones with first priority on your list. Avoid working on minor tasks to the neglect of high-payoff, essential activities. Don't be concerned about the priorities of others to the point of neglecting your own tasks. Concentrate first on your own job assignments. You cannot do everything and be everybody.

Develop a game plan

You cannot do everything yourself

Delegate Effectively. Supervisors often say, "I'll do it myself, and it will be done right." You cannot take the time to do your employees' work; you would just find yourself assuming additional work loads. Furthermore, your failure to delegate provides few incentives for employee development. Skill at delegation, with a resultant savings in time, can be improved if you recognize that many tasks can be assigned to others. Be sure that employees have the necessary abilities and expect a reasonable level of performance from them. Your workers may not do the job as well as you can, but they likely will do an acceptable job. Make sure you also give requisite authority to do the work you have delegated.

Gain control of yourself

Self-discipline. Self-discipline, which requires persistence in efforts to reach objectives, is the key to success in any activity. It is a combination of attitude, desire, and confidence. To maintain enthusiasm, remember to reward yourself for completing tasks. A break to participate in a recreational activity or to eat lunch at your favorite restaurant can increase incentive and promote productivity. Here are some self-discipline strategies to minimize wasted time:

- ☐ Do more challenging tasks while you are fresh. Save routine work for later in the workday.
- ☐ Reduce the impact of distractions.
- ☐ If possible, do work requiring uninterrupted concentration in another room.
- ☐ Learn to use idle time wisely.
- ☐ Use waiting time for doing small tasks, like reading nonpriority correspondence.

Consider This

1. Why do so many supervisors have difficulty managing their time?
2. In supervision, what is the most troublesome time waster?
3. How can supervisors discourage the practice of time theft?

Personal Dimensions of Time Management

Rules, guidelines, and suggestions are all valuable to developing your time-usage skills; yet, results depend on each individual. What about the supervisor as an interrupter of others? How about the relationship between time and human nature? How does one develop a good time log? Larry D. Alexander once observed that "time management is a very personal matter . . . Changing behavior takes time, and it may involve setbacks along the way; but, it can eventually be successful if there is an ongoing commitment."[8]

Supervisors as Interrupters

Do you interrupt others? People think of "time intruders" as being other persons. Supervisors who are guilty of this rarely realize it, and most workers will not tell them. (When you are quite involved in a task, how do you react when the boss appears?) Thinking about the other person is a good idea, but it is seldom practiced to the fullest extent, at least in terms of minimizing interruptions. From your experiences, note how interruptions always consume more time than anticipated. Think of benefits to the other person as well as yourself, if you learn to control them.

Do you cause others to waste time?

    Measure yourself by answering these questions?

- ☐ Do I spend coffee breaks or slack time in areas where others are working?
- ☐ Do I get directly to the message in each communication, especially in phone conversations and personal contacts, without excessive socializing?
- ☐ Do I communicate clearly and completely to avoid interruptive callbacks or return visits?
- ☐ Do I keep greetings — hellos and good-byes — short, especially while at somebody's office or workstation?
- ☐ Do I leave a message, instead of interrupting with "I need just a minute to . . ." when I see that the person appears busy?

Developing a Time Log

"Where does my time go?" is a question many supervisors ask. The answer is to develop a **time log,** which is a record of how time is spent. It shows priorities placed on time and who initiates various activities. Time is usually recorded in 15-to-30-minute intervals, and it is helpful to keep a time log for a three- or four-day period to recognize how time is actually used.

What is a time log?

    Figure 5.4 shows a nursing supervisor's time log, which can be adapted as a model for your own use. Note the simplicity — short notations on how time is spent as well as brief comments. It is important to record actions promptly; otherwise, you're likely to forget exactly what happened. The greatest benefit of a time log is this: It allows you to go back and review details of how time was used each workday. After recording information for several days, review each log and ask yourself these questions.

- ☐ Am I allocating time appropriately?
- ☐ What time-consuming activities can I eliminate?
- ☐ Are there any activities I can delegate?
- ☐ Where am I wasting time?

Time and the Nature of People

"You're taking too much time doing it that way." "That's a big waste of time." These are typical comments about using time. Realize that people have different ways of doing things. A time-saving method for you may be confusing

Try to understand human nature

Figure 5.4   **Example of a Time Log**

Date: 12/1/90

Time	How time is spent	Initiated by	Priority	Results/comments
8:00–8:30	Worked on next week's work schedule; due this afternoon.	S	1	Answered three telephone calls, but task was completed.
8:30–8:45	Meeting with director of nursing to discuss revision of work procedures.	B	1	Will get input from subordinates and prepare recommendations; due in three days (12/4/90).
8:45–9:00	Stopped by nurse's lounge.	S	3	Drank coffee and visited.
9:00–9:30	Checked inventory of supplies; tried to repair malfunctioning equipment.	S	2	Checking could have been delegated; wasted too much time on trial and error solutions—equipment still does not work.
9:30–9:45	Responded to important question from a subordinate and gave directions; noticed interesting magazine article and read several pages.	O/S	1/3	Should not have gotten side-tracked with article.

Initiated by: S = Self   Priorities: 1 = Top
                 B = Boss   2 = Average
                 O = Others   3 = Low

to another person. Also, we become accustomed to our own routines and frequently do things in a certain way because that is how they have always been done. Attitudes as well as feelings affect our productivity. Let's examine how time use relates to habits, attitudes, and feelings.

Habits are difficult to change

Habits. Established patterns of behavior are hard to change. Success comes only with an understanding that change is necessary and with a real desire to make needed corrections. Try to discipline yourself. Do not make a single exception that allows a return to past ineffectiveness. Reward yourself for getting things done on schedule, and try to experience a feeling of accomplishment that will reinforce your efforts to continue effective time-management practices.

People can learn time-management skills. Those who practice them have corrected many nonproductive habits. They have learned to overcome the common problem of needless worry about past decisions and situations. They do not dwell on past failures or circumstances beyond their control. They concentrate on necessary work, not just tasks that appear to be interesting or enjoyable.

Attitudes and Feelings. How you think and feel influences your accomplishments. All types of personal and job-related events trigger either positive or negative reactions. As a rule, work goes more smoothly when positive attitudes and feelings prevail. When you encounter difficulties sticking with a task or when concentration wanes, try doing something different. The change to a more routine, less demanding task will help, as would taking a break to refresh yourself. Key thoughts occur at such moments. You might look for shortcuts and better ways of doing things. Consider training others to do work that you dislike but which may properly be delegated to people who might enjoy it. You might dislike adding long columns of figures, but an employee may consider the assignment an enjoyable challenge.

Attitudes and feelings affect productivity

Views abound concerning mastery over the management of time. Perhaps you have heard comments involving how to get more done with less effort or observed people who always anticipate the completion of tasks but consistently meet failure. Many people feel overburdened and frustrated by attempts to balance their personal and professional lives. Gaining control over time is a key to accomplishing more. Do not get sidetracked by commonly accepted myths about the use of time.

Understanding Myths about Time

1. With more time available, work is likely to get completed sooner. (Frequently, extended deadlines simply encourage procrastination.)
2. People who look busy get a lot accomplished. (Appearances can be deceiving. The person who seems to be busy could be muddling along without getting much accomplished.)
3. By working faster, more assignments will get finished. (An old adage holds that "haste makes waste." Completing work within a minimum amount of time does not imply quality job performance.)
4. There's seldom time for personal activities. (If an activity is really meaningful, it's safe to bet that time will be found for it.)
5. Time is not money. (The loss of 5 minutes each hour amounts to 40 minutes per 8-hour day and 3⅓ hours per week.)

Communication and Time-Management Skills

Effective communication
saves time

Communication and time-management skills must be developed. Too often, insufficient effort is given to building these skills. Assumptions are incorrect, actions are poorly planned, and paperwork is allowed to accumulate. Effective reading and listening skills improve communication and lessen the likelihood of misunderstandings. Finally, time must be viewed as an important concern. Figure 5.5 indicates several factors to recognize in managing time.

Assumptions and Timing. As a supervisor, it is easy to assume workers know as much as you do about work-related issues and topics. You take for granted that your staff knows the necessary details and possesses relevant background data. Avoid these assumptions by taking care to provide needed information and opportunities for questions, even though some may be emotional or complex. Make sure to follow up. Get back to employees with answers to any questions you cannot answer now.

Figure 5.5   **Factors to Recognize in Managing Time**

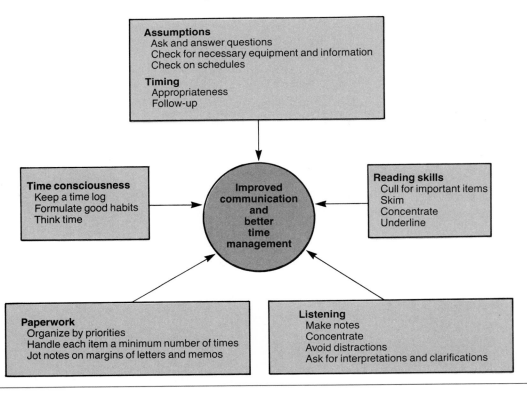

Do not assume that everything is in order. You need to check and recheck so that things work out as scheduled. Equipment and supplies are not always shipped as anticipated. Facilities may not be arranged as planned. People confuse dates, places, and times. Sometimes the unexpected happens. Assume that a meeting has been scheduled to hear an out-of-town speaker. Arriving, employees discover that the building is locked. After a 40-minute wait, somebody arrives with a key, unlocks the front door, and leaves. Does everything work out fine? No. No one has keys to the inside doors. More time is wasted.

Assumptions may be incorrect

Timing, the selection of an appropriate moment to begin an action, can enhance the likelihood of getting desired responses with a corresponding savings of time. When is the best time to see the instructor of a course you are taking? It probably is not just before class or lunch. The instructor will likely be most approachable early in the day while fresh or just after a class.

How's your timing?

Reading Skills. Vast amounts of written communication are produced, and we expect this to continue. Yet much written matter is irrelevant — junk mail, material of no interest to you, or information you already have. You must learn to cull unimportant reading matter and expediently allocate your reading time.

Read for results

Seize every chance to develop reading skills. A rapid reading rate is a plus, but you must also comprehend what you read. These guidelines can save you time: skim for concepts but read carefully for details; concentrate and, whenever possible, avoid distractions or interruptions that destroy thought continuity; underline key concepts, phrases, or terms to help you review and locate pertinent points.

Listening Skills. Are you a good listener? If so, you will not spend time contacting others for missed information. Supervisors do not always listen carefully when they disagree with a speaker's philosophy or viewpoint. Several suggestions save time. Try not to argue mentally. Train yourself to concentrate on what is said rather than on the speaker's distracting mannerisms, speech habits, or philosophical differences. Take brief notes as you listen, or at least jot down pertinent information as soon as possible. Request interpretations and clarifications to reduce chances of misunderstanding. When someone speaks too rapidly or tends to get sidetracked in conversations, ask him or her to speak more slowly or make a comment to redirect their attention to the topic.

Listen for key points

Paperwork. Is your desk covered with forms, letters, and reports demanding attention? Paperwork can accumulate rapidly, and you can waste a lot of time just shuffling through it. A key time saver is to control the flow of paperwork. Categorize paper according to priorities (daily, weekly, and monthly) or topics, whichever is most useful. Prompt filing of papers reduces chances of misplacing them. If you take action as

Reduce piles of paperwork

paperwork crosses your desk, piles of paper remain at a minimum. Do not procrastinate until it gets the better of you and seems insurmountable. Handle each piece of paper a minimum number of times — if possible, just once. This is mostly a matter of self-discipline. In many instances, you can reduce your response time by making a phone call. Jot down notes on margins of letters and memos. Keep photocopies if they are needed. Put the burden of further communication on the other person. For example, say, "If I don't hear from you, I'll assume the schedule is satisfactory."

Learn to think about time

Time Consciousness.   Think time. This is critical to using time well and communicating time concerns to others. As you think and plan time, opportunities will arise to get things done more efficiently. You will also find that your workers become more time conscious by observing your time-saving methods. Charles J. Ferderber observes that the bottom line for time management involves three "ates": eliminate, insulate, and concentrate.[9]

☐ Eliminate unnecessary activities.
☐ Insulate yourself to maximize time usage that can be controlled.
☐ Concentrate on the most important priorities.

As you continue to be time conscious, distinguish between anticipated and actual outcomes. When you're busy, it is easy to assume that tasks are getting accomplished. If you look back later, you may be surprised to discover that all the busyness failed to generate worthwhile results.

Consider This

1. What is the most important factor to recognize in gaining control over time?
2. How can supervisors avoid wasting their subordinates' time?
3. What is the greatest obstacle to overcome in using a time log?

Looking Back

Consider how to apply the concepts and suggestions in the chapter to become a better time manager. By exercising control over time, you will be more productive and encounter fewer frustrations. As you review, launch your own plan to attack time waste and take control of both personal and supervisory job time.

☐ **Emphasize the importance of time as a valuable resource.** Time cannot be replaced and is available only in limited supply. People have different peak working periods and a wide variety of ways to do their jobs. It is crucial that time be used wisely. Time theft is widespread, costly, and causes a loss in productivity. Through increased awareness and exemplary behavior, supervisors can help alleviate this problem. Bosses as well as workers place demands on a supervisor's time. Unforeseen events and problems arise, and you must plan for them. Supervisors must clearly understand what tasks need to be done and how results will be used.

☐ **Recognize common time wasters.** Most people do not recognize how much time is actually wasted during a workday. Failure to attain goals or meet deadlines is often due to needless mistakes and misunderstandings. Common time wasters include indecisiveness, procrastination, crisis management, failure to set priorities, inability to delegate, and lack of self-discipline. Also, drop-in visitors, excessive socializing, lack of or poor communication, ineffectively handled phone calls, and meetings are a source of wasted time.

☐ **Understand the purpose of time logs.** Time logs help you recognize how time is actually spent and create awareness of priority assignments for work activities. Also they allow you to know who initiates these activities. This information provides a way for you to determine proper allocation of time, know what items can be eliminated or delegated, and understand where time is wasted.

☐ **Identify strategies to improve time management.** Concentrate on how time is used. Arrange tasks into A, B, and C priorities. Make to-do lists, which serve as valuable memory aids. Do different tasks while you are fresh and have a high energy level. Before obligating yourself to do more than can reasonably be accomplished, learn to say no. Divide projects into small parts to avoid being overwhelmed at the amount of work that needs to be done. Ask questions and seek clarifications before proceeding with assignments.

☐ **Explain how effective communication skills save time.** Opportunities to save time are a part of all aspects of supervision. They include expedient handling of paperwork, improvement of listening as well as reading skills, careful examination of assumptions, and timing—the selection of proper moments to initiate actions. Supervisors need to "think time" and develop time consciousness.

Key Terms

agenda	socializing
crisis management	time log
effectiveness	time theft
efficiency	time wasters
meeting plan	to-do lists

Review and Discussion Questions

1. Why are people, especially supervisors, not better time managers?

2. How can supervisors overcome reluctance to begin working on tasks that are new, different, or involve uncertainties concerning possible outcomes?

3. Discuss the time wasters supervisors encounter.

4. Excessive socializing is a common source of wasted time. How can supervisors avoid this?

5. Before working on easier tasks, why should supervisors try to complete difficult assignments?

6. How can supervisors overcome the waste of time resulting from procrastination and indecisiveness in decision making?

7. What steps can be used to reduce wasted time in meetings?

8. What actions can supervisors take to help workers improve their time management practices?

9. What essential items should be included in time logs?

10. Discuss the relationship between communication skills and effective time management.

Action Incident 5.1

What Happens to My Time?

Connie Smith is a nursing supervisor at Newsome Hospital. She is energetic, constantly on the move, and always volunteers assistance to patients, nurses, and other members of the staff. Connie wonders what happens to her time, and she is concerned about how to use it better. At the end of a recent workday, she listed time allocated for various activities and time actually spent on them.

Minutes Allocated	Minutes Actually Spent	Activity
30	45	1. Meeting with the director of nursing to discuss the new operations policy and two minor problems with subordinates. (Fifteen minutes were spent in the director's office waiting for another meeting to end.)
40	30	2. Completing necessary reports and daily paperwork.
45	50	3. Interviewing job applicants.
15	20	4. Trying to repair equipment that failed to function properly. (Connie is unfamiliar with repair procedures and relies on trial-and-error techniques.)

Minutes Allocated	Minutes Actually Spent	Activity
15	0	5. Reading an assignment for an in-service seminar and glancing through a professional nursing magazine.
55	55	6. Attending an in-service seminar, part of the hospital's continuing education program.
0	15	7. Socializing with other supervisors and subordinates.
40	40	8. Accompanying doctors on visits to patient rooms.
40	20	9. Checking facilities to be sure that everything is functioning properly and that workers are doing their jobs.
30	40	10. Morning and afternoon coffee breaks.
30	30	11. Lunch in the hospital cafeteria.
20	30	12. Searching through files to locate needed information.
40	50	13. Responding to employee questions about procedures and handling minor problems involving patients, doctors, and others.
20	15	14. Writing memos to nurses and higher-level managers.
45	30	15. On the phone.
15	10	16. Reading mail and internal hospital correspondence.

Discussion Questions

1. Did Connie actually spend her time in the manner she had expected?
2. If an emergency had occurred, which activities might have been postponed or eliminated?
3. For each of the activities consuming more time than anticipated, list two factors that Connie might consider to improve time usage.
4. Should Connie consider a daily time log? If so, what might help her use it properly?

Action Incident 5.2

It's a Madhouse

Bob Collins is office manager for Dome Products. The staff consists of four others, including Ann Henderson, the secretary. It's Tuesday, and Bob has been at work for about two hours. Before leaving for work, he had an argument with his teenage daughter because she had left the family car low on gas and had disregarded curfew. As he left home, she was crying. On the way to work, Bob had a flat tire. He arrived 10 minutes late.

It's a busy day. Two staff members have been deluged with phone orders and are getting testy with Ann because she isn't typing orders fast enough. Ann says she still has six letters left from yesterday. She is becoming frustrated.

Jan Jones, a staff assistant, has misplaced the file for Alto Enterprises. Earlier, Alto's bookkeeper called and was less than pleased with statements that have been incorrect for three consecutive months. To add to the confusion, Jan has just told Bob that she is not feeling well and must go home. Just as Bob learned this, a sales representative who is seldom in town arrived and is waiting to see Bob. The salesperson wants to discuss purchases of office equipment.

Even though interrupted twice by phone calls, Bob has spent the past 15 minutes rummaging through his desk and file drawers trying to locate a brokerage-house confirmation, which contains important income tax information, for 100 shares of recently purchased stock.

Bob pauses for a moment, and the thought crosses his mind — this office is a madhouse.

Discussion Questions

1. What can Bob Collins do to improve use of (a) his time and (b) the staff's time?
2. As to time management, what is Bob's most urgent task?
3. Considering the importance of time, human relationships, and effective job performance, what should Bob do about:
   a. his unhappy child at home?
   b. the sales representative?
   c. Jan's absence due to illness?
   d. The misplaced file?
4. Who is responsible for the conflict between Ann Henderson and the two staff members who are upset with her?

Action Incident 5.3

I Manage My Time

Jane Dillon, a supervisor at King Industries, regards herself as an organized person. One day, she was bragging about her time management skills and commented to Roy Gilligan, her boss, "It's other people who waste most of my time." Roy, the company's self-proclaimed authority on time, asked her to choose a day and note how time was actually spent. Partly to satisfy him and partly out of curiosity, Jane recorded the following information.

Time	Activity
8:00–8:15 A.M.	1. Started to collect materials for the weekly report due in two days; made two phone calls.
8:15–9:00	2. Glanced at a summary report of last week's sales; called for a dental appointment; arranged to have lunch with a friend.
9:00–9:30	3. Stopped at employee lounge; socialized with colleagues and drank coffee.
9:30–10:30	4. Weekly meeting with subordinates; meeting lasted 15 minutes longer than anticipated.
10:30–11:00	5. Meeting requested by Roy to discuss a personnel matter.
11:00–12:00 P.M.	6. Made a trial-and-error attempt to repair a malfunctioning computer.
12:00–1:00	7. Lunch with the friend; arrived late because of a discussion with an employee over a personal problem.
1:00–1:15	8. Returned two telephone calls.
1:15–2:00	9. Developed purchase specifications for new equipment (used the wrong forms).
2:00–2:30	10. Attempted to resolve a problem with a dissatisfied customer.
2:30–3:00	11. Revised the work schedule for next week.
3:00–3:40	12. Unintentionally took time to read two interesting periodical articles.
3:40–4:00	13. Called a sick friend.
4:00–4:20	14. Took a coffee break.
4:20–5:00	15. Once again, started to gather material for the weekly report.

Discussion Questions

1. How well does Jane manage time?
2. To what extent are interruptions by others a problem for Jane?
3. How might Jane be a better time manager?
4. Why should Jane continue to use a time log?

Notes

1. Peter F. Drucker, *The Effective Executive* (New York: Harper & Row, 1967), p. 51.
2. Susan T. Parker, "How the Boys in the Office Mishandle Time," *Iron Age* 225 (March 1, 1982), p. 44.
3. Paul Scelsi, "Time Is Money—Lots of It," *Management World* 17 (November–December 1988), p. 19.

4. Donald S. Miller and Stephen E. Catt, *Human Relations: A Contemporary Approach* (Homewood, Ill.: Richard D. Irwin, 1989), p. 381.
5. Alec Mackenzie, *The Time Trap* (New York: AMACOM, 1972), p. 61.
6. Drucker, *The Effective Executive,* p. 31.
7. "How to Make the Most of Your Time," *U.S. News & World Report* 75 (December 3, 1973), p. 47.
8. Larry D. Alexander, "Effective Time Management Techniques," *Personnel Journal* 60 (August 1981), p. 640.
9. Charles J. Ferderber, "10 Techniques for Managing Your Time More Effectively," *The Practical Accountant* 14 (August 1981), p. 68.

Suggested Readings

Bryne, John A. "Don't Let Time Management Be a Waste of Time." *Business Week* No. 2997, May 4, 1987, p. 144.

"Get It Done Today," *Supervision* 48, June 1986, pp. 6, 11.

Goode, Erica E. "Help for Procrastinators." *U.S. News & World Report* 103, November 9, 1987, p. 106.

Harris, Marlys J. "The Theory of the Busy Class." *Money* 16, April 1987, pp. 203–6, 208, 210, 212, 214, 216, 218, 220.

Martin, Wallace. "Taking Control of Time Off." *Personnel Administrator* 32, June 1987, pp. 195–96, 198–200.

Matejka, J. Kenneth, and Richard J. Dunsing. "Time Management: Changing Some Traditions." *Management World* 17, April 1988, pp. 6–7.

Oncken, William. "The Manager's Time Machine." *Success* 34, October 1987, p. 14.

Phillips, Steven R. "The New Time Management." *Training and Development Journal* 42, April 1988, pp. 73–77.

"Spending Time Wisely." *Management Review* 76, February 1987, p. 9.

Wilkinson, Roderick. "Don't Spend It—Invest It." *Supervision* 49, July 1988, pp. 3–6.

Training and Professional Development

Chapter

6

Learning Objectives

Training is vital because job knowledge is a key to successful performance. Supervisors play important roles in training. These objectives have been developed to assist your study. Much of the content of this chapter has dual application. It applies as you train and develop your workers and also applies to your own development as a supervisor.

1. Understand the elements involved in learning.
2. Discuss ways to improve training effectiveness.
3. Know how to determine training needs.
4. Discuss methods of training.
5. Explain techniques used to evaluate training.
6. Understand the role of professional development.

The Role of Training and Learning

Training refers to acquiring skills needed to do job tasks. New workers must understand company policies as well as know how to operate equipment and complete required paperwork. More experienced employees need training to keep up with technological advances, adapt to revised work procedures, and acquire information about new products and services. Well-trained employees play vital roles in improving productivity and maintaining quality. They are less likely to make costly errors or needlessly waste time in deciding proper courses of action. Supervisors have the major responsibility for training subordinates. Therefore, it is necessary to know how people learn and select appropriate methods for training them.

Training is essential

Growth in the service and information sectors of the economy has changed the nature of many jobs. For numerous manufactured products, the United States has lost much marketshare to other nations.

> Less than 20 years ago, the United States manufactured about 50 percent of the world's television sets, 90 percent of the world's radios, 76 percent of the automobiles, and 47 percent of the world's steel. Now we produce barely 6 percent of the world's TV sets and radios combined, 28 percent of the cars and 20 percent of the world's steel.[1]

Even though the creation of many new jobs is anticipated, a gap will exist between qualifications demanded by employers and skills possessed by job applicants. Of necessity, business and industry will assume an increasingly greater role in training employees. It is estimated that corporate America spends over $40 billion annually to train 8 million workers.[2] The cost of remedial education has reached $21 billion per year.[3]

Over the years, viewpoints toward the field of training have changed considerably.[4] Sixty years ago, training was accorded little recognition. Trainers simply demonstrated or explained various skills. Training grew in importance during World War II. By the 1970s, it broadened into management development and career planning, and trainers reported to officer-level positions. In the future, the emerging global economy, emphasis on competitiveness, continued technological advancements, and greater complexity of human interactions will contribute to the need for increased training.

Training has grown in importance

Illiteracy in the workplace is a growing concern. David Kearns, chairman and CEO of Xerox Corporation notes:

> The American work force is in grave jeopardy. If current demographic and economic trends continue, American business will have to hire a million new workers a year who can't read, write, or count.[5]

The Learning Process

Learning, which is a complex process, is the acquisition of knowledge and skills resulting in a change of behavior. The learner goes from having little or no background about a concept or operation to mastery. People possess

Learning involves behavioral change

various background experiences and differ in their abilities to learn. A mechanically oriented person may quickly learn how to repair an item of equipment but at the same time be less adept at collecting data and writing a report.

Active participation encourages learning. Assume that an employee must know how to remove and clean the blade on an electric band saw. Verbal instructions alone may be insufficient. The process can be learned more effectively by combining explanations with actual practice of the procedure. Supervisors sometimes fail to recognize the extent of knowledge possessed by learners. It is easy to take too much for granted. Through understanding elements in the learning process, supervisors can develop training to be of maximum benefit to learners. Figure 6.1 shows several of these elements.

Goals provide reasons to learn

Goals. Job-related goals include a desire to upgrade work skills, become more knowledgeable, attain job security, and prepare for promotion. Clearly established goals provide direction to the learner and make learning a worthwhile activity. Otherwise, the learner may wonder, "What is the purpose of this training? Why should I pay attention to these instructions?"

Learning requires effort

Motivation. Ideally, the goal is important enough for people to want to learn. Having a goal, however, is not enough. The learner must want to exert enough effort to achieve it. To motivate learning, you must specify and emphasize benefits that are important to the employee. An employee may want to become a first-line manager but not desire to spend extra time gaining the needed knowledge and skills. Consequently, lack of motivation is detrimental to successful learning.

Figure 6.1   **Elements in the Learning Process**

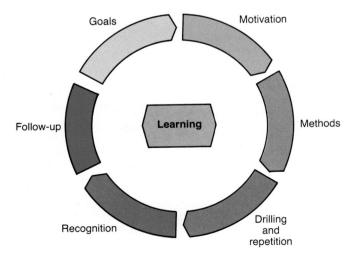

Methods. Learning involves reading, seeing, hearing, thinking, and a variety of methodologies. The method selected depends on the learning task. The demonstration method is useful for learning how to service an air conditioning unit. A role-playing exercise, involving a buyer and seller, is better for learning sales techniques. The lecture, including handouts and question-answer opportunities, is appropriate for explaining work rules and procedures. Later in the chapter, you will study several instructional methods.

Consider instructional methodology

Drilling and Repetition. To be learned adequately, concepts need to be reviewed and skills must be practiced. Nobody comprehends the content of a lengthy document or learns to operate a word-processing system through observation alone. Drilling and repetition are necessary to develop a high level of skill. The amount of drilling and repetition needed depends on the complexity of a task. For example, computer technicians must possess a vast amount of technical knowledge to perform successfully.

Practice makes perfect

Recognition. Praise makes workers more self-confident and provides an incentive for them to continue their efforts to learn. This can be as simple as saying, "Jill, you really made progress today." In cases where learning is complex, sit down with the learner and discuss performance. Positive recognition may make a difference between success and failure to a learner who is striving to master a new technique or procedure.

Recognize progress and provide encouragement

Follow-up. Even though learners seem to grasp concepts and appear ready to apply their new knowledge, you need to check on how they are doing. Too often, learners are left on their own without opportunities to ask questions or have their work examined. When this occurs, the likelihood of incorrect work practices increases dramatically. By promptly checking on performance, any improper application of learning can be corrected. Note the following pointers on how to make learning relevant.

Have desired learning outcomes occurred?

Make Learning Relevant

1. Explain why it is important for learners to know about each topic or issue. *Emphasize how the learner benefits.*
2. Recognize the extent of prior knowledge possessed by learners. *Be certain the level of instruction is not too complex or too simplistic.*
3. Determine if learners are grasping key points. *Summarize major concepts and ask questions.*
4. Provide feedback and correct misunderstandings. *Compliment learners on their progress.*
5. Consider the pace of explanatory presentations. *Remember, you are familiar with the material, and learners are not.*
6. Allow sufficient time for learning. *Avoid shortcuts that confuse learners.*
7. Explain how topics relate to each learner's job. *Stress on-the-job applications.*

Determining Training Needs

Who should be trained?

To train effectively, first determine needs. While there is no single procedure to follow, assessing needs is essential in developing well-trained employees. According to a national survey sponsored by the American Society for Training and Development, over two thirds of U.S. firms use these assessment techniques: interviews, direct observation, examination of work/productivity measures, and questionnaires.[6] Let's examine several ways for determining who should be trained.

Appraise work performance

Formal Appraisals. A formal employee appraisal system serves to identify strengths and weaknesses in job performance. Your review of evaluations can indicate where additional training is necessary. For instance, a consistent pattern of low evaluations on product knowledge shows a need for several training sessions or a short course to help workers gain more knowledge about the products they are selling. Also, at the time appraisal results are discussed with employees, they can be asked to suggest training activities.

Note improper work habits

Observation. Since you work closely with subordinates, you have a firsthand opportunity to observe and note instances where training can improve operations. In the hectic pace of daily activities, this approach to gathering data is frequently overlooked. Be alert; when you see inferior work, unsafe practices, or unnecessary waste, note it on a file card. You can use these data to develop training recommendations and perhaps justify a request for additional monies in the training budget.

Quality is a top priority

Quality of Work. In today's competitive marketplace, there is no substitute for quality. Businesses cannot afford to alienate customers or risk lawsuits. Examine how well products are manufactured, and observe how well services are performed. You may learn of errors and shoddy work. Note the number of consumer complaints. By keeping accurate records, you will be aware of problems that can be solved through training.

Listen to employees

Employee Suggestions. Few people know more about a job than the person who does it. Employees possess a wealth of information about job requirements and how training can improve performance. Questionnaire surveys and interviews can help you gather worker suggestions and recommendations. A tabulation of comments and opinions might indicate consistency in their views toward needed training. If so, appropriate training activities can be developed. Remember to provide feedback. When employees perceive that you consider their views to be important, they are more likely to continue sharing them with you. This can be a vital factor in improving training.

Training Priorities

Conduct effective training

Setting priorities enhances your ability to develop effective training. When management, trainers, and learners view training as a valuable experience, the best results are possible. Remember, trainees will have differing views. Some might eagerly anticipate the challenge of learning new concepts. Others may be somewhat hesitant, often because they question their abilities as learners. Awareness of the following priorities increases the likelihood of getting successful results.

Planning. The best training involves carefully thought-out objectives, methods of presentation, and means of evaluation. Ask relevant questions. What will the training accomplish? Who should participate? Which topics are essential? What instructional methodology is most appropriate? How can the training be evaluated? Answers to these questions provide information necessary to design and implement training activities.

Plan ahead

Essential content. Material presented must be relevant. Through needs assessment, deficiencies can be determined. According to the national survey noted earlier in the chapter, 80 percent or more of the respondents regularly provided training in the areas of employee orientation, supervisory skills, and management development. For supervisors and new managers, the top four topics included performance appraisal, discipline, motivation, and communication skills.[7]

Examine the content

Scheduling. Training activities must stay on schedule. When formal training is conducted, the length of each session and amount of time between them are relevant concerns. When training covers detailed topics, such as accounting procedures or computer techniques, be careful not to present too much subject matter at any one session. Enough time should be allowed between meetings for learners to review material and understand major concepts.

Schedule realistically

Repetition and practice. To master tasks, trainees need to practice. It is difficult to learn even a simple task, such as tying a knot, without repetition. Since trainers know the subject matter, it is easy for them to assume incorrectly that learners possess more knowledge than they actually do. Be sure to include opportunities for practice in your training program.

Repetition and practice are necessary

Practicality. Trainees have a natural incentive to learn concepts that will improve job performance. Frequently, explanations are too complicated or too abstract, and learners do not understand the relationship between training and their job responsibilities. Trainers must consistently emphasize *how* training applies to the job.

Be practical

Formal structure. In our daily lives, many lessons are learned informally through interactions with others. However, a formal structure (including trainers, assignments, and scheduled sessions) increases the likelihood that specific subject matter will be studied and discussed. When possible, therefore, consider implementing a formal approach to training.

Formal structure enhances learning

Understand Priorities. Let's consider an example of how to recognize training priorities. You have just hired a new receptionist/bookkeeper who must know how to schedule appointments, provide information, and keep records. Knowledge of how to transfer calls, use call forwarding, and initiate intraoffice calls is essential. Also, he or she has to practice proper telephone

Set priorities

etiquette. This person must be capable of giving correct information and understanding the company's bookkeeping system. Each of these activities necessitates training. You will plan learning experiences and provide practice opportunities, concentrating on practical applications.

Consider This

1. Why is it essential for supervisors to understand how people learn?
2. What can supervisors do to determine training needs?
3. How can supervisors plan effective training presentations?

Training Considerations

Train to improve performance

The most obvious benefit of training is the acquisition of job knowledge. However, other, possibly less obvious, benefits also exist. Training improves employee attitudes toward the job and firm. It serves to develop confidence and security and reduces unnecessary costs and waste. When personnel are well trained, fewer conflicts will arise between supervisors and subordinates or among workers themselves. Also, training is instrumental in gaining the skills and knowledge needed to handle additional job responsibilities.

Seldom, if ever, is job competency a chance occurrence. It requires a capability to learn and is aided by proper presentation of instructional materials. Greater competitive pressures and rapid advances in technology increase the need for a well-trained labor force. Let's review several essentials to help you become a capable trainer.

Consider content and methodology

Instructional Considerations. Remember, effective instruction combines knowledge of content with a proper teaching technique. Both factors are vital. Perhaps you've had instructors who knew their subject but were poor in conveying knowledge to students, and you probably have had teachers who used excellent methods but lacked a firm grasp of their subject. Constantly review and, if necessary, upgrade your own job knowledge. Should weaknesses become apparent, get further education and training. Later in the chapter, you will study several widely used methods of training. Strive to understand them and know how they are used to develop workplace skills.

Prepare to train

Preparation is an essential characteristic of successful training. Consider the learner's prior knowledge and experience and focus on the best means to convey subject matter. To be prepared, think of why, who, what, how, when, and where. Then you will more likely present instruction that is organized and to the point. Review the following instructional considerations and use them as a guideline.

Instructional Considerations

Why: First, recognize reasons for holding training sessions. The rationale should be obvious, realistic, and focused on definite objectives.

Who: Decide who is to take part in the training. It is likely to be mandatory for new personnel. For others, you must select persons to participate.

What: Specify the content to be presented. Make a written plan or outline of topics and subtopics. Recognize the need to reinforce learning.

How: Choose the methods you will use. Consider tasks and decide on the best methods — lectures, discussions, demonstrations, role playing. Also, consider use of films, handouts, and audio/visual aids that might be useful.

When: Decide on the time of day or evening and the number of sessions as well as their length.

Where: If there is a choice among locations, select facilities that best accommodate trainees. Focus attention on attractiveness, physical arrangements, ventilation, lighting, and comfort.

Training in the Supervisory Environment

From your study of the supervisory environment and functions in earlier chapters, you know that a wide variety of relationships and experiences influence human behavior. Many factors — attitudes, assigned responsibilities, relationships, and prior experiences — contribute to the atmosphere in which training is conducted. Look out for behaviors that hamper job success. Avoid the temptation to ignore problems in the hope they will go away or at least not get any worse. Observe and correct poor work habits.

Create a positive environment

Link suggestions for improvement with criticism. Too often, supervisors do not understand that a worker may not realize the importance of correcting unproductive work practices. For example, an equipment operator may need to work faster but not recognize how much time is consumed through his or her present method of changing machine settings or repairing jammed equipment. You can give suggestions for improvement and encourage use of proper work practices.

Suggest how to improve

Remember to monitor the trainee's progress and evaluate whether your actions have corrected errors or changed undesired behaviors. Even though you have given explanations and demonstrated the correct way to do things, further guidance may be necessary. Consistent interactions with trainees enable them to ask questions and give you opportunities to acknowledge progress that occurs. Some workers resist change or attempts to correct improper work practices. A positive end result is likely if you:

Do not neglect your trainees

☐ Concentrate on the issues at hand and not on the employee's personality.

☐ Allow sufficient time to hear the worker's viewpoint.

☐ Respond to questions or concerns that arise. When questions are answered, your employees are more likely to feel they are working in a positive environment.

☐ Stick to the facts of issues. Do not prejudge or base actions on rumors.

☐ Try to arrive at an agreement on future commitments.

Training Methods

Select an appropriate
method

A variety of training methods are available. Selection of one or a combination of methods depends on objectives and availability of resources. Simulation of an airplane cockpit, for instance, is quite sophisticated and expensive but is necessary to train pilots. However, an inexpensive videotape can be rented to assist in explaining the benefits of positive interaction among supervisors and subordinates. Job Instruction Training is useful to teach repetitive job duties, but job rotation is more appropriate to provide relevant learning experiences in various departments of a firm. Regardless of the method chosen, well-planned activities and competent trainers are essential.

Some training methods are
widely used

What methods of training do companies use? According to a national survey sponsored by the American Society of Training and Development, lectures/discussions, discussion groups, films/slides, and audiocassettes were used by over 70 percent of the respondents to teach technical skills. In addition to case studies and role playing, the top-ranked methods for management development were the same as those used for technical training. Newer, more costly high-tech methods (videodiscs, interactive video programs, and teleconferencing) were among the least-utilized training techniques.[8]

Job Instruction Training

Job Instruction Training (JIT) features a four-step approach—preparation, presentation, performance, and follow-up. It relates instruction to principles of learning and structures training around motivation, understanding, participation/feedback, and application of knowledge.[9] Figure 6.2 shows the four steps that characterize JIT.

JIT is a four-step approach

Preparation of learners encourages receptiveness to instruction, stimulates interest, and helps to overcome anxieties about learning new and different tasks. The presentation step is the essence of JIT and involves providing explanations in a manner that is understandable. Next, learners try out their skills under supervision. This provides an opportunity to ask questions and lets instructors correct any misunderstandings. Finally, follow-up involves letting learners be on their own with the instructor still checking to determine that work is performed correctly.

Use JIT for teaching
repetitive tasks

Since it breaks operations into repetitive operations, JIT is useful for teaching repetitive tasks. Give special attention to putting trainees at ease. Take care to organize your presentation. Plan the presentation and make sure that needed materials and instructional aids are ready and in working order. Gear the pace of explanations to your learners. Explanations can be given so rapidly that learners simply have too much material to absorb. Do not neglect

---

The Job Instruction Training Method   **Figure 6.2**

Step 1: Preparation (of the learner)
  1. Put the learner at ease.
  2. Find out what is already known about the job.
  3. Get the learner interested and eager to learn the job.
Step 2: Presentation (of the operations and knowledge)
  1. Tell, show, illustrate, and question in order to put over the new knowledge and operations.
  2. Instruct slowly, clearly, completely, and patiently, one point at a time.
  3. Check, question, and repeat.
  4. Make sure the learner really learns.
Step 3: Performance (try out)
  1. Test by having the learner perform the job.
  2. Ask questions beginning with why, how, when, or where.
  3. Observe performance, correct errors, and repeat instructions if necessary.
  4. Continue until you are confident that the learner knows.
Step 4: Follow-up
  1. Put learners "on their own."
  2. Check frequently to be sure they are following instructions.
  3. Taper off extra supervision and close follow-up until the learner is qualified to work with normal supervision.
Remember: If the learner hasn't learned, the teacher hasn't taught.

Source: *The Training Within Industry Report, War Manpower Commission* (Washington, D.C.: Bureau of Training, War Manpower Commission, 1945), p. 195.

follow-up. Additional questions nearly always arise, and trainees are often put on their own too soon.

Other Training Methods

You can think of many ways to train and probably have experience with lectures, films, and classroom discussions. In the workplace, these and other methods are commonly used to help learners update knowledge and prepare for new assignments. Each method has advantages and limitations. Select the one method or combination of methods that best suits the workers or problems at hand. Supervisors may be required to use training methods already implemented by employers. If other methods appear to be more appropriate, however, suggestions for change (along with clearly explained rationales) may be recommended to higher management.

Special Assignments.   When an employee has some control over the flow of work, you can make **special assignments,** which involve delegating nonroutine work duties to develop experience and build job skills. You assign a special project, report, or information-gathering activity. The task may be to find ways to improve safety or research what other businesses do to assure

Special assignments involve nonroutine tasks

a safe workplace. Other special assignments might be examining the merits of changes in scheduling procedures or preparing justification for new equipment recommendations. Special assignments broaden an employee's knowledge and understanding of the firm.

> However, assignments should not be made haphazardly. As a practice, it's unwise to further obligate persons who are struggling to meet current performance expectations. Also, personal interests and capabilities of trainees merit consideration. Regardless of circumstances, clear explanations are necessary to let learners know what is expected and how each experience will benefit them.[10]

Delegation, or giving responsibility and authority to perform a task, is an excellent method of training. Before delegating, though, examine the extent of an employee's ability to perform. Never assign responsibilities of a confidential nature, such as discipline or performance appraisal, that you yourself should handle. The purpose of making assignments is to train, not a way for you to avoid doing disliked tasks. You will still need to provide guidance, as questions will inevitably arise.

Job rotation broadens experience

Job Rotation. Training that involves moving workers from job to job to provide experiences in various units or departments of an organization is called **job rotation.** It is a good way for employees to gain firsthand insight into the firm's different functions. The success of job rotation depends on how it is structured. Trainees do gain knowledge by observing others, but to make the experience more meaningful, active involvement is advantageous. For example, it's one thing to review a completed accounting report but a quite different challenge to collect data and do the calculations necessary to prepare the report.

Trainees should stay on each job long enough to gain an overview of duties and responsibilities. However, learners possess different experiential backgrounds, and some jobs are more complex than others. At each job, enough time should be allowed to enable them to gain a realistic perspective of the position. Job rotation facilitates cross-training of personnel. In the event of resignations, promotions, or even layoffs, an employee can perform a different job assignment with greater knowledge of the work responsibilities that must be performed. Sometimes job rotation opens up exciting career possibilities. As a result of working in the marketing department, a person might discover a career interest in becoming a market researcher.

Simulations replicate real jobs

Simulation. An artificial learning exercise designed to replicate a real job-related situation is called **simulation.** This method is especially appropriate when the cost of equipment or safety implications are major concerns. For example, air traffic controllers must know exactly how to give proper directions and respond to emergencies. Until a learner knows how to operate equipment and is accustomed to technical jargon used on the job, it is impractical to train in real situations. The consequences of potential errors are simply too great. Therefore, trainees learn on simulated control panels that replicate real situations.

The *case study* approach, an application of simulation, provides opportunities to analyze problems. Learners are given information and asked to study the data, exchange viewpoints, discuss alternatives, and recommend solutions. Often, no one correct solution exists, and learning results from interaction among participants—explanations of thoughts, justification of rationales, responses to questions, and comments about the views of others. Case study enables trainees to improve analytical abilities, communication skills, and understanding of decision making.

Role-Playing. A training method in which participants are assigned roles, given background information, and then act out the roles is known as **role-playing.** One trainee might be asked to play the role of a supervisor and two others the roles of employees involved in a dispute over job duties. From this point, they act out the respective roles. Role-playing is designed to see how players react to evolving circumstances. In effect, they are forced to ask questions, answer questions, and make judgments without a script. It is an excellent method to gain practice in handling the uncertainty of situations encountered in the workplace.

Role-playing develops insights

The value of role-playing is enhanced by taping sessions and then giving the players an opportunity to observe their performance. They can note strengths and weaknesses, and trainers can then make suggestions as well as reinforce desired learning. Role-playing makes productive use of time and equipment and provides realism. The person who has just role-played the supervisor more readily understand how to handle similar on-the-job situations.

Seminars and Workshops. Training methods that provide concentrated study of topics are **seminars** and **workshops.** They range from a few hours to several days in length. Professional or trade associations, universities, commercial training organizations, and firms themselves sponsor them. While themes vary, seminars and workshops emphasize acquisition of job knowledge. They provide opportunities to share information, exchange ideas, and gather suggestions for improving work skills.

Seminars and workshops focus on specific topics

Often, topics are presented in a general manner. Supervisors may find it useful to have follow-up sessions and further discuss how the subject matter can be applied. This aspect is often overlooked, but it clarifies possible misunderstandings and reinforces how employees can apply the knowledge to their jobs.

Before recommending approval for workers to attend seminars and workshops, examine the content to be presented. The training should address relevant topics. Check the reputations of instructors you do not know. Find out how well they know their subject and whether they present it effectively. This procedure increases the probability that training will be worthwhile for employees and decreases the likelihood of experiencing poorly conducted sessions.

Make classes meaningful

Formal Classes. Another training method is **formal classes,** classroom sessions held on company premises or at other locations. Professional groups, vocational-technical schools, colleges, or businesses themselves may offer classes. Generally, presentations are either lectures or a combination of lecture and discussion. Through discussion, learners share experiences, clarify concerns, and express viewpoints. To initiate discussion, pose a question and invite responses. (Questions prefaced by what, why, or how are most appropriate.) If nobody chooses to respond, call on a person individually (not always the same person), and others will usually become involved and volunteer comments. It is useful to summarize key points, which can be listed on a chalkboard.

From your school experience, you have insight into the pros and cons of classroom instruction. When text and other reading materials are combined with knowledgeable, organized instructors, this method is appropriate for learning concepts. Handouts, overhead transparencies, chalkboards or flip charts, and films or videotapes can be used as supplemental aids. Instructors do need to recognize that people have different learning capabilities and direct instruction to the needs of class members. This is difficult to accomplish in courses consisting of persons whose experiences and abilities vary widely.

Audiovisual methods enhance learning

Audiovisual Methods. The use of **audiovisual methods** (films, tapes, or cassettes) plays an important role in training. Video as well as audiocassettes can be purchased or developed. They can be used over and over and can easily be sent to any location. Flexibility enables firms to adapt content to specific needs and tailor presentations to production, sales, or any other functional area. "Circumstances, which are not easily replicated, can be taped . . . Examples include demonstrations of surgical procedures, handling of radioactive substances, and paving of highways."[11]

Programmed instruction lets learners pace themselves

Programmed Instruction. A method of learning in which content is divided into steps requiring learners to answer questions about what they have just read or observed is known as **programmed instruction.** For example, Job Instruction Training consists of four steps. After study, the learner might be asked to complete this statement: "_____ is the second step in the JIT process." To determine the correct answer, the learner turns to the reverse side of the page (formats vary) and notes the correct answer, which is "presentation of material." This method provides quick reinforcement, as the proper response is known immediately.

Content may be presented through computers, teaching machines, texts, or manuals. Programmed instruction is most useful for teaching terminology or procedures and least suitable for teaching concepts. For instance, it lends itself to learning the sequence of steps in the communication process (develop ideas, create the message . . . interpret the message). However, programmed instruction is not appropriate for learning the role of supervision in an environment characterized by rapid change. Since there is no opportunity for discussion, learners are on their own to derive an understanding of study materials.

Study Circles. An increasing number of firms have become interested in **study circles,** which are employee groups that discuss work-related concerns as well as personal, educational, and social needs.[12] These circles use a democratic approach to decide what topics will be discussed and provide a forum for exchanging ideas and viewpoints. The study-circle leader, called a facilitator, organizes sessions and helps members obtain materials or speakers on certain topics.

Study circles actively involve learners

Firms often provide for meetings on company time, as long as the circle discusses work-related issues. Otherwise, meetings are held during off-work hours. Suggestions or concerns are usually submitted to management. However, there is usually no obligation for management to implement results. The use of study circles is likely to increase because of the potential to develop closer employee-employer relationships.

Consider This

1. In the future, how is the supervisor's responsibility for training likely to change?
2. What factors should supervisors consider in selecting a particular method of training?
3. Considering the importance of training, why do some employees resist efforts to improve their job skills?

Evaluation of Training

Are training activities effective? This is a most important question because of the time and expense committed to training. Productivity, workplace safety, and job satisfaction are related to the capability of employees to do their jobs. In an era of increased competitive pressures that necessitates the wise use of resources, greater attention is likely to focus on evaluation. Whatever your training method, you must examine the learning progress of your trainees. You will want to check on:[13]

Is the training effective?

☐ How well they plan work assignments during training.
☐ How well they apply what has been taught.
☐ How well they retain what has been taught.
☐ Whether they are at ease in performing what they have learned.

Answers to these questions help supervisors judge how well learners are prepared to handle job responsibilities. Due to the variety of training activities, learning variables, and problems in measuring behavioral changes, assessment is difficult. It can be classified into formal processes, observation and informal comments, and comparisons with records. Keep in mind that some methods of training are more readily assessed than others. Measuring how well an employee masters computer skills is easier than evaluating the results of training in customer relations.

Formal Processes. Questionnaires are a common method of evaluating training. They are used to solicit opinions about the value of information studied, learn how well instructors performed, and determine favorable and unfavorable views toward training experiences. Figure 6.3 illustrates an assessment questionnaire. Note how some questions (numbers 2, 3, and 4) request a simple yes or no response. However, open-ended questions (numbers 9, 10, and 11) provide an opportunity for trainees to note their own comments. When summarized, results indicate whether revisions in format, content, or methods of instruction are necessary. Frequently, respondents make valuable comments and suggestions that improve future training sessions.

Examinations, which are usually in a written format, provide evidence as to how well the subject matter has been mastered. Learners must demonstrate their capabilities and attain specified levels of competency to receive a passing score. Documentation of attained levels of proficiency is a key facet of examinations. Stockbrokers, insurance agents, and real estate salespersons must earn satisfactory exam scores to practice their professions. Some employers require periodic training to upgrade job performance and use examinations as a measure of results. A series of rigorous examinations must be passed to earn professional designation as a Certified Public Accountant or Certified Financial Planner.

Observation and Informal Comments. Supervisors have many opportunities to observe if subordinates benefit from training, and trainees can easily make before and after comparisons about training experiences. For example, a cosmetics salesperson who attends a skill-building seminar knows whether the demonstrated sales techniques are helpful by applying them in dealings with customers.

Workers are usually willing to share opinions about training. These can be gathered simply by asking for them. However, you should hesitate to form conclusions based on one or a few comments because people vary in their reactions to experiences. Have you ever asked two people about an instructor and received entirely different opinions?

Comparisons with Records. Comparing job accomplishments of workers who are given training with those who have not been trained aids evaluation. A number of criteria can be used; the number of accidents, amount of absenteeism, or extent of personnel turnover are examples. For instance, records may show that trained workers incur significantly fewer accidents and

Questionnaires and examinations are widely used

Note behaviors and listen to comments

Keep good records

Figure 6.3   **Example of an Assessment Questionnaire**

Title of Program _____

Date _____ Job Title _____

Directions: Please indicate your response to each question and return this questionnaire to the program leader. Your responses are confidential. DO NOT SIGN YOUR NAME ON THIS EVALUATION INSTRUMENT.

1. In my opinion, this program was: (check one)
    _____ Excellent   _____ Very good   _____ Good   _____ Fair   _____ Poor
2. Did the program meet the objectives stated in the outline given to you? (check one)
    _____ Yes   _____ No
3. Did the program meet *your* expectations? (check one)
    _____ Yes   _____ No   If you checked no, please explain. _____
    _____
4. Were the training facilities adequate? (check one)
    _____ Yes   _____ No   If you checked no, please explain. _____
    _____
5. In my opinion, the instructor was: (check one)
    _____ Excellent   _____ Very good   _____ Good   _____ Fair   _____ Poor
6. How important was each of these training elements? (check one for each element)
    Videotapes   _____Very important _____Worthwhile _____Not important
    Role-playing   _____Very important _____Worthwhile _____Not important
    Lecture   _____Very important _____Worthwhile _____Not important
    Handouts   _____Very important _____Worthwhile _____Not important
    Group discussion _____Very important _____Worthwhile _____Not important
7. To what extent did you participate in the program? (check one)
    _____ A lot   _____ Just enough   _____ Somewhat   _____ Not at all
8. How much will the content of this program help you to perform your job responsibilities? (check one)
    _____ A lot   _____ Just enough   _____ Somewhat   _____ Not at all
9. What other types of training programs are of interest to you? Indicate your preferences. _____
    _____
10. How can this program be improved? Indicate your suggestions. _____
    _____
11. Other comments and suggestions. Please indicate any other comments/suggestions that you feel will be useful in planning future training programs.

Source: Donald S. Miller and Stephen E. Catt, *Human Relations: A Contemporary Approach* (Homewood, Ill.: Richard D. Irwin, 1989), p. 330.

lost workdays. You can report these results to your boss and perhaps recommend that more monies be budgeted for additional training. Your records provide justification to support the request. It is necessary to maintain an accurate, updated recordkeeping system and focus attention factors that critically affect on-the-job performance.

Supervisors' Professional Development

Consider your career goal

Professional development includes the use of educational opportunities and other experiences to further career potential. It involves using your abilities to the greatest extent possible to fulfill job expectations, prepare for future jobs, and achieve personal growth. Professional associations, community activities, and special interest organizations provide many developmental opportunities. Service as chair of a community fund drive or membership on local committees, councils, and boards enables you to learn how to organize people and gain their support. Observe how leaders of these and other groups handle human relations problems and solicit cooperation necessary to attain objectives. Many persons do not fully recognize the potential to gain knowledge and greater understanding of human behavior that result from both on- and off-the-job experiences.

Professional development strategies

Because of their ability to accomplish tasks, some supervisors are offered more responsibilities. Acceptance of these duties affords insights, develops self-assurance, and serves to gain the confidence of superiors and peers. Because of an already heavy workload or inability to control the flow of work, you may not be able to assume additional duties. Before making a commitment, be reasonably sure you can meet expectations. Do not accept more than you can handle. Often, however, the opportunity to gain on-the-job developmental experiences cannot be obtained otherwise. If responsibilities are successfully performed, they provide greater recognition as an added benefit.

Looking Back

You have studied the major concepts of learning and training. It is important to understand how people learn and use proper training methods. Well-trained employees are a key to high productivity. Now let's review the objectives listed at the beginning of the chapter.

☐ **Understand the elements involved in learning.** The learning process consists of goals, motivation, methods, drilling and repetition, recognition, and follow-up. Supervisors must recognize the importance of these elements and be aware that people possess different background experiences and differ in their abilities to learn. Managers need to encourage active involvement of learners and accurately assess the extent of their previous knowledge about topics or issues.

☐ **Discuss ways to improve training effectiveness.** Knowledge of the subject and selection of proper training techniques are important. However, training activities should be adapted to the work environment itself. Employees must perceive benefits of training and be able to apply what they learn. Supervisors must be aware that not all workers are eager learners. Recognize that some employees will resist change, some will be openly critical, and some will need greater amounts of individual attention. To get maximum benefits from training efforts, supervisors must adjust instructional strategies to the employees to be trained.

☐ **Know how to determine training needs.** These needs are determined by examining employee appraisal forms, observing job performance, listening to employee suggestions, and noting the quality of work produced. Before starting training activities, carefully conider needs so that proposed training can be properly designed and implemented.

☐ **Discuss methods of training.** Job Instruction Training consists of four steps: preparation of learners, presentation of content, trying out performance, and follow-up. Figure 6.2 explains the details of each step. Other training methods include: special assignments, job rotation, simulation, role-playing, seminars and workshops, formal classes, audiovisual methods, programmed instruction, and study circles. Remember, selection of a method depends on your objectives. You might not have the flexibility to make special assignments or be able to implement job rotation. But you may have facilities available to hold formal classroom sessions.

☐ **Explain techniques used to evaluate training.** Evaluation of training is complex because many variables influence the learning process. Nevertheless, appraisal generally consists of formal evaluations, observation and informal comments, and comparison of performance between trained and untrained workers. In an era of increased competitive pressures, it is necessary to use resources wisely.

☐ **Understand the role of professional development.** Professional development involves the use of educational opportunities and other experiences to further career potential. Developmental activities are valuable to improve job capabilities and prepare for career advancement. Supervisors can assume additional job responsibilities to broaden their knowledge. Professional associations, community activities, and special interest organizations provide many opportunities to learn.

Key Terms

audiovisual methods	programmed instruction
formal classes	role-playing
Job Instruction Training	seminars and workshops
job rotation	simulation
learning	special assignments
professional development	study circles
	training

Review and Discussion Questions

1. Why is it important for supervisors to understand how people learn?
2. What is the most important element in the learning process? Why?
3. In terms of determining training needs, compare the merits of gathering information through formal appraisals to getting data by simply requesting informal employee comments.
4. Why should trainers consider such things as: (a) the learner's receptiveness to training; (b) providing training in a consistent, continuous manner; and (c) participant involvement in learning experiences?
5. How can a supervisor encourage employees to participate in training activities?
6. Explain types of training situations for which each of these methods is appropriate:
   a. Job Instruction Training
   b. Job rotation
   c. Simulation
   d. Role playing
   e. Seminars and workshops
7. How can supervisors evaluate the effectiveness of training?
8. How do relevant job-related experiences contribute to supervisors' professional development?
9. Before making special task assignments to workers, what concerns should supervisors consider?
10. How will advances in technology and increased emphasis on productivity influence the supervisor's training responsibilities?

Action Incident 6.1

The Impatient Trainer

Judy Hillis, a new word processing employee at the Federal National Bank got the job by responding to an ad stating "no experience necessary—will train." She has been on the job for two weeks and is becoming discouraged about her training. Jim Astle, her supervisor, believes that learning by observation is the best approach. He says, "Watch me. See how easy it is." Highly skilled himself, he tends to be impatient and overlook her inexperience.

Frequently Judy asks, "Could you slow down? I don't understand." Jim does slow down momentarily but is soon back to his rapid-fire explanations and shouting, "Haven't I already told you how to do these things?" Judy discussed her situation with a co-worker who emphasized that Jim is temperamental but the only person with knowledge that is adequate to do the training. Lately Jim is becoming more impatient and irritable. He believes explanations should not need to be repeated so often and thinks Judy should try harder to remember.

Judy feels she is doing her best and is convinced Jim is actually hindering her ability to master job skills. She thinks, "I do want to keep this job and I know Jim's competent. I just wish he could improve his training skills. Maybe

I should tell him that he's hindering my learning and causing me to make needless mistakes."

Discussion Questions

1. How can Jim become a better trainer?
2. What can Judy do to improve her ability to perform necessary job skills? Which training methods might help Judy become more proficient at word processing?
4. Should Judy tell Jim how she feels about his approach to training? Explain your response.

Action Incident 6.2

The Defective Shutters

Shutters International manufactures decorative shutter panels for homes. Recently, there has been a great increase in complaints from retailers. In addition to returning products to Shutters International, many retailers have said they will purchase no more unless these problems cease. The difficulties involve unglued frames, failure to include hinges and other hardware items, and wrong or different sizes placed in the same box.

At this time, there is no formal training for production-line employees. New hires acquire skills by observing employees on the jobs. Each supervisor is responsible for one area of the production line and is also in charge of quality. There are no formal inspection procedures.

The plant manager has informed you of the existing situation and asks that you suggest ways to alleviate these difficulties. In forming your remarks, consider responses to the following questions.

Discussion Questions

1. How would you characterize the existing training for employees at Shutters International?
2. What type of training should the company consider?
3. What roles should supervisors assume to implement changes in training procedures?
4. In the future, how should quality control be handled?
5. What training priorities need to be recognized and included in the suggestions you recommend?

Action Incident 6.3

It's Your Predicament

You are responsible for meeting the training and development needs of five employees in the department. You have the following brief description of each employee.

Omar: A new employee with some experience at a job similar to his current position, he is not up-to-date on how to operate new equipment being used. Omar seems willing to learn but has a "know-it-all" attitude.

Roberto: Roberto has six years' experience with the company. He has acquired sufficient capability to be promoted, but no position is expected to open in the near future. Roberto meets all job-related expectations. However, he seems increasingly restless and shows symptoms of burnout.

Wilma: Wilma is a happy-go-lucky person who hopes to become a supervisor some day but is slow at learning new things. Even though she has been with the company five years, she has always held her current job. Her performance is satisfactory, and she is well liked by her peers. Nevertheless, Wilma is insecure about her own abilities.

Gerado: Gerado has been with the company for 10 years, during which time he has held four different jobs in the department. He performs his work in a satisfactory manner and has no aspirations for a management position. Gerado's chief interest is to learn anything related to the work he does.

Molly: Molly's main ambition seems to be doing as little as possible without getting fired. She is careless, has little formal education, and is reluctant to learn anything new. Actually, Molly has trouble reading and writing and in her efforts to disguise feelings of insecurity, she is rather flippant.

Discussion Questions

1. What training method, or combination of methods, is most appropriate for each employee?
2. Assume that you are to train these persons as members of a group. What concerns should you recognize?
3. What approaches can be used to evaluate training results for these persons?

Notes

1. John D. Ong, "Workplace 2000—Managing Change," *Vital Speeches of the Day* 54 (May 15, 1988), p. 471.
2. Constance Mitchell, "Corporate Classes: Firms Broaden Scope of Their Education Programs," *The Wall Street Journal* (September 28, 1987), p. 29.
3. "Remedial Education—A Rising Corporate Concern," *Behavioral Sciences Newsletter* 16 (August 22, 1988), p. 3.
4. Glenn H. Varney, "Productivity in the '80s—Are You Ready?" *Training and Development Journal* 35 (March 1981), pp. 13–17.
5. Ron Zemke, "Workplace Illiteracy: Shall We Overcome?" *Training* 26 (June 1989), p. 35.
6. "Employee Training in America," *Training and Development Journal* 40 (July 1989), p. 35.
7. "Employee Training in America," p. 36.
8. "Employee Training in America," p. 37.
9. Leon Gold, "Job Instruction: Four Steps to Success," *Training and Development Journal* 35 (September 1981), p. 29.
10. Donald S. Miller and Stephen E. Catt, *Human Relations: A Contemporary Approach* (Homewood, Ill.: Richard D. Irwin, 1989), p. 323.
11. Miller and Catt, *Human Relations,* p. 321.
12. Karen Quallo Osborne and Renee Scialdo Shevat, "Study Circles: Personal and Professional Fulfillment for Employees," *Management Review* 71 (June 1982), pp. 37–42.
13. Ronald Brown, *The Practical Manager's Guide to Excellence in Management* (New York: AMACOM, 1979), p. 109.

Suggested Readings

Broadwell, Martin M. "Training Supervisors—Before the Fact." *Training* 23, August 1986, pp. 47–49.

Buonocore, Anthony J. "Reducing Turnover of New Hires." *Management Solutions* 32, June 1987, pp. 5–10.

Fleming, Laura K., and Ann M. Apking. "The Supervisor's Role in Training Needs Analysis." *Supervisory Management* 31, May 1986, pp. 40–42.

Goddard, Robert. "Workforce 2000." *Personnel Journal* 68, February 1989, pp. 65–71.

Knox, Alan B. "Helping Adults Apply What They Learn." *Training and Development Journal* 42, June 1988, pp. 55–56, 58–59.

Lansing, Rick L. "Training New Employees." *Supervisory Management* 34, January 1989, pp. 16–20.

Lloyd, Terry. "Winning the Budget Battle." *Training* 26, May 1989, pp. 57–62.

Pine, Devera. "Action Learning." *Psychology Today* 23, July–August 1989, pp. 25–26.

Smith, Melvin. "Training—Supervisory Responsibility or Not?" *Supervision* 48, May 1986, pp. 3–5.

Zemke, Ron. "Workplace Illiteracy: Shall We Overcome?" *Training* 26, June 1989, pp. 35–39.

Promoting Job Satisfaction

Learning Objectives

After reading and studying the material in this chapter, you should be able to:

1. Define job satisfaction.
2. Identify ways in which job satisfaction influences important elements of employees' work lives.
3. Indicate important work attributes that contribute to job satisfaction.
4. Explain the three stages employees often progress through in response to irritations on the job.
5. Identify different techniques that a supervisor can use to recharge an employee's job interest.
6. Explain the concept of flextime.
7. Explain the concept of compressed workweeks.
8. Describe the concept of job sharing.

The Importance of Job Satisfaction

First, what does the term *job satisfaction* typically mean? **Job satisfaction** can be defined as the level of enjoyment or contentment individual employees feel toward their jobs. That is, if you are pleased with your job because it meets your wants and needs, you will likely experience high job satisfaction. Conversely, if you have negative feelings about your job, you will probably experience low job satisfaction. Some students view employee morale as being synonymous with job satisfaction. The two terms, however, have different intended meanings. **Morale** generally refers to the job satisfaction of a group of employees rather than the attitude of a single individual toward a job. Supervisors should be concerned about the job satisfaction and morale of employees. Imagine, for example, that your subordinates have low job satisfaction and poor morale. You would expect little, if any, good to come out of the situation. Justifiably, you would be concerned. Consider the influence of job satisfaction on the following elements of employees' work life.

There is a difference between job satisfaction and morale

Absenteeism and Turnover

Suppose two employees each wake up one morning with a headache. Both employees begin to contemplate calling in sick and then going back to bed. One of the employees really likes his job, while the other dreads going to work. Guess which employee will probably not show up for work! There is little doubt that the employee who is unhappy with his job is more likely to call in sick. College students enrolled in early morning classes sometimes experience a similar situation. After all, it is easier to get up and attend a class you like than it is to drag yourself off to a class you dislike. Regarding absenteeism on the job, research shows that job satisfaction is closely related to absenteeism and turnover. That is, the higher employees' satisfaction with their jobs, the less likely they are to be absent from work. Furthermore, research indicates that the higher employees' job satisfaction, the less likely they are to resign.[1] Certainly, low job satisfaction is not the only reason employees may be absent or resign from a job. However, considering the high cost of absenteeism and turnover, the research findings on job satisfaction should be of interest to supervisors.

High turnover can be expected among unhappy workers

Safety

Employees who experience low job satisfaction are usually in a hurry to complete their required tasks. When job procedures are rushed, mistakes are more likely to occur, and in some cases mistakes on the job can cause accidents and other safety problems. Even if employees who dislike their jobs do not rush through their work, they are likely to show little interest in what they are doing. This lack of concentration invites errors and in-

Unhappy workers are prone to making mistakes that can affect job safety

creases the likelihood that safety problems will go unnoticed until an accident does occur. The employees' lack of interest in their work also decreases the likelihood that they will identify and suggest ways to improve safety on the job.

Physical Health

Can job satisafaction contribute to a healthier life for employees? The tentative answer appears to be "yes." Granted, physical health is influenced by many factors. However, several studies have provided evidence to indicate that workers who are dissatisfied with their jobs are prone to physical ailments ranging from headaches to heart disease.[2] Specifically, one study found fairly strong relationships between job dissatisfaction in different occupations and the incidence of death due to heart disease in those occupations.[3]

Mental Health

Most individuals have noticed that when they must perform tasks they do not enjoy, they sometimes become irritable and short-tempered. On the other hand, people generally experience a sense of accomplishment and worth when performing a job they find satisfying.[4] Can satisfying work enhance the mental health of employees? Research findings appear to indicate that more satisfied employees do tend to be psychologically healthier.[5]

Satisfying work can enhance mental health

Life Satisfaction

Suppose someone agreed to take care of your basic needs for food, clothing, and shelter for the rest of your life. The only catch is that you must agree not to get a job; instead, you must stay at home and just relax. This offer may sound tempting on days when things do not go well. However, most of us would not find our lives to be very meaningful if we did not engage in some type of productive work. As a matter of fact, a person's self-concept can be influenced by the type of job he or she has. That is, if we have an important and prestigious job, we will generally feel better about ourselves than if we are employed in a very low-level job. Furthermore, research studies find that job satisfaction has a spillover effect on employees' satisfaction with life.[6] For example, in one four-year study, approximately 1,000 workers were interviewed about their job satisfaction. Interestingly, the study found "that workers who are more, rather than less, satisfied with supervision, pay, and promotion also are more satisfied with life."[7] Can improvement in job satisfaction enhance workers' satisfaction with life? The answer appears to be a resounding "yes."

Productivity

The relationship between
job satisfaction and
productivity is not
straightforward

The impact of job satisfaction on the behavior of workers is not always straightforward. This observation is especially true when it comes to analyzing the relationship between job satisfaction and employee productivity. For example, some satisfied workers are unproductive and enjoy their jobs because they are under little pressure to produce. On the other hand, dissatisfied workers may work hard in hopes that their hard work will help them win a promotion to a better job. If workers are already productive, there may be little possibility of improvement, even if job satisfaction is increased. Therefore, it is inappropriate to make the generalized statement that "a happy worker is always a productive worker" or the reverse. However, most supervisors intuitively believe that enhancing the job satisfaction of employees will also increase productivity. The answer to resolving this dilemma appears to lie in how productivity or performance is viewed. "Defined narrowly as quantity of output or quality of craftsmanship . . . performance does not consistently or appreciably follow from satisfaction in a direct functional relationship."[8] However, an employee's performance usually is viewed in broader terms than simply quantity of output.

For lack of a better term, **organizational citizenship behavior** is the label given to several broad behaviors in defining performance.[9] Examples of employee behaviors that fit this label include:[10]

Workers engage in
organizational citizenship
behavior

- [ ] Helping co-workers with a job-related problem.
- [ ] Accepting orders without a fuss.
- [ ] Tolerating temporary impositions without complaint.
- [ ] Helping to keep the work area clean and uncluttered.
- [ ] Making timely and constructive statements about the work unit or its head to outsiders.
- [ ] Promoting a work climate that is tolerable and minimizes the distractions created by interpersonal conflict.
- [ ] Protecting and conserving organizational resources.

Organizational citizenship
behaviors can improve
productivity

Supervisors value these types of employee behaviors because they usually make their own jobs easier. Such behaviors also often free up supervisors' time, allowing them to focus on work that is important to them. The organizational citizenship behaviors described above *can* improve the narrow, traditional measures of productivity. For example, when one employee, Carol, helps another employee, Jeff, with a job-related problem he is experiencing, Jeff's performance in terms of quantity and quality of production may improve. Furthermore, the organizational citizenship behavior of conserving company resources may translate into more being produced using fewer expensive resources.

High job satisfaction can be especially important in jobs where the productivity or success of employees hinges on them being able to satisfy others by providing personal services. Ready examples include service jobs in the areas of health care and direct sales. Specifically, research supports the view that people who experience high job satisfaction are likely to engage in behaviors that show consideration and sensitivity toward others, and these types of behaviors are likely to be especially important in many kinds of jobs. One study, for example, showed that managers with high job satisfaction were likely to:[11]

□ Listen carefully to others.
□ Show awareness and concern for the needs and feelings of others.
□ Show good emotional control.
□ Accept criticism.

Satisfied workers tend to show sensitivity toward others

Consider how these behaviors affect jobs that involve extensive contact with people. To be a good supervisor, for example, you need to be a good listener to better understand and assist with problems your subordinates may be experiencing. Furthermore, supervisors should show awareness and concern for the needs and feelings of others. Especially when dealing with customers, employees need to be tactful, maintain emotional control, and accept legitimate criticism in order to be productive.

Therefore, the relationship between job satisfaction and productivity is intricate. On the one hand, high job satisfaction cannot be shown to automatically lead to increased productivity, at least not in the narrow sense of precise changes in the quantity and quality of what is being produced. For instance, when a supervisor's actions increase the workers' job satisfaction, some of the workers may not have the ability or opportunity to increase their work output. However, workers usually do have control over their citizenship behavior, and research reports significant relationships between employees' job satisfaction and their organizational citizenship behavior.[12] That is, workers who are satisfied with their jobs are likely to demonstrate good organizational citizenship behavior, and this behavior, in turn, can have many positive effects on the productivity of organizations in general.

The relationship between job satisfaction and productivity is intricate .

Workers have control over their citizenship behavior

Work Attributes Contributing to Job Satisfaction

As has been discussed, organizations can benefit in several ways when employees find their jobs to be satisfying. Consider the list, shown on the next page, of seven specific attributes of the work environment that contribute to job satisfaction.

Satisfied workers benefit organizations in many ways

Mentally Challenging Work

Research has shown that there are several work attributes that are related to work interest and satisfaction. For example, employees like to see their skills and abilities put to good use on the job, and they enjoy having an opportunity to be creative. Furthermore, employees want to have some control over their work methods and the pace at which they work. It is hard to say which of these attributes and others related to job satisfaction are most important to

Key Factors Contributing to Job Satisfaction

1. Mentally challenging work with which the individual can cope successfully.
2. Personal interest in the work itself.
3. Work which is not too physically tiring.
4. Rewards for performance which are just, informative, and in line with the individual's personal aspirations.
5. Working conditions which are compatible with the individual's physical needs and which facilitate the accomplishment of his or her work goals.
6. High self-esteem on the part of the employee.
7. Agents in the workplace who help the employee to attain job values such as interesting work, pay, and promotions, whose basic values are similar to his own, and who minimize role conflict and ambiguity.

Source: Edwin A. Locke, "The Nature and Causes of Job Satisfaction," *Handbook of Industrial and Organizational Psychology,* ed. Marvin D. Dunnette (New York: John Wiley & Sons, 1983), p. 1328.

Stress can reduce job satisfaction

employees. However, one element which many of the attributes share in common is that of mental challenge. After all, making judgments, being creative, and learning on the job all require mental effort. The less employees have to exert mental effort at work, as when a job is very routine and simple, the easier it is for them to experience boredom. However, when employees have meaningful responsibilities on the job and have an opportunity to make decisions, they are likely to show interest and involvement in their work. Furthermore, when employees exercise individual judgment and make decisions on the job, they are likely to feel committed to the job. For example, there is less reason to care about a job in which you are told what to do than a job in which you have some control over the situation. Of course, as a job becomes more challenging mentally, a point can be reached at which the job becomes too difficult to handle and employees become stressed out. As a result, job satisfaction will decline at this point. The objective, therefore, should be to provide employees with work that is mentally challenging without becoming overwhelming. Naturally, individual workers differ in their capabilities. A task that may be mentally challenging for one worker may seem boring to another. However, workers will experience a sense of pride and accomplishment when they have succeeded in doing something that is a challenge. Furthermore, this sense of pride and accomplishment is likely to translate into high satisfaction with the job.

Personal Interest in the Work

As just discussed, there is an important positive relationship between job satisfaction and mentally challenging work. However, employees will not necessarily enjoy their job simply because it is mentally challenging. For example, college students often find math courses to be mentally challenging.

However, math courses are seldom ranked among the most popular courses, even by many students who received above average grades in required math courses. College advisors know that promoting the values of a strong mathematics education to students does not necessarily excite them into taking math courses. Likewise, employees will not automatically like their job just because someone tells them they should like it. For high job satisfaction to exist, employees must like a job because they take a personal interest in the work itself.

The ideal situation is where employees take personal interest in their work

Work That Is Not Too Physically Demanding

Some jobs involve much taxing physical work. When this demanding work continues day after day, it often produces physical and mental stress. Some employees who work in front of computer display terminals, for example, complain of eye strain after a few hours. This eye strain, if not reduced by work breaks, can produce headaches and other physical ailments. Managerial work can also be physically demanding in that it often requires long hours in the office, much concentration, and attention to personnel problems. The stress from these demands can cause managers to experience burnout. Regardless of the job, when employees find their work to be too physically demanding, their level of job satisfaction is likely to decline. Conversely, employees who leave a job due to burnout and take another job that is less physically demanding often show greater job satisfaction with their new job.

Job burnout can occur under stress

Appropriate Rewards for Performance

Three aspects of rewards on the job are often considered by employees. First, they look at how fair a reward appears to be. An employee will consider a reward as being fair if its value appears to be commensurate with the quality of his or her performance. For example, if your performance on the job is the same as another employee doing the same job, you would expect to receive the same pay. It would not seem just or fair if you received less pay than the other employee. Second, verbal recognition can be important to employees. For instance, most employees value receiving praise for their good work and being given credit where credit is due. Furthermore, verbal recognition from a supervisor lets the subordinate know that the supervisor is aware of the subordinate's good performance. Employees like knowing that someone in a position of responsibility in the organization is aware of their hard work and the results it has produced. Third, employees view their pay in terms of how well it allows them to achieve their personal aspirations. The most obvious needs employees have are for such necessities as food, shelter, and clothing. However, money can also represent a symbol of achievement in that if you are paid a lot, you interpret the pay as recognition that you do a lot on the job. Money can also act as a status symbol to some. Furthermore, pay allows employees to obtain or purchase other things they value. Therefore, the

Reward systems should be perceived as fair

greater the extent to which employees' pay allows them to achieve their personal aspirations, the more likely employees are to be satisfied with their level of pay.

Pleasant Working Conditions

Employees generally prefer pleasant working conditions for two reasons. First, they wish to have physical comfort while they are performing their work. Elements of the work environment such as temperature, humidity, ventilation, lighting, and noise can all affect the physical needs of employees. For example, employees are likely to become easily fatigued if they are required to work under conditions of high temperature and high humidity, and they naturally want to avoid being exposed to dangerous working conditions. As a result, any extreme working conditions that cause physical discomfort to employees or are perceived as dangerous will likely cause the employees' level of job satisfaction to decline. Second, employees desire working conditions that aid them in attaining their work goals. For example, most employees will experience difficulty in performing their job if they must work under conditions of poor lighting. In addition, they need adequate tools and equipment. When working conditions provide employees with physical comfort and facilitate attainment of work goals, the employees' job satisfaction will be enhanced.

Pleasant working conditions are important to job satisfaction

High Self-Esteem

It is believed that an employee's level of self-esteem can influence his or her level of job satisfaction. For example, employees with high self-esteem tend to be less defensive and display fewer defense mechanisms on the job compared to employees with low-esteem. Employees with high self-esteem also are likely to experience fewer conflicts and feelings of anxiety. As a result, when employees with low self-esteem become defensive and experience conflicts and anxiety, it is likely that their level of job satisfaction will decline. Conversely, it is believed that employees with high self-esteem find it easier to enjoy their jobs.

Workers with high self-esteem are more likely to be satisfied with their jobs

Helpful Individuals on the Job

When others on the job help an employee to achieve goals and create a desired work environment, the employee's level of job satisfaction will likely be enhanced. For example, subordinates respond positively when their supervisor demonstrates friendliness, praises good performance, listens to their opinions, and takes a personal interest in them. In addition, a supervisor's efforts to free subordinates from interruptions, provide them with good equipment, and help them attain work goals will be well received. Likewise, when a supervisor helps a productive subordinate get a promotion, the subordinate will be appreciative, and this appreciation will usually show up in increased job satisfaction for the employee. In short, we enjoy people who assist us on the job and who are easy to be around, and we tend to be satisfied while in the presence of people who help us to create a pleasurable work environment.

Workers appreciate helpful assistance from their supervisor

Promoting High Job Satisfaction

What can supervisors do to promote and maintain high levels of job satisfaction among subordinates? Countless items mentioned and discussed throughout this book can affect job satisfaction. For example, some of the broad supervisory actions that enhance job satisfaction but that have not been emphasized so far in this chapter are listed in Figure 7.1. However, as a supervisor, you should also realize that an accumulation of little things on the job can also affect employees' level of satisfaction with their work.

Little things on the job can be important to employees

Sweat the Details

Consider the plight of Joe Robbins, a trainer for a financial services company in Michigan. As Joe pulls into the company parking lot one winter morning, he notices that fresh snow remains in the parking area. The city street leading up to the parking lot had been cleared of snow early that morning. Even the path from the parking lot to his building entrance contains snow through which he must walk. Once in the building, he begins to walk down the corridor leading to his department. He soon realizes that the temperature in the building is much too hot. Joe and his co-workers do not enjoy complaining about the heating system that seems to work only in extremes. When he enters through the main doorway to his department,

---

Broad Supervisory Actions that Enhance Job Satisfaction   **Figure 7.1**

---

1. Provide effective leadership.
2. Encourage upward communication.
3. Act on suggestions made by employees.
4. Keep employees informed on important matters.
5. Be sensitive to the needs of employees.
6. Treat employees with respect.
7. Hire capable co-workers.
8. Protect employees from discrimination on the job.
9. Find win-win solutions to conflicts.
10. Encourage creativity.

Figure 7.2   **Effects of "Little Things" on Job Satisfaction**

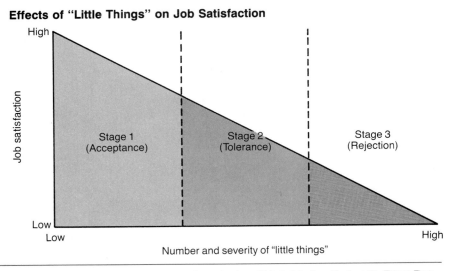

Joe notices that the photocopier is disassembled. Apparently, routine cleaning and maintenance of the photocopier has been scheduled for that morning—the time the machine is most needed by him and others. Soon after Joe begins working, a maintenance worker arrives in Joe's office. The worker says he is there to replace the ceiling panels in the office that were damaged last week by a water leak. Joe received no advance notice of this scheduled work, and he has to leave the office while the work is being completed. The small but numerous irritations Joe is experiencing on the job are frustrating him and reducing his job satisfaction. Increasingly, Joe is becoming more receptive to job offers from other companies.

Too often, supervisors and other managers believe that it is the big things that determine employee job satisfaction. Certainly, big things, such as having mentally challenging tasks and working in a safe physical environment, are important to employees. However, it is not only the big things that influence job satisfaction. Joe is not thinking about working for another company due to dissatisfaction with any big things at work. It is the mounting number of little things that is causing Joe to become dissatisfied with his job. Supervisors need to realize that when trying to improve the job satisfaction of subordinates, it is the little things that often count.[13] Employees begin to wonder why a company may be willing to address the big things but is not making an effort to deal with the little ones. Figure 7.2 depicts the effects of an accumulation of little things or irritants on employee job satisfaction. It shows that the greater the number and severity of irritants, the lower an

Little problems on the job can also increase job turnover

Workers notice the attention you give to little problems they experience

employee's job satisfaction level. It also illustrates that employees progress through three stages in response to these irritants: the acceptance stage, the tolerance stage, and the rejection stage.[14] In the **acceptance stage,** employees view irritants on the job as normal, not as the result of uncaring management. They believe that their supervisor will act on the "little things" that need to be corrected once he or she is informed of them.

As the number and severity of irritants increase, however, there is a decline in job satisfaction and the employees move into the **tolerance stage.** Now they begin to question the supervisor's competence, sincerity, and willingness to correct the problems. Employees begin to complain to each other about the problems that exist and the supervisor's slowness in dealing with them. Grievances may be filed to put more pressure on management to address the problems. If the number and severity of irritants continue to increase, employees eventually move into the **rejection stage.** Once they reach this stage, employees' job satisfaction is minimal. They now believe management does not care, is incompetent, or both. As a result, dissatisfied employees may seek employment elsewhere or develop a "who gives a darn" attitude and put in only a minimum amount of work. At this point, management has lost the great potential of important human resources. It is unfortunate when a problem situation is allowed to deteriorate to this point. However, faced with employees who are in the rejection stage, the first step to improve employee job satisfaction is for the supervisor to examine the causes of employee dissatisfaction. One way of doing this, of course, is to talk with the employees directly about what things aggravate them on the job. Ask them about their job frustrations, especially the "little things" that aggravate them, and how severe they perceive these problems to be. Another approach is to watch employee behaviors for an indication of whether they seem to be in the acceptance, tolerance, or rejection stage. For example, what types of complaints do they have? How strong is the tone of their complaints? How committed do they seem to be to their work?

As a supervisor, you should not wait until things have deteriorated so badly that subordinates reach the rejection stage. A responsible supervisor acts on problems early. For example, if your subordinates are in the acceptance stage, they view you as being on their side, and they believe that you will act on the little things that need correcting. Don't let the employees down. Address the things that need changing, and make sure the employees know you are working on these problems. Once employees have reached the tolerance stage, it should be realized that they are questioning management's competency, credibility, and concern for them. As a supervisor, you need to restore this declining perception by reassuring employees that you do care. Find out the little things that are bothering them and begin to correct them. Many times the difficulty and costs of correcting small problems is minimal,

Grievances may be filed due to little problems

Avoid letting little problems get out of hand

Find out what frustrates your subordinates on the job

Address the problems that need correcting

yet the payoff can be significant. Once employees reach the rejection stage, they no longer are just questioning management's concern for them. Now they seem convinced management is unconcerned about the problems that have been voiced. At this stage, the supervisor must realize that actions speak louder than words. One valuable technique is to hold meetings in which the supervisor meets with employees to develop a list of their job frustrations. Input from the employees should also be solicited regarding what changes need to be made and how the changes will be implemented. The employees who are most directly affected by the problems discussed at meetings are often able to provide excellent solutions.

▼
Consider This

1. Think about a job you have had that you enjoyed. What was it about the job that gave you such a high level of job satisfaction?

2. Why do you think some people prefer jobs that require them to accept many responsibilities, while other individuals prefer jobs that are not demanding? Which type of job situation would you prefer for yourself?

Recharging an Employee's Job Interest

There probably is no such thing as the perfect job, but some employees, finding their jobs to be far from exciting, eventually become bored with their work. In some cases, they may perceive that there are few opportunities for promotion or advancement in their present jobs. As a result, there is an increased likelihood that they will lose interest in their jobs. For some employees, there may not be much a supervisor can do to improve the jobs they perform and make them more exciting. However, this does not mean that supervisors are powerless to help in all situations where employees are losing interest in their work. In some instances, it is a matter of revitalizing and renewing the interest of employees in their jobs. Fortunately, as discussed below, there are several relatively inexpensive techniques that can be used by a supervisor to recharge an employee's job interest.[15]

Low job interest can be revitalized

Encourage Job Development. The satisfaction of acquiring new, job-related knowledge can by itself be an experience that results in increased personal and professional satisfaction for employees. If possible, therefore, offer employees current journals in their area to read. It may also be possible to offer them vendor publications and newsletters. Encourage them to attend job-related seminars; as a supervisor, perhaps you can persuade the company to pay part of the seminar fee. Also, notify these employees of relevant in-house presentations they may attend. Emphasize to

Professional growth is possible in most jobs

employees that there is no dead end when it comes to professional growth and development and that the company believes they are worth its investment.

Promote Involvement in Professional Activities. Many professions have professional associations that sponsor meetings and activities for individuals employed in specific areas. Encourage employees to join these organizations and attend their meetings. After becoming involved in professional associations, the employees may even decide to serve on committees or be officers in the associations. Such involvement and the interaction with other members in the associations can stimulate the employees' interest and enthusiasm in their areas of employment. Your efforts as a supervisor to make subordinates feel important will be complemented by reinforcement they will receive from members of the professional associations.

Encourage professional involvement

Offer Involvement in Interdepartmental Activities. Some employees can become very isolated in their own departments. This situation can compound any problem of declining interest and enthusiasm that an employee may be experiencing. However, one effective way to break that isolation is to provide employees in this situation with an opportunity to become involved in interdepartmental activities. For example, you may offer a subordinate the opportunity to attend an interdepartmental meeting on ways to reduce waste and inefficiencies in the organization.

Offer Cross-Training in Other Jobs. **Cross-training** offers employees the opportunity to learn how different jobs in the organization are performed. However, offering cross-training does not mean that an employee will be performing the new jobs on a regular basis. The employee stays with his or her regular job but may perform the other jobs on an as-needed basis, such as when another employee is sick or on vacation. Cross-training provides employees with some opportunity to engage in job development and to participate in new challenges.

Cross-training can enhance job interest

Consider Delegating More Responsibility. Remember, not all subordinates are interested in accepting more responsibility. However, for some employees, it is an effective method for enhancing their interest and enthusiasm on the job. Obviously, there are some key responsibilities that would be inappropriate for most supervisors to delegate to inexperienced employees. However, if they think carefully about the situation, most supervisors can probably identify some meaningful responsibilities that could be transferred to some subordinates on a trial basis. For example, to make decisions supervisors may need to request information from different individuals or departments. It may be possible to entrust some of this investigative work to different subordinates. This type of delegation will help

Consider what responsibilities can be delegated

subordinates understand that they are doing something important and that they have worth. When a subordinate reports the information he or she has acquired, ask the subordinate's opinion about the situation. This type of participation in analyzing situations will likely enhance the employee's interest and enthusiasm on the job.

As has been discussed, there are different low-cost methods available to help supervisors address situations where the job interest of subordinates is waning. Supervisors do not have to accept those employees who are losing interest as unavoidable casualties to boredom. When your efforts to recharge an employee's job interest do succeed, everyone involved benefits.

Alternative Work Schedules

Creative work schedules can be designed

In recent years, organizations have been focusing more attention on ways to modify traditional work schedules. In a number of experiments and settings, new kinds of work schedules have been associated with improved job satisfaction, morale, and performance.[16] Therefore, many organizations believe they benefit from the increased job satisfaction employees often experience when they are provided with greater flexibility in their work schedules. Organizations are looking for ways to adjust work schedules to

Work schedules can influence job satisfaction

provide employees with more convenient time for leisure, family, education, personal errands, and household tasks.[17] Three methods for modifying traditional work schedules that will be examined here are flextime, compressed workweeks, and part-time employment.

Flextime

Flexible working hours, or **flextime,** provides employees the option of choosing daily starting and quitting times provided that they work at other set times and for a prescribed number of hours per day. Although flextime work schedules can be set up in different ways, the basic format is fairly simple. To illustrate how the concept works, consider Figure 7.3. Under this flextime arrangement, workers are free to choose at what time they wish to start work, as long as it falls between 7 and 10 A.M. During the "core times" in the morning and afternoon, all workers must be on the job. However, they can elect to take either a half-hour or one-hour lunch break any time between 11:30 A.M. and 1:30 P.M. Workers are free to end work anytime between 3:30 and 6:30 P.M. The only stipulation is that the total hours worked per day or week must meet the minimum specified by management. Flextime is more commonly found in offices that have large clerical operations than in factories or on construction

Flextime works best in independent jobs

sites. The major reason for this pattern is that flextime works best when employees are not highly dependent on each other to complete their work. For example, office employees can often complete their work by themselves. Automobiles, on the other hand, cannot be assembled correctly without the proper number of employees working together at the same time.

The Flextime Schedule   **Figure 7.3**

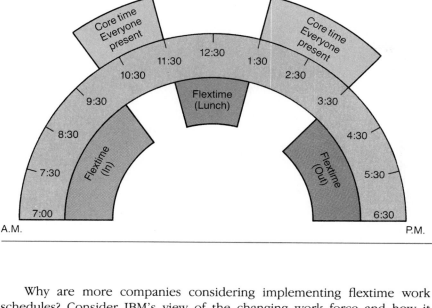

Why are more companies considering implementing flextime work schedules? Consider IBM's view of the changing work force and how it is adapting.[18] IBM believes that the future work force will be filled with working women, dual-career couples, single parents, and retirees who want second careers and that there will be a shortage of young, skilled workers. As a result, IBM has introduced a new plan that provides most of its employees with the option to begin or end their workdays an hour later or earlier than normal. Furthermore, labor experts say changing workplace demographics will require more companies to consider flextime as a way to meet the needs of workers. In one study, for example, 900 firms from the three areas of banking, insurance, and public utilities were surveyed regarding their flextime programs.[19] The focus was on clerical workers employed by the firms. The study showed that in all three industries, an overwhelming majority of respondents (94.1 percent in banking, 93 percent in insurance companies, and 100 percent in gas and electric companies) reported greater levels of job satisfaction under flextime. Employee lateness also decreased under flextime. Furthermore, the companies surveyed were asked to assess the overall effectiveness (worker and organizational improvement) of flextime. In this regard, flextime received high marks in all three industries.

The future work force will change

Flextime can enhance job satisfaction

Advantages of Flextime. Employees like flextime because it gives them more flexibility over how they spend their time during the day compared to traditional work schedules. As a result, it makes it easier for each employee to develop a work and life schedule that best suits him or her. Some of the advantages to employees of flextime are:

- ☐ Working hours can be set to avoid rush-hour commuting problems.
- ☐ Working hours can be adjusted to accommodate a person's internal body clock. For example, people who find it difficult to wake up early can elect to start work later than the traditional 8 A.M.

Flextime makes it easier to take care of personal business

- ☐ It is easier to take care of necessary personal business. Under flextime, it is easier to visit a physician or dentist. Also, employees do not have to rush off during lunch breaks to deal with public agencies, sign forms at a mortgage company, or meet with a banker.
- ☐ Nonessential personal errands can be run during normal working hours. An employee can use flextime in the morning to take pants to the cleaners or help a child fix a flat bicycle tire. Otherwise, these tasks would have to wait until later in the day when the employee got off work.
- ☐ Personal leisure time can be scheduled during the day. An employee can actually leave work relatively early in the afternoon to go fishing!
- ☐ Psychologically, it is comforting to know that part of a workday can be rearranged if it becomes necessary to do so.

Employers can benefit from offering flextime schedules

Employees, however, are not the only ones who can benefit from flextime. A company itself can also benefit from implementing a flextime work schedule. Consider the advantages of flextime listed below that are often cited by companies:[20]

- ☐ Increases production.
- ☐ Decreases tardiness.
- ☐ Decreases absenteeism.
- ☐ Decreases turnover.
- ☐ Helps in recruiting personnel.

Although there are advantages to flextime, there are also disadvantages associated with it. The task of dealing with these disadvantages often falls squarely on the shoulders of supervisors. Several of the disadvantages of flextime are listed below.[21]

Flextime may require more work for supervisors.

- ☐ To supervise during all hours of work requires the supervisor to work longer than any employee.
- ☐ Key employees may be gone at a time when they are needed.
- ☐ Understaffing may occur.
- ☐ It is difficult to coordinate the work of employees who are coming and going at different times.
- ☐ It is hard to schedule meetings at convenient times.
- ☐ Knowing whether all employees are actually working the required number of hours per day is difficult.
- ☐ Overhead costs can increase because the office is open longer, requiring more electricity for lighting, heating, etc.

However, in general, the more a supervisor can trust his or her subordinates to be conscientious in completing work assignments each day and not abusing the system, the greater the likelihood that flextime will work.[22] Should a flextime program seem appropriate for an organization, the program's chances of succeeding are increased if the following steps are taken.[23]

1. *Get the support of top management.* As a supervisor, you should make suretop managers support flextime before attempting to implement a flextime program. Without such support, the program is likely to fail.

2. *Request employee involvement at all levels.* In doing so, valuable input is received. The employees will also be more committed to the change because they shared in the decision. Specifically, involve employees in the planning, design, and operation of the flextime program.

3. *Designate a project director.* This person is responsible for working out all of the details of the flextime program. Duties may include coordinating work assignments, holding meetings to explain procedures, and answering questions. Needless to say, this person should have the respect of both management and the employees.

4. *Establish a flextime training program.* The purpose of this training program is to acquaint supervisors and others about their responsibilities under the flextime system. A flextime manual or handbook covering key points of the program may be developed and distributed in the training program.

5. *Start out with a trial run.* Before implementing a flextime program companywide, first try it out on a small scale in one area of the company. Bugs in the program can be removed, and its suitability for the company can be assessed without taking much risk.

6. *Establish flextime guidelines.* Of course, appropriate flextime policies and procedures should be developed before such a program is actually implemented. However, existing guidelines may need to be expanded or made more specific as any problems with flextime develop and are settled.

7. *Determine how work schedules will be monitored.* With employees coming and going at differnt times, how do you know that the prescribed number of hours is being worked each day by each employee? This is a question that frustrates many individuals who must supervise under a flextime program. Some companies use a time clock to keep track of starting and quitting times. Based on their experience with employees, some supervisors use the honor system. Some system, however, needs to be established.

In a **compressed workweek,** employees work fewer days but more hours each day than in a traditional workweek. The most common compressed workweek schedule is one in which employees work four 10-hour days each

---

Trust is important in flextime

All workers need to understand their flextime guidelines

week; this is referred to as a 4-40 system. Under such a system, a company or department is only open four days a week and usually closed on either Mondays or Fridays.

Reactions of Employers. Those employers who have experienced success with the use of compressed workweeks point to several benefits of the system. Apparently, compressed workweeks often increase job satisfaction for many workers because they like having three consecutive days off from work. This finding explains why absenteeism and employee turnover often decline under a compressed workweek system. Furthermore, for some companies, recruiting is reported to be easier when they can offer applicants a shorter workweek. In addition, a compressed workweek is reported to help some companies improve their plant and equipment utilization.[24]

Reactions of Employees. Employees quickly notice that shorter workweeks reduce commuting costs because they commute one less day per week to work. Also, as mentioned earlier, many employees like having three consecutive days off under a compressed workweek schedule. Consider, for example, how a four-day workweek improved things for the Henrico County, Virginia, police force.[25] Due to long workweeks, there was a morale problem among the uniformed officers. Furthermore, the officers' personnel records revealed a relatively high turnover rate, excessive use of sick time, and mounting absenteeism. A committee formed to investigate the problem found that a four-day workweek was being used by several other police departments. Those police departments using a compressed workweek schedule praised the system. Specifically, they reported a reduction in sick leave taken, increased morale, and preference for the four-day workweek by most of the officers. As a result, the Henrico County police department adopted a four-day workweek. Six months after the system was adopted, Henrico County police officers reported very favorable reactions. Furthermore, there was a decrease in the sick leave taken by the officers and an increase in their productivity and efficiency.

Drawbacks. The compressed workweek is not without its drawbacks, however, for both employers and employees. For instance, it is very difficult for many factories and offices to close completely on the first or last day of the regular workweek. They find that customers and suppliers expect them to be open Monday through Friday. Also, for working parents, child-care arrangements are often based on an eight-hour workday. Another problem is that the longer employees work, the more fatigued they become. For some jobs, 10-hour shifts are just too long and fatiguing. A 10-hour day in these situations just adds two more inefficient hours to an 8-hour day. For some companies, a compressed workweek offers special benefits for everyone involved. However, the concept is not universally appropriate and beneficial to all companies.

Compressed workweeks can reduce absenteeism and turnover

Workers often like having three consecutive days off

A 10-hour workday may be too fatiguing

Part-Time Employment

Any job requiring less than a full-time work schedule is defined as **part-time employment.** Specifically, individuals who work less than 35 hours a week, or less than 32 hours for federal employees, are classified by the U.S. government as part-time employees.[26] It is estimated that more than 25 percent of the nation's work force is employed on a part-time basis.[27] Part-time jobs can be designed and classified in several different ways. One general classification, job sharing, is gaining in popularity.

Many employees work part-time jobs.

Job sharing is an arrangement whereby two or more part-time employees share a job that would otherwise be performed by one full-time employee. Frequently, in a job sharing situation, one person works from 8 A.M. to noon each day and another person works the same job from 1 to 5 P.M. For many reasons, some employees prefer to share a job with another. Due to family responsibilities, for example, some individuals only want to work on a part-time basis. Other individuals who are semiretired do not want to work a full eight-hour workday. Hiring people to work part time at certain jobs can also be advantageous to employers. Turnover, for instance, may be high in certain jobs that are tedious, but sharing such jobs may reduce the turnover. Also, the energy level of an employee who only works a few hours each day can be expected to be high. As a result, two employees working part-time may actually be more productive in some cases and more efficient than one employee working full-time. In other cases, both employees sharing a job may work at the same time. This situation might occur when a job has peaks of work. Two part-time employees can be scheduled to work when these peaks occur and accomplish more than a single employee. Furthermore, for employees working part-time, absenteeism and tardiness tend to be low.[28] In job sharing, when one employee is absent due to illness, at least half the work gets done by the other employee.

---

1. To a certain extent, college students live under flextime schedules. That is, they often schedule their courses at times that are convenient for them. However, how comfortable do you think you would be in supervising employees who had flextime schedules?
2. Beyond the alternative work schedules of flextime, compressed workweeks, and job sharing, what changes in traditional work schedules would you like to see tried?

Consider This

Job sharing, however, is not without its drawbacks. Employees naturally earn less working fewer hours than if they were employed full-time. Company benefits provided to full-time employees may not be available to part-time workers. Also, in an economic downturn, part-time employees are the first to be dismissed. For employers, it is more difficult and expensive to train two or more employees to do a particular job than to train one full-time employee. Furthermore, employers complain that there often is a lack of loyalty and interest by part-time employees in helping their company achieve its goals.[29] The use of part-time employees unavoidably increases the number of subordinates a supervisor must supervise. As a result, more effort on the part of supervisors is required to communicate with and to coordinate the increased number of employees. Suppose, for example, that an employee arrives for work in the afternoon and notices that she cannot finish the work started by a morning employee. Specifically, part of the work the morning employee was supposed to have completed is missing, and the morning employee is gone for the rest of the day! What is the supervisor supposed to do? To straighten things out, the work may need to be delayed until the next morning when the other worker returns. Other difficulties that may arise when part-time employees are hired can also cause delays on the job.

Alternative work schedules are not appropriate for all organizations. As a supervisor, however, you should be aware of the existence of these different work schedules any time you are considering ways to improve the job satisfaction of employees.

Looking Back

Of all the resources organizations have available, their human resources are usually the most important in accomplishing their goals. An organization's efforts to promote high job satisfaction among its employees can be just as critical to the organization's success as its attention to any of its resources. As a result, it is now appropriate to briefly review the objectives concerning job satisfaction established at the beginning of this chapter.

☐ **Define job satisfaction.** For individual employees, job satisfaction is the level of enjoyment or contentment associated with a job.

☐ **Identify ways in which job satisfaction influences important elements of employees' work lives.** In general, employees who have a high level of job satisfaction, compared to those with a low level, are more likely to have a low rate of absenteeism and turnover, to have a good on-the-job safety record, and to have good physical and mental health. Furthermore, employees with high job satisfaction are more likely to be satisfied with life in general and may be more productive on the job.

☐ **Indicate important work attributes that contribute to job satisfaction.** Some important working conditions that lead to job satisfaction include providing employees with mentally challenging work and providing work that interests employees and is not too physically demanding. It is also important to provide appropriate rewards for performance and to offer pleasant working conditions. Furthermore, when employees have high self-esteem and receive help from others at work, their job satisfaction will be enhanced.

☐ **Explain the three stages employees often progress through in response to irritations on the job.** Employees progress through three stages. In the acceptance stage, employees view irritants on the job as normal and not the result of uncaring management. As the number and severity of irritants increase, however, there is a decline in the job satisfaction of employees, and they move into the tolerance stage. If the number and severity of irritants continue to increase, employees eventually move into the rejection stage.

☐ **Identify different techniques that a supervisor can use to recharge an employee's job interest.** To recharge the job interest of an employee, encourage job development, promote involvement in professional activities, and offer involvement in interdepartmental activities. Furthermore, it is also helpful to offer cross-training in other jobs and to delegate more responsibility where appropriate and possible.

☐ **Explain the concept of flextime.** Flextime provides employees with the option of choosing daily starting and quitting times provided that they work at other set times and for a prescribed number of hours per day.

☐ **Explain the concept of compressed workweeks.** In a compressed workweek, employees work fewer days but more hours each day than in a traditional workweek. The most common compressed workweek schedule is one in which employees work four 10-hour days each week; this is referred to as a 4-40 system. Under such a system, a company or department is only open four days a week and is usually closed on either Mondays or Fridays.

☐ **Describe the concept of job sharing.** Job sharing is an arrangement whereby two or more part-time employees share a job that would otherwise be performed by one full-time employee.

Key Terms

acceptance stage	job sharing
compressed workweek	morale
cross-training	organizational citizenship behavior
flextime	rejection stage
job satisfaction	tolerance stage

Review and Discussion Questions

1. What is the difference between job satisfaction and morale?
2. What is the relationship, according to research, between job satisfaction and absenteeism and turnover?
3. Explain the controversy over whether job satisfaction influences employee productivity.

4. Explain the three aspects of rewards on the job that are often considered by employees and that contribute to job success.

5. What is the difference between the acceptance stage and the tolerance stage for irritants on the job?

6. How should a supervisor deal with a situation in which employees have progressed to the rejection stage for irritants on the job?

7. How does the concept of cross-training work as a method of recharging an employee's job interest?

8. What is the difference between core time and flextime in a flextime work schedule?

9. What steps should an organization take to enhance the chances that a flextime work schedule will succeed?

10. How does the compressed workweek schedule work?

Action Incident 7.1

No Compensation

Two years ago Carol Ross interviewed for a job in the personnel department of a medium-size insurance company. The duties of the job included preparing files on job applicants, scheduling employees for in-house seminars, and assisting with responsibilities in public relations. It was the type of work she knew she would enjoy from the very beginning. Getting a job with duties she would enjoy was important to Carol. Although she expected to earn a fair salary, money is not a big consideration to Carol. As she is fond of saying, "A large salary just isn't worth working all day at a job you dislike!" Therefore, Carol did not interview for a lot of the higher-paying jobs her friends pursued because she did not perceive the required work in those jobs to be very meaningful to her. When she did interview for the personnel job, she made a special effort to clarify the duties of the job with the interviewer. Carol liked the answers she received to her questions, and at the end of the interview she said, "As long as I won't be working in the area of compensation in the personnel department, it sounds like I am a perfect fit for the job you have open." The interviewer agreed that Carol was well suited for the job, and Carol was hired. From the start, Carol excelled in her work. It was obvious that she enjoyed her job.

Two years after Carol started her job, the company began a large reorganization plan. Kelly Meyer, Carol's supervisor, is responsible for making sure the personnel department can meet the new demands placed upon it by the reorganization. To meet this challenge, Kelly reassigned Carol to work in the compensation division. When Carol learned of her reassignment, she complained to Kelly and reminded her that in her interview she had indicated that she did not want to work in compensation. However, Kelly knew that Carol was a hard worker and she insisted that she needed Carol's help in the compensation area.

The first problem Carol experienced upon being reassigned was with the math and statistics she needed to do on the new job. Specifically, she needed to compute modifications in benefits and salary due to changes in such things as sick leave taken, early retirement, etc. However, these tasks were too difficult for her, due to her limited math training. As a result of the difficulties she experienced, Carol worked many more hours to complete her tasks than before. She received little help with her demanding tasks due to personnel cutbacks. When Carol complained about her difficulties, Kelly said, "I know your new job isn't easy, but keep in mind that you got a $1,000 salary increase when you went to the compensation area." Carol does not think the extra money is worth the frustration. This morning, Kelly received a notice that Carol had accepted a position in the personnel department of another company in town.

Discussion Questions

1. How did Carol's attitude toward her job change after she was reassigned?
2. Not everyone who is reassigned to a new job in a company quits. What probably prompted Carol to resign?
3. How should Kelly have handled the situation differently?

Action Incident 7.2

A New Idea

The Western Block Company manufactures masonry blocks for use in building block fences and residential houses. The work required by employees to manufacture and handle the masonry blocks is very demanding. For example, the machinery in the manufacturing process requires a lot of physical effort to operate, and the temperature in the manufacturing plant itself is usually hot. If the employees do not concentrate on their work, several problems can develop. For example, if due to inattention too few blocks of a particular style are produced during a particular production schedule, supply agreements with commercial customers cannot be met. As a result, a new production run for a small quantity will need to be scheduled at great expense. Due to the physically demanding nature of the work, it is not uncommon for the workers to get fatigued toward the end of their eight-hour workday. For this reason, most of the workers in the plant are young men, and they often complain about the low wages they are paid. A recent increase in the number of accidents and injuries at the company's manufacturing plant has the workers and company officials concerned. A single cause for the worsening safety record has not been identified. Although the increased accident rate may be the result of a string of bad luck, company officials are watching the situation carefully.

The metropolitan area that Western Block serves has been experiencing a lot of economic growth over the last year. As a matter of fact, the population of the area is growing faster than expected. New residential housing construction is on the increase, which is placing increased demand on Western Block to produce more masonry blocks each day. To meet this increased demand, the company has decided to install new equipment and expand its production capacity. One problem that threatens to keep production well below capacity is the high turnover rate among plant workers. Even when new replacement workers are hired, their productivity is low while they are being trained and while they gain experience. Kevin Sandburg, a supervisor at the manufacturing plant, has been reading about the advantages of a compressed workweek as an alternative work schedule. He thinks a 4-40 work schedule will help solve the problems being experienced at the plant, and he plans to make his recommendation to his superior.

Discussion Questions

1. How well does the situation at the Western Block Company lend itself to a compressed workweek schedule?

2. What problems do you predict the company will face if it accepts Kevin's recommendation to adopt a compressed workweek schedule?

3. If you were Kevin's superior, how would you try to solve the turnover problem?

Action Incident 7.3

Changing Times

Craig Dexter and Edith Hopkins both work as design engineers for the Hansen International Corporation. The Hansen Corporation designs large power plants for utility companies that provide electricity. Craig and Edith have a new supervisor, Doyle Parks, but they have not had an opportunity to get to know Doyle well. In early January, Craig and Edith meet in Edith's office to discuss some engineering designs they have been working on. Toward the end of their meeting, the following conversation occurs.

Craig: I see that one of your neon ceiling lights is flickering on and off. A light in my office is doing the same thing. It is very distracting to work under.

Edith: My bad ceiling light distracts me, too. This type of problem happens periodically; it's nobody's fault. I mentioned it to Doyle, and I expect it will get fixed this week.

Craig: Since you called the problem to Doyle's attention, I'm sure the maintenance worker he sends up here to fix it will also notice and repair my light. I won't bother Doyle by mentioning my problem light to him. By the way, have you been having any trouble understanding the phone messages left for you by our new secretary? Some of my phone messages are very confusing.

Edith: I've been experiencing the same problem. I also mentioned that to Doyle.

Craig: Okay.

A couple of weeks later, Craig and Edith have lunch together. During their conversation at lunch, the following comments are made.

Craig: Has the flickering light in your office been fixed yet?

Edith: No. What about your light?

Craig: Nothing has been done on it! Are your phone messages still incomprehensible?

Edith: If anything, they have gotten worse. You wouldn't believe the problems they have caused me. I talked to Doyle about it; I don't know why nothing is being done. Do you think Doyle is just lazy?

Craig: Even lazy people are faster than he is. When he says he will correct a problem, I don't think he is sincere. He just doesn't care, and he's not willing to help. Maybe he just isn't smart enough to deal with these problems!

Edith: I'm scared to think how he would react if a really big problem developed.

Craig: I'm beginning to think that if Doyle isn't willing to put in the extra effort to help us, why should we work hard to make him look good?

Edith: I agree. Has he been hassling you over little supply items you order to do your work?

Craig: Yes he has; it is ridiculous. I talked to Doyle about it, and he said, "All costs have to be controlled around here and that also includes the little expenses."

In April, Craig meets Edith in the elevator. She notices that he appears angry, but she doesn't know what is wrong.

Edith: You seem upset. What's wrong?

Craig: Remember the funding Doyle approved for me to travel to the seminar this month? Well, he withdrew the money this morning.

Edith: What reason did he give?

Craig: He mentioned something about our department being over budget, but I don't believe him.

Edith: Since you are already upset, I might as well tell you now that the design review department needs us to make a lot of changes in the plans we submitted last month. They are so slow in reviewing work submitted to them. If we had known earlier about the changed specifications, it would have saved us a lot of wasted time and energy. I don't know about you, but my level of job satisfaction has just hit a new low.

Craig: I'm at the point now where I just don't give a darn anymore.

Discussion Questions

1. What three stages did Craig and Edith progress through in response to job irritations?
2. How did you determine they were in each specific stage?
3. How should Doyle have handled this situation as it developed?

Notes

1. Charles L. Hulin, "Effects of Changes in Job-Satisfaction Levels on Employee Turnover," *Journal of Applied Psychology* 52 (April 1968), pp. 122–26.

2. Edwin A. Locke, "The Nature and Causes of Job Satisfaction," in *Handbook of Industrial and Organizational Psychology,* ed. Marvin D. Dunnette (New York: John Wiley & Sons, 1983), pp. 1328–29.

3. S. M. Sales and J. House, "Job Dissatisfaction as a Possible Risk Factor in Coronary Heart Diseases," *Journal of Chronic Diseases* 23 (1971), pp. 861–73.

4. Gary Johns, *Organizational Behavior: Understanding Life at Work,* 2d ed. (Glenview, Ill.: Scott, Foresman, 1988), p. 134.

5. Michael J. Kavanagh, Michael W. Hurst, and Robert Rose, "The Relationship Between Job Satisfaction and Psychiatric Health Symptoms for Air Traffic Controllers," *Personnel Psychology* 34 (Winter 1981), p. 704; Muhammad Jamal and Vance F. Mitchell, "Work, Nonwork and Mental Health: A Model and a Test," *Industrial Relations* 19 (Winter 1980), pp. 88–93.

6. R. W. Rice, J. P. Near, and R. G. Hunt, "The Job-Satisfaction/Life-Satisfaction Relationship: A Review of Empirical Research," *Basic and Applied Social Psychology* 1 (1980), pp. 37–64.

7. Thomas I. Chacko, "Job and Life Satisfactions: A Causal Analysis of Their Relationships," *Academy of Management Journal* 26 (March 1983), pp. 166–67.

8. Thomas S. Bateman and Dennis W. Organ, "Job Satisfaction and the Good Soldier: The Relationship Between Affect and Employee 'Citizenship'," *Academy of Management Journal* 26 (December 1983), p. 587.

9. Dennis W. Organ, "A Restatement of the Satisfaction-Performance Hypothesis," *Journal of Management* 14 (1988), p. 548.

10. Bateman and Organ, "Job Satisfaction and the Good Soldier," p. 588.

11. Stephan J. Motowidlo, "Does Job Satisfaction Lead to Consideration and Personal Sensitivity?," *Academy of Management Journal* 27 (December 1984), p. 914.

12. Organ, "A Restatement of the Satisfaction-Performance Hypothesis," p. 550.

13. Material in this section based on material from R. Bruce McAfee and Myron Glassman, "Job Satisfaction: It's the Little Things That Count," *Management Solutions* 33 (August 1988), pp. 32–37.

14. McAfee and Glassman, "Job Satisfaction," p. 34.

15. Marcia Ann Pulich, "Revitalizing an Employee's Job Interest," *Supervisory Management* 34 (March 1989), pp. 3–10.

16. John M. Ivancevich and William G. Glueck, *Foundations of Personnel: Human Resource Management,* 4th ed. (Homewood, Ill.: BPI-Irwin, 1989), p. 828.

17. Ivancevich and Glueck, *Foundations of Personnel,* pp. 828–29.

18. "IBM Writes the Book on Liberal Leave," *U.S. News & World Report* (October 31, 1988), pp. 13–14.

19. J. Carroll Swart, "Clerical Workers on Flexitime: A Survey of Three Industries," *Personnel* 62 (April 1985), pp. 40–44.

20. Adapted form Edward G. Thomas, "Flexible Work Keeps Growing," *Management World* 15 (April–May 1986), p. 45.

21. Thomas, "Flexible Work Keeps Growing," p. 45.

22. Andrew J. DuBrin, *The Practice of Supervision: Achieving Results Through People,* 2d ed. (Plano, Tex.: Business Publications, 1987), pp. 72–73.

23. Adapted from Philip I. Morgan, "Taking a Look at Flexitime," *Supervisory Management* 29 (February 1984), pp. 41–42.

24. Arthur W. Sherman, Jr., George W. Bohlander, and Herbert J. Chruden, *Managing Human Resources,* 8th ed. (Cincinnati, Ohio: South-Western Publishing, 1988), p. 118.

25. Robert H. Crowder, Jr., "The Four-Day, Ten-Hour Workweek," *Personnel Journal* 61 (January 1982), p. 26.

26. Ivancevich and Glueck, *Foundations of Personnel,* p. 838.

27. Daniel Forbes, "Part-Time Work Force," *Business Month* 130 (October 1987), p. 45.

28. Ivancevich and Glueck, *Foundations of Personnel,* p. 841.

29. Forbes, "Part-Time Work Force," pp. 46–47.

Suggested Readings

Bernstein, Paul, "The Ultimate in Flexitime: From Sweden, By Way of Volvo." *Personnel* 65, June 1988, pp. 70–74.

Chacko, Thomas I. "Job and Life Satisfactions: A Causal Analysis of Their Relationships." *Academy of Management Journal* 26, March 1983, pp. 163–69.

Cregar, Michael. "Flextime Continues to Edge Upward." *Management World* 17, July–August 1988, pp. 14–15.

Forbes, Daniel. "Part-Time Work Force." *Business Month* 130, October 1987, pp. 45–47.

Kiechel, Walter, III. "How Important Is Morale, Really?" *Fortune,* February 13, 1989, pp. 121–22.

Locke, Edward A. "The Nature and Causes of Job Satisfaction." In *Handbook of Industrial and Organizational Psychology,* ed. Marvin D. Dunnette. New York: John Wiley & Sons, 1983, pp. 1297–1349.

McAfee, R. Bruce, and Myron Glassman. "Job Satisfaction: It's the Little Things That Count." *Management Solutions* 33, August 1988, pp. 32–37.

Olsten, William. "Effectively Managing Alternative Work Options." *Supervisory Management* 29, April 1984, pp. 10–15.

Organ, Dennis W. "A Restatement of the Satisfaction-Performance Hypothesis." *Journal of Management* 14, December 1988 pp. 547–57.

Pulich, Marcia Ann. "Revitalizing an Employee's Job Interest." *Supervisory Management* 34, March 1989, pp. 3–10.

Part III

Applying Supervisory Communication Skills

▼

Supervisors as Communicators

Chapter

8

Learning Objectives

After reading and studying the material in this chapter, you should be able to:

1. Define communication.
2. Explain the communication process.
3. Identify the major causes of miscommunication.
4. Discuss strategies for avoiding miscommunication.
5. Identify techniques for effective communication.

To Supervise, You Must Communicate

Supervision and communication are intertwined. Workers rely on you as supervisor for directions and guidance in work-related activities. You must also share information with other supervisors. Likewise, you may need to interact with customers, and, of course, your boss will expect you to keep him or her informed on the progress of your work unit. Your boss will also observe how you communicate with others.

In a recent study, the job performance evaluations of people who were considered to be either good or poor communicators were analyzed. The study found that individuals who were judged to be good communicators also received high job-performance evaluations. Conversely, employees who were judged to be poor communicators received low overall job-performance evaluations. The findings of this study indicate that communication competencies are good predictors of overall performance evaluations.[1] Clearly, supervisors who are good communicators are likely to be judged as doing a better overall job than those supervisors who are perceived as poor communicators. Without a doubt, to be successful as a supervisor in meeting the expectations of others on the job and customers, you must be able to communicate effectively with them.

Good supervisors are good communicators

What Is Communication?

Specifically, **communication** is the sharing of meaning between the sender and receiver of a message. If the receiver understands exactly what you mean, then you have communicated very well. However, if he or she misunderstands what you mean, then miscommunication occurs. When miscommunication does exist, all kinds of problems can develop. For example, Figure 8.1 shows the results of miscommunication when a customer ordered a teeter-totter.

Communication is the sharing of meaning

After experiencing problems caused by miscommunication, supervisors show great interest in becoming better communicators. The first step in learning how to communicate more effectively is to understand how the communication process works.

Many communication problems can be avoided

The Communication Process

The **communication process** involves the sending and receiving of messages for the purpose of sharing meaning. Figure 8.2 shows the six basic stages of the communication process.

Stage 1: Develop an Idea

Communication is not random behavior. Instead, you have a purpose when you communicate with another person. The main purpose is to have the receiver of your message understand your message as you intended

Figure 8.1   **Processing Teeter-Totter Order**

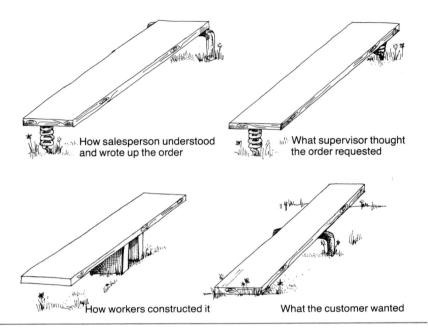

How salesperson understood and wrote up the order

What supervisor thought the order requested

How workers constructed it

What the customer wanted

it to be understood. To start this process, you must have an idea you wish to express. It is at this point that a big problem in communication often emerges. How can you communicate well if *you* are not especially clear about what you want to say? Give careful thought to what you wish to express. Otherwise, you handicap the communication process.

Stage 2: Create Your Message

You cannot expect the other person to read your mind. To get your idea across, you must put it into message form. You may do this verbally or nonverbally or both. However, special care should be taken in forming your message. You could have the greatest idea in the world, but if you choose vague or confusing words to express it, communication between you and the receiver will be poor.

Stage 3: Send Your Message

You can send your message in various ways. For example, you may speak to a person, send a memo, or use gestures. Unless you send a message in some

The Communication Process   **Figure 8.2**

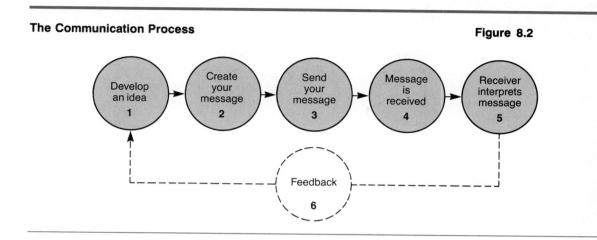

manner, however, no communication will occur between you and the other person.

Stage 4: Message Is Received

People use some or all of their five senses to receive messages. For example, you can hear oral messages and see visual messages, such as gestures or memos. Your senses of taste, touch, and smell can also provide you with information about what is going on around you. Sometimes, just part of a message is received. For example, the receiver may not hear everything you say, and this will hamper your attempt to communicate.

You receive messages through your five senses

Stage 5: Receiver Interprets the Message

Once received, the message must be interpreted. This may be easy or difficult. If, for example, you use words your subordinates are familiar with, they will have little trouble understanding what you mean. However, employees may not understand your directions if you use jargon or words they do not know.

Interpreting a message is called decoding

Stage 6: Feedback

Through feedback from the receiver, you discover how well you have communicated. In some cases, the receiver's response to your message will clearly indicate that miscommunication has occurred. The way an employee carries out your instructions also provides feedback on whether he or she correctly understood what you wanted done. Without feedback, you do not

Feedback can be very helpful

know how your message was interpreted and how well you communicated with the other person.

Consider This

1. Some college students believe that they must be good communicators because they claim they have been communicating all their lives. What is your reaction to this logic?
2. How good do you think you are as a communicator? In what ways would you like to improve as a communicator?

Causes of Miscommunication

Watch out for miscommunication

When the receiver of your message interprets it differently than you intended, **miscommunication** occurs. For supervisors, there is the constant danger that miscommunication will occur on the job. When you give a worker instructions, he or she might misunderstand what you wanted and make a costly mistake. Likewise, you may misunderstand an important request made by an employee. This problem can create ill will between you and the employee. You may also misunderstand instructions from upper management, or you may fail to express yourself clearly to your boss. As a result, top management may lose confidence in you. To guard against miscommunication as a supervisor, you should know the factors that promote miscommunication. These include inferences, word-meaning confusion, and differing perceptions.

Inferences

Inferences can cause communication problems

An **inference** is the act or process of drawing a conclusion based on facts or indications. The process works as follows: You observe something. As a result, you gain information. You then analyze the information and draw a conclusion about what you have observed. Your conclusion, or inference, may be correct or incorrect. The exercise on page 195 will help you better understand the material in this section. Read the instructions and complete the exercise now.

At first, inferences seem correct

    Turn to page 196 to find the answers to the above exercise. How did you do? For any items you may have missed, think of the inferences you made. If you missed very many, don't feel bad, because the statements were designed to play on your inferences. Although this exercise is harmless, the inferences supervisors make on the job can cause damaging miscommunication.[2]

Instructions

Read the short story below. Assume that all the information in the story is accurate. After reading the story, you will find seven statements about it. "T, F, ?" follows each statement. If you think the statement is true, based on the information in the story, circle T. If you think the statement is false, based on the information, circle F. If you are not sure whether the statement is true or false, circle the question mark. Circle only one answer at the end of each statement. Please feel free to refer back to the story in responding to the statements.

The Story

A prisoner was being fed when suddenly a man appeared with a gun to help free him. The convict made a run for it and escaped. The highway patrol immediately set up roadblocks around the area.

Statements about the Story

1. A man with a gun appeared as the convict was being fed.   T   F   ?
2. The man who appeared did not have a gun.   T   F   ?
3. The man who escaped was a convict.   T   F   ?
4. The man who appeared with a gun helped the convict escape.   T   F   ?
5. The highway patrol set up roadblocks to help capture the   T   F   ?
   convict.
6. Roadblocks were set up around the area.   T   F   ?
7. The following events occurred: A prisoner was eating dinner   T   F   ?
   when a man with a gun suddenly appeared. An escape was
   made, and the highway patrol set up roadblocks.

How Inferences Cause Miscommunication. When reading, you sometimes read between the lines. That is, you assume the writer is really saying certain things even though the information is not actually stated. Reading between the lines can lead you to unwarranted and incorrect interpretations. Likewise, the inferences you make while interacting with others on the job can lead you to incorrectly interpret their statements. Miscommunication then results.

Inferences can lead to incorrect conclusions

In one company, a supervisor learned that the boss would return by airplane the next day. When the supervisor was asked to pick up the boss at the airport, he replied, "Sure, what time does she arrive?" He was informed that the airplane would get in a 8 o'clock. The supervisor inferred that the airplane would arrive at 8 P.M. the next day. Unfortunately, it landed at 8 A.M., and the supervisor was not there! Miscommunication occurred because the supervisor inferred evening even though no one said that it was an evening flight.

Strategies for Avoiding Miscommunication Due to Inferences. It is natural to make some inferences when you communicate with others. However, miscommunication due to false inferences can be avoided by using the following strategies.[3]

Be aware of your inferences. The first step in avoiding miscommunication due to inferences is to realize when you are making them. If you do not realize you are making one, there is always the risk that you will treat the inference as a known fact. In the example of the boss left waiting at the airport, the supervisor acted on the inference as if it were fact.

As a supervisor, you need to realize that you are not expected to know or observe everything that goes on in your work area. But you are expected to distinguish between what you know and what you are inferring.[4] When you make a conscious effort to be aware of inferences, you are better able to isolate them. That way, you are less likely to mistakenly treat the inferences as actual statements made by the speaker, thus causing miscommunication.

Label the important inferences you make. When you label your inferences, you make them clear to the other person. If your inferences are incorrect, the other person can point that out. Going back to the earlier example, the supervisor should have labeled the inference by saying, "I'm inferring that you mean the airplane arrives at 8 o'clock in the *evening.*" The supervisor would then have been informed that the airplane arrived in the *morning,* and miscommunication would have been avoided.

Answers to "The Story" Exercise

To see how you did on the exercise you completed, compare your responses to the statements about the story with the answers below:

1. ? You do not know if the "prisoner" and the "convict" are the same person. For example, a civilian could be held prisoner by an escaped convict. The prisoner and the convict may or may not be the same person; you simply do not know, and that is why ? is the correct answer. To conclude otherwise would be to make an inference.
2. F The story clearly states that the man who appeared had a gun.
3. ? Do you know that the convict was a man? The story does not say whether the convict was a man or a woman, so ? is the correct answer.
4. ? You do not know that the man who appeared actually helped the convict escape. This does not make the statement false; it just makes it uncertain. To say the man helped the convict escape, you would also have to infer that the prisoner and the convict are one and the same, which is not certain.
5. ? The story does not say why the highway patrol set up roadblocks; you are uncertain as to the reason.
6. T The story specifically states that roadblocks were set up around the area.
7. ? Do you know what meal the prisoner was eating? Could it have been breakfast? Due to the uncertainty, ? is the correct answer.

Word-Meaning Confusion

When a sender and a receiver give the same word different meanings or different words the same meaning, **word-meaning confusion** occurs. In either case, as will be shown, miscommunication will result.[5]

Same Word—Different Meanings. Miscommunication commonly occurs when two people fail to realize that they are giving different meanings to the same word. Consider the following conversation between a daughter and her mother.

Different people may interpret the same word differently

Daugther: Mom, George just got a new Blazer.
Mother: Oh, that's nice. What color is it?
Daughter: It's white and very pretty.
Mother: I can't wait to see it.
Daughter: You'll like it. It's red on the inside.
Mother: Isn't that a little bold?
Daughter: I don't think so. Mom, it's a lot of fun to get into—it sets up so high.
Mother: How can a sport coat set up high?
Daughter: Mom, it's not a coat. It's a Chevrolet Blazer truck!

Miscommunication also occurs on the job when the meaning a supervisor and a worker give to a word differs. Consider the following example. A worker who had grown up in a large city moved to a small rural town and got a job in a manufacturing company. One day his supervisor asked him, "Can you finish the project you are working on by dinner?" The worker answered yes. At noon, the supervisor asked to see the finished project. Surprised, the worker complained, "You said you wanted it by dinner. That still gives me until 6 P.M. to finish." In response, the supervisor exclaimed, "Around here dinner is at noon and supper is at 6 in the evening!" A further example of miscommunication between a supervisor and a worker is illustrated in Figure 8.3.

Different Words—Same Meaning. Miscommunication can also occur when two people fail to realize that they are using different words to mean the same thing. The argument between the two supervisors in the following incident occurred because of that.

Different words may be used to mean the same thing

Supervisor A: If you ask my opinion, the workers in our division are of a *higher caliber* than the workers in any other division.
Supervisor B: I disagree. Our workers may be *more capable,* but they are not any better than anyone else.
Supervisor A: If they are more capable, they are better.
Supervisor B: I think you are making an unfair value judgment!

As the argument progressed, supervisor A explained that when he used the phrase *higher caliber* he meant better educated. Upon learning this, supervisor B explained that she meant the same thing by *more capable.*

Figure 8.3   **An Example of Miscommunication**

Supervisor B was annoyed because she thought supervisor A was referring to the character of the other workers.

Strategies for Avoiding Miscommunication Due to Word-Meaning Confusion. Miscommunication resulting from word-meaning confusion plagues many supervisors. However, by using the strategies listed below, you will be able to avoid most forms of miscommunication resulting from word-meaning confusion.[6]

Consider the person with whom you are communicating. Words do not carry meaning as they are transmitted from one person to another. Instead, as you receive words or messages, *you* must give them meaning. Therefore, when communicating with other people, think about what they probably mean by the words they use, and when you send a message to others, consider how they will interpret your words. Failure to consider the person with whom you are communicating invites miscommunication. Read the following exchange of letters between a foreign-born plumber and officials with the National Bureau of Standards.[7]

You can send a message, but you can't send meaning

Bureau of Standards
Washington, D.C.

Bureau Director:

As a plumber, I recently found that hydrochloric acid opens up clogged drainage pipes very quickly. Is it safe for me to use this substance?

Sincerely,

Guilo Giordano, Plumber

Mr. Guilo Giordano, Plumber
Anytown, U.S.A.

Dear Mr. Giordano:

The efficacy of hydrochloric acid is indisputable, but its chloric residue renders it incompatible with metallic permanence.

Sincerely,

Director, Bureau of Standards

Mr. Giordano appreciated the fast reply to his letter and sent the following to the Bureau of Standards thanking them for answering his question.

Bureau of Standards
Washington, D.C.

Bureau Director:

In response to my recent inquiry, thank you for recommending hydrochloric acid as a substance for cleaning out drains.

Sincerely,

Guilo Giordano, Plumber

The Bureau director was greatly disturbed at the plumber's failure to understand the dangers in using hydrochloric acid for cleaning drains. As a result, she asked a new staff scientist to do what he could to help the plumber understand the inadvisability of using hydrochloric acid in pipes. To resolve the communication problem, the staff scientist sent the following letter.

Mr. Guilo Giordano, Plumber
Anytown, U.S.A.

Dear Mr. Giordano:

Don't use hydrochloric acid. It eats the hell out of drainage pipes!

Sincerely,

Scientist, Bureau of Standards

Ask questions. If you do not understand a statement, or you realize that more than one interpretation would be plausible, ask a question to clarify. For example, another supervisor may tell you that the supplies you ordered will cost "a little more" than you expected. If you are uncertain about how much more the supplies will cost, ask her how much more money she means by "a little more." Too often supervisors fail to follow the simple practice of asking questions when in doubt.

Paraphrase important statements. When you **paraphrase,** you restate in your own words what another person has said. Upon hearing the message rephrased, the sender of the message can tell you if you interpreted the message correctly. Paraphrasing important statements can reduce miscommunication and help avoid costly mistakes resulting from misunderstood directions.

Differing Perceptions

Your **perceptions** represent how you interpret or view what goes on around you. However, individual perceptions can differ. When you look at the picture in Figure 8.4, do you see an old woman or a young woman? Some people see an old woman; others see a young woman. To help you understand how the picture can be viewed as either an old or young woman, Figure 8.5 shows a separate picture of each.

Your background and past experiences influence your perceptions. Viewing the crosses in Figure 8.6, for example, an airplane pilot may see a

Don't be afraid to ask questions

An Aid for Demonstrating Differences in Perception   **Figure 8.4**

Source: Edwin G. Boring, "A New Ambiguous Figure," *American Journal of Psychology*, July 1930, p. 444. Also see Robert Leeper, "A Study of a Neglected Portion of the Field of Learning—the Development of Sensory Organization," *Journal of Genetic Psychology*, March 1935, p. 62. Originally drawn by cartoonist W. E. Hill and published in *Puck*, November 8, 1915.

formation of airplanes. Viewing the same crosses, a lineman for a telephone company may see a string of telephone poles. In contrast, a minister may see religious or cemetery crosses. The pilot, lineman, and minister all see the same crosses, but their perceptions as to what the crosses represent differ because of their different backgrounds.

When another person's differing perception causes him or her to interpret your message differently than you intended, miscommunication can result. For example, if you said, "My sister looks just like the woman pictured in Figure 8.4," you would probably mean that your sister was young and attractive. However, if the other person saw an old woman in the picture, he or she would think you meant your sister was old and unattractive!

Strategies for Avoiding Miscommunication Due to Differing Perceptions. There are several strategies you can use to avoid miscommunication due to differing perceptions.

Make your message specific. Messages that are vague increase the likelihood of miscommunication. It is important to make your important points clear to the other person.

Clarify important points. Major problems can develop on the job when important points in a message are misinterpreted. Therefore, when

Bring differing perceptions into the open

Figure 8.5   **Pictures of the Old and Young Woman**

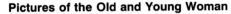

Source: Robert Leeper, "A Study of a Neglected Portion of the Field of Learning—the Development of Sensory Organization," *Journal of Genetic Psychology,* March 1935, p. 62.

sending messages to others, clarify your meaning on important points.

Seek feedback. Asking for feedback is especially important when you realize that the other person's background differs a lot from yours. Feedback will give you information on how your message is interpreted.

Consider This

1. We give meaning to spoken words and nonverbal cues based on our experiences. Think of a person you have had trouble communicating with in the past. To what extent might different backgrounds or experiences help explain part of the communication problem between you and this person?

2. Think of an inference you made that caused a communication problem. In looking back at the situation, what should you have done to avoid the communication problem?

Techniques for Effective Communication

Impress others with your communication skills

The ability to communicate effectively is a requirement for successful supervision. As a supervisor, you must be able to communicate effectively with others on the job in order to achieve organizational goals. The following techniques will help you.

**An Aid for Demonstrating How Different Backgrounds Can
Influence Perception**   **Figure 8.6**

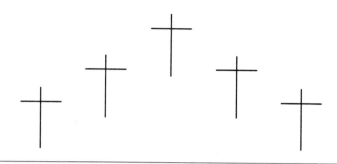

Give Careful Thought to What You Wish to Say.   Before speaking, consider
what you are about to say. If what you are about to say is not clear to you,
it will not be clear to the other person. Take the time to form statements that
will be easy for others to understand and strive to make your statements
concise. Statements that ramble and are vague or poorly organized often
cause miscommunication.

Use Appropriate Lanaguage.   "Language, a basic tool of communication, is
a delicate, sensitive instrument through which we attempt to convey the most
simple to the most complex of ideas."[8] When speaking to a person, adapt
your words to that person. Keep in mind that just because a word is clear to
you does not mean it will be clear to the other person. For instance, technical
terms may be clear to your boss but confusing to new employees or customers
outside the company. Thus, when communicating with others, use language
they understand.

Word choice is important

Make Sure Your Message Is Necessary.   Some supervisors think that the
more messages they send, the better they are communicating with their
workers. Too many messages, however, can lead to communication overload.
When workers are faced with this, they cannot give proper attention to all of
the messages. If some of the messages that go unattended are especially
important, major problems can arise. Therefore, before sending messages,
make sure they are necessary.

*Communication overload
creates problems*

Time Messages Properly.   The timing of a message can influence its impact.
For example, a message requiring employees' careful consideration should be
sent early enough to permit them to give proper attention to it. If an employee
makes a mistake, you should discuss it as soon as possible. In general, the

timing of a message should enhance the chances that it will be successful in accomplishing its purpose.

Others notice your body language

Watch Your Body Language.   Your facial expressions, eye movements, and gestures send messages that are often just as communicative as the words you speak. Therefore, make sure your body language does not contradict your oral messages. If you compliment a worker's performance, you should maintain good eye contact, smile, and appear pleased. Otherwise, the worker may wonder if your words are sincere.

Listen Attentively.   As a supervisor, you are expected to keep up with important developments and what is going on in your work area. You get much of this knowledge by listening. However, you should realize that there is a difference between listening and just hearing. To listen, you must concentrate on what is being said. If you listen carefully to what others say and do not interrupt, you will be better informed. You also will be respected for your interest and courtesy.

Let others know how you are interpreting their important messages

Give and Seek Feedback.   When talking, you should realize that the other person may not give your words the meaning you intended. When you speak, get feedback on important points to make sure you are not misunderstood. Likewise, when you receive a message on the job, clarify the important points in it that could cause serious problems if miscommunication occurred.

Sometimes, it is the little things that count

Watch for Subtle Messages.   Before signing agreements, it is often recommended that you "read the fine print." The same caution can be adapted to apply to subtle messages sent by others you work with on the job. Suppose, for example, you explain a new procedure to a subordinate. In response, the subordinate says, "I'll give it a try." Some subtle messages that may have gone unnoticed were that the subordinate did not ask any questions or take any notes. In light of these subtle messages, an appropriate response by you might be "Before rushing off, please tell me your understanding of the new procedure."

Also, realize that although people may nod their head and say "uh-huh" while you speak, they may not necessarily agree with you.[9] They may only be signaling that they understand you, while other subtle messages indicate disagreement. Furthermore, realize that hidden agendas may exist which need to be taken into account when interpreting what others say.[10]

Looking Back

Now that you have studied the concept of communication and techniques for effective communication, it is appropriate to review the objectives restated from the beginning of this chapter.

☐ **Define communication.** Communication is the sharing of meaning between the sender and the receiver of a message.

☐ **Explain the communication process.** You develop an idea that you put into message form and send to a receiver. The receiver receives the message and interprets it. Feedback from the receiver allows you to determine how well you have communicated.

☐ **Identify the major causes of miscommunication.** Miscommunication frequently results from inferences, word-meaning confusion, and differing perceptions.

☐ **Discuss strategies for avoiding miscommunication.** To avoid miscommunication, you should be aware of your inferences and label them. It is also important to consider the person with whom you are communicating. In addition, you should ask questions and paraphrase important statements. Make your message specific, clarify your meaning on important points, and seek feedback.

☐ **Identify techniques for effective communication.** In order to communicate effectively on the job, give careful thought to what you wish to say and use appropriate language. Also, make sure your message is necessary, time your message properly, and watch your body language. You should listen attentively and give and seek feedback. In addition, watch for subtle messages.

Key Terms

communication

communication process

inference

miscommunication

paraphrase

perceptions

word-meaning confusion

Review and Discussion Questions

1. Beyond sending a message, what else is needed for communication to take place?
2. What is the danger in thinking that words carry meaning by themselves?
3. How does the communication process work?
4. What are the main causes of miscommunication?
5. How can inferences cause miscommunication?
6. What are the main forms of word-meaning confusion?
7. What strategies can you use for avoiding miscommunication due to word-meaning confusion?
8. How does feedback promote effective communication?

Action Incident 8.1

Broken Promises

The Westwood Company manufactures kitchen cabinets and counter-tops in a variety of styles. Chris Henrick is the supervisor in charge of the cabinet department, and Sam Westfall supervises the countertop department.

Recently, Chris received an order for Westwood's premium line of kitchen cabinets from Russell Johnson, a local builder. Russell also requested that the company supply the countertops. Both Chris and Sam developed production schedules for their departments to make sure the cabinets and countertops would be finished on time.

Russell then contacted Chris and requested an earlier delivery date. Chris knew that he could meet the earlier date, but he did not know whether Sam could. Therefore, Chris told Russell he would contact him as soon as he knew whether they could meet the earlier delivery date.

Chris quickly called Sam to see if he could have the countertops ready earlier than expected. Sam said he would have to check a few things before he could commit to the new delivery date and asked Chris to call him back later.

That afternoon, Chris called Sam's office, but Sam was not in. The following conversation with Sam's assistant, Ralph Wyatt, took place.

Chris: I just called to check on Russell's order.

Ralph: There's no problem. Russell's order will be finished on schedule.

Chris: Then I can tell Russell there's no problem?

Ralph: We won't have any problem finishing his order on time.

Chris: That's great. Thanks for your help.

Chris then called Russell to tell him everything would be ready by the earlier delivery date. Unfortunately, Ralph did not know anything about Russell's new request, and the countertops were not ready on the early delivery date as Chris promised.

Discussion Questions

1. What major inferences did Chris make?
2. What communication problems occurred from his inferences?
3. How could Chris have avoided the communication problems?

Action Incident 8.2

High Flier

As a supervisor for a large electronics company in Kansas City, Kansas, Alice Potter needed to fly to Phoenix, Arizona, on company business. Alice was concerned about her inner ear condition, which became aggravated by the pressure changes of an airplane landing. Therefore, she hoped she could get a *nonstop flight* with no landings before arriving in Phoenix.

After explaining her travel dates to the travel agent, Alice was informed that a *direct flight* to Phoenix was available each morning and afternoon. Alice bought a ticket for the morning flight.

Before leaving the agent's office, Alice looked at her ticket. The ticket showed that her flight left at 9 A.M. and arrived in Phoenix three hours later. Alice was pleased that she had been able to get a flight that did not make any landings before arriving in Phoenix. Soon after the airplane left Kansas City, Alice learned that the plane would make a scheduled landing in Denver before proceeding to Phoenix!

Discussion Questions

1. How did the phrase *direct flight* cause miscommunication between Alice and the travel agent?

2. As discussed in the chapter, what type of miscommunication took place in this case?

3. What could Alice have done to avoid the miscommunication that occurred?

Action Incident 8.3

Problem Cupcakes

Doug Smith was recently hired as a production supervisor for a large baking company. His first assignment was to schedule production of chocolate and vanilla frosted cupcakes for a supermarket chain. The order called for each box of cupcakes to be either all chocolate or all vanilla, with six cupcakes per box.

After checking his supplies of ingredients, Doug called in his packaging foreman, Alan Gray, to discuss the order. To explain how he wanted the order produced, Doug said, "Alternate chocolate and vanilla frosted cupcakes during packaging." After production started, Doug inspected the critical stages. He was pleased with everything he saw until he looked into some crates of packaged cupcakes. To his surprise, Doug discovered that each box of cupcakes contained both chocolate and vanilla cupcakes.

Doug quickly called Alan to find out why his order on packaging had been disobeyed. "I didn't disobey your order," Alan protested. "You told me to alternate the cupcakes during packaging, so I alternated them in each box." Doug exclaimed, "By 'alternate' I meant that the boxes were to alternately contain all chocolate and then all vanilla cupcakes!"

Discussion Questions

1. What type of miscommunication did Doug experience with Alan?

2. What should Doug have done to reduce the chance of miscommunicating with Alan?

3. What should Alan have done to minimize the chance that he would misunderstand Doug's order?

Notes

1. Joseph N. Scudder and Patricia J. Guinan, "Communication Competencies as Discriminators of Superiors' Ratings of Employee Performance," *Journal of Business Communication* 26 (Summer 1989), p. 224.

2. William V. Haney, *Communication and Interpersonal Relations: Text and Cases,* 5th ed. (Homewood, Ill.: Richard D. Irwin, 1986), pp. 213–23.

3. Haney, *Communication and Interpersonal Relations,* p. 223.

4. Haney, *Communication and Interpersonal Relations,* p. 226.

5. Haney, *Communication and Interpersonal Relations,* p. 251.

6. Haney, *Communication and Interpersonal Relations,* p. 273.

7. Adapted from Haney, *Communication and Interpersonal Relations,* p. 281.

8. Richard F. Whitman and Paul H. Boase, *Speech Communication: Principles and Contexts* (New York: Macmillan, 1983), p. 139.

9. Ken Matejka and Jay Liebowitz, "Five Critical Challenges to Communicating Clearly," *Supervision* 51 (February 1989), pp. 9–10.

10. Ken Matejka, "Ten Key Strategies for Communicating More Clearly," *Management Solutions* 33 (December 1988), pp. 22–23.

Suggested Readings

Farrant, Don. "The 'Stanley Syndrome'." *Supervision* 43, October 1981, pp. 8–9.

Goyer, Robert S. "Communication, Communicative Process, Meaning: Toward a Unified Theory." *Journal of Communication* 20, March 1970, pp. 4–16.

Haney, William V. *Communication and Interpersonal Relations: Text and Cases,* 5th ed. Homewood, Ill.: Richard D. Irwin, 1986.

Hunsicker, F. R. "How to Approach Communication Difficulties." *Personnel Journal* 51, 1972, pp. 680–83.

Lindo, David K. "Why Are You Afraid of Your Subordinates?" *Supervision* 45, March 1983, pp. 3–5.

Matejka, Ken, and Jay Liebowitz. "Five Critical Challenges to Communicating Clearly." *Supervision* 51, February 1989, pp. 9–10.

Scudder, Joseph N., and Patricia J. Guinan. "Communication Competencies as Discriminators of Supervisors' Ratings of Employee Performance." *Journal of Business Communication* 26, Summer 1989, pp. 217–25.

Tubbs, Stewart L., and Sylvia Moss. *Human Communication,* 3d ed. New York: Random House, 1980.

Verderber, Rudolph F., and Kathleen S. Verderber. *Inter-act: Using Interpersonal Communication Skills,* 5th ed. Belmont, Calif.: Wadsworth, 1989.

Practicing Effective Communication

Chapter

9

Learning Objectives

After reading and studying the material in this chapter, you should be able to:

1. Define listening.
2. Explain the difference between hearing and listening.
3. Identify the stages in the listening process.
4. Define comprehensive listening.
5. Identify strategies for comprehensive listening.
6. Define nonverbal communication.
7. Identify the functions of nonverbal messages.
8. Define downward communication.
9. Identify downward communication skills.
10. Define upward communication.
11. Identify ways to facilitate upward communication.
12. Define horizontal communication.
13. Identify ways of facilitating horizontal communication.
14. Define grapevine.
15. Identify ways to deal with the grapevine.
16. Identify five principles of effective written communications.

Listening, the Key to Staying Informed

Listening is paying attention to what is said and giving meaning to what you have heard. To supervise effectively, you need information from various sources. Much of that information comes to you in verbal form. Therefore, to benefit from spoken information, you must be skilled at listening. Research shows that many listeners remember only about 25 *percent* of what they hear.[1] Figure 9.1 illustrates how poor listening can distort messages as they pass from one person to another. Because you spend much of your work time as a supervisor listening to others, you must develop effective listening skills to do your job well.

Supervisors spend much of their time listening

Hearing versus Listening

There is a great difference between hearing and listening. Since your ears are open all the time, you automatically *hear* most of the sounds around you. However, *listening* only occurs when you pay attention to what is said and give meaning to what you have heard. Hearing is just the passive receiving of sounds, while listening is an active process that requires you to use your ears *and* your mind. Effective listening requires extra effort beyond just hearing. In learning how to listen effectively, it is necessary to understand how the listening process itself works.

Hearing and listening are different

Stages in the Listening Process

The **listening process** requires you to attend to what you hear in order to give meaning to the verbal message and consider a reaction. As Figure 9.2 shows, listening involves four stages.

Stage 1: Hear.   Of course, you must hear before you can listen. If you have a hearing impairment, or if other noises drown out the message, it will be difficult for listening to occur. Once the message has been heard, though, the first step in the listening process is complete.

Stage 2: Pay Attention.   After hearing the verbal message, you must pay attention to it. To do this, you may have to ignore other sounds or messages occurring at the same time. Hearing takes place whether or not you attend to a verbal message. For listening to occur, however, you must pay attention to the verbal message.

Stage 3: Assign Meaning.   Next, you must give meaning to what the speaker is saying. If the speaker uses words you are familiar with, you will probably do this automatically and have no trouble understanding the speaker.

Verbal messages don't carry meaning; it is assigned

Figure 9.1   **An Example of the Effects of Poor Listening**

Stages in Listening

Figure 9.2

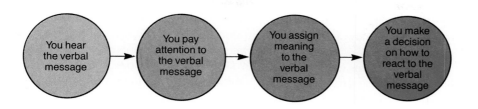

However, if the message is complex and contains unfamiliar words, you will likely have trouble understanding it. As a result, listening and communication will suffer.

Stage 4: Decide How You Will React.   Once you have given meaning to the message, you must decide how you are going to deal with it. You may decide to respond to the verbal message, or you may simply retain the information. Of course, you do not have to respond or commit the message to memory for listening to occur. However, you must at least give some thought to how you plan to deal with what the speaker has said.

The Importance of Effective Listening in Business

Firms value effective listening. For example, in commercials and ads, the Sperry Corporation detailed the benefits of effective listening and stated, "We're convinced that effective listening adds a special dimension to what we can do for our customers."[2] Being a good listener also adds a special dimension to what you can do for the people with whom you work. J. Paul Lyet, the former chairman of Sperry, acknowledges that poor listening is a major problem facing most businesses and that listening mistakes can be costly.[3] It has been estimated that with over 100 million workers in the United States, a $10 mistake by each worker due to poor listening could amount to over one billion dollars.[4] Unfortunately, listening mistakes occur daily in business. One company lost a million-dollar sale because of poor listening.[5] In another case, a broker placed a large order to *buy* after being told to *sell*. The mistake proved costly for the stock brokerage firm. A supervisor in a different company approved the shipment of a large piece of equipment to a city in the wrong state. The supervisor had failed to listen to the shipping instructions. The cost of reshipping was sizable.

Fortunately, effective listening skills can be learned, and improvement in the listening ability of employees can lead to increased productivity. To

Listening mistakes can be costly

Listening skills can be learned

illustrate, it is reported that approximately 30 percent of the new computer systems organizations purchase either fail to improve their operations or are severely underutilized because employees cannot adjust to the new ways of performing their work.[6] Specifically, one large manufacturing company in New York State was studied by listening researchers. The company planned to introduce a new computer system that would influence the jobs of many employees in two divisions. One week before introduction of the new computer system, 204 employees in Division B participated in a 15-hour listening training program. The 187 employees in Division A did not receive the training. The results of the study indicated that "the employees who received the listening training program performed at significantly higher levels with the new technology than employees who did not receive training."[7] To perform well with the new computer system, the employees in the company studied needed to be able to listen well to the information and directions given them about the new system, and the employees who received listening training were helped to do so.

Large firms offer listening training programs

Understanding the importance of listening, many large firms—Sperry, Xerox, Pfizer, 3M, General Electric, and IBM, to name a few—offer training in effective listening skills for employees.[8] One area of listening training that is especially appropriate for supervisors is *comprehensive* listening.

Comprehensive Listening

Specifically, **comprehensive listening** is listening for the purpose of understanding and remembering the information contained in a verbal message.[9] Placed between workers and higher-level management, the supervisor faces many situations calling for comprehensive listening.

Strategies for Comprehensive Listening

Comprehensive listening is not easy. However, you can become skilled at it by using certain strategies.

Ask Questions to Enhance Understanding. If a speaker's statements are confusing, or you are uncertain if your interpretation is correct, ask questions. Suppose a worker says, "I had to make some changes in the specifications you gave me. But the changes will allow us to finish the job faster." In this situation it would be appropriate for you to ask, "What changes did you make?" "How much faster can the job be finished?" The answers might help you better understand what the worker meant. They will also help you decide whether the changes the worker made were sound.

When listening, make sure your understanding is correct

Confirm Your Understanding. The best way to make sure you are interpreting the speaker's message correctly is to confirm your understanding. Explain your understanding of what the speaker said. Then ask if your interpretation is correct. This strategy is especially important when the consequences of a misunderstanding are high. To confirm your understanding you might say, "Let me see if I understand you correctly. You're saying that. . . . Is that right?" If you are going to take the time to listen, make sure you understand the message correctly.

Maximize Your Excess Thought Time. An inherent difficulty listeners experience is that they can think much faster than people speak. Specifically, we think at a rate of about 500 words per minute, while the typical speaker talks at a rate of about 125 to 150 words per minute.[10] So you mentally process words almost four times as fast as people normally talk. This leaves **excess thought time,** the extra time you have while listening to think about things while the speaker is talking.

You can mentally process words quickly

Excess thought time can hinder listening or aid it, depending on how the time is used. If the extra time is used to think about things unrelated to the speaker's comments, you may take a permanent mental detour. As a result, you will miss out on what the speaker says. This danger can be avoided if you use the excess thought time to review what has been said. In doing so, think of relevant questions to ask or comments to make. While using excess thought time in this manner, "tune back in" to the speaker often enough to avoid missing important information.

Listen for the Speaker's Main Idea. No one expects you to remember everything you listen to on the job. Of all the information you may remember, however, comprehensive listening emphasizes that it is most important to identify and retain the speaker's main idea. Suppose an employee says, "We have found the missing supplies. I always thought we had received them, but they never showed up on the records. It seems that the delivery truck driver forgot to unload them with the other equipment. When the driver returned with them, they weren't recorded with the items unloaded the first time." The most important item to retain here is the speaker's main idea—that the missing supplies have been found. Compared to the other information in the message, the speaker's main idea is the most useful for making decisions. Listening would be less effective if other points of information were retained at the expense of remembering the speaker's main idea.

Make sure you get the main idea

Listen for Supporting Details. You should also listen for relevant details that *support* the speaker's main idea.[11] These details can help you better understand the main idea. Suppose, for example, that an employee says, "We need to correct the fire code violations in the assembly plant. Just this morning, I noticed that our fire extinguishers are overdue for inspection. Also, we never repaired the fire escape ladder after it was damaged during the last storm. On top of all this, many of the smoke detectors are not working." Clearly, you should remember the speaker's main idea—the fire code violations need to be corrected. But it is also important to recall the supporting details. The speaker gave three examples of violations: the fire extinguishers, the fire escape ladder, and the smoke detectors. All three represented details backing up the main idea. By listening for the supporting details, you discovered the specific fire code violations that existed.

Listen for Key Words.   Words that help you recall parts of what the speaker said are called *key words*.[12] Imagine that an employee says, "I think we should stop buying lumber from our present supplier. I've noticed that their prices are higher than any other supplier in town. That would be all right if we were getting quality lumber, but what they ship us is often warped, and they are undependable. Half the time, we don't get the lumber when we need it. It doesn't make any sense to continue buying lumber from them." The employee's main idea was that the firm should stop buying lumber from its present supplier. Three key words — *price, quality,* and *undependable* — can help you remember much of what the worker said to support the main point. For example, the word *price* would probably help you recall that the employee said the lumber supplier's prices were too high. What about *quality?* You would likely recall that the quality of the lumber was poor. The word *undependable* would help you recall that the employee said the lumber often did not arrive on time. Key words allow you to recall most of a verbal message without memorizing the complete message.

Mentally Organize the Material.   When listening, try to find an organizational pattern in the speaker's message. Then use the pattern to remember what was said. For example, another supervisor may say to you, "There are advantages and disadvantages in renting more equipment to handle the extra work load." Immediately, you should begin to listen for *advantages* and *disadvantages.* Later, when you need to remember what was said, you can use the same pattern. That is, recall the information by first remembering the advantages, then the disadvantages.

Take Notes.   Too often listeners fail to take notes on the job when a speaker is presenting important information. When appropriate, do not hesitate to take notes; they can be a great memory aid. Taking notes is easy, and speakers generally find it flattering to know that you are interested enough in what they are saying to write it down. Notes are especially valuable for recalling what was discussed in telephone conversations.

Nonverbal Communication, an Important Part of Supervision

Whether you realize it or not, as a supervisor you send many nonverbal messages. When you wave your hand at someone, nod your head while listening, or smile at others, you are sending nonverbal messages. Even the

Remembering key words
can aid recall

Mentally organizing groups
ideas together

Taking notes can aid
listening

appearance of your office can send nonverbal messages about how organized or efficient you are. You also receive nonverbal messages. Another supervisor may point to a box to indicate where certain parts are stored. A worker might fail to complete a job on time. This behavior can signal an inability to accept responsibility. A worker listening to your instructions might look confused. This signal is a reliable nonverbal cue that the worker does not understand your instructions.

You communicate nonverbally on the job

It is safe to say that supervisors send and receive countless nonverbal messages on the job each day. As a matter of fact, it has been estimated that 93 percent of the total impact of our messages is influenced by our nonverbal behavior, with only 7 percent due to word selection.[13] Therefore, you must be aware of nonverbal communication and understand how it words.

Nonverbal Communication Defined

Specifically, **nonverbal communication** is communication other than through spoken words. You can communicate without speaking by using facial expressions, gestures, eye movements, or other forms of nonverbal messages. Nonverbal messages are rich in information, but nonverbal communication is not a precise language. For example, in some cultures nodding the head indicates agreement, whereas in other cultures it indicates disagreement.[14] Other than the universal sign language for the deaf, there is no documented nonverbal language system.[15] As a result, one often must consider the context of the situation, and the accompanying verbal language, when interpreting nonverbal messages.

There are no standard nonverbal dictionaries available to define nonverbal signals. Yet supervisors still engage in nonverbal communication on a daily basis. Whether you like it or not, you are *always* sending nonverbal messages. Your hairstyle, your clothing, even your gait sends nonverbal messages that others use in forming an impression of you.

There are no nonverbal dictionaries

Functions of Nonverbal Messages

From a communication standpoint, nonverbal messages serve many functions. The following ones are of special importance to supervisors.

Provide Clarification. Nonverbal messages can help you clarify verbal messages. Suppose you are explaining to a worker where to move a shipping crate. While giving verbal instructions, you may also provide some nonverbal messages. For example, you may *point* to the new location and *emphasize* certain words in your instructions. Your *facial expression* may make it clear to the worker that the task is to be taken seriously. Your nonverbal messages, then, clarify your verbal instructions. What about situations where nonverbal messages appear to *contradict* verbal messages? When this contradiction occurs, many experts say it is appropriate to believe the nonverbal messages. For example, you may notice a friend frowning and ask, "What's wrong?" Your friend answers, "Nothing is wrong!" Do you believe the verbal or the nonverbal message? Most likely, you will focus on the frown and conclude that your friend is upset even though he or she denies it verbally.

Express Emotion.   Sometimes it is easier to show another person how you feel by using nonverbal messages. For example, it may be better to use nonverbal facial expressions instead of words to express dissatisfaction with another supervisor's actions. Your message still gets across, but nothing is ever spoken. Likewise, if you give an employee an award, the award itself is a nonverbal sign that you appreciate the employee's work.

Others learn much from your nonverbal messages

Regulate Conversation.   Nonverbal messages help you regulate the order in which people speak. In group discussions, some people may raise their hands at the same time, all wishing to speak. As the leader, you point to a person, signaling who should speak first. Nonverbal messages can also indicate when a person's time to speak is up, or they may signal whether it is appropriate to discuss a certain topic.

Substitute for Verbal Message.   Nonverbal messages permit you to communicate with others without using spoken words. On a noisy construction site, for example, you can direct a bulldozer operator with only hand gestures. Furthermore, without saying a word, your eyes can show excitement or fear.

There are many different sources of nonverbal messages on the job. One is the face.

The Face

The face is very expressive. Sometimes, we judge a person's mood or personality simply by looking at his or her face. Facial features may even be used to stereotype individuals. On the job, you should be alert to facial expressions. For example, when explaining new policies or procedures to workers, be alert to facial expressions showing uncertainty or confusion. A confused worker may be reluctant to ask questions for fear of looking stupid or being accused of not paying attention. So if you see a bewildered look on an employee's face, *encourage* him or her to ask questions.

A worker's facial expressions may signal confusion

Certain facial areas show particular emotions. For example, research has shown that the lower face and the eye area are the most expressive in conveying happiness. The eyes do the most to show sadness, and the eye area and lower face most often reveal surprise. The lower face and eyebrows-forehead area register anger. The lower face area expresses disgust, and fear is predominantly shown through the eyes.[16]

The Eyes

The eyes are probably the most revealing source of nonverbal messages for most individuals. For example, downward glances may make you appear modest. Wide-open eyes can show terror or frankness. Rolling the eyes upward can signal you think a person's behavior is strange, and excessive blinking may indicate anxiety.[17]

Appropriate Use of Eye Contact. In face-to-face conversations on the job, it is important to look the other person in the eye. Engaging in direct eye contact is often interpreted as a sign of credibility.[18] Failure to maintain good eye contact when *speaking* can cause the listener to perceive you as untrustworthy or lacking confidence. If you fail to maintain good eye contact while *listening,* the speaker may conclude that you are not interested in what he or she is saying. Sometimes, workers remark that they find it difficult to respect a supervisor who does not maintain good eye contact. Good eye contact, it should be noted, is generally perceived as a sign of openness and honesty.[19] Give your undivided attention to the other person instead of trying to watch everything around you. If you engage in a lot of eye movement while interacting with workers, your "shifty eyes" may cause them to be suspicious of you. At the very least, you will be considered inattentive. Caution, however, should be taken not to engage in gazing that is perceived negatively.

    Civil inattention. The practice of gazing momentarily at someone for about one second, then switching attention to another person or object is referred to as **civil inattention.**[20] When you are with strangers, it is usually civil to glance at them. It is considered uncivil to stare. Prolonged gazing can irritate others.

    The unimportant-person gaze. Whenever you give another person a blank or indifferent gaze as if he or she did not exist, you are using the **unimportant-person gaze.**[21] The recipient of such a gaze is made to feel low in status or unimportant and he or she will resent it. Due to their position of power and status over workers, some supervisors develop overinflated egos. This condition can lead them to use the unimportant-person gaze on workers. Such nonverbal behavior can cause the receiver to feel insulted, and you should resist it. At times, you may have a lot on your mind and use this gaze unintentionally, meaning no disrespect. Even then, however, the unimportant-person gaze can leave a bad impression. Therefore, you should be careful to acknowledge those around you at work, especially when doing otherwise could leave the impression that they are being treated rudely.

The Voice

When speaking, you send nonverbal as well as verbal messages. The words you speak represent messages the listener receives and interprets. However, the *way* you vocalize the words you speak can represent a nonverbal message

The eyes are expressive

Good eye contact is important

Staring is perceived negatively

that is also received and interpreted by the listener. **Paralanguage** refers to the way something is said, which influences how the verbal message is interpreted. Therefore, the way you say something can be just as important as what you say. Figure 9.3 illustrates this point. You use your voice to emphasize certain words. By changing your tone of voice, you can alter the way your verbal messages are interpreted.

Touching

On the job, supervisors often engage in one common form of touching—the handshake. The typical handshake occurs quickly. However, it is amazing how a simple handshake can influence how others perceive you. A firm handshake usually leads them to make positive inferences about your fortitude and character. A weak handshake can make you appear submissive and leave a negative impression, especially for men. In general, it is risky to make judgments about personality or ability solely on the basis of a person's handshake. You should realize, however, that your handshake does send nonverbal messages that others use to form an impression of you.

Other than shaking hands with someone, it is wise to avoid physical contact with others at work. Consider, for example, the plight of a Fort Wayne, Indiana, man, Henry. Apparently, a female co-worker helped him clean his office. To show his appreciation to the woman, Henry said, "I'll give you a kiss

Figure 9.3   **The Influence of Paralanguage on Meaning**

Consider the following statement: "The supervisor gave Susan an increase in pay." Examine how the interpretation of this statement is influenced by emphasizing the different words in capital letters.

"The SUPERVISOR gave Susan an increase in pay." Emphasizing the word *supervisor* stresses the fact that the supervisor, not anyone else, gave Susan the increase in pay.

"The supervisor GAVE Susan an increase in pay." Emphasizing the word *gave* could easily imply that Susan did not deserve the increase in pay. It was given to her.

"The supervisor gave SUSAN an increase in pay." Here, the vocal emphasis is on *Susan*. As a result, the speaker appears to imply that Susan was the last person who should have received an increase in pay.

"The supervisor gave Susan an INCREASE in pay." Susan did not stay at the same level of pay or have her pay cut. Instead, she actually received an *increase* in pay.

"The supervisor gave Susan an increase in PAY." Susan did not receive an increase in work, status, or vacation time. She received an increase in *pay*.

on the cheek." However, she held out her hand, so Henry assumed she was offering her hand instead, and he kissed her hand. Within an hour, Henry was handcuffed and escorted from the building by five police officers. He was charged with sexual battery.[22]

Space

You usually do not have to occupy or work in an area long before you feel protective about it. The physical area in which you work is often categorized in terms of "territory" and "personal space."

Territory. The fixed space and the objects therein that you lay claim to is your **territory.** As a supervisor, you may have your parking space, your office, your desk, and your chair. After establishing your territory, you expect others to respect it. For example, they should knock before entering your office. The territory you establish may intimidate some workers. As a result, they may hesitate to visit your office to talk about important matters for fear of invading your territory. Therefore, you should stay in touch with your employees to learn about the important job-related thoughts and ideas they have.

Respect the territory of others

Personal Space. The movable space you carry around with you is your **personal space.** This space acts as a buffer zone between you and others, and it surrounds you like a bubble. Personal space is comprised of different zones or distances that are reserved for various types of interactions with others. The different zones are intimate distance, personal distance, social distance, and public distance.[23] Figure 9.4 shows the relationship of these distances.

Personal space has different zones

    Intimate distance ranges from actual physical contact to about 18 inches. On the job, you generally do not want others to invade your intimate zone. There are special exceptions, of course. For example, you freely allow others to come close to you to shake hands, to whisper a message in your ear, or to stand next to you in a crowded elevator. Exceptions aside, you will likely feel uncomfortable if others invade your intimate zone, and you should be cautious about invading the intimate zones of others at work.

    Personal distance ranges from 18 inches to 4 feet. Most personal and casual conversations take place within this distance. For example, if you compliment an employee for doing a good job, you will probably stand within 4 feet of him or her during the conversation.

There is a difference between personal distance and personal space

    Social distance extends from 4 to 12 feet. On the job, you may find it necessary to call a few other supervisors together to discuss an issue. In the small-group discussion, it is likely that most participants will sit within 4 to 12 feet of each other. Also, while socializing during coffee breaks, employees often congregate in circles roughly the size associated with social distance.

    The widest zone, **public distance,** ranges from 12 feet to whatever

Figure 9.4   **The Zones of Your Personal Space**

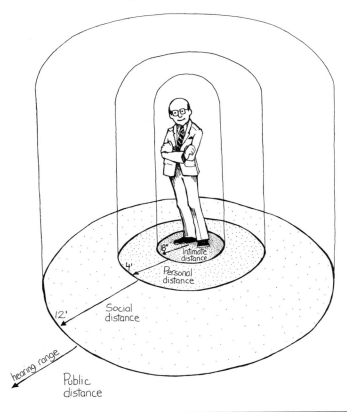

distance the people involved can still hear and see each other. You would typically use this distance when giving a public speech or calling out to someone who was more than 12 feet away.

When interacting with others at work, be aware of each person's personal space. Respect it, and you will enhance your efforts to interact effectively with others and be more successful as a supervisor.

Consider This

1. It has been said that listening takes more than two good ears. Why is it often difficult, even fatiguing, to be a good listener?
2. Think of a situation in which your nonverbal actions or messages were misinterpreted. What did you learn from this incident?

Formal Communication Paths

Communication networks in organizations are commonly identified as being either formal or informal in nature. **Formal communication** refers to communication between individuals in the organization about formal work-related matters. To plan, organize, control, and delegate as a supervisor, you must communicate with others at work through formal communication. In the formal system, messages travel along official paths dictated by the organizational hierarchy or by job function.[24] The formal communication you engage in on the job occurs along downward, upward and horizontal paths. To supervise well, you must understand the appropriate use of the different formal communication paths.

Formal communication is necessary in organizations

Downward Communication

In an organization, **downward communication** refers to the flow of messages from superiors to subordinates. When you send messages to employees who work under your supervision, you are engaging in downward communication. What types of messages are sent to employees as part of downward communication? Typical examples include job instructions and information on the importance of an assigned task. Other examples are explanations of procedures, policies, and practices, feedback on performance, and statements of company missions and goals.[25] Good downward communication includes information that:

Employees rely on downward communication

- ☐ Is needed by employees.
- ☐ Is wanted by employees.
- ☐ Is accurate.
- ☐ Flows quickly to employees.
- ☐ Is provided by the employees' supervisor (the preferred source).

Robert J. Keith, former president and board chairman of the Pillsbury Company, identified some familiar phrases that represent old and outdated attitudes toward downward communication. For each familiar phrase, Keith proposed a more appropriate alternative for effective downward communication (see Figure 9.5).

Adopt a positive attitude toward downward communication

Downward Communication Skills. The alternative views of downward communication Robert Keith identified stress the importance of maintaining good downward communication in firms. To complement the alternative views of downward communication articulated by Robert Keith, you should practice the following skills in communicating with subordinates.[26]

Acquaint workers with company goals. Before workers can be motivated to achieve company goals, they must know and understand them. To illustrate, consultants made an important discovery when analyzing a retail store that was having problems. Interestingly, they found that the

Inform employees of company goals

Figure 9.5   **Attitudes on Downward Communication**

Familiar Phrase	Alternative
Significant communications with hourly employees must flow through union channels.	We must build a commonality of interests between the company and the employee without relying on a third party. We should continue to talk to the unions, but not through them.
We don't acknowledge mistakes or failures of management.	Pretentions to infallibility damage credibility.
First-line supervisors are responsible only for task-oriented communications.	First-line supervisors are the hourly workers' preferred channel for receiving information. We can meet this information demand through proper selection, training, and evaluation of supervisors, and through adequate communication with them.
If we tell employees what's going on, it will leak out to our competitors.	Our concern for security should not become an excuse to say nothing.
Don't tell them any more than you have to.	Employees want to know how what they are doing fits into a larger framework. Unless the company satisfies this need, they will construct a framework from other sources.
Task-oriented communication is the responsibility of local management; all other information comes either through corporate media or from the plant manager.	We must develop each level of production management, including our first-line supervisors, as an important source of general information about the company, its objectives, its opportunities, and its problems.
Communication is OK, but it takes too much time and too much money.	Communication is a management accountability, of equal priority with quality, cost control, and sanitation.
Yes, we communicate, and we do it our own way. We know what our employees are thinking and what they want to know.	These are sincere and honest beliefs; but, nevertheless, we need periodic, objective measurement of employee attitudes and information needs.

Source: Reprinted by permission of the *Harvard Business Review,* Excerpts from "Communicate Through Your Supervisors" by Louis I. Gelfand (November/December 1970). Copyright © 1970 by the President and Fellows of Harvard College; all rights reserved.

employees believed the owner, who had other business interests, was operating the store simply as a hobby. Therefore, the employees approached their jobs with the same carefree attitude that most people have toward hobbies. Many people, understandably, do not expect their hobbies to be profitable. The workers, however, had the wrong understanding of the owner's motives. The owner viewed the retail store as a business venture and he wanted it operated in an efficient and profitable manner.

Explain company policies and practices. Employees should be informed of important company policies and practices. Your subordinates will look to you for this information. If you ignore this responsibility, an employee may work conscientiously but unknowingly violate company policies.

Explain why specific rules exist. Rules are not always popular. However, if employees understand the reasons for different rules, they can more easily see the need for them. As a result, there is a greater likelihood that they will accept and follow the rules.

Give the reasons for rules

Explain to workers the importance of their jobs. Employees are more likely to be motivated to do well if they understand how their work relates to the operation of the entire organization. For example, hospital orderlies may be responsible for keeping patients' rooms sanitary. If they do not think their work is important, they probably will not be motivated to do it well. To motivate them, you must change the orderlies' perception of their work. You might explain that their efforts to keep rooms sanitary could save the lives of patients. Realizing the importance of their work, the orderlies would be motivated to do well.

Keep workers informed of things they need to know. You will periodically receive information from your boss to pass on to your workers. It is your responsibility to make sure they receive it. Withholding information from employees can result in major problems, and you will be held accountable.

Clearly state downward messages. When workers fail to follow instructions correctly, it is often because they misunderstand what is requested. As you start to send messages downward, consider who will be receiving them. Then, make sure the messages are phrased clearly so they will be easily understood and interpreted correctly. Also, seek feedback on how important messages are being interpreted. Getting feedback helps you to identify and resolve misunderstandings that may exist. In addition, make sure your orders are appropriate and reasonable, based on the employee's job description and ability.

Make it easy for employees to interpret your messages

Provide workers with feedback on performance. Workers need to be kept informed on how well they are performing their jobs. Even if they are doing excellent work, they might interpret a lack of feedback as a sign that you are dissatisfied with their performance. The opposite is also possible. In the absence of feedback, workers who are doing poor work may conclude that they are performing satisfactorily. Cut off from information about how they are doing, workers lose their motivation and often miss the mark on performance.

Let workers know how they are doing

Keep the following guidelines in mind when providing feedback. Make sure it concerns an issue the worker can do something about or control. Do not overwhelm the worker with too many issues at one time. State what is factual and has been observed. For example, don't say, "The people in quality control are complaining about your work." Instead, state that, "Ten percent of the radios you assembled were missing volume-control knobs."[27]

Upward Communication

Communicate upward

In the formal communication system, **upward communication** refers to the flow of messages from subordinates to superiors. Your subordinates engage in upward communication whenever they send you messages. Two-way communication is important in organizations; upward is just as necessary as downward communication. The results of a survey by the Opinion Research Corporation indicate that "management appears to be taking upward communication from employees more seriously today and acting upon it."[28] Respondents in the survey predicted a continued shift from top-down to bottom-up decision making.[29]

Facilitating Upward Communication. As a supervisor, you can benefit in many ways from receiving upward communication. However, barriers to upward communication can cause the valuable ideas and thoughts of employees to go untapped. Fortunately, you can minimize these barriers and

Promote upward communication

promote appropriate upward communication by utilizing the following suggestions.[30]

Show a positive attitude. Demonstrate an interest in your subordinates and in the work they do. Employees are more likely to keep you informed about important work-related matters if they sense that you care. Otherwise, they will wonder why they should make the effort if it does not matter to you.

Indicate what information workers should send. Be specific in explaining the type of information that you need to receive and that is most helpful to you. For example, you need to know periodically how work is

Let workers know what information is helpful

progressing and what workers have achieved. Your subordinates will appreciate it if you show an interest in learning about their achievements. Also, indicate that you want to know about any work-related problems employees experience and about any assistance they need. Make sure they understand that you are interested in knowing how they feel about their work and the company in general.

Listen to what workers say. You cannot expect to benefit from upward communication if you do not listen to workers' comments. Pay attention to

Pay attention to what workers tell you

what subordinates say and ask questions to clarify and to encourage elaboration. In addition, while listening, make sure your facial expressions and other nonverbal messages signal your interest in their comments. Be willing to listen to *all* workers who wish to communicate upward.

Be open-minded. You may disagree with some of your worker's suggestions, but it is important to be open-minded in considering new ideas. Workers will make suggestions only if they are convinced their ideas will be given fair consideration. The same applies to constructive criticism. Workers will hesitate to offer it if they sense you are unwilling to change.

Respond.   When workers make the effort to send messages upward, they expect you to respond. Would you continue trying to communicate with your boss if you never got a response? Probably not, and neither will your workers. In responding, you obviously do not have to agree with all comments or suggestions you receive. For example, you may not want or be able to make a change a worker recommends. However, in responding, you should explain why the change cannot or will not be made.

Workers want a response to their upward communication

Establish a formal means for upward communication.   If you want information to flow upward to you in a company, you must help pull it in. Various techniques and programs are available to encourage this communication in organizations. These include suggestion boxes, question and answer sessions, and procedures for employees to voice concerns and ideas anonymously. Of course, an excellent way is to maintain good daily communication with your subordinates.

Horizontal Communication

In an organization, **horizontal communication** refers to the lateral exchange of messages among people on the same level of authority. When you communicate directly with another supervisor, for example, you are engaging in horizontal communication. As a matter of fact, an important advantage of horizontal communication is that it is very effective in allowing supervisors to communicate with each other. For instance, as Figure 9.6 illustrates, it would be frustrating for supervisor A to send a message to supervisor B through upward and downward channels. The message would have to go to the top of the firm and back down to get to the other supervisor. To avoid this detour, horizontal communication allows the two supervisors to communicate directly with each other.

Horizontal communication is important

Advantages of Horizontal Communication.   Organizations cannot function very effectively without horizontal communication. For supervisors, horizontal communication offers the following advantages.

Coordinates efforts.   Supervisors understand their subordinates and the work done in their units better than anyone else. Horizontal communication allows supervisors whose departments must work together to discuss plans directly with each other.

Facilitates problem solving.   The problems experienced by one department in a company may also eventually affect the operations of other

Figure 9.6   **Upward, Downward, and Horizontal Communication Paths**

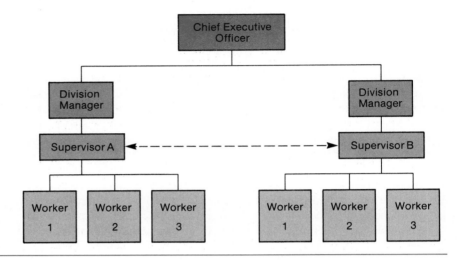

Horizontal communication
helps solve problems

departments. If, however, the leaders in the different departments work together, the chances of containing and resolving the problems are increased. When employees from different work groups who have different skills discuss together ways to solve company problems, creativity is enhanced.

Promotes information sharing. New information that becomes available in a company and needs to be known by many of the company's

Needed information can be
shared through horizontal
communication

employees is of little use unless it is disseminated. Bureaucratic structures can make it time consuming and difficult for employees in different groups to share relevant information through vertical communication channels. Horizontal communication eliminates these difficulties and, therefore, promotes the sharing of information.

Enhances working relationships. Sometimes, it may not be what you know but who you know that helps you get things accomplished. It is through direct, personal interaction and communication that we develop productive working relationships with others. These relationships create and foster a spirit of camaraderie among employees, which helps them to be effective on the job.

Horizontal communication
does not always occur
when it should

Facilitating Horizontal Communication. Too often, appropriate horizontal communication does not occur in organizations unless it is encouraged. There are two techniques commonly used to encourage it.

Schedule direct communication.   Upper management may decide that it would be helpful for supervisors from two departments to meet. It should then schedule a meeting. Not only will horizontal communication result, but the supervisors may also find that they gain from sharing ideas and information. Horizontal communication will then probably continue without being scheduled again.

You can promote horizontal communication

Emphasize company goals.   Management should stress the importance of working together to achieve goals. It should also be made clear that in this endeavor, the problems of one department are the problems of all. Stressing the interrelationship of departmental and company goals can further enhance cooperation and horizontal communication.

The Grapevine

Just as companies have a formal structure represented by the chain-of-command, they also have an informal organization that is served by the grapevine. The **grapevine** represents a firm's informal communication system or the unofficial flow of information about people and events. Information not official or required by job conditions, company rules, or procedures is considered grapevine information.[31] It is only natural for employees to communicate with each other on an informal basis while at work. When, for example, workers have lunch together, meet during coffee breaks, or congregate in hallways, there is ample opportunity for informal communication. As a matter of fact, psychologists consider a firm to be psychologically sick if its employees are so uninterested in their work that they do not engage in shoptalk. However, grapevine activity can be expected to increase beyond its normal level when:

The informal communication system is called the grapevine

☐ Formal communication channels restrict the flow of important information.
☐ Information the employees want to know is withheld from them.
☐ Employees feel insecure about the future of their jobs or how they will be affected by organizational change.[32]

Increased grapevine activity has many causes

If any of these conditions prevail, employees will speculate about what is going on in the company. Failing to receive the desired information from their supervisors, they speculate among themselves about what is happening. The more the needs of workers to receive and give information are not met by the formal communication system, the greater will be grapevine activity. Although the grapevine is beneficial in certain respects, employees feel uneasy getting important, job-related information from it. The problem is that they do not know whether such information is correct and believable. As a piece of information or a story is told from one person to the next, distortions frequently occur; workers know that the grapevine is no exception. Even when the majority of information is correct, most of the stories the grapevine carries are incomplete in detail.[33] The parts that are incorrect or missing can be and often are very important. These problems, therefore, frustrate workers and cause them to be cautious about believing hearsay.

The grapevine will always exist

Since the grapevine allows employees to communicate with each other in an unrestricted manner, it will always exist. However, due to the drawbacks, it is in the best interests of workers and management to minimize speculative activities of the grapevine.

▼

Consider This

1. An organization may have too much horizontal communication. What type of horizontal communication would be inappropriate or bad?

2. Suppose a subordinate gossips to his superior. Why is this grapevine communication even though the information went from a subordinate to a superior through the formal chain of command?

Dealing with the Grapevine

Supervisors must deal with the grapevine

On the job, workers prefer to get job-related information from their supervisor because they usually know they can believe him or her. In a survey of 10,000 General Electric employees, the company found an important relationship between communication and worker satisfaction. Employees who received their information from immediate supervisors were much more satisfied with their jobs than were those who got their information from the grapevine.[34] The finding of this survey confirms the fact that an effective way to deal with the grapevine is to establish an open communication climate. Stated simply, if a supervisor keeps his or her workers informed, they will have less need to rely on the grapevine. What type of work-related information should supervisors give to employees? The answer is information that affects them, that they want to know, and that is current.

Another way to deal with the grapevine is to be approachable. If you are approachable as a supervisor, you encourage upward communication and show empathy toward subordinates. Being a good listener, showing sincerity through nonverbal cues, and giving feedback are also important aspects of being approachable. When you are perceived as an approachable person, subordinates will likely feel comfortable contacting you to discuss work-related issues. As a supervisor, how does being approachable help you deal with the grapevine? If subordinates see you as approachable, they will more likely seek information from you rather than from hearsay. As a result, grapevine activity is reduced and you have the opportunity to provide workers with information they can trust. In addition, workers will also likely bring new work-related information to you, which keeps you informed on what is going on.

Handling Rumors. When rumors are spread, they travel through the grapevine. Since they can be damaging to an organization, it is important to understand how to deal with them. A **rumor** is unofficial information without evidence to confirm. Although rumors can be true, they are frequently either partially or completely false. In most cases, the best way to handle a false rumor is simply to release the correct facts as quickly as possible and let the facts speak for themselves. However, in doing so, do not restate the rumor itself, because this will just call more attention to it and cause people who haven't heard the rumor before to start thinking about it. Employees who have heard the rumor will wonder why it is being mentioned with a denial. If they believe you have a vested interest in denying the rumor, they may even speculate that perhaps it has some truth to it. Such an effort to squelch a rumor, therefore, could backfire.

Rumors can create problems

The appropriate technique for dealing with most rumors is illustrated in the following example. In one company, a worker cut two fingers on his left hand one morning while operating a machine. He was sent to the dispensary for first aid. As the story traveled through the company, it became more gruesome. Finally, a rumor was circulating that the worker had lost his entire left hand; this had a negative effect on employee morale. Upon learning of the incorrect rumor, management responded using the public-address system. Specifically, management notified employees that the most serious injury treated that morning was two cut fingers suffered by a machine operator. The statement also indicated that the worker received treatment and returned to his job. No mention, however, was made of the rumor itself.[35]

Rumors can be controlled

Written Communications

For many individuals, including supervisors, the most difficult method of communication is through written messages. Supervisors can take some consolation in knowing that writing generally only takes up about 14 percent of their total communication time. However, the writing you do as a supervisor can play an important role in influencing how competent you are perceived to be by others in your organization. There are several reasons for the extraordinary influence of written messages. Written messages are permanent until destroyed. As a result, mistakes in writing can be around for a long time to haunt you. Also, written messages can be re-read frequently and scrutinized closely. Under this close examination, even small inadequacies in your ability to express yourself in written form can become glaring. Furthermore, most individuals are more critical of written messages that are wordy, disorganized, or poorly phrased than they are of these same problems in spoken messages. It is assumed that you have more time to consider what you wish to say if it is transmitted in written form. Do not let poorly

You are judged by your writing

Mistakes in writing can haunt you for a long time

constructed written messages discredit you. Understand that the quality of your writing will be noticed by others and used in part to judge your performance as a supervisor. Consider your attitudes or practices as a business writer. Specifically, take a moment to complete the quiz on the next page to see how you rate as a business writer. After you have completed the quiz, add your score from the 10 statements and compare that score with the explanation of scores contained on page 235.

Principles of Effective Written Communications

The five Cs of good writing will improve written communications

Whenever you must put your thoughts into writing, careful consideration should be given to the construction of the written message. If you follow the **five Cs of good writing** listed below, many common flaws associated with written messages can be avoided.

1. Clarity. The goal of clarity is to make it easy for the reader to understand your written message as you intended it to be understood. Be straightforward and use terms with which the reader is familiar. The following example demonstrates how an unclear message can be rewritten for clarity.

What's clear to you may not be clear to others

Unclear: One of our production schedules invites comparison with a comparable one that has been enhanced.

Clear: The production schedule of paper sacks could be increased if we modernized that equipment, as we did with the equipment that produces plastic sacks.

2. Courtesy. A courteous message gets your point across in a manner that promotes goodwill. Much is to be gained by being courteous; rudeness is seldom excusable. Consider the following discourteous message that has been rewritten as a courteous message.

Discourteous: This is the fifth day of the month, but you have not paid your rent. I am filing the necessary eviction papers in the morning.

Courteous: I have not received your rent payment, which was due by today. Please contact me tomorrow to let me know when I can expect to receive the payment.

Brief messages are often best

3. Conciseness. Although brief, concise messages make their meaning clear without forfeiting courtesy. In the following example, a wordy message is rewritten more concisely.

Wordy: When we ordered the metal desks from you, we placed the order because we were assured of a special price, which was omitted unfairly from invoice 246 when the desks arrived.

Concise: Please recompute invoice number 246 to reflect the discount authorized on our purchase order.

How Do You Rate as a Business Writer?

Here are some statements about business writers. If a given statement describes your attitudes or practices as a business writer, give yourself 10 points. If it differs completely from your attitudes or practices, give yourself a 0. If it partially describes your attitudes or practices, give yourself a 5.

1. I have developed one specific style of expressing how I say things, as well as a specific organizational pattern by which to present these messages.

    ☐ 0   ☐ 5   ☐ 10

2. I treat all types of messages alike. I do not change my writing style and organization to suit passing situations.

    ☐ 0   ☐ 5   ☐ 10

3. I do not concern myself much about style and organization when writing down in the organization or laterally to peers.

    ☐ 0   ☐ 5   ☐ 10

4. I try to perfect every memo or letter I write.

    ☐ 0   ☐ 5   ☐ 10

5. I generally "set the stage" early in a memo or letter, before stating my purpose for writing and what I want of the reader.

    ☐ 0   ☐ 5   ☐ 10

6. I do not allow my writing to be influenced by the image of the company I work for, the type of industry or profession I work in, or the particular position I hold.

    ☐ 0   ☐ 5   ☐ 10

7. I generally avoid putting negative information in writing. Instead, I deal with such situations face to face.

    ☐ 0   ☐ 5   ☐ 10

8. For every assertion made, I give supporting evidence in the body of a memo or report.

    ☐ 0   ☐ 5   ☐ 10

9. I expect that letters written for my signature really sound as if they were written by me personally.

    ☐ 0   ☐ 5   ☐ 10

10. I let subordinates and secretaries worry about basic mechanics of proper English grammar, punctuation, and spelling. I concentrate on the message and let the mechanics take care of themselves.

    ☐ 0   ☐ 5   ☐ 10

Source: John S. Fielden and Ronald E. Dulek, "What Is Effective Business Writing?" Reprinted from *Business Horizons* 30 (May–June 1987), p. 63. Copyright 1987 by the Foundation for the School of Business at Indiana University. Used with permission.

4. Completeness. Written messages that are complete provide the reader with the necessary information to take appropriate action without needing to ask questions. If important information is omitted, however, clarity will not overcome the problem. Examine the following incomplete message that has been made complete.

Incomplete: Make sure the employees know about the seminar.

Complete: Please notify the sales staff that they may attend the time management seminar tomorrow from 9:00–10:00 A.M. in the training room.

5. Correctness. To make good decisions, those individuals receiving written messages from you need accurate, correct information. The following example compares an incorrect message with the rewritten, corrected message.

Make sure your information is correct

Incorrect: Nothing should prevent the recommended plan from working.

Correct: Although the recommended plan has been researched carefully and should work, it must be realized there is a 20 percent chance that bad weather will cause it to fail.

Bad writing is bad business

Remember, bad writing in companies is bad business. Needless to say, confusing messages can cause havoc in organizations. Consider how the five Cs of good writing are violated in the following memo.

MEMO

TO: Fred Ruger
        Parts Department Supervisor

FROM: John Iverson
        Production Department Supervisor

RE: Parts Problem

DATE: Monday

Your poor performance is inexcusable and will not be tolerated. How do you expect us to meet our production schedules with the problems you have created for us? The first time it happened, I didn't say anything because I thought you wouldn't let the problem continue. I was obviously wrong, and I am suffering the consequences of *your* mistake. The error on your part had to have been intentional, and you failed to send us a written notice explaining that the computer access codes we normally use had changed. As a result, we had difficulty checking on the inventory levels of different parts. I realize outside suppliers are available, but it did not appear necessary to use them because we wanted everything to be taken care of in-house. However, I don't know if outside suppliers could have met all our needs. We must meet next Wednesday after my production committee meeting to work on ways of improving the quality control of parts delivered to my division. Once we solve the parts problem, I'm sure our customer satisfaction ratings will improve.

How You Rate

(Explanation of scores for writer's quiz on page 233.)

 0–10   Your attitudes and practices are those possessed by truly effective and successful writers in business.

15–30   You are an effective business writer, but you may want to change some of your attitudes and practices to achieve even greater effectiveness.

30–50   You are about average in your attitudes and practices when it comes to effective business writing. Although you are in no particular trouble as a writer, there is room for improvement.

55–100 Your attitudes and practices about business writing need modification. There is no way of proving in any given case that less than effective attitudes and practices will hurt anyone's career advancement, but they certainly won't help. To achieve maximum success, you would be well advised to consider improving your business writing attitudes and practices.

An analysis of the above memo indicates that *clarity* suffers because Fred does not know what the specific problem is. Also, John indicates that "We must meet *next* Wednesday. . . ." Does John mean Wednesday of this week or Wednesday of *next* week? In addition, it is immediately obvious that the memo is not *courteous.* Furthermore, the memo is wordy instead of being *concise.* The memo rambles, and the reference to outside suppliers is probably irrelevant. Certainly, the memo lacks *completeness,* since it does not provide Fred with the necessary information to take action. Last, the memo contains statements that may not be entirely *correct.* For example, how does John know for sure that the error was intentional? Also, maybe John did send a written notice to Fred concerning the new computer codes. However, the written notice may have been lost in the company mail room.

To complement the five Cs of good writing, consider the person to whom you are writing and use appropriate vocabulary. Help the reader understand by using words he or she is familiar with and keep most of your sentences short. Also, use correct punctuation.

Looking Back

Clearly, communication in organizations is multifaceted. It is now appropriate to review the objectives established at the beginning of the chapter.

☐ **Define listening.** Listening is paying attention to what is said and giving meaning to what you have heard.

☐ **Explain the difference between hearing and listening.** Hearing takes little effort; it is just the passive receiving of sounds. Listening, however, is an active process that requires you to use your ears and your mind.

☐ **Identify the stages in the listening process.** For listening to occur, the listener must hear the verbal message, pay attention to it, assign meaning, and decide how to react to the message.

☐ **Define comprehensive listening.** Comprehensive listening is listening for the purpose of understanding and remembering the information contained in a verbal message.

☐ **Identify strategies for comprehensive listening.** To be effective at comprehensive listening, ask questions when in doubt and confirm your understanding. Also, maximize your excess thought time. In addition, listen for the speaker's main idea and supporting details. Furthermore, listen for key words, mentally organize material in the verbal message, and take notes.

☐ **Define nonverbal communication.** Nonverbal communication is communication other than through spoken words.

☐ **Identify the functions of nonverbal messages.** As a supervisor, you should realize that nonverbal messages can serve several functions. They can provide clarification, express emotion, regulate conversation, and substitute for verbal messages.

☐ **Define downward communication.** Downward communication refers to the flow of messages from superiors to subordinates.

☐ **Identify downward communication skills.** As a supervisor, you should acquaint workers with company goals and explain company policies and practices. It is also important to explain to workers why specific rules exist and how their work is important to the firm. In addition, you should keep workers informed of information they need, provide clearly stated downward messages, and give workers feedback on how well they are doing their job.

☐ **Define upward communication.** Upward communication refers to the flow of messages from subordinates to superiors.

☐ **Identify ways to facilitate upward communication.** Show a positive attitude toward upward communication and indicate the type of information that should be sent upward. Also, listen to what workers say, be open-minded, and respond to messages workers send. In addition, you should establish formal means for soliciting upward communication.

☐ **Define horizontal communication.** Horizontal communication refers to the lateral exchange of messages among people on the same level of authority.

☐ **Identify ways of facilitating horizontal communication.** When considered necessary, appropriate horizontal communication that is not occurring should be scheduled. Also, the importance of working together to achieve company goals should be emphasized to employees.

☐ **Define grapevine.** The grapevine represents a firm's informal communication system or the unofficial flow of information about people or events.

☐ **Identify ways to deal with the grapevine.** An effective way for a company to deal with the grapevine is to establish an open communication climate. Also, grapevine activity is reduced when supervisors are considered approachable by subordinates.

□ **Identify five principles of effective written communications.**
According to the five Cs of good writing, your written communications should be clear, courteous, concise, complete, and correct.

Key Terms

civil inattention

comprehensive listening

downward communication

excess thought time

five Cs of good writing

formal communication

grapevine

horizontal communication

intimate distance

listening

listening process

nonverbal communication

paralanguage

personal distance

personal space

public distance

rumor

social distance

territory

unimportant-person gaze

upward communication

Review and Discussion Questions

1. What is the difference between hearing and listening?
2. How does the listening process work?
3. What strategies should you use for effective comprehensive listening?
4. What are the primary functions of nonverbal messages?
5. Why is it important to be cautious when interpreting nonverbal messages?
6. Why is it important to maintain good eye contact in face-to-face conversations?
7. What is a person's personal space, and what are its forms?
8. What are the characteristics of good downward communication?
9. As a supervisor, how can you facilitate good upward communication?
10. As a supervisor, how can you facilitate appropriate horizontal communication?
11. How can you, as a supervisor, deal with grapevine activity?
12. In the five Cs of good writing, what is the difference between conciseness and completeness?

Action Incident 9.1

The False Rumor

The city of Melville recently began the process of incorporating the area of Eastchester. Bill Wilson, a supervisor at the Eastchester Hospital, realized that the incorporation would subject the hospital to new city regulations and policies. Bill understood that, as a result, reorganization of the hospital would be necessary to avoid duplicating certain services other medical facilities in Melville offered. Other employees were also aware that a reorganization would take place and that a loss of some jobs was inevitable. However, Bill was the only person in his department who knew the details of the reorganization and which jobs would be eliminated. Bill believed that many of his employees were overpaid and not working as hard or efficiently as they could. Although only a few jobs were actually in jeopardy, he realized that almost every employee feared that his or her job might be terminated. Bill decided not to announce which jobs were vulnerable. He believed that withholding this information would cause everyone to work harder to try to save his or her job.

The personnel director had enough experience with the structure of Melville's existing medical facilities to understand the type of reorganization that was necessary. However, Bill asked the director not to answer any questions from his employees about the matter. Instead, all inquiries from them were to be directed to his office. A few days later, Bill was informed that a competent technician in his department had resigned and taken a similar position at another hospital. Bill was dismayed because he realized it would be difficult to replace the technician with someone as well qualified and efficient. In an exit interview, the technician explained that he had heard rumors that his job might be eliminated. To be safe, he felt he should take the new job while it was still open. Upon learning this information, Bill exclaimed, "Your job was never in jeopardy! It's irresponsible for anyone to spread such a rumor!"

Discussion Questions

1. What probably caused the grapevine to carry such a rumor?
2. How did Bill contribute to the problem?
3. From a communication standpoint, how should Bill have handled the upcoming reorganization?

Action Incident 9.2

No News Is Good News

Diane King, a retail store supervisor, was busy in her office when a salesclerk knocked on her door. Angrily, Diane yelled, "What do you want?" The clerk said she was concerned because some of the pants on display were incorrectly marked in size. Diane exclaimed, "Don't bother me with those kinds of problems!" Startled, the clerk returned to her sales area.

That week, other salesclerks made suggestions to Diane regarding ways to improve operations in the store. However, they did not receive a response from Diane about how she viewed their suggestions, so they didn't bother to offer any more. About a month later, Diane had lunch with a supervisor of another retail store. When asked how things were, Diane responded, "I haven't heard anything from my salesclerks lately, so everything must be going well."

Discussion Questions

1. How would you describe Diane's attitude toward upward communication?
2. What happened when Diane failed to respond to her salesclerks?
3. Do you think Diane's assessment that everything must be going well is correct? Why?

Action Incident 9.3

A Rail Job

The B & L Welding and Fabricating Company recently received an order to manufacture a wrought-iron railing for a two-story apartment complex. Soon after receiving the order, the company hired Bob Crowell for his experience in welding iron railings. One day, Bob contacted Stan Arnold, his supervisor, to point out a problem with the plans for the railing. The following conversation took place in Stan's office.

Bob: I've been going over the railing plans and. . . . *(Interrupted by Stan)*

Stan: Yeah, I know the plans are hard to read. The architect didn't draw them very clearly.

Bob: I can read the plans all right, but my main concern is. . . . *(Interrupted again by Stan)*

Stan: Oh, I was also concerned about where we would store all the railing when it was finished. The owner of the apartment complex said we can just leave the railing outside.

Bob: I figured you would let me know where to store the railing when the time came. I'm concerned with the builder's decision to use wooden stairways instead of the metal stairways the plans show. According to the plans, the railing was supposed to be welded to the side of the stairways, but I can't do that with wooden stairways.

Stan: Yeah, that will be a problem. *(Stan looks out the window and notices a bulldozer clearing trees from the vacant lot next door to make way for new construction. He is fascinated with what is going on next door.)*

Bob: We will need to come up with a way to attach the iron railing to a wooden stairway. It would be easy to drill holes in the railing supports and the wooden stairways and bolt the two together. But that technique violates Brownsville's building code, since the side holes can weaken the stairways. The contractor wouldn't accept the railing that way, and we'd have to go back and fill in all the holes we drilled. A better way to attach the metal railing would be to. . . . *(Interrupted by Stan)*

Stan: Oh, gee, it's almost 5 o'clock, and I have to call in an order for new material. I haven't got any more time to discuss the railing. When you get older and more experienced, you will realize that where you can't weld, you bolt! I'll tell you what to do. Drill holes in the side of the railing supports so the contractor can bolt them to the wooden stairways at the job site. Oh, yeah, hand this receipt to the secretary on your way out, would you?

Discussion Questions

1. Would it be appropriate to call Stan a poor listener? Why?
2. Why was Bob unable to explain his idea for solving the problem?
3. What should Stan have done to listen effectively to Bob?

Notes

1. Lyman K. Steil, Larry L. Barker, and Kittie W. Watson, *Effective Listening: Key to Your Success* (Reading, Mass.: Addison-Wesley Publishing, 1983), p. 51.
2. Sperry advertisement, *The Wall Street Journal,* March 11, 1980, p. 17.
3. Raymond S. Ross and Mark G. Ross, *Relating and Interacting: An Introduction to Interpersonal Communication* (Englewood Cliffs, N.J.: Prentice-Hall, 1982), p. 208.
4. Lyman K. Steil, "Secrets of Being a Better Listener," *U.S. News & World Report* 88 (May 26, 1980), p. 65.
5. Steil, "Secrets of Being a Better Listener," p. 65.
6. Michael J. Papa and Ethel C. Glenn, "Listening Ability and Performance With New Technology: A Case Study," *Journal of Business Communication* 25 (Fall 1988), p. 6.
7. Papa and Glenn, "Listening Ability and Performance With New Technology: A Case Study," p. 5.
8. Papa and Glenn, "Listening Ability and Performance With New Technology: A Case Study," p. 5.
9. Andrew D. Wolvin and Carolyn Coakley, *Listening* (Dubuque, Iowa: Wm. C. Brown, 1982), p. 85.
10. Wolvin and Coakley, *Listening,* p. 88.
11. Wolvin and Coakley, *Listening,* p. 92.
12. Florence I. Wolff, Nadine C. Marsnik, William S. Tacey, and Ralph G. Nichols, *Perceptive Listening* (New York: Holt, Rinehart & Winston, 1983), p. 161.
13. A. Mehrabian, *Silent Messages: Implicit Communication of Emotions and Attitudes,* 2d ed. (Belmont, Calif.: Wadsworth, 1981), p. 77.
14. Loretta A. Malandro and Larry Barker, *Nonverbal Communication* (Reading, Mass.: Addison-Wesley Publishing, 1983), p. 7.
15. Malandro and Barker, *Nonverbal Communication,* p. 7.
16. Paul Ekman, Wallace W. Friesen, and Silvan S. Tomkins, "Facial Affect Scoring Technique: First Validity Study," *Semiotica* 3 (1971), pp. 37–58.
17. Mark L. Knapp, *Nonverbal Communication in Human Interaction,* 2d ed. (New York: Holt, Rinehart & Winston, 1978), pp. 294–95.
18. J. K. Burgoon and T. Saine, *The Unspoken Dialogue: An Introduction to Nonverbal Communication* (Boston: Houghton Mifflin, 1978).

19. Jane Whitney Gibson and Richard M. Hodgetts, *Organizational Communication: A Managerial Perspective* (New York: Academic Press, 1986), p. 96.

20. Ken Cooper, *Nonverbal Communication for Business Success* (New York: AMACOM, 1979), p. 74.

21. Cooper, *Nonverbal Communication for Business Success,* p. 75.

22. Carlee R. Scott, "If Chivalry Hasn't Died Already, the End Must Surely Be at Hand," *The Wall Street Journal,* August 29, 1989, p. B1.

23. Edward T. Hall, *The Hidden Dimension* (Garden City, N.Y.: Doubleday Publishing, 1966), p. 116.

24. Gerald M. Golhaber, *Organizational Communication,* 3d ed. (Dubuque, Iowa: Wm. C. Brown, 1983), p. 154.

25. Daniel Katz and Robert L. Kahn, *The Social Psychology of Organizations,* 2d ed. (New York: John Wiley & Sons, 1978), p. 440.

26. Katz and Kahn, *The Social Psychology of Organizations,* 2d ed., pp. 440–43.

27. Sharon Nelton, "Feedback to Employees Can Nourish Your Business," *Nation's Business* 73 (July 1985), p. 63.

28. "Relying on Bottom-to-Top Communications," *Employee Benefit Plan Review* 41 (October 1986), p. 30.

29. "Relying on Bottom-to-Top Communications," p. 30.

30. Early Planty and William Machaver, "Upward Communications: A Project in Executive Development: Using the Syndicate Method," *Personnel* 28 (January 1952), pp. 304–17.

31. Keith Davis, "Grapevine Communication among Lower and Middle Managers," *Personnel Journal* 48 (April 1985), p. 7.

32. John W. Newstrom, Robert E. Monczka, and William E. Reif, "Perceptions of the Grapevine: Its Value and Influence," *Journal of Business Communication* 11 (Spring 1974), p. 12.

33. Keith Davis, "The Care and Cultivation of the Corporate Grapevine," *Dun's Review* 102 (July 1973), p. 47.

34. "G.E. Campaigns to Boost Execs' Job Satisfaction," *World of Work Report* 9 (March 1984), pp. 1–2.

35. Davis, "Corporate Grapevine," p. 47.

Suggested Readings

Chase, Andrew B., Jr. "How to Make Downward Communication Work." *Personnel Journal* 49, June 1970, pp. 478–83.

Cohen, Lynn Renee. "Nonverbal (Mis) Communication Between Managerial Men and Women." *Business Horizons* 26, January–February 1983, pp. 13–17.

Cooper, Ken. *Nonverbal Communication for Business Success.* New York: AMACOM, 1979.

Fuller, Rex M. "How to Improve Your Listening." *Supervision* 45, July 1983, pp. 8–10.

Glauser, Michael J. "Upward Information Flow in Organizations: Review and Conceptual Analysis." *Human Relations* 37, August 1984, pp. 613–43.

Halatin, Ted. "Upward Communication." *Supervisory Management* 27, October 1982, pp. 7–10.

Harriman, Bruce. "Up and Down the Communication Ladder." *Harvard Business Review* 52, September–October 1974, pp. 143–51.

Imundo, Louis V. "Getting Commitment by Soliciting Employee Ideas." *Supervisory Management* 27, November 1982, pp. 23–29.

Simmons, Donald B. "How Does your Grapevine Grow?" *Management World* 15, February 1986, pp. 16–18.

Van Tell, Terry. "Communicating With Your Employees and Boss." *Supervisory Management* 34, October 1989, pp. 5–10.

Weaver, Carl H. *Human Listening: Process and Behavior.* Indianapolis, Ind.: Bobbs-Merrill, 1972.

Developing Effective Interpersonal Relations

Chapter

10

Learning Objectives

After reading and studying the material contained in this chapter, you should be able to:

1. Identify common cultural problems that often exist when supervising a multicultural work force.
2. Indicate ways that supervisors can improve their intercultural communication.
3. Define self-concept.
4. Explain how self-concepts are generally formed.
5. Define self-esteem.
6. Identify strategies for improving subordinates' self-esteem.
7. Indicate techniques for building trust.
8. Identify the appropriate steps involved in counseling troubled employees.
9. Explain the difference between counseling and coaching.

Supervising in a Multicultural Work Force

North American organizations are changing. New competitive forces and mergers and acquisitions have, without a doubt, altered the way many firms operate. However, changes in the composition of the U.S. work force are also having a significant impact. Specifically, the number of foreign-born professional, technical, and semi-skilled individuals joining the ranks of white- and blue-collar workers is steadily increasing. Consider, for example, the population changes expected in California, the most populus state in the Union. Projections based on census data indicate that, before the year 2000, the majority of the population of California will no longer be white and may not necessarily speak English.[1]

The U.S. work force is becoming more multicultural

In California, "Some firms literally would have to pack it in if their foreign-born engineers—not to speak of their production-line workers— decided to leave the country en masse. In some Silicon Valley companies, the percentage of engineers from other countries is as high as 30 percent and their contribution to the success of the industry is immeasurable."[2] How supervisors deal with multicultural work forces can influence how efficient and productive those employees become.

Be Aware of Cultural Differences

Supervisors who interact with a multicultural work force must understand that values and behaviors may differ among employees of different cultures. Misinterpreting these differences can create problems for supervisors. Figure 10.1 provides examples of values and behaviors that may be misinterpreted by supervisors. **Culture** refers to the customs of the groups that have influenced an employee.[3] On the job, cultural differences among employees can affect the way they are treated by their supervisor, and the way they are treated can affect their morale and productivity. As a result, supervisors need to be aware of key elements that influence supervisor-employee interactions in a multicultural work force context.

The values and behaviors of employees from different cultures may be misinterpreted

Cultural Problems Facing Supervisors

Those individuals responsible for supervising a multicultural work force face special problems. Foremost among these problems are difficulties associated with language, stereotyping, nonverbal behavior, and differing values.

Language. Obviously, if a supervisor and a subordinate do not speak the same language, their ability to interact will be severely hampered. However, even if they speak the same language, their levels of familiarity with the language may differ greatly. English, for example, may be the subordinate's second and least used language. Furthermore, culture influences the way individuals use their language. This point is demonstrated by the fact that

Culture can influence the way language is used

Figure 10.1	**Examples of How Culturally Influenced Behaviors May Be Misinterpreted by a Supervisor**

Description and explanation of employee's behavior	**Supervisor's interpretation of employee's behavior**
Park Lee Kim, a South Korean immigrant, seldom participates in critical discussions of proposals in company meetings but will talk to colleagues individually. Criticizing ideas in an open meeting represents alien, insensitive, and unacceptable behavior to Kim.	His supervisor considers Kim to be aloof and arrogant.
Hussein Shabaz was born and raised in Iran. When talking to his American colleagues, Hussein stands close to them to show friendship. He stares at female employees because he is not accustomed to seeing women employed in a company.	His supervisor considers Hussein to be aggressive and offensive because he stands so close. The women judge Hussein to be ill-mannered.
Hecter Gonzalez, born and raised in Mexico, arrived for work at his first job in the United States after the scheduled time for arrival. However, Hecter did not believe he was actually "late" based on his culturally-influenced perception of time.	His supervisor judges Hecter to be late. As a result, the supervisor concludes that Hecter is lazy and can't be trusted.
Mary Cheng, an immigrant from Taiwan, was hired as a box-office clerk to sell tickets for various entertainment events. She was furnished with an electronic machine to check credit cards, but she does not use it. Even though her white, male, older supervisor has explained to her how to use the machine, Mary continues to check credit cards in the "lost and stolen" book available. This time-consuming method causes lines to form at the box office. Mary is embarrassed and believes her supervisor will "lose face" if she mentions that she doesn't understand his explanation.	Her supervisor believes she is guilty of insubordination for not using the electronic machine after he explained how to operate it. The supervisor also considers Mary to be inconsiderate of the customers by holding up the line while checking credit cards the slow way.

Source: Adapted from Fathi S. Yousef, "Human Resource Management: Aspects of Intercultural Relations in U.S. Organizations," pp. 176–78; and John Condon, ". . . so near the United States: Notes on Communication between Mexicans and North Americans," pp. 114–15 in Larry Samovar and Richard E. Porter, *Intercultural Communication: A Reader*, 5th ed. (Belmont, CA: Wadsworth Publishing Co., 1988).

people from Western cultures favor precision in language, whereas, people from Eastern cultures favor ambiguities.[4] Even if you speak the same language as a subordinate from a different culture, different meanings may be given to the same words. To illustrate, in England a joint is a roast (meat), a wing is a car fender, and braces are suspenders.[5] However, in the United States other, different meanings are usually given to these words.

Stereotyping.   It is common for people to develop stereotypes while working in intercultural settings. **Stereotyping** is the act of making an oversimplified judgment about persons solely on the basis of their class or culture. It is very tempting to engage in stereotyping because it represents a shortcut in thinking. That is, once you meet people, you may think you automatically know and understand hem if you use stereotypes. For example, if they are of a certain race, they must be lazy. If they are of a particular ethnic background, you may conclude that they are hotheaded. And if they are a member of a specific group, they are racist. Therefore, without taking the time to talk to these individuals or to do much thinking, your stereotyping has supposedly allowed you to "know" them. As a result, you may also conclude that you know how to treat them. In reality, you do not know these new acquaintances very well at all, and your stereotypes of them may be wrong.

Unfortunately, prejudice and racism are common companions of stereotyping. As a supervisor, you must be cautious to avoid behaviors that may be interpreted as racist. For instance, consider the following examples.[6] Do you vary the space between youself and others in the company cafeteria depending on their race? Do you tell, listen to, or encourage jokes that demean people of other races? Do you ignore the presence of others who are of a different race? Even if you do not mean anything negative by these and other questionable behaviors, your actions may be perceived as racist, and this perception will greatly undermine your ability to perform effectively as a supervisor.

Engaging in stereotyping can cause problems on the job

Nonverbal Behavior.   Many of the messages sent and received by individuals at work are nonverbal. It should be realized that culture and nonverbal communication are learned. For instance, individuals born and raised in the United States are taught to greet people by shaking hands, yet in most Oriental countries it is customary to bow when greeting others. Our use of space is also influenced by culture. To illustrate, in the United States, the space of 18 inches around people is generally considered their "intimate distance." On the job, employees typically do not want others to invade their intimate distance. People from other countries, including Europeans and those from the Middle East, may tend to stand close to each other when conversing. However, when individuals from other cultures stand too close to Americans, intimate distance is violated and a feeling of uncomfortableness results.

Perceptions and the use of time are also culturally influenced. In the United States we view time monochronically by emphasizing the neat scheduling of appointments, segmentations, and promptness.[7] Those with **monochronic-time values** focus on completing one task at a time. However, not all cultures view time in this manner. Some Latin American countries, for example, view time polychronically. According to this view, life involves many things happening at once, so a more flexible perception of what is "on time" seems appropriate. As a matter of fact, in some cases tardiness is a sign of respect.[8] Those with **polychronic-time values** believe

Culture can influence an individual's view of time

that interruptions and delays are to be expected and that human activities seldom proceed like clockwork.[9] If something does not get finished today, it can be done tomorrow—there is always more time.

Values.   A **value** refers to the worth, utility, or merit we give to something. Examples of values include judging a behavior to be right or wrong, or considering a product to be desirable or undesirable. Without a doubt, value and culture are inextricably connected. Cultural values are learned by members of a culture when they are taught what is good or bad, positive or negative, etc. These values set standards and guidelines for what behaviors are deemed appropriate and inappropriate.

For example, what constitutes corruption in an organization? In the United States, a behavior that is viewed as corrupt in a company may not be considered corrupt by people of a different culture in another country. To illustrate further, Americans generally believe that it is important to show a willingness to compromise with others. However, the Japanese prefer to go back to the drawing board if compromise is suggested, and the Mexicans and French do not see much virtue in compromising per se.[10] The intensity with which a value is held can also vary among cultures. For example, Western cultures place far greater value on efficiency than do Muslim or Eastern cultures.[11] In general, therefore, supervisors must realize that values are not universal. Values can and often do vary among employees from different cultures.

Values are learned and may differ among cultures

Improving Your Intercultural Communication

Supervisors who are responsible for directing the activities of a multicultural work force face special challenges. However, the cultural problems they often experience can be minimized by practicing the following suggestions.[12]

Have a Sincere Desire to Improve Your Cultural Awareness.   Supervisors who suffer from ethnocentrism experience difficulty supervising a multicultural work force. **Ethnocentrism** is the belief that one's own culture or ethnic group is better than all others. Supervisors with this belief tend to dislike those from other cultures because they are different; this attitude tends to manifest itself in poor superior-subordinate relations. However, those who demonstrate an honest and sincere desire to learn about and seek mutual understanding with culturally different subordinates promote effective working relationships.

Understand Your Cultural Conditioning.   There is more to improving your intercultural communication than just learning more about people from other cultures. A very important prerequisite is for you to understand your own cultural conditioning.[13] What are your dominant values and behavior expectations? What are your cultural biases and assumptions? By answering these questions, you can better understand how and why you communicate and behave the way you do around others from different cultures. Once you become more aware of these issues, you can work on improving the way you interact with others on the job who are from different cultures. As a result, you will be better able to relate to diversity and cultural plurality on the job.[14]

To improve your intercultural communication, you must be aware of your cultural conditioning

Communicate Effectively. To communicate effectively, the sender and receiver must give similar meanings to messages. However, our backgrounds and experiences influence how we interpret messages, and people from different cultures typically come from different backgrounds and experiences. As a result, a message developed by a supervisor from one culture and interpreted by a subordinate from a different culture is especially vulnerable to miscommunication. To avoid this problem, select your words carefully. For example, say "next to" rather than "adjacent." Also, avoid slang and compressed speech like "Whaddya' doin?"[15]

Be Careful When Drawing Conclusions. Jumping to conclusions when supervising subordinates from different cultures can cause problems. Within your culture, you have learned how to interpret certain statements and behaviors. A different interpretation, however, may be appropriate for the same statements and behaviors made by subordinates in a multicultural work force. In these situations, you need to suspend judgment, because more time is needed to consider relevant cultural influences. For example, in Hong Kong people show little or no emotion when they receive a compliment.[16] Once this cultural conditioning is known, however, it is easy to understand why a worker from Hong Kong may appear aloof after being paid a compliment.

Encourage Feedback. Feedback is important in many communicative situations. However, feedback is especially important for promoting more effective intercultural communication. For example, feedback between people from different cultures allows miscommunication to be identified early. As a supervisor, you should realize that to get feedback, you must create an environment where subordinates in your multicultural work force feel comfortable providing feedback. For instance, asking questions is a good way to get feedback. Also, watch for nonverbal feedback.

Show Empathy. "Empathy comes from the German word *Einfühling*, which means 'to feel with.'"[17] When you demonstrate empathy, you imagine yourself in the other person's situation. This effort may be difficult when the other person comes from a different cultural background. However, practicing empathy is crucial to understanding and appreciating the point of

Practicing empathy helps
you to better understand
the cultural conditioning of
others

view and cultural orientation of others. As a supervisor, your efforts to empathize will be noticed and appreciated by your multicultural work force. Furthermore, your sensitivity to the needs, values, and views of your subordinates will help you to develop a good working relationship with them, regardless of their cultural background.

Your Self-Concept

Supervisors with a positive self-concept find that this trait aids them in developing effective interpersonal relations and good working relationships with others on the job. **Self-concept** refers to the relatively stable perceptions people have about themselves. It includes our conception of what is unique about ourselves, what distinguishes us from others, and what makes us similar to others.[18] In many respects your self-concept is like a mental mirror that reflects how you view yourself. In the mental mirror you observe more than just your physical features. You also are aware of your emotional states, talents, likes and dislikes, values, and roles.[19]

Your self-concept reflects
how you view yourself

Forming Self-Concepts

How are self-concepts formed? They are derived primarily from four sources. First, we are influenced by our social interactions with others. For example, we consider how other individuals treat us and react to our traits and characteristics. Second, we compare ourselves with others. On the job, you may consider how intelligent, motivated, and physically fit you are compared to others. Third, what others say about us has an impact. They may or may not like our beliefs or behaviors. Fourth, we examine how we see ourselves. We study our feelings and observe our behaviors.[20]

Self-Esteem

Self-esteem refers to the evaluation a person makes of his or her self-concept.[21] A positive evaluation of your self-concept will provide you with high self-esteem. Conversely, a negative evaluation frequently results in low self-esteem. Some of the characteristics that may be associated with high and low levels of self-esteem are shown in Figure 10.2.

In addition, research studies have shown that individuals with low self-esteem, as compared to those with high self-esteem, perform less effectively under stress. They have also been shown to be more persuasible, to lack confidence, and to have depressed aspirations.[22]

Characteristics that Are Sometimes Associated with High and Low Levels of Self-Esteem

Figure 10–2

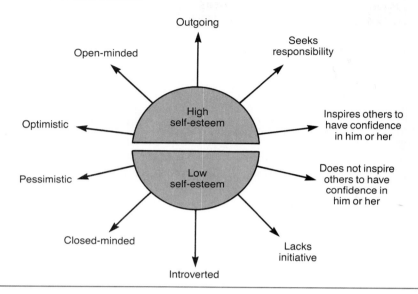

Conduct a Self-Analysis

The Oracle at Delphi offered valuable advice: "Know thyself." It is amazing how some supervisors are so observant of what goes on around them at work but are unaware of what makes them tick. To improve your self-concept, you need to engage in an examination process usually referred to as self-analysis. You may, for example, ask yourself the following questions: What is my leadership ability? How well do I communicate with others? To what extent am I sensitive and understanding of others? How knowledgeable am I about work-related matters? What are my job skills? What are my goals? Your answers to these and other similar questions will help you better understand yourself and what you like and do not like about the way you function as a supervisor. When conducting your self-analysis, carefully note your strengths. By focusing on your strengths, you can often build upon them in a way that will help you overcome weaknesses. Remember, having a positive self-concept works wonders in helping you achieve your potential as a supervisor. "People take you at the value you put on yourself. If you believe you are successful, if you believe in your own power, then people will believe you and treat you with the respect you've provided for yourself."[23]

Make the most of your strengths

Developing a Positive Self-Concept

With a positive self-concept, you have a lot going for you on the job. The following ways of developing a positive self-concept as a supervisor can apply to you.[24]

Give Yourself Credit for Making Good Decisions.   You are responsible for making decisions in your job as supervisor. Too often, however, supervisors give themselves little credit for their good decisions but they place a lot of blame on themselves for bad decisions. This tendency promotes low self-esteem. Although mistakes should not be ignored, and bad decisions need to be analyzed so they are not repeated, do not let them consume you. Learn from them but also focus on good decisions you make and give yourself credit for them. In order to develop a positive self-concept, it is important to congratulate yourself when you experience an achievement.

View Problems as Challenges.   Your attitude in approaching problems can influence how successful you will be in dealing with them. Individuals with a low self-concept may not attempt to solve certain problems they face. Others realize that you cannot win a race unless you enter it, and if nothing is ventured, nothing is gained. Accept problems as challenges to which you can apply your abilities and from which you can learn.

A positive self-concept will help you deal with challenges on the job

Be Willing to Change.   It is hard to grow and develop if you are unwilling to change. People with a positive self-concept want to grow and develop. As a result, they are willing to accept the changes that may be required to do so. Being open-minded also goes along with willingness to accept change. If you make a mistake, be willing to admit it. Give new ideas careful consideration; you may benefit from them, which will enhance your self-concept.

Be Future Oriented.   What has happened in the past cannot be changed. However, the knowledge you gain from past experiences can be applied to the future. Have a strategy to accomplish your goals and begin to put it into action. As the adage says, "Each day is the beginning of the rest of your life." Focus on the future to make the most of it.

Obtain the Skills Needed to Improve.   Two years from now you will be two years older, and you have no control over that. However, you do have a lot of control over what you do in that period of time. If you want to improve your self-concept, but make no effort to do so, two years later you will simply be an older person with the same low self-concept. Part of the difficulty in improving a poor self-concept is getting started. However, once you start you will gain momentum. For example, if becoming better at writing reports will improve your self-concept, get started. There are books you can read, seminars you can attend, and other activities you can engage in that will help you achieve your goal. As you progress in developing your skill, you will become more encouraged. Remember, a self-concept can be improved if you make the effort to do so.

1. Sometimes, people sell themselves short and discount their abilities. What is a strength or ability you possess that you should give yourself more credit for having?
2. If you believe you have a good self-concept, how well do you think it shows to others? Do you think your level of confidence in yourself is strong enough to inspire others to follow you as a leader?

Improving Subordinates' Self-Esteem

When employees' feelings of self-worth as members of an organization are built up, the result is an improvement in labor-management relations.[25] As a supervisor, you should attempt to foster high self-esteem among subordinates by using the following strategies.

Listen Carefully to Your Subordinates. When you make an effort to listen, you indicate that you value employees' comments. Also, show empathy for their situation. Subordinates will notice these efforts on your part and will appreciate and benefit from them.

Show an Interest in and Concern for Employees. In the Hawthorne studies, the productivity of workers in the investigation increased while they were being observed by the researchers. Why did just the presence of the researchers have this effect? Interestingly, it was learned that the workers liked the special attention they received. Their favorable reaction, in turn, motivated them to be even more productive.[26] If you show an interest in and concern for your subordinates, it is likely that the workers will feel better about themselves and their self-esteem will be enhanced. This behavior is also likely to improve their motivation and productivity.

Express Confidence in Your Subordinates. Part of building up employees' self-esteem is to express confidence in them. When they do a good job, acknowledge it and express your appreciation.

Praise subordinates for their accomplishments

Provide Employees with Some Decision-Making Responsibilities. It is hard to develop high self-esteem when you are always told what to do, when to do it, where to do it, and how to do it. Give subordinates all the responsibility they can handle. Besides enhancing their self-esteem in most cases, it will help them develop on the job.

Help Your Subordinates Succeed. There is nothing that builds up a worker's self-esteem like actually succeeding at something important on the job. Provide your subordinates with all the information and support they need to succeed. Not only will their success enhance their self-esteem, but they will gain additional confidence to be even more successful.

Model High Self-Esteem Yourself. As their supervisor, you need to be ready and willing to accept the role of mentor to your subordinates. They will naturally look to you to see how you deal with different situations, and they will notice whether or not you have high self-esteem. If you do have high self-esteem, it will be easier for subordinates to admire and trust you. They will be receptive to you showing them how to identify their strong points and how to use their abilities. In turn, their self-esteem will be enhanced.

Trust

Supervisors find that they can accomplish much when they develop a cooperative working relationship with subordinates. However, it is difficult to develop such a relationship if employees do not trust their supervisor. Therefore, it is important for you to develop and maintain mutual trust between yourself and your subordinates. The degree of trust that develops on the job between a supervisor and subordinates depends on several factors. Subordinates, for example, make judgments concerning the character of a supervisor. In doing so, they evaluate the supervisor's integrity, motives, consistency of behavior, and openness.[27] Goals also affect the degree of trust in a working relationship. "To trust another is to know that the two of you share basic goals in the long run so that left to your own devices, each will behave in ways that are not harmful to the other."[28]

Barriers to Developing Trust

Although trust is a very important part of productive interpersonal relations, it requires effort to develop. Supervisors may find that their efforts to enhance the level of trust their subordinates have for them are hindered by the following barriers.

Inconsistent Behavior. Considering that it usually takes time for trust to develop, a supervisor whose behavior is hard to predict thwarts the development of trust. A supervisor at a large hospital, for example, was described as "moody" by his subordinates. Apparently, workers never knew from one day to the next whether the supervisor would be in a good, bad, or indifferent mood. When the supervisor is in a good mood, he believes he is gaining the subordinates' trust. What he fails to realize is that his inconsistent behavior causes his subordinates to hesitate to trust him.

Manipulation. Even when a strong level of trust exists between subordinates and their supervisor, attempted manipulation by the supervisor can tarnish that trust. Workers typically feel manipulated when they conclude that their supervisor's motive is concealed and that they have been misled. In one

Supervisors can accomplish much if they have the trust of subordinates

Inconsistent behavior by supervisors thwarts trust in them

organization, when a problem developed, the supervisor often assembled a group of subordinates to study it and make a recommendation. The supervisor did not participate in the discussion. Recently, however, the supervisor did attend one of the group meetings and exerted great pressure on the subordinates to make a particular recommendation. Her efforts at manipulating the group lost her much respect and trust.

Lack of Dependability.   Subordinates learn from experience whether or not their supervisor is dependable. Supervisors who are viewed by their subordinates as always coming through for them will be considered dependable. When these supervisors ask for support on certain issues by saying, "Trust me," their subordinates will do so in most cases. However, supervisors who do not have a good track record of being dependable and competent will not succeed if they make the same appeal for trust.

Authoritarian Leadership.   Authoritarian leaders are very task oriented. This characteristic often hinders them from developing much rapport with their subordinates. In addition, authoritarian leaders are criticized for not keeping subordinates well informed and for not encouraging upward communication. As a matter of fact, employees who have authoritarian supervisors often fear the negative consequences of making suggestions and being open with their supervisor.[29] The nature and quality of communication between a supervisor and his or her subordinates can influence the level of trust in the working relationship. As a result, the level of trust that subordinates have for authoritarian leaders is often low.

Authoritarian leaders do not encourage upward communication

Building Trust

Any fear, distrust, or other defensive feelings subordinates may have toward their supervisor will naturally reduce the level of trust they have for their supervisor. The deeper these feelings, the longer it will take for a supervisor to turn the situation around and gain the subordinates' trust. In general, of course, the best way for a supervisor to gain the trust of others is to behave in a trustworthy manner. The following suggestions are offered to help you build trust as a supervisor.

Promote Common Goals.   It is easier to build trust when subordinates perceive that they are working with you, not just for you. As a supervisor, you should explain the goals of the work unit and indicate how you will work with the subordinates to help them achieve those goals. Not only is this approach part of being a good leader, as discussed in Chapter 3, it is also helpful in building trust.

Keep Your Subordinates Well Informed.   As mentioned elsewhere, subordinates prefer to get important, job-related information from their

Subordinates trust
supervisors who keep
them well informed

supervisor. The more you meet your subordinates' need to be kept informed, the more they will respect and trust you for doing so. That is, such actions show that you are trustworthy.

Be Open with Your Subordinates. Develop rapport with your subordinates; do not remain aloof. Some supervisors are secretive and remain distant from workers. They seem unapproachable. It is as if they want to make certain their employees are always aware of the status difference. However, such behavior hinders the development of trust for the supervisor. Developing rapport and being open with your subordinates does not mean that you will stop enforcing performance standards or company rules. Instead, it means that you want the subordinates to feel comfortable in bringing their ideas, concerns, and suggestions to you for consideration. That is, by being open and developing rapport, you are indicating that you want to promote mutual trust.

Show Genuine Interest in Your Subordinates. Workers soon decide whether their supervisor values their opinions. When supervisors who do not appear to value the opinions of their subordinates start asking for them, their requests are met with suspicion.[30] In these cases, the subordinates usually conclude that the supervisor is insincere. As a result, they are not very responsive. On the other hand, if the supervisor's interest is perceived as genuine, the ice will begin to thaw. Trust is usually gained gradually. When your interest is perceived as genuine, your efforts at building trust will be enhanced.

Trust often takes time to
develop

Supervisors as Role Models

As a supervisor, you have many duties, such as setting goals, delegating work, following the progress of work, and evaluating the performance of subordinates. However, in performing such duties on the job, you also serve as a role model for others with whom you work. For example, think back to some of your first jobs. Like most new employees, you probably felt a little uncertain about what the norms of behavior were in these unfamiliar situations, and you probably watched the behavior of your supervisor to better understand the appropriate work tone and attitudes. Remember, your subordinates will be looking for the same cues from you.

People in organizations learn much by merely looking at and observing what goes on around them.[31] It has been said that actions speak louder than words. Certainly, subordinates will listen to what you say as a supervisor. However, they will also pay close attention to your actions and the way you behave. As a result, an important part of being a good supervisor is setting a positive example.[32] Supervisors who arrive on time for work and are courteous to customers send a message to their employees that this is the type of behavior expected of them. Furthermore, your attitude toward controlling costs, being honest, and setting high standards will have a greater influence on your subordinates than written policies. You cannot escape this fact by saying, "Do as I say, not as I do." Determine the behaviors and attitudes you want to promote in your work unit and model them for others to observe.

Supervisors are expected to practice what they preach

---

1. Think of a person, other than a member of your family, who you trust a lot. What is it about this person that leads you to trust him or her? Which of these qualities do you think you should display as a supervisor to help you gain the trust of subordinates?

2. Have you ever worked for someone who was a good role model for you? What did this person do that caused you to view him or her as a good role model?

Consider This

The Supervisor as Counselor

Supervisors who are unwilling or ill prepared to accept the role of counselor on the job frequently complain that employees should leave their personal problems at home. They believe that employees should not let personal problems interfere with their work. Supervisors with this attitude are expecting their subordinates to be robots, not human beings. The reality of the modern work force is that employees, like everyone else, do experience personal problems occasionally, and those problems may affect their work performance. It is not the case that employees want to bring their personal problems with them to work. They would welcome the opportunity to escape from the problems by leaving them at home, but it is much easier said than done. Only recently have supervision textbooks offered more than a single paragraph concerning ways to help employees with personal problems. However, there is an increasing need for supervisors to be aware of ways they can deal with this issue. "Authoritative estimates place the number of potentially mentally disturbed employees at one out of every four or five American workers."[33]

Personal problems experienced by employees can affect work performance

Why Should the Supervisor Counsel?

There are several reasons to justify having a supervisor become involved with the problems of employees. First, personal problems that affect job performance become company problems, and the supervisor is the first member of management to become aware of these difficulties. When employees' personal problems cause their own work performance to slack off, the performance of their co-workers may also be dragged down as a result. The fact of the matter is that personal problems can have a domino effect as difficulties experienced by troubled employees eventually have a negative impact on the organization. This domino effect is illustrated in Figure 10.3. Second, personal interest and attention shown toward employees can have a positive in-

Figure 10.3   **The Domino Effect of Personal Problems**

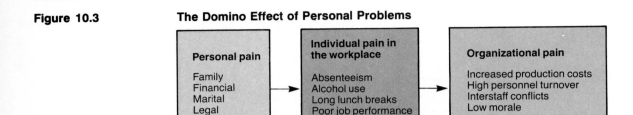

Source: Adapted from "The Supervisor as Counselor—How to Help the Distressed Employee," by John H. Meyer and Teresa C. Meyer, *Management Review* 71 (April 1982), p. 45.

Counseling can help employees with personal problems

fluence on their morale and performance. This attention can have especially beneficial results if an employee is suffering from a personal problem. Third, supervisors typically have frequent interaction with employees. If the supervisor has established a good working relationship with subordinates, then they will often confide in the supervisor and seek his or her counsel. Fourth, through counseling, valuable human resources can often be salvaged.

The approach used by some supervisors in dealing with employees who are suffering from personal problems is to fire them. This approach is certainly an option. However, before selecting this option, a supervisor should consider the time and effort spent training and developing employees. Before they developed personal problems, these subordinates were often very productive workers. If they can be helped, it does not make good business sense to automatically fire them; the cost of retraining a replacement can be considerable. Successful counseling by supervisors, therefore, can give their companies a competitive edge over companies whose supervisors simply fire employees with potential. Fifth, counseling is a very humanitarian approach. Supervisors are not only responsible for helping new employees develop on the job, they also have a responsibility to help established employees deal with new problems that affect their job performance. To ignore personal problems that fall into this category is to deny any obligation to supervise in a humane manner.

Counseling can be defined as the process of understanding the personal problem an individual is experiencing and helping the person deal with that problem. Supervisors must realize that their role in motivating subordinates extends beyond the basic managerial functions. Many psychological factors influence worker performance, and counseling is the most effective way to deal with most of the psychological factors.[34] For example, "an AT&T study of 110 counseling programs found that 86 percent of all cases showed improvement with a total annual saving of $448,000."[35] Many leading companies require their supervisors to understand the essentials of performing this helping role.[36]

Companies often benefit from establishing counseling programs

Understanding When to Counsel

In most cases, supervisors are not considered to be professional counselors. The typical supervisor should not try to play this role, particularly when dealing with personal problems that are traditionally reserved for professional counselors. For example, personal problems relating to marital difficulties, divorce, difficult children, poor financial investments, or severe mental depression are best referred to professional counselors. Also, if you make recommendations concerning the above areas, you may be legally responsible for any negative consequences an employee experiences by following your recommendations. When the scope of an employee's personal problem is beyond the supervisor's ability to help, the supervisor should encourage the employee to see a professional counselor. Some companies actually provide in-plant counseling services with outside professional counselors. Kennecott Copper, for example, provides the services of professional counselors to employees. Those employees who have received help from these counselors in dealing with personal problems experienced a 75 percent decrease in work-related costs. They also showed a 55 percent decrease in health-care costs. In addition, their attendance improved by 52 percent.[37]

Some companies provide professional counselors in-house

In some situations, however, direct counseling by the supervisor can help a troubled employee. What do you look for to determine whether a subordinate may be in need of counseling from you or others? Unfortunately, there is no easy formula available for making this decision. Instead, you must observe how employees perform and behave on the job in order to identify clues that may indicate that problems exist. Other individuals from within and outside the organization may also notify you about an employee who appears to be experiencing difficulties. Troubled employees may even voluntarily seek counseling from their supervisor if good rapport and trust exists in their working relationship. Note the following changes in an employee's behavior that may signal a need for counseling.

Some Employee Behavior Changes That May Indicate That Counseling Should Be Considered

Decline in performance	General depression
Absenteeism	Indecisiveness
Engaging in unacceptable behavior	Poor concentration
Carelessness at work	Uninterested in job
Involved in accidents on the job	Sadness
Chronically late	Dereliction of duties
Sloppy work	Withdrawal
Poor relations with customers	Moodiness
Shows tension	Irritableness

Basic Counseling Skills

Even though they are not trained psychologists or psychiatrists, supervisors should become aware of basic counseling principles. By doing so, supervisors are in a better position to assist troubled employees. Richard Walsh identifies 10 counseling skills as particularly helpful.[38]

Attending Behavior.   Here, "attend" refers to taking care of the troubled employee. As a supervisor, you want to convey to the troubled subordinate that you are concerned about his or her situation. You should also indicate your commitment to helping the employee find a solution. When you meet with the employee, make him or her feel at ease and be relaxed yourself. Also, demonstrate good eye contact. In general, your behavior should show that you want to work with the employee and help in any way you can.

Active Listening.   Make a special effort to listen attentively to the employee. To help, you must first listen to the employee's description of the problem. Concentrate on what is said and paraphrase periodically to make sure you are on track. For example:

Employee: "It's hard for me to get with it right now."

Supervisor: "You seem to be preoccupied, is that what you mean?"

You want the employee to know that you are trying hard to understand the situation correctly.

Support Responding.   Through your verbal and nonverbal responses, you can convey support and encouragement to the troubled employee. For example, appropriate head-nodding and verbal promptings can indicate support. To encourage the employee to continue speaking and open up, respond with statements such as, "Please continue," "Go on," "Tell me how you felt," and "I understand." These verbal promptings also indicate that you are interested.

Proper Questioning.   It is through the asking of questions that you are able to get the employee's perspective on what is actually troubling him or her. Properly phrased questions can influence the quality and amount of information you receive from a troubled employee. For example, as indicated in Chapter 13, open questions are designed to gain more information than are closed questions. To illustrate, it is generally better to ask "Why do you have trouble concentrating on your work?" instead of "Do you know why you are having trouble concentrating on your work?" The second question only

requests a yes or no answer. In contrast, the first question encourages the employee to express thoughts and emotions.

Reflection of Feelings.   Part of counseling a troubled employee is determining the key emotion being experienced. For example, is the employee experiencing anger, sadness, loneliness, fear, or some other emotion? To illustrate, suppose the employee says, "I liked the way we operated before the merger, but the new policies aren't fair." In response, you may say, "You seem to be angry about the changes." Here, you are reflecting your understanding of the employee's feeling. The employee can then let you know if you are correct.

Reflection of Content and Meaning.   Beyond determining what emotion the employee feels, you should also reflect your understanding of the content of the employee's concern. Suppose, for example, the employee says, "In the past I have always felt in control of my job, but things are starting to become so technical. And I feel so much more pressure on me now." In reflecting your understanding of the content of the employee's statement, you may say, "You're saying, then, that you are feeling much more stress on your job now." Your reflection of content should help the employee better understand the problem.

Summarizing Feeling and Content.   Periodically, you should summarize your understanding of the feeling and content of the subordinate's comments. Your job, through condensing and clarifying, is to pull together often diverse important feelings and elements of the conversation. This technique helps you demonstrate that you are in tune with what the employee is saying. As a result, the employee will be encouraged to continue and open up even more.

Interpretation Responding.   This skill enables the supervisor to share his or her viewpoint or frame of reference with the subordinate. As a result, the subordinate is provided with a new and perhaps more functional perspective from which to view his or her problem. In essence, you are offering your understanding of why the employee feels or acts a certain way. For example, you might say, "You seem to be discouraged because your productivity and effectiveness are declining even though you believe you are working just as hard. Perhaps you are having trouble adjusting to the changes that were implemented and you need some help." Here the idea is to assist the employee in coming up with a solution to the problem.

Assist the troubled employee in developing a solution

Rendering Advice.   In most counseling situations, the often unspoken question being asked by troubled employees is, "What can I do to resolve this problem?" Remember, however, that subordinates usually feel better about a solution they helped develop, compared to one imposed by the supervisor. As a supervisor, you should be willing to assist troubled employees. However, in doing so, present your ideas in such a way that the subordinates can be involved in shaping the information into a final solution.

Gaining a Commitment to Change.   Even when troubled employees have an understanding of their problem and have identified a solution, they may still continue aimlessly as before. What is necessary for positive

The employee must be
committed to make the
solution work

change? A definite commitment from the employee to change and implement the solution is needed; that is, the employee must follow through. The challenge for the supervisor is to use questions and tactful comments to guide the subordinate in a way that will help him or her put the solution into action.

Engaging in Counseling

Not all supervisors make good counselors; and counseling is often as much the practice of an art as it is a form of applied science.[39] However, to enhance success, some training in counseling is advisable for all supervisors who are willing to accept the responsibility. Although each counseling situation is unique, the counseling technique offered in this section can be applied by supervisors in many circumstances.

A Technique for Counseling

Keep in mind that counseling requires the cooperation of the troubled employee for it to be successful. Therefore, no pressure should initially be placed on the troubled employee to participate in counseling, although it may be necessary later.[40] Once you are faced with a situation in which you believe counseling would be appropriate, you will usually benefit from following the steps discussed below.

Step 1: Prepare notes on the problem you have observed or that has been called to your attention. Document your concerns as much as possible, and review this information prior to meeting with the employee.[41] If an employee seeks your guidance concerning a problem of which you are not aware, you obviously will not have material to review. Otherwise, you need to do your homework.

Confidentiality is an
important part of
counseling

Step 2: Make the employee feel comfortable. Select a location for counseling that is nonthreatening and where the employee will feel relaxed. The site for the session should be relatively private, free from interruptions, and quiet. Emphasize that you and the company care about the welfare of employees who may be experiencing difficulties. Also, assure the employee of complete confidentiality. As much as possible, foster and encourage mutual trust in the counseling session.

Step 3: Describe your concern or the problem as you see it. In a nonjudgmental fashion, present the relevant facts and information that you have. Observations made by others can also be mentioned. Of course, you do not want to threaten or intimidate the employee while describing problem behavior.

Step 4: Solicit the troubled employee's interpretation and perception of his or her behavior and actions. Once again, indicate your personal concern for the employee and express your desire to better understand the situation by getting his or her perspective. If the employee denies experiencing inner turmoil or indicates that nothing is wrong, focus again on the facts. However, in doing so, your tone of voice and facial expressions should emphasize that you are concerned and want to help instead of argue. Ask the employee for his or her reaction to the facts you present. Although an employee may find it difficult to recognize or accept a problem, inappropriate behavior must be pointed out to the employee. Emphasize that the employee is responsible for his or her actions but that help is available to any troubled employee who is willing to accept it. At the very least, the employee needs to understand that the behavior or actions you have identified are unacceptable and cannot continue.

Step 5: If you lack the specific training or experience to deal with a particular problem that is troubling an employee, ask whether the employee is willing to seek professional counseling. Excellent psychiatric and counseling services are often available in the community and are listed in the Yellow Pages of most cities. To enhance your ability to be helpful, acquaint yourself in general with the professional services available before meeting with the troubled employee. Employees who realize they are experiencing personal problems may perceive a stigma associated with seeking professional counseling. As a result, they do not avail themselves of the help available. A persuasive effort by you to dispel this concern and to promote the benefits of professional counseling may be all that is needed to get the employee to seek professional help.

Professional counseling is needed for some troubled employees

If, on the other hand, you can help counsel the employee, discuss with the employee what seems to be causing the problem. Also, discuss how the employee's behavior or action is affecting the employee. Do your best to help troubled employees see that in most cases their inappropriate behaviors and actions are only hindering them from achieving their goals. Once you and the employee appear to have a good understanding of the causes of the problem, you need to get a commitment from the employee to work toward improving the situation. Then you are ready to consider solutions.

Determine what is causing the problem

Step 6: Assist the troubled employee in developing an action plan to deal with the problem. Help guide the employee in considering possible solutions, but avoid telling him or her exactly what to do. As mentioned earlier, the action plan developed should be one the employee helps create. As a result, the troubled employee will be more committed to working to implement the plan or solution.

Step 7: Establish an appropriate date in the future to review how the action plan is working for the employee. At that meeting, be prepared for the possibility that the employee may have experienced difficulties that will necessitate changing part of the action plan. Remember that your continued support and encouragement is an important part of the action plan.

Coaching

In organizations, **coaching** is the job-related guidance and instruction supervisors provide to their employees. Today, whether they realize it or not, all supervisors engage in coaching while they direct the activities of their subordinates. Furthermore, coaching goes hand-in-hand with the principles of counseling just discussed. As to the distinction between the two, counseling focuses on enhancing the emotional well-being of employees, whereas coaching generally attempts to build work competency.[42]

Coaching helps to improve job performance

For supervisors, the purpose of coaching is to help employees reach desired performance levels.[43] Therefore, through coaching, supervisors help accomplish organizational goals by guiding the work of their subordinates and by helping them understand when a problem exists. In addition, when problems exist, the supervisor makes suggestions, provides instruction, assists the employees in improving, and provides relevant feedback. Therefore, by developing employees, coaching helps them prepare for greater responsibility. Furthermore, through coaching, the supervisor helps employees set goals, encourages them to ask questions, and provides them with needed information. Separating coaching from the daily interaction supervisors often have with their workers is frequently difficult because the coaching can be informal in nature.[44] However, when coaching does occur, it generally involves five phases. First, observe and analyze the employee's behavior or performance. Second, determine the area of performance that needs improvement. Third, identify how the employee's performance can be improved and the actions that need to be taken. Fourth, guide the employee in making the necessary improvement. Fifth, periodically review the employee's performance.[45]

Coaching requires cooperation

When an employee's job performance does not meet expectations, the appropriateness of coaching to close the gap depends in part on what is causing the gap. In analyzing the situation as a supervisor, ask yourself the following questions.[46] Does the employee know what is expected of him or her? Does the employee know how to perform the job well? Is the employee working toward goals that are realistic and challenging? If the answer to any of these questions is no, coaching will likely help the situation. However, for coaching to be successful, the employee must also recognize that a problem exists. Most employees are receptive to coaching if they sense that it will help them develop on the job.

Closing the Performance Gap

Coaching involves working with employees, not just dictating orders to them. In working with an employee whose performance is poor, you should meet with the subordinate and discuss his or her performance. At the end of this meeting, you should have reconfirmed or established the following items of understanding.[47]

☐ Get agreement on what the employee's job is and what major activities are to be performed. It is difficult to be successful in coaching someone on how to do something if there isn't agreement on what is to be done.

☐ Determine the criteria against which performance will be judged and measured. For example, greater priority may be given to the quality of the work performed than to the quantity of work completed. How quality will be measured should also be understood.

☐ Determine the standards for success on the job. A common understanding of what the employee needs to accomplish to succeed is important. Make sure the standards are realistic but challenging.

The need for the supervisor and the employee to reach agreement in their discussion of the above three items is critical in coaching. Without a common understanding of performance criteria, for example, the employee may misunderstand which criteria you consider to be of highest priority. As a result, the employee may incorrectly devote only a moderate effort on tasks you consider important. Unfortunately, sizable discrepancies between what managers and subordinates consider to be the key responsibilities of subordinates are common in organizations.[48]

The supervisor-employee discussions that take place in coaching need to occur in a special climate of open, candid, two-way communication.[49] When providing feedback while coaching employees, give careful consideration to the suggestions that follow.[50]

Provide helpful feedback when coaching

Generally, it is best to focus on changing or improving only one or two aspects of an employee's behavior at a time. Otherwise, the coaching may suffer because you and the employee took on too much too fast. Make sure your recommendations concern behavior that can be changed. Also, as mentioned earlier, include the employee as much as possible in developing a strategy for improving performance. This approach will enhance the employee's receptiveness to your coaching. Furthermore, make certain you and the employee understand each other clearly. For example, be as specific as possible to avoid the confusion that often results from statements that are vague and general in nature.

As a supervisor, you must work with and through your employees to accomplish organizational goals. Through coaching, you help your employees develop in ways that enhance their ability to accomplish important goals and to be productive.

Supervisors cannot isolate themselves from their subordinates and be effective in their job. Instead, it is necessary for them to interact with others at work and to promote effective interpersonal relations in the process. It is now appropriate to briefly review the objectives for promoting effective interpersonal relations established at the beginning of this chapter.

Looking Back

☐ **Identify common cultural problems that often exist when supervising a multicultural work force.** Those individuals responsible for supervising a multicultural work force face special problems. Foremost among these problems are difficulties associated with language, stereotyping, nonverbal behavior, and differing values.

☐ **Indicate ways that supervisors can improve their intercultural communication.** To improve their intercultural communication, supervisors should have a sincere desire to improve their cultural conditioning. They also need to communicate effectively, be careful when drawing conclusions, encourage feedback, and show empathy.

☐ **Define self-concept.** Specifically, self-concept refers to the relatively stable perceptions people have about themselves. It includes our conception of what is unique about ourselves, what distinguishes us from others, and what makes us similar to others.

☐ **Explain how self-concepts are generally formed.** Self-concepts are derived primarily from four sources. First, we are influenced by our social interactions with others. Second, we compare ourselves with others. Third, what others say about us is considered. Fourth, we examine how we see ourselves.

☐ **Define self-esteem.** Specifically, self-esteem refers to the evaluation a person makes of his or her self-concept.

☐ **Identify strategies for improving subordinates' self-esteem.** As a supervisor, you can help foster subordinates' self-esteem by being a good listener and showing concern for them. Also, express confidence in them and provide subordinates with some decision-making responsibilities. In addition, help subordinates succeed and model high self-esteem yourself.

☐ **Identify techniques for building trust.** As a supervisor, your ability to gain the trust of subordinates will be enhanced if you promote common goals and keep subordinates well informed. In addition, you can encourage trust by being open with subordinates and showing a genuine interest in them.

☐ **Identify the appropriate steps involved in counseling troubled employees.** First, prepare notes on the problem you have observed or that has been called to your attention. Second, when you meet with the troubled employee, make him or her feel comfortable by selecting a location for counseling that is nonthreatening and where the employee will be relaxed. Third, describe your concern or the problem as you see it. Fourth, solicit the troubled employee's interpretation and perception of his or her behavior and actions. Fifth, if you lack the specific training or experience to deal with a particular problem that is troubling an employee, ask whether the employee is willing to seek professional counseling. Sixth, assist the troubled employee in developing an action plan to deal with the problem. Last, establish an appropriate date in the future to review how the action plan is working for the employee.

☐ **Explain the difference between counseling and coaching.** Counseling and coaching go hand-in-hand. As to the distinction between the two, counseling focuses on enhancing the emotional well-being of employees, whereas coaching generally attempts to build work competency.

Key Terms

coaching	polychronic-time values
counseling	self-concept
culture	self-esteem
ethnocentrism	stereotyping
monochronic-time values	value

Review and Discussion Questions

1. How can stereotyping cause cultural problems on the job?
2. Explain how viewing time from a monochronic-time perspective is different than viewing time from a polychronic-time perspective.
3. How can differing values create intercultural communication problems?
4. Why is it a mistake to think that all you need to do to improve your intercultural communication is to learn more about people from other cultures?
5. In order to develop a positive self-concept as a supervisor, why is it important to give yourself credit for making good decisions?
6. Why does providing employees with some decision-making responsibilities often help them to improve their self-esteem?
7. In order to gain the trust of subordinates, why is it important to be open with them?
8. What are some of the drawbacks to firing troubled employees instead of attempting to counsel them?
9. Before attempting to counsel a troubled employee, why is it important to first prepare notes on the problem that appears to exist?
10. Why is it necessary for an employee to recognize that there is a problem with his or her performance before coaching can help the employee?

Action Incident 10.1

I Get No Respect

Ben Wilson sees himself as a no-nonsense supervisor. Others who work around him are less charitable in their description of him. At best, they characterize him as an authoritarian leader. One thing both Ben and his critics would probably agree on is that he does not funnel much downward communication to his subordinates. As Ben is fond of saying, "What they don't know won't hurt them." He makes little effort to encourage upward communication. This behavior leaves subordinates with the impression that Ben does not care what they think. When Ben does request information from subordinates, they are often uneasy about how he might react to their comments. In any case, subordinates view any encouragement of upward communication as inconsistent behavior on the part of Ben. As a matter of fact, Ben's subordinates find him to be unpredictable in general. They note, for example, that Ben will leave workers with the impression that certain project deadlines are flexible. Suddenly, however, after a project has been delayed due to unavoidable problems, he may change his view and insist that a deadline be met. The workers view this tactic as an attempt by Ben to pressure them to work harder to meet a deadline.

The workers would like to believe they can depend on Ben, but they are leery to do so. Too often, they believe, he just does not come through for them. For example, last year top management announced that some departments would experience budget cuts. Although there was compelling evidence for sparing Ben's department from the budget axe, his budget was cut. Workers in his department blame Ben for their current budget woes. They believe Ben did not come through for them when he defended the department's budget to his superiors. As a result, they do not think they can rely on him, and they wonder sometimes if they and Ben are working toward the same goals. Occasionally, they are convinced that different goals exist. The workers sense that when Ben's superior says jump, Ben's only response is "How high?" They wonder, for example, why Ben cannot work as hard in presenting their views to top management as he does in manipulating them into accepting the ideas of top management. Recently, Ben's superior expressed concern that Ben did not have the trust of his workers. Ben replied, "That's not true. I've been their supervisor for several years!"

Discussion Questions

1. Why is length of time as a supervisor not necessarily a good determinant of whether subordinates trust a supervisor?
2. Why has Ben been unsuccessful in gaining the trust of his subordinates?
3. What should Ben do to better gain the trust of his subordinates?

Action Incident 10.2

Thanks for Nothing

Carol Arnold has worked as a bookkeeper for a large automobile dealership for the last four years. She has always been a good employee, but recently the quality of her work has declined. Specifically, she is often late for work, has trouble concentrating, seems depressed, and shows tension. Unknown to her co-workers, Carol is experiencing mounting financial problems since her husband's business failed. In particular, she has credit-card debts that are no longer manageable for her. Carol's current supervisor, Sally Daniels, is relatively new to the job and has only known Carol for a few months. However, Sally is aware that something is bothering Carol. The following dialogue occurs as Sally attempts to counsel Carol.

Sally: Carol, I've noticed that you seem to be very preoccupied lately. If I can help, I will be glad to do so, but I hope things will improve soon.

Carol: I hope so, also.

Sally: Hoping isn't going to get the job done. What do you plan to do to change the situation?

Carol: Well, I'm working on a budget to follow and. . . . *[Interrupted by Sally]*

Sally: I'm not talking about a budget—I'm talking about the quality of your work. I think you need to make your job top priority while you are at work.

Carol: My job is important to me.

Sally: Then you have a strange way of showing it. Do you think showing up late is a good way to indicate that your work is important to you?

Carol: You just don't understand.

Sally: I understand that your behavior and performance have changed. I guess only you can help change things back around again.

Carol: I guess so.

Discussion Questions

1. Do you agree with Sally's statement that only Carol can help change things back around again? Explain.
2. What mistakes did Sally make in her attempt to "counsel" Carol?
3. What procedures should Sally have used in attempting to counsel Carol?

Action Incident 10.3

Setting a Poor Example

Betty Watson is a supervisor for the catalogue sales department of a large department store. In her job, Betty has several responsibilities, one of which is to evaluate the performance of catalogue sales operators who work under her supervision. It is time consuming to monitor the performance of the operators, and Betty does not like to make the necessary observations. Therefore, her evaluations of the operators' performance are often incomplete. As a result, poor performance by operators is slow to be identified and corrected. In addition, Betty's behavior on the job often fails to set a positive example. For instance, Betty often takes excessively long breaks for lunch, and the operators notice that she occasionally takes office supplies home with her. In addition, the goals Betty sets for her department are not very challenging, and she does not show much concern for controlling costs. For example, operators are occasionally paid extra to work overtime on tasks that Betty failed to assign while the operators were not especially busy. Work is also delayed because Betty does not follow the progress of assignments very closely. As a result, the subordinates do not see much urgency to many of the tasks.

Recently, Betty disciplined an operator for not being courteous to a customer on the telephone. During the discussion, the operator said to Betty, "You are not always courteous to difficult customers." Betty's response was, "We are talking about your behavior, not mine!"

Discussion Questions

1. Is Betty's behavior partly responsible for the discourteous actions of the operator? Explain.
2. In what ways did Betty act as a poor role model?
3. What recommendations would you make to Betty in regard to becoming a better role model?

Notes

1. Fathi S. Yousef, "Human Resource Management Aspects of Intercultural Relations in U.S. Organizations," in *Intercultural Communication: A Reader,* 5th ed., eds. Larry A. Samovar and Richard E. Porter (Belmont, Calif.: Wadsworth, 1988), p. 176.
2. Ann Clarke Cessaris, "When Employees Don't Speak English Well," *Training and Development Journal* 40 (October 1986), pp. 58–61.
3. Robert G. King, *Fundamentals of Human Communication* (New York: Macmillan, 1979), p. 247.
4. William B. Gudykunst and Young Yun Kim, *Communicating With Strangers: An Approach to Intercultural Communication* (Reading, Mass.: Addison-Wesley Publishing, 1984), p. 142.
5. Larry A. Samovar, Richard E. Porter, and Nemi C. Jain, *Understanding Intercultural Communication* (Belmont, Calif.: Wadsworth, 1981), p. 50.
6. Kathleen S. Verderber and Rudolph F. Verderber, *Inter-Act: Using Interpersonal Communication Skills,* 4th ed. (Belmont, Calif.: Wadsworth, 1986), p. 230.
7. Samovar, Porter, and Jain, *Understanding Intercultural Communication,* p. 183.
8. Samovar, Porter, and Jain, *Understanding Intercultural Communication,* p. 183.
9. John Condon, "'. . . So Near the United States': Notes on Communication

between Mexicans and North Americans," in *Intercultural Communication: A Reader,* 5th ed., eds. Larry A. Samovar and Richard E. Porter (Belmont, Calif.: Wadsworth, 1988), p. 114.

10. Glen Fisher, "International Negotiation," in *Intercultural Communication: A Reader,* 5th ed., eds. Larry A. Samovar and Richard E. Porter (Belmont, Calif.: Wadsworth, 1988), p. 198.

11. Samovar and Porter, *Understanding Intercultural Communication,* p. 43.

12. Adapted from Samovar and Porter, *Understanding Intercultural Communication,* pp. 202–9.

13. Yousef, "Human Resource Management," p. 180.

14. Yousef, "Human Resource Management," p. 181.

15. James B. Stull, "Giving Feedback to Foreign-Born Employees," *Management Solutions* 30 (July 1988), p. 45.

16. Stull, "Giving Feedback to Foreign-Born Employees," p. 43.

17. Judy C. Pearson, *Interpersonal Communication: Clarity, Confidence, Concern* (Dubuque, Iowa: Wm. C. Brown, 1987), p. 172.

18. Anthony G. Athos and John J. Gabarro, *Interpersonal Behavior: Communication and Understanding in Relationships* (Englewood Cliffs, N.J.: Prentice-Hall, 1978), p. 140.

19. Ronald B. Adler and George Rodman, *Understanding Human Communication,* 2d ed. (New York: Holt, Rinehart & Winston, 1985), p. 25.

20. Robert A. Baron, *Understanding Human Relations: A Practical Guide to People at Work* (Boston, Mass.: Allyn and Bacon, 1985), pp. 162–63.

21. Phyllis Tharenou, "Employee Self-Esteem: A Review of the Literature," *Journal of Vocational Behavior* 15 (December 1979), p. 317.

22. Kevin W. Mossholder, Arthur B. Bedeian, and Achilles A. Armenakis, "Group Process-Work Outcome Relationships: A Note on the Moderating Impact of Self-Esteem," *Academy of Management Journal* 25 (September 1982), p. 577.

23. Ron Zemke, "How to Gain Power and Support in the Organization," *Training* 19 (January 1982), p. 13.

24. Adapted from Barry L. Reece and Rhonda Brandt, *Effective Human Relations in Organizations,* 2d ed. (Boston, Mass.: Houghton Mifflin, 1984), p. 105.

25. "Stroke Your Folks: Build Subordinates' Self-Esteem," *Training* 23 (January 1986), pp. 13–14; and "Common Expectations Through Self-Esteem," *Management World* 16 (January 1987), p. 17.

26. F. J. Roethlisberger and W. J. Dickson, *Management and the Worker* (Cambridge, Mass.: Harvard University Press, 1939).

27. Teri Kwal Gamble and Michael Gamble, *Contacts: Communicating Interpersonally* (New York: Random House, 1982), p. 201.

28. "William Ouchi on Trust," *Training and Development Journal* 36 (December 1982), p. 71.

29. J. Clifton Williams and George P. Huber, *Human Behavior in Organizations,* 3d ed. (Cincinnati, Ohio: South-Western Publishing, 1986), p. 361.

30. Williams and Huber, *Human Behavior in Organizations,* p. 362.

31. Alan W. Farrant, "Be Your Own Supervisor," *Supervision* 49 (November 1987), p. 4.

32. Rogala and Associates, "Steps to Successful Employee Relations," *Supervision* 49 (September 1987), p. 17.

33. Lester R. Bittel, *What Every Supervisor Should Know: The Basics of Supervisory Management,* 5th ed. (New York: McGraw-Hill, 1985), p. 329.

34. George L. Frunzi and Joseph R. Dunn, "Counseling Subordinates: It's Up To You," *Supervisory Management* 19 (August 1974), p. 2.

35. Leslie W. Rue and Lloyd L. Byars, *Supervision: Key Link to Productivity,* 2d. ed. (Homewood, Ill.: Richard D. Irwin, 1986), p. 238.

36. Thomas J. Peters and Robert H. Waterman, Jr., *In Search of Excellence* (New York: Harper & Row, 1982), pp. 235–78.

37. "Employee Counseling Pays Off," *Behavioral Sciences Newsletter* (November 13, 1978).

38. Richard J. Walsh, "Ten Basic Counseling Skills," *Supervisory Management* 22 (July 1977) pp. 4–9.

39. Robert Culpepper and Larry R. Smeltzer, "When Personnel Problems Get Personal or How to Get Personal with Your Personnel," *Supervision* 46 (May 1984), p. 7.

40. Culpepper and Smeltzer, "When Personnel Problems Get Personal," p. 7.

41. John H. Meyer and Teresa C. Meyer, "The Supervisor as Counselor—How to Help the Distressed Employee," *Management Review* 71 (April 1982), p. 45.

42. Thomas J. Von der Embse, *Supervision: Managerial Skills for a New Era* (New York: Macmillan, 1987), p. 331.

43. Lynn Mcfarlane Shore and Arvid J. Bloom, "Developing Employees Through Coaching and Career Management," *Personnel* 63 (August 1986), p. 36.

44. Christina Christenson, Thomas W. Johnson, and John E. Stinson, *Supervising* (Reading, Mass.: Addison-Wesley Publishing, 1982), p. 343.

45. Adapted from Shore and Bloom, "Developing Employees Through Coaching and Career Management," p. 36, and Bittel, *What Every Supervisor Should Know,* p. 265.

46. Adapted from Richard V. Concilio, "Will Coaching Pay Off?," *Management Solutions* 31 (September 1986), p. 21.

47. Concilio, "Will Coaching Pay Off?," pp. 19–20.

48. Chip R. Bell, "Coaching for High Performance," *Advanced Management Journal* 52 (Autumn 1987), p. 27.

49. *Behavioral Sciences Newsletter,* September 28, 1987, p. 1.

50. Concilio, "Will Coaching Pay Off?," p. 20; and *Behavioral Sciences Newsletter,* September 28, 1987, p. 1.

Suggested Readings

Brockner, Joel, and Ted Hess. "Self-Esteem and Task Performance in Quality Circles." *Academy of Management Journal* 29, September 1986, pp. 617–23.

Cessaris, Ann Clarke. "When Employees Don't Speak English Well." *Training and Development Journal* 40, October 1986, pp. 59–61.

Concilio, Richard V. "Will Coaching Pay Off?" *Management Solutions* 31, September 1986, pp. 18–21.

Longenecker, Clinton O., and Patrick R. Liverpool. "An Action Plan for Helping Troubled Employees." *Management Solutions* 33, July 1988, pp. 22–27.

Meyer, John H., and Teresa C. Meyer. "The Supervisor as Counselor—How to Help the Distressed Employee." *Management Review* 71, April 1982, pp. 42–46.

Mossholder, Kevin W., Arthur G. Bedeian, and Achilles A. Armenakis. "Group Process-Work Outcome Relationships: A Note on the Moderating Impact of Self-Esteem." *Academy of Management Journal* 25, September 1982, pp. 575–85.

Samovar, Larry A., and Richard E. Porter. *Intercultural Communication: A Reader.* 5th ed. Belmont, Calif.: Wadsworth, 1988.

Schwartz, Andrew E. "Counseling the Marginal Performer." *Management Solutions* 33, March 1988, pp. 30–35.

Stull, James B. "Giving Feedback to Foreign-Born Employees." *Management Solutions* 30, July 1988, pp. 42–45.

Tharenou, Phyllis. "Employee Self-Esteem: A Review of the Literature." *Journal of Vocational Behavior* 15, December 1979, pp. 316–46.

Working with Groups

Learning Objectives

After reading and studying the material contained in this chapter, you should be able to:

1. Define group.
2. Identify the benefits of group homogeneity.
3. Identify the benefits of group heterogeneity.
4. Identify possible benefits of group decision making.
5. Identify possible problems of group decision making.
6. Define groupthink.
7. Identify remedies to groupthink.
8. Explain the risky-shift phenomenon.
9. Explain the spectrum approach.
10. Indicate the advantages of the spectrum approach.
11. Identify techniques for conducting effective meetings.

What Is a Group?

In an organization, a **group** can be defined as two or more people working together and satisfying needs through interaction. A supervisor, for example, may request that a few employees meet together to analyze a particular problem the company is experiencing. The supervisor requests that the employees make recommendations to her for solving the problem. In this case, the employees in the group are all working on the same problem. Their individual needs, however, may differ. For example, one employee may like being in the group because it gives him a break away from his regular work. His need for a change of pace is being satisfied. Another employee has accepted the group task in order to become more experienced at dealing with company problems. His need to enhance his qualifications for promotion is being satisfied. Other group members may join the group to meet different needs. By working together, they deal with the company problem and satisfy their individual needs.

What about a group member whose needs are not being satisfied? Maybe this person does not want to leave his work to serve on the group or does not consider the group task to be important. In short, she considers the group to be a waste of time. Difficulties will develop as a result. That is, she probably will not take much interest in the group task and will contribute little to the group discussions. Therefore, due to these types of negative consequences, it is important for you to make sure members of a group see the need for the group. It is also important to explain why their involvement in the group is needed. At a minimum, the needs of the group members to be valued and to perform meaningful work should be touched upon.

Group members must work together

Consider the needs of your group members

Are Groups Necessary?

Without a doubt, for modern companies to operate effectively, groups are necessary to make and implement different company policies. However, although groups are necessary, they are not always beneficial. As a matter of fact, most employees can identify groups in their organizations that are not needed. They notice that these groups have nothing important to do and serve no important purpose.

If a group is not needed, then it is a waste of the members' time. It has been said that, in business, time is money. For example, an employee earning $20,000 a year may cost a company $25 per hour when all company benefits are accounted for. If five of these employees have a two-hour meeting, it costs the company $250. The same meeting with an equal number of $40,000-per-year supervisors attending will cost the company $500. Are these costs worth it? In today's competitive environment, when a group meets in a company, executives are asking, "Are we spending $500 to solve a $200 problem?" Clearly, many groups are productive and allow their companies to profit from their efforts. It just depends on the situation.

Group meetings can be expensive

Group Composition

The productivity of a group, especially in problem solving, can be influenced by how homogeneous or heterogeneous the group is.[1] **Homogeneous** groups have members who are much alike in traits and characteristics. The group members, for example, may be alike in interests, abilities, personalities, age, work experience, and education. Conversely, **heterogeneous** groups contain members who differ in traits and characteristics. The group members may differ in their training, opinions, cultural background, jobs, and attitudes.

Group composition is important

Benefits of Group Homogeneity

In an organization, you may wish to form a small group of employees to discuss a particular situation the company is experiencing. If the employees assembled represent a homogeneous group, they are likely to realize the following benefits.[2]

More Influence. Group members who are alike, as compared with those who have little in common, find it easier to influence each other. They feel an affinity with each other, so they are more receptive to each other's ideas.

Greater Satisfaction. It is natural for us to like other employees who have the same opinions we do and who are similar to us in many ways. As a result, you will likely find it satisfying to be in a group with others who share your views on issues being discussed.

Higher Productivity for Simple Tasks. Homogeneous groups can mobilize to do a job quickly. They are especially effective in performing simple group tasks.

Much Cooperation. If the group task requires coordinated efforts among the members, then a homogeneous group is desired. High cooperation occurs here primarily because the members of homogeneous groups are generally very compatible and get along well together. Homogeneity in technical speciality is considered by hospitals, for example, in assigning nurses to task groups.[3]

Homogeneous groups are very compatible

Well-Performed Sequential Tasks Sequential tasks, where each employee performs a separate task and one task is completed after another in a chain, are performed well by homogeneous groups. Homogeneous groups, for example, are seldom faced with a deviant member who tries to hold things up, and the abilities of members in homogeneous groups are not greatly varied. Therefore, it is unlikely that one member will be unfamiliar with the group task and drag down performance.

Figure 11.1   **Benefits Associated with Homogeneous and Heterogeneous Groups**

Homogeneous Groups	Heterogeneous Groups
Members are influential with each other.	Deal well with complex problems.
Members find the group experience satisfying.	Members examine issues thoroughly.
Productivity in performing simple tasks is high.	Produce creative ideas and solutions.
Members are cooperative.	
Perform sequential tasks well.	

Source: Adapted from Bernard M. Bass and Edward C. Ryterband, *Organizational Psychology*, 2d ed. (Boston, Allyn & Bacon, 1979), pp. 260–64.

Benefits of Group Heterogeneity

There are also advantages that are unique to heterogeneous groups. Some of the benefits associated with these groups are discussed below.[4]

Ability to Deal with Complex Problems.   In heterogeneous groups, the members have varied skills and training. These varied assets give the group needed breadth and depth to deal with complex problems.

Heterogeneous groups have varied strengths

Thorough Examination of Issues.   When group members have differing points of view and perspectives on an issue, each will want his or her position considered. As a result, in most cases heterogeneous groups thoroughly examine the issue being discussed.

Enhanced Creativity.   When the members of a group are very similar, they are prone to reach agreement too easily and too often on the same incorrect decisions. This result is due to the fact that the group fails to examine the situation very thoroughly; they do not consider many alternative courses of action. Heterogeneous groups may experience some discord in their discussions. However, members who are different are likely to be creative as a group because their diversity causes them to examine problems in many different ways.

It may not always be possible to control the membership of groups. However, when you can influence group composition, Figure 11.1 provides a convenient summary of the benefits associated with homogeneous and heterogeneous groups.

Possible Benefits of Group Decision Making

Especially in the area of problem solving, small groups have several advantages to offer organizations. Some of the benefits of using small groups for this purpose will now be discussed.[5]

Individual Member's Knowledge Expands Group's Knowledge in Different Directions

Figure 11.2

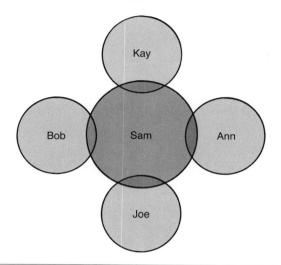

Greater Total Knowledge and Information

Each member in a group is a potential source of valuable knowledge and information for analyzing a particular problem. One member may be more knowledgeable than any other individual in the group. However, lesser-informed members may have unique knowledge to offer the group that can fill in certain gaps in understanding. For example, in designing a new product, an engineer may have the most technical knowledge about the product. However, a lesser-informed individual on the planning committee may have valuable information about how the product should be styled to sell well. Therefore, by sharing information in the group, the product will be technically sound and well styled.

Each group member brings new knowledge to the group

As Figure 11.2 illustrates, Sam's circle of knowledge about a problem may be greater than each of the other four group members. However, the specialized, unique knowledge of Kay, Ann, Joe, and Bob expand on Sam's knowledge in different directions. In short, groups know more than their individual members.

More Approaches to a Problem

Individually, when faced with a problem, we analyze it from the way we see it. Our perspectives, however, are influenced by our experiences, and people have different experiences in life. As a result, it is not uncommon for several people to see the same problem in different ways. On at least one occasion, you have probably heard about a creative solution to a problem and thought, "I would never have come up with that." You may, however, have been able to develop the new idea had you viewed the problem differently. That is, locked into your perspective of the issue, *you* did not see the problem from other angles.

Group decisions are often better than individual ones

When you work on a problem individually, you will persist in developing a solution that makes sense to you. In a group, however, others will likely have different ideas that make sense to them for dealing with the problem. By sharing ideas, group members can help each other remove themselves from the rut of looking at a problem in just one way.

Involvement in Problem Solving Increases Acceptance

Group decisions may be better accepted in organizations than decisions made by one person

It's fairly simple; individuals who participate in making decisions tend to support them. As a result, when members of a group work together in developing solutions, they are usually unified in supporting the solutions they formulated. In addition, if just one person makes the decisions in a company, he or she alone must sell others on accepting and implementing them. All the members of a group, however, can be used to sell a decision made by the group. For this reason, it is important that the members of problem-solving groups be selected carefully. They should be respected by others in the company and able to represent departments affected by the group's decisions. With these characteristics, the persuasiveness of the group members is enhanced.

Better Comprehension of Decisions

When a decision by a supervisor needs to be carried out by subordinates, the decision must first be relayed to the subordinates. In the process of conveying this information, communication problems can develop. These problems, however, are greatly reduced when the employees who must work together to implement the decision also helped develop it. If they participated as a group in making the decision, they understand it and realize why alternative solutions were not used.

▼

Consider This

1. How comfortable do you generally feel working on a project with others in a group? Why do you feel this way?
2. In your opinion, what should the leaders and members of groups do to make it more enjoyable and productive to work on a problem as a group?

Possible Problems of Group Decision Making

As just discussed, there are certain benefits associated with group decision making. However, there are also drawbacks to consider.[6]

Social Pressure

The desire to be viewed as a good group member and to be accepted encourages conformity in many groups. This tendency occurs as part of the groupthink phenomenon. Specifically, **groupthink** occurs when a group avoids critically testing, analyzing, and evaluating ideas in order to minimize conflict and reach a consensus.[7] As a result, majority opinions tend to be accepted regardless of whether or not they are very logical or technically sound.

Group members may feel pressured to conform

Symptoms of Groupthink.   To the trained observer, there are a number of signs that can signal when a group is becoming a victim of groupthink. Consider the following ones.[8] Sometimes, as groups become cohesive and members are amiable, a norm develops that critical thoughts should be suppressed. Members, therefore, voluntarily refrain from disagreeing with each other's ideas in order to avoid creating disunity. If a group member does not voluntarily refrain from critical thinking, other members will pressure him or her to conform. The group may permit some dissension from a member. However, a norm is quickly established as to how much criticism will be tolerated.

With little dissension, groups may be lulled into thinking that once a consensus is reached, all of the members support it. There may, however, be unvoiced disagreement that has not surfaced. A group prone to groupthink also often ignores warnings that its assumptions or decisions in some cases may be wrong. It is as if the group has blind faith in its actions. When making policy decisions that will affect subordinates, for example, the group does not consider the views of employees. Group members may also be quick to apply negative stereotypes to outsiders who disagree with their actions. Leaders who like to be surrounded by group members who agree with them create the perfect environment for groupthink.

Watch out for groupthink

Remedies to Groupthink.   All groups are not automatically doomed to suffer through the difficulties associated with groupthink. In order to reduce the likelihood that your group will be hindered by groupthink, practice the following strategies.[9]

1. *Request that each group member be a critical evaluator.* Also, encourage an open airing of objections and doubts in group discussions. As a leader of a group, you should reinforce your request for openness by demonstrating a willingness to accept criticism of your own views.

2. *Adopt an impartial stance when you request that a group analyze a particular problem and propose a solution.* That is, refrain from telling the group what you think should be done. Be neutral in giving group members their assignment so they will not be influenced by your views. Otherwise, they may feel pressured to propose a solution for which you have indicated a preference.

3. *If appropriate and possible, consider having two groups work on the same problem.* Sometimes a second group outside a department can be more open-minded in discussing a particular problem than an inside group.

4. *Have group members get the opinions of members in the departments they represent about solutions being considered by the group.* These reactions can then be considered by the group before making a final decision.

5. *If appropriate and possible, have an outside person attend some of the group meetings.* This person should be knowledgeable about the topic being discussed. Also, encourage this person to play the role of devil's advocate on key issues being discussed. If an outside person is not brought in, have a group member play the role of devil's advocate. In doing so, this group member should challenge the arguments of those who advocate the majority position.

An outside person can give a neutral view of the group's decision

Individual Domination

In many groups, a dominant individual member emerges, who frequently interjects his or her ideas in group discussions. Through active participation, persuasion, or persistence, this person attempts to exert significant influence on the group. However, although dominant individuals may participate a lot in group discussions, this does not mean that they are skilled at problem solving. As a matter of fact, their dominance may intimidate some members who *are* skilled at problem solving.

Overemphasis on Winning

Once a group is confronted with a problem, it is natural for group members to suggest their own solutions. Most people dislike having their suggestions rejected. Therefore, when their ideas are criticized or when competing suggestions are offered, they may become defensive. Too often, personal energies are directed more toward refuting others and winning than on finding the best solution. As a result, the group's ability to develop superior solutions is hindered.

Greater Risk Taking

You have probably heard of the old adage "There is strength in numbers." One person, for example, may not wish to go out on a limb or take a particular stand alone regarding certain issues. This same individual, however, may be willing to do so if a group of others also goes along. We have all seen situations where people we knew well acted differently in a group than they would have otherwise. Sometimes people become bolder in groups and appear more risk oriented when they have the support of their group.

It is easier to take risks in a group

Research also indicates that it is not uncommon for individuals to advocate greater degrees of risk in a group discussion than they would have in private.[10] This tendency of individuals to be greater risk takers when participating in a group than when acting alone is referred to as the **risky-shift phenomenon.** Four prominent explanations offered by researchers to explain this phenomenon are discussed below.[11]

1. *Group discussion allows group members to become more familiar with the situations being discussed.* This increased familiarity with an issue involving risk can cause the members to become more risky on that issue. For example, a group of people who attempt to operate a sailboat for the first time will probably do so with caution. After they become more familiar with the boat, however, they may likely attempt more daring maneuvers.

2. *Risk takers are often dominant individuals.* In a group setting, these individuals will attempt to lead and have significant influence on the group. As a result, they are more likely to persuade other more conservative-minded, but less vocal, members to accept their point of view.

3. *In a group there is a diffusion of responsibility among the members.* This diffusion of responsibility has been used to explain the risky actions sometimes taken by individuals in mobs and crowds. Within organizations, for example, members of a problem-solving group may be willing to suggest riskier solutions than when acting alone. After all, a group member knows that he or she does not have to accept all the blame if the risky solution fails.

4. *Moderate risk taking is a valued trait in our society.* Many individuals view themselves as being just as willing as their peers to take risks. In a group discussion, a member may notice that his or her private positions are less risky than the group average. As a result, the person may recognize his or her relative cautiousness and accept the challenge of being just as big of a risk taker as the other members. The person, therefore, goes along with a riskier position taken by the group than was his or her original inclination.

It is important to note, however, that it is not always bad for the risky-shift phenomenon to occur in a group. Sometimes, difficult situations in companies call for bold, untested solutions. After all, nothing ventured, nothing gained. When groups help individual members to consider a broader range of options, some of which may be risky, the results can be good. However, we all realize the dangers inherent in making imprudent or rash decisions. If, for example, you bet the company each time you make a very risky decision, you may reap spectacular rewards for each successive success. However, under this approach there will not be any company left after the first mistake. In essence, risk needs to be tempered by the situation, and groups should be aware of any temptations to throw caution to the wind.

The riskiness of group decisions needs to be considered

Team Building

The purpose of team building is to help group members work together in a spirit of cooperation to improve the efficiency and effectiveness of their performance. The goals of team building usually include one or more of the following:

1. To establish group goals and/or priorities.
2. To analyze how work is performed and/or to allocate tasks.
3. To examine how the norms, decision-making process, and communication style of the group affect how the group functions.
4. To examine working relationships among group members.[12]

When a group engages in team building, it first analyzes its current level of performance or functioning. Many sources, ranging from attitude surveys to open discussion sessions, can provide information for this analysis. Through this analysis, strengths and weaknesses of the group are identified. A list of ways to improve team functioning and strategies for making the needed changes are then developed. Ideally, this form of team building is a continuing process that involves regular evaluation sessions and making necessary changes in the way the group functions.[13]

Team building should occur on a continuing basis

Fostering Creativity in Groups

People working together in groups to solve problems in their company benefit by being creative, and companies are always interested in techniques that will help groups to develop creative ideas. In many cases, however, groups hinder creativity by the way they approach problem-solving discussions.

A common hindrance is antagonism toward new ideas.[14] That is, when a new idea is offered in a group, the other members often begin to focus on what might be wrong with the idea. Why is there this tendency? In some cases, the rules of competition are partly to blame. Other members of the group, for example, may reason that if the idea suggested for solving a problem is

Antagonism toward new ideas hinders creativity

accepted, their ideas will not be used. They look at it as a win-lose situation where they lose if someone else's idea wins. Therefore, they attempt to discredit ideas that compete with their ideas. Habit is another reason that group members tend to focus initially on what might be wrong with an idea. That is, most people naturally look for weaknesses in an idea when evaluating it and deciding whether to accept the idea. As a result, weaknesses associated with an idea frequently determine whether an idea is adopted or thrown out. This approach seems very logical to most people. However, it is important to note that all ideas have some weaknesses, and this type of cold reception causes many new ideas to be abandoned or discarded quickly in group discussions.

A better approach that fosters creativity in group discussions is to view all ideas as having both weaknesses and strengths. When you focus on weaknesses, there is the danger that the weaknesses will cause the idea to be discarded before its strengths are fully appreciated. That is, when you throw out an idea, its strengths are also lost.

To illustrate, suppose the internal combustion gasoline engine has not been developed yet and your group is discussing different possible ways of powering a carriage. One group member, Richard, suggests an idea he has just imagined—an internal combustion engine. Richard's newborn idea is still hazy in his mind. He has only a general notion of how it might work. Figure 11.3 indicates a few of the idea's weaknesses and strengths.

The weaknesses associated with Richard's idea are glaring. Who would want to get near a contraption that contained exploding gasoline, got very hot, made a lot of noise, and produced noxious fumes? By focusing on the obvious weaknesses, it is very possible that Richard's idea would be rejected by the group. New ideas, especially novel ones, are usually in embryonic form when first presented; that is, they are not fully formed yet. As a result, they need to be nurtured and fostered for them to become fully developed.

Don't focus on the weaknesses of ideas

Since Richard's newborn idea is still hazy in his mind, he is not prepared to give details about it. If the weaknesses of the idea are focused on, Richard may even back away from it. When an idea is thrown out, its strengths go along with it! By using the spectrum approach, this problem can often be avoided.

---

1. Have you ever worked in a group that experienced problems with groupthink? What were the problems and how should the group have dealt with these problems?

2. How do you feel when you are working in a group and the other members of the group reject a suggestion or a recommendation you make? How does your reaction to this treatment affect the way you respond to suggestions made by others in the group?

Consider This

Figure 11.3   **Some Strengths and Weaknesses Associated with the Idea of Creating an Internal Combustion Gasoline Engine**

Internal Combustion Gasoline Engine Idea

↓ Weaknesses ↓	↑ Strengths ↑
1. Exploding gasoline is dangerous. 2. Engine will get very hot. 3. Engine will make a lot of noise. 4. Engine will produce noxious fumes.	1. Exploding gas will create a powerful force. 2. More than one piston could be used. 3. Engine could be mounted on a carriage. 4. Engine power could be transferred to the wheels.

The Spectrum Approach

The **spectrum approach** focuses on the strengths of ideas to promote the development of creative ideas in groups.[15] Figure 11.4 shows the steps group members should follow when using the spectrum approach to discuss ideas presented in group discussions.

Each idea, in the view of the spectrum approach, has a spectrum that ranges from weaknesses on one end to strengths at the other end. Based on this view, each group member is encouraged to focus first on the strengths of an idea that is presented. In other words, you should first look for the idea's good points or what you like about it. If you cannot find anything you like about it, ask for the idea to be repeated and re-evaluate it. Remember, every idea has some good aspects to it. Group members sometimes find this first step difficult. They are used to looking for weaknesses and once they identify what they consider to be a major problem, they stop listening. Weaknesses of ideas should not be ignored. However, it is easier to develop creative solutions when the strengths of ideas are considered first.

After identifying an idea's strengths, you can then indicate your concerns. Next, the spectrum approach encourages you to focus again on the idea's strengths. In doing so, you should ask yourself, "How can I build upon the idea's strengths?" Here is where you and the other group members can really let your creative energies flow. It is very possible, for example, that the proposed idea will not be adopted by the group in its original form. However, by pulling out some of its good points and building on them, the idea may be modified by the group into a new *creative* solution. In its modified form, the new solution may retain the original idea's strengths but not its weaknesses. Without this approach, the original idea may have been

Each idea has strengths and weaknesses

Build upon an idea's strengths

The Steps Involved in Using the Spectrum Approach   **Figure 11.4**

1. Indicate what you like about the idea presented.
2. Express your concerns about the idea.
3. Build upon the strengths of the idea.

---

discarded, since the group members may have focused initially on its weaknesses. As a result, the new, modified, creative idea would probably never have been developed.

The following example illustrates in a simple fashion how the spectrum approach can be utilized. The Capital Manufacturing Company designs and manufactures replacement radiators and mufflers for various brands and models of automobiles. In a warehouse district near one of its manufacturing plants, the company owns two separate warehouse buildings. One building is large; the other is small. The company has improved the efficiency of its manufacturing process to the point where it no longer needs the smaller warehouse building for storing raw materials. As a result, the company eventually plans to sell the building. Recently, Capital Manufacturing purchased Valco, a local metal fabricating company. Several years ago, Valco purchased a small vacant lot next to Capital's small warehouse. Specifically, the west side of the lot borders the east side of Capital's smaller warehouse. Valco originally intended to build a small storage building on the lot, but it never did so. Eventually, part of the east side of the lot was taken by the city to widen a side street. The reduction in the lot's size means that it is no longer of a buildable size. That is, the city will no longer allow a separate, minimum-sized warehouse to be built on the vacant lot. Capital wants to sell the vacant lot it acquired through its purchase of Valco. Bud, Cal, and Deb, who are supervisors at Capital, are asked to discuss how to best dispose of the vacant lot. They use the spectrum approach to develop a creative solution.

The spectrum approach will work in many situations

Bud: I don't think the vacant lot is good for anything except a warehouse. Maybe we could build a very small specialty warehouse on it.

Cal: The city has made it clear that no freestanding warehouse of any kind will be approved for that lot. That decision includes even the smallest warehouse. You can't build a warehouse on the lot, and there is no sense in even making such a suggestion.

Deb: Wait a minute. We are supposed to be using the spectrum approach! Don't focus on the weaknesses first. Cal, what do you *like* about Bud's idea?

Cal: Well, I like the fact that a warehouse of some kind is the perfect use for the vacant lot. As a matter of fact, the city zoning for that area makes it almost impossible to build anything else there.

Deb: Ok, now what are your concerns about Bud's idea?

Cal: The city says the lot is no longer of a buildable size. That means you can't get a building permit from the city to build even a small storage building on it.

Deb: All right, now let's see if we can build on the strength. A warehouse is the best building for the vacant lot. How can we build on that strength in a way that eliminates or reduces Cal's concern?

Bud: I've got it; add on to the east side of our small warehouse. An extension of our building onto the vacant lot would not be a freestanding building. Therefore, the city would issue a building permit for the construction. The enlarged warehouse would be worth a lot more than the construction cost of the extension, and we want to sell the warehouse.

Cal: That sounds great. I never thought of using the land to get more for our small warehouse after we enlarged it.

Advantages of the Spectrum Approach

For employees working in groups to solve company problems, use of the spectrum approach can benefit the group discussion. Specific advantages of the spectrum approach are as follows.[16]

The spectrum approach requires you to listen carefully

Better Listening.   Most people have little difficulty identifying weaknesses in ideas. However, knowing that you are going to identify the strengths of an idea first, you tend to listen more carefully to what is said.

Maintenance of Self-Esteem.   When an idea is strongly criticized, the person offering the idea may feel his or her self-esteem is threatened. However, employees are less apprehensive about making suggestions when the spectrum approach is used. Therefore, it is easier to save face and maintain self-esteem when ideas are discussed in this manner.

Reduction of Defensiveness.   The spectrum approach embodies a spirit of cooperation. The manner in which group members' ideas are treated under this approach reduces defensiveness in group discussions.

Building upon Strengths.   The strengths of ideas presented are automatically identified and built upon in a manner that produces creative solutions.

Meetings

What is a meeting? A **meeting** is a group of people assembled to discuss issues in a structured setting according to an agenda. In this definition, *structured* means a leader is in charge who conducts the discussion in an orderly manner. In fact, some meetings are so structured that formal rules govern recognizing speakers and handling motions. Another key term, **agenda,** refers to a list of items or issues to be discussed in a meeting. The purpose for which a meeting is called and the agenda also structure what is discussed.

Meetings are structured

The Value of Meetings

Meetings allow people to interact, share information, and solve problems. The participants benefit from "putting their minds together." In a meeting, members can clarify and evaluate policies, goals, or expectations face-to-face. For example, it is usually easier to get agreement on a plan by bringing the interested parties together than by going to them individually. Meetings can also make it easier for you to coordinate the work of various groups. For instance, if you bring key people together, you can quickly assess each group's progress and delegate new tasks.

Meetings allow people to put their minds together

Common Meeting Problems

When people in organizations experience frustration due to ineffective meetings, they may think that many of the problems they face are unique to their situation. That is, problems in meetings are often blamed on the behavior of certain individuals, the specialized goals of the firm, or the bureaucratic structure that exists. As a result, it is tempting to believe that other organizations with different employees, goals, and bureaucratic structures do not have the same meeting problems. In reality, however, certain meeting problems commonly occur in many firms, regardless of their design. Several of these common meeting problems are discussed below.[17]

Ineffective meetings breed frustration

Getting Off the Subject. Time is often wasted in meetings when discussions get off the subject. Therefore, when a supervisor allows discussions in a meeting to get off the subject, group members get frustrated, and the wasted time can be costly to the organization.

Meeting without Goals or an Agenda. Every day, some meetings occur that are unnecessary. In some cases, these unnecessary meetings occur because the organization has a policy that "There will be a staff meeting every Monday morning." As a result, the Monday meetings occur even though there may not be a need for a meeting every Monday.

Meeting Too Long.   If a meeting is scheduled to last one hour, for example, the supervisor should develop an agenda of items that requires an hour to discuss. However, group members will resent an hour of their time being taken if the items on the agenda could easily have been addressed in half the time. Dissatisfaction will also occur if the items scheduled to be discussed in the meeting are so complex that the meeting will inevitably run overtime.

Poor or Inadequate Planning.   If you lead a meeting, those attending the meeting will expect you to be well prepared. Too often, however, individuals who lead meetings try to "wing it" without doing their homework. For example, they do not anticipate questions that will be asked in the meeting and what information they should obtain to answer the questions. They also fail to prepare and bring necessary handouts. In general, they do not give careful consideration to what will be needed in the meeting.

Inconclusive Meeting.   People attending meetings in organizations do so in the hope that the meetings will conclude with something worthwhile having been accomplished. After all, they do not want the time and effort they exert in attending a meeting to have been wasted with nothing accomplished. Too often, however, their hopes are dashed by attending meetings that are inconclusive; that is, they leave the meetings wondering what, if anything, was decided. Agreements developed in the meetings are vague and imprecise, no assignments were made, and no one seems to know who is supposed to be doing what.

Disorganized Meeting.   On the job, most individuals behave in a professional manner and take their work seriously. In a meeting, however, attitudes may become less serious and disruptive behaviors can emerge. For example, group members who would never think of interrupting a client may frequently interrupt each other in a meeting. Such behavior can harm the continuity and development of ideas presented, resulting in some ideas being lost. Poor listening can lead to false assumptions that take valuable time to straighten out, and hidden agendas can wreak havoc in any meeting. Furthermore, disorganization in a meeting breeds dissatisfaction and a lack of interest by participants.

When a Meeting Is Appropriate

Used properly, meetings can be productive. As a matter of fact, they can aid you as a supervisor in many ways. For example, meetings are especially appropriate when members will benefit from the interaction and sharing of

Subordinates expect you to be prepared for meetings

Make sure something gets accomplished in your meetings

New information can be disseminated in meetings

ideas. A meeting is often the most effective way for workers to get needed information. Meetings may also help you to gain information from workers. In addition, meetings can be invaluable when problems need to be solved or ideas must be discussed before a decision is made. In some cases, face-to-face interaction through a meeting is necessary to express feelings and explore questions thoroughly. Meetings can also be used to publicize and explain rules, policies, and goals. Furthermore, a meeting may be the best choice when viewpoints need to be reconciled or immediate feedback on new ideas is required. Last, if you need to build support for a certain goal, program, or idea, a meeting is appropriate.

Meetings allow face-to-face interaction

Preparing for a Meeting

To conduct a smooth and successful meeting, you must be prepared. The following checklist will help you plan your meetings.

Have You	Yes	No
1. Clearly determined your objectives for the meeting?	_____	_____
2. Arranged for an appropriate place for the meeting?	_____	_____
3. Checked to see if the meeting room is set up correctly?	_____	_____
4. Prepared all the necessary materials for the meeting?	_____	_____
(a) Diagrams prepared?	_____	_____
(b) Handouts prepared?	_____	_____
(c) Audiovisual material ready?	_____	_____
5. Notified participants of the time, place, and agenda for the meeting?	_____	_____
6. Decided what you wish to say when you begin the meeting?	_____	_____
7. Determined a strategy for completing all the agenda items?	_____	_____
(a) Set time limits?	_____	_____
(b) Identified priorities among the agenda items?	_____	_____
(c) Developed relevant questions to guide the discussion?	_____	_____
(d) Noted important facts or ideas to be discussed?	_____	_____
(e) Anticipated the reactions from group members to the agenda items and how to address those reactions?	_____	_____

Techniques for Conducting Effective Meetings

Many people in organizations hate to attend meetings because, as mentioned earlier, the meetings are too often poorly run and accomplish little. The use of the techniques discussed below, however, will help you conduct well organized and productive meetings.

Successful meetings don't happen by chance

Create a Seating Arrangement that Aids Communication.   Seating arrangements can affect conversation and the flow of information. Therefore, make certain that the seating arrangement in your meeting room allows people to see and hear each other easily. Also, select a meeting room that has a comfortable temperature, is free from distractions, and allows the participants to concentrate on the topics to be discussed in the meeting.

Set goals and priorities for your meetings

Have a Clear Understanding of the Meeting's Purpose.   As the person in charge of the meeting, you should prepare an agenda. *Set specific goals and priorities for achieving them.* Also, make sure these goals are realistic. Having a clear purpose before starting will give you confidence in conducting the meeting.

Make Sure the Participants Understand the Meeting's Purpose.   Those attending a meeting need to be informed of the meeting's purpose and understand the importance of the items to be discussed. Indicate that you appreciate the help of participants. Clarify issues to be discussed or decisions that must be made. Show interest and enthusiasm for the meeting and the agenda items. The group will then be more likely to respond with interest and enthusiasm.

Prepare Discussion Questions.   As will be discussed in Chapter 13, open questions do a much better job in gaining information and generating responses that are rich in content than do closed questions. Therefore, make use of open questions when conducting meetings. Also, phrase your questions in a way that makes it easy for them to be understood as you intended. Raising appropriate questions in the meeting can help keep the discussion on track and aid the group in accomplishing its objectives.

Raise appropriate questions when necessary

Follow the Agenda.   The intended purpose of the agenda you prepared is to help you achieve the goals you set for the meeting. If you have given careful thought to preparing a realistic agenda, you should be able to complete it in the time alloted for the meeting. Special circumstances may require some deviation, but those aside, stay with the agenda and request that the other members of the meeting also adhere to it.

A well-prepared agenda will help you run your meeting

Provide Relevant Background Material.   Those attending your meeting will be of the most assistance when they are well informed on the topics that are scheduled for discussion. For example, suppose the group must discuss ways to deal with new regulations imposed on your department. Before starting the discussion, clarify the regulations the group will consider. This technique assures that each member has the same facts and understanding of the issue being discussed.

Finish One Agenda Item before Going On to Another.   It is pointless to rush through an agenda just to make sure every item is addressed. If you have misjudged the amount of time necessary to cover all the items listed, you may have to schedule another meeting. This does not mean that you cannot set time limits for discussion. It just means that the relevant aspects of an issue should be addressed before moving on to another agenda item.

Don't rush through important topics

Take Notes on What Is Said.   This technique will help you to periodically summarize the discussion and remember important points afterward. In some cases, such as when the group is seeking solutions to a problem, list suggestions on a chalkboard or chart for everyone to see.

Watch Out for Miscommunication.   When leading meetings, there may be times when you sense that the group has misinterpreted a member's comments. For example, you may notice verbal reactions or nonverbal cues suggesting that miscommunication has occurred. When you believe miscommunication exists, stop the discussion and clarify what you believe the speaker meant. People usually appreciate it when you help them get their points across to the other members in the meeting.

Miscommunication is a danger in meetings

Stay Clear of Irrelevant Issues.   Sometimes, people become involved in discussing issues that are really irrelevant to the item being considered. These issues may be somewhat related to the topic, but they do not help the group understand the item at hand or arrive at decisions. If such a situation arises, stop the discussion. Point out why the issue is not germane to the topic being considered, and get the discussion back on track.

Summarize Major Points.   The discussion of an important issue may become involved and last a long time. As a result, group members may feel overwhelmed by the number of different points presented and lose their direction. When this type of overload occurs, stop the discussion and summarize the major points that have been covered. Explain the direction in which the discussion seems to be heading and point out whether the discussion is achieving what the group set out to accomplish. Also, once the group has reached a consensus on an issue or the meeting is about to end, summarize what has been discussed and agreed on in the meeting. This technique ensures that there is no confusion.

The Nominal Group Technique

As a supervisor, you may need to call a meeting to get opinions on how to deal with certain problems on the job. One procedure that can aid you in doing so is the Nominal Group Technique. Andre L. Delbecq and Andrew H. Van de Ven developed this technique as a problem-solving device in 1968.[18] The **Nominal Group Technique** (NGT) helps members interact in meetings and develop practical yet creative solutions to problems.

A problem-solving device for meetings

Conducting a Nominal Group Technique Meeting

The NGT works best in meetings of no more than nine people. If more are present, break the group up into smaller groups to promote greater interaction. In using the NGT, first develop a question for the group to work on. The question should focus on the problem you want discussed. Make the question specific. For example, "How can things in the sawmill department be improved?" is too vague. However, "How can the accident rate among the sawmill workers be reduced?" is better. After developing a question, conduct the meeting according to the following four steps.[19]

Formulate a good question for group consideration

Step 1: Generate Individual Ideas in Writing.   At first, have group members work silently by themselves. Specifically, have them write down as many answers as they can to the question posed. The individuals in the nominal group work in the presence of others but do not interact verbally during this step. Limit this activity to about five minutes.

Step 2: Record Each Member's Ideas.   You may act as recorder as well as leader for the group. Have each member give one idea at a time until all have been presented. Write the ideas on a flip chart or chalkboard so everyone can see them. There should be no discussion of the strengths or weaknesses of any of the ideas at this point. However, going from member to member for ideas, you give everyone a chance to participate. As the list grows and one idea sparks another, a number of practical yet creative solutions often arise.

Don't discuss ideas as they are recorded

Step 3: Discuss Each Idea.   After all ideas have been listed, discuss them. Taking one at a time, get members' reactions. Here, the ideas are discussed for the purpose of clarification, elaboration, and evaluation. However, no ideas are eliminated from the list. Depending on the time available, you may need to limit discussion of each idea.

Step 4: Vote on the Ideas Listed.   Of course, you will not be able to accept all the ideas the group members come up with as solutions to the question. The list must be reduced to a few for final consideration. To narrow the list, first number the ideas. Then have the group members select the five they like best and rank them in order of preference. Analyzing those ideas selected and their rank order will show members which seem most acceptable. The idea ranked the highest then becomes the recommended solution to the question you posed at the beginning of the meeting.

The Nominal Group Technique can be better than brainstorming

The NGT is a variation of the brainstorming technique used in group discussions. The nature of a brainstorming session may inhibit some group members. However, the NGT allows members to write out their ideas silently and independently in step one. Then, in step two, their ideas are presented without discussion or criticism. As a result, intimidation is less likely to occur.

That is, the NGT makes it difficult for dominant individuals to unduly influence the group, and minority opinions are less susceptible to social pressure for conformity. In addition, low-status members are less subject to being influenced by high-status members.[20] Interestingly, nominal groups have been found to be significantly superior to brainstorming groups in the number of ideas developed, the number of unique ideas created, and the quality of the ideas produced.[21]

Every day, various groups of employees meet to address important issues in organizations. Therefore, understanding group behavior and how to utilize groups effectively in organizations is a necessary aspect of the study of supervision. At this point, it is appropriate to review key issues associated with groups by reexamining the objectives established at the beginning of the chapter.

Looking Back

- ☐ **Define group.** A group is two or more people working together and satisfying needs through interaction.
- ☐ **Identify the benefits of group homogeneity.** Members of homogeneous groups generally find that they have a lot of influence on each other. They also usually find it satisfying to be members of such groups. In addition, homogeneous groups are highly productive in completing simple tasks and usually have high cooperation among members. Furthermore, sequential tasks are performed well in these groups.
- ☐ **Identify the benefits of group heterogeneity.** Groups that are heterogeneous can deal well with complex problems. Issues considered by such groups are typically examined thoroughly. In addition, the makeup of heterogeneous groups frequently helps them to be creative.
- ☐ **Identify possible benefits of group decision making.** For the purpose of solving problems, small groups have greater total knowledge and information than any individual member. Members offer different approaches for the group to consider for solving problems. In addition, group involvement in problem solving increases acceptance and comprehension of decisions.
- ☐ **Identify possible problems of group decision making.** Group members may feel social pressure from other members toward conformity. Individual domination by some group members may allow them to exert undue influence over group decision making. Too often, there is also an overemphasis on winning that causes group members to push their ideas while criticizing others' ideas. As a group, members may take greater risks in the solutions they suggest than they would when acting alone.
- ☐ **Define groupthink.** Specifically, groupthink occurs when a group avoids critically testing, analyzing, and evaluating ideas in order to minimize conflict and reach a consensus.
- ☐ **Identify remedies to groupthink.** Request that each group member be

a critical evaluator. Adopt an impartial stance when you request that a group analyze a particular problem and propose a solution. If appropriate and possible, consider having two groups work on the same problem. Have group members get the opinions of members in the departments they represent about solutions being considered by the group. Also, if appropriate and possible, have an outside person attend some of the group meetings.

☐ **Explain the risky-shift phenomenon.** This phenomenon refers to the tendency of individuals to be greater risk takers when participating in a group than when acting alone.

☐ **Explain the spectrum approach.** When using the spectrum approach in group discussions, you should first indicate what you like about the idea presented. Next, express your concerns about the idea. Last, build upon the strengths of the idea.

☐ **Indicate the advantages of the spectrum approach.** As a result of using the spectrum approach, you are likely to listen carefully to what is said. This approach also helps group members maintain self-esteem and it reduces defensiveness. In addition, the spectrum approach allows the strengths of ideas to be built upon.

☐ **Identify techniques for conducting effective meetings.** When you conduct a meeting, create a seating arrangement that enhances communication and interaction within the group. You must have a clear understanding of what you are trying to accomplish. Make sure the participants understand the purpose of the meeting, too. Have discussion questions prepared to help guide it. In addition, follow the agenda you have prepared and provide relevant background material on each item being discussed. Finish discussing one agenda item before going on to another. Also, take notes on what is said, watch out for miscommunication, stay clear of irrelevant issues, and summarize major points.

Key Terms

agenda	meeting
group	Nominal Group Technique
groupthink	risky-shift phenomenon
heterogeneous	spectrum approach
homogeneous	

Review and Discussion Questions

1. Why is it important for you to make sure your group members see a need for the group?

2. Why do heterogeneous groups have an advantage over homogeneous groups in solving complex problems?

3. Why do groups often develop better solutions to problems than individuals working alone?

4. Why is it often easier to get group decisions accepted and implemented in organizations than decisions handed down by one person?

5. To what does the concept of groupthink refer?

6. Why does groupthink sometimes occur in groups?

7. To what does the concept of the risky-shift phenomenon refer?

8. Why is it best to focus first on the strengths of an idea suggested in a group?

9. When is it appropriate to summarize major points in a meeting?

10. Why shouldn't ideas presented in step two of the Nominal Group Technique be evaluated at that stage?

Action Incident 11.1

The Loner

The company where Tom works was recently purchased by a few successful businessmen. The previous owners of the company showed little interest in receiving upward communication from the employees. The new owners, however, believed the company would benefit by soliciting ideas from employees, and they immediately began to encourage upward communication in the company.

Specifically, the new owners requested that employees suggest ways to improve efficiency and reduce costs in each department. As supervisor of one department, Tom does not like to work in groups. He believes he is most productive when he works alone. Tom is fond of saying, "The only type of group I want to work in is a group of one!" Therefore, Tom decided he would work alone in creating ideas for improving efficiency and reducing costs. However, to meet the new owners' request, he also formed a small group of employees in the department and asked them to prepare their own list of ideas.

After Tom completed his list, he gazed upon it with much pride and satisfaction. He thought his experience and position as supervisor gave him an advantage in suggesting a lot of good ideas. He was also pleased that the new owners were interested in receiving upward communication.

Soon after completing his list, Tom received the list of ideas prepared by the group of employees. He considered it unlikely that their list would be as comprehensive or contain as many good ideas as his list. To his amazement, Tom quickly noticed that the list of ideas prepared by the group was superior to his. As a matter of fact, he was very impressed with the quality of ideas developed by the group. He thought he had an advantage in being able to work alone and concentrate on being creative. In frustration, Tom mumbled to himself, "How could they do so well working as a group?"

Discussion Questions

1. Why does Tom prefer not to work in a group to solve company problems?
2. Why was Tom incorrect to expect that the group's list of ideas would be inferior to his list?
3. What should Tom learn from this experience?

Action Incident 11.2

The Pessimistic Group

The Allied Roofing Material Supply Company sells roofing materials to roofing contractors throughout the state in which it is located. The company manufactures some of the roofing materials it sells, and it stores large quantities of just about every supply or material roofing contractors purchase. Recently, the company has been plagued with the theft of materials at one of its regional locations which doubles as a warehouse and retail store operation.

The owner of the company, John Parker, asked the regional store manager, Dale Noble, to discuss the theft problem with a group of staff members at the store. Dale decided to include such a discussion at the end of the next staff meeting he scheduled. The dialogue of that segment of the meeting follows.

Dale: As you know, Mr. Parker wants us to come up with some suggestions for eliminating or reducing the theft problem we have been experiencing. Does anybody have any ideas?

Fred: I think we could reduce a lot of the thefts by installing more floodlights.

Carl: We have lights now and that hasn't stopped the thieves. Determined thieves will just break out the lights.

Jane: Maybe we could unleash a guard dog in the warehouse area at night.

Bill: There are big problems with a guard dog. What if it bites the wrong person? The company could be exposed to a major lawsuit.

Saul: An easy thing to do would be to put larger padlocks on the gates leading into the storage areas.

Beth: Bigger locks won't work. The last thief must have had training as a locksmith because the lock was picked, not broken open.

Jane: Maybe we could get a security guard.

Carl: Security guards are expensive. There must be a cheaper way to deal with the problem.

Fred: We could put in an electronic security system that would sound an alarm if the system was violated.

Bill: Electronic security systems are notorious for false alarms. Do you want to come down here at 3 in the morning to turn the alarm off?

Dale: It doesn't look like we are getting very far today. Let's put the discussion on hold until we meet again next week. Maybe we can come up with some better ideas then.

When Dale reported back to Mr. Parker later that day, he indicated that the group was still working on ways to deal with the theft problem. In frustration, Dale said, "Maybe a group discussion is a bad way to generate good ideas for solving this problem."

Discussion Questions

1. Do you agree with Dale's assessment that a group discussion is probably a bad way to deal with the problem? Explain.
2. What is the main problem the group is experiencing?
3. How should the group attempt to resolve the problem?

Action Incident 11.3

A Group Effort

Leslie manages a large furniture store in a major metropolitan area. In addition to selling furniture for homes, her store also sells carpet, tile, drapes, and office furniture. She must decide soon what items she will order to replenish her dwindling stocks. Knowing that Leslie will be placing large orders, sales representatives from many manufacturers have left her samples and literature promoting their merchandise.

Leslie has decided to meet with a small group of her employees to discuss what types and styles of merchandise should be purchased. She has decided to include in this group only staff members with whom she gets along well. In describing the group, Leslie says, "We all think alike." Referring to the group, another member says, "We trust each other. Sometimes I have concerns about a strategic plan that is developed by the group. However, if the other members favor the idea, I figure it must be okay, so I don't raise any objections." Consider the following group discussion as Leslie begins the meeting.

Leslie: As you know, we need to add a new line of carpeting. I'm sure all of you have had a chance to look at the carpet samples we received. I think we should go with the carpet produced by the Olson Mills, but I am interested in your opinions. What do you think?

George: I also like that carpet. The price on it isn't as competitive as some of the other carpets, but I think we will do fine with it.

Steven: An article I read in the newspaper the other day indicated that Olson Mills is experiencing financial problems. I don't think we should rely upon them.

Andrew: You don't know for certain that they are having problems. You can't believe everything you read in the newspaper!

Leslie: I don't know of any store that has had trouble receiving carpet from Olson Mills. Let's not look for problems where none exist yet.

Andrew: If we avoided doing business with every manufacturer that experienced an economic downturn, there wouldn't be anyone to buy from. *(Everyone laughs)* I also like the carpet samples by Olson.

Leslie: Then are we in agreement that Olson Mills will supply our new line of carpeting? *(Pause)* Hearing no objections I'll place the order with them. I appreciate your input.

Discussion Questions

1. Why do you think Leslie really met with the small, select group of employees?
2. To what extent did the group experience groupthink?
3. What should Leslie have done to protect the group from experiencing groupthink?

Notes

1. Marvin E. Shaw, *Group Dynamics: The Psychology of Small Group Behavior,* 3d ed. (New York: McGraw-Hill, 1981), p. 255.
2. Bernard M. Bass and Edward C. Ryterband, *Organizational Psychology,* 2d ed. (Boston: Allyn & Bacon, 1979), pp. 260–62.
3. Peggy Leatt and Rodney Schneck, "Criteria for Grouping Nursing Subunits in Hospitals," *Academy of Management Journal* 27 (March 1984), pp. 150–65.
4. Bass and Ryterband, *Organizational Psychology,* pp. 262–64.
5. Norman R. F. Maier, "Assets and Liabilities in Group Problem Solving: The Need for an Integrative Function," *Psychological Review* 74 (July 1967), pp. 239–41.
6. Maier, "Assets and Liabilities in Group Problem Solving," pp. 241–42.
7. Steven A. Beebe and John T. Masterson, *Communicating in Small Groups: Principles and Practices* (Glenview, Ill.: Scott, Foresman, 1982), p. 168.
8. Irving L. Janis, "Groupthink," *Psychology Today* 5 (November 1971), pp. 43–46, 74–76.
9. Janis, "Groupthink," p. 76.
10. Russell D. Clark III, "Group-Induced Shift Toward Risk: A Critical Appraisal," *Psychological Bulletin* 76 (October 1971), p. 251.
11. Clark, "Group-Induced Shift Toward Risk," pp. 253–61.
12. Richard Beckhard, "Optimizing Team-Building Efforts," *Journal of Contemporary Business* (Summer 1972), pp. 23–27, 30–32.
13. Gary Johns, *Organizational Behavior: Understanding Life at Work,* 2d ed. (Glenview, Ill.: Scott, Foresman, 1988), pp. 592–93.
14. George M. Prince, *The Practice of Creativity* (New York: Collier Books, 1976), p. 4.
15. Adapted from George M. Prince, *The Practice of Creativity* (New York: Collier Books, 1976).
16. Prince, *The Practice of Creativity.*
17. Roger K. Mosvick and Robert B. Nelson, *We've Got to Start Meeting Like This!* (Glenview, Ill.: Scott, Foresman, 1987), pp. 151–65.
18. Andre L. Delbecq, Andrew H. Van de Ven, and David H. Gustafson, *Group Techniques for Program Planning: A Guide to Nominal Group and Delphi Processes* (Glenview, Ill.: Scott, Foresman, 1975), p. 7.
19. Delbecq, Van de Ven, and Gustafson, *Group Techniques for Program Planning,* pp. 44–61.

20. David L. Ford, Jr., and Paul M. Nemiroff, "Applied Group Problem-Solving: The Nominal Group Technique," in *The 1975 Annual Handbook for Group Facilitators* (La Jolla, Calif.: University Associates, 1975), pp. 179–82.

21. Thomas Bouchard, Jr. and Melana Hare, "Size, Performance, and Potential in Brainstorming Groups," *Journal of Applied Psychology* 54 (February 1970), pp. 51–55.; Marvin Dunnette, John Campbell, and Kay Jaastad, "The Effect of Group Participation on Brainstorming Effectiveness for Two Industrial Samples," *Journal of Applied Psychology* 47 (February 1963), pp. 30–37.

Suggested Readings

Beebe, Steven A., and John T. Masterson. *Communicating in Small Groups: Principles and Practices.* Glenview, Ill.: Scott, Foresman, 1982.

Blake, Robert R., and Jane Srygley Mouton. "Don't Let Group Norms Stifle Creativity." *Personnel* 62, August 1985, pp. 28–33.

Cartwright, Dorwin. "Risk Taking by Individuals and Groups: An Assessment of Research Employing Choice Dilemmas." *Journal of Personality and Social Psychology* 20, December 1971, pp. 361–78.

Clark, Russel D., III. "Group-Induced Shift Toward Risk: A Critical Appraisal." *Psychological Bulletin* 76, October 1971, pp. 251–70.

Delbecq, Andre L., Andre H. Van de Ven, and David H. Gustafson. *Group Techniques for Planning: A Guide to Nominal Group and Delphi Processes.* Glenview, Ill.: Scott, Foresman, 1975.

Janis, Irving L. "Groupthink." *Psychology Today* 5, November 1971, pp. 43–46, 74–76.

Mosvick, Roger K., and Robert B. Nelson. *We've Got to Start Meeting Like This!* Glenview, Ill.: Scott, Foresman, 1987.

Raudsepp, Eugene. "How to Make the Most of Meetings." *Supervision* 45, February 1983, pp. 6–8.

Wilkinson, Roderick. "Should You Run a Meeting—or Forget It?" *Supervision* 50, October 1989, pp. 9–11.

Part IV

Developing an Effective Work Environment

▼

Motivation

Chapter

12

Learning Objectives

Why do some people promptly complete assignments while others do not? What stimulates employees to high productivity? How can top performance be encouraged? As they deal with motivation, supervisors seek answers to these questions.

This chapter discusses several theories and explores the nature of motivation. You will learn how to encourage employees to work toward satisfying personal and company needs. You will also consider how communication aids motivation. The following objectives will assist you.

1. Understand the concept of motivation.
2. Explain several commonly recognized theories of motivation.
3. Discuss Theory Z management principles.
4. Examine quality circles and how they function.
5. Explore the relationship between effective communication and motivation.

Motivation: A Crucial Concern

Motivation is vital to top performance. People are motivated in different ways and have varying degrees of tolerance for frustration. One person will be happy doing structured, routine work, while another will be totally unhappy with such a job. He or she may like to do a variety of tasks in an unstructured work atmosphere.

Motivation is complex

The topic of motivation is complex. It includes factors such as job content, satisfaction of worker needs, and emotions that affect performance. Workers spend half or more of their waking hours on the job. If company and employee goals correspond, the ideal motivational opportunity exists. This situation does not always prevail, though, and you must work to tap your employees' potential.

Understanding Motivation

Understanding human behavior is seldom an easy task. A certain goal may be perfectly logical and worth seeking to one person but illogical and meaningless to another.

Motivation is an internal process through which needs and desires are satisfied. Needs, desires, drives, motives, and goals all influence motivation. Figure 12.1 illustrates the relationships among these and barriers to goal attainment.

Motivation is an internal process

Relationships among Needs, Drives, and Goals

Figure 12.1

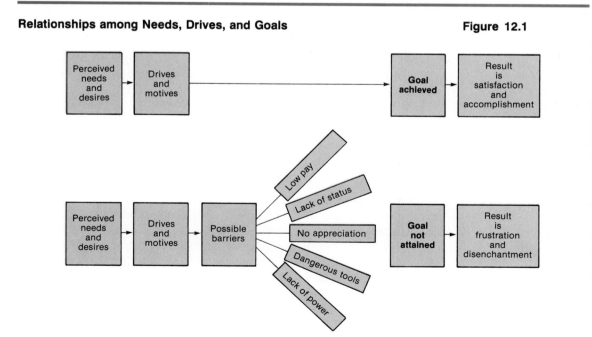

Motivation—Forty Years Later

In 1946, a sample of industrial workers was asked to rank 10 "job reward" factors. A similar survey was repeated in 1986. Results of the two studies are listed below.

1946	**1986**
1. Full appreciation of work done	1. Interesting work
2. Feeling of being in on things	2. Full appreciation of work done
3. Sympathetic help with personal problems	3. Feeling of being in on things
4. Job security	4. Job security
5. Good wages	5. Good wages
6. Interesting work	6. Promotion and growth in organization
7. Promotion and growth in organization	7. Good working conditions
8. Personal loyalty to employees	8. Personal loyalty to employees
9. Good working conditions	9. Tactful discipline
10. Tactful discipline	10. Sympathetic help with personal problems

Source: Kenneth A. Kovach, "What Motivates Employees? Workers and Supervisors Give Different Answers," *Business Horizons* 30 (September–October 1987), p. 59.

Firms must be competitive

To survive and prosper, firms must serve customer needs and be profitable. Consequently, they are vitally concerned with being competitive and getting the maximum efficiency from human and equipment resources. Concerns of workers may not coincide with those of employers. People work for many reasons, including their own need to survive and attain a desired standard of living. Today's labor force is increasingly well educated, demonstrates more loyalty to professions than to employers, and evidences concern for attaining personal objectives.[1] The baby-boom generation— those between the ages of 20 and 39—places considerable importance on autonomy, individual achievement, and the importance of being challenged.[2]

Differences among Workers

You will work with persons who have different experiential backgrounds, job expectations, and career goals. It is necessary to understand some of the factors that motivate your employees. This requires keeping channels of communication open and determining workers' priorities as well as interests.

People are different

It means providing opportunities for employees to show their abilities and be recognized. Do not assume that what motivates you also motivates your subordinates. Money rewards and chances for career advancement are major incentives to some people. Challenging assignments, freedom to pace themselves on the job, and short working hours appeal to others.

Are supervisors generally aware of what motivates workers? Table 12.1 shows results from a survey of 75 supervisors and 100 employees. Notice the

Comparison of Supervisor and Employee Rankings on Various Motivators   Table 12.1

Personal Motivator	Employees' Rating		Supervisors' Rating	
	Rank	Percentage Selecting	Rank	Percentage Selecting
1. Rating on your next performance appraisal.	9	49%	9	59%
2. Possibility of an award.	16/17	32	14	37
3. Personal work-related goals.	4	83	5	72
4. Good physical working conditions.	15	34	15	33
5. Feelings of loyalty and friendship for your supervisor.	18	18	16	31
6. Doing interesting work.	5	78	8	60
7. Possibility of higher salary.	8	51	13	41
8. Not wanting to let the group down.	13	38	10	53
9. Recognition by your peers.	12	40	2/3	79
10. The possibility of promotion.	6	71	4	73
11. Feelings of achievement from doing challenging work well.	1	96	6	69
12. The possibility of disciplinary action by your supervisor.	20	3	17	23
13. Being part of a team.	16/17	32	11	52
14. Inner need to always try to do a good job.	2	94	7	68
15. Strong job security.	14	36	18	20
16. Appreciation and recognition from your supervisor.	10	42	2/3	79
17. Doing work you feel is important.	3	88	1	81
18. Desire to help the agency attain its goals.	7	57	20	7
19. The possibility of increased freedom on the job.	11	41	12	48
20. Being appointed the leader of a work group.	19	10	19	11

The results indicate that "achievement" is a primary motivator of subordinates. While underrating the "achievement" motive, supervisors overrate the "recognition" motive.

Source: Richard E. Wasiniak, "Employees, Supervisors Don't Agree: What Really Motivates Workers?" *Management* 1 (Summer 1980), p. 17. Reprinted with permission of the author.

difference between what supervisors thought to be motivators and those workers rate as highest. High ratings for "feelings of achievement from doing challenging work well" and "your inner need to always try to do a good job" suggest that workers consider achievement an important motivator. However, supervisors gave high ranking to "recognition by your peers" and "appreciation and recognition from your supervisors." Both are recognition-oriented factors. In a 1986 survey of 1,000 industrial workers and 100 supervisors, employees ranked "interesting work," "full appreciation of work done," and "feeling of being in on things" as the top three motivators. Yet supervisors ranked them fifth, eighth, and tenth, respectively. The researcher

Employee motivators are not recognized

concluded that "supervisors have a very inaccurate perception of what motivates employees."[3]

You must recognize that the same motivational factors may not predominate thoughout an employee's life. A person might be motivated to seek employment because of a need for income. Later, he or she ceases to exert effort because the job becomes boring, personality differences with a boss become apparent, or family-related activities take precedence. Recognizing such changes is a vital factor in encouraging good job performance.

Attitudes and Behavior

What attitudes and behaviors motivate you? Are you motivated by people who display an attitude of superiority, who delight in telling you your opinions are all wrong, or who are negative about almost everything? Such attitudes discourage motivation and create a negative atmosphere in which productivity is likely to decline.

> Managers need to find ways to build into the daily life of the organization more of the zesty, exhilarating spirit that characterizes crisis situations. If they do it in the right way, they can capture more of the readiness, willingness, and ability of their people to achieve better results.[4]

To encourage motivation in employees, display concern for them. Recognize their accomplishments and have realistic expectations. Workers react positively and enthusiastically to supervisors who are receptive to ideas or suggestions and who respond to questions or needs. Subordinates want to be kept informed about issues affecting their jobs and are interested in being involved in the decision-making process. Strive to develop a positive work environment and show a personal interest in events important to employees.

Another key factor is the concept of **leveling,** which means being open, honest, and sincere in communication with workers.[5] Leveling lets workers know where they stand, makes expectations clear, and removes doubts and misunderstandings. The concept does not mean overlooking poor performance. It recognizes the importance of earning trust, acknowledging good work, and administering constructive criticism. This technique reduces fears, many of which may be unfounded. It provides a supportive environment where people can concentrate on productivity and goal achievement.

Attitudes and behaviors form the basis from which workers perceive supervisors. There is an old saying: "Actions speak louder than words." As a supervisor, you must give more than lip service to obtain results. If your words and actions do not match, employees will consider your efforts insincere and manipulative. Also, do not give employees "mixed signals," which create confusion and anxiety. For example, you assign a work project and tell the subordinate, "You are in charge; I'm depending on you." However, authority for making necessary decisions is not granted. The employee faces a difficult

Supervisors can motivate

Level with subordinates

Words and actions may differ

Motivational Sabotage   **Figure 12.2**

Constraint 1: A supervisory attitude that tells an employee that he or she is much more capable than they are.

Constraint 2: An organizational belief about increasing performance that makes employees feel they are on a treadmill.

Constraint 3: Supervisory behavior that is influenced by the supervisor's view of the nature of mankind and personal biases and prejudices.

Constraint 4: Rules and practices within the organization that compartmentalize employees and are seen by them as demeaning.

Source: Excerpted from John Nirenberg, "Constraints to Effective Motivation," *Supervisory Management* 26 (November 1981), p. 27. © 1981 by AMACOM, a division of American Management Associations, New York. All rights reserved. Reprinted with permission of the publisher.

situation and will soon discover that he or she is not really in charge. Figure 12.2 summarizes constraints that can sabotage motivation.

Motivation Theories

What motivates people? Over the years, researchers have sought answers to this question. Theories have emphasized such concerns as need satisfaction, the structure of jobs themselves, and reward achievement. Abraham Maslow examined the role of need satisfaction. Frederick Herzberg focused on the work environment and the nature of jobs themselves. Victor Vroom investigated how motivation is influenced by achievement expectations and the value of rewards. Douglas McGregor, known for Theory X and Theory Y, recognized the importance of assumptions in motivating performance. Reinforcement theory focused on the use of reinforcers to encourage or extinguish certain behaviors. Now let's examine each of these widely accepted theories.

Are you motivated?

Maslow's Hierarchy of Needs

Abraham H. Maslow based a theory of motivation on a hierarchy of needs.[6] He divided human needs into the five levels shown in Figure 12.3. The basic needs for food, clothing, and shelter are **survival needs.** Once these are satisfied, **safety needs**—the desire to avoid physical harm or economic misfortune—come into play. The third level, **social needs,** involves the desire for acceptance by others and may be fulfilled by developing personal and group relationships. **Esteem needs** are satisfied by gaining self-respect and respect from other people. The highest rung on the hierarchy, **self-actualization,** evolves from an aspiration for development to your maximum potential.

Five levels of human needs

How does Maslow's hierarchy apply in practice? Assume you got lost on a hiking trip, spent two days in the wilderness, and have just been found. What

Figure 12.3   **Maslow's Hierarchy of Needs**

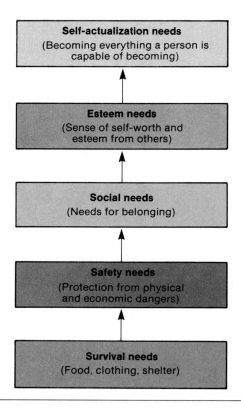

needs do you want to satisfy — social, esteem, or self-actualization? It is likely that none of these is motivational because you are cold, hungry, and thirsty. Compare this situation to an employee working at a job. Does he or she have predominant needs for survival and safety? No. The worker is more likely motivated to satisfy social and esteem needs. The major point is: Successful motivational efforts are directed toward unsatisfied, rather than satisfied, needs.

Emphasize incentives

The process of fulfilling needs varies among individuals. You can learn a lot by observing workers' behaviors. Whenever possible, emphasize incentives that are meaningful. For example, an employee who always wants to work overtime might place a greater value on money rewards than does a person who refuses to work beyond minimum hours. Under Maslow's hierarchy, more than one need level can motivate at the same time. An employee can want to be admired by peers (a social need) and also seek personal recognition (an esteem need).

Examples of Hygiene and Motivator Factors   **Figure 12.4**

Sources of Job Satisfaction — Motivator Factors	Sources of Job Dissatisfaction — Hygiene Factors
Job advancement	Salary
Additional responsibility	Supervisors
Achievement	Company policies
Nature of work itself	Working conditions
Recognition	Interpersonal relations

Herzberg's Two-Factor Theory

Frederick Herzberg looked at motivation from the perspective of job environments and jobs themselves.[7] His research indicated that factors such as company policies, salary, quality of supervision, interpersonal relations, and working conditions related to job dissatisfaction — not to motivation. He labeled these variable **hygiene factors.** According to Herzberg, work itself, achievement, more responsibility, advancement, and recognition are sources of job satisfaction. He called them **motivators.** Figure 12.4 groups factors as either hygiene (job dissatisfiers) or motivators (job satisfiers). Many supervisors focus attention on hygiene factors without sufficient regard for the potential of motivators to encourage greater employee efforts.

What really motivates people?

An important conclusion from Herzberg's work is that positive hygiene factors — good salary, adequate supervision, and good working conditions — will not by themselves produce motivation. Employee attitudes toward the work environment (hygiene factors) may create unpleasant feelings about jobs they perform. These dampen motivation, and job performance suffers.

Herzberg's motivational factors are like Maslow's esteem needs. In understanding what motivates workers to produce more effectively, an important point becomes clear. Attention and emphasis must be directed toward factors workers themselves consider relevant. In other words, managers who stress hygiene factors may not realize that these alone will not stimulate workers to be more motivated and hence more productive. Even though supervisors are limited in their ability to improve many workplace conditions, they can be motivators by recognizing excellent job performance, preparing subordinates for promotion, and delegating meaningful responsibilities.

Workers determine what motivates

Vroom's Expectancy Theory

The essence of expectancy theory is that people are motivated if they believe their efforts will be rewarded and if they value the reward offered.[8] According to Vroom, the amount of effort exerted depends on two factors — expectancy

Expectations and values affect efforts

and valence. **Expectancy** means the likelihood of being successful. **Valence** is perception of the value attached to an expected reward for the effort put forth.

Workers exert their best efforts when they believe tasks can reasonably be done and where the payoff is meaningful to them. Assume you are working in an office and the copier breaks down. Your boss wants to have some important papers copied and says, "I'd be willing to give $50 to get this thing working in the next hour." Are you motivated by this seemingly generous offer?

If you can do the repair job and value the reward, you'll likely be motivated and eager to get started, but even if you have the know-how, the reward possesses little value if you do not have a strong need for $50. You will not be motivated to exert effort and fix the machine, especially if the boss does not know you can fix it. If you do not know how, you cannot perform, even though you place high value on the money.

Motivation depends on a worker's perception of both the amount of effort needed and the value of the reward. Supervisors should not assume their valuation of a reward is the same as that of a subordinate. Figure 12.5 illustrates relationships among employee perceptions, motivated performance, and satisfied expectations. It is essential to understand this process of fulfilling expectations. Workers need to know how performance relates to attainment of desired rewards.

McGregor's Theory

Douglas McGregor is known for Theory X and Theory Y. Both involve assumptions about human behavior.[9] According to **Theory X,** which reflects the traditional approach to management, these assumptions are:

Theory X stresses management by control

- ☐ People do not like to work.
- ☐ Workers are not ambitious. They must be directed and controlled.
- ☐ People do not want to assume responsibilities. They work mainly for money and highly value security.

Managers who practice this theory use coercion, control, and threats of punishment to assure tasks are properly and promptly completed. They do not provide opportunities for employees to express views or make suggestions. As you can see, the approach is autocratic and based on the premise that managers know what is best. **Theory Y** makes a different set of assumptions:

Theory Y recognizes human initiative

- ☐ People enjoy work. It is a natural activity.
- ☐ Workers are ambitious, self-directed, and demonstrate self-control.
- ☐ People are willing to assume responsibilities. They get much satisfaction from work and are willing to accept challenge.

The Theory Y approach is more democratic and not focused on controlling worker behavior. It involves delegation of duties, less emphasis on

Vroom's Expectancy Theory   **Figure 12.5**

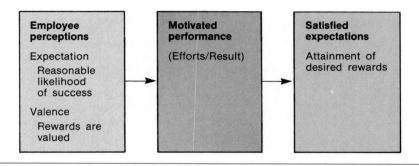

close supervision, and greater employee involvement in job-related concerns. Despite its apparent potential to motivate, validity of the theory is difficult to determine. "While Theory Y sounds good and appeals to the more humanistic preferences held by many of us in our relationships with others, we are espousing a philosophy rather than supporting our beliefs with evidence from research."[10]

What do these differences imply about motivation? Simply that your attitudes and assumptions are important in influencing results. When you assume workers are lazy, when you expect little beyond minimal efforts, and when you overcontrol employees, do not be surprised to see your assumptions realized. Supervisors must recognize the favorable factors that will motivate workers and ensure they exist.

Attitudes and assumptions influence behavior

Figure 12.6 compares the communication behaviors of a Theory X and a Theory Y supervisor. Notice differences in the flow of communication and extent of openness. Theory X communication is more restricted. It concentrates on "necessary" data with a one-way flow. The Theory Y pattern is interactive, involving a two-way exchange of information. Which type of supervisor is likely to have greater employee interest and enthusiasm and a more productive work atmosphere? Most likely, one who follows Theory Y has the most productive work team. This is because employee involvement is more likely to bring greater cooperation, a greater degree of trust, and more sincerity in working relationships.

Theory X and Theory Y practices differ

Reinforcement Theory

Reinforcement theory, which is sometimes referred to as operant conditioning, focuses attention on the consequences of behavior. If a behavior leads to desired or pleasurable results, it is likely to be repeated, but whenever negative consequences occur, it will not be repeated. According to this theory, people learn from previous experiences and consequently behave

Rewarded behaviors will be repeated

Figure 12.6

Communication Behaviors: Theory X and Theory Y Supervisors

Theory X Behaviors	Theory Y Behaviors
1. Messages flow downward.	1. Messages flow up, down, and across the organization.
2. Upward communication is restricted to suggestion boxes, grapevines, and spy systems.	2. Feedback is encouraged; no supplemental upward communication system is necessary.
3. Little interaction with employees.	3. Frequent interactions produce an atmosphere of confidence and trust.
4. Downward communication consists of informative memos and an-	4. Downward communication is usually adequate for satisfaction of needs.

Source: Adapted from Gerald M. Goldhaber, *Organizational Communication*, 3d ed. (Dubuque, Iowa: Wm. C. Brown Publishers, © 1974, 1979, 1983), pp. 84–86.

accordingly. Assume you believe that your boss has fewer hassles and is a more receptive listener during the early hours of the workday. When will you schedule an appointment to discuss a budget request? Obviously, it will be during the time period in which you are most likely to get the request approved. Should you be successful, your behavior is reinforced, and future meetings will be scheduled for the same time period.

How is behavior reinforced?

This theory recognizes four methods of reinforcement—positive, negative, extinction, and punishment.[11]

☐ *Positive reinforcement.* Positive rewards are given to acknowledge demonstration of preferred behaviors. (Example: You praise a subordinate who completes an assignment much quicker than anticipated.)
☐ *Negative reinforcement.* This method of reinforcement involves avoiding unpleasant outcomes. (Example: When a job is done properly, you quit nagging at an employee.)
☐ *Extinction.* Through extinction, rewards are withdrawn to discourage repetition of behaviors. (Example: An individual sends you several memos, but no response is returned. The sender's efforts to continue writing them will likely soon diminish.)
☐ *Punishment.* When a penalty is imposed, the frequency of an undesired behavior declines. (Example: An employee who is over five minutes late to work incurs a pay deduction for one fourth of an hour.)

Positive reinforcers work best where a close link exists between performance and corresponding rewards. A difficulty with negative reinforcement is that it may not motivate performance above the threshold necessary to avoid undesired consequences. Punishment offers the potential for a temporary remedy to change unacceptable behavior, but it often generates hostility and anger, which may outweigh the benefits gained.[12]

   Reinforcers can be applied in either a continuous or partial manner. With a *continuous* schedule, each correct response is reinforced. A more common approach is to apply the concept of *partial* reinforcement, which does not reward every correct behavior. There are four types of partial reinforcement schedules.[13]

□ *Fixed interval.* With this schedule, reinforcers are administered at specific intervals of time. The reward of a set salary per week or month illustrates an application of the fixed-interval approach.

□ *Variable interval.* Reinforcers are given over irregular intervals of time, and workers do not know when the reinforcer will occur. Assume you manage employees at several locations and tell them of your intention to visit each work unit periodically. It is impossible for the subordinates to know exactly when you will arrive. While this method does encourage performance, there is a possibility that it will decline immediately after the visit.

□ *Fixed ratio.* Reinforcement is offered after a predetermined number of correct responses. A worker might be rewarded for every 15 units produced without defects. This schedule encourages a steady rate of performance, but desired behaviors can decline quickly after reinforcers are withdrawn.[14]

□ *Variable ratio.* With variable ratio reinforcement, a random number of correct responses must be given before recognition is received. An employee does not know how often to expect reinforcement. Praise might be given after 8 units are finished but not be given again until 17 more are assembled. "Variable ratio schedules tend to produce a very high rate of response that is vigorous, steady, and resistant to extinction."[15]

   Successful use of reinforcement theory requires consideration of each circumstance and the nature of human behavior. Figure 12.7 illustrates four alternatives to improve an absenteeism problem. Judgment must be exercised to determine which reinforcer, or combination of reinforcers, is most likely to produce optimal outcomes. You can use positive or negative reinforcement to encourage desired behavior or extinction and punishment to discourage undesired behavior. "Application of reinforcement theory suggests that the most efficient combination of reinforcers involves extinction and positive reinforcement."[16]

It's impractical to reinforce all correct behaviors

▼

Consider This

1. Why do many supervisors fail to recognize factors that employees consider motivational?
2. Which theory of motivation has the most potential to motivate today's workers?
3. Why do motivational needs of employees differ?

Figure 12.7   **Example of Reinforcement Theory on the Job**

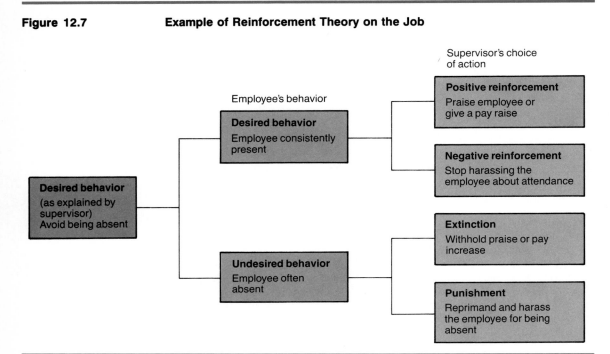

Source: W. Alan Randolph and Richard S. Blackburn, *Managing Organizational Behavior* (Homewood, Ill.: Richard D. Irwin, 1989), p. 103. Used with permission of the publisher.

Perspectives on Motivation

How do some people get so much accomplished? Why are some supervisors so adept at handling people? Despite obstacles, what makes some individuals so persistent and dedicated to getting things done? These questions are asked repeatedly about highly motivated people. Consider the four Cs of motivation, which characterize achievement-oriented persons. *Confidence* involves being sure of abilities to handle job-related demands. *Competence* refers to possession of knowledge of how to carry out assignments. *Commitment* means dedication to completion of necessary work demands. Finally, *challenge* is the willingness to accept and devote effort to finishing new or different tasks.

The four Cs of motivation are very relevant

Motivating Yourself and Others

If you are not motivated, you cannot motivate others. Supervisors must understand themselves. Some people find that they really do not enjoy supervision, while others view it as a step on the way to higher management. Still others consider being a supervisor the greatest thing in their lives.

Ten Commandments of Human Relations   **Figure 12.8**

1. Speak to people. There is nothing as nice as a cheerful word of greeting.
2. Smile at people. It takes seventy-two muscles to frown, only fourteen to smile.
3. Call people by name. The sweetest music to anyone's ear is the sound of his or her own name.
4. Be friendly and helpful. If you want to have friends, be a friend.
5. Be cordial. Speak and act as if everything you do is a genuine pleasure.
6. Be genuinely interested in people. You can like almost everybody if you try.
7. Be generous with praise and cautious with criticism.
8. Be considerate of the feelings of others. There are usually three sides to a controversy: your side, the other fellow's side, and the right side.
9. Be alert to giving service. What counts most in life is what we do for others.
10. Add to this a good sense of humor, a big dose of patience, and a dash of humility, and you will be rewarded many times.

Source: Paul Preston and Thomas W. Zimmerer, *Management for Supervisors*, 2d ed. (Englewood Cliffs, N.J.: Prentice-Hall, Inc., © 1983), p. 133. Reprinted by permission of the publisher.

Self-understanding involves recognizing goals, expectations, and aspirations. Your inner satisfaction comes from a variety of personal and professional concerns — feelings of a job well done, chances for advancement, recognition, and money rewards. These are the same things that motivate workers. Before you attempt to motivate them, consider your own level of motivation.

Understand yourself and others

You must understand your employees. Many workers infrequently express motivational needs. They do not always recognize or acknowledge what motivates them, so it is not surprising that you may not always recognize, or respond to, their needs.

How can you develop a climate for motivation? Human relations skills are important in motivating others. The Ten Commandments of Human Relations are presented in Figure 12.8. Notice that each of these carries an appeal for caring, which is a key to development of mutual trust and respect. A positive work environment, good working conditions, and pride in the company are worthy of consideration in approaching, motivating, and understanding workers.[17] Employees appreciate and generally respond favorably to supervisors who:

Practice effective human relations

- ☐ Actively listen to them.
- ☐ Promptly recognize their achievements.
- ☐ Provide, whenever possible, incentives and valued rewards.
- ☐ Remedy annoyances before they become problems.
- ☐ Support workers by inquiring how to improve their jobs.

Understanding how to motivate others involves being receptive to their perceptions and concerns. You will encounter workers who are difficult to handle, who are absent too often, and who disregard rules. There are others with various types of personal difficulties. You cannot overlook these problems, which seldom disappear, usually get worse, and may give rise to undesirable behaviors. You must learn to consider appropriate responses for each special situation that arises. The objectives are to correct deviant behavior, prevent future problems, and get workers to perform in a capable manner. Most supervisors are not trained counselors. Such things as alcohol, drug, or emotional problems should be referred to professionals for proper treatment. However, several strategies are useful in handling incidences of subordinate misconduct.

Be certain that rules and policies are understood. In some instances, an employee really may not be aware of infractions. Have specific facts available. Accusations should be justifiable, not based on hearsay or rumor. Documentation is essential. Provide an opportunity for the employee's side of the story to be heard. Explain why the infraction must not recur. For example, some workers may not perceive the relationship between absences and operational effectiveness. Be positive and volunteer to be of assistance. Your main concern is to avoid future problems. Always try to end a discussion on a positive note and reassure employees of their value to the company. Review the following myths of motivation.

Myths of Motivation

Employees can always be motivated by money

Money is a useful incentive to fulfill lower-level needs, such as survival and security, but individuals differ in their attitudes toward money. For a person with a good income and money left for savings and discretionary purchases, the chance to work a six-day week might not be motivational.

Opportunities for large rewards stimulate workers' efforts

People may perceive success to be unattainable or not worth the extra effort required. An offer of a paid vacation to double sales in the next quarter may sound great. But can it be done? To be motivated, a person must view success as reasonably attainable.

A high level of desire translates into high-level performance

Desire alone is not enough to attain results. Know-how, ability, and equipment resources must be combined effectively to demonstrate performance excellence.

Training and educational seminars ensure motivated employees

Training and education are key factors. However, too many managers assume that employees who take part in educational programs will automatically become motivated and direct their energies toward desired objectives.

Contented employees are always highly motivated

Workers can be happy with their jobs and still not exert much effort. People may have many years of experience with a company and build up numerous job-related benefits without ever exerting anything close to their maximum efforts.

Theory Z

Since the early 1980s, much interest has centered on **Theory Z,** which holds that improved productivity and greater job satisfaction are attained by involving employees in the decision-making process and having a shared responsibility for those decisions. William Ouchi, a professor at the University of California, has popularized the theory. "Z" organizations combine traits found in both American and Japanese management styles. Hewlett-Packard Co., Honeywell, IBM, and Eastman Kodak are examples of corporations that have integrated Theory Z concepts. Concern over declining productivity in the United States caused much of the interest in Japanese management. For several decades, Japan's productive capability has excelled. Even so, productivity per worker in the United States remains the highest of any country in the world.

Theory Z emphasizes involvement

The Japanese Perspective

Consider some differences between Japan and the United States. In area, Japan is smaller than California. It has few natural resources and suffered ruin in World War II, yet Japan has become one of the world's industrial powers. There are vast differences between Japanese and American traditions, child-rearing practices, valuation of education, and attitudes toward work. In Japan, the group tends to supersede the individual. The Japanese stress conformity, and close relationships prevail among workers and employers.

Japan and America are dissimilar

Japanese supervisors work closely with employees who are devoted to employers in a way that makes the firm sort of an extended family. People who work together also socialize off the job. As a result, workers and employees acquire greater understanding of one another as individuals, rather than as superiors and subordinates. J. P. Alston, a professor of sociology, notes:

> Workers give the company a loyalty similar (or greater) to what they owe their families and villages . . . Such loyalty means that workers do whatever is needed for the company's benefit, even if this means working overtime or taking evening courses in order to become a more valuable member.[18]

Theory Z Concepts

Theory Z holds that employee involvement is an important factor in motivating productivity. Participation gives workers opportunities to express views, improve job attitudes, and promote loyalty to the firm. While productivity increases, absenteeism and turnover decline. Successful application of Theory Z requires supportive managerial attitudes throughout a firm. These do not necessarily develop over a short period, and some people

Management support is essential

may be unable or unwilling to make commitments. William G. Ouchi listed these features of "Z" firms.

Characteristics of "Z" firms

□ Stable, long-term employment obligations.
□ Holistic concerns for employees involving both social and economic aspects of life.
□ Implied, informal approaches to control in combination with specific, formal measurements.
□ Patterns of career development not strictly specialized in one job function.
□ Relatively slow processes of evolution and promotion.
□ Consensus decision making.[19]

Implementing and using these practices represent a departure from traditional management thinking. In the United States, evaluation and promotion tend to be based on short-term performance. Many firms limit their concern solely to the worker's "job-life" and focus little attention on off-the-job aspects of life. Career paths are specialized (such as accounting, finance, or marketing), with few, if any, opportunities to gain perspectives on the entire organization. Supervisors who demonstrate concern for employees as people, are willing listeners, and encourage teamwork can successfully apply Theory Z concepts. These supervisory practices summarize a "Z" orientation.

Theory Z supervisory practices

□ Involvement of employees, whenever possible, in decisions that affect them.
□ Provision of sufficient freedom for employees to perform job duties. Oversupervision is avoided.
□ Demonstration of sensitivity toward needs and feelings.
□ Formulation of plans with long-term goals in mind.
□ Communication with workers reflects openness to their ideas and suggestions.
□ Consideration of worker viewpoints and absence of autocratic direction.
□ Awareness of the need for quality work output and prevention of errors.

Adaptive Potential. Can American firms adapt Japanese management techniques? This question has generated much attention and numerous opinions. Differences in cultures, values, and views make copying Japanese practices unlikely.[20] However, a hybrid Theory Z viewpoint recognizes that many Americans are concerned about "a greater degree of job security, social cohesiveness, and holistic concern for employees."[21]

Nissan builds trucks in Tennessee, Sanyo makes television sets in Arkansas, and Auburn Steel turns out steel products in New York State. These are examples of companies using an amalgam of American-Japanese management concepts.[22] The Auburn plant does not use time clocks or job descriptions and employs the team approach. Supervisors coordinate work activities, help workers with jobs, and assist with personal problems. Japanese techniques are more likely to be applied in larger, stable firms committed to long-term employment and having greater financial resources to train and develop employees.

What aspect of Theory Z has the greatest promise to motivate American workers, improve productivity, and increase job satisfaction? It is likely greater management awareness of the value of human resources. Coupled with American know-how, the Japanese concern for quality, welfare of employees, and use of teamwork appears to have considerable potential. Peters and Waterman, authors of *In Search of Excellence,* illustrate an interesting example of employee commitment. On his way home every night, a Honda worker stops to straighten the windshield-wiper blades on Honda vehicles he encounters. "He just can't stand to see a flaw in a Honda."[23]

Theory Z values human resources

Practicing Theory Z. Understanding and awareness are key aspects of Theory Z. Information flows are multidirectional, even crossing different areas of responsibility. Since there is much interaction among workers, interpersonal skills are of great importance in "Z" firms.[24]

Key aspects of Theory Z

Job rotation allows workers to gain firsthand knowledge of how different departments function and an understanding of problems encountered in various subunits. They learn different job skills and how to work cooperatively with a variety of individuals.

Japanese management places great emphasis on participation. Closeness of supervisors and subordinates reinforces teamwork and strengthens relationships. Theory Z's basic premise emphasizes trust through mutual recognition of worker and management interests in achieving goals. Employee involvement in decisions provides a basis for generating ideas and exchanging viewpoints. This results in a greater degree of commitment and encourages efforts to reach objectives.

Quality Circles

Quality circles (QC) are groups of workers who meet periodically to identify and recommend solutions for job-related problems. Most circles have from 7 to 15 members, meet weekly during work hours, and are led by a supervisor. H. Edwards Deming, an expert in statistical quality control, originated the concept, which was first introduced at Lockheed Corporation in the 1970s. During the 1980s, QC programs were started by many firms. According to a national survey sponsored by the New York Stock Exchange, 44 percent of responding firms with over 500 employees have quality circle programs.[25]

QCs can solve job problems

Many managers do not provide opportunities for ideas and suggestions from subordinates. Since employees are most familiar with tasks they perform, quality circles demonstrate management's concern about resolving work-related problems. They have the potential to encourage involvement, promote job satisfaction, and develop motivation. Quality circles cannot remedy all difficulties in a short time or grow in a nonparticipative work environment. The firm must be committed to the concept at all levels, and it must train personnel to understand how circles function and what results they might bring. Management is obliged to respond to recommendations submitted by circle members.

Fundamental Considerations

Quality circles should not be established to promote management's views. Group members should set priorities and decide which problems to tackle. Circle membership should be voluntary, free from any compulsion or penalties for not joining. Before setting quality circles up on a companywide basis, it is advisable to introduce them on a limited scale into areas led by capable supervisors. The number of circles can then grow and expand. A gradual approach lets employees become familiar with how the concept works. Later circles can avoid pitfalls encountered by early groups.

Supervisors usually serve as circle leaders, and their performance is critical to success. It is necessary to see that all members have opportunities to voice concerns. Supervisors should focus attention on workers' problems at the job level rather than on such broad issues as salary or overall policies. The best solutions are generated when participants are free from fear that ideas and suggestions will be ridiculed by other circle members. Personality differences must not overshadow discussion of issues. Circle members should dwell on one problem and not become involved with many issues at the same time. Supervisors must not dominate meetings or force acceptance of their own views.

Supervisors play a key role

QC groups generally encounter few difficulties in deciding on problem areas. As leaders, supervisors prepare agendas, schedule regular meetings, and stress cooperation. A key concern is to maintain a proper flow of information among circle members and with management. At times, middle managers resist formulation of quality circles because they perceive a possible loss of power. "Many are uncomfortable about getting ideas from subordinates and either reject them out of hand or respond slowly and unenthusiastically."[26] Application of the QC approach is not restricted to any job classification. Circles have evolved in a wide variety of job categories. For example, Westinghouse has QC groups that consist of secretaries and janitors.

Supervisors are leaders

While suggestions flow upward to management, information from management is also needed. As a leader, you must be adept at working with others. The greatest challenge you will face is to maintain interactions within the circle itself. You must be skillful at encouraging participation and minimizing internal friction. Recognize the merits of listening. The art of asking questions is vital to draw out ideas. You must consolidate views, gain commitment for suggestions, and keep the circle on course toward accomplishments. Group problem solving requires time and patience. You must not be threatened by sentiments members express. Otherwise, circles will exist in name only, never reaching maximum potential.

QC Trends and Benefits

The Japanese adopted quality circles to improve productivity and build an image of quality. In the 1930s, "made in Japan" did not imply quality. Today, the Japanese have a reputation for producing products that are well built and without defects. The QC concept is increasingly being adopted by U.S. firms. Compared with the Japanese, American companies use QCs at higher organizational levels and place greater emphasis on money rewards for increased performance results. Greater awareness of the need to be competitive in the world marketplace and a concern for cost reduction should contribute to the growth of quality circles in America.

Use of QCs is growing

Quality circles can be implemented without revising or otherwise changing existing organizational structures. To management, this is a definite advantage and is a major reason for widespread interest in the technique. Not all organizations have had similar experiences. However, QCs can contribute to bottom-line results. At Verbatim Corporation, a new method of coating floppy disks saved $100,000, and improved efficiency at Blue Cross of Washington and Alaska resulted in savings of $430,000.[27] The Norfolk Naval Shipyard has been a leader among government agencies developing QCs and saved $3.75 for every dollar invested. Net savings of $150,000 appeared during the first year of use.[28]

QCs save money

Remember, the mere existence of quality circles does not automatically guarantee beneficial outcomes. They cannot be established and then ignored. Active management support, commitment of participants, realistic expectations, and thorough understanding of QC fundamentals are necessary for success. Management must value employee involvement and capabilities. Workers need to be sincere in meeting responsibilities of circle membership. They must attend sessions, volunteer suggestions, and recognize the need for improved productivity.

The QC concept must be supported

Benefits of Quality Circles

---

1. Employee job satisfaction, morale, and motivation are increased.
2. Organization structures need not be altered to accommodate quality circles.
3. Costs and defects are reduced with corresponding increases in productivity.
4. Cooperative attitudes and a spirit of teamwork exist between management and employees.
5. Commitment to achievement of objectives is strengthened.
6. Opportunities are provided to develop problem-solving abilities and increase job skills.

Communication and Motivation

Communication is
important

Is communication an important aspect of motivation? It is, according to results of a nationwide study sponsored by the Balfour Company.[29] The study involved people in several different industries. Employees valued both verbal and nonverbal (a pat on the back) communication as forms of recognition. Merit raises and bonuses were perceived as relevant, but two factors were found to be of equal or greater importance — interpersonal relationships and a sense of accomplishment.

Open communication is essential to development of trust and confidence. Your help in building workers' confidence is especially important to good performance. Many supervisors fail to note that some subordinates do not feel confident of their abilities. A lack of confidence is not conducive to motivation. For example, consider a job activity where you feel quite unsure about your ability. You may be somewhat hesitant to get started and feel quite relieved when the task is completed.

Effective communication can remove vagueness and uncertainty, which impede motivation. When they understand, workers are less reluctant to express concerns, and a more positive work atmosphere prevails. Personnel turnover will be reduced and efficiency increased. The company will attract capable employees. Would you enjoy working for a supervisor who provides little or no feedback, or do you prefer a supervisor who keeps you informed?

Effective communication
strategies

How can you communicate to enhance motivation? You can give prompt recognition for accomplishments — phone calls, short notes, items in the company newsletter, and personally expressed sentiments. These involve little time and cost but have great potential to motivate.

Let subordinates know that you and the company value their efforts. Good performance is often taken for granted. Communication often occurs only when something has gone wrong, or progress is slow. Examine the tone as well as the sincerity of your message. Workers listen to how you say things. Have you known a supervisor who begins with the "I'm not mad, but . . ." approach? Some supervisors do not convey their real views and then become critical when subordinates act on what they perceive is wanted. Level with employees about inadequate performance. Do not hestiate to let them know where you and they stand. Early discussion about small problems prevents them from becoming big problems.

Obstacles: Communication and Motivation

Miscommunication creates
problems

Miscommunication is often a major obstacle to motivation. Communication should emphasize goals and actions in a manner *both* senders and receivers of messages comprehend. When they understand not only the *meaning* but also the *process* of what should be done, workers respond more favorably. Have you ever received directions but encountered confusion in trying to get a task completed? If this happens frequently, your enthusiasm for doing the task declines.

Several practical concerns can reduce obstacles caused by poor communication. These concerns are within supervisors' control and have the potential to improve productivity and develop positive attitudes toward job duties.

☐ *Communicate at an understandable level.* Inexperienced or insecure supervisors often try to impress subordinates with their knowledge. They use big words and technical jargon that confuse listeners.

☐ *Give clear explanations.* Avoid showing resentment to questions, even though they might seem ridiculous or repetitive. Discussion of an explanation provides feedback and ensures that both sender and receiver are understood.

☐ *Do not be overly forceful or pushy.* Encouragement, not pushiness, motivates most workers. Directions can be given without making them orders.

☐ *Avoid being too critical.* When mistakes or oversights occur, get all available data to determine what actually happened. Restrict your comments to inappropriate behaviors, not personality traits of the offender.

☐ *Recognize good performance.* Consistent performance above expectations often goes unrecognized. Let employees know when they have done a good job.

☐ *Be consistent.* Inconsistency leaves workers not knowing what to expect. They will be confused if you recognize them sometimes and ignore them at other times. Openness and sincerity will strengthen employees' desires to achieve. Miscommunication, lack of clarity, and even errors cannot always be avoided. Your primary concern is to provide needed information, correct errors, and recognize the importance of not creating obstacles to accomplishment.

You have gained insights into motivation and learned that it is a complex topic. The various theories of motivation, Theory Z, and quality circles are designed to improve productivity, encourage greater employee involvement, and promote a sense of accomplishment. It is now time to review the objectives stated at the beginning of the chapter.

Looking Back

☐ **Understand the concept of motivation.** Motivation is individual internal effort directed toward satisfying human needs and desires. Motivations among people do differ because they have a wide variety of expectations, backgrounds, and personal priorities. Needs/desires, actions/behaviors, barriers, and goals are all involved in the process of motivation. As a supervisor, you must recognize that needs and desires change. Also, what motivates you does not necessarily encourage subordinates to exert greater efforts.

☐ **Explain several commonly recognized theories of motivation.** Maslow's hierarchy involves satisfaction of needs: survival, safety, social, esteem, and self-actualization. Herzberg examined motivation from the perspective of the job environment and jobs themselves. He developed a two-factor theory based on hygiene and motivator factors. Vroom's expectancy theory emphasizes that people are motivated if they believe their efforts will be rewarded and if the reward itself is valued.

McGregor's Theory X and Theory Y stress assumptions about human behavior. Theory X assumes people avoid work and do not accept responsibilities. According to Theory Y, people accept responsibility, are committed to jobs, and enjoy work. Finally, reinforcement theory focuses attention on the consequences of behavior. The central idea of this theory is that behaviors leading to desired outcomes will be repeated.

☐ **Discuss Theory Z management principles.** Compared to American management, Japanese techniques emphasize close cooperation and open communication. Theory Z firms are characterized by long-term employment, holistic concern for employees, informal controls, involvement of employees in decision making, and generalized patterns of career development. In American firms, the greatest potential for benefits from applying Theory Z concepts involves greater awareness of the value of human resources, improved quality, and use of teamwork strategies.

☐ **Examine quality circles and how they function.** Quality circles are composed of workers who perform similar job duties. Membership is voluntary and usually involves from 7 to 15 persons who meet regularly. These circles identify various job-related problems, study alternative approaches for improvement, form recommendations, and forward them to management. Benefits of quality circles include increased job satisfaction, reduced costs, more cooperative work attitudes, and greater problem-solving skills.

☐ **Explore the relationship between effective communication and motivation.** Communication is an essential factor in building relationships, forming trust, and developing confidence. Good communication practices remove vagueness and uncertainty, which impede motivation. Obstacles can be avoided through consistent and understandable communication that is not overly forceful or critical. Openness and sincerity strengthen desires of workers to perform and achieve.

Key Terms

esteem needs

expectancy

hygiene factors

leveling

motivation

motivators

quality circles

reinforcement theory

safety needs

self-actualization

social needs

survival needs

Theory X

Theory Y

Theory Z

valence

Review and Discussion Questions

1. Practically everyone wants to be successful. Why, then, must supervisors motivate employees?
2. What is the relationship between a supervisor's attitude and the level of worker motivation?
3. Distinguish between Theory X and Theory Y. Discuss implications of these theories for motivating employees.
4. How can Herzberg's theory be used to encourage improved performance?
5. In motivation, what is the relationship between incentives and rewards?
6. Why is it important for supervisors to understand the role of communication in motivation?
7. What can supervisors do about company policies and practices which are perceived to be motivational obstacles?
8. Why does application of Theory Z concepts require commitment and support of the entire organization?
9. What aspects of Theory Z have the most potential to increase the productivity and job satisfaction of Amerian workers?
10. Explain the supervisor's role in quality circles.

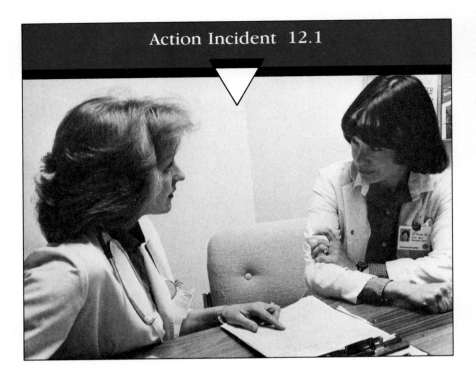

Action Incident 12.1

Just Getting By

For the past six months, Patty Solano has been a nursing supervisor at Mountain Grove Hospital. Earlier, she worked as a nurse for a hospital in another city. She also has had nursing experience in a doctor's office. Most of her subordinates respect Patty, and she has not encountered any unusual problems on her job. She thinks that employees should be concerned with professional development and believes that improvement in productivity is important.

Patty is concerned about one of her employees, Betty Harkness. Betty has held the same job for the past six years and is a close friend of Jennifer Green, director of nursing. Jennifer's husband, John, is chairman of the hospital board of directors.

On various occasions, Betty has been encouraged to participate in professional development activities. However, she is willing only to meet the minimal training requirements for maintaining her nursing license. She has no aspirations for advancement. On the job, she does the minimum amount of work to get by.

To motivate Betty, Patty has attempted cordiality and tried to get involvement by asking her for suggestions. Neither of these approaches was successful. Finally, Patty was frank in discussing Betty's mediocre performance record with her and even threatened to inform Jennifer about the situation. Betty responded, "What do you want, perfection? Besides, I'm getting by. Anyway, why waste your time going to see Jennifer?"

Patty agonizes over Betty's performance and feels that she is capable of doing a better job.

Discussion Questions

1. What actions should Patty take regarding Betty's performance?
2. Should Patty have threatened to discuss the situation with the director of nursing? Explain your response.
3. Suppose Patty does contact Jennifer and she replies, "I'm aware of Betty's situation; just ignore it." How should Patty respond?
4. Should Patty permit Betty's mediocre effort to continue without attempting to improve it? Explain your response.

Action Incident 12.2

A Deterioration in Productivity

The office employees of Barnard and Smith Enterprises are responsible for handling orders, invoices, typing, and recordkeeping. Elsie Graves, supervisor of the office staff, recently recognized that a number of problems hinder productivity.

1. Employees fill out forms in widely different ways. This includes specification of data they consider pertinent rather than information that is requested.
2. Customer files are frequently misplaced, and time is wasted trying to locate them.
3. Messages do not get delivered. Consequently, some customer orders are not received, calls are not returned, and confusion results.
4. During the past several months, absenteeism has increased significantly, and three employees have quit.
5. Employees complain about being overworked.
6. Staff members say they are not consulted about ways to do the work.
7. Several workers insist some tasks are practically impossible to complete within deadlines.
8. There are problems coordinating work responsibilities between full- and part-time employees.

Discussion Questions

1. Why are these problems occurring?
2. How can principles of motivation be applied to remedy apparent difficulties?
3. Before implementing the Theory Z approach, what factors should Elsie Graves consider about the Barnard and Smith organization?
4. Are quality circles appropriate for Elsie's situation?

Action Incident 12.3

The Superperformer

Dawn Moore, an employee of Amalgamated Enterprises, has established an enviable performance record and has consistently received merit increases. A year ago, Dawn was featured as employee of the month in recognition of her outstanding abilities.

While her productivity has not visibly slipped, Dawn seems to have changed her attitude toward work. She is increasingly irritable and seems to take the job for granted. She devotes less effort to tasks, is more abrupt with co-workers, and seems reluctant to accept directions.

When compared to the merit salary increases her co-workers received, Dawn feels she has not been properly recognized for her performance. She considers herself more capable than her co-workers and perceives that they resent the seemingly effortless manner in which she does things, as well as her intellectual abilities. Also, Dawn believes that she was slighted in being passed over for a supervisory position that opened a couple of years ago. The person selected turned out to be ineffective and later left the company.

Ilene Wyrick, her supervisor, respects Dawn but realizes that some employees consider her arrogant and somewhat antagonistic. While believing that she has the potential to become even more effective and valuable to the company, Ilene has said nothing to her. Nevertheless, Ilene recognizes that Dawn has become less outgoing and quieter than in the past.

Discussion Questions

1. What are the signals that Dawn is not motivated to do the best possible job?
2. Considering what she knows about Dawn's situation, should Ilene talk with Dawn? If so, what should Ilene say?
3. What can Ilene do to renew the motivation Dawn once showed?

4. What can Dawn do to become motivated and possibly even improve relationships with her co-workers?
5. Should Dawn consider leaving her job? Explain your response.

Notes

1. Robert W. Goddard, "Motivating the Modern Employee," *Management World* 13 (February 1984), p. 9.
2. "Baby Boomers Have the Work Values to Meet the Japanese Challenge," *Behavioral Sciences Newsletter* 6 (March 25, 1986), p. 2.
3. Kenneth A. Kovach, "What Motivates Employees? Workers and Supervisors Give Different Answers," *Business Horizons* 30 (September–October 1987), p. 60.
4. Robert N. Schaffer, "Built-in Barriers to High Performance," *Management Solutions* 33 (November 1988), p. 43.
5. Frank Stagnaro, "The Benefits of Leveling with Employees: ROLM's Experience," *Management Review* 71 (July 1982), pp. 16–20.
6. Abraham H. Maslow, *Motivation and Personality* (New York: Harper & Row, 1954).
7. Frederick Herzberg, *Work and the Nature of Man* (New York: Thomas Y. Crowell, 1966).
8. Victor H. Vroom, *Work and Motivation* (New York: John Wiley & Sons, 1964).
9. Douglas McGregor, *The Human Side of Enterprise* (New York: McGraw-Hill, 1960).
10. Thomas A. Kirkpatrick, *Supervision: A Situational Approach* (Boston: Kent Publishing, 1987), p. 325.
11. Gregory Moorhead and Ricky W. Griffin, *Organizational Behavior,* 2d ed. (Boston: Houghton Mifflin, 1989), pp. 44–46.
12. Moorhead and Griffin, *Organizational Behavior,* p. 52.
13. Robert P. Vecchio, *Organizational Behavior* (Hinsdale, Ill.: Dryden Press, 1988), pp. 148–49.
14. David J. Cherrington, *Organizational Behavior: The Management of Individual and Organizational Performance* (Boston: Allyn & Bacon, 1989), p. 140.
15. Cherrington, *Organizational Behavior,* p. 140.
16. W. Alan Randolph and Richard S. Blackburn, *Managing Organizational Behavior* (Homewood, Ill.: Richard D. Irwin, 1989), p. 103.
17. John Nirenberg, "Motivation as if People Matter," *Supervisory Management* 26 (October 1981), p. 25.
18. J. P. Alston, "Three Principles of Japanese Management," *Personnel Journal* 62 (September 1983), p. 761.
19. William G. Ouchi, *Theory Z: How American Business Can Meet the Japanese Challenge* (New York: Avon Books, 1982), pp. 60–79.

20. William H. Franklin Jr., "What Japanese Managers Know That American Managers Don't," *Administrative Management* 42 (September 1981), p. 36.

21. Robert R. Rehder, "What American and Japanese Managers Are Learning from Each Other," *Business Horizons* 24 (March–April 1981), p. 65.

22. Paul Cathey, "Japanese Managers Find Best Way to Direct U.S. Workers," *Iron Age* 225 (May 21, 1982), pp. 69–74.

23. Thomas J. Peters and Robert H. Waterman, Jr., *In Search of Excellence* (New York: Warner Books, 1982), p. 37.

24. Ouchi, *Theory Z,* p. 91.

25. "Quality Circles: From America to Japan and Back Again," *Psychology Today* 20 (March 1986), p. 44.

26. Mitchell Lee Marks, "The Question of Quality Circles," *Psychology Today* 20 (March 1986), p. 46.

27. Marks, "The Question of Quality Circles," p. 46.

28. Joe M. Law, "Quality Circles Zero in on Productivity," *Management* 1 (Summer 1980), p. 5.

29. Robert L. Mathis, "Effective Employee Recognition: Concepts and Considerations," *Personnel Administrator* 26 (January 1981), pp. 71–76.

Suggested Readings

Arnold, Vanessa Dean. "Motivation in Today's Office Environment." *The Balance Sheet* 68, May–June 1987, pp. 31–34.

Feinberg, Martin, "Inviting Involvement." *Management World* 17, September–October 1988, p. 27.

Gabor, Andrea. "The Leading Light of Quality." *U.S. News & World Report* 105, November 28, 1988, pp. 53–54, 56.

Hall, Jay. "Putting Your Power to Work." *Management World* 17, November–December 1988, pp. 21–23.

Harper, Stephen C. "Now That the Dust Has Settled: Learning from Japanese Management." *Business Horizons* 31, July–August 1988, pp. 43–51.

Lewis, John W. "Breaking the Quality Circle." *Personnel Administrator* 34, October 1988, pp. 72–76, 78–79.

Merchant, John E. "Motivating Entry-Level Service Employees." *Management Solutions* 33, March 1988, pp. 43–45.

Nelson, Andre. "The Need for Recognition." *Management Solutions* 33, April 1988, pp. 33–36.

Quick, Thomas L. "Expectancy Theory in Five Simple Steps." *Training and Development Journal* 42, July 1988, pp. 30–32.

Wayne, Sandy J., Ricky W. Griffin, and Thomas S. Bateman. "Improving Effectiveness of Quality Circles." *Personnel Administrator* 31, March 1986, pp. 79–88.

Conducting Interviews and Selecting Employees

Chapter

13

Learning Objectives

After reading and studying the material in this chapter, you should be able to:

1. Define interviewing.
2. Explain the distinction between directive and nondirective interviewing.
3. Identify tips for asking questions.
4. Explain how to conduct informational interviews.
5. Indicate the steps used in selecting employees for employment.
6. Identify key aspects of conducting the final selection interview.
7. Explain how to conduct exit interviews.

Supervisors Coordinate by Asking Questions

Supervisors need to gain information

To do their jobs well, supervisors need information from many individuals. As a supervisor, you must seek information from workers about how their work is progressing. In addition, when changes are needed or problems arise, you may need information from your boss before making decisions. You may also need information from other supervisors. Furthermore, questions must be asked of job applicants, and it can be helpful to learn why employees resign. Therefore, you must understand how to interview to gain needed information.

Interviewing Defined

Interviewing is a process in which two people with a specific purpose share information through asking and answering questions.[1] In a panel interview, more than two people may participate; however, at any one time, attention is focused primarily on two people: the person asking a question and the person answering it. It is also important to realize that successful interviews require careful planning. Therefore, you should have a *specific purpose* to guide you in developing questions and conducting an interview.

Two Interviewing Approaches

The directive approach gives the interviewer control

In conducting an interview, you can employ two approaches: directive and nondirective. In a **directive interviewing approach,** you establish the purpose of the interview and control it through a structured set of questions. A directive approach works well when you know exactly what information you want. Your questions guide the respondent in the direction you want to go. In the following exchange, an airline baggage supervisor uses a directive interviewing approach.

Supervisor: When does Flight 300 arrive?

Worker: In 30 minutes.

Supervisor: Will you have time to transfer the baggage to Flight 400 without delaying it?

Worker: No.

Supervisor: How many extra workers will you need to make the transfer and keep things on schedule?

Worker: We can make it fine if we get three extra workers.

Supervisor: All right, who do you want?

The nondirective approach gives the interviewee control

As a supervisor, you can gain information quickly with the directive approach. However, the respondent has little opportunity to provide information beyond that requested. In the **nondirective interviewing approach,** you allow the respondent to control the direction of the interview and what is discussed. This approach encourages the respondent to open up and explain how he or she feels. The following is an exchange in which a supervisor uses a nondirective interviewing approach with a customer.

Supervisor: We regret that you are having trouble with our product. What problems do you want to discuss?

Customer: When the product works, it's great; but we can't depend on it.

Supervisor: In what way can't you depend on it?

Customer: Well, we're cautious about using it in the field away from the plant.

Supervisor: Go on.

Customer: Occasionally it overheats.

Supervisor: What do you think causes this problem?

The nondirective approach allows the respondent to explain his or her viewpoints on an issue. However, in using this approach, you must have patience and listen carefully to what the respondent says. Is one approach better than the other? Not really. In fact, a combination of approaches is often used in many interviews. For example, you might use a nondirective approach at the beginning of an interview to put the respondent at ease and help establish rapport. Later, you may switch to a directive approach to make sure certain questions are answered.

Open and Closed Questions

In conducting an interview, you must use your "toolbox" of questions. As an analogy, imagine a carpenter replacing a screw in a door hinge.[2] The carpenter has a number of tools for this task, for example, a hammer to drive the screw in or pliers to turn the screw. It would be more appropriate, though, to use a screwdriver. However, the toolbox holds many different types of screwdrivers. To do the job right, the carpenter must select the screwdriver that will work best in this case.

Likewise, as a supervisor, you have different types of questions at hand to use in an interview. Selecting the appropriate question is crucial to gaining the information desired. Two broad types of questions commonly used for gaining information are open questions and closed questions.

Different types of questions are available

Open Questions. Generally, **open questions** provide the respondent with a great deal of freedom in responding. The following are examples of open questions:

☐ What do you think of the new work rules?
☐ Why did you change the dimensions?
☐ How should the factory be designed?

Note the following advantages and disadvantages of open questions.

Advantages of Open Questions

1. The respondent is encouraged to open up and give a detailed response.
2. They demonstrate the respondent's ability to think and organize material.
3. The respondent has flexibility in answering.
4. They can reveal the respondent's depth of knowledge and feelings concerning a topic.

Disadvantages of Open Questions

1. The respondent may take a lot of time to answer.
2. The interviewer has little control over how the respondent will answer.
3. Due to the broad nature of the questions, the respondent may not know what information to provide.
4. Lengthy answers may force you to interrupt.

Closed Questions. By their nature, **closed questions** restrict or limit the answer options available to the respondent. Closed questions often request very specific information. Some examples of closed questions are:

Closed questions limit answer options

- ☐ What is the first name of the new supervisor?
- ☐ How many new employees will be hired?
- ☐ What was your blood pressure the last time it was checked?

Multiple-choice questions and bipolar questions requesting a yes or no answer are also closed questions. Consider the following advantages and disadvantages of closed questions.

Advantages of Closed Questions

1. They are easy to create.
2. Many can be asked in a short amount of time.
3. Specific information can be gained easily.
4. Little effort is required of the respondent to answer.

Disadvantages of Closed Questions

1. They provide limited information.
2. They restrict the respondent from elaborating.
3. The respondent can still answer yes or no, even though he or she may know little or nothing about the subject.
4. The respondent has little opportunity to explain an answer.

Tips for Asking Questions

There are various ways to ask questions. The following suggestions will help you acquire desired information.

Make open questions specific.   Open questions that are too broad often appear vague and are difficult to answer. For example, asking a patient, "How are you doing?" or "How are *we* today?" may not provide the information you are seeking. Instead, a supervising nurse may ask such specific questions as:

☐ "How is your arm today?"
☐ "How well did you sleep last night?"
☐ "What effect did the medicine have on you?"[3]

Preface a question if that will make it easier to answer.   If you ask an employee "Which project do you think we should start next?" the employee may need clarification before he or she can answer. The question's intent will be more understandable if you preface it. For example, you might ask, "Considering that we're running low on supplies, which project do you think we should start next?"

Ask a follow-up question to explore an answer.   If you want the respondent to expand on an answer, ask a follow-up question. This technique allows you to explore answers that may seem incomplete, confusing, or incorrect.

Consider using indirect questions.   If the respondent hesitates to answer, try indirect questions. For example, if you ask an employee to comment on the quality of another's work, the employee might be reluctant to respond directly. However, the worker may be more likely to respond if you ask, "How do the other workers feel about the quality of Jim's work?" Here, the employee might actually answer the question according to his or her own personal feelings.[4]

Use appropriate language.   In phrasing questions, use words the other person will understand. When your words could easily be given a different meaning than you intend, clarify the information you seek. For example, suppose you ask another supervisor, "Can we meet for a few minutes after the seminar to review the plans?" Miscommunication could easily result. In agreeing, the other supervisor may think you want to meet for only five minutes. However, you may have meant 15 minutes. To avoid confusion, ask "Can we meet for about 15 minutes after the seminar to review the plans?"

Keep your questions simple.   Complex questions do not necessarily show sophistication. Instead, they are often a sign of poor preparation.

Use compound questions cautiously.   A question that contains two or more queries is a compound question. "*When* and *how* did the accident occur?" is one. At times, compound questions can be appropriate. However, there is always the chance that the respondent may answer one part of the question but not the other. When this happens, you may forget to request an

Vague questions can hinder interviews

Follow-up questions can be helpful

Break up compound questions

answer to the other part. Therefore, it is usually advisable to break compound questions up into two or more separate queries.

Avoid add-on questions.   Too often a supervisor spoils a good question by adding other questions to it. Consider the following:

Supervisor: What will you do with the cracked part? Will you weld it? Could you glue it?

Employee: I guess I could weld it.

The first question was great. Had the supervisor stopped there, he or she would have received an answer. However, the supervisor couldn't quit while ahead! Sometimes, add-on questions can bias the respondent's answer. The employee may have believed that the cracked part should have been replaced. However, he or she may have interpreted the supervisor's add-on questions as suggestions on how to repair the crack. The worker may have chosen to weld the part to please the supervisor when it would have been better to replace it.

The Informational Interview

The **informational interview** is used to gather information for the purpose of analyzing siutations and making decisions. As a supervisor, you will frequently need to conduct informational interviews because you cannot observe everything that goes on in your work area. Therefore, you must obtain much of the information you need by asking questions through informational interviews.

An interview needs a goal

Determine information needed.   To conduct a successful informational interview, first determine the information you wish to acquire. If you fail to do this, you will probably end up groping blindly through the interview.

Develop questions.   Once you determine the information you want, you need to develop relevant questions to gain that information. Careful consideration must be given to the construction of questions in an informational interview. You can use both open and closed questions, but open questions are usually more appropriate and productive. As a rule, they provide much more information than do closed questions. For example, if you want to know how much of a project has been completed, don't ask, "Is the project going all right?" This question is closed. It calls for a yes or no answer. If the respondent says "Yes," you have obtained no information about how much work has been completed. In fact, if you actually knew how much of the project had been completed, you might disagree with the assertion that everything was all right! Instead, ask "What parts of the project have been completed?"

Sometimes you may find that the respondent's answer to your question is inadequate, or you may want more detailed information. To probe for more information, use a **follow-up question.** Follow-up questions like those below can help clarify vague answers.

- ☐ How could that happen?
- ☐ Just how "expensive" is it?
- ☐ What do you mean by "minor defects"?
- ☐ What is your idea of "a reasonable period of time"?

If the respondent fails to complete an answer or hesitates, you can use the following **"nudging"** probes.

Nudging questions encourage the interviewee to continue

- ☐ What else?
- ☐ And then?
- ☐ What happened next?
- ☐ Yes?[5]

When you think the respondent's answer is superficial, begin your follow-up questions with a phrase similar to these:

- ☐ How did you deal with . . . ?
- ☐ What was your reaction when . . . ?
- ☐ What action did you take after . . . ?
- ☐ Explain further why you decided to . . . ?

Respondents may occasionally give incorrect answers unintentionally. For example, an answer may contain the wrong name, date, price, time, or address. In cases where a real or suspected inaccuracy occurs, a reflective follow-up question is appropriate.[6] A **reflective question** reflects or incorporates part of the respondent's answer in the follow-up to clarify. The following questions demonstrate how reflective follow-up questions can be used to clarify a suspected inaccuracy.

Reflective questions seek clarification

- ☐ Was it Kansas City, *Missouri,* or Kansas City, Kansas?
- ☐ Didn't we agree to offer a *5 percent* discount instead of 10 percent?
- ☐ Do you mean *1988* instead of 1989?
- ☐ Didn't he check *any* of the receipts?

After you believe you have finished delving into an area, one last question may still be appropriate—the clearinghouse question. A **clearinghouse question** seeks additional relevant information the respondent may have to offer but has not presented. The following questions are examples of clearinghouse questions.

- ☐ Is there anything else I should know about . . . ?
- ☐ What else, if anything, should I ask you about the proposal before I make a decision?
- ☐ Is there anything else you want to tell me about the problem?
- ☐ Well, I guess that wraps it up. Did I miss anything?

Clearinghouse questions
are asked near the end of
the interview

Occasionally, you can gain valuable additional information by using a clearinghouse question. To illustrate, Jim Royer, a supervisor, needed to replace the worn tires on the company's fleet of automobiles. Jim contacted a local tire dealer and asked questions about the quality, mileage expectancy, and prices of several brands of tires. Having all the information he thought he needed, Jim asked, "What else, if anything, do you think I should be aware of in making a decision?" The dealer replied, "I understand that the original equipment spare tires in the automobiles have never been used. If you would be willing to use the best of the worn tires for spares, I will buy your unused spare tires." Jim had never thought of selling the spare tires. In addition, he probably would not have considered the idea had it not been for his clearinghouse question. Jim's boss liked the idea, and the firm saved money as a result. By using a clearinghouse question at the end of an informational interview, you have nothing to lose and you may gain valuable information.

▼

Consider This

1. It is not uncommon for novice interviewers to experience trouble in phrasing their questions properly. What suggestions would you give to a novice interviewer for overcoming this difficulty?
2. What communication problems would you caution supervisors to be alert for when conducting informational interviews?

Staffing: The People Ingredient

Supervisors usually need
to make staffing decisions

Staffing involves selecting capable employees for the organization. The importance of choosing the right people for the right jobs cannot be overstated. Supervisors should view the staffing function as critical and take care to fill positions with the most qualified applicants. How much do supervisors participate in the staffing function? The answer often depends on the size of the company. In small firms, supervisors may be responsible for the entire staffing process. Large firms have specialists who perform many of these duties. In any case, as a supervisor, you will usually have some involvement in the process of obtaining competent, qualified employees for your work unit, and whenever staffing is not given proper attention, organization effectiveness is diminished.

Job Description and Job Specification

To do the most professional job in staffing, you must begin with a good job description and a job specification. A **job description** lists the duties and responsibilities of a particular job. To further aid in the staffing process, a **job**

specification indicates the required knowledge, skills, and attributes desired in the job holder.

If you have a job description for a job that is vacant, review it to make sure it is still current and accurate. When no description exists for a new job or one that is vacant, you will need to develop an appropriate job description. This task requires you to consider the makeup of the job. In other words, you need to decide what the successful applicant will be expected to do on the job *before* he or she is hired. Suppose, for example, that you are responsible for supervising the work of several systems analysts, and you wish to hire a new analyst. A possible job description for such a position is shown in Figure 13.1.

Periodically, it is a good idea to review job descriptions and compare them with what employees actually do. If over time a job changes to the extent that it is no longer adequately represented by the job description, the description should be updated.

Once the content of a job has been determined, or re-evaluated, you then need to determine the knowledge, skills, and attributes which are required of the job holder. In preparing this material, you should be realistic. Setting specifications or standards which are too low will set some candidates up for failure if they get the job. On the other hand, if specifications are set too high, it may be very difficult or impossible to fill the job. Figure 13.2 shows a possible job specification for the systems analyst position discussed earlier.

Job Description for Position of Systems Analyst　　　　　　　　　　**Figure 13.1**

Job Title
　　Systems Analyst
Department
　　Programming and Systems Analysis
General Description
　　Responsible for systems analysis and design, programming specifications
　　and development, and systems implementation and documentation.
Duties and Responsibilities
　　1. Prepare complete studies of assigned systems including:
　　　　a. review of work assignments.
　　　　b. analysis of work flow.
　　　　c. study of work load pattern.
　　　　d. study of backlogs and overload points.
　　2. Prepare feasibility studies.
　　3. Prepare programming specifications for the necessary programs for the system(s).
　　4. Prepare complete systems documentation for assigned systems.
　　5. Work with the programming staff to make certain that programming specifications
　　　　are completed in an efficient manner.
　　6. Maintain appropriate files in a professional fashion.

Figure 13.2			**Job Specification for Position of Systems Analyst**

Job Title
  Systems Analyst
Qualifications
  Education:	Minimum of baccalaureate degree in a field such as
  		business, accounting, or management information systems.
  Experience:	At least 2 years as a systems analyst. Programming experience in widely
  		used computer languages.
  Skills:	Technical writing ability required.
  		Ability to identify alternative courses of action and make timely decisions
  		based on factual information and logical assumptions.
  		Ability to retain perspective while working on detail.
  		Demonstrate creativity and initiative in completing work assignments.
  		Develop and maintain good working relations with system users.

With a job description and a job specification prepared, you are ready to begin recruiting. Furthermore, this information will guide you in determining which candidate represents the best fit for the job.

Recruitment and Selection

Recruitment involves activities aimed at soliciting potential job applicants for available positions. This process is usually the responsibility of the personnel (human resources) department. Supervisors, however, need to understand that effective recruitment is the basis for selecting qualified candidates. If personnel does not recruit good people, you cannot make a good choice for your department. Therefore, it is to your benefit as a supervisor to assist the personnel staff in their effort to find and select good candidates.

Job openings can be advertised in many ways

Sources for informing potential employees about your job openings include newspaper and trade journal ads, referrals, government employment services, employment agencies, colleges, high schools, and vocational schools. For example, representatives of some firms travel to colleges, job fairs, and trade shows to inform prospective employees about the company and available jobs. If done properly, recruiting activities produce a pool of qualified persons from which to make employment choices. After preliminary screening by the personnel department, the supervisor usually makes the final selection. In some cases, the personnel department may want to make the final selection. However, even in this situation, the supervisor should have a voice in hiring.[7]

Selection includes a number of steps with decisions about the applicant made at each of them. The sequence varies with the firm, but the objective remains the same — to get the best match between job requirements and applicant abilities. Figure 13.3 illustrates steps in employee selection.

Application and First Interview. After learning of an opening, interested workers contact the firm and fill out an application form. The first interview is brief. This interview is meant to eliminate candidates who obviously do not qualify.

Second Interview and Testing. At this stage, the personnel department often interviews those people who seem most promising, and two-way communication is important here. For example, the interviewer may seek to clarify data placed on the application form. He or she asks questions about the applicant's qualifications and provides information about the job. The applicant can ask questions about the job and the employer. Furthermore, the applicant may be asked to take one or more tests. There are a variety of tests available to increase the likelihood of successful job placement. The five general types of tests are:

- ☐ Achievement tests, which measure performance involving particular abilities, such as computer or word processing skills.
- ☐ Aptitude tests, which measure potential for learning how to perform various kinds of tasks, such as selling or doing mechanical tasks.
- ☐ Intelligence tests, which measure capacity for reasoning as well as verbal and quantitative abilities.
- ☐ Interest tests, which measure an individual's preferences for certain types of work.
- ☐ Personality tests, which measure such personality variables as emotional or psychological status.

Checking: Work Record and References. Employers usually look at the applicant's work record and request references. Employment histories can reflect performance of assignments, growth in job skills, and responsibilities held by the applicant. A person's past employment record is considered a basis for predicting success in a new position. References are usually checked by phone or mail. When weighing the value of references, recognize two cautions. First, the applicant has chosen the references, so what is not stated may be more important than what is. If you were not fairly sure of getting good support from a certain person, would you give that person as a reference? Second, some people hesitate to make negative comments about an applicant, even if such comments are pertinent. In fact, some employers will only confirm dates of employment. Many employers are especially cautious

The goal is to find the right person for the job

Many job placement tests exist

Important information on resumes should be checked

Figure 13.3   **Illustration of Representative Steps in the Selection Process**

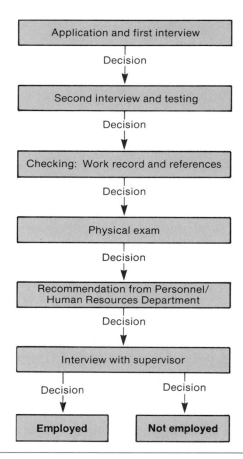

about putting negative remarks in writing. Therefore, you must carefully interpret responses from references.

Physical Examination. Physical examinations are designed to determine whether a prospective employee is physically able to do the job. Physicals may reveal illness that can prevent people from performing work duties. The timing of physicals varies among companies and may depend on specific jobs. Some firms hire persons contingent upon passing physicals. Others require that the examination be passed before any further steps are taken.

Recommendation from Personnel/Human Resources Department. Procedures vary among firms, but a common approach involves the personnel department recommending several candidates for the first-line supervisor to consider. Firms that use this approach ask supervisors to take part in selection because they are the ones with whom the employees will work, and the supervisor is likely to make a further investment in training and developing the new worker.

Interview with the Supervisor. Before interviewing, supervisors should carefully read application forms, test results, and any other data from the personnel department. Interview time is limited, so use it wisely. Do not waste time on information already available. As a matter of fact, the only reason for an interview is to gain information you cannot get otherwise. After the final selection interview, a decision on whether to hire is made.

Avoid asking unnecessary questions

Conducting the Final Selection Interview

It is best to hold your selection interview in a location where you will not be subjected to frequent interruptions. The interruptions hinder your ability to gain the information you need from the applicant, and when interruptions occur, desirable applicants may be left with a bad impression of your organization. If you have no control over the location of the interview, do what you can to minimize the chances that interruptions will occur during the time you have scheduled for the interview. Start out by making a good impression so your chances of getting the best candidate to accept your job offer are increased. For example, do your best not to keep the candidate waiting past the time the interview is scheduled to start, and, if possible, greet the applicant in the waiting room. Introduce yourself and then escort the applicant into the interviewing room.[8] Applicants are more impressed with this approach than being told to enter a room where they find you sitting behind a desk.

Make a good initial impression

When you conduct a selection interview as a supervisor, you should attempt to learn two things. First, determine if the applicant is qualified for the job. Do not assume the applicant is well qualified for the job just because the resume indicates that the applicant has the appropriate degree and relevant work experience. Probe into the applicant's education and work experience to make sure he or she really has the ability to do your job well. Some people look good on paper, but when they are asked how they would handle a particular situation or perform a certain task, their inability shows through. Second, determine if the applicant is right for the job. That is, will the person likely be able to get along well with the other employees and fit in with the personality of the department and/or organization? If the job requires the applicant to be articulate, for example, consider how articulate the applicant is when he or she speaks. If the job requires much traveling, find out how the applicant feels about traveling. If the job requires the applicant to be a good listener, observe how well the interviewee listens to your questions. If the job requires the applicant to work closely with others, consider how cooperative and open-minded he or she appears to be. An

Learn if the applicant is qualified

Learn if the applicant is right for the job

applicant may have the appropriate education to do the job, for example, but lack the maturity to accept certain responsibilities associated with the job. In one study, every manager interviewed stressed how important it is that the prospective employee fit into the personality of the organization.[9] Only after you have determined whether the applicant is qualified for the job and right for the job can you say that you have conducted a successful selection interview.

In the selection interview, you must focus on the applicant's responses to your questions in order to determine if the applicant is a good fit for the job. Therefore, as the interviewer, do not go into the interview unprepared. Have your key questions developed ahead of time. How do you determine what your key questions should cover? First, decide what levels of education and experience are required to be a success at the job. However, do not ask interview questions that can be answered simply by reviewing the interviewee's letter of application, resume, and application form. For example, it is a waste of time to ask what jobs the applicant has held over the past five years if that information is shown on the applicant's resume. Instead, it would be more relevant to ask what the applicant learned from his last job that will help him do this job well. Most likely, that information is not on the resume. Therefore, decide what *specific* information you need to learn about the applicant's education and experience that you do not already have, and then develop focused questions to gain that information. Writing these questions ahead of time helps you examine the best way to phrase them so you get the exact information you desire. Also, when you conduct an interview with key questions written out, there is less chance that you will forget to ask some of the questions and you minimize the risk that you will get off track and run out of time before asking some important questions.

Second, decide what characteristics a candidate should possess in order to be considered right for the job. Do not be unreasonable, but do be realistic. When new employees do not work out in a job, it is not necessarily due to deficiencies in education or job skills. Often, it is because they are not right for the job in terms of their personality and the way they conduct themselves around clients and others on the job. Therefore, decide what the characteristics of a person who fits in well with the culture of the organization should be. Then develop questions that will probe into these areas. For example, suppose a willingness to work overtime during the Christmas holiday season is desired in employees. Ask the applicants how they feel about working overtime during the Christmas holidays. On important issues, do not assume you know an interviewee's views; ask for that information. Once you have prepared a list of the key questions you wish to ask, prioritize them so the most important questions will get asked first.

When inquiring into an applicant's background, you must be aware of guidelines for selection interviewing. The 1972 Equal Opportunity Act, amending Title VII of the Civil Rights Act of 1964, established the Equal

Prepare key questions in advance

Determine what exact information you need

Prioritize your questions

Employment Opportunity Commission. The objective here is to prevent employment discrimination on the basis of religion, color, race, sex, or natural origin. To ensure compliance with the spirit and intent of the law, you must know the types of questions that are permissible in conducting interviews. Figure 13.4 compares areas of inquiry which are generally considered appropriate and inappropriate.

Do not ask illegal questions

The Opening

Once you have reviewed the applicant's credentials and have prepared your key questions, you are ready to interview the individual. When conducting a selection interview, the opening serves two important purposes.[10] First, as the interviewer, you should attempt to develop rapport with the interviewee and create a warm and supportive atmosphere that will motivate the candidate to participate actively. That is, through your greeting and the small talk that often follows, you are trying to create goodwill and trust between you and the applicant. However, it is best to keep the small talk brief. If the small talk in the opening is lengthy, the applicant may become uneasy wondering when the important questions will start. Second, orient the interviewee on how the interview will proceed and what to expect. For example, you might point out that you will be asking questions about certain items of information you need and explain that you will reserve time at the end of the interview for the interviewee to ask questions. Some anxiety is reduced, for example, if the applicant knows that the interviewer will be asking about his or her training and views on selling. The applicant also feels more at ease after learning that his or her questions will be answered near the end of the interview.

Explain how the interview will proceed

Asking Questions

The body of the selection interview involves the asking of questions. Unfortunately, however, a common selection problem is the failure of supervisors to seek information on all of the important aspects needed for successful job performance. As mentioned earlier, do your homework before the interview in order to determine what attributes are most needed by the successful applicant to do the job well. Create good questions that request the important information you need and ask those questions before asking lower-priority questions. Too often, interviewers do not do their homework and try to "wing it" in the interview. They may have fun talking to the applicant and enjoy the interview, but the interview is usually unproductive because the information needed to make a sound hiring decision is not obtained. The supervisor then wonders why he or she has so many personnel problems. As Walter Wriston, the former chairman of the board and chief executive officer of Citicorp, once stated: "I believe the only game in town is the personnel

Figure 13.4   **Guidelines for Pre-Employment Inquiries**

	Permissible inquiries	**Inquiries which must be avoided**
Name	"Have you worked for this company under a different name?" Is any additional information relative to change of name, use of an assumed name or nickname necessary to enable a check on your work and educational record? If yes, explain."	Inquiries about the name which would indicate applicant's lineage, ancestry, national origin or descent. Inquiry into previous name of applicant where it has been changed by court order or otherwise. Indicate: Miss, Mrs., Ms.
Marital and Family Status	Whether applicant can meet specified work schedules or has activities, commitments or responsibilities that may hinder the meeting of work attendance requirements. Inquiries as to duration of stay on job or anticipated absences which are made to males and females alike.	Any inquiry indicating whether an applicant is married, single, divorced, engaged, etc. Number and age of children. Information on child-care arrangements. Any questions concerning pregnancy, any such questions which directly or indirectly results in limitation of job opportunity.
Age	If a minor, require proof of age in the form of a work permit or a certificate of age. Inquiry as to whether or not the applicant meets the minimum age requirements as set by law and requirement that upon hire proof of age must be submitted in the form of a birth certificate or other forms of proof of age. If age is a legal requirement: "If hired, can you furnish proof of age?"/or statement that hire is subject to verification of age. Inquiry as to whether or not an applicant is younger than the employer's regular retirement age.	Requirement that applicant produce proof of age in the form of a birth certificate or baptismal record. BASIS The Age Discrimination in Employment Act of 1975 forbids discrimination against persons between the ages of 40 and 70.
Handicaps	For employers subject to the provisions of the Rehabilitation Act of 1973, applicants may be "invited" to indicate how and to what extent they are handicapped. The employer must indicate to applicants that: 1) compliance with the invitation is voluntary; 2) the information is being sought only to remedy discrimination or provide opportunities for the handicapped; 3) the information will be kept confidential; and 4) refusing to provide the information will not result in adverse treatment. All applicants can be asked if they are able to carry out all necessary job assignments and perform them in a safe manner.	Asking job applicants general questions about whether they are handicapped or asking them about the nature and severity of their handicaps. BASIS An employer must be prepared to prove that any physical and mental requirements for a job are due to "business necessity" and the safe performance of the job. Except in cases where undue hardship can be proven, employers must make "reasonable accommodations" for the physical and mental limitations of an employee or applicant. "Reasonable accommodation" includes alteration of duties, alteration of work schedule, alteration of physical setting, and provision of aids.
Sex	Inquiry or restriction of employment is permissible only where a bona fide occupational qualification exists. (This BFOQ exception is interpreted very narrowly by the courts and EEOC.) The burden of proof rests on the employer to prove that the	Sex of applicant. Any other inquiry which would indicate sex. BASIS Sex is not a BFOQ because a job involves physical labor (such as heavy lifting) beyond the capac-

Figure 13.4   **Guidelines for Pre-Employment Inquiries (continued)**

	Permissible Inquiries	**Inquiries which must be avoided**
Sex (continued)	BFOQ does exist and that all members of the affected class are incapable of performing the job.	ity of some women nor can employment be restricted just because the job is traditionally labeled "men's work" or "women's work". Sex of applicant may be requested (preferably not on the employment application) for affirmative action purposes but may not be used as an employment criterion. Avoid questions concerning applicant's height or weight unless you can prove they are necessary requirements for the job to be performed.
Race and Color	Race may be requested (preferably not on the employment application) for affirmative action purposes but may not be used as an employment criterion.	Applicant's race. Color of applicant's skin, eyes, hair, etc., or other questions directly or indirectly indicating race or color.
Address or Duration of Residence	Applicant's address. Inquiry into place and length of current and previous addresses.	Specific inquiry into foreign addresses which would indicate national origin. Names and relationship of persons with whom applicant resides. Whether applicant owns or rents home.
Ancestry or National Origin	Languages applicant reads, speaks, or writes fluently, if another language is necessary to perform the job.	Inquiries into applicant's lineage, ancestry, national origin, descent, birthplace, or native language. National origin of applicant's parents or spouse.
Birthplace	"Can you, after employment, submit a Birth Certificate or other proof of U.S. citizenship?"	Birthplace of applicant. Birthplace of applicant's parents, spouse, or other relatives. Requirement that applicant submit a birth certificate before employment. Any other inquiry into national origin.
Religion	An applicant may be advised concerning normal hours and days of work required by the job to avoid possible conflict with religious or other personal conviction. However, except in cases where undue hardship can be proven, employers must make "reasonable accommodation" for religious practices of an employee or prospective employee. "Reasonable accommodation" may include voluntary substitutes, flexible scheduling, lateral transfer or change of job assignments.	Applicant's religious denomination or affiliation, church, parish, pastor, or religious holidays observed. Applicants may not be told that any particular religious groups are required to work on their religious holidays. Any inquiry to indicate or identify religious denomination or customs.
Military Record	Type of education and experience in service as it relates to a particular job.	Type of discharge.
Photograph	May be required after hiring for identification.	Requirement that applicant affix a photograph to their application. Request that applicant, at their option, submit photograph. Requirement of photograph after interview but before hiring.

Figure 13.4	**Guidelines for Pre-Employment Inquiries (continued)**	
	Permissible Inquiries	**Inquiries which must be avoided**
Citizenship	"Are you a citizen of the United States?" Statement that if hired, applicant will be required to submit proof of employability. "If not a citizen are you prevented from lawfully becoming employed because of visa or immigration status?"	"Of what country are you a citizen?" Whether applicant or his parents or spouse are naturalized or native-born U.S. citizens. Date when applicant or parents or spouse acquired U.S. citizenship. Requirement that applicant produce his naturalization papers. Whether applicant's parents or spouse are citizens of the U.S.
Education	Applicant's academic, vocational, or professional education; school attended. Inquiry into language skills such as reading, speaking, and writing foreign languages, if job related.	Any inquiry asking specifically the nationality, racial or religious affiliation of a school. Inquiry as to how foreign language ability was acquired.
Experience	Applicant's work experience, including names and addresses of previous employers, dates of employment, reasons for leaving, salary history.	
Conviction, Arrest and Court Record	Inquiry into actual convictions which relate reasonably to fitness to perform a particular job. (A conviction is a court ruling where the party is found guilty as charged. An arrest is merely the apprehending or detaining of the person to answer the alleged crime.)	Any inquiry relating to arrests. Ask or check into a person's arrest, court, or conviction record if not substantially related to functions and responsibilities of the particular job in question.
Relatives	Names of applicant's relatives already employed by this company if needed for compliance with nepotism policy.	Name or address of any relative of adult applicant.
Notice in Case of Emergency	Name and address of persons to be notified in case of accident or emergency after selection is made.	Name and address of relatives to be notified in case of accident or emergency.
Organizations	Inquiry into the organizations of which an applicant is a member, providing the name or character of the organization does not reveal the race, religion, color, or ancestry of membership. "List all professional organizations to which you belong. What offices are held?"	"List all organizations, clubs, societies, and lodges to which you belong." The names of organizations to which the applicant belongs if such information would indicate through character or name the race, religion, color, or ancestry of the membership.
References	"By whom were you referred for a position here?" Names of persons willing to provide professional and/or character references for applicant.	Require the submission of a religious reference. Request conferences from applicant's pastor.
Credit rating		Any questions concerning credit rating, charge accounts, etc. Ownership of automobile.
Miscellaneous	Notice to applicants that any misstatements or omissions of material facts in the application may be cause for dismissal.	

Source: "A Guide for Pre-Employment Interviewing." Prepared by the Kansas Division of Personnel Services. This chart was compiled by Clifford Coen, University of Tennessee, and was originally published in the December 1976 newsletter of the American Association for Affirmative Action and revised in March 1980.

game. . . . If you have the wrong person in the job, there is no management system known to man that can save you."[11]

After you have prepared your questions, review them before the interview to be familiar with their purpose and wording. Do not try to memorize them. There is nothing wrong with having your list of written questions in front of you in the interview. However, do not be tied to the list. Some interviewers, for example, are so tied to their list of questions that they think after asking question three, they must automatically ask question four on the list. However, suppose the interviewee's response to question three is confusing, a surprise, or inadequate. In this situation, you should momentarily abandon your prepared list and ask a probing question that will help you investigate and learn more about the applicant's previous answer. Some supervisors are so dependent on their list that it does not seem to matter how the interviewee responds to a question; they just automatically ask the next question on their list. Much valuable information may be lost by this shortsighted approach.

Utilize Open Questions. In the interview, you want the candidate to be open and responsive to your questions. Although you may enjoy talking, a general rule of thumb in interviewing is that if you do more than 30 percent of the talking, you are giving a speech, not an interview. A good way to get interviewers to open up is to ask open questions. As mentioned earlier, closed questions often can easily be answered with a single word. For example, the closed question "Can you deal with upset customers?" requests a yes or no answer and may not get much more than that as a response from the applicant. However, the open question "How do you deal with upset customers?" requests a detailed and open answer. From this open question you not only learn how the applicant responds to upset customers, but, based on the answer, *you* decide whether the candidate really knows how to deal with upset customers. If the applicant answers yes to your closed question, you have gained very little information. If you knew how the interviewee planned to deal with upset customers, you might strongly disagree that he or he knows the proper way to respond to your customers! Your ability to make that important decision is hindered when you rely on closed questions to gain information in a selection interview.

Also, when developing open questions, consider using hypothetical questions. In a selection interview, a **hypothetical question** describes a job-related situation and asks how the interviewee would react. For example, as the interviewer, you may ask the applicant "Suppose the equipment you will be operating starts to overheat. What procedure would you follow in this situation?" Hypothetical questions allow you to better understand how the applicant would react to job-related situations rather than waiting until he or she gets on the job to find out. However, you should be careful not to ask leading questions. A **leading question** directly or indirectly leads the

Review your questions before the interview

Let the interviewee do most of the talking

Avoid asking leading questions

interviewee to believe that he or she should give a particular answer that is desired by the interviewer. For example, if you ask "You can take dictation, can't you?" the applicant senses that yes is the correct answer and may give that answer because you appear to desire that response. Even if the applicant can't take dictation, he or she may answer yes in hopes of getting the job and then learning dictation skills. Instead of asking this leading question, simply ask the candidate to take some dictation. The candidate's performance in this task will demonstrate whether he or she can take dictation. As another example, do not ask "You like working overtime, don't you?" Instead, ask "How do you feel about working overtime in this job?" This open question does less to signal a desired answer. As a result, the interviewee's answer is more reliable.

In addition, be cautious about asking compound questions. As mentioned earlier, a **compound question** is a question that includes two or more queries. Consider the following compound question: "How did you obtain the jobs you have held, how interesting did you find the work, and what were your responsibilities in those jobs?" Or, a compound question can be more than one unrelated question asked quickly together. For instance, "How much of your educational expenses did you earn while in college?" "How would you describe personal success?" Compound questions have several disadvantages. First, seldom does the interviewee answer *all* of the separate questions contained in a compound question. Second, the interviewer usually forgets to repeat the parts that were unanswered. Third, the parts of the question that go unanswered are wasted. Fourth, due to their rambling nature, compound questions are often given little thought and are poorly constructed. Therefore, it is advisable to avoid asking compound questions in selection interviews. As mentioned before, it is best to ask one distinct, well-phrased question at a time and give the interviewee sufficient time to answer it before asking your next question. Also, try to get all the information you need on one topic before you switch to a different topic in the interview.

Keep in mind that, in interviewing, a request for information does not have to end with a question mark to be considered a question. To illustrate, grammatically, the following is considered a question: "Do you have any welding experience?" However, it is a closed question, and a response of yes to the question is limited in value. For example, you do not know anything about the amount or quality of welding experience the applicant has when he answers yes to the closed question. On the other hand, the question could be refined to read "Please tell me about the welding experience you have." Since this statement requests information, it is still considered a question in interviewing even though it ends with a period, not a question mark. This rephrased version represents an open question that is likely to gain more valuable information concerning the applicant's welding experience than is the closed question.

Compound questions may not be answered completely

Examine whether your questions request the information you really want. Suppose, for example, you want to know how much training in management the applicant has had through her college courses. In this case, do not say, "Tell me about your education at Metropolitan College." This question may or may not get you the information you wanted. For instance, the interviewee may answer by talking about her overall grade point average and what she learned from being involved in student government. This information may be interesting, but it is not what you really wanted. A more refined question, such as "What management courses have you completed at Metropolitan College?" is more specific and more likely to get you the information you want. As a further example, suppose a supervisor wants to learn more about any special qualifications the applicant has for the job. The supervisor may say, "Tell me about yourself." However, the supervisor does not really want to know the shortened version of the applicant's life history. Such an answer, however, may occur in response to the above question. Instead, it would be better to say, "Tell me what qualifications you believe you have that make you well suited for this job." Therefore, before you create a question, ask yourself what information you are trying to obtain. Then, after creating your question, analyze it to see if it really gets at what you were trying to accomplish. If it does not, rethink the question.

Phrase your questions properly

Make sure your questions will do what you intended

Next, after the question is worded properly, ask yourself what you plan to do with the information once you get it. In one company, the interviewing skills of a supervisor were observed and evaluated by a consultant while the supervisor interviewed several applicants. One of the questions the supervisor asked each applicant was "What does the word 'ameliorate' mean to you?" Many of the applicants had to admit that they were unfamiliar with the word, and it was obvious that the question made several of them more nervous. When the interviews had been completed, the consultant asked the supervisor why he asked the above question. The supervisor explained that when he was interviewed by the company several years ago, he was asked that question. "I squirmed then when I didn't know the answer, so I make the interviewees squirm now by asking the same question," the supervisor admitted! This situation represents an unfortunate abuse of the interviewing process. However, it also demonstrates the point that questions unrelated to relevant aspects of the job or the applicant's abilities should not be asked in selection interviews.

As another example, Helen is interviewing Kathy for a sales representative position with the Atlas Company, which sells personal computers. During the interview, Helen asks, "Kathy, what changes do you expect in the computer industry over the next five years?" This is called a "so what" question. That is, once Helen has Kathy's answer, so what? Does the answer to Helen's question help in any significant way to determine if Kathy will be a good sales representative for the company? The answer is no. What is especially

Watch out for "so what" questions

important is Kathy's ability to persuade customers that their computer needs can be met by Atlas computers. Interviewing time should be used wisely to ask relevant and meaningful questions.

When the applicant answers a question, you may need to ask a follow-up or probing question to gain more information beyond that provided in the interviewee's original answer. Suppose, for example, you ask the applicant, "What have you learned in your college course on supervision that you think will help you on this job?" In response, the applicant says, "I think the material on how to avoid miscommunication will be especially helpful to me." An appropriate probing question would be "Based on what you learned, how do you plan to avoid miscommunication with others on the job?" As a result, you get the applicant to expand on his or her answer. You then have a better understanding of how good a communicator the applicant will likely be on the job.

Listen carefully to the interviewee's answers

Regardless of the type of question you ask in the interview, listen carefully to the interviewee's response. However, do not verbally judge the interviewee's answers. For example, in answering one of your questions, suppose the interviewee mentions why she quit a job. If you think it is a poor reason to quit a job, do not respond by saying, "That's not a very good reason to quit a job, is it?" Such a response will create a negative interview climate. Instead, a more appropriate response in this case would be "Tell me more about why you think that situation necessitated that you quit your job." Furthermore, while you are maintaining a neutral stance in the interview, take notes on what the interviewee says in response to your questions. Otherwise, you may forget some important comments made by the interviewee. After interviewing several applicants, if you did not take notes during each interview, you can easily get confused on which candidate made certain comments.

Take notes in the interview

The Closing

Although the closing for a selection interview should be brief, it is nonetheless important. When you decide to close the interview, keep the following principles in mind. First, make it clear that the interview is over. Do not confuse the applicant on whether or not the interview is actually coming to a close. A false closing where you act like the interview is coming to a close and then suddenly ask more questions is inappropriate and avoidable. Avoid abrupt closings that can leave the applicant with the impression that, since you now have all the information you want, he or she is no longer important to you. Second, thank the interviewee for his or her help. That is, express to the interviewee your appreciation for the opportunity to interview him or her. Third, indicate when the applicant will be notified of your hiring decision. Even if you do not hire the applicant, a proper closing can help leave the applicant with a favorable impression of you and your company.

Avoid false closings

1. Some supervisors complain that restrictions against asking questions considered to be illegal hinder their ability to conduct selection interviews. Why is it that supervisors usually do a better job of interviewing when they avoid asking illegal questions?
2. Think of a time when you applied for a job and the interviewer did a poor job of interviewing you. What mistakes did the interviewer make?

The Exit Interview

The **exit interview** is used to learn why an employee is leaving a job voluntarily and to collect other information that might be valuable to the company. Whenever an employee leaves a job for any reason other than being laid off, fired, or retired, it is usually considered voluntary. Although personnel departments often conduct exit interviews, supervisors may also do so. Therefore, you should understand how to conduct these interviews.

Exit interviews can provide valuable information

The Value of Exit Interviews

Learning why workers quit their jobs can be important to a company. Specifically, the information obtained from exit interviews can aid organizations in the following ways.

Help Retain Good Employees. Once the causes of turnover are learned, steps can be taken to reduce it. Overcoming problems that cause turnover will help the company retain good employees.

Identify Employee Selection Weaknesses. Information from exit interviews can identify needed changes in selection procedures. The information obtained from these interviews may help explain why certain employees leave while others stay. For example, suppose a company's work procedures require employees to work at various jobs. Some employees may feel comfortable with this procedure, while others may dislike it and resign. As a result, more thorough screening of future job applicants to make sure those hired accept job rotation seems appropriate.

Provide Documentation. Information from exit interviews helps to document why employees leave their jobs. This information is also used to complete employment files on departing workers and it remains available for future reference should questions arise later regarding an employee resignation.

Preparing for the Exit Interview

Advanced preparation greatly increases the likelihood that the exit interview will be smooth and productive. The following suggestions will help you prepare for any exit interviews you may need to conduct.

Learn why the employee is leaving

Listen Attentively.   Remember, your goal is to learn the employee's reason for leaving, not to give a speech or lecture. Therefore, let the departing employee do most of the talking, and listen carefully.

Review the Personnel or Employment Record. What is the employee's educational level? Maybe he or she is overeducated for the job and has become bored with it. Has the employee's physical condition affected his or her ability to do the job? By reviewing the employee's personnel record before the interview, you may detect hidden reasons that could explain the departure.[12] Also, when reviewing the employee's record, make sure you are familiar with the job and the people with whom the employee works.

Schedule a Private Room. As mentioned earlier, you should arrange for a room that is free from interruption, distraction, and observation by others. Privacy is essential for obtaining open and candid answers from the departing employee.

Select a convenient time for the exit interview

Hold the Interview before the Last Workday. Schedule the interview any time within the last two weeks of employment, except on the departing employee's last day. He or she will probably be too busy to participate in an exit interview then.

Develop a List of Questions. In preparing a list of questions, consider some of the common reasons for leaving a job. Also, look at the specific nature of the departing employee's job for possible areas to explore. Questions frequently asked in exit interviews are:

- ☐ Why are you resigning?
- ☐ What did you like about your job?
- ☐ What did you dislike about your job?
- ☐ How fairly do you believe you were paid for the work you did?
- ☐ How well did your job fit your career plans?
- ☐ How completely and fairly do you believe your performance was evaluated?
- ☐ How well do you believe your contributions on the job were recognized and appreciated?[13]

It is also important to use follow-up questions to probe into the departing employee's answers. Once you have developed your list of questions, you are ready to conduct the exit interview.

Conducting the Exit Interview

In most companies, a departing worker needs to be given certain information. For example, the worker needs to know about such matters as the amount of the final paycheck and when insurance coverage ends. You can begin the exit interview by providing this kind of information. Then, explain that you need to determine why the worker is leaving. In requesting reasons for the departure, explain that the information will be used only for improving working conditions in the firm.[14] Point out that the departing worker is in a unique position to provide valuable information that may result in improvements that will benefit other workers. To motivate the departing worker to respond openly, appeal to his or her concern for the welfare of other employees. It would even be helpful if you cited a few examples of improvements that had been made based on information gained from exit interviews.[15] Be sure to point out that any information the worker provides will be kept confidential and given serious consideration. Maintain a climate of mutual trust and confidence throughout the interview. This approach will help encourage the departing worker to be open and candid. Assure the person that the information will not affect his or her employment references from the company.

Seek open and honest answers

Without making any evaluation or judgment, carefully and objectively probe the reasons given for leaving. Next, ask about the strengths and weaknesses the worker sees in the firm and probe into the answers given. Throughout the interview, treat the departing worker with respect. Do not become defensive if he or she criticizes the company or anyone in it. You want the worker to be honest and identify any major problems that may exist. Arguing will only create a defensive climate, which will discourage frankness. Continue to encourage the worker to express his or her true feelings. As you conduct the exit interview, be a good listener. A successful exit interview will reward you with valuable information.

Don't argue with the employee

You have studied the concept of interviewing and the techniques for conducting informational, selection, and exit interviews. It is now time to briefly review the objectives established at the beginning of the chapter.

Looking Back

☐ **Define interviewing.** Interviewing is a process in which two people with a specific purpose share information through asking and answering questions.

☐ **Explain the distinction between directive and nondirective interviewing.** A directive interviewing approach allows you to establish the purpose of the interview and control it through a structured set of questions. A nondirective interviewing approach permits the respondent to control the direction of the interview and what is discussed.

☐ **Identify tips for asking questions.** Make your open questions specific. Preface a question if that will make it easier to answer. Ask a follow-up question if you want the respondent to expand on an answer. In addition, consider using indirect questions if the respondent seems reluctant to answer directly. Use appropriate language and keep your questions simple. Last, use compound questions cautiously and avoid add-on questions.

☐ **Explain how to conduct informational interviews.** An informational interview is used to gather information for the purpose of analyzing situations and making decisions. To conduct one, determine the specific information you wish to acquire. Then develop relevant questions to obtain it.

☐ **Indicate the steps used in selecting employees for employment.** The selection process begins with an application form and a brief interview. A second interview and testing follow. Next, the applicant's work record and references are checked. A physical exam is often required. Then comes a recommendation from personnel, an interview with the supervisor, and the decision to hire or not to hire.

☐ **Identify key aspects of conducting the final selection interview.** Hold your selection interview in a location where you will not be subjected to frequent interruptions. Have appropriate and legal questions prepared before the interview. The opening you use should help develop rapport and orient the applicant. Then, determine if the applicant is qualified and right for the job. In doing so, make appropriate use of open questions, hypothetical questions, and follow-up questions. Make your closing brief, but thank the interviewee for participating in the interview and indicate when a hiring decision will be made.

☐ **Explain how to conduct exit interviews.** An exit interview is used to learn why a worker is leaving a job voluntarily and to collect other information that might be valuable to the company. To obtain this information, you should establish a climate of mutual trust and confidence with the departing worker and maintain it throughout the interview. Ask questions that will solicit information on why the worker is leaving. In addition, seek suggestions from the departing employee on ways to improve working conditions or efficiency in the organization.

Key Terms

clearinghouse question

closed question

closing

compound question

directive interviewing approach

exit interview

follow-up question

hypothetical question

informational interview

interviewing

job description

job specification

leading question

nondirective interviewing approach

nudging probe

open question

opening

recruitment

reflective question

selection interview

selection procedure

Review and Discussion Questions

1. What is the difference between directive and nondirective interviewing?

2. What are the advantages and disadvantages of open and closed questions?

3. Why should you be cautious in using compound questions in an interview?

4. What is a clearinghouse question? When should it be asked?

5. What are the steps involved in selecting new employees?

6. As the interviewer, how do you know whether you have conducted a successful selection interview?

7. What basic functions should the opening serve in a selection interview?

8. What are hypothetical questions? What is their purpose in selection interviews?

9. What types of valuable information can an exit interview provide the supervisor?

10. How should you motivate a departing employee to answer your questions candidly in the exit interview?

Action Incident 13.1

Nothing Changes

Supervisor: Hi, Ron. I wanted to get some information on the changes that were made in the blueprints. How long ago were they made?

Draftsman: Which changes?

Supervisor: The ones for the second floor of the building.

Draftsman: Those changes were made three weeks ago.

Supervisor: Which of the changes. . . ? I mean, would there be any. . . ? Could we get by without all of those changes?

Draftsman: Yes.

Supervisor: What would happen if we took out the center wall? Oh, before I forget, how difficult would it be to extend the balcony?

Draftsman: It would be fairly easy to extend the balcony because it's narrow. All we need to do is lengthen the supporting beams a little.

Supervisor: If we couldn't make all of the changes requested by the city building department, which ones would we have the option of not making? I guess we wouldn't have to put in a skylight or storm windows. What kind of smoke detectors do we have to install?

Draftsman: We are required to install electric smoke detectors.

Supervisor: With the air conditioning duct work extending from the heat exchanger through the first floor and branching off at other points, will there be a problem with the return-air duct since the thermostat is near the doorbell transformer?

Draftsman: *[Hesitates.]* I guess not.

Supervisor: Can the balcony be extended?

Draftsman: Yes.

Supervisor: Should we use copper or aluminum wiring?

Draftsman: You can use either, but it probably would be wise to use copper wiring.

Supervisor: Will the new building codes require us to make additional changes in the blueprints?

Draftsman: No.

Supervisor: Thanks a lot for your help. I guess that's all the questions I have.

Discussion Questions

1. What problem did you notice with the first two questions the supervisor asked? How could both questions be improved?
2. Why do you think the draftsman failed to answer the supervisor's question concerning what would happen if they took out the center wall?
3. What other mistakes did the supervisor make in conducting the informational interview? How could these mistakes have been avoided?

Action Incident 13.2

Where's the Exit?

Supervisor: Well, Judy, what's on your mind?

Employee: What do you mean?

Supervisor: Something must be bothering you, or you wouldn't be leaving the company.

Employee: Actually, I'm going to miss the short drive to work. However, I inherited some money, and I am planning to start a small business on the other side of town with my cousin. I know it won't be easy, but now I will be paid fairly, and I won't have to follow inefficient policies. However, I don't hold any grudges against the other employees.

Supervisor: In other words, you're leaving because you don't get along with the other employees. Isn't that right?

Employee: No, it isn't. I don't think there's any evidence to indicate that I don't get along with the other employees. However, I do think there's evidence that some of the company's policies are inefficient. For example, we have computerized a lot of our operations, but some of the departments don't use their computers to keep track of inventory. So only part of the company's inventory shows up on the computer. It's hard to coordinate production when you don't know the actual size the inventory. Unfortunately, company policy allows this problem to go on.

Supervisor: I don't agree that it's a major problem. Each department knows what's going on in its area, and if people in other departments want to know about current inventory levels, they can ask.

Employee: You have to remember that there are times when an employee in one department needs to know . . . *[interrupted by supervisor.]*

Supervisor: What are some of the strengths you see in the company?

Employee: *[Hesitates.]* Well, maybe working conditions and flexible deadlines are strengths. The facilities are certainly clean and modern.

Supervisor: You would agree that another strength would be good employee morale, wouldn't you?

Employee: Oh, some of the employees are satisfied with their jobs, but I've noticed a lot of resentment over certain policies.

Supervisor: What changes would you suggest to increase production?

Employee: I think the level of quality is good right now. That's something I'm sure you feel is important. I would keep that as a high priority.

Supervisor: In your opinion, do the other employees seem fairly satisfied with their jobs?

Employee: Yes.

Supervisor: What type of business do you plan to start with your cousin?

Employee: She has some experience as a travel agent, so we are going to start a travel agency.

Supervisor: How effective did you feel your training program with the company was?

Employee: It was well designed and provided a lot of practical information I could use on the job. The main problem was that we didn't have time to practice the skills we learned because the training program went so fast.

Supervisor: *[Looks at watch.]* Well, I'm afraid I have a meeting I must attend. I'm glad we had a chance to talk before you left. Good luck in your new business.

Discussion Questions

1. How appropriate is the supervisor's opening in the exit interview?
2. How skillful is the supervisor in probing into the answers the employee gave?
3. To what extent does the supervisor find out why the employee is leaving or what strengths and weaknesses the employee sees in the company?
4. What mistakes in interviewing did the supervisor make?

Action Incident 13.3

Who Should Be Hired?

Wanted: Management Trainee

City's largest retailer of office products seeks person to train for management in new store. Experience in retail sales preferred.

Compensation includes salary, profit sharing, medical benefits, and paid vacation. Excellent advancement opportunity.

Send resume and three references to:

Personnel Department
Enterprise Office Products

Twenty applicants responded to this advertisement. From this group, the human resources department selected three for you to consider. You have interviewed them and must recommend one for the position. Your notes show the following information:

PEDRO ALVARADO

Work experience:	1 year — clerk at Hopkins Hardware.
	3 years — retail salesperson for Schmidt Office Supply (current employer).
Aptitude test score:	75 (100 possible).
Comments by references:	Pleasant personality; average work performance; gets along well with people; average in terms of initiative; dependable; willing to learn.
Your interview comments:	Interested in career progress; likes sales; excellent appearance; answers questions without hesitation; desires a higher salary.

MARY HUSTON

Work experience:	1 year — retail sales at Jones Shoe Store.
	½ year — salesclerk at Wolf's Variety Store.
	2 years — retail sales consultant for Betty Lou's Cosmetics.
	1 year — advertising salesperson for McCune Advertising Agency.
	1 year — office supervisor at Boone's Office Supply (current employer).
Aptitude test score:	95 (100 possible).
Comments by references:	An aggressive person; gets work accomplished; has a tendency to be somewhat abrupt; difficult to manage at times — has own ideas regarding how things should be done.
Your interview comments:	She feels there is no future at Boone's; likes job challenges; doesn't waste words — seems to say what she thinks; indicates that she tends to become bored with routine assignments; extremely favorable personal appearance.

ROY BRYAN

Work experience:	6 years — sales representative for Newmont Printing Company.
	1 year — assistant manager at Willow Office Products Company.

Aptitude test score: 85 (100 possible).

Comments by references: A likeable person; excellent at working with others; does not tend to be a self-starter; willingly accepts responsibilities; is not especially innovative.

Your interview comments: Seeks a more challenging position; seems to be people oriented; tends to answer questions in generalities; appears to be somewhat unsure of himself; somewhat sloppy in personal appearance.

Discussion Questions

1. What are the strengths and weaknesses of each applicant?
2. Examine your interview comments. What additional questions might you have asked?
3. Based on available information, which applicant will you select? Why?

Notes

1. Adapted from Charles J. Stewart and William B. Cash, Jr., *Interviewing: Principles and Practices,* 5th ed. (Dubuque, Iowa: Wm. C. Brown, 1988), p. 3.
2. Analogy provided by Charles J. Stewart, Purdue University.
3. From seminar notes provided by Charles J. Stewart, Purdue University.
4. Cal W. Downs, G. Paul Smeyak, and Ernest Martin, *Professional Interviewing* (New York: Harper & Row, 1980), p. 49.
5. Stewart and Cash, *Interviewing,* p. 64.
6. Stewart and Cash, *Interviewing,* p. 83.
7. Harry E. Williams, "The Elements of Supervision," *Supervision* 43 (May 1981), p. 5.
8. Robert Half, "How to Conduct a Successful Interview," *The Practical Accountant* 21 (September 1988), p. 97.
9. Barbara LaBarbara, "Recruiting and Interviewing: The Trump Card of the Personnel Game," *Supervision* 49 (December 1988), p. 16.
10. Stewart and Cash, *Interviewing,* pp. 39–41.
11. LaBarbara, "Recruiting and Interviewing," p. 14.
12. S. Bernard Rosenblatt, T. Richard Cheatham, and James T. Watt, *Communication in Business,* 2d ed. (Englewood Cliffs, N.J.: Prentice-Hall, 1982), p. 203.
13. Downs, Smeyak, and Martin, *Professional Interviewing,* p. 241.
14. Felix M. Lopez, *Personnel Interviewing: Theory and Practice,* 2d ed. (New York: McGraw-Hill, 1975), p. 332.
15. Lopez, *Personnel Interviewing,* p. 332.

Suggested Readings

Bahn, C. "Expanded Use of the Exit Interview." *Personnel Journal* 44, December 1965, pp. 602–23.

Bell, James D.; James Castagnera; and Jane Patterson Young. "Employment References: Do You Know the Law? *Personnel Journal* 63, February 1984, pp. 32–36.

Campion, Michael A.; Elliott D. Pursell; and Barbara K. Brown. "Structured Interviewing: Raising the Psychometric Properties of the Employment Interview." *Personnel Psychology* 41, Spring 1988, pp. 25–42.

Gorden, Raymond L. *Interviewing: Strategy, Techniques, and Tactics.* Homewood, Ill.: Dorsey Press, 1980.

Grossman, Morton E. "Hire Spending." *Personnel Journal* 68, February 1989, pp. 73–76.

Half, Robert. "How to Conduct a Successful Interview." *The Practical Accountant* 21, September 1988, pp. 96–98, 100, 102.

Hergenrather, Edmund R. "32 Points No Interviewer Should Miss." The Recruitment Supplement of *Personnel Journal* 67, August 1988, pp. 28–32.

Hinrichs, John R. "Employees Going and Coming: The Exit Interview." *Personnel* 48, January–February 1971, pp. 30–35.

LaBarbara, Barbara. "Recruiting and Interviewing: The Trump Card of the Personnel Game." *Supervision* 49, December 1988, pp. 14–16.

Stewart, Charles J., and William B. Cash, Jr. *Interviewing: Principles and Practices.* 5th ed. Dubuque, Iowa: Wm. C. Brown, 1988.

Appraising and Compensating Employees

Learning Objectives

Appraisal and compensation of employees are important concerns. How can job performance be appraised? Is there any way to avoid frustrations of the appraisal process? What happens if attention is not given to salary and benefit issues? The tasks of appraisal and compensation merit careful examination. When performed improperly, serious difficulties arise. Complaints of unfairness, possible legal complications, and negative attitudes can occur. This chapter's objectives, listed below, are designed to strengthen your knowledge of appraisal and compensation.

1. Understand the purpose of performance appraisal.
2. Specify the steps involved in the appraisal process.
3. Discuss several commonly used appraisal techniques.
4. Explain the basic purposes of compensation and benefits.
5. Understand the concept of job evaluation.
6. Discuss the supervisor's role in compensation.

Appraising Employees

Appraisal is the process of evaluating work accomplishments that involves comparing actual performance to standards or expectations. While discussion of job performance should be an ongoing process, formal appraisals are usually held at least annually. Performance of new employees should be formally evaluated more frequently, usually at three- or six-month intervals. The concept of appraisal is certainly not new, and a wide variety of techniques are used. You will study many of them later in this chapter. Some supervisors are not keen about appraising subordinates, often because they have not been trained to conduct appraisals and are hesitant to discuss negative ratings with employees.

The appraisal process serves as a technique to review how well subordinates have performed their duties, to counsel about future job expectations, and to encourage professional development. Appraisal programs are of much value when making plans, giving useful feedback, and encouraging communication. When used properly, they encourage supervisors and subordinates to work cooperatively toward greater productivity and increased understanding of their duties. Successful appraisal systems are:

Goal directed. Emphasis is placed on measurement of the extent to which goals are met or exceeded during an appraisal period.

Understandable. Supervisors and subordinates know how the system operates.

Fair. The process is perceived as beneficial to evaluators and administered in an equitable manner.

Positively oriented. Attention is focused on employee development and improvement rather than on a routine that must be tolerated.

Performance: The Primary Consideration

Performance measures whether an employee accomplishes or fails to complete job assignments. For example, a secretary who always must retype letters because of typing errors has a low performance level. If the secretary fails to type the letters, there is no performance at all. When the letters are typed correctly in a reasonable amount of time with no errors, a level of excellence is attained.

A worker's desire, ability, and understanding of the job influence performance. An employee must be capable of doing the job and knowing what is expected. Your failure to clarify expectations is a prelude to unsatisfactory job accomplishments. "We are excellent at telling employees where they fell short of our expectations after the fact, but we are utterly terrible at informing our employees of what is expected ahead of time."[1] Desire is a most important concern. It depends on motives, which vary among people. For instance, a person may have a strong compulsion to achieve success or avoid unpleasant events. Figure 14.1 illustrates factors that influence a worker's job performance.

Too many supervisors do not fully consider how employee attitudes affect performance outcomes. It is human nature to expect a payoff for hard work, yet a study conducted by the Public Agenda Foundation concluded that a majority of job holders do not believe extra effort is rewarded in the workplace. Only 20 percent of those surveyed believed a direct relationship existed between hard work and pay.[2] Also, some supervisors do not clearly distinguish between demonstrated *performance* and the *potential* to perform. Achievements are quite different from the possibility that desired productivity will occur. Many employees possess the potential to excel but do not actually get tasks accomplished.

Attitudes influence performance

Purposes of Performance Appraisal

Appraisal serves as a method to evaluate how well employees do their jobs and discuss ways to improve performance. Results influence decisions on promotion, termination, job reassignment, and salary increases.

Appraisals provide needed information

> A good performance review system increases employee motivation and job-related communications between subordinates and managers. It provides a vehicle for discussing current performance, determining an individual's self development and training needs, and for talking about advancement desires and opportunities.[3]

Appraisals provide a chance to develop long-term joint efforts for meeting objectives. Let's review several important purposes of appraisals.

Planning and Goal Setting. Appraisals help supervisors measure progress toward goals and plan future activities. Workers do not always know how their duties relate to overall goals. They may need clarifications and more information. Also, employees may have useful ideas or suggestions.

Training and Development. Since appraisals measure performance, more training may be needed. Supervisors can suggest educational and/or work experiences to develop competence and help subordinates become more productive.

Employee Concerns. Subordinates want feedback on their performance and information about future expectations. Appraisals are used to give feedback, provide recognition, and respond to questions. By listening and explaining your actions, you avoid many problems. You may discover that a subordinate has trouble because needed materials are not available. You can then make necessary changes to create a better work environment.

Figure 14.1   **Factors Influencing Performance Outcomes**

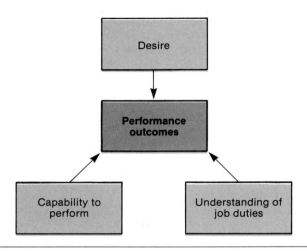

Documentation. Appraisal is a formal method of recording evaluation results. These data will be available for future recognition decisions, grievance proceedings, or even legal actions. It is important for you to keep good records and follow company guidelines for evaluating employees.

Correcting Weaknesses. Some employees' job performance will be inadequate. This situation cannot be overlooked, and you must point out shortcomings. Subordinates need to be told exactly what problems exist. Have facts to justify the evaluation and offer suggestions for improvement. Your sincere willingness to help overcome weaknesses can turn a poor or marginal employee into a good performer.

Steps in the Appraisal Process

Appraisal is a continual process. Each day, you will give advice, observe work behaviors, correct mistakes, provide encouragement, and give recognition for good work. Such actions are *informal* performance appraisals. The *formal* appraisal process requires time to be set aside for a careful examination of each employee's work accomplishments. You may discover that personal opinions differ from facts or that a well-liked employee is not the most productive. According to studies conducted by Opinion Research Corporation, half of the employees surveyed perceived evaluations to be unfair.[4]

Informal versus formal appraisals

Successful appraisals depend on your ability to be objective and clearly explain evaluations. It is necessary to plan ahead and focus attention on all factors involved in making appraisals. Now let's examine four steps of a typical appraisal process.

☐ *Step 1.* Based on each worker's job duties, which are specified in the job description, determine performance expectations.

☐ *Step 2.* Compare actual job accomplishments to these expectations.

☐ *Step 3.* Complete the appraisal form. Comply with organizational guidelines for appraising workers. Examine available information about the performance of each worker. (If necessary, request additional information.) Be consistent in applying evaluation criteria, and review the results to assure yourself that they are justifiable and accurate.

☐ *Step 4.* Hold a review session and discuss results with each subordinate. Later in the chapter, you will study how to conduct appraisal interviews.

Understand the essentials of performance appraisal

Appraisal Techniques

Many appraisal techniques are available, but no single one of them is ideal. Each has advantages and disadvantages. Well-known methods of evaluation include checklists, graphic rating scales, the forced-choice technique, ranking, and MBO. As a supervisor, you will likely have little choice in selection of a method. Progressive middle managers, however, will welcome your ideas and suggestions for improvement.

Checklists.   This technique uses a series of statements or questions that are checked to describe job performance of the person being evaluated. Figure 14.2 illustrates the **checklist technique,** which is easy to use. The evaluator simply checks either yes or no for each item. No comments are included, as the process is simply a method to record observations. With the checklist, a separate group of questions may be needed to provide more detailed information.

Checklists are easy to use

Graphic Rating Scales.   Among the most widely used methods of appraisal, **graphic rating scales** employ a range of indicators (such as poor to excellent or 1 to 5) on which raters make a mark to show their evaluation for each job-performance factor. Like the checklists, graphic rating scales are easy to use and take little time. Figure 14.3 illustrates a graphic rating scale, which includes space for comments. This is advantageous because the rater can include explanations or make additional comments. In practice, raters need to exercise caution so that a high (or low) rating on one factor does not influence evaluation of other factors.

Graphic rating scales are widely used

Forced-Choice Technique.   With the **forced-choice technique**, the evaluator must choose among "most" and "least" likely descriptive statements to indicate how a subordinate does his or her job. In Figure 14.4, for example,

The Forced-Choice technique has limited application

Figure 14.2 **Illustration of the Checklist Technique**

	Yes	No
1. Does the employee willingly cooperate with others in completing work assignments?	____	____
2. Does the employee have adequate job knowledge to perform duties in a satisfactory manner?	____	____
3. In terms of quality, is the employee's work acceptable?	____	____
4. Does the employee meet deadlines for the completion of work assignments?	____	____
5. Does the employee's record indicate unexcused absences?	____	____
6. Does the employee follow safety rules and regulations?	____	____

the human resources department has predetermined two favorable choices (follows directions and promptly completes work duties). There are two unfavorable items (wastes time and work assignments contain errors). To reduce the tendency to give high ratings, you do not know which traits the human resources department considers "best" or "worst." So you cannot be sure of the exact meanings of appraisals. Consequently, this method has limited value for enhancing workers' development.

Critical Incidents. The **critical-incident technique** involves recording especially strong or weak incidents of job performance. Records of these events are essential and enable you to be specific in discussing work behaviors with subordinates. Include dates, details, persons involved, actions taken, and relevant comments. Keep such records secure; never leave them lying around, as they are confidential.

Record both strong and weak incidents

When used properly, an opportunity is provided for employees to express their viewpoints. Unknown to you, there may be good reasons for behaviors. For example, you notice an employee idly sitting and drinking a soda pop. What do you think of this? Is this person lazy and wasting time? Not necessarily. This person may just be resting after making several sales calls that generated more than $10,000 in company profits.

Ranking. The process of **ranking** includes a number of approaches that involve comparing employees according to performance abilities. When you have few employees, you can use *simple ranking*. Position workers from top to bottom, best to worst. As the number of people increases, ranking becomes more difficult. Assume you are ranking 10 service representatives. You will likely have little difficulty picking the most and least outstanding

Rankings involve comparisons

Illustration of Graphic Rating Scales   Figure 14.3

	Excellent	Above Average	Average	Below Average	Poor
Job Knowledge Understanding of duties and responsibilities necessary to perform. Comments:	[ ]	[ ]	[ ]	[ ]	[ ]
Dependability Promptness in completing job duties, thoroughness, punctuality, consistency in following directions. Comments:	[ ]	[ ]	[ ]	[ ]	[ ]
Cooperation Willingness to work with co-workers and supervisors in accomplishing work tasks. Comments:	[ ]	[ ]	[ ]	[ ]	[ ]

people. What about those in the middle? What reasons exist for placing persons in the fifth or sixth position? This situation illustrates the difficulty in ranking performance.

In *alternative ranking*, you list all workers and then rank them according to their job performance. You alternately assign a name to a high and low position. For example, rank the most outstanding performer first and worst performer last. Then, place the person with the next-to-highest performance second and the name of the next-to-lowest performer just above the worst. Continue this process until all people are ranked. The results are a high-to-low placement that is somewhat more objective than the simple ranking process.

With the *paired-comparison* approach, all workers' names are listed. Each person's performance is compared to that of all the others. For each comparison, the better performer is noted. People are then ranked according to the number of preference choices received.

Essay Technique.   The **essay technique** involves writing statements about positive and negative aspects of job performance. Since each supervisor

---

Figure 14.4   **Illustration of the Forced-Choice Technique**

Indicate the statement that "most likely" and "least likely" describes the work performance of the employee that you are appraising.

	Most Likely	**Least Likely**
1. Follows directions.	_____	_____
2. Promptly completes work duties.	_____	_____
3. Wastes time.	_____	_____
4. Work assignments contain errors.	_____	_____

Essays are written statements

has leeway to describe work behaviors and some supervisors are better than others at expressing themselves in writing, it is difficult to compare various appraisals. The extent of detail varies considerably. While some appraisals are specific and comprehensive, others are cursory and general. Despite all this, the essay method forces supervisors to think carefully about their evaluations.

Management by Objectives. This concept was discussed in Chapter 4. **Management by Objectives (MBO)** emphasizes interaction between supervisors and subordinates to set mutually agreeable objectives. It enables you to compare performance with job targets. A major advantage of MBO is that employees do know the basis on which their work will be judged. Such awareness helps to overcome a common complaint of those who say, "Until my appraisal, I thought that I was doing the right things." Caution must be taken to write realistic, quantifiable objectives and, when necessary, demonstrate a willingness to adjust objectives.[5] Because of equipment breakdowns, it may be impossible to attain an established quota, or unanticipated personnel turnover can delay introduction of a new product or service.

Worker participation is a characteristic of MBO

Other Appraisal Techniques. The most common method of appraisal involves direct evaluations by supervisors. Although not as widely used, other appraisal systems include *peer, self,* and *subordinate* assessments. Peer ratings are rather uncommon in business. Self-appraisals are worthwhile for encouraging employees to gain personal insights into how well job duties are accomplished; supervisors can compare these results with their own evaluations. Subordinate appraisals involve worker ratings of their bosses.

Such evaluations give supervisors a greater understanding of how workers view their administrative abilities. This information is useful in correcting weaknesses and developing managerial skills.

Obstacles to Effective Appraisals

There is no perfect appraisal system, yet supervisors must make every effort to judge employees in an accurate and fair manner. Without continual awareness, it is easy for mistakes to distort ratings. Evaluators make errors for many reasons.[6] They may lack an understanding of the appraisal instrument, have personal biases, or feel uncomfortable about doing evaluations. Common obstacles to effective appraisals, often called effects, are noted in Figure 14.5.

Halo Effect.   Raters may give either high or low evaluations based on liking or disliking one aspect of an employee's work. This tendency is called the **halo effect**. A supervisor may allow such things as a pleasant personality, impressive appearance, or lack of complaints to overshadow assessment of actual work. By examining each aspect of job performance, supervisors can reduce the likelihood of making broad generalizations that do not represent actual job accomplishments.

Avoid the tendency to generalize

Leniency or Strictness Effect.   Supervisors who are either too hard or too easy in evaluating subordinates illustrate the **leniency or strictness effect**. Some are too lenient with appraisals. When this occurs, productivity deteriorates because employees are rewarded for putting forth less than their best efforts. Others are too strict, frequently to the point of being unreasonable. A strict rater needs to focus attention on the goal-setting process. "Goals that are measurable, obtainable, and realistic must be set with subordinates, and the rater must recognize achievement when appropriate."[7] Evaluators who are too strict or lenient do not address the real issue — quality of work performed.

Know evaluation criteria and be realistic

Central-Tendency Effect.   Rather than rate high or low, some supervisors do not differentiate among employees; they are inclined to rate all persons toward the middle of the scale. This describes the **central-tendency effect**. Many times, it occurs because of a reluctance to treat workers differently and possibly upset some of them. Most employees have a fairly accurate understanding of how well they do their jobs. So the central-tendency effect can cause misgivings about the appraisal process.

Do all workers perform similarly?

Personal-Bias Effect.   Letting personal feelings interfere with objectivity in conducting appraisals is termed the **personal-bias effect**. We tend to like

Figure 14.5   **Common Obstacles to Appraisals**

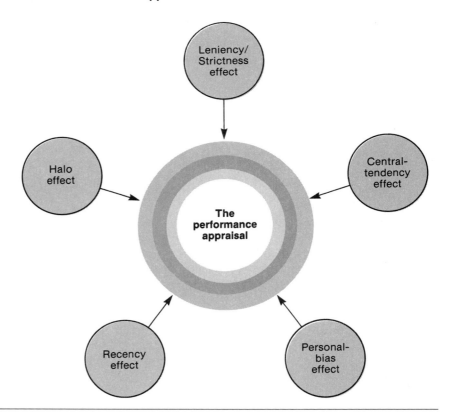

Appraise performance, not
personal feelings

some people more than others and generally feel closer to those whose thoughts and actions correspond to our own. Some of the most productive members of your staff, however, often are among those who are most difficult to manage. On the other hand, some of your personable and cooperative subordinates may be marginal in terms of their productivity. Nevertheless, personal likes and dislikes should not be a part of evaluations. Base judgments strictly on information related to job performance.

Past results should not be
overlooked

Recency Effect.   It is easy to forget events that happened several months ago. The **recency effect** refers to the influence of recent events on judgments affecting job effectiveness. For example, subpar performance can be overshadowed by acceptable or even excellent execution of job duties just before evaluation. On the other hand, the process is frequently reversed. Earlier accomplishments are overlooked due to recent problems. Be careful to not let the latest positive or negative example of subordinate behavior unduly influence performance ratings.

Consider This

1. What is the most important characteristic of successful job appraisal?
2. Why should subordinates participate in evaluation of their own job performance?
3. Which appraisal technique has the fewest number of disadvantages?

Performance Appraisal Interviews

After completing the evaluation instrument, the next step is to conduct an interview with each worker. This has several purposes. One is to discuss the evaluation, while another is to clarify work expectations. Still others are to offer ideas for improvement and to form plans for the future.

Why have appraisal interviews?

A positive attitude is a key factor. Supervisors often view appraisal interviews as necessary but unpleasant tasks. They fail to seize chances to coach, counsel, and help subordinates improve performance.[8] Strengthened supervisor-employee relationships result from increased awareness of the other person's perspectives. The interview process is an excellent means for exchanging ideas, concerns, and suggestions.

Have a positive attitude

Successful interviews require thorough preparation. Too often, supervisors do not allocate enough time to review rationales for their ratings. Consequently, they are not prepared to answer employee questions and concerns. Should this happen, the interview often evolves into fruitless accusations and defensiveness.

Preparation is essential

Each worker should be informed about the interview's purpose and given sufficient advance notice. Do not say, "When you have a few minutes I need to see you." The employee has no idea of what to expect. It is much better to say, "Jane, are you available for a meeting this afternoon at 3? I want to go over your appraisal and discuss plans for next year." Hold the interview in a place that provides privacy, without interruptions from the phone and other people.

Keep people informed

You establish an "atmosphere" for the discussion. Strive to be friendly and congenial to encourage sincere two-way communication. Since the purpose is to give feedback and prepare for the future, do not view the interview as an occasion to "unload on employees" and "put them in their place." Also, it is a mistake to create an impression that appraisals are just something that must be tolerated. This causes the discussion to lose much of its importance and can encourage employees to take an indifferent, or even negative, attitude toward evaluations. The following pointers are worth considering as you plan for appraisal interviews.

Prepare for Appraisal Interviews

1. Review the evaluation given on each item of the appraisal form.
2. Identify strengths and weaknesses to be discussed with each worker.
3. Document and be prepared to justify performance ratings.
4. Anticipate the employee's reaction to factors brought to his or her attention, especially negative aspects of performance.
5. Prepare possible responses to questions and comments likely to be expressed by the employee.
6. Give specific suggestions and recommendations to improve the worker's performance.

Conducting Appraisal Interviews

Many supervisors are not enthusiastic about a face-to-face meeting with employees, especially those who are low performers. As noted previously, however, a positive attitude toward the process and thorough preparation can go a long way toward reducing anxieties about the interview itself. This is not to say that the task is easy. It does imply that you can add to difficulties encountered in discussing job performance. Let's examine several essential steps for conducting successful interviews.

Keys to successful interviews

Develop Rapport and Establish the Tone.   A congenial, positive tone must prevail. Do not overlook basic psychological needs: "the need to feel important, the need for self-esteem, the need to be liked and appreciated."[9] Establish a relaxed atmosphere, briefly review the purpose of the meeting, and explain procedures. You might begin by saying, "Jane, please sit down. I'm glad we could set aside some time. I'd like to review last year's performance, hear your comments or suggestions, and make some plans for next year."

A congenial atmosphere is important

Go Over the Evaluation.   This step involves discussing performance. Have facts at hand, cite specific instances rather than talk in generalities, and recognize both positive and negative aspects of job performances. In a straightforward manner, explain the rationale for evaluations.

Explain reasons for your evaluations

Invite Questions and Comments. Give ratees time to express their viewpoints and reactions. Listen carefully to what they say. Based on these comments, it is possible that ratings may need to be revised. Do not let the discussion become an argument. Before reacting to remarks, think about

Solicit questions and comments

what you will say and plan your comments. (Once expressed, comments cannot be retracted.) Concentrate on available facts and do not make allegations you cannot support.

Offer Suggestions for Improvement.   When criticism is necessary, also give suggestions for improvement. These recommendations can be given verbally, but it is wise to note them in a follow-up memo. Remember to keep a copy of the memo in your file. Should a future disagreement arise, you have documentation of your actions. Sincere willingness to help employees meet expectations is of great value in strengthening supervisor-employee relationships.

Help workers attain performance excellence

Establish Future Goals.   Planning for the future is a vital part of the appraisal interview. When employees take part in setting goals, there is greater likelihood of gaining their commitment. Clearly specify goals and actions to be taken. This will help to avoid confusion and misunderstanding. As a result of employee participation, you will have greater knowledge of what subordinates actually expect to accomplish.

Look to the future

Summarize the Interview. Besides written notes, oral summaries of interviews are advantageous.[10] These let you know how well key points are understood. Summaries give employees an opportunity to review the main concerns supervisors deem important. Review the following suggestions, which increase your effectiveness as an evaluator.

A summary reinforces important conclusions

Actions to Avoid in Appraisals

1. Do not argue with employees or put them on the defensive.
2. Do not discuss other people's performance. The only exception is a circumstance involving dependence on the work of another person.
3. Do not make promises that cannot be kept.
4. Do not overlook weaknesses.
5. Do not criticize the employee as a person. Direct criticism toward performance.
6. Do not lose your temper.
7. Do not display indifference or dislike of the appraisal process.
8. Do not hurry through the interview. Consider it to be a building tool for working with subordinates.

Compensating Employees

Compensation includes direct monetary remuneration for employment and a variety of indirect benefits, such as insurance, pensions, educational allowances, and paid vacations. A perception of fairness is a major concern in the design, implementation, and administration of compensation programs.

What is compensation?

It is human nature for people to compare their compensation to that of colleagues and persons holding similar positions at other firms. Frequently, dissatisfaction arises due to a lack of understanding about how jobs are priced in the workplace. Some persons conclude that organizations, especially in the private sector, are too secretive about salary data. Since such information can cause friction among workers, many firms do not make salaries of specific individuals known to others. Another concern is the difficulty supervisors encounter in justifying relatively minor salary differences.[11]

What affects the amount of compensation paid by employers? Major factors include the value of jobs and level of employee skills needed to perform them. A highly computerized company depends on trained personnel who know how to operate sophisticated equipment and handle the breakdowns that inevitably occur. Computer skills are essential to maintain uninterrupted operations. Compared to many types of jobs, therefore, the salary for computer specialists is likely to be rather high. Other factors influencing compensation include salaries paid by other companies, the firm's ability to pay, contributions of individual workers, and perceptions of equity.[12]

Purposes of Compensation

The basic purposes of compensation are to attract, retain, and motivate personnel. When considering employment or contemplating a job change, salary and benefits are important considerations to most people, and firms use them as incentives to employ capable workers. A comfortable income represents a symbol of accomplishment and reinforces feelings of personal pride and achievement. Higher incomes provide greater discretionary purchasing power to upgrade a person's standard of living.

Compensation serves several purposes

Once hired, a good compensation package is an inducement to keep and motivate capable employees. Employers avoid costly turnover problems and retain people who possess needed job skills. Workers maintain continued employment and have opportunities to develop professionally and advance their careers. While money helps to satisfy human needs, its importance as a motivator tends to decline as these needs are satisfied. Once you have attained a desired standard of living, you might not want to work an extra day each week because personal time becomes more meaningful. Yet, an individual with an insecure employment future or large personal debt may forgo any days off to earn extra money. To motivate successfully, employees must have a clear understanding of the link between money and performance.[13] Otherwise, disenchantment is probable because of uncertainty regarding how efforts will be rewarded or a feeling that hard work is not recognized appropriately.

Objectives of compensation programs can conflict with one another.[14] If the pay for a capable performer is increased to retain his or her services, morale of other employees may decline. Retention can have a detrimental impact on motivation. Therefore, it is necessary to analyze the reasons for selecting specific methods of compensation. Relevant concerns include how to communicate with personnel regarding compensation issues and whether pay should be uniform throughout an organization. It is also important for compensation practices to correspond with management's philosophy.[15]

Recognize the complexity of compensation issues

Discussion of the many compensation issues is beyond the scope of this book. However, supervisors do need to be familiar with the role of compensation in the workplace, so we will examine several methods for compensating employees, identify types of benefits, discuss the rationale of job evaluation, and provide an overview of comparable worth. Also, you will learn about the supervisor's role in compensation.

Compensation and Benefits

People are compensated according to the amount of time they spend on the job or according to their productivity.[16] **Time wages** are based on a number of hours worked. **Salary** refers to monetary payment on a weekly or monthly basis. A key aspect of **incentive pay** is its direct link to performance. Consider an example of a piecework incentive program. A drill-press operator received 20 cents for each metal part processed. When the person produces 20 units per hour, he or she is paid $4.00, but if the hourly output increases to 40 units, pay doubles to $8.00. Incentive pay is a common practice in direct sales. A real estate salesperson may earn a 3 percent commission based on the selling price of property sold.

Incentives. In addition to piecework and commissions, other types of incentives include individual bonuses, group production incentives, profit sharing, and cost-reduction plans.[17] The essence of incentive plans is to encourage productivity. Nevertheless, they can be complicated and difficult for workers to understand. "The administration of an incentive system can be complex. . . . For many jobs, the standards and measures are too imprecise or too costly to develop. This means that the incentive system may result in inequities."[18]

What is the purpose of incentives?

Bonuses. A bonus is additional compensation for production that exceeds an established standard. Frequently, it is based on the number of "extra" units produced or amount of time saved by job-performance excellence. While bonuses have the potential to stimulate initiative, employees often believe that management will increase standards if too many people qualify for bonus payments.

Production incentive plans. This approach is similar to individual bonuses. However, it is designed to reward group effort and is especially useful for encouraging cooperation in situations where individual contributions are difficult to identify.

Profit sharing. The main theme of profit sharing is for employees to receive a portion of the profits earned by a firm. It is intended to reward productivity and develop commitment to an employer. According to a survey of members belonging to the American Productivity Center and the American Compensation Association, profit sharing is the most widely used nontraditional reward system.[19] However, it does have drawbacks. Rewards are not immediately paid to workers, and despite their productivity, a firm may not be profitable because of economic or competitive conditions.

Cost-reduction plans.   The idea behind cost reduction is to compensate employees for suggestions that reduce expenses. The Scanlon plan, which originated in the 1920s, is perhaps the most popular of these plans. Here, a committee of management and employee representatives evaluates proposals to reduce costs, and incentives are based on the difference between actual productivity and established standards or norms.[20]

Benefits. You probably have heard workers discuss benefits provided by employers or, when considering employment, have compared the appeal of various benefit arrangements. **Benefits** refer to a "wide range of indirect forms of compensation usually provided to make employment attractive."[21] As illustrated in Figure 14.6, numerous types of benefits exist, and the employee who has most or all of them is quite fortunate. Benefits are not inexpensive to employers and may amount to as much as 30 to 40 percent of total compensation expenses. In 1985, for instance, U.S. firms spent slightly over $2,500 per worker on health care.[22]

Benefits are expensive to employers

Considerable growth in the variety of benefit plans has occurred since World War II. In the 1940s, pensions were used as an alternative to monetary payments because of limits imposed by wage controls. Today, many employees regard benefits as "rights" of employment.[23] We can conclude that a majority of workers think of compensation in terms of money actually earned and are probably unaware of the total cost of their employment. The value of insurance coverages, retirement plans, paid vacations, and paid sick leaves is substantial, even though it is not directly reflected in paychecks.

People value benefits differently

People place different values on benefits and view them from their own perspectives. A person without health problems may give only slight attention

---

Figure 14.6   **Examples of Employee Benefits**

Medical insurance	Professional development allowances
Life insurance	Clothing allowances
Disability insurance	Child care
Workers' compensation	Recreational activities
Vacations	Transportation allowances
Paid holidays	Maternity/paternity leaves
Sick leaves	Credit union facilities
Paid personal days	Stock purchase plans
Retirement pensions	Relocation expenses

to the number of accumulated sick-leave days. However, an individual with severe health complications will highly value this benefit.

If given a choice, some younger persons may prefer contributions toward retirement plans be paid directly to them. The perceived importance of retirement income increases as a person reaches middle age and faces the reality of a limited worklife.

During the 1980s, considerable interest in flexible benefits, called **cafeteria plans**, evolved. With these plans, an employee allocates a set amount of benefit dollars according to personal choice. According to a 1988 Administrative Management Foundation survey, 24 percent of responding firms had flexible-benefit plans, an increase of 7 percent since 1986. The most frequently offered benefit choices were medical coverage, life insurance, and dental care.[24]

Cafeteria plans provide choices

Let's examine the rationale for cafeteria benefits. Assume you and your spouse are middle-aged, employed at different firms, and have no dependent children. Your employer provides medical coverage for both of you. If your spouse participated in a cafeteria plan, he or she may not be required to take medical coverage and could apply an allocated dollar amount to other types of preferred benefits, such as disability income protection or a retirement annuity. A Louis Harris Associates survey indicated reasons why firms adopted flexible benefits.[25] The most important reason was to control accelerating costs. Other reasons were a concern for differing needs of workers and a desire to increase job satisfaction. Flexible benefits are not without disadvantages for workers.

The rationale for flexible benefits

> When flexible benefits are introduced, many companies raise the deductible and copayment levels that are paid by employees . . . Employers define how much they will contribute toward benefits, not what benefits they will pay for . . . . Employers might direct their employees' choices by pricing some benefit options disproportionately higher than others.[26]

1. What is the most important purpose of job compensation?
2. How can compensation practices decrease job satisfaction?
3. Which type of job incentive will experience the greatest increase in usage during the next decade?

▼

Consider This

Job Evaluation

Job evaluation is a process used to determine the relative value of jobs. It serves to develop equitable wage scales, provide a method for establishing pay increases, specify qualifications for personnel decisions, and meet equal employment opportunity guidelines.[27] Nevertheless, job evaluation methods

What is job evaluation?

Figure 14.7   **Comparison of Job Evaluation Methods**

Method	Basis for Comparison	Scope of Comparison
Point	Predetermined scale.	Compensable factors (quantitative).
Factor comparison	Other jobs.	Compensable factors (quantitative).
Job classification	Predetermined classes of jobs.	Job as a whole (non-quantitative).
Job ranking	Other jobs.	Job as a whole (non-quantitative).

Source: Lloyd L. Byars and Leslie W. Rue, *Human Resource Management*, 2d ed. (Homewood, Ill.: Richard D. Irwin, 1987), p. 319. Used with permission of the publisher.

do have problems. They "typically suffer from all sorts of biases—both in the structure of the measurement devices themselves and in the ways in which they are used."[28]

How are jobs evaluated? Four methods of evaluation are commonly used: ranking, classification, factor comparison, and the point method.[29] *Ranking*, which is the simplest method, involves comparing the worth of jobs and placing them in order of importance. In *classification*, various pay grades or ranges are established, and jobs are positioned accordingly. The other two methods are more quantitative in nature. *Factor comparison* focuses on identifying critical job factors (such as level of skill, amount of responsibility, and degree of difficulty) and individually comparing them among all jobs. Finally, the *point method* is based on "the selection and definition of job factors, the assignment of point values to each factor, and the evaluation of each job to determine the total points for the job."[30]

Evaluation methods do differ

Figure 14.7 presents a comparison of job evaluation methods. While classification and ranking focus on the job as a whole, factor comparison and the point method examine compensable factors within a job. Also, notice differences among the bases used for comparisons. Factor comparison and ranking compare a job to other jobs, rather than use predetermined scales or classes. Another difference among evaluation methods is whether comparisons are quantitative or nonquantitative. For factor comparison and the point method, the scope of comparison is quantitative. "Although both methods are analytical, neither technique is necessarily statistically valid. Points or dollar values can easily be manipulated to create shifts in the positioning of jobs in the wage schedule."[31]

The specifics of factor comparison and the point method are somewhat complicated and will not be discussed in detail. A major concern for supervisors is to recognize the importance of job evaluation and contact the personnel/human resources department or seek specialized expertise for conducting job evaluations. Employees do have a legitimate concern about equity in relation to jobs and rewards.

A recent survey by Research Institute Recommendations revealed the startling fact that only two in 10 U.S. workers believe that performance and pay are related. This is a sad commentary indeed for employers who have allowed their compensation programs to deteriorate to this extent.[32]

Comparable Worth

A gap exists between earnings of men and women. The U.S. Census Bureau has estimated that women earn approximately 65 cents for every dollar earned by men.[33] **Comparable worth** involves comparing pay for jobs that are not identical but are of equivalent value. For example, a predominately female nursing job and a largely male carpenter position would be rated equally on a job evaluation point-rating scale but be unequal in terms of compensation. Proponents conclude that lower salaries characterize traditionally female fields of employment (such as teaching, nursing, and office work) and discriminate against women. Opponents argue that the marketplace sets salaries; they emphasize the difficulty of comparing jobs requiring different types of skills. The following list summarizes pros and cons of the comparable worth issue.

Equal pay for comparable work?

Should Jobs of Comparable Worth Receive Comparable Pay?

The arguments *for* comparable pay for comparable work are:
1. If one employee contributes as much to the firm as another, he or she should be paid the same.
2. It is needed to raise women's pay.
3. It will give women greater internal job mobility.
4. This is one way to further women's career ambitions.
5. It would serve to motivate women to be more productive.

The arguments *against* comparable pay are:
1. Federal law only requires equal pay for equal work.
2. It violates a firm's structured job evaluation system.
3. Employers must pay salaries competitive with those of other employers, which are based on what employees produce and the economic value of work performed.
4. Women receive less than men because two thirds of new employees are women, and they always receive less than more senior employees.
5. It is practically impossible to determine accurately the real value of a job.

Source: Leon C. Megginson, *Personnel Management: A Human Resources Approach*, 5th ed. (Homewood, Ill.: Richard D. Irwin, 1985), p. 479. Used with permission of the publisher.

In a 1981 decision, *County of Washington v. Gunther*, the Supreme Court ruled that discrimination on the basis of sex for jobs not requiring identical work duties could violate Title VII of the Civil Rights Act; yet the Court clearly stated that the ruling did not relate to the issue of comparable worth.[34] A federal court awarded a union between $500 million and $1 billion because of sex-based discrimination in *AFSCME v. State of Washington*. Later, an appeals court reversed the decision, and the parties ultimately reached an acceptable agreement.

> In early 1985, EEOC issued its first policy statement on comparable worth, stating that unequal pay for work of a similar value wasn't by itself proof of discrimination. The agency stated that it would not pursue "pure" comparable worth cases but would act in cases where it can be shown that employers intentionally paid different wages to women and men in comparable jobs.[35]

The Supervisor's Role in Compensation

Most supervisors have little, if any, responsibility for designing compensation and benefit plans. As a supervisor, your primary role is to function within policies and guidelines established by upper management and implemented through the personnel/human resources department, yet you can do a lot to assure that pay and benefit issues are handled properly within your work unit. Several recommendations will help alleviate potential problems and increase employees' confidence in your ability as a manager.

Understand the compensation program

Strive to understand compensation and benefit practices used by your employer. When in doubt, contact your boss or the personnel administrator. Many employee handbooks specify how workers are to be paid and benefits to which they are entitled. A major concern is educating subordinates; be certain they understand compensation practices. Clear explanations help to avoid difficulties caused by misinformation or misunderstanding.

Inform workers about changes in pay or benefits being contemplated by management. Whenever possible, solicit their views and report them to management. If you become aware of ways to improve compensation procedures, do not hesitate to recommend them. For example, a supervisor for a processing firm became concerned because many employees immediately spent their profit sharing checks and suggested that a financial planning seminar be held just before the money was distributed. Review your subordinates' compensation. If obvious salary inequities are discovered, inform your boss and try to remedy them. Finally, it is very important to evaluate personnel in an objective, unbiased way and clearly communicate the rationale for evaluations.

Looking Back

This chapter discussed employee appraisal and the basics of compensation. To subordinates, these topics are more important than many supervisors realize. Time taken to understand the appraisal process and compensation practices is seldom, if ever, wasted. Now let's review several key points and relate them to the chapter objectives.

☐ **Understand the purpose of performance appraisal.** Appraisal is the process of evaluating how well an employee has done his or her job. It serves as a basis for promotion, termination, job reassignment, and salary decisions. Appraisal is useful in setting goals, recognizing training needs, encouraging employee development, and providing documentation. Successful appraisal systems are understandable to supervisors and subordinates and are perceived as being equitable in terms of measuring performance.

☐ **Specify the steps involved in the appraisal process.** Appraisal involves four steps: determining performance expectations, establishing measurement criteria, completing the evaluation form, and conducting an appraisal interview. This interview follows a certain pattern. First, it is important to establish rapport. Subsequent steps are: review the evaluation, provide an opportunity for questions and comments, and then offer suggestions for improvement. Finally, future goals are established, and the interview is summarized.

☐ **Discuss several commonly used appraisal techniques.** There are a variety of techniques available to evaluate job performance. They include checklists, graphic rating scales, the forced-choice approach, the critical-incident method, essays, and management by objectives. No technique is ideal, and each has its own advantages and disadvantages. Supervisors must make every effort to judge job performance in an accurate and fair manner.

☐ **Explain the basic purposes of compensation and benefits.** Compensation and benefits are designed to attract, retain, and motivate employees. When considering employment or contemplating a job change, salary and benefits are important considerations to most people. Once hired, a good compensation package is an inducement to keep and motivate capable workers. While employees maintain continued employment, employers avoid costly turnover and retain people who possess needed job skills. For compensation to be motivational, employees must have an understanding of the direct relationship between money and performance accomplishments.

☐ **Understand the concept of job evaluation.** Job evaluation is a process for determining the relative value of jobs. It enables firms to establish salary scales and pay increases and set qualifications for personnel decisions. Four methods of job evaluation are: ranking, classification, factor comparison, and the point method. Review Figure 14.7, which compares these various methods of job evaluation.

☐ **Discuss the supervisor's role in compensation.** Most supervisors have little, if any, responsibility for designing compensation plans, yet they must understand compensation practices and educate subordinates about them. Clear explanations help to avoid difficulties caused by misinformation or misunderstanding. Employees need to be informed about changes in compensation arrangements that are contemplated by management. Whenever possible, supervisors should elicit employees' views and report them to management.

Key Terms

appraisal	halo effect
benefits	incentive pay
cafeteria plans	job evaluation
central-tendency effect	leniency or strictness effect
checklist technique	management by objectives (MBO)
comparable worth	performance
compensation	personal-bias effect
critical incident technique	ranking
essay technique	recency effect
forced-choice technique	salary
graphic rating scales	time wages

Review and Discussion Questions

1. Why do many supervisors lack enthusiasm and have negative attitudes toward evaluating workers' job performance? What can be done to change these sentiments?

2. How does an employee's desire, capability to do a job, and understanding of the job influence performance outcomes?

3. Which appraisal techniques are appropriate for evaluating the following positions in a large grocery store?
    a. Shelf stocker
    b. Checkout clerk
    c. Store manager
    d. Produce manager

4. Since supervisors usually have frequent contacts with workers, why is it important that they prepare for appraisal interviews?

5. Name the obstacle or effect each of the following comments displays.
    a. "In terms of ratings, Joe always considers everyone to be average."
    b. "Most likely, Sara gives the lowest ratings of any supervisor in the organization."
    c. "Sam just doesn't like fat people. They don't have a chance of getting good evaluations."
    d. "All you have to do is keep a clean workstation, and you have it made in Jane's department."
    e. "Harold is a good supervisor who always gives his people high evaluations."

6. What is your reaction to these comments a supervisor made during an appraisal interview?

a. "You have made considerable improvement in reducing the number of errors. Is there any way I can be of assistance to you?"

b. "We have received several compliments on your performance, but you still need to work harder."

c. "I need to discuss your future with the organization. Where should I begin?"

d. "Let's try to determine the cause of the performance problems. Remember, I'm here to help you."

7. Why should a supervisor understand his or her employer's compensation system?

8. What factors affect the amount of compensation paid to workers?

9. Why is comparable worth an issue in the workplace?

10. What is the purpose of job evaluation?

Action Incident 14.1

The Rating Game

Robert Greene, an employee of Consolidated Office Systems, has received excellent job appraisals and salary raises during the past several years. However, his colleagues consider him a gossip, troublemaker, and bad influence on other workers, especially the younger ones.

Ann Morris, Robert's supervisor for the past eight months, is preparing for the annual employee appraisal. In all fairness, she believes he has earned an average performance rating for each category on the appraisal form. But Ann has heard rumors that the former supervisor usually rewarded Robert rather than argue with him.

Robert is a persuasive person, often getting his own way. Ann is unsettled at having to interview him, knowing she is no match for his verbal skills. She has asked each worker to complete a self-rating prior to the appraisal interview.

Robert arrives promptly for the interview and gives Ann the completed self-appraisal form. She immediately notices that, with the exception of an above-average rating on "employee creativity," he has rated his performance as excellent in every category.

Discussion Questions

1. What should Ann do to prepare for this appraisal interview?
2. How should Ann react to Robert's self-appraisal of his job performance?
3. If Robert challenges Ann's appraisal on the basis of his experience and previous ratings, how should she respond?
4. How can Ann handle Robert's ability with words and his ability to persuade?
5. What should Ann do about allegations that Robert is a gossip, troublemaker, and bad influence on other workers?

Action Incident 14.2

I Deserve More

Dave Howerson is a supervisor at Pyramid Educational Systems and manages a staff of 18 people. He has held this position for three years and is respected for his knowledge and ability to get things accomplished. One of his subordinates, Doreen McCollum, transferred into the work unit two years ago. Doreen is a rather quiet, reserved individual who is not known as a troublemaker.

Pyramid uses a merit-based incentive system, which is designed to encourage and reward individual job-performance excellence. Each year, employees submit an annual report describing in detail their accomplishments for the previous year. Dave reviews these reports and accordingly prepares salary recommendations. Procedures do not require Dave to conduct appraisal interviews with each subordinate and none of the supervisors hold them. However, every supervisor must give employees a written letter to summarize evaluations for the appraisal period. For the past two years, Dave has not experienced any problems with this procedure and no employee complaints have been received. Two weeks ago, however, the first problem emerged.

Doreen requested an appointment to discuss her appraisal. She insisted that the evaluation was inaccurate and unduly influenced by Dave's personal dislike for her and sex-based bias against her. Completely surprised, Dave tried to explain the rationale for his evaluation and reassure her that she had not been discriminated against. Nevertheless, the discussion evolved into a defensive standoff. Dave said, "I've recommended an above-average percentage salary increase for you. You should be quite pleased; only three people received a higher percentage recommendation." Doreen responded, "I'm not buying this percentage stuff. I'm concerned about the dollar amount, and it is too low. Besides, I try harder than most of the others and deserve a greater reward for my efforts."

Since the discussion, relations between Dave and Doreen have become strained. They converse only when absolutely necessary. Dave believes that the evaluation was fair. In fact, he thinks she was given every benefit of the doubt and probably rated too highly. Doreen is convinced the appraisal was not equitable and has vented her feelings to her colleagues, who in turn have informed Dave.

Discussion Questions

1. What is your opinion of the appraisal process at Pyramid?
2. How might Dave have avoided the problem with Doreen?
3. What course of action can Doreen pursue to remedy her belief that she was treated unfairly?
4. Given the present situation, what can Dave do to improve his relationship with Doreen?

Action Incident 14.3

It Isn't Fair

Melodie Hansen has been employed as an administrative assistant at Midwestern Communications for the past five years. Her duties require extensive knowledge of word processing and an understanding of several computer languages. In addition, she is responsible for preparing the monthly company newsletter and contacting the telephone company to assure that all telephones operate properly.

Jake Wolford is also an employee at the firm. For five years, he has been a maintenance technician. His job includes making minor repairs on the heating and cooling system. Also, he responds to requests for fixing broken electrical switches, installing light fixtures, and replacing fluorescent tubes.

Recently the personnel department revised the wage ranges for all jobs. For Melodie's position, the range was increased from $5.00-$8.00 per hour to $6.00-$9.00 per hour. Since her hourly wage was already $6.25, Melodie received no increase in pay. The wage scale for Jake's position was also increased from $6.00-$9.00 to $8.00-$11.00. As he previously earned $7.75 per hour, Jake's pay was automatically increased 25 cents for each hour of employment.

At coffee breaks, Melodie learned that many employees appear to have benefited from the revised plan. As a loyal, dedicated worker, Melodie concluded there was probably a logical rationale why others seemed to get more pay. Yesterday, however, Jake stopped by to install a new electrical cord. While working, he brought up the topic of the new schedule and asked how much of an increase she received. When she replied, "Jake, I didn't get anything," he began kidding her and said, "That's probably because secretarial types have it pretty easy anyway." Then Melodie became upset, especially since she considers Jake to be overpaid and lazy.

This morning, Melodie decided to discuss the situation with her supervisor, Emma Parks. Emma indicated that the change was due to action taken by the personnel department and said, "I understand your concern, but there's nothing I can do about it." Melodie responded, "But Emma, this just doesn't seem to be fair." "That's the way it is. A lot of things in life aren't fair," replied Emma.

Discussion Questions

1. Is Melodie a victim of sex-based wage discrimination? Explain your response.

2. How does the concept of comparable worth apply to Melodie's situation?

3. At the time the revised wage schedule was implemented, what might Emma have done to alleviate potential difficulties?

4. Did Emma respond appropriately to Melodie's concern? If not, how should she have responded?

Notes

1. John F. Bache, "Performance Appraisals — Let's Quit Appraising and Begin Reviewing," *Supervision* 48 (March 1986), p. 11.

2. Carey W. English, "'Pay for Performance' — Good News or Bad?" *U.S. News & World Report* 98 (March 11, 1985), p. 74.

3. Ron Zemke, "Is Performance Appraisal a Paper Tiger?" *Training* 22 (December 1985), p. 24.

4. Gerald Graham, "Management File," *Wichita Eagle-Beacon* (February 3, 1986), p. 3D.

5. Charles M. Kelly, "Reasonable Performance Appraisals," *Training and Development Journal* 38 (January 1984), p. 80.

6. Terry R. Lowe, "Eight Ways to Ruin a Performance Review," *Personnel Journal* 65 (January 1986), p. 60.

7. Lowe, "Eight Ways to Ruin a Performance Review," p. 62.

8. Don Caruth, Bill Middlebrook, and Frank Rachel, "Performance Appraisals: Much More Than a Once-a-Year Task," *Supervisory Management* 27 (September 1982), pp. 32–33.

9. Kaye Loraine, "How Effective Are Work Evaluations?" *Supervision* 45 (May 1983), p. 8.

10. Peter G. Kirby, "A Systematic Approach to Performance Appraisal," *Management World* 10 (December 1981), p. 14.

11. Wendell L. French, *Human Resources Management* (Boston: Houghton Mifflin, 1986), p. 426.

12. French, *Human Resources Management*, pp. 401–02.

13. Douglas T. Hall and James G. Goodale, *Human Resource Management: Strategy, Design, and Implementation* (Glenview, Il.: Scott, Foresman, 1986), p. 490.

14. Hall and Goodale, *Human Resource Management*, p. 491.

15. Hall and Goodale, *Human Resource Management*, pp. 491–492.

16. Leon C. Megginson, *Personnel Management: A Human Resources Approach*, 5th ed. (Homewood, Ill.: Richard D. Irwin, 1985), p. 467.

17. William B. Werther, Jr. and Keith Davis, *Personnel Management and Human Resources* (New York: McGraw-Hill, 1985), pp. 334–337.

18. Werther and Davis, *Personnel Management and Human Resources*, p. 333.

19. Carla O'Dell and Jerry McAdams, "The Revolution in Employee Rewards," *Management Review*, 76 (March 1987), p. 32.

20. Lloyd L. Byars and Leslie W. Rue, *Human Resource Management*, 2d ed. (Homewood, Ill.: Richard D. Irwin, 1987), p. 348.

21. Hall and Goodale, *Human Resource Management*, p. 495.

22. Richard P. Sloan and Jessie C. Gruman, "Does Wellness in the Workplace Work?" *Personnel Administrator* 33 (July 1988), p. 42.

23. Gerald A. Ferris and Kendrith M. Rowland, *Human Resource Management*, (Boston: Allyn & Bacon, 1986), p. 225.

24. Jeffrey E. Long, "Flexible Benefits Move Ahead," *Management World* 17 (March–April 1988), pp. 12–13.

25. Carolyn A. Baker, "Flex Your Benefits," *Personnel Journal* 67 (May 1988), p. 56.

26. Baker, "Flex Your Benefits," p. 59.

27. Leon C. Megginson, *Personnel Management*, p. 481.

28. Leonard R. Burgess, *Compensation Administration*, 2d ed. (Columbus, Ohio: Charles E. Merrill Publishing, 1989), p. 145.

29. George T. Milkovich and William F. Glueck, *Personnel/Human Resource Management: A Diagnostic Approach*, 4th ed. (Plano, Tex.: Business Publications, 1985), pp. 522–28.

30. Burgess, *Compensation Administration*, p. 139.

31. Judith R. Gordon, *Human Resource Management: A Practical Approach* (Boston: Allyn & Bacon, 1986), p. 378.

32. John F. Bache, "Merit Increase Programs—Do We Really Pay for Performance?" *Supervision* 48 (May 1986), p. 14.

33. Ted Gest, "The Women Win—Again," *U.S. News & World Report* 102 (April 6, 1987), p. 18.

34. Byars and Rue, *Human Resource Management*, pp. 63–64.

35. Byars and Rue, *Human Resource Management*, p. 64.

Suggested Readings

Eyres, Patricia S. "Legally Defensible Performance Appraisal Systems." *Personnel Journal* 68, July 1989, pp. 58–62.

Grider, Doug, and Mike Shurden. "The Gathering Storm of Comparable Worth." *Business Horizons* 30, July–August 1987, pp. 81–86.

Hunter, William L. "Relieving the Pain of Performance Appraisals." *Management World* 17, May–June 1988, pp. 7–9.

Jacobs, Dorri, "Coaching to Reverse Poor Performance." *Supervisory Management* 34, July 1989, pp. 21–28.

Kirkpatrick, Donald L. "Performance Appraisal: When Two Jobs Are Too Many." *Training* 23, March 1986, pp. 65–69.

Lawrie, John. "Steps Toward an Objective Appraisal." *Supervisory Management* 34, May 1989, pp. 17–24.

Lee, Chris. "Using Customers' Ratings to Reward Employees." *Training* 26, May 1989, 40–46.

Ost, Edward. "Gain Sharing's Potential." *Personnel Administrator* 34, July 1989, pp. 92–96.

Sape, George P. "Coping with Comparable Worth." *Harvard Business Review* 63, May–June 1985, pp. 145–52.

Wehrenberg, Stephen B. "Train Supervisors to Measure and Evaluate Performance." *Personnel Journal* 67, February 1988, pp. 77–79.

Handling Conflict

Learning Objectives

After reading and studying the material in this chapter, you should be able to:

1. Define conflict.
2. Identify common conflict management strategies.
3. Outline a problem-solving procedure.
4. Describe a strategy for intervening in conflicts between others.
5. Explain organized labor's approach to dealing with conflict.
6. Define union.
7. Indicate the supervisor's role where a union exists.
8. Offer suggestions for working with the union steward.

Chapter

15

Understanding Conflict

Specifically, a **conflict** exists between two people when one person believes the other is preventing him or her from achieving a goal. Figure 15.1 illustrates this situation. As a supervisor, you may have goals that conflict with those of persons with whom you interact on the job. Suppose, for example, you are a quality-control supervisor. As a result, your goal of maintaining high quality might conflict with the production supervisor's goal of increasing output. Unfortunately, a key reason some supervisors are unable to handle a supervisory position is that they lack effective conflict management skills.

Expect some conflict on the job

Like it or not, conflict is an inevitable part of the job for any supervisor and for managers in general. As a matter of fact, research indicates that managers generally spend 24 to 49 percent of their time dealing with conflict.[1] The outcome of conflict is not always predictable; that is, conflict may be destructive or constructive.

Destructive Conflicts

Conflict can hurt productivity

A conflict is said to be destructive when those involved are dissatisfied with the outcome and believe they are worse off as a result of the conflict.[2] If employees go on strike because of a conflict with management, both sides will likely be worse off as a result. After all, during a strike *both* employees and management lose money. In addition, conflict can distract people from the important goals of an organization and cause valuable time to be wasted on nonproductive arguing. The consequences of destructive conflicts may also include a decline in morale and the refusal of those experiencing conflict to talk to each other. Furthermore, the people involved in a conflict may resort to threats, coercion, and deception. If they do—instead of focusing on persuasion, cooperation, and conciliation—the conflict will probably be destructive.[3]

Constructive Conflicts

Sometimes conflicts can be constructive, benefiting those involved. Consider Wally, a newly hired supervisor who quickly found that he did not get along well with Paul, another supervisor. As time went on, Wally became more annoyed with Paul. Specifically, Wally resented the fact that Paul never accepted responsibility for his mistakes or for production problems caused by his inattention to detail.

One day, while discussing certain production quotas, Wally and Paul got into an argument over what type of production schedule was best. Suddenly, Paul asked, "Why can't you see it my way?" In response, Wally explained the specific problems with Paul's production schedule, after which Wally became

Conflict As a Result of Differing Goals   **Figure   15.1**

more open. He pointed out that Paul had not accepted responsibility for errors that had resulted from other decisions he had made on the job. Wally also gave examples of how Paul's inattention to detail had caused problems. Wally explained he was concerned that this trend would continue if Paul's flawed idea was accepted and failed. There was silence for a few moments. Then Paul agreed that Wally was right. As a result of the conflict and their candid discussion, Wally and Paul developed a better working relationship and Paul became a more conscientious supervisor.

You can probably recall situations where you, too, developed a better relationship with someone as a result of a conflict. When conflict does produce a better working relationship, it is usually because open, candid communication between the people involved finally occurred. In most cases, communication is a key element in preventing, managing, or resolving conflicts in companies.[4] Granted, you do not need conflict before you can engage in open communication with others, but issues are often clarified and responsibilities better defined as a result of it. Sometimes, therefore, conflict can expose and eliminate factors that hinder working relationships.

Discussing problems often helps resolve them

When people work together, some conflict is inevitable. Some of the most common causes of conflict that supervisors experience on the job are listed below.

Common Causes of Conflict

1 Poor communication.
2 Style of supervision.
3 Incompatible goals.
4 Differing ideas about how a task should be performed.
5 Differences in perceptions.
6 Differences in values and philosophies.
7 Personality differences.
8 Work assignments.
9 Change.
10 Competition.

Conflict Management Strategies

There are different conflict management strategies

There are several strategies used by supervisors for dealing with conflicts on the job. Supervisors engage in conflict management when they select and use a strategy that seems most appropriate for dealing with a particular conflict. It should be noted, however, that there is always the danger that a particular conflict management strategy will not actually resolve the conflict. Consider the common conflict management strategies discussed below.

Avoidance.   Some supervisors use **avoidance** as a strategy for dealing with conflict by simply doing nothing and ignoring the conflict. They may view the conflict as hopeless and useless, and they see no need to get involved. By doing nothing, they just hope the conflict will go away or resolve itself. In either case, they remove themselves mentally and physically from the conflict. In some cases, avoidance may be appropriate. Interestingly, research indicates that "Managers with poor conflict management skills incur high performance costs if they bring their subordinates together to resolve conflict. 'Don't rock the boat' appears to be good advice to such managers."[5] Sometimes conflicts do blow over without anything being said or done, but an avoidance strategy can also be risky. What if the conflict does not go away? The conflict may become even more intense over time and even more difficult to resolve. Therefore, before selecting avoidance as a strategy for dealing with conflict, ask yourself the following questions:[6] What do you risk by not confronting the conflict and letting the problem continue? What will be the impact of this strategy on your subordinates, on your ability to supervise, and on the attainment of department goals?

Smoothing.   When a supervisor uses a **smoothing** strategy, he or she attempts to eliminate conflict by trying to get along with others at all costs. To maintain harmony, differences with others are played down and areas of agreement are emphasized. The assumption behind this strategy is that conflict is bad and that differences between people only drive them apart.[7] Some conflicts are minor and it may be appropriate to smooth over them and not get concerned. However, attempting to smooth over major problems in organizations is usually inappropriate. Such problems need to be addressed, even if some feathers get ruffled in the process.

Compromise.   A **compromise** strategy selects a solution that satisfies some of the needs of both parties to a conflict. This strategy may even be forced on subordinates by their supervisor. Regardless of how it occurs, however, compromise is fine if the solution meets most of both parties' needs. Unfortunately, sometimes a compromise solution is not good for either individual. As a result, neither person will be satisfied or committed to it. In other cases, "Compromise may be the only practical way of handling a conflict situation in which two equally strong and persuasive parties attempt to work out a solution."[8] As a supervisor, however, be leery about compromising on issues that are critical to the success of your work unit.[9]

Forcing.   Under a **forcing** strategy, a supervisor uses position power to force others to accept his or her solution. Supervisors may end a conflict with a subordinate by ordering things to be done a certain way. As a result, the subordinate who disagrees loses. Not surprisingly, this strategy often leads a subordinate to conclude that the supervisor does not care about the subordinate's perceptions or needs. When something must be done a certain way, it may be necessary for you to require that a particular procedure be followed. However, in such cases, ask yourself, "Is forcing the only way to gain compliance?" Unfortunately, forcing can create bad feelings and even cause a decline in worker morale. Forcing can produce quick results; however, over the long run, its continued use hinders the development of effective interpersonal relations with subordinates.

Consider This

1. Have you ever experienced conflict with a teacher because you misunderstood the teacher's instructions? If so, how did you feel? In retrospect, how might you have avoided or corrected the misinterpretation?
2. Consider a recent conflict situation you experienced in which you used a smoothing strategy for managing the conflict. Were you satisfied with the results? If not, what other conflict management strategy do you think might have produced better results?

Conflict Suppression or Resolution

There are different ways in which conflicts are ended. An individual, for example, may simply defeat the other person in a conflict. In such cases, although one person wins in the disagreement, the conflict itself may only be suppressed. This outcome is referred to as a **win-lose situation.** That is, one person achieves his or her objective, but the other does not. When subordinates lose a conflict because their supervisor uses position power to get his or her way, the subordinates often resent it. As a result, the employees' motivation and performance on the job may decline. A **lose-lose situation,** on the other hand, occurs when both parties in a conflict fail to get what they want. As a result, both sides lose and each person is dissatisfied. However, when both parties in a conflict reach a mutually acceptable agreement, the conflict is said to be resolved. This outcome is referred to as a **win-win situation.** A win-win solution satisfies the goals of both people involved in a conflict. Although it may be time

Win-win solutions are best

consuming, a win-win solution to a conflict is usually the most beneficial approach over the long run. A solution that benefits both parties in a conflict enhances their morale, and they will be committed to making the solution work. Using a problem-solving procedure is one common means available to supervisors for developing a win-win solution to a conflict.

Problem-Solving Procedure

Problem solving represents more than a method; it represents an attitude or perspective.[10] If you do not want to deal with a conflict, you can use the avoidance strategy mentioned earlier. To be a problem solver, however, you must take an interest in the problem, desire to cooperate, and seek to find a solution to the problem. The following **problem-solving procedure,** shown in Figure 15.2, is one approach to problem solving that can have beneficial results for supervisors in resolving conflicts.

Create a Positive Environment

The old adage "You can catch more flies with honey than with vinegar" applies very much to problem solving in conflict situations. Avoid making the other person in the conflict feel defensive. For example, defensiveness will be triggered in others if they believe they are being controlled, manipulated, ignored, or talked down to by you.[11] To arrive at an acceptable solution, both parties in a conflict must work together. Also, you must control your own anger. People who handle anger well have learned to mentally step back and further analyze the situation.[12] Problem solving is especially difficult when both individuals approach the process showing hostility, disrespect, and vindictiveness toward each other. Such a combative environment does not foster agreements; it often only produces more conflict. Two parties in a conflict may not be fond of each other, but they need to show a willingness to consider each other's needs and cooperate for the problem-solving process to work.

Characteristics of a positive environment for problem solving include meeting in a location that is comfortable to both individuals and engaging in open communication. The neutral meeting location should be free of distractions and allow confidentiality to be maintained.[13] Open and honest communication helps both individuals understand each other's perspective and intentions. In addition to being candid in expressing themselves, both individuals must be willing to listen carefully to each other. When past relations between two parties in a conflict have not been good, their success in using the problem-solving process will be enhanced if they approach it as a new start. Any effort toward developing or improving the level of trust and confidence existing between the two parties will help create a positive environment for resolving a conflict.

Cooperation helps to resolve conflicts

The Problem-Solving Procedure   **Figure 15.2**

       Evaluate the Solution
          Did the solution accomplish what it was intended to do?
         ↑
      Implement the Agreement
        Determine how it will be implemented.
        ↑
     Reach an Agreement
       Review the list of possible solutions.
       Make any revisions necessary.
       Select a solution that meets the needs of both parties.
       ↑
    Propose Different Solutions
      Brainstorm a list of possible solutions.
      Don't evaluate the ideas at this point.
      ↑
   Determine What Results are Desired
     What are the parties trying to accomplish?
     Depersonalize the conflict.
     ↑
  Identify Relevant Facts and Opinions
    Determine what happened.
    Identify the key issues.
    How do the parties feel about the situation?
    ↑
 Define the Problem
   Agree on what is the problem.
   Focus on each other's needs.
   ↑
Begin: Create a Positive Environment
  Demonstrate a willingness to cooperate.
  Indicate an interest in finding an equitable solution.

Define the Problem

A wise adage states that "a problem well defined is half solved."[14] Therefore, early in the problem-solving process, the parties in the conflict should agree on the nature of the problem. In doing so, the individuals need to be specific and concrete in defining the problem. Even though individuals in a conflict may realize they are experiencing a problem, the problem may be vague, abstract, and confusing. If you are uncertain as to why an issue is a problem or a concern for the other person, consider expressing "a feelings commentary."[15] For example, you might say, "I don't understand why this issue troubles you. Please tell me more about your concerns." Once the problem is carefully analyzed and its dimensions understood, it is much easier to get a grip on it. Solutions that address the causes of a problem can then be developed.

A problem must be understood before it can be resolved

Identify Relevant Facts and Opinions

In many cases, problems are best viewed as a jigsaw puzzle. The pieces to the puzzle or problem must be collected, analyzed, and put together to produce a solution. These pieces usually show up in the form of facts and opinions. To gather this information, key questions need to be asked. For example, What is the actual situation? How did it develop? What are the key issues? How does the other person feel about what has happened? Understanding the relevant facts and opinions helps you begin to see what the solution to the problem will probably need to look like.

Determine What Results Are Desired

When using the problem-solving process, both individuals should think carefully about what they are trying to accomplish and the results they are seeking. That is, what are the end results desired from whatever solution is eventually developed? In answering this question, the individuals involved in the conflict must be honest with themselves, candid with each other, and realistic. Be hard on the problem and soft on the other person.[16] Do not be

Be clear on what you want

reserved in expressing your interests or what you want. Also, do not worry if the interests expressed by you and the other person appear incompatible at first. Creative solutions are developed every day to sticky problems. Separate the people from the problem. Different personalities may be present and a part of the problem. However, you should attempt to depersonalize the conflict to avoid judging each other. Blaming should be avoided. Instead, be supportive of the other person as much as possible.[17] As shown in Figure 15.3, you want to focus your energies on the problem instead of allowing anger to exhaust you. The expectations established at this stage in the problem-solving procedure represent standards for evaluating possible solutions.

Propose Different Solutions

Both parties in the conflict are encouraged to offer different ideas for solving the problem—a process frequently referred to as "brainstorming." Don't worry about producing the perfect solution at this point. There will likely be general solutions that will quickly come to mind, but also exercise creativity. Be spontaneous; the more ideas, the better. Through hitchhiking on ideas,

Brainstorm new ideas

one suggestion may spawn others. During brainstorming, possible solutions should not be criticized, judged, or rejected, no matter how impractical they may appear at the time. Just focus on generating ideas. People are more likely to express new ideas and be imaginative if they know they will not be ridiculed or criticized. Look at the problem in as many different ways as possible. Write down the ideas as they are presented, preferably on a large sheet of paper where all parties can easily see them.

Depersonalize Conflicts and Focus on the Problem   **Figure 15.3**

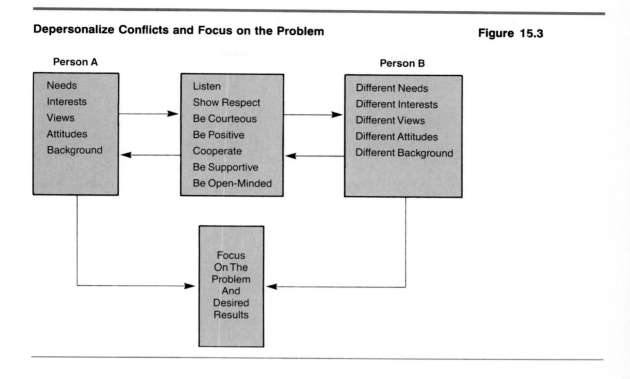

Person A		Person B

Needs	Listen	Different Needs
Interests	Show Respect	Different Interests
Views	Be Courteous	Different Views
Attitudes	Be Positive	Different Attitudes
Background	Cooperate	Different Background
	Be Supportive	
	Be Open-Minded	

Focus
On The
Problem
And
Desired
Results

Reach an Agreement

After the two parties have recorded all of the possible solutions they can think
of, the items listed should be reviewed. In doing so, the individuals may
decide to revise different solutions or combine some of them; however, it is
important to keep in mind the interests of the two parties and what they are
trying to accomplish. At this point, there is a natural tendency to craft a
compromise. This strategy can produce acceptable solutions, but only if key
interests of the two parties are satisfied. Compromises which do not satisfy
critical needs of one or both individuals will leave them unhappy and
disenchanted. As a result, there will be little motivation to make the
compromise work. Eventually, it may even be abandoned. The key is to select
a solution that satisfies the major interests of both parties and that enables
them to accomplish what they wanted to achieve.

For example, consider two supervisors, Jack and Ken, who are working
on a project. Jack wants to increase the inventory of parts to be used in the
project. Ken is against the idea. The two positions appear incompatible. That
is, either they do or they do not increase the inventory of parts. Focusing on
their opposing positions will only cause Jack and Ken to reach an impasse or

Not all compromises are good

decide to compromise. A compromise might involve increasing inventories some, but less than what Jack wanted. As a result, neither of their demands would be satisfied completely.

A better approach would be for both of them to consider each other's interest. What is Jack's interest in increasing the inventory? He wants to avoid price increases on the parts they will need. Jack knows that by building up the inventory now, he can avoid future price increases. Unfortunately, Ken does not have room to store more parts. Ken's interest is in keeping the inventory at a manageable level. The best solution to this conflict will address both supervisors' interests. An examination of their interests shows that their positions are not necessarily incompatible; there is a possible solution. Jack could pay for the needed parts in advance and have the supplier stagger the shipments. As a result, price increases could be avoided and new parts would arrive as the inventory dwindled and space became available for new ones. Focusing on the interests of the two individuals produced a satisfactory solution.

Once an agreement appears to have been reached, make sure you and the other person clearly understand it. For example, you may summarize or paraphrase in your own words the major aspects of the agreement.

Implement the Agreement

A solution is of little benefit unless it is put into action. Too often, however, considerable time and effort are spent developing an acceptable solution for resolving a conflict without determining how it will be implemented. Instead of relaxing and going off in different directions once an agreement has been reached, the two parties must realize that there is more to do. It would be appropriate, for example, to consider the following questions. What are the individuals going to do next? How are their behaviors going to change? When will they act? What, if anything, do the individuals need to acquire to implement the agreement? How long should it take to implement the solution?

Remember, solutions do not implement themselves; people must put them into practice. The design of a particular football play may be well thought out, but it will fail if it is executed poorly. Do not stop short in the problem-solving process. If you are going to work hard to develop a good solution, spend time analyzing how it should be implemented. Then go ahead with the implementation.

Evaluate the Solution

Solutions that looked satisfactory before they were implemented may not always appear very good afterward. To determine if a solution is working satisfactorily, you should evaluate it periodically after it is put into practice. How are solutions best evaluated? The outcome from the solution must be compared with the desired results established earlier in the problem-solving process. That is, what were you and the other person trying to accomplish and does the solution allow these objectives to be met? Also, is the solution being implemented as expected? Are both parties doing what they agreed to do? In short, has the solution truly allowed the conflict to be resolved? If problems still exist, refinements in the solution will be in order. Otherwise, the conflict will still exist and it may worsen. Assuming the solution works, you can begin to enjoy the fruits of your labor in the problem-solving procedure.

Make sure the solution really works

The problem-solving procedure for resolving conflict may appear to be rather time consuming, but let us look at how the time is spent. Specifically, time is spent analyzing and understanding the problem, determining what is to be accomplished, and working together to develop an acceptable solution. After the solution is implemented, it is evaluated. It is, therefore, time well spent, because a carefully designed solution emerges. The solution usually has a good chance for long-term success because both parties to the conflict have developed the solution and will be committed to making it work. "Quick fixes" may not take long to develop, but they often are just stop-gap measures providing only short-term relief. On the other hand, the problem-solving procedure does more than just enable individuals to resolve conflicts. By interacting and cooperating, a better environment for working more effectively with others on the job is created for the supervisor.

Be leery of quick fixes

Intervening in Conflicts between Others

As a supervisor, you may on occasion need to intervene in conflicts between others at work. Two of your subordinates, for example, may get into an argument over how to do a job. As a result, they turn to you to settle the issue. Or, even without being asked, you may have to intervene in a conflict just to maintain order on the job. Regardless of the reason, it is helpful to understand the important aspects of conflict intervention.

Intervention Strategy

There is no perfect strategy that guarantees successful intervention. However, using the following **intervention strategy** will greatly enhance your chances of success.

Establish Order. When intervening in a conflict, quickly stop any name-calling or destructive bickering. Hate begets hate in most cases. A pattern of blaming and counterblaming will not solve the conflict. If possible, you want the two parties in the conflict to come up with an acceptable solution they can support. They will probably show less commitment for a solution that you impose.[18] However, to get them to work together, you have to establish order and develop a climate that is conducive to cooperation.

Identify the Problem. Do not assume that you understand what is the problem. If you are wrong in your assumption, the participants may gang up on you by saying, "That's not the problem!" To avoid false assumptions about the conflict, simply ask both participants to explain the problem. Listen carefully—people involved in conflicts often have a tendency to speak in generalities and make vague statements. For example, one worker may complain that another is not following established procedures. To get a better grasp of the problem, ask the worker to explain which procedure is not being followed and to what extent. By getting the worker to be specific, you have something concrete with which to work.

Get Answers Instead of Countercharges. Try to get the parties in the conflict to communicate with each other rather than just throw charges back and forth. For example, suppose you intervene in a conflict between two workers, Jerry and Vernon. Jerry says, "I don't understand why Vernon never returns the tools he borrows from me." Reacting to Jerry's comment, Vernon says, "Well, I don't understand why Jerry never cleans up the workbench when he finishes using it." At this point, the two are only exchanging charges, which just escalates the conflict. More sharing of information is needed.

Help the two parties to communicate

   To correct this situation, get each person to respond to the other's concerns. For example, ask Vernon to explain why he has not returned Jerry's tools and have Jerry explain why he has not been cleaning up the workbench. Both workers may have good reasons for their actions, but they will not be known until each substitutes *communication* for charges.

Have Participants State Their Goals. Sometimes the people involved in a conflict are not exactly certain what they are trying to accomplish or what it will take to satisfy them. How can you help resolve a conflict if even the people involved do not know what they want? Help them clarify what they are trying to accomplish. If you find that a worker wants something that cannot be achieved or desires a change that cannot be made, you need to help the worker see the reality of the situation. In such cases, be direct and explain why the goal is unrealistic or why something cannot be changed.

Restate the Positions. Once you think you understand each person's position and concern, summarize your understanding. You might say something like, "Let me see if I have this right. Carol, you feel that Jane can't accept constructive criticism. You also charge that Jane fails to take care of mistakes she has promised to correct. Jane, you say that Carol's criticism of your work is unjustified and that she hasn't given you time to correct the mistakes. Is this summary correct?" In some cases, your restatement may be the first time the participants have heard a clear explanation of the other person's position or concern.

Explore the Options. People sometimes become so involved in a conflict that they cannot see the forest for the trees. As a result, they frequently consider only two positions, one of which always seems to be unacceptable to the other. By being less involved in the conflict and standing away from it, however, you may see more than two options. As a result, you are in a good position to help find creative options for resolving the conflict. Direct the participants in the conflict toward identifying possible solutions and encourage them to consider changes they would like to see made for the future rather than dwelling on the past.[19]

Have Participants Select a Solution. Encourage each person to consider the strengths and weaknesses of every solution presented. However, avoid taking sides. Do not make it appear that you and one participant are ganging up on the other. Instead, sell both individuals on the value of choosing a solution that benefits each and point out how certain solutions meet this objective.

Summarize and Seek Commitment. When concluding a conflict intervention, summarize what has been discussed and agreed on. Make sure there are no loose ends or unresolved issues. Seek commitment from each person to implement the decision, and make sure they know *how* to implement it.[20] Intervention in conflicts is seldom easy. However, you are responsible for planning, directing, and controlling what occurs in your work unit, so you may have to engage in conflict intervention now and then.

Seek commitment from both parties

Organized Labor's Approach to Dealing with Conflict

When one person in an organization has a conflict with another, each person speaks for himself or herself. The case where many workers appear to have demands or needs that conflict with those of management is a much different situation, however. In this case, management is usually united and able to coordinate its actions and comments. Individually, the worker's voice may seem faint to management. As a matter of fact, when management holds more power than labor, communication regarding worker needs and grievances may be minimal.[21] Through unions, however, workers attempt to increase their power and influence. When their voices are in unison and magnified as one voice, the workers expect to have greater success in gaining management's attention.

Understanding Unions

A **union** is an organization that represents employees to management and tries to protect the workers' rights and improve their economic status through collective bargaining. Specifically, **collective bargaining** is the

Unions negotiate through collective bargaining

process through which representatives of management and the union negotiate an employment contract for workers. Usually, issues such as wages, hours of work, fringe benefits, and working conditions are discussed during collective bargaining talks. The U.S. labor force has approximately 18 million union workers. The number of workers who hold membership in a union, however, has been declining in recent years. In 1980, for example, unions represented 23 percent of the work force. By 1986, union membership represented less than 18 percent of all workers.[22] And, as Figure 15.4 shows, the degree to which different industries are unionized varies widely.

Why is union membership declining? The answer to this question is fairly straightforward. Labor unions' share of the nonfarm, private work force is declining annually by 3 percent. This shrinkage occurs as union members retire or lose their jobs in smokestack industries. Unions are winning only .3 percent of the work force yearly in representation elections.[23] Union leaders are even starting to offer services such as low-interest credit cards and inexpensive health insurance to attract new members.[24] Experts predict that, as the nature of the modern work force changes, organized labor will need to be more creative in order to attract new members.

Union Goals

Organized labor unions have four goals and specific strategies for achieving them.[25] First, they seek to provide economic security and improve members' economic status. In order to achieve these objectives, unions engage in collective bargaining with employers. Second, unions attempt to protect their members against adverse conditions resulting from market and technological changes or management decisions. To achieve this objective, unions seek rules which protect members' job rights, and they request a system of due process. Third, unions attempt to influence political decisions in ways that will favor them. A common approach used by unions in this endeavor is to lobby for favorable legislation. Fourth, unions desire to improve the welfare of all workers, whether or not they belong to a union. In attempting to do so, unions promote political policies that will lead to a stable economy and fair treatment of workers.

Unions have several goals

Consider This

1. Employees in many companies are content not belonging to a union. In what ways might the working relationship between employees and management be different in these companies compared to those in which employees want a union?

2. Have you ever worked in a company in which the employees belonged to a union? If so, how much did you feel the union benefited the employees?

Unionization in Various Industries Figure 15.4

Industry	Percentage of Work Force that is Unionized			
	0–24%	25–49%	50–74%	75% or More
Agriculture and fishing	X			
Apparel			X	
Chemicals	X			
Construction				X
Electric, gas utilities		X		
Electrical machinery		X		
Fabricated metals		X		
Federal government			X	
Finance	X			
Food and kindred products		X		
Furniture		X		
Instruments	X			
Leather		X		
Local government		X		
Lumber		X		
Machinery, except electrical		X		
Manufacturing			X	
Mining				X
Nonmanufacturing	X			
Paper			X	
Petroleum refining		X		
Primary metals			X	
Printing, publishing	X			
Rubber		X		
Service	X			
State government		X		
Stone, clay, and glass products		X		
Telephone and telegraph		X		
Textile mill products	X			
Tobacco manufacturers			X	
Trade	X			
Transportation				X
Transportation equipment			X	

Source: Adapted from U.S. Department of Labor, Bureau of Labor Statistics, *Directory of National Unions and Employee Associations,* 1979 (Washington, D.C.: U.S. Government Printing Office, 1980), p. 86.

Development of Unions

The beginnings of the union movement in the United States can be traced to the late 1700s when skilled artisans formed local groups called societies. Those individuals who joined these societies provided financial aid to each other during times of need. In 1799, the Philadelphia shoemakers and their employers held the first recorded meeting in which worker and employer representatives discussed specific labor demands.[26]

The right of workers to unionize, however, did not come easily. In order to counter union pressures, employers sought relief from the courts. A series of legal rulings set the principle that a combination of workers exerting pressure on an employer amounted to a criminal conspiracy.[27] As a result, until 1926, the courts often issued injunctions restricting the freedom of workers to organize or engage in strikes. Federal legislation then began to redefine the balance of power between workers and employers.

The Railway Labor Act, 1926

Early attempts by railroad workers to organize and conduct strikes resulted in bloody battles with authorities. Congress believed that peaceful railroad labor-management relations would be best served by collective bargaining between railroad workers and management. As a result, it passed the **Railway Labor Act** in 1926. The act contained the following key provisions.

☐ Railroad workers were permitted to join unions.
☐ Railroads could not discriminate against union members.
☐ Railroads were required to bargain with the unions.
☐ Railroads were required to give prompt attention to employee grievances.

Although the Railway Labor Act was limited at first to railroads, it marked a turning point in U.S. labor law. Today, the act also applies to airlines.

The Wagner Act, 1935

The refusal of some employers to grant workers the right to organize and engage in collective bargaining displeased Congress. This type of behavior was viewed as restricting the free flow of commerce because it led to industrial unrest, strikes, and business instability by depressing wages.[28] As a result, in 1935 Congress passed the National Labor Relations Act, also known as the **Wagner Act.** In essence, this law extended the rights provided under the Railway Labor Act to other nonmanagerial employees in private business. Specifically, the Wagner Act gave workers the right to:

☐ Form and join unions.
☐ Engage in collective bargaining with an employer.
☐ Strike.

The Wagner Act also forbade employers from engaging in certain unfair labor practices. Employers, for example, are prohibited from interfering with or restraining workers from exercising their right to form and join a union. In addition, employers may not dominate or interfere with union affairs. Employers also cannot discriminate against a worker in any way because of union membership.

As a result of the Wagner Act, the National Labor Relations Board (NLRB) was established. The NLRB has the authority to investigate and correct unfair labor practices. In addition, it oversees elections on unionization and representation. When a union wins such election, the NLRB certifies it as the workers' exclusive bargaining agent. Once this occurs, the employer is required to recognize and bargain with that union. After the NLRB was created, union "ballot box organizing" began; it continues today.

Union representation is decided by elections

The Taft-Hartley Act, 1947

Prior to the Wagner Act, employers clearly held the upper hand in labor-management struggles. The Wagner Act, however, strengthened labor unions and many new unions were formed as a result. Soon, employers began to complain that the act gave labor an unfair advantage over them. From the end of World War II in 1945 to July of 1946, there were a total of 43 strikes in the United States involving 10,000 or more workers.[29] This wave of strikes dampened public sympathy for unionism. As a result, Congress passed the **Taft-Hartley Act** in 1947 in an attempt to bring the power of unions and employers back into balance.

Just as the Wagner Act prohibited certain unfair labor practices by employers, the Taft-Hartley Act had the same effect for unions. As a result, the rules regulating labor-management relations and activities became more clearly defined. Specifically, the Taft-Hartley Act prohibited unions from engaging in the following unfair labor practices:

☐ Pressuring employers to discriminate against employees denied admission to the union or expelled from it.
☐ Coercing employees to join or not join a union.
☐ Refusing to bargain in good faith with an employer.
☐ Engaging in secondary boycotts, that is, trying to force employer A to stop doing business with employer B because the union has a dispute with employer B.
☐ Pressuring employers to bargain with a union other than the one duly elected or to assign work to members of a particular union.
☐ Engaging in featherbedding, that is, requiring employers to pay for work not performed.

The Landrum-Griffin Act, 1959

While the Wagner Act strengthened labor unions by restricting the actions of management and the Taft-Hartley Act benefited management by controlling the actions of unions, the **Landrum-Griffin Act** was designed to protect union members by placing checks on the actions of union leadership. By 1959, Congress was particularly concerned with the lack of democratic procedures in several unions and the corruption that existed

Unfair labor practices must be avoided

in the internal operations of some unions. As a result, key provisions of the act included:

- ☐ A bill of rights for union members. Workers were guaranteed equal rights in elections, the rights of free speech and assembly, the right to vote on proposed increases in dues and initiation fees, and protection against arbitrary discipline.
- ☐ A requirement that unions had to regularly report on their finances.
- ☐ A tightening of the secondary boycott provision of the Taft-Hartley Act. "Hot cargo" agreements, whereby employer A refused to handle the products of employer B, were prohibited.[30]

The Supervisor's Role When a Union Exists

If a union exists in your workplace, you must accept and work with it. The contract between management and the union spells out the rules you must follow. Study the agreement carefully. Be familiar with its provisions and stay abreast of any changes made in the agreement. You may be unsure about certain parts of the agreement or the restrictions some provisions may place on you as a supervisor. If so, seek clarification from higher management. When a union represents your workers, both the *union* and *management* watch you. So you must be careful to meet certain responsibilities.

Uphold the Labor Contract. You are expected to uphold the provisions management has agreed to in the contract. If it requires that only employees with a specific skill classification perform a task, you must abide by that. If you find it necessary to lay off workers, the labor contract may require you to start with those who have the lowest seniority. Failure to follow contract provisions can bring labor problems. If you find the union committing any unfair labor practices, address that problem quickly.

Be Consistent and Fair in Interpreting Contract Provisions. Sometimes you may have to interpret provisions of a labor contract. For example, how tardy can an employee be before he or she is "late"? Whatever interpretations you make, be consistent and do not play favorites in applying rules. Otherwise, you will have complaints from union representatives.

Communicate with Management and the Union. As a first-line manager, you are an important link between management and workers. You are expected to keep higher-level management informed about how your work unit is functioning and what issues are important to employees. You are also responsible for informing workers and union representatives of information coming from management.

How you interact with union workers has a great impact on your firm's management-union relations. Very simply, if you make life difficult for the union, the union may make things difficult for you and management. Bickering and conflicts with union employees will not produce high productivity and strong morale. Where a union exists, try to foster a spirit of cooperation in communicating with it. Usually, the key to productive relations with a union is for you to maintain a good working relationship with the union steward.

Cooperate and communicate with the union

Working with the Union Steward

The **union steward** is a union worker elected by other union members to protect their rights on the job. The steward acts as the union's watchdog. Besides being a union official, the steward may also be an employee working under you. Treat the steward fairly as an employee and show him or her the same respect given other workers. Strive to maintain a good working relationship with the steward as a union official. The suggestions offered below can help you here.

Develop a good working relationship with the steward

Keep the Union Steward Informed. Communicate with the steward and let him or her know of any new developments that might concern the union. The steward should understand how management interprets various aspects of the labor contract. If changes are going to be made that will affect employees, notify the steward. Do not try to slip work-rule changes by. Doing so will probably cause the steward to file grievances, which will be time consuming to handle.

Indicate an Understanding of the Difficulty of the Steward's Job. As shown in Figure 15.5, the union steward must meet demands placed on him or her as an employee *and* as a union official. This is not an easy role to maintain. Do not treat him or her differently from other workers, but let the steward know you are aware of the special demands he or she labors under. The steward will appreciate your sensitivity to this unique situation.[31]

Work to Gain the Steward's Trust and Confidence. You will likely enjoy greater latitude working within union restraints if the steward trusts you. Then the steward will be inclined to help you solve many labor problems. Just being fair in interpreting and carrying out the labor contract will bring you the steward's trust and confidence.

Show a Willingness to Cooperate with the Steward. The steward monitors your actions to make sure workers' rights are not violated, but you gain nothing by treating the steward as an enemy or refusing to cooperate

Figure 15.5   **The Dual Role of the Union Steward**

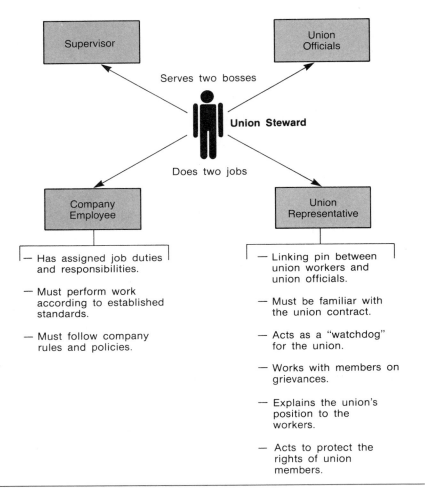

with him or her. When the steward makes a suggestion, show a willingness to listen. The suggestion may be worth adopting. In discipline matters, information the steward presents may help you better understand the problem and determine an appropriate form of discipline. Remember, the union wants the company to succeed. Employees' jobs depend on it. A good relationship between you and the union steward enhances the prospects for the firm's success.

You have studied how to handle conflict and how to work with unions. It is now appropriate to briefly review the objectives established at the beginning of the chapter.

- ☐ **Define conflict.** Conflict exists between two people when one person believes the other is preventing him or her from achieving a goal.
- ☐ **Identify common conflict management strategies.** Some common conflict management strategies include avoidance, smoothing, compromise, and forcing.
- ☐ **Outline a problem-solving procedure.** Initially, there is a need to create a positive environment, define the problem, identify relevant facts and opinions, and determine what results are desired. Then it is important to propose different solutions, reach an agreement, and implement the agreement. Last, you should evaluate the solution.
- ☐ **Describe a strategy for intervening in conflicts between others.** When intervening in conflicts between others on the job, you should establish order, identify the problem, and get answers instead of countercharges. In addition, you should have the participants state their goals. Restate each person's position, explore the options available, and have the participants select a solution. Then, summarize and seek a commitment from each person to implement the solution selected.
- ☐ **Explain organized labor's approach to dealing with conflict.** When management holds more power than labor, communication regarding workers' needs and grievances may be minimal. Through unions, however, workers attempt to increase their power and influence. When their voices are magnified through the one voice of a union, workers expect to have greater success in gaining management's attention. Through collective bargaining, the union negotiates an employment contract for the workers it represents.
- ☐ **Define union.** A union is an organization that represents employees to management and tries to protect the workers' rights and improve their economic status through collective bargaining.
- ☐ **Indicate the supervisor's role where a union exists.** To supervise effectively where a union exists, you must uphold the labor contract. Be consistent and fair in interpreting contract provisions and communicate with management and the union.
- ☐ **Offer suggestions for working with the union steward.** To develop and maintain a good working relationship with the union steward, you should keep him or her informed. Indicate that you understand the difficulty of the union steward's job and work to gain his or her trust and confidence. Last, show a willingness to cooperate with the union steward.

Key Terms

avoidance

collective bargaining

compromise

conflict

forcing

intervention strategy

Landrum-Griffin Act, 1959

lose-lose situation

problem-solving procedure

Railway Labor Act, 1926

smoothing

Taft-Hartley Act, 1947

union

union steward

Wagner Act, 1935

win-lose situation

win-win situation

Review and Discussion Questions

1. How can conflict actually be constructive or benefit a company?
2. Although it may be unintentional, how can poor communication cause conflict on the job?
3. What are some of the main problems with using a "forcing" strategy to manage conflict on the job?
4. What are the differences between conflict situations that result in "win-lose," "lose-lose," and "win-win" outcomes? Which outcome is usually the best approach over the long run for a supervisor to use and why?
5. Why is it important to focus on the interests or needs of the other person, in addition to your own interests, when attempting to resolve conflicts?
6. What are the goals of unions, and how do unions try to achieve them?
7. What unfair labor practices did the Taft-Hartley Act make illegal?
8. What responsibilities should you meet as a supervisor when working with a union?
9. How should you go about developing a good working relationship with the union steward?

Action Incident 15.1

Where's the Union Steward?

Rex Brown has been a supervisor for the Bedrock Cement Manufacturing Company for 10 years. About three years ago, the employees voted to be represented by a union, which infuriated Rex. He doesn't like the idea of working under the restrictions of a union contract. As Rex is fond of saying, "The only good union is *no* union!"

The company has recently acquired a new cement truck, and Rex is responsible for assigning a driver. According to the union contract, only employees with a heavy-equipment skill classification are eligible for the job. Rex enjoys hunting with Kent Richards, a nonunion employee, and decided to assign him to drive the truck. When he learned of this, Kent reminded Rex that he didn't have the appropriate skill classification to drive the truck. Rex said, "Don't worry about it. I can sneak it by the union steward."

That afternoon a young man entered Rex's office and said he wanted to apply for a job. Rex explained that he had an opening for someone to operate a conveyor belt. When the young man showed interest in the job, Rex said, "Fine, I'll hire you if you'll agree not to join the union."

Discussion Questions

1. How did Rex violate a provision of the Wagner Act?
2. How might Rex's other actions get him into trouble with the union?
3. What does Rex need to do to supervise more effectively now that a union exists?

Action Incident 15.2

A Splintered Relationship

Craig Jones, a supervisor for the Evergreen Lumber Company, oversees loading and delivery. Ben Whyte, a company salesperson, has had complaints from some customers about damaged lumber that was delivered to them. Improper loading of delivery trucks was the apparent root of the problem, so Ben made some suggestions to Craig's workers about how to load lumber in such a way as to avoid damage. Ben's actions irritated Craig, who confronted Ben.

Craig: Who do you think you are, telling my workers how to load lumber? You must be an idiot to think you can get away with that!

Ben: Look, this problem all started because. . . . *(Interrupted by Craig.)*

Craig: I don't care what the problem is; my workers take orders from me, not you.

Ben: Sure, you're their supervisor, but it doesn't hurt for me to make some suggestions for improving things.

Craig: There's no need for any suggestions from you on loading procedures because there's nothing wrong with the way we load lumber.

Ben: When lumber gets damaged during delivery, something's wrong. And I think the loading procedure is at fault.

Craig: Hey, the stuff's bound to get messed up on the way sometimes. Our loading procedure is just fine, and I'm not making any changes. Case closed!

Discussion Questions

1. What mistakes did Craig make in the way he handled the conflict with Ben?

2. How appropriate was it for Ben to make suggestions to Craig's workers?
3. How should Craig have handled the conflict with Ben?

Action Incident 15.3

A Conflict over Building Codes

Carl Spalding has been a supervisor in the city of Thomasville's building inspection department for 10 years. He supervises inspection of new construction within the city limits. Carl is against the adoption of stricter building codes, because he feels the existing codes are adequate. He also opposes the extra inspection work any new codes would create for his staff of inspectors. Carl is known to have a short temper.

A few months ago, a windstorm caused structural damage to a number of new homes in town. As a result, Shirley Clark, a supervisor in the engineering department, has encouraged the city council to adopt stricter building codes for new construction. One day, Carl rushed into Shirley's office where the following discussion took place.

Carl: You have a lot of nerve trying to increase my inspectors' work loads when I'm already understaffed!

Shirley: What are you talking about?

Carl: You know what I'm talking about! Those silly building codes you're pushing will double the time it takes us to make inspections.

Shirley: There are a lot of good reasons for the code changes I have proposed.

Carl: There couldn't be because you've never built anything in your life. All you know about construction is what you got from some textbook, which is worthless.

Shirley: Let me explain my position. That last storm caused structural damage to many homes in Thomasville. However, the homes in towns around us with stricter building codes haven't experienced any structural damage from storms. I don't have anything against your inspectors. I think they're doing the best job they can.

Carl: Just as I thought. When you say, "They're doing the best job they can," you're saying my inspectors aren't very capable.

Shirley: I didn't say that.

Carl: Look, you're just argumentative. I'm going to contact *my* friends on the city council.

Discussion Questions

1. How would you rate Carl's communication skills?
2. What mistakes did Carl make in attempting to resolve the conflict with Shirley?
3. How should Carl have tried to resolve the conflict?

Notes

1. Gordon Lippitt, Ronald Lippitt, and Clayton Lafferty, "Cutting Edge Trends in Organization Development," *Training and Development Journal* 38 (July 1984), p. 60.

2. Morton Deutsch, "Conflicts: Productive and Destructive," *The Journal of Social Issues* 25 (January 1969), p. 10.

3. Deutsch, "Conflicts: Productive and Destructive," p. 11.

4. Gerald R. Miller, "Epilogue," in *Perspectives on Communication in Social Conflict,* eds. Gerald R. Miller and Herbert W. Simon (Englewood Cliffs, N.J.: Prentice-Hall, 1974), pp. 206–19.

5. Andrew Crouch and Philip Yetton, "Managing Behavior, Leadership Style, and Subordinate Performance: An Empirical Extension of the Vroom–Yetton Conflict Rule," *Organizational Behavior and Human Decision Processes* 39 (June 1987), p. 395.

6. M. Michael Markowich and JoAnna Farber, "Managing Your Achilles' Heel," *Personnel Administrator* 32 (June 1987), p. 142.

7. Michard L. Weaver II, *Understanding Business Communication* (Englewood Cliffs, N.J.: Prentice-Hall, 1985), p. 123.

8. Gordon L. Lippitt, "Managing Conflict in Today's Organizations," *Training and Development Journal* 36 (July 1982), p. 70.

9. Ronald H. Hermone, "Resolving Differences," *Supervisory Management* 28 (May 1983), p. 33.

10. Weaver, *Understanding Business Communication,* p. 124.

11. Jaine Carter, "How to Handle Disagreement," *Management Solutions* 32 (September 1987), p. 30.

12. John Lawrie, "Handling Anger by Reducing Its Cause," *Management Solutions* 33 (May 1988), p. 12.

13. Weaver, *Understanding Business Communication,* p. 125.

14. Barry L. Reece and Rhonda Brandt, *Effective Human Relations in Organizations,* 2d ed. (Boston: Houghton Mifflin, 1984), p. 346.

15. Robin Gourlay, "Negotiations and Bargaining," *Management Decision* 25 (1987), p. 21.

16. Roger Fisher and William Ury, *Getting to Yes* (Boston: Houghton Mifflin, 1981), p. 55.

17. Fisher and Ury, *Getting to Yes,* p. 56.

18. Dan DeStephen, "Mediating Those Office Conflicts," *Management Solutions* 33 (March 1988), p. 5.

19. DeStephen, "Mediating Those Office Conflicts," p. 9.

20. Joyce Hocker Wilmot and William W. Wilmot, *Interpersonal Conflict* (Dubuque, Iowa: Wm. C. Brown, 1978), p. 167.

21. Peter Drucker, *Managing in Turbulent Times* (New York: Harper & Row, 1980), p. 201.

22. Thomas O. Kirkpatrick, *Supervision* (Boston: Kent, 1987), p. 299, and "New-Collar Jobs: Unions Court People in Service-Type Work to Stem Fall in Ranks," *The Wall Street Journal,* September 19, 1986, p. 1.

23. "Beyond Unions," *Business Week,* July 8, 1985, p. 74.

24. "Big Labor Tries the Soft Sell," *Business Week,* October 13, 1986, p. 126.

25. Edwin F. Beal and James P. Begin, *The Practice of Collective Bargaining,* 6th ed. (Homewood, Ill.: Richard D. Irwin, 1982), p. 91.

26. U.S. Department of Labor, Bureau of Labor Statistics, *A Brief History of the American Labor Movement,* Bulletin 1000 (Washington, D.C.: U.S. Government Printing Office, 1970), p. 1.

27. Sanford Cohen, *Labor in the United States* (Columbus, Ohio: Charles E. Merrill Publishing, 1979), p. 48.

28. Cohen, *Labor in the United States,* p. 358.

29. *A Brief History of the American Labor Movement,* p. 40.

30. Sar A. Levitan, Peter E. Carlson, and Isaac Shapiro, *Protecting American Workers* (Washington, D.C.: Bureau of National Affairs, 1986), p. 135.

31. Leslie W. Rue and Lloyd L. Byars, *Supervision: Key Link to Productivity,* 2d ed. (Homewood, Ill.: Richard D. Irwin, 1986), p. 326.

Suggested Readings

Cliff, Gordon. "Managing Organizational Conflict." *Management Review* 76, May 1987, pp. 51–53.

DeStephen, Dan. "Mediating Those Office Conflicts." *Management Solutions* 33, March 1988, pp. 5–10.

Estey, M. *The Unions.* 3rd ed. New York: Harcourt, Brace, Jovanovich, 1982.

Fossum, J. A. *Labor Relations: Development, Structure, Process.* Dallas: Business Publications, 1982.

Hocker, Joyce L., and William W. Wilmot. *Interpersonal Conflict.* 2d ed. Dubuque, Iowa: Wm. C. Brown, 1985.

Holley, W. H., Jr., and J. M. Jennings. *The Labor Relations Process.* 2d ed. Hinsdale, Ill.: Dryden Press, 1984.

Lawrie, John. "Handling Anger by Reducing Its Cause." *Management Solutions* 33, May 1988, pp. 11–14.

Levitan, Sar A.; Peter E. Carlson; and Isaac Shapiro. *Protecting American Workers.* Washington, D.C.: Bureau of National Affairs, 1986.

Martin, Philip L. *Contemporary Labor Relations.* Belmont, Calif.: Wadsworth, 1979.

Morgan, Philip I. "Resolving Conflict Through 'Win-Win' Negotiating." *Management Solutions* 32, August 1987, pp. 5–10.

Muniz, Peter, and Robert Chasnoff. "Assessing the Causes of Conflict—and Confronting the Real Issues." *Supervisory Management* 3, March 1986, pp. 34–39.

Phillips, Eleanor, and Ric Cheston. "Conflict Resolution: What Works?" *California Management Review* 21, Summer 1979, pp. 76–83.

Powell, Jon T. "Stress Listening: Coping with Angry Confrontations." *Personnel Journal* 65, May 1986, pp. 27–30.

Rahim, M. Afzalur. "A Measure of Styles of Handling Interpersonal Conflict." *Academy of Management Journal* 26, June 1983, pp. 368–76.

Weiss, Laurie. "Revisiting the Basics of Conflict Intervention." *Training and Development Journal* 37, November 1983, pp. 68–70.

Dealing with Grievances and Discipline

Learning Objectives

After reading and studying the material contained in this chapter, you should be able to:

1. Define grievance.
2. Explain how to prevent many grievances from occurring.
3. Describe how grievances are typically handled in unionized companies.
4. Identify three grievance procedures used by nonunion firms.
5. Indicate why grievance systems sometimes fail.
6. Define discipline.
7. Explain progressive discipline.
8. Explain the discipline-without-punishment approach.

Chapter

16

The Reality of Labor Relations

When an employer hires an employee, there is the expectation that a good match has been made. The employer anticipates that a positive working relationship will develop and that the employee will be productive. After all, nobody hires someone in the belief that the working relationship will be unpleasant or that the employee will fail. Likewise, applicants typically approach new employment opportunities with positive expectations.

Be prepared for personnel problems

The reality of labor relations, however, is somewhat different. That is, even in the most cooperative work groups, grievances or complaints and discipline problems may occur. As a student of supervision, you need to understand the basics of these issues.

Grievance Defined

A **grievance** is any formal complaint, usually written, by an employee related to some aspect of a labor agreement or an employment policy. Whenever employees believe they have been treated unfairly or some condition of employment has been violated, relations between labor and management can become strained. Grievances often result. Some of the common causes of grievances are identified in Figure 16.1.

Avoiding Grievances

Practicing good supervision skills can help you avoid many grievances. Treat employees with respect and dignity. Acknowledge good work and give credit to any employee who makes a good suggestion. When interacting with employees on the job, be sensitive to the way they feel about working

---

Figure 16.1   **Common Causes of Grievances**

1. Inequities in wages paid for the same job.
2. Disagreement over how certain provisions of the labor contract are interpreted and implemented.
3. Mistakes caused by poor communication or vague orders.
4. Failure to honor provisions in the labor contract.
5. Passing an employee over for a promotion.
6. Violating established work procedures.
7. Failure to provide adequate supplies or equipment to do the job properly.
8. Disciplinary action too severe for the violation.
9. Treating an employee unfairly.
10. Discrimination in rule enforcement.
11. Unsafe working conditions.
12. Breaking a law.
13. Failure to consider seniority for overtime and job assignments.

conditions, job assignments, and other aspects of employment. When you are notified of labor problems, show a willingness to help resolve them. In addition, be open-minded and listen to your subordinates' points of view. Make certain they receive proper training in how to do their jobs. Give clear instructions and be fair in administering discipline; do not show favoritism. Finally, make sure you understand and follow the labor contract.[1]

Many grievances can be avoided

In spite of precautions taken, some grievances may still occur in an organization. Therefore, most organizations have procedures for resolving employee grievances. However, these procedures differ depending on whether or not the employees are unionized.

Handling Grievances in Unionized Organizations

Generally, grievance procedures in firms with union contracts are more formal and structured than those in nonunion firms. In unionized companies, the steps in the grievance procedures are usually spelled out in the labor agreement. Although the procedure may vary, Figure 16.2 shows the traditional way a grievance proceeds in both large and small firms where workers are unionized.

Step 1: File the Formal Grievance. Generally, employees file formal grievances for one of two reasons. They feel they have been treated unfairly on the job, or they believe a condition of their employment contract has been violated. If a union member desires to file a grievance, he or she may request help from the union steward to do so. The employee files the grievance orally or in writing with his or her supervisor.

After receiving the formal grievance, the supervisor must review it. The employee and supervisor then need to calmly discuss the grievance and listen carefully to each other. Next, the supervisor must make a decision on it. If you are the supervisor and you conclude that the grievance was justified because a mistake was made, admit it. Once you make your decision, be tactful and considerate in explaining your decision, especially if it is unfavorable to the employee.[2]

Most grievances are settled during the discussion between the employee and the supervisor. However, when an early resolution does not occur, the employee can take step 2.

Step 2: Appeal to Appropriate Department Head. Any grievance appealed to a department head must be in writing. Both sides must document their positions. The employee and a union representative meet together with the department head to discuss the grievance. The department head then renders a decision. If not satisfied, the employee can continue to appeal upward.

Figure 16.2   **Procedure for Processing a Grievance for Unionized Workers**

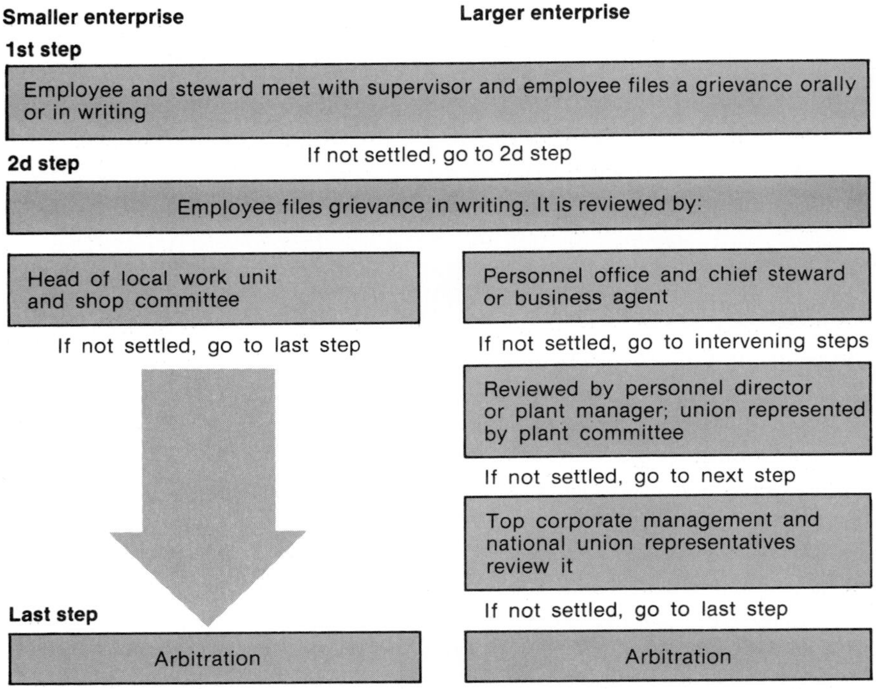

Smaller enterprise   Larger enterprise

1st step

Employee and steward meet with supervisor and employee files a grievance orally or in writing

2d step   If not settled, go to 2d step

Employee files grievance in writing. It is reviewed by:

Head of local work unit and shop committee	Personnel office and chief steward or business agent

If not settled, go to last step   If not settled, go to intervening steps

Reviewed by personnel director or plant manager; union represented by plant committee

If not settled, go to next step

Top corporate management and national union representatives review it

Last step   If not settled, go to last step

Arbitration	Arbitration

Source: William F. Glueck and George T. Milkovich, *Personnel: A Diagnostic Approach* (Plano, Tex.: Business Publications, 1982), p. 607.

Step 3: Appeal to Higher-Level Management. In a large company, the worker can appeal to many levels of authority. Each level naturally involves people who hold higher positions of responsibility in the union and the company. Specialists on both sides may also be asked to review the evidence and present arguments.

The Final Step: Arbitration. Union contracts generally provide for **arbitration** if the union wishes to appeal top management's decision on a grievance. Once a union decides to take a grievance to arbitration, a disinterested third party acceptable to both sides is brought in to hear it. When binding arbitration is used, both sides agree in advance to accept the arbitrator's decision. Otherwise, the arbitrator's decision is considered nonbinding. It is the arbitrator's responsibility to listen to both sides of the case, consider the evidence, and then make a decision. Under binding arbitration, that decision is considered final and marks the end of the formal grievance procedure.

A grievance may lead to arbitration

Handling Grievances in Nonunion Organizations

Labor unions represent less than 18 percent of the American work force. In the past, companies with nonunion employees often showed little interest in grievance procedures. Today, however, attitudes are changing, and these firms are placing greater value on grievance procedures for three reasons.

First, nonunion firms often view the establishment of a grievance procedure as an effective way to avoid unionization. They believe that if a grievance procedure is available to employees, interest in seeking unionization to get such a system will be eliminated.

Second, increasing numbers of firms are being sued by former employees who claim they were wrongfully discharged. The courts set limits on the power of companies to fire nonunion workers without cause. These limits are forcing companies to reevaluate and change certain personnel policies.[3]

Third, top management in many nonunion firms realizes that it is just good business to provide employees with a grievance procedure. The logic is very simple. Employees who believe they have received inequitable or unfair treatment naturally want some way to voice their concerns. If no grievance procedure is available to them, the employees are likely to become dissatisfied. As a result, morale usually declines, work performance typically drops, and turnover frequently increases.

For these reasons, increasing numbers of nonunion organizations are establishing grievance procedures for their employees. The following procedures represent examples of innovative approaches that have been developed by progressive organizations for processing complaints or grievances.

More nonunion companies are developing grievance procedures

The Open-Door Grievance Procedure. The **open-door grievance procedure** permits employees to take their grievances to top management. An employee with a grievance is encouraged to take it to his or her supervisor initially.[4] If the employee and supervisor together cannot resolve the grievance, the employee must contact a higher-level manager. Some companies even allow employees to take a grievance all the way to the chief executive officer.[5] Employees using this procedure receive assurances that reprisals will not be taken against them for voicing a grievance.

An Ombudsman. Some nonunion firms assign a single person, called an **ombudsman**, as a referee to help resolve grievances. An ombudsman is a respected, neutral person who investigates an employee's complaint and recommends action to management. There is a special need for an ombudsman if the employee's supervisor is arrogant or the company has an immense bureaucracy containing cumbersome appeals procedures. In these cases, the employee may want someone to call upon who has the power to investigate complaints—i.e., the ombudsman. The existence of the ombudsman is also a deterrent to the misuse of administrative powers that strain management-labor relations.[6]

It is recommended that the ombudsman be an outside, independent individual who will be neutral and objective. To maintain independence, it has even been suggested that, when possible, the employees pay half the salary of the ombudsman.[7] It should also be noted that some organizations appoint someone from within the company to act as an ombudsman. This approach can also be successful when the company provides the individual with necessary autonomy and employees have trust and confidence in the ombudsman.

Peer-Review Panels. Generally, **peer-review panels** consist of three hourly workers and two managers who consider an aggrieved employee's complaint and render a decision. General Electric and Control Data Corporation are two major companies that have adopted peer-review panels. At GE, for example, the aggrieved employee selects three individuals from a pool of hourly workers who have volunteered for peer-review duty. Two other members from management, one of which is usually a plant manager, are also assigned. The panel members receive training in basic law and in peer-review guidelines.[8]

Consider This

1. It has been said that employees like to work with others, not for others. How can an understanding of this philosophy help supervisors avoid the filing of grievances by subordinates?
2. How do you think supervisors react to the concept of peer-review panels.

In most cases, employees and management see benefits in peer review. Employees, for example, tend to trust a complaint system that allows them to present their case to a panel that contains peers who listen to them. Some executives believe that peer review puts managers on their toes. The executives claim that supervisors do a better job when they know that their subordinates can go before a peer-review panel if problems develop.[9]

Seek Out Employee Dissatisfaction

As a supervisor, you do not have to wait for complaints to be called to your attention. To promote effective human relations, you should be observant of what is going on around you, including concerns of subordinates. There are many opportunities for supervisors to elicit opinions and concerns from subordinates. Staff meetings can be used to learn the concerns of employees and what suggestions they may have. Employee performance appraisals also provide an opportunity to gain important employee feedback. Whenever an

Watch for employee
concerns that are
developing

employee's behavior subjects him or her to discipline procedures, employee dissatisfaction may be partly to blame, which should be investigated.[10] The sooner concerns of employees can be identified and addressed, the better it is for the employees and the organization.

Why Grievance Systems Sometimes Fail

Grievance systems may be set up with good intentions, but they are not always effective. When they fail, the result may be employee dissatisfaction, poor morale, and reduced productivity. Four of the most common reasons that grievance procedures fail are identified below.[11]

Employees Do Not Understand It. If a grievance procedure confuses employees, they will probably not use it. In addition, to make sure employees are aware of an existing grievance procedure, a company must encourage its use when employees have a legitimate complaint. Creating a grievance system but not publicizing or explaining it has almost the same effect as not having it at all.

Employees Do Not Trust It. Whenever employees become convinced that they will not be treated fairly by an existing grievance procedure, they will not trust it. As a result, they will no longer use it. One reason General Electric developed the peer-review panels mentioned earlier was that employees did not trust the previous grievance procedure that existed at the company.[12] As a supervisor, you can avoid this problem by showing a genuine interest in employees' complaints and taking them seriously. Also, take action on them.

Supervisors Do Not Understand It. It has been said that a grievance system succeeds or fails on the shop floor. To make a grievance system work, supervisors must be adequately trained in problem-solving techniques. Otherwise, a lot of complaints that could be resolved early on mushroom into full-blown grievances. When the grievance system is used, a supervisor who mishandles the complaint because of unfamiliarity with the procedure can make the problem worse.

Expectations Are Too High for the Grievance System. A grievance system can help expose significant problems that exist in an organization. By itself, however, a grievance system cannot solve problems. Only people working together with a sincere desire to make improvements where possible can actually solve labor-management problems. If top management is insensitive to the concerns of the employees, the best grievance system will prove inadequate. In addition, employees must realize that there are advantages and disadvantages to any job. Expecting a grievance system to address simple dislikes associated with a job is unrealistic.

Grievance systems require cooperation to work

Administering Discipline

In organizations, **discipline** is any action directed toward an employee for failing to follow company rules, standards, or policies. Traditional disciplinary procedures are established to promote compliance with rules and to deal with any infractions. The best situation of course, and one that should be promoted, is where employees willingly comply.

Self-Discipline

Employees demonstrate **self-discipline** whenever they voluntarily follow established company policies and rules. There is a natural desire by most individuals to succeed on the job, so they usually do their best to avoid infractions. Success in promoting self-discipline is enhanced when supervisors put into practice the following suggestions.

Self-discipline can and should be promoted

Engage in Two-Way Communication.   As a supervisor, you need to do more than just inform employees of rules and regulations. You should also solicit feedback from them. This type of two-way communication allows you to clarify any confusion the employees may have regarding policies or what is expected of them.

Explain the Reason for Specific Rules. Help employees understand that established rules are reasonable and logical. The motivation to follow rules simply because they exist may not be great. However, once you explain why specific rules exist and the need for them, employees will be more likely to follow them.

Set a Good Example. You should practice what you preach. Your subordinates cannot be expected to take rules seriously if they see you breaking them.

The Responsibility to Discipline

Disciplining employees is not a pleasant task. However, when you are responsible for the performance of subordinates, you are also expected to deal with infractions of rules and policies. When is discipline required? A variety of situations can occur that may require you to take disciplinary action. Figure 16.3 lists several of them.

Reclaiming Your Rights to Discipline

Suppose, for whatever reason, you become lax in enforcing a certain rule. Later, you decide that you must begin to enforce it. In any situation like this one, by overlooking violations, you lose your right to discipline an employee

---

Common Reasons For Disciplining Employees   **Figure 16.3**

Disruptive Behaviors on the Job:	**Unethical Behaviors on the Job:**	**Attendance Behaviors on the Job:**
Insubordination	Stealing	Absenteeism
Fighting	Falsifying employment application	Tardiness
Gambling	Falsifying company and work records	Leaving early
Intoxication	Willful damage to company property	
Horseplay	Disloyalty to employer	
Smoking in unauthorized areas		
Failure to follow safety procedures		
Sleeping		
Possession or use of drugs		
Abusive language or threatening actions		
Negligence		
Refusal to accept job assignment		
Refusal to work overtime		

Source: Adapted in part from Frank Elkouri and Edna Elkouri, *How Arbitration Works*, 3d ed. (Washington, D.C.: Bureau of National Affairs, 1973), pp. 652 – 66.

---

for breaking the rule. Before you discipline an employee for breaking the rule, you must first reclaim the right to do so.

For example, suppose your firm has a rule against gambling on the job. However, you have permitted subordinates to run a baseball pool because you consider the activity harmless. Sometimes, you even collect the money for the pool! Imagine the outcry if you suddenly decided to discipline an employee for gambling because he participated in the baseball pool. This action would be considered to be unreasonable. It would be improper to suddenly punish the worker for gambling on the job. Instead, you would first need to reclaim your right to discipline for that particular rule infraction. To do so requires that the following three things be done.

Be consistent in applying discipline

☐ Publicize the rule and make sure all employees are aware of it.
☐ Inform them that you are now going to enforce the rule.
☐ Explain what will happen if they break the rule.[13]

Once you have reclaimed your right, you may discipline an employee who violates the rule. When you must discipline, the traditional approach for dealing with such problems has been to use a procedure of progressive discipline.

Progressive Discipline

In organizations, **progressive discipline** is a procedure that sets increasingly stiffer penalties for repeated or serious misconduct. Its purpose is to apply corrective measures in increasing degrees to get an employee to voluntarily correct inappropriate behavior. A guiding principle of progressive discipline is the belief that when misconduct occurs, the seriousness of the infraction should determine the severity of the corrective measure. That is, the punishment should fit the crime.

Consider This

1. Why is it better to convince an employee to voluntarily change or correct inappropriate behavior than for you to force the employee to change?
2. In administering discipline, why is it important to make sure that "the punishment fits the crime"?

Most progressive discipline programs in companies have six steps. In order they are:

- ☐ Informal talk.
- ☐ Oral warning.
- ☐ Written warning.
- ☐ Suspension.
- ☐ Demotion.
- ☐ Discharge.

Informal Talk. An **informal talk** with the offending employee will often correct many relatively minor violations. At this stage, you inform the employee of the misconduct and try to find out what is causing the problem. The goal is to get a commitment from the employee to correct the misconduct or to stop violating a certain rule.

Promptly address disciplinary problems

In most cases, it is not necessary to document in the employee's personnel record that the informal talk occurred. If the problem continues, or if the violation is more serious, an oral warning may be necessary.

Oral Warning. The **oral warning** represents a higher level of concern with an infraction. You should be firm and direct in discussing the misconduct with the employee. Give him or her an opportunity to explain the action. If your understanding of the facts differs from that of the employee, clear it up immediately. Make sure the employee understands that the misconduct must be corrected. Also let the employee know that you are willing to help him or her solve the problem. When you issue an oral warning, observe the following guidelines.

- ☐ Issue the warning as soon after the incident as possible when things are still fresh in everyone's mind.
- ☐ Focus on the facts; do not make personal comments. Avoid a remark such as, "You were really stupid to do something like that." Focus attention on what the employee did wrong.

☐ Indicate how much time the worker has to make the necessary improvement.
☐ Explain what will happen if the employee does not improve.

You should be brief and to the point when delivering an oral warning. Record when the oral warning occurred, the reason for it, how the employee reacted, what the employee said, and the agreements made. Inform the employee that this information will be placed in his or her personnel record.

Written Warning. If violations continue, or if an infraction is considered to be fairly serious, the next step in progressive discipline is to issue a **written warning.** Before doing so, however, you should discuss matters with the employee. Discussing the problem before disciplining is important for several reasons. The discussion warns the employee of what to expect so that he or she is not surprised by the disciplinary action. It also gives him or her an opportunity to respond to the charges. Last, face-to-face oral communication encourages and enhances the exchange of feelings and thoughts. Candid discussion is especially helpful in dealing with disciplinary problems.

At this step, however, more than a discussion is required. When preparing the written warning, you should:

☐ Summarize the problem and indicate whether it has occurred before.
☐ Explain the detrimental effect the employee's actions have on the company.
☐ Identify the forms of progressive discipline that have been taken so far.
☐ Explain what improvement the employee is expected to make.
☐ Explain what form of disciplinary action is now being taken.
☐ Point out what will happen if the employee does not improve.[14]

Make certain the warning is clear and easily understood. For example, if an employee has an attendance problem, avoid a vague comment like "Your attendance record must improve." What is considered to be an acceptable improvement? Ambiguous statements can add their own problems to the situation because of the potential for miscommunication.

Avoid ambiguous statements in written warnings

You should request that the employee acknowledge the written warning by signing it. If the employee refuses to do so, note this on his or her personnel record along with the written warning.

Suspension. In cases where previous forms of discipline fail, or the employee commits a major rule violation, **suspension** may be necessary. Even if the misconduct would appear to justify firing the employee on the spot, it is usually best to suspend first. This action gives you time to make sure you have all of the facts straight.

Suspensions generally range from a day to a month, with the length of time depending on the severity of the offense. Unfortunately, a few employees simply fail to appreciate that certain behaviors will not be tolerated until they have been shocked by a suspension.

Demotion.   As the next step in progressive discipline, **demotion** has both a positive and a negative side. On the positive side, demotion may occasionally be the best thing for an employee. For example, an employee holding a certain position in a company may be in constant conflict with others because his or her temperament is not right for that position. The employee may actually be better off being demoted to a position for which he or she is better suited. Occasionally, an employee will even request demotion to a position where he or she feels more comfortable. In some cases, therefore, demotion can have a positive outcome for an employee.

More often, though, such a decision produces negative effects. Some employees view demotion as a continuous form of punishment due to the loss of income and position. Demotion, therefore, may produce permanent discontent and low morale. If you expect a negative outcome, it is probably best to rule out demotion.

Discharge.   When an employee continues to violate certain rules or commits a very serious offense, there may be no other alternative but to fire him or her. **Discharge** is unfortunate, but you must be prepared to take the last step in progressive discipline if it becomes necessary. However, you must also make certain that you have made the right decision before putting it into effect. Suspending before discharging gives you a chance to review all the relevant evidence. Furthermore, you may be required to obtain the approval of the personnel department and/or higher-level management before firing an employee. While this approval is being sought, suspension is appropriate.

Offenses that generally warrant discharge include hitting a supervisor, fighting on the job, stealing, willful damage to company property, or falsification of records. Regardless of the reason for firing an employee, the circumstances should be carefully documented. The need for specific documentation is especially important if the employee is represented by a union and can appeal the decision to arbitration.

It is best to suspend before discharging

Discipline without Punishment

There is a growing trend in organizations toward the use of nonpunitive disciplinary methods. These methods are based upon the belief that employees themselves must be the real source of discipline. Therefore, they emphasize self-discipline.

Discipline without punishment works like this:[15] Employees who behave in a manner that requires disciplinary action get an oral reminder. That is, the supervisor meets with the offending person to discuss the problem and to get a commitment from the employee to resolve the problem. The employee is not warned of more serious disciplinary action to come. Instead, the supervisor reminds the employee of the personal responsibility he or she has to meet reasonable standards of behavior and performance.

If the problem continues, the next step is for the supervisor to issue a written reminder. Once again, the supervisor discusses the problem with the employee. Together they agree on how the employee is going to go about eliminating the gap between actual and desired behavior or performance. Should the disciplinary discussions fail to produce the desired changes, the employee is instructed to take a day off from work with full pay. This day off is also referred to as a "decision-making leave." The employee is told to return on the day following the leave and to have made a decision either to change and stay or to quit. The paid day off, therefore, represents the employee's last chance for reform. If the employee does not shape up after agreeing to do so, he or she is discharged. The supervisor documents the discussions that occurred during all stages of the discipline-without-punishment procedure.

Both Approaches to Discipline Have Supporters

Those who support the procedure of progressive discipline acknowledge that no method of discipline is perfect. However, some of the advantages of progressive discipline commonly cited are as follows.

☐ It is consistent. Employee discipline problems are handled according to the same procedure throughout an organization that subscribes to progressive discipline.
☐ Offending employees are notified as to the specific consequences they will face if their unsatisfactory behavior is not corrected.
☐ It is a fairly uncomplicated procedure.
☐ The discipline becomes more severe if the problem continues.[16]

Proponents of discipline without punishment, however, believe that their method is superior. Some of the major advantages they associate with this method of discipline are as follows.

☐ Emphasis is placed on convincing offending employees that they have a personal responsibility to meet reasonable standards of behavior and performance. The main objective is gaining an employee's agreement to change.
☐ An action plan for the future is created in consultation with the offending employee to resolve the problem.
☐ An offending employee is given a paid day off instead of an unpaid suspension. This action eliminates the resentment and hostility that punitive actions too often produce.[17]

The Hot-Stove Rule

An effective way to remember important principles concerning discipline is to apply the **hot-stove rule**. This simple rule emphasizes four key elements in administering discipline, as illustrated below.

1. Heat radiating from the hot stove provides a *warning* that you will get burned if you touch it. As a supervisor, you should make sure employees are aware of important rules and warn them against violating them.

2. The hot stove *immediately* burns anyone who touches it. Similarly, you should administer discipline quickly after an infraction occurs.

3. The hot stove *consistently* burns those who touch it. Correspondingly, you should be consistent in how you discipline for similar offenses.

4. The hot stove is *impersonal* in that it will burn anyone. You should also be impersonal in administering discipline. Discipline the act; don't play favorites.

Looking Back

Understanding the nature of grievances and discipline problems and knowing how to deal with them is an important part of knowing how to work with and supervise others in organizations. To emphasize these concepts, it is now appropriate to briefly review the objectives established at the beginning of the chapter.

☐ **Define grievance.** A grievance is any formal complaint, usually written, by an employee related to some aspect of a labor agreement or an employment policy.

☐ **Explain how to prevent many grievances from occurring.** Practicing good communication skills can help you avoid many grievances. Treat employees with respect and dignity, acknowledge good work, and give credit to anyone who makes a good suggestion. Be sensitive to the way employees feel about working conditions, job assignments, and other aspects of employment. When you are notified of labor problems, show a willingness to cooperate in resolving them. Be open-minded and listen to your employees' points of view. Make sure employees receive proper training for their jobs and give clear instructions. Be fair in administering discipline; do not show favoritism. Last, make sure you understand and follow the labor contract.

☐ **Describe how grievances are typically handled in unionized companies.** Grievance procedures in unionized companies usually are highly structured. An aggrieved employee, with the help of the union steward, files a grievance with the supervisor. The employee and the supervisor discuss the grievance and try to resolve it. The employee can appeal the supervisor's decision to the appropriate department head. In a large organization, the employee can appeal the department head's decision to many higher levels of authority. Arbitration is the final step in the grievance procedure.

☐ **Identify three grievance procedures used by nonunion firms.** Three innovative approaches include the open-door grievance procedure, use of an ombudsman, and peer-review panels.

☐ **Indicate why grievance systems sometimes fail.** A grievance procedure may fail if employees do not understand or trust it, if supervisors do not understand it, or if expectations are too high for it.

☐ **Define discipline.** In organizations, discipline is any action toward an employee for failing to follow company rules, standards, or policies.

☐ **Explain progressive discipline.** There are six steps in most progressive discipline programs. They include: informal talk, oral warning, written warning, suspension, demotion, and discharge.

☐ **Explain the discipline-without-punishment approach.** Employees who behave in a manner that requires disciplinary action get an oral reminder. If the problem continues, the next step is for the supervisor to issue a written reminder. Employees who then fail to meet reasonable standards of behavior and performance are instructed to take a day off from work with full pay. Last, employees who do not shape up after agreeing to do so are discharged.

Key Terms

arbitration	ombudsman
demotion	open-door grievance procedure
discharge	oral warning
discipline	peer-review panels
discipline without punishment	progressive discipline
grievance	self-discipline
hot-stove rule	suspension
informal talk	written warning

Review and Discussion Questions

1. What behavior or supervision skills help prevent many grievances from occurring?
2. What procedure is typically used for handling grievances in unionized organizations?
3. Why are companies with nonunion employees showing increased interest in developing grievance procedures?
4. Why do employees tend to like peer-review panels for resolving grievances?
5. What can supervisors do to promote self-discipline in employees?
6. As a supervisor, how should you go about reclaiming your right to discipline for breaking a rule that has not been previously enforced?
7. What are the steps involved in progressive discipline?
8. What are the key differences between progressive discipline and discipline without punishment as procedures for handling disciplinary matters?

Action Incident 16.1

Trouble Ahead

Dale and Phil work for the same manufacturing company and are both supervisors in different departments within the company. On Tuesdays and Thursdays they usually meet for lunch in the company cafeteria. At noon on a recent Thursday, the following conversation occurred between the two men after Dale arrived late for lunch.

Dale: I'm sorry I'm late. I had to spend extra time explaining something for a second time to a dumb subordinate. It never ceases to amaze me; if I have 10 subordinates, I'll have 15 problems.

Phil: What was the problem?

Dale: Oh, the subordinate keeps putting off a job assignment I gave him. I confronted him about it and he brought up the lame excuse again that the ventilation is bad in the area in which he would have to do the work. He claims he has some respiratory difficulty. I doubt that there is a ventilation problem.

Phil: Have you checked?

Dale: No, not yet. I'll get around to it eventually.

Phil: Is he a good worker most of the time?

Dale: He's not any lazier than the others. And believe it or not, another one of my subordinates is mad at me for just doing my job.

Phil: What do you mean?

Dale: I only passed on a good suggestion she had to the plant manager. She's upset because I didn't mention that it was her idea. What does it matter whose idea it was if it works and everyone at the company benefits?

Later that afternoon a new supervisor, Eric, mentioned to Phil that one of Dale's subordinates had filed a grievance. Phil replied, "That's not the first grievance against Dale, and it probably won't be the last!"

Discussion Questions

1. What examples of poor supervision skills demonstrated by Dale can you identify in this case?
2. What is Dale's perception of subordinates? How does this perception increase the likelihood that grievances will be filed against him in the future?
3. What changes in the way Dale supervises would you recommend to reduce the likelihood of grievances being filed?

Action Incident 16.2

The Joke That Backfired

The Northwestern Forest Products Company owns vast tracts of timberland. From the timber it harvests, the company produces large quantities of lumber in its huge sawmill. Paul Wagner is a young man who has worked for the company in its sawmill for two years. Paul has never missed a day of work with the company, and he has learned a lot about the sawmill operation. On several occasions, Paul has sent in suggestions, which have impressed the top manager, for improving the efficiency of the sawmill. As a matter of fact, the manager expects that Paul may be able to advance in the company if his employment record continues to show outstanding performance.

Paul works hard and enjoys his job. He says the people he works with make his job fun. It is not a high-pressure job, and Paul admits that there is a lot of horseplay that occurs on the job. Employees in the sawmill often play tricks on each other and enjoy having a good laugh on the job. Paul claims it is all harmless, and the horseplay helps some tedious tasks go faster. As a matter of fact, Paul believes you can tell a lot about employees by finding out if they can take a little ribbing at work.

Fred Walden, Paul's supervisor, has tolerated the horseplay among the sawmill employees. In some cases, Fred even participates in the horseplay that occurs. He enjoys it and does not believe that his involvement will undermine his authority or respect with the sawmill employees. Lately, however, Fred has been in a somber mood. Unknown to his subordinates, Fred has experienced large financial losses from poor investments and has been receiving demands from his creditors to make delinquent payments. Unfortunately, he is unable to do so.

Arriving one morning after a sleepness night, Fred finds himself the object of one of Paul's practical jokes. Reacting angrily, Fred points his finger at Paul and shouts, "That's it, you're suspended for two days without pay!" "Why are you so touchy?" Paul responds. "Don't challenge me," Fred continues. "This continuous horseplay hurts our performance, it can be dangerous, and it is going to cease. I could have been injured if I had tripped as a result of your practical joke. Your suspension starts now!"

Discussion Questions

1. Was Fred correct in pointing out that frequent horseplay can hurt performance and be dangerous? Explain.
2. Was Fred correct in disciplining Paul for engaging in inappropriate behavior on the job? Explain.
3. How should Fred have handled the situation if he wanted horseplay on the job to cease?

Action Incident 16.3

Unfair Treatment

Employees at the Allied Manufacturing Company have time cards they must punch in the time clock when they arrive at work. They must also punch out at the time clock when they leave work. If an employee fails to follow this procedure, there is no specific record of the hours worked, and the employee will not be paid for the undocumented hours. In addition, the company has a policy that forbids an employee from punching a time card for another employee. That is, each employee must punch in his or her own time card.

Karl Mains is a new employee at the company. One morning when Karl arrived for work he saw another employee, Tina, punch in for a friend. Karl's supervisor, Gene, also noticed what Tina did. As a result, Gene approached

Tina and reminded her about the company policy against punching another employee's time card. Tina apologized and indicated she would not do it again. At the same moment, Tina's friend joined her. Gene accepted the apology and walked away to attend a scheduled meeting.

Due to a reorganization at the company, Gene has been assigned additional duties and responsibilities. Gene is dissatisfied with the change because he does not believe he has the time to meet the new demands in a satisfactory manner. One of Gene's duties is to train new employees. However, due to the time pressures placed upon him, Gene did a poor job training Karl. Inadequately trained, Karl performed poorly on the job and became frustrated with his work. Karl realized he needed help and requested additional training, but Gene did not act on his request.

One morning Karl shared a ride to work with another co-worker, Ralph. That day Ralph had to carry a large box into the company building. To be helpful, Karl punched in for Ralph so he would not have to set the box down to do so.

Suddenly, Gene confronted Karl and asked him if he was punching in for another employee. Karl said yes. Before Karl could explain, however, Gene said, "You're suspended without pay for the day!" Karl protested that Tina had not been suspended for doing the same thing. Gene replied, "We're not talking about Tina, we're talking about what you did. Do you deny that you just violated company policy?" Karl answered, "No, I guess I did something wrong, but . . ." Gene interrupted and said, "No buts about it, you can't escape responsibility for your actions. You're still suspended for the day." In response, Karl exclaimed, "I'm filing a grievance about my suspension, and I'm filing a second grievance because I haven't received adequate training!"

Discussion Questions

1. Is Karl justified in filing his grievances? Explain.
2. Did Gene's behavior contribute to the filing of the grievances? Explain.
3. What should Gene have done that would have helped him avoid this situation and the filing of the grievances?

Notes

1. Maurice S. Trotta, *Handling Grievances: A Guide for Management and Labor* (Washington, D.C.: Bureau of National Affairs, 1976), pp. 48–49.
2. Trotta, *Handling Grievances*, pp. 79–80.
3. "Legal Challenges Force Firms to Revamp Ways They Dismiss Workers," *The Wall Street Journal*, September 13, 1983, p. 1.
4. Ronald Berenbeim, *Nonunion Complaint Systems: A Corporate Appraisal* (New York: The Conference Board, 1980), p. 11.
5. Berenbeim, *Nonunion Complaint Systems*, p. 11.
6. Kim E. Clark, "Improving Employee Relations with a Corporate Ombudsman," *Personnel Journal* 64 (September 1985), p. 12.

7. Clark, "Improving Employee Relations with a Corporate Ombudsman," p. 13.

8. Jonathan Tasini, "Letting Workers Help Handle Workers' Gripes," *Business Week* (September 15, 1986), p. 82.

9. Tasini, "Letting Workers Help Handle Workers' Gripes," p. 82.

10. Roger Madsen and Barbara Knudson-Fields, "Employee-Employer Relationships: When They Have Cause to Complain," *Management Solutions* 32 (April 1987), pp. 39–40.

11. "Why Grievance Systems Fail," *Training and Development Journal* 39 (November 1985), p. 20.

12. Tasini, "Letting Workers Help Handle Workers' Gripes," p. 82.

13. George W. Bohlander, "Employee Discipline and Complaint Handling," Seminar presented by the Center for Executive Development at Arizona State University, November 20, 1980.

14. Bohlander, "Employee Discipline and Complaint Handling."

15. David N. Campbell, R. L. Fleming, and Richard C. Grote, "Discipline Without Punishment—at Last," *Harvard Business Review* 63 (July–August 1985), pp. 162–78. Also Laurie Baum, "Punishing Workers with a Day Off," *Business Week* (June 16, 1986), p. 80.

16. Adapted from Jill Hauser, "In Defense of Traditional Discipline," *Personnel Administrator* 31 (June 1986), pp. 42–43, 156.

17. Campbell, Fleming, and Grote, "Discipline Without Punishment—at Last," pp. 162–78.

Suggested Readings

Baroni, Barry J. "A Complaint Processing System That Will Work for Your Business." *Management Solutions* 31, July 1986, pp. 22–26.

Belohlav, James A. "A Comparative View of Employee Disciplinary Practices." *Public Personnel Management* 14, Fall 1985, pp. 245–51.

Campbell, David N.; R. L. Fleming; and Richard C. Grote. "Discipline Without Punishment—At Last." *Harvard Business Review* 63, July–August 1985, pp. 162–78.

Caruth, Don. "This Matter of Discipline." *Supervisory Management* 28, April 1983, pp. 24–31.

Florey, Peter. "A Growing Fringe Benefit: Arbitration of Nonunion Employee Grievances." *Personnel Administrator* 30, July 1985, pp. 14–18.

Fossum, John A. *Labor Relations: Development, Structure, Process.* Rev. ed. Plano, Tex.: Business Publications, 1979.

Harvey, Eric L. "Discipline vs. Punishment." *Management Review* 76, March 1987, pp. 25–29.

List, Jill Hauser, "In Defense of Traditional Discipline." *Personnel Administrator* 31, June 1986, pp. 42–43, 156.

Martin, Philip L. *Contemporary Labor Relations.* Belmont, Calif.: Wadsworth, 1979.

Mauer, George W., and Jeanne Flores. "From Adversary to Advocate." *Personnel Administrator* 31, June 1986, pp. 53–58.

Part V

Understanding Workplace Concerns

Maintaining Safety and Health

Chapter

17

Learning Objectives

Maintaining a safe and healthy work environment is of utmost importance to managers. Accidents and illnesses cause lost workdays, increased absenteeism, and decreased productivity. In this chapter, you will learn why supervisors must be concerned about alcohol and drug abuse, stress, safety, smoking, and a major illness called AIDS. The objectives of the chapter are to help you:

1. Understand the nature of substance abuse in the workplace.
2. Identify strategies for alleviating employee stress.
3. Recognize the importance of being knowledgeable about AIDS.
4. Discuss the potential health dangers caused by smoking.
5. Explain the importance of safety and accident prevention.

Alcohol and Drugs

How much is the annual cost of drug and alcohol abuse to American business? Most people vastly underestimate the amount, which is an astounding $43 billion.[1] Almost one fourth of all workers use harmful drugs in the workplace.[2] The exact number of employed alcoholics is unknown; however, various sources estimate it to be between 10 and 15 percent of the labor force. **Alcoholism** involves drinking to the extent that a person ceases to function effectively in social and work situations. **Drug abuse** refers to improper use of a variety of substances, such as stimulants or depressants, and may include alcohol. Have you ever thought about the size of the illegal drug industry? In terms of annual revenue, it ranks second only to Exxon, one of the world's largest corporations.[3]

What is substance abuse?

Alcoholism does not occur suddenly. It develops gradually over time, shortens life expectancy, and does not cure itself. Without intervention and proper care, the disease gets progressively worse. Denial is a common characteristic of alcoholics. The most difficult aspect of treatment is to get the alcoholic to acknowledge that a problem exists. Usually, they do not respond to appeals from family, friends, or even doctors. The workplace is generally a last resort for help because the loss of a job and income is a major concern. In such a crisis situation, the choice between seeking help or losing a job can force a person to seek aid.

Alcoholism evolves over time

The cost of alcoholism (absenteeism, health complications, accidents, and lost productivity) is enormous. Forty percent of industrial deaths and 47 percent of industrial injuries are related to alcohol.[4] Research Triangle Institute estimates that, in a single year, substance abuse costs the economy $177 billion.[5] Consider also the impact of alcohol and drug abuse on the personal lives of victims—broken family relationships, financial problems, and lack of dependability.

Alcoholism is expensive

The roots of substance abuse are deep and complex. Abuse may stem from a desire for others' approval or a fear of disapproval. Compared to drugs, alcohol has greater social acceptance. It is often served at social functions and is readily available at many restaurants. Some people associate alcohol with both favorable and unfavorable events. Celebrations of promotions and others types of accomplishments frequently include alcohol. When things go wrong, it is also an excuse for a drink. To some, alcohol is a means to escape the realities of life—marital difficulties, job problems, or death of a loved one. The effects of poor childhood relations with parents or rejection by others can influence the consumption of alcohol.

Regardless of sex, income, or occupation, anyone is susceptible to illnesses caused by substance abuse. Alcoholism or drug dependency are not new problems, and both are treatable. Many companies use **employee assistance programs (EAPs)** to help employees cope with alcohol, drug, personal, or emotional problems. These programs provide professional counseling and guidance to rehabilitate afflicted workers. Some firms have

EAPs help troubled workers

developed their own EAPs; however, it is common for services to be arranged through outside providers, which are available in most communities. "Most substance abusers accept help, and approximately 80 percent of those individuals resolve their problems and return as productive workers."[6]

Watch for symptoms of substance abuse

What are the symptoms of alcohol and drug abuse? Several common symptoms are noted in Figure 17.1. Do not forget that these are only symptoms, not conclusive evidence of problematic use of alcohol or drugs. Nevertheless, they are signs that should not be ignored. Deterioration of job performance is a major clue to indicate the possibility of substance abuse. It is important for you to keep accurate records and document specific instances of poor work or violation of rules. Without such data, potential abusers will likely deny the existence of problems or allege that you dislike them and are biased in your judgment. Always restrict comments to work-related issues and do not try to cover up or protect abusers because the difficulties will only get worse.

When initially confronting a suspected abuser, you might say, "John, I've noticed you had three unexcused absences in the past six weeks and continue to have the highest product-defect rate in the department. Is there anything wrong?" Should John have a problem, do not expect him to admit it. He likely will have a plausible excuse to explain his actions. Without making accusations or trying to be a counselor, give John a definite time period to demonstrate improved performance and warn him that continued absenteeism and poor

Figure 17.1   **Symptoms of Alcohol and Drug Abuse**

Symptoms of Alcohol Abuse

1. Excessive absenteeism, especially following weekends or holidays.
2. Odor of alcohol on the breath.
3. Slurred speech and stumbling mannerisms.
4. An unusual amount of time spent away from work station—visits to the restroom or trips outside of the work area to secluded places.
5. Inability to explain failures for not completing work adequately, particularly when performance fluctuates.

Symptoms of Drug Abuse

1. Variation in moods for no apparent reason.
2. Appearance of confusion, possibly combined with an attitude of indifference or apathy.
3. Deterioration in physical condition, especially weight loss and apparently poor eating habits.
4. A "dreamy or spacey" appearance accompanied by lack of awareness of reality.
5. Compulsive talking or extreme quietness and withdrawal, depending on the type of drug.
6. Unnatural sleeping and periods of apparent forgetfulness.

Do You Have a Cocaine User in Your Workplace?

If you do, you may be making it possible, even easy, for the drug abuser to continue to use the drug. Supervisors often unknowingly contribute to cocaine abuse through a process known as enabling. For example, supervisors *enable* cocaine use when they let an employee repeatedly function below standards out of fear, guilt, or personal loyalty to the user. You are no longer a part of the problem when you:

- Pay attention to the warning signs of cocaine abuse by watching for excessive absenteeism and tardiness on Mondays, Fridays, and the day after payday, erratic performance, errors in judgment, and frequent accidents.
- Make it clear that drug use is unacceptable in the workplace.
- Consistently enforce the company's work standards.
- Refuse to be an enabler.

Source: *Cocaine in the Workplace: What You Can Do.* © 1986 by Krames Communications, 312 90th Street, Daly City, CA.

work may lead to dismissal. Hopefully, John will get the message, but ultimately, he may have to make a choice — seek professional treatment or be terminated. The pointers noted above are useful for a supervisor who manages a cocaine user.

Increasingly, media attention has focused on the detrimental impact of alcohol and drugs in America. During the 1980s, concerns about declining productivity, safety, and the need for a healthy workplace led greater numbers of employers to adopt drug testing programs. In 1982, fewer than 5 percent of Fortune 500 firms used drug testing, but by 1988, the figure had increased to nearly 50 percent.[7] Various views prevail about the appropriateness of drug testing. Some stress the importance of protecting personal privacy and emphasize that results are not always reliable. Others note the possibility of physical harm to innocent persons caused by errors of persons using alcohol or drugs. As a part of the pre-employment screening process, drug testing is legal. For current employees, courts have ruled tests can be administered if there is "reasonable or individualized suspicion that an employee is abusing drugs or alcohol."[8]

Use of drug testing is increasing

The workplace often serves as a "last resort" to remedy alcohol and drug abuse. This occurs because jobs provide the money to sustain these habits, and the threat of job loss becomes a major concern to abusers. Your task is to maintain a drug-and-alcohol-free workplace. You must know the firm's policy toward these substances and also make certain employees understand it. Furthermore, it is necessary for you to enforce the policy. Should you be in doubt about how to handle a specific situation, consult with your boss before taking action. Although it might be hard for you to realize why abusers deliberately harm their bodies, substance addiction is a reality of today's workplace. Whenever possible, the primary concern is to rehabilitate afflicted workers so they can be healthy and productive employees.

Managing Stress

Stress is a part of everyday life. When personal or job-related stress becomes too great, however, problems arise. "I'm trapped." "It's hard to face another day at this dead-end job." "After work, I've got to stop at a bar and wind down." "I'm exhausted; it's tough putting up with this place." These comments reflect reactions to feelings of frustration, anger, or fatigue. **Stress** involves an individual's inability to respond adequately without undue emotional or psychological strain. Failure to cope with stress leads to **burnout** — emotional and physical exhaustion that brings feelings of chronic frustration and depression.

What causes stress? How individuals choose to react to an event or situation determines whether it will be stressful. For example, assume you feel quite comfortable holding two jobs or working in commission sales, a field which offers opportunities for an unlimited income. To another person, however, the pressures of a second job might be unduly frustrating, and the insecurity of an uncertain income could provoke much anxiety. Stress is attributed to both positive and negative events. Marriage, a promotion, or winning an election are positive events, but each situation necessitates personal adjustments and can be stressful. The death of a spouse, divorce, and a major health problem are examples of negative events that invoke high stress.

Some people thoroughly enjoy their jobs and eagerly look forward to each workday. Nevertheless, jobs are a source of anxiety and frustration to many workers. According to one survey, major job-related worries include not doing preferred kinds of work, coping with a job, working too hard, colleagues, and a difficult boss.[9] Employees who cannot control the flow of work, such as persons holding assembly-line jobs, are likely to experience greater stress than those having flexibility to set their own pace.

Many new supervisors do not realize the amount of time and effort spent preparing reports, maintaining records, and interacting with subordinates. Also, they are no longer responsible only for their own work; they now bear responsibility for the performance of subordinates. Doing a job yourself and overseeing others require different sets of skills. Consequently, a promotion to supervision involves an adjustment, especially for those promoted from the ranks. Such a transition can be stressful because actual experiences often differ considerably from prior expectations.

Stress involves both personal and organizational factors. Feelings of career stagnation, fears of job-skill obsolescence, or worries about personal problems are sources of stress. Organizational causes of stress include unclear, unreasonable, and conflicting expectations. To reduce vagueness, ask questions and give directions in a clear, straightforward manner. Assign reasonable amounts of work, set realistic deadlines, and whenever possible, do not try doing too many things at once.

Symptoms of Stress

Changes in behavior evidence stress. A good-natured, gregarious person becomes withdrawn and easily irritated. One who has always been aggressive and competitive displays a passive, indifferent attitude. Smokers consume even more cigarettes, and people who drink alcohol rely on it to a greater extent. With too much stress, job performance eventually will deteriorate. Perceived physical ailments signal stress-related problems. Headaches, stomach disorders, changes in sleeping or eating habits, and chronic tiredness (even when rested) are common symptoms.

Stress affects behaviors

> When suffering from excessive stress, people question their own decision-making abilities, values, and goals. They may attempt to alter behaviors and become even more depressed. Despite working harder and longer, less may be accomplished. Enjoyable assignments and challenges turn into obstacles.[10]

Some people believe that stress is entirely negative. This view is incorrect because acceptable levels of stress are motivational. In the absence of stress, much work simply does not get accomplished. A key concern is to remember the need for keeping a balance between too little and too much stress. Differences in individual tolerance levels complicate efforts to maintain this balance. Medium levels of stress encourage maximum work output.

Some stress is beneficial

It is important to keep records and observe behaviors. Excessive absenteeism and turnover can indicate the presence of too much stress. Listen to employee complaints, which often indicate a need to provide more training, alter workloads, or hire additional personnel. Exit interviews are a source of valuable information to provide greater understanding of why employees leave jobs. Figure 17.2 summarizes symptoms that signal excessive stress.

Strategies for Managing Stress

Successful stress reduction focuses on several key strategies, including proper dietary habits, regular physical exercise, and relaxation. Drinking too much coffee, eating too many sweets, smoking excessively, and consuming liquor are counterproductive to stress relief. Nutritious, well-balanced meals provide sufficient nourishment without the drawback of excessive caffeine or sugar. In addition to serving as an emotional release, regular exercise promotes physical fitness and builds self-confidence. Learning to relax is a most effective strategy.

Harmful stress can be managed

Figure 17.2   **Symptoms of Stress**

---

 1. An increase in the consumption of alcohol.
 2. For smokers, an increase in the number of cigarettes smoked.
 3. Difficulty concentrating on the job.
 4. A continual feeling of excessive tiredness.
 5. A growing sense of irritability, especially for relatively minor reasons.
 6. Either a greatly increased or decreased desire for food.
 7. An increasingly negative attitude toward colleagues, clients, or the organization.
 8. Loss of confidence in personal abilities.
 9. A feeling of personal hopelessness and a negative outlook toward the future.
10. A gnawing sense of boredom.
11. Conjuring up feeble reasons for being absent from work.
12. An inability to sleep without interruptions.
13. An attitude of general unhappiness.
14. An increase in frequency of headaches or stomach disorders.
15. A decline in relationships with family members.
16. A feeling of apathy toward performing work duties that were once exciting and challenging.
17. Increasing rigidity in expectations.
18. An excess amount of competitiveness without a sense of personal satisfaction that comes from achievement.

Unfortunately, many people try to relax at the same pace that they lead the rest of their lives. For a while, tune out your worries about time, productivity, and "doing right." You will find satisfaction in just *being*, without striving. Find activities that give you pleasure and that are good for your mental and physical well-being.[11]

"Get that job finished." "I'm sick of your work." "You'll pay for those actions." These statements are antagonistic and are likely to be received negatively. Too many supervisors "demand" rather than "request," "hurt" instead of "help," and "punish" but do not "praise." Freedom of expression without undue fear of retaliation minimizes stress. Trust in and respect for workers and their views encourages open communication. Any disagreements can then focus on issues and not be perceived as attacks on personalities. Greater receptiveness to ideas and suggestions becomes possible, and workers are more likely to make desired contributions without feeling unduly stressed.

To reduce stress, you need to make changes, as it does not generally alleviate itself. Many people have found these strategies to be useful.

Take Brief Breaks.   Preparation of reports, budgets, schedules, or appraisals requires mental concentration. When your concentration begins to wane, take a break—stand up and stretch your arms, go get a drink of water, or walk down the hall.

Pause and renew your energy

> If unable to leave your workstation, close your eyes, breathe deeply, and exhale slowly. Another useful technique is to rotate your head slowly in one direction and then the other. Also, you can relax by alternatively moving your shoulders up and down.[12]

Talk Out Problems. Discuss anxieties with a trusted friend, colleague, or counselor. Talking about a concern relieves frustration, and the other person may have suggestions to help reduce stress. Through conversation, people often are able to gain insights that previously were never considered.

Seek insights

Develop a Sense of Humor. Generally, things are not as bad as they may seem to be. Laughter is relaxing, and humor can improve difficult, tense situations. Instead of bottling up anger toward an employee who repeatedly enjoys minor hassles, it is worthwhile to chuckle to yourself, ''Well, Joe's at it again; how am I so fortunate to have him on my staff?''

Laugh a little

Get Sufficient Rest. A well-rested person is better able to handle stress in a positive manner. Work schedules might be revised to provide relief from constant stress. When possible, organize work activities to allow enough time for getting assignments completed.

Get enought rest

Avoid Procrastination. Do not put off doing difficult or disliked tasks until the last minute. Reverse the process, and do them first. When the work is finished, you will experience a sense of relief and feel more energetic about doing the remaining tasks.

Tomorrow comes all too soon

▼

1. What can supervisors do to help subordinates with alcohol or drug problems?
2. Considering the negative effects of alcohol and drugs, why do some people continue to abuse these substances?
3. Why is stress likely to be a major concern in the workplace of the future?

Consider This

AIDS

AIDS, formally known as acquired immune deficiency syndrome, attacks the neurological system and destroys the body's ability to fight infection. In the United States, the first cases of this incurable disease were reported during 1981. From 1981 to 1987, 32,000 AIDS cases were diagnosed in America, and over 50 percent of these victims have died. By 1987, 50,000 to 125,000 people evidenced signs of the AIDS virus, and another 1.5 million individuals were categorized as carriers who had not yet evidenced symptoms of the disease.[13]

AIDS has no known cure

> The task of coping with AIDS sufferers in the workplace can only grow in the years ahead. Scientists predict a total of 271,000 diagnosed cases in the U.S. by 1991—at a medical-care cost to the nation of $66.4 billion annually by then—and a million American AIDS cases by the year 2000.[14]

Since the mid-1980s, much media attention has focused on AIDS. The severity of the problem resulted in a mandate from the U.S. Congress for distribution of an informational brochure about AIDS to all households in the country. In five years (1982–1987), Public Health Service spending on AIDS programs increased from $5.5 million to $411 million.[15]

Symptoms of AIDS

Many fears surround the AIDS issue, largely because it has not been understood. Evidence indicates that AIDS cannot be acquired through casual contacts with others or from using public facilities — telephones, drinking fountains, restrooms, or restaurants. High-risk candidates include those having sexual intercourse with infected partners, drug addicts using contaminated needles, and hemophiliacs depending on blood transfusions. Also, it is believed that pregnant mothers with AIDS can transmit it to their babies before or during the birth process. Approximately 90 percent of those having AIDS are concentrated among homosexual and bisexual males and intravenous drug users.[16]

Some people are high-risk candidates

An AIDS carrier can unintentionally transmit the disease, since he or she may reveal no signs of infection. "It is possible to be infected for years, feel fine, look fine, and have no way of knowing you are infected unless you have a test for the AIDS virus."[17] A positive test result does not actually show infection with AIDS but indicates presence of the virus. Figure 17.3 presents several possible symptoms of AIDS that are not conclusive evidence of the disease but nonetheless indicate a need for caution and further inquiry.

What Behavior Puts You at Risk?

Risky Behavior

Sharing drug needles and syringes.
Anal sex, with or without a condom.
Vaginal or oral sex with someone who shoots drugs or engages in anal sex.
Sex with someone you don't know well (a pickup or prostitute) or with someone whom you know has several sex partners.
Unprotected sex (without a condom) with an infected person.

Safe Behavior

Not having sex.
Sex with one mutually faithful, uninfected partner.
Not shooting drugs.

Source: "Understanding AIDS," U.S. Department of Health and Human Services, Publication No. (CDC HHS-88-8404), May 1988, p. 5.

AIDS and the Workplace

Because of negative reactions by customers and co-workers, some firms have terminated employees with AIDS. In the mid-1980s, the Department of Health and Human Services recommended placing no restrictions on employees having the disease and encouraged employers not to screen out job applicants having AIDS. In 1986, the Justice Department took the position that discrimination on the basis that a victim might spread the disease was justifiable. A year later, a U.S. Supreme Court decision involving employers who receive federal funds assured protection against job discrimination for persons having contagious diseases. "A person with an infectious disease and a record of impairment from that illness is considered "handicapped" under the Federal Vocational Rehabilitation Act of 1973."[18]

Under this act, employers must make "reasonable accommodations" for handicapped employees. For example, workers with life-threatening illnesses may be permitted to complete job assignments at home. The philosophy at International Business Machines is that "IBMers affected by AIDS will be encouraged to work as long as they are able, and their privacy will be respected."[19] Levi Strauss and Company does not differentiate among workers having illnesses and treats employees with AIDS like those afflicted by other diseases.

Employers must respond to employees with AIDS

As greater numbers of people are diagnosed as having AIDS, it is likely that more cases will be filed with the courts. Already, many AIDS complaints involve smaller firms that do not have established personnel policies.[20] New York State and three California cities are among the first to adopt legislation aimed at preventing AIDS-based job discrimination. "Although specific AIDS legislation at the state or local level is limited, AIDS may constitute a handicap under state disability and handicap laws. Every state in the union has some sort of disability law."[21]

Employers have legal concerns

Let's review several questions regarding AIDS and the workplace. Is it legally defensible for co-workers to refuse to work with a person having AIDS?

Possible Symptoms of AIDS **Figure 17.3**

1. Swollen lymph glands
2. Loss of weight for no apparent reason
3. Unexplained, persistent coughing
4. Night sweats
5. Tiredness and fatigue
6. Running a fever for no apparent reason
7. Loss of appetite
8. Continuous diarrhea

Source: Donald S. Miller and Stephen E. Catt, *Human Relations: A Contemporary Approach* (Homewood, Ill.: Richard D. Irwin, 1989), p. 398.

If an employee has AIDS, can he or she be terminated to avoid costly medical-expense claims? Can you refuse to hire an AIDS victim because the person is expected to have a short life expectancy? The answer to each question is no, as courts are unlikely to uphold such actions.[22]

How is the AIDS issue addressed in company policies? One of three options can be chosen.

> One approach is to view AIDS as any other life-threatening illness and write a policy addressing the rights of employees with such illnesses. A second approach is to address AIDS in and of itself. A third approach is to create no special policy if existing corporate policies already cover the rights of employees with life-threatening illnesses.[23]

According to a *Business Week*/Harris executive poll, only 10 percent of the firms surveyed had a specific policy for dealing with AIDS. Eighty-nine percent of the executives reported their firms had not established such a policy.[24]

Bank of America, a leader in the development of a corporate response to AIDS, has a comprehensive policy covering life-threatening illnesses. Several key provisions relate to concerns of employees with AIDS.[25] They are assured their health status will be kept confidential and are given the opportunity to work, as long as performance meets standards. Also, the bank pledges to make reasonable accommodations, which may involve flexible schedules or transfers to jobs better suited to health conditions. These alternatives coincide with the views of AIDS counselors, who recommend that, when possible, afflicted workers remain on the job and encourage employers to provide flexible work accommodations.[26]

Education is a major part of the strategy to provide correct information about AIDS and dispel myths. Medical experts can be invited as guest speakers. Pamphlets and brochures explaining the disease can be distributed to employees. Articles can be included in company newsletters, and films and videotapes can be used to disseminate information in a nonthreatening way without embarrassment to anybody. Companies taking the initiative to educate workers are likely to encounter fewer problems because of misunderstanding about the disease.

Smoking: A Health Hazard

In the 1960s, the surgeon general warned of harmful health consequences from smoking. Cigarette packages have carried a label to note potential health hazards for over two decades. Television and radio advertisements for cigarettes have not been aired since the early 1970s, yet 55 million Americans, approximately 31 percent of adults, continue to smoke.[27] According to the American Lung Association, the premature death each year of 350,000 Americans is caused by cigarette-related illnesses. This organization considers smoking to be "the greatest cause of preventable deaths in America."[28] William Weis, a business professor at Seattle University, calculated that a smoker costs an employer $5,740 more per year than a nonsmoker.[29] The cost of cigarettes themselves continues to escalate as governments level additional "sin" taxes.

Increased attention has focused on the danger of smoking to people who do not smoke. Passive smoking—breathing of air contaminated by smoke—possibly contributes to the development of lung cancer in non-smokers. Some data show that infants of parents who smoke heavily at home experience an unexpectedly high frequency of colds and other respiratory complications. Although the evidence is not substantial, exposure to passive smoking may increase the risk of heart disease. The passive-smoking issue could be more problematic for tobacco companies than active smoking.[30]

Smokers can harm others

During the past 30 years, consumption of cigarettes has decreased. In 1963, the peak year, Americans consumed 4,345 cigarettes per person, but by 1986, usage had declined to 3,274 per person.[31] Several factors contributed to this trend. In 1964, the surgeon general issued a major statement about the impact of smoking on lung cancer and other respiratory illnesses. Negative publicity, increasing health consciousness, and growth of stop-smoking programs have helped to reduce the number of smokers. Also, nonsmokers are becoming more intolerant of smokers. Results of a *Wall Street Journal*/NBC News poll indicated that nonsmokers are increasingly more prone to consider their rights as nonsmokers than previously. Forty percent of smokers surveyed noted they received more complaints about smoking from co-workers than they had five years earlier.[32]

Smoking of cigarettes has declined

Smoking is an age-old practice in our society. It was introduced to Christopher Columbus by the Indians of San Salvador, but the tobacco industry came into prominence with the introduction of the first blended cigarette in 1911.[33] Unlike alcohol and drugs, smoking has enjoyed greater social acceptability. Historically, smokers encountered few restrictions, and cigarettes were smoked practically anywhere, except around potentially flammable products or chemicals. During the 1980s, however, greater limits were placed on where cigarettes could be smoked. For example, smoking in many public buildings and on commercial airlines was severely restricted.

Smokers will encounter greater restrictions

Smoking in the Workplace

While the tobacco industry emphasizes the lack of direct scientific proof, much data suggest a link between smoking and employee health complications. Poor health causes absenteeism, turnover, and declining productivity, while carelessness with cigarettes causes accidents and fires. Data from the

National Center for Health Statistics show the magnitude of complications attributed to smoking in the United States.

> Smoking was the cause of 8½ percent of the cost of all illnesses. . . . Male workers who smoked lost about 40 percent more days at work than did nonsmoking workers. Also, male smokers spent 63 percent more days in the hospital than nonsmokers.[34]

Legislation and smoking

Are employers liable for claims of injury caused by smoking in the workplace? The answer appears to depend on whether the cause was job related or due to a smoker's own consumption of cigarettes.[35] In a 1987 court decision *(McCarthy vs. Washington Department of Social and Health Services),* a worker successfully sued an employer because of exposure to smoke in the job environment. By 1988, 15 states had laws to regulate smoking for private-sector employers. More firms seemingly are becoming concerned about their obligation to provide a safe and healthy workplace.

In a 1987 survey of 2,000 companies employing large numbers of office workers, 68 percent had adopted smoking policies.[36] The most commonly used policy limited smoking to certain areas, such as cafeterias or private offices. The number of firms adopting such policies will increase in the next few years, especially in office environments. AMS Foundation studies on regulation of smoking in offices revealed that the percentage of employers adopting policies more than tripled between 1980 and 1987.[37]

Smoking policies cannot be implemented haphazardly. Communication with employees is necessary to provide explanations, answer questions, and prevent misunderstandings. Support by all levels of management is necessary, and employees must know that, once adopted, a policy will be enforced. Many kinds of questions will arise. "It's my decision to smoke; why should the company tell me what to do?" "Does the policy apply to everybody, even managers?" "If the policy is violated, what are the penalties?" "Will the policy *really* be enforced?" As a supervisor, you should be prepared to answer these kinds of questions.

How can smoking be regulated

Successful regulation of smoking should allow sufficient time for smokers to make adjustments to a newly established policy. Also, employers can make a commitment to pay for stop-smoking programs to help workers break the habit. Company-sponsored in-house programs are advantageous. Some data suggest that smokers participating in such programs experience more success than those who attend sessions at outside clinics.[38] Contests, cash awards, or reduction in health insurance premiums can be used to promote a smoke-free workplace. Persons who do not smoke may not realize the addictive power of nicotine. Consequently, support, encouragement, and recognition for overcoming the habit are important considerations. Most supervisors have close contact with subordinates and can play a vital role in helping them kick the habit. Note the following summary of reasons for smoking tobacco products.

Why Do People Smoke?

1. Stimulation—a belief that smoking helps to increase energy.
2. Handling—a desire to handle or manipulate things.
3. Pleasure—the feeling associated with a state of well-being.
4. Reduction of Negative Feelings—a reaction to anger, anxiety, and other stressful circumstances.
5. Psychological Addiction—a craving for cigarettes.
6. Habit—an established pattern of repetitive smoking.

Source: "Why Do People Smoke?" U.S. Department of Health, Education, and Welfare, National Institutes of Health, Publication No. (NIH) 79-1822.

Consider This

1. What responsibilities do supervisors have toward subordinates who have AIDS?
2. How can supervisors educate employees about AIDS?
3. What factors should be recognized in formulation of a policy to regulate smoking in the workplace?

Safety: Protecting Human Resources

Imagine the trauma of losing a limb or eye at work or even suffering a lesser injury. We tend to say, "It won't happen to me." Yet, as shown in Table 17.1, there were almost 6 million occupational injuries in private-sector employment during 1987, resulting in over 49 million lost workdays. Some people link dangerous working conditions with jobs in mining and construction, but over 1 million cases were reported in finance-insurance-real estate and service sectors. Employees incur risks of all kinds on the job, but many injuries can be avoided by exercising caution.

Practice safe work habits

When injuries occur, nobody wins. Workers suffer pain and lost workdays. Employers must replace injured workers, and they face the possibility of lower productivity, decreased morale, and higher insurance costs. From 1973 to 1983, the average cost per disabling injury tripled from $5,600 to almost $18,000.[39] It is essential to assure equipment functions properly, avoid careless use of machines, and constantly exercise caution.

Injuries are costly

Causes of Accidents

Safety practices are measures taken to protect people from injuries and accidents. Research data show that over 90 percent of injuries and accidents in the workplace happen because of unsafe acts.[40] Accidents can happen

Unsafe acts: major causes of accidents

Table 17.1   **Number of Private-Sector Occupational Injuries by Industry, 1987**

Industry	Total Cases (thousands)	Lost Workday Cases (thousands)	Lost Workdays (thousands)
Agriculture, forestry, and fishing	95.0	49.3	823.4
Mining	59.3	34.6	1,028.9
Construction	631.2	292.3	5,854.2
Manufacturing	2,087.2	923.2	16,293.7
Transportation and public utilities	422.5	247.5	5,422.7
Wholesale and retail trade	1,456.2	648.3	10,592.8
Finance, insurance, and real estate	112.2	49.9	802.8
Services	981.9	476.0	8,231.1
TOTAL	5,845.5	2,721.1	49,049.6

Source: *Occupational Injuries and Illnesses in the United States by Industry, 1987* (U.S. Department of Labor, Bureau of Labor Statistics, May 1989), p. 19.

because of unsafe working conditions, which include absence of safeguards on machines, poorly maintained equipment, and improper lighting or ventilation systems. The nature of jobs themselves, work schedules, and psychological climates also contribute to the possibility of accidents.[41] Some jobs involve greater exposure to injuries than others. Greater numbers of accidents are likely to happen during the latter part of a workday. Stress factors, including hostility toward managers or co-workers or an uncomfortable (too hot or too cold) work environment, affect the likelihood of accidents happening.

Indeed, causes of accidents include employees and job-related activities, the work environment, and a combination of both. People do not deliberately plan to have accidents, but their unsafe actions contribute to them. It is impossible to list all of the individual acts that lead to accidents and injuries. Contributing causes include carelessness caused by daydreaming, failure to pay attention, and taking shortcuts that involve unnecessary risks. All-too-frequent causes of accidents are insufficient care in performing assignments involving lifting, climbing, or handling heavy materials. Failing to use proper equipment and wearing jewelry, rings, or clothing, which can get caught in moving parts of equipment, are other common causes of accidents. Faulty communication while doing tasks requiring coordination among several workers is a contributing factor in accidents.

Why do people have accidents

Accident Prevention

Prevention is the best remedy for accidents

Prevention is the best safety measure. As a supervisor, you must make sure that employees are trained to do their jobs and emphasize the importance of practicing safe work habits. Safety training programs, regular safety meetings, safety committees, and constant monitoring of safety regulations are vital to accident prevention. To help assure a safe workplace, it is essential for all levels of management to make a commitment to safety. According to a DuPont Safety Services study of companies making safety a priority, lost workday cases were reduced by an average of 37 percent during the first year of a safety program.[42]

Congress passed the **Occupational Safety and Health Act** in 1970 to assure safe and healthy working conditions for employees. This Act covers practically all businesses and established the Occupational Safety and Health Administration. OSHA is responsible for increased emphasis on safety by both employees and employers. If workers believe unsafe or unhealthy working conditions exist, the Act provides a means for them to request inspections of their workplaces. Workers cannot be penalized or discriminated against for reporting possible violations.

What is OSHA?

OSHA guidelines require employers to provide a work environment free from hazards that are likely to cause injuries. Employers must permit OSHA personnel to inspect workplaces and provide information on recordable illnesses or injuries — such as events resulting in death, lost work time, medical treatment, interrupted work flows, or unconsciousness. OSHA has been the target of criticism. Some guidelines have been nonspecific, and employers aren't sure if they are in compliance. Other regulations have been complex and difficult to interpret. As compared to the probability of injuries, some employers consider the cost of compliance to be excessive.

As a supervisor, your subordinates often regard you as "the management." Your responsibilities for accident prevention include being certain that workers understand how to operate equipment. This applies especially to new personnel or those performing new jobs. You must be a role model of safety consciousness. Follow safety regulations and promptly correct any violations. Seek opinions about safety matters and recommend necessary changes. Promote "think safety." Many firms have award programs to recognize workers for safety achievements and suggestions. "Recognition not only serves to reward deserving employees, but it also underscores the safety effort through continuous reminders to work, drive, and live safety."[43]

Do your part; practice safety

A **safety audit** is a process to determine if safe workplace behaviors are being practiced. An audit provides valuable information to you. Accumulated data show the types of unsafe acts, indicate which equipment is unsafe, and reveal where additional training is necessary. Conducting an audit forces you to be safety conscious. Time given to an audit is certainly not wasted. Periodic audits can uncover unsafe work practices and equipment problems before potential accidents and injuries occur. A successful audit depends on your knowledge of safe work habits and involves four steps.[44]

What is a safety audit

1. *Decision.* You must decide to audit compliance with safety expectations, preferably on a regular basis.
2. *Observation.* Watch employees do their jobs and question whether safer methods are possible.

3. *Action.* Correct unsafe acts as soon as they are noted. Your tone and approach are important, as the objective is to ensure that unsafe acts are not repeated and faulty equipment is repaired.

4. *Records.* Keep written records to document observations and follow up to correct any problems that are noted.

Protection of human resources will continue to be a workplace issue. **Ergonomics,** which examines the relationship among people, the work environment, and equipment, involves safety concerns in many areas. One area is the possible effect on eyesight from VDTs (visual display terminals). Another is the design of machines to accommodate human needs. Still another is the structure of seats better adapted to human bodies.

Advancing technology raises many concerns about safety. For example, animal research involving pregnant mice has indicated a possible link between magnetic pulses found in VDTs and malformed offspring. As American firms have some 15 million VDTs operated by approximately five million females of child-bearing age, implications of such research become quite important.[45]

Looking Back

This chapter has discussed several topics of special concern in today's workplace: alcohol and drugs, stress, AIDS, smoking, and safety. It is essential for every supervisor to be knowledgeable about these subjects and understand the importance of maintaining a safe and healthy work environment. Review the objectives stated at the beginning of the chapter and consider how the content can be applied on the job.

☐ **Understand the nature of substance abuse in the workplace.** A decline in work performance may be the first symptom of alcohol or drug problems. Symptoms of possible substance abuse are shown in Figure 17.1. Initially, comments to suspected abusers should relate only to observable job performance. If poor job performance continues, supervisors should document records of work deficiencies. They can then confront the employee with evidence and recommend that the person seek assistance from counselors or specialists outside of the organization.

☐ **Identify strategies for alleviating employee stress.** Stress is attributed to any number of events and circumstances. Figure 17.2 indicates symptoms of excessive stress. Supervisors should consider the impact of job expectations on subordinates. Unclear, unreasonable, and conflicting requests are instrumental in creating stress. Realistic attitudes and rational perspectives are great assets to stress reduction. Strategies to manage stress include taking brief breaks, forming proper eating habits, engaging in physical exercise, talking out problems, developing a sense of humor, and getting sufficient rest.

☐ **Recognize the importance of being knowledgeable about AIDS.** AIDS attacks the neurological system and destroys the body's ability to fight infection. In the workplace, many fears surround the AIDS issue, largely because it has not been understood. Evidence indicates it cannot be acquired through casual contacts with others or from using public facilities. High-risk candidates include those having sexual intercourse with infected partners, drug addicts using contaminated needles, and hemophiliacs depending on blood transfusions. Also, it is believed that pregnant mothers with the disease can transmit it to their babies before or during childbirth.

☐ **Discuss the potential health dangers caused by smoking.** Approximately 31 percent of American adults smoke. While the tobacco industry emphasizes the lack of direct scientific proof, much data suggest a direct link between smoking and employee health complications. Poor health causes absenteeism, turnover, and declining productivity, while carelessness with cigarettes causes accidents and fires.

☐ **Explain the importance of safety and accident prevention.** Safety is of extreme importance. When injuries occur, employers as well as employees suffer losses. The best safety measure is prevention. Supervisors are instrumental in creating an awareness of safe working practices. They must be sure that employees are trained properly, and it is essential to correct all violations of safety regulations. Supervisors act as role models by "thinking" and "acting" safety.

Key Terms

AIDS	ergonomics
alcoholism	Occupational Safety and Health Act
burnout	safety audit
drug abuse	safety practices
employee assistance programs	stress

Review and Discussion Questions

1. Identify common symptoms of alcohol and drug abuse.
2. Upon learning that an employee might be an abuser of alcohol or drugs, what should a supervisor do?
3. How does a lack of stress contribute to low productivity?
4. What symptoms indicate that stress is reaching dangerous proportions and is likely to cause difficulties?
5. Explain how a supervisor's manner of communicating can be influential in creating or alleviating stress.

6. What can supervisors do to emphasize accident prevention in the workplace?
7. What is the primary purpose of the Occupational Safety and Health Act?
8. How can a firm educate personnel about AIDS?
9. What behaviors characterize persons who are high-risk candidates for becoming afflicted with AIDS?
10. Why will greater restrictions likely be placed on smoking in the workplace?

Action Incident 17.1

Is There Anything Else?

Glenn Niebling is a capable employee who has received numerous recognitions for his performance during the past 10 years at Avco Company. Al Butcher, his supervisor, feels that Glenn can be counted on to get things done.

During the past year, Glenn has become increasingly negative, especially toward his co-workers. He does not seem nearly as cooperative as before. At meetings, he is withdrawn, and unless specific requests are made of him, he volunteers little. Nevertheless, Glenn's productivity has not declined, even though he considers himself to be "just going through the motions."

Glenn feels that he is more capable than his colleagues but not rewarded accordingly, at least not in salary. He considers himself in a dead-end position but really does not want to leave the company and have to build a reputation all over again. Glenn keeps a mental file on everything that happens and quietly holds resentments against those persons who disagree with him.

Glenn has few close friends and no hobbies. Nearly all of his professional associates consider him a competitive individual and are most respectful of his performance.

In the past couple of months, Glenn has been feeling increasingly tired, eating more and smoking more than usual. He wonders where all of his earlier efforts have gotten him and continually asks himself: "Is there anything else?"

Discussion Questions

1. What symptoms of stress are exemplified in Glenn's behavior? Should Al, his supervisor, recognize these symptoms?
2. What would you recommend to help Glenn alleviate the stress that he apparently is encountering?
3. If he continues to work at his present job, what will likely happen to Glenn?
4. Since he apparently has mastered his current position, does Glenn have the necessary abilities to become a successful supervisor?

Action Incident 17.2

It Happened So Suddenly

After two years of repairing printing presses, Jane Norris decided to leave her position at Standard Equipment for a similar job, which paid a higher salary, at Superior Printing Services. Since Jane was familiar with all types of presses, Sara Laughlin, the new supervisor, considered her ideal for the job.

Jane always arrived promptly for work, but whenever she remained at company facilities to make repairs, Sara noticed that she disappeared for 10- to 15-minute intervals several times each day. Nevertheless, her work seemed satisfactory, and Sara thought nothing more about these incidents.

After a few weeks, several customers called to complain that Jane had arrived late for appointments. When Sara confronted her, Jane explained that her schedule was overloaded, and several jobs had taken more time than anticipated. She agreed to do everything possible to keep more on schedule in the future.

When returning from lunch one day several weeks later, Sara had a note to call the emergency room at Midland Hospital. She learned that Jane had accidentally gotten her right hand caught between two rollers on a press and was in surgery for amputation.

As Sara entered Jane's hospital room that evening, Jane's first remark was, "It happened so suddenly."

Discussion Questions

1. Considering the aspect of safety, what might Sara have done differently in her supervisory relationship to Jane?
2. What might be possible reasons for Jane's frequent disappearances from her workstation?
3. Since Jane agreed to keep more on schedule, what should Sara have done about Jane's seemingly overloaded work schedule?
4. As Jane always arrived promptly for work, it is apparent that she was not experiencing any behavior problems. Explain your response to this statement.

Action Incident 17.3

I've Got AIDS

Doug Whitehall, a supervisor at National Brokerage, arrived for work promptly at 8 A.M. A few minutes later, Herb Kizer, last year's top account executive, asked to see him. After he sat down, Herb said, "About a month ago, I tested positive for AIDS. I'm scared and don't know what lies ahead." Doug was caught by surprise. Although his sales had declined for the past few months, there had been no indication that Herb was experiencing any problems. Soon, the conversation ended. As Herb left, Doug's parting words were, "Herb, I'm sorry, but I do appreciate knowing about your health. I'll treat the matter as confidential and check into the company policy on AIDS."

As he entered the restroom at midmorning, Doug heard Bill Heinz make a remark about Herb's deteriorating sales to Marvin Thompson. Then Bill turned to Doug and asked, "Is there any truth to the rumor about Herb having AIDS?" Unsure of how to respond, Doug replied, "I make it a practice never to comment about rumors." "Is that so?" shrugged Bill as he opened the door to leave, "Just wait until you want to know something and see how much I tell you."

Shortly before lunch, Pat Sullivan appeared at Doug's office door. Pat shut the door and sternly asked, "I've heard from very reliable sources that Herb has AIDS. Is this true?" Doug hesitated and responded, "Well, you hear a lot of things in an office like this." "If it's true," shouted Pat, "you should tell us and fire him." Then Pat stomped out the door.

As he went to lunch, Doug wondered if he had properly handled the situations that had occurred during the morning. While eating, he spotted Sue Hamlin, his boss, and asked her how the company responded to the AIDS issue. Sue indicated that National Brokerage did not have a specific policy on AIDS but treated AIDS like any other life-threatening illness and recommended educating all employees about the nature of AIDS.

Discussion Questions

1. What is your opinion of Doug's responses to Bill Heinz and Pat Sullivan?
2. Should Doug inform all employees about Herb's affliction with AIDS? Explain your response.
3. Should National Brokerage have a specific policy covering employees with AIDS? Explain your response.
4. What can Doug do to help employees become more knowledgeable about AIDS?

Notes

1. "What Illness Costs Business Annually," *Wichita Eagle-Beacon* (September 22, 1986), p. 1D.
2. William E. Lissy, "Drug/Alcohol Testing in the Workplace," *Supervision* 49 (July 1988), p. 19.
3. *Let's All Work Together to Fight Drug Abuse* (Addison, Tex.: L.A.W. Publications, 1985), p. 20.
4. Miriam Rothman, "Random Drug Testing in the Workplace: Implications for Human Resource Management," *Business Horizons* 31 (March–April 1988), p. 24.
5. "Battling the Enemy Within," *Time* 127 (March 18, 1986), pp. 53, 58.
6. Wayne Mondy, Shane R. Premeaux, and Larry Worley, "People Problems: Substance Use and Abuse," *Management Solutions* 32 (February 1987), p. 24.
7. Rothman, "Random Drug Testing in the Workplace," p. 23.
8. Susan R. Mendelsohn and Kathryn K. Morrison, "Testing Applicants for Alcohol and Drug Abuse," *Personnel* 65 (August 1988), p. 58.
9. Michael J. McCarthy, "Stressed Employees Look for Relief in Workers' Compensation Claims," *The Wall Street Journal,* April 7, 1988, p. 27.

10. Donald S. Miller and Stephen E. Catt, *Human Relations: A Contemporary Approach* (Homewood, Ill.: Richard D. Irwin, 1989), pp. 406–7.

11. "Plain Talk about Handling Stress," U.S. Department of Health and Human Services, Public Health Service, Publication No. (ADM) 83-502, 1983, p. 2.

12. Miller and Catt, *Human Relations: A Contemporary Approach,* pp. 407–8.

13. "The AIDS Epidemic in Business," *Business Week,* March 23, 1987, p. 126.

14. Gordon Witkin and Joseph Carey, "AIDS: A Job-Rights Victory," *U.S. News & World Report* 102 (March 16, 1987), p. 11.

15. Joe Davidson, "Need to Alert Youth to AIDS Danger Is Dilemma for Administration Cautious on Sex Education," *The Wall Street Journal,* November 21, 1986, p. 56.

16. "The AIDS Epidemic in Business," p. 123.

17. "Understanding AIDS," U.S. Department of Health and Human Services, Public Health Service, Publication No. (CDC) HHS-88-8404, May 1988, p. 5.

18. Ira D. Singer, "AIDS in the Workplace," *Nation's Business* 75 (August 1987), p. 37.

19. Marilyn Chase, "Corporations Urge Peers to Adopt Humane Policies for AIDS Victims," *The Wall Street Journal,* January 20, 1988, p. 25.

20. Singer, "AIDS in the Workplace," p. 37.

21. Frank Kuzmits and Lyle Sussman, "Twenty Questions about AIDS in the Workplace," *Business Horizons* 29 (July–August 1986), p. 38.

22. Kuzmits and Sussman, "Twenty Questions about AIDS in the Workplace," p. 41.

23. William H. Wagel, "AIDS: Setting Policy, Educating Employees at Bank of America," *Personnel* 25 (August 1988), p. 7.

24. "BW/Harris Executive Poll: The Corporate Response to AIDS Is Slow," *Business Week* (March 23, 1987), p. 132.

25. Wagel, "AIDS: Setting Policy, Educating Employees at Bank of America," p. 7.

26. Singer, "AIDS in the Workplace," p. 39.

27. Alix M. Freedman, "Smokers' Rights Campaign Suffers from Lack of Dedicated Recruits," *The Wall Street Journal,* April 11, 1988, p. 17.

28. "Do Employees Have the Right to Smoke?" *Personnel Journal* 67 (April 1988), p. 80.

29. "Do Employees Have the Right to Smoke?" p. 80.

30. Alan L. Otten, "Movement to Restrict Smoking in Public Places May Gain Momentum as U.S. Releases New Data," *The Wall Street Journal,* October 14, 1986, p. 62.

31. Daniel P. Wiener, "Puffing Up a Second Wind," *U.S. News & World Report* 103 (July 28, 1987), p. 80.

32. Alix M. Freedman, "Cigarette Smoking Is Growing Hazardous to Careers in Business," *The Wall Street Journal,* April 23, 1987, pp. 1, 14.

33. " 'No Smoking' Sweeps America," *Business Week* (July 27, 1987), p. 41.

34. "Economic Cost of Smoking in the United States Topped $38 Billion in 1980, New Study Finds," *Chronicle of Higher Education* 33 (April 1, 1987), p. 7.

35. "Do Employees Have the Right to Smoke?" pp. 76–77, 80–81.

36. J. Carrol Swart, "Corporate Smoking Policies: Today and Tomorrow," *Personnel* 65 (August 1988), pp. 63–64.

37. Joseph E. McKendrick, "Smoking Policies Take Off," *Management World* 17 (January–February 1988), p. 12.

38. "Do Employees Have the Right to Smoke?", p. 82.

39. "Disabling Injuries," *Supervision* 48 (April 1986), p. 11.

40. Dwight Monk, "Conducting a Safety Audit in Your Workplace," *Management Solutions* 33 (September 1988), p. 16.

41. Gary Dessler, *Personnel Management*, 4th ed. (Englewood Cliffs, N.J.: Prentice-Hall, 1988), pp. 664–66.

42. "Companies Can Improve Safety," *Supervision* 50 (March 1988), p. 25.

43. Donald R. Crane, *Personnel: The Management of Human Resources*, 4th ed. (Boston: Kent Publishing, 1986), p. 633.

44. Monk, "Conducting a Safety Audit in Your Workplace," pp. 16–17.

45. Bill Paul, "Latest Study on VDTs Adds to Safety Fears," *The Wall Street Journal*, October 20, 1988, p. B4.

Suggested Readings

Comarow, Avery. "AIDS: A Time of Testing." *U.S. News & World Report* 102, April 20, 1987, pp. 56–59.

Dimond, Diane. "Up in Smoke." *Insurance Review* 48, February 1987, pp. 32–36.

Finney, Martha I. "The Right to be Tested." *Personnel Administrator* 33, March 1988, pp. 74–75.

Hingsburger, David. "Learning How to Face That Stressful Situation." *Management Solutions* 33, February 1988, pp. 41–45.

Kiely, Janet E. "Repetitive Motion Trauma—the Injury of High Technology." *Supervision* 48, October 1986, pp. 9–10.

Levine, Hermine Zagat. "AIDS in the Workplace." *Personnel* 63, March 1986, pp. 56–64.

Redeker, James R., and Deborah J. Tang. "Criminal Accountability for Workplace Safety." *Management Review* 77, April 1988, pp. 32–36.

Spruell, Geraldine. "Work Fever." *Training and Development Journal* 41, January 1987, pp. 41–45.

Strechert, Kathryn. "Your Best Defense Against Office Stress." *Working Woman* 13, August 1988, pp. 60–64.

Wrich, James T. "Beyond Testing: Coping with Drugs at Work." *Harvard Business Review*, January–February 1988, pp. 120–22, 124, 126–27, 130.

Special Concerns for Supervisors

Chapter

18

Learning Objectives

Is there a difference between prejudice and discrimination? How does a supervisor's ethics influence workers' behaviors? Can staring, joking, or gesturing constitute sexual harassment? What is involved in office or shop politics? Supervisors must know the answers to these questions; an understanding of special concerns is essential to effective supervision. These objectives have been developed to assist your study of them.

1. Understand how discrimination affects women, minorities, older workers, and the handicapped.
2. Recognize the importance of ethical behavior.
3. Explain the nature of sexual harassment.
4. Discuss the practice of office or shop politics.

Understanding Prejudice and Discrimination

The workplace is characterized by diversity—people with different experiences, beliefs, and abilities. However, women, minorities, older workers, and the handicapped have been victims of prejudice and discrimination. **Prejudice** is an *attitude* toward an individual or group that is based on incomplete information. Many times, it originates because of incorrect stereotypes, hearsay, and inaccurate generalizations. **Discrimination** involves either favorable or unfavorable *actions*. While it is necessary to hire personnel and assign duties, unfairness exists if decisions are based on a person's race, sex, or national origin.

What is the difference between prejudice and discrimination?

Life experiences influence our opinions and views. While children, parents help to mold our perspectives and beliefs. Later, teachers and classmates influence how we think and respond to others. As adults, our experiences with others at work, within the community, and in personal interactions further help shape our attitudes. Peers, bosses, friends, and acquaintances play a role in our philosophy toward life, people, and the workplace. Sometimes, inaccurate stereotypes exist; unfortunately, these are not easily changed.

A problematic aspect of discrimination is its subtle nature. Subjective performance appraisals, inaccurate assumptions about job capabilities, and vague rationales used to promote personnel increase the likelihood of discrimination. **Equal employment opportunity legislation** forbids unfair discrimination in the job selection process and in the performance of job duties. The Civil Rights Act of 1866 protects the rights of all persons, regardless of race, to make and enforce employment contracts. However, major federal legislation to protect rights of disadvantaged groups emerged during the past thirty years.

Legislation protects disadvantaged groups

Equal Pay Act of 1963. It is unlawful to use sex as a basis for discrimination in employment compensation. This legislation mandates equality of pay between sexes for performance of equal work duties.

Title VII of the Civil Rights Act of 1964. In employment decisions, it is illegal to discriminate because of race, color, sex, religion, or national origin.

Age Discrimination in Employment Act of 1967. Employment discrimination against people between 40 and 70 years of age is forbidden. The intent of this law is to assure competitiveness of job opportunities for those within the designated age range. As amended, the upper age limit has been eliminated for most occupations.

Rehabilitation Act of 1973/Executive Order on the Handicapped of 1974. As an employer, the federal government, including contractors and subcontractors of the federal government, cannot discriminate against the handicapped.

Pregnancy Discrimination Act of 1978.   Discrimination against females because of "pregnancy, childbirth, or related medical conditions" is prohibited.

The labor force is diverse

Table 18.1 shows the civilian labor force classified by occupation, sex, race, and Hispanic origin. White employment predominates in managerial/professional and technical sales/administrative support positions. Blacks and persons of Hispanic origin are employed to a greater extent in service occupations and as operators, fabricators, and laborers. This disparity is of concern to blacks and members of other minority groups who believe that discrimination is a factor in denying them opportunities to hold higher-level, better paid positions. Women average approximately two thirds of the salary earned by men and want greater representation in management jobs. Alleged unfairness is a major issue to those who believe sex and racial or ethnic background unfairly influence job selection and promotion decisions.

For those who are not familiar with problems encountered by members of disadvantaged groups, their concerns may be somewhat difficult to understand. Once again, discrimination is subtle and can be based on

Discrimination is subtle

inaccurate stereotypes. For example, consider how these stereotypes are wrong. Blacks (or some other minority) are undisciplined. (Are members of other races disciplined?) Women are passive and temperamental. (Are men assertive and even tempered?) American Indians (or some other minority) are lazy. (Do members of other ethnic groups work diligently?)[1]

Table 18.1   **Employed Civilians Classified by Occupation, Sex, Race, and Hispanic Origin, 1988**

Occupation	Male	Female	White	Black	Hispanic
Managerial and professional	25.5%	25.2%	26.5%	15.4%	13.2%
Technical sales/ administrative support	19.7	44.6	31.2	27.8	25.0
Service occupations	9.6	17.9	12.1	23.2	18.9
Precision production, craft and repair	19.7	2.3	12.3	8.9	13.5
Operators, fabricators, and laborers	20.9	8.9	14.7	22.9	23.9
Farming, forestry, and fishing	4.6	1.1	3.2	1.8	5.5
TOTAL	100.0%	100.0%	100.0%	100.0%	100.0%

Source: *Handbook of Labor Statistics,* U.S. Department of Labor, Bureau of Labor Statistics, August 1989, p. 78.

Employed Persons Classified by Sex Table 18.2

	1959	1969	1979	1983	1988
Males	67.3%	62.7%	58.3%	56.4%	55.0%
Females	32.7	37.3	41.7	43.6	45.0

Source: *Handbook of Labor Statistics*, U.S. Department of Labor, Bureau of Labor Statistics, August 1989, pp. 63–65.

Women in the Workplace. The number of working women continues to increase. As noted in Table 18.2, this growth pattern has existed for the past 30 years. Between 1979 and 1988, female employment grew by 3.3 percent and increased 1.4 percent in the most recent (1983–1988) five-year period. Increasingly, more women have gone to college. Since 1979, female students have outnumbered males, and females have earned over half of the bachelor's degrees awarded since 1982.[2] Despite greater representation in the labor force, relatively few women have attained top-management positions. A 1985 survey of 1,362 top managers revealed that only 2 percent were female, and only one woman (Katharine Graham of *The Washington Post*) headed a Fortune 500 company.[3]

More women are employed

Various explanations are cited regarding obstacles encountered by working women. According to one view, women and men have a different perception of organizational cultures—rituals, myths, and legends.

> The male model traditionally emphasized competition, dominance, and survival of the fittest. Aggressive management philosophies and behavior are the norm in most successful companies. . . . Organizational cultures may not only help us to understand why women are having difficulty ascending the managerial ranks but also to understand the prevalent attitude towards women in management. Although women are certainly accepted by men in the managerial ranks, men are confused when women behave in ways that are characteristically female and conclude that women don't know how to behave.[4]

Georgia P. Childress of Western Kentucky University believes women must overcome commonly accepted myths.[5] According to one myth, women do not make good managers and have little power. Childress points out that management is a generic activity and stresses that women gain power just like men do. Women do not need preferential treatment to rise up the managerial hierarchy, but it is important for them to receive the same treatment as males.

Myths must be overcome

A survey of 722 women executives focused attention on sex-related considerations.[6] Respondents felt that men treat women differently, fail to include them in social activities, and underestimate their experience. These views illustrate the type of concerns held by females. Katharine Graham, a corporate executive, concludes, "I believe women will get to the top and gain power the same way men do, not with artificial aids or special deals, but by working harder, knowing more, taking risks, and being better than their competitors, male and female."[7]

Blacks are the largest
minority

Blacks and Other Minorities.   Blacks are America's largest minority and comprise approximately 12 percent of the population. Compared to the percentage of black lawyers, engineers, and dentists, more than three times as many blacks work as practical nurses, social workers, and law enforcement officers.[8] Higher education is a prerequisite for many professional careers. Unfortunately, fewer black students are going to college. In 1976, a third of the blacks who graduated from high school went to college. By the late 1980s, slightly over 25 percent continued their education.[9]

Government legislation and affirmative action programs were designed to enhance equal employment opportunities. In a 1988 *Business Week*/Harris Survey of 531 black adults, participants were asked to indicate factors most responsible for the progress of blacks over the previous thirty years.[10] Highest ratings were given to individual initiative (21 percent), government laws against discrimination (18 percent), companies trying to hire blacks (11 percent), and a decline in white discrimination (7 percent).

Compared to their white colleagues, blacks are underrepresented in managerial positions. Consequently, they have fewer role models to emulate and less opportunity to establish mentor relationships. "To achieve career success, blacks may need to excel at levels above expectations for whites. In terms of expected benefits, it's possible that some may believe that the effort — frustration and pressure for excellence — may not be worthwhile."[11]

The number of Hispanics
is increasing

Hispanics, America's fastest growing minority group, represent almost 8 percent of the population and are expected to increase by another 3 percent by 2010. Lack of schooling is a major difficulty encountered by Hispanics. Estimates indicate that over 40 percent of Hispanic high school students do not receive their diplomas.[12] Hispanic employment is concentrated in lower paying jobs, partially because they lack education and encounter language barriers. The influx of illegal immigrants from Mexico has created a controversy. While these illegal aliens are a source of unskilled labor, some believe they take jobs that otherwise could be held by Americans.

About 3 percent of the population is Asian. In the years ahead, the number of Asians in the United States will increase considerably. Economically, they have not suffered like other minorities because of the value their

Asians value education

culture places on education. Asians, especially the Japanese and Chinese, are more prepared to compete for better jobs, but they still encounter discrimination in the workplace.

Discrimination affects our
"first" Americans

American Indians comprise less than 1 percent of the population and have been discriminated against partially because of a failure on the part of white Americans to understand their culture and traditions. Prejudiced stereotypes have prevailed for many years. During the 1800s, Indians lost their homelands, and the government placed them on reservations. In the movies, cowboys and the military were portrayed as victors in battles against Indians. Recently, however, some tribes have proudly proclaimed their heritage and sought to gain greater recognition for our "first" Americans.

Older Workers.   At what age are workers considered old? There is nouniversal answer to this question. Ronald Reagan, a former actor and governor of California, served as President of the United States in his 70s. In his 80s, Konrad Adenauer led West Germany, and Charles deGaulle, at age 79, was leader of France. Claude Pepper, a noted crusader for concerns of older citizens, was over 80 years old while serving in the U.S. Congress. Even though a professional athlete is considered old at age 40, a corporate executive is regarded as being young at that same age.

America's labor force is growing older. Between 1984 and 1995, 16 million additional workers will be 40 years of age or older. In 1950, 17 Americans were working for each retired person; by 1992, the ratio will be 3 to 1. Increasingly, workers have taken advantage of early-retirement opportunities. In the late 1960s, 83 percent of persons from 55 to 64 years old continued to work. By 1988, however, only 68 percent were in the labor force.[13] From 1989 to 1996, the number of workers in the 35–54 age group will increase by 4.2 percent, or slightly over 14 million people.[14]

The labor force is aging

The Age Discrimination in Employment Act of 1967 prohibits discrimination against older workers in terms and conditions of employment and makes it illegal to compensate on the basis of age, yet age discrimination is the most rapidly escalating source of bias claims in the workplace. In 1986, nearly 27,000 complaints were filed with government agencies — twice as many as received six years earlier.[15] In managing subordinates, supervisors must avoid references to age and not condone age-related comments expressed by workers. For example, a comment that the company is "going to get rid of the 'good ole Joes' and get some younger folks in" or "for men (or women) your age, there isn't going to be a future" can result in discrimination charges.[16] The following myths often stereotype older workers.

Age discrimination is a concern

Myths about Older Workers

Myth No. 1: Older workers are less productive than the average worker.
Myth No. 2: It costs more to prepare the older worker for the job than it does to prepare other workers.
Myth No. 3: The costs of employee benefits outweigh any possible gain from hiring older workers
Myth No. 4: Older workers do not get on well with others.
Myth No. 5: Older workers are prone to frequent absences because of age-related infirmities and above-average rates of sickness.
Myth No. 6: Older workers have an unacceptably high rate of accidents at work.
Myth No. 7: Older people are unwilling to learn new jobs and are inflexible about the hours they will work.

Source: "Older Workers: Myths and Reality," Publication No. (AoA) 84–20516, U.S. Department of Health and Human Services, Office of Human Development Services Administration on Aging, pp. 2–6.

The Handicapped.   Thirty-six million Americans are disabled, and only a third of the 15 million who are of working age have secured employment.[17] According to census data, only 16 percent of disabled persons hold managerial and professional positions. The 1986 Report of the President's Committee on Employment of the Handicapped concluded that many disabled persons may be pigeonholed in lower-salaried jobs offering little possibility for advancement.[18]

Handicap discrimination is illegal

According to Sections 503 and 504 of the Rehabilitation Act of 1973, it is illegal for employers to discriminate based on a handicap. A **handicapped person** is an individual who has a physical or mental impairment that substantially limits one or more of such person's major life activities, has a record of such impairment, or is regarded as having such an impairment. Some employers believe that employment of the handicapped will lead to increased costs, greater absenteeism, and more workplace accidents. Data tend not to support these views. In a U.S. Department of Labor survey, 367 federal contractors were asked to report costs of making accommodations for handicapped employees. Seventy percent of the needed accommodations cost $100 or less.[19]

Understanding is a key to supervising the handicapped

To manage handicapped workers, supervisors should "avoid stereotyping, recognize abilities, focus on positive attitudes, implement new communication skills, and watch out for barriers."[20] Some modification of facilities may be necessary. Try to understand the nature of the disability and remember to encourage acceptance by co-workers of a handicapped colleague. It may take some time for disabled workers to make adjustments and overcome preconceived negative attitudes. "What is needed is simply more information, more familiarity with disabled people of all kinds, and more rubbing of shoulders with people who have disabilities."[21]

Guidelines for Working with the Handicapped

---

1. If you are not familiar with handicapping conditions, be willing to learn.
2. Be helpful. Like all employees, handicapped persons sometimes require help in getting started with new tasks.
3. Be willing to learn new communication skills.
4. Introduce the handicapped employee to other members of the work group.
5. Focus your attention on the skills and positive attributes of the handicapped employee.
6. Be aware of worksite modifications that may help the handicapped employee complete tasks. These modifications mean changing the *way* work is done, not the *amount* of work that is done.

Source: "Working with Handicapped Employees," The President's Committee on Employment of the Handicapped (1984), p. 2.

The Role of Ethics

Standards governing behavior and dictating choices between appropriate or inappropriate actions are called **ethics**. What is appropriate can vary, and choices are not always easy. Imagine that you receive a phone call from a prospective employer about your worst-performing employee. You have been hoping this worker will quit before he or she must be fired. Will you recommend this person, or will you be honest?

Society is governed by norms, customs, and traditions. However, each of us is influenced by life experiences, individual concerns, and personal motives. At work, the boss, subordinates, and colleagues have an impact on ethical judgments. If rewards are given only for results (without any concern for how they were attained), the likelihood of unethical conduct will increase. A need to "look good" on performance appraisals, the desperate need for money, or a belief that "nobody will know the difference" can lead to improper actions. When an individual is caught, the customary explanation tends to prevail. "Everybody does it."[22]

Some years ago, Albert Z. Carr wrote in the *Harvard Business Review* that business ethics differ from those of society at large. He compared the business environment to a game of poker with its own rules and concluded that the test for business "moves" often involved legality and profit.[23] In practice, the difference between legality and morality can pose a dilemma. Supervisors who have firm personal convictions, yet remain flexible enough to be realistic, will usually handle ethical issues well. A sense of judgment about proper courses of action develops as you do your job. Figure 18.1 illustrates how societal and organizational factors influence ethical judgments and consequential behavior.

There is no universal agreement on what constitutes ethical behavior. **Codes of ethics**, formal written policy statements establishing ethical guidelines for an organization, provide guidance. To be successful, codes must be supported by management. Also, penalties for infractions and a method of enforcement should be clearly specified. Figure 18.2 presents the ethic commitment of the Martin Marietta Corporation. It includes the firm's commitment to employees, customers, communities, shareholders, and suppliers. Should you be pressured to comply with an unethical request, a code of ethics provides justification for refusal. Such a circumstance can be quite delicate and provoke much thought. Should you ultimately elect to be a whistle-blower (report the improper request), be prepared to encounter personal stress and frustration, which ultimately may lead to employment elsewhere.

Training can enhance ethical awareness and develop insights into ethical choices. Several factors merit consideration.[24] First, training promotes recognition and awareness of value systems. Examples of proper behavior, codes of conduct, and knowledge of the consequences of misconduct serve to encourage desired behavior. Alert supervision, demonstrated manage-

Ethics govern behavioral choices

What influences ethics

Training increases ethical awareness

Figure 18.1   **Factors Influencing Ethical Behavior**

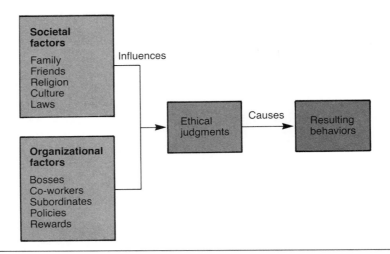

Source: Donald S. Miller and Stephen E. Catt, *Human Relations: A Contemporary Approach* (Homewood, Ill.: Richard D. Irwin, 1989), p. 189.

Figure 18.2   **Illustration of an Ethic Commitment**

Martin Marietta demonstrates its ethic through these commitments:
- To our employees we are committed to just management and equality for all, providing a safe and healthy workplace, and respecting the dignity and privacy due all human beings.
- To our customers we are committed to produce reliable products and services at fair prices that are delivered on time and within budget.
- To the communities in which we live we are committed to be responsible neighbors, reflecting all aspects of good citizenship.
- To our shareholders we are committed to pursuing sound growth and earnings objectives and exercising prudence in the use of our assets and resources.
- To our suppliers we are committed to fair competition and the sense of responsibility required of a good customer.

Source: "Corporation Schedules Workshops in Ethics Program," *Martin Marietta Today,* No. 1 (1986), p. 1.

ment concern, and rapid responses to unethical actions reduce the likelihood of infractions. Use of videotapes, case studies, and role playing provides opportunities to examine ethical choices. Learners discuss possible alternative solutions and gain an understanding of how to make ethical decisions. Ideally, knowledge gained from these learning experiences will be applied to on-the-job ethical considerations.

Practice good ethical conduct

Ethical conduct involves upholding company standards as well as your own. The employment relationship requires loyalty and commitment to company objectives. You must consider the best interests of your employer and your workers in the decisions you make. Ethical awareness does not imply that your judgments are always right. It does suggest that decisions are not deliberately deceitful. For example, you might permit a worker to take a piece of equipment home for work on a personal project. If for some reason you did not know that company policy forbids this, your action could not be considered unethical.

The Supervisor and Ethics

Is there a relationship between your ethics and those of your workers? Yes. You are a leader and a role model. Your actions set examples for workers. If you are dishonest or steal from your employer, subordinates can say, "If my supervisor does it, why shouldn't I?" Trustworthiness and respect are earned. You communicate standards and values to others through your decisions, attitudes, and daily behaviors. You can minimize workers' ethical dilemmas by, whenever possible, avoiding questionable practices that place impossible expectations on subordinates. If it is clearly not possible for an employee to do a quality check on every 10th item produced, do not place him or her in the position of having to record that such inspections have been completed.

Supervisors are ethical role models

Supervisors are human and have to live with themselves. Each person's conscience and value system provide guidance in determining what is right or wrong. Suppose you are under pressure to promote a worker who is marginally qualified but has a close personal relationship with your boss and several upper-level managers. Your evaluation of the employee's performance and a potentially harmful effect on your own career aspirations conflict. When confronted with difficult choices, ask this question: "Would I make the same decision if I had to make a full and public disclosure of my actions?"[25]

Job pressures influence behaviors

People, including supervisors, have different perspectives about the appropriateness of behavior. Figure 18.3 lists several questions about job-related behavior. Rate yourself on each of these questions. If possible, ask a friend or colleague to answer these questions. Then compare responses and discuss dissimilarities among responses. Without being critical, try to understand reasons for the differences. Perhaps you will discover for yourself how experiences, opinions, and values influence personal views toward ethical conduct.

Consider your own ethics

1. What actions can women, minorities, older workers, and the handicapped take to minimize discrimination in the workplace?
2. Many incidents of unethical behavior in business and government have been publicized by the media. How can supervisors promote greater awareness of proper ethical conduct?
3. Codes of conduct can alleviate unethical misconduct. How do you respond to this statement?

Consider This

Figure 18.3   **Rate Your Behaviors**

	Yes	No	Occasionally
1. Even if it creates difficulties, are you honest with your boss?	____	____	____
2. Do you take materials or supplies from the office for personal use?	____	____	____
3. Even if it's clearly unethical, will you follow instructions from the boss?	____	____	____
4. Do you withhold information that reflects poorly on your job performance?	____	____	____
5. Do you criticize the work of others to gain personal advantage?	____	____	____
6. During work hours, do you take time to run personal errands?	____	____	____
7. Even though not ill, do you use sickness as an excuse for absenteeism?	____	____	____
8. On the job, do you work at less than the best of your ability?	____	____	____
9. Do you fail to volunteer ideas to improve job effectiveness?	____	____	____
10. Is the future welfare of your employer personally unimportant to you?	____	____	____

Source: Donald S. Miller and Stephen E. Catt, *Human Relations: A Contemporary Approach*
(Homewood, Ill.: Richard D. Irwin, 1989), p. 193.

Sexual Harassment in the Workplace

The key is unwelcomed behavior

Sexual harassment, which involves unwelcome sexually oriented annoyances, negatively affects emotions, causes productivity to decline, and creates an unhealthy work environment. Harassment includes staring, gesturing, touching, joking, and pressures for dates or sexual intimacy. How widespread is sexual harassment? In 1980, the Merit Systems Protection Board surveyed federal workers to determine the extent of sexual harassment encountered on their jobs. Compared to 15 percent of the males, 42 percent of the females had been sexually harassed. The survey was repeated seven years later with the same results. The cost (lost employees, sick leave, and reduced productivity) of sexual harassment to the federal government over a two-year period was estimated to be $267 million.[26]

Sexual harassment is costly

While large, the total cost of sexual harassment and the number of actual cases is not known. Many victims do not report harassing incidences, largely because they fear reprisals, publicity, or possible loss of their jobs. Aside from costs measured in dollars, sexual harassment is costly in terms of frustrations and emotions for both employers and workers. "In addition to litigation fees and possible court awards to plaintiffs, harassment can lead to job turnover, morale difficulties, interruption of work performance, and a poor public image for the company. Victims experience embarrassment, stress, lowered productivity, and health problems."[27]

In 1980, the Equal Employment Opportunity Commission established guidelines covering inappropriate sexual conduct in the workplace. Sexual behavior is discriminating and unlawful if it

What actions constitute sexual harassment

1. requires submission to sexual advances as a condition of employment;
2. is a part of employment decisions;
3. causes interruption of or interference with performance of an employee's job duties; or
4. creates an offensive working environment.

Six years later, the first sexual harassment case (*Meritor v. Vinson*) was decided by the U.S. Supreme Court. According to the court ruling, a victim need not suffer monetary or job loss to establish a Title VII discrimination claim. It was concluded that a key factor is whether the sexual activity is "unwelcomed."

If unaware of sexual harassment by an employee, is an employer liable? The Supreme Court issued divided opinions. A majority of the judges believed an employer's liability should be determined on a case-by-case basis. However, a four-justice minority opinion stated that "employers are responsible for supervisors' acts regardless of whether those acts were authorized or even forbidden by the employer and regardless of whether the employer knew or should have known of the acts."[28]

Preventing Sexual Harassment

Management's attitude and education of employees are key factors in prevention of sexual harassment. All managers must adopt a serious stance toward this issue and communicate that harassing behavior will not be tolerated. Information can be disseminated through brochures, notices on bulletin boards, company newsletters, and presentations at meetings attended by employees. A professional attitude, not merely lip service, conveys the message that sexual harassment is an important concern. As a supervisor, emphasize the "unwelcome" aspect of sexually oriented comments and behaviors and be a role model for subordinates. Think before speaking and avoid behaviors that may be misinterpreted. At Chase Manhattan Bank, for example, employees are directed not to touch others, even to congratulate them for accomplishments.[29]

Management views and education are important

A policy evidences
concern

Formulation of a policy to address sexual harassment is a key step in prevention of undesirable behaviors. Such a policy should define offensive actions, explain the company's position, and provide a procedure to handle complaints. For instance, AT&T's policy defines improper conduct as "offensive sexual flirtation, advances, propositions, continual or repeated abuse of a sexual nature, graphic verbal commentary about an individual's body . . . and the display in the workplace of sexually suggestive objects or pictures."[30] Inform subordinates about policy provisions and grievance procedures.

Handling Allegations of Sexual Harassment

Sexual harassment can
involve complexities

Human behavior is complex, and sometimes motives are expressed in subtle, even misleading, ways. Sexually oriented remarks, jokes, or placing an arm around another person convey different messages — depending on the people involved and previous events or interactions between them. Sexual harassment evokes anxieties and requires personal courage to report, especially if the offender is the claimant's boss. Dealing with the issue is seldom easy and necessitates gathering information to establish what did or did not happen. It is possible for a harassment claim to be contrived as a way to "get at" a person who is disliked. Frequently, offenders deny improper conduct or emphasize that their actions were misunderstood. Sometimes, allegations are met with countercharges without either party having any documentation. In other instances, a person files an allegation of sexual harassment and later withdraws it.

Know how to handle
complaints

Generally, policies provide for reporting misconduct to an employee's immediate boss. If the supervisor is a harasser, procedures can provide for reporting abuses to his or her boss or the personnel/human relations office. Often, a verbal warning to the offender is sufficient to stop the unwelcomed behavior. Another approach is for the victim to write a letter to the harasser. It should state the nature of the improper conduct, ask that it cease, and specify actions to be taken if such behavior continues. This communication can be confidential without third-party intervention. When delivery is documented, the victim has a record to show an effort was made to stop the harassing behavior.

Should management action become necessary, procedures usually call for collecting information and taking corrective actions. First, listen carefully to the claimant's explanation of what occurred. Is there a sound basis for the allegation? Is the alleged misconduct a violation of company policy? Is there evidence, such as witnesses or written material, to support the claim? Based on these data, inquiries can substantiate or refute the allegations. It is important to determine whether persons are willing to speak for the record and, if necessary, provide testimony. Should the claim have merit, the accused person must be confronted and given an opportunity to present his or her side of the issue.

The problem might be misperceived intentions that can be remedied at this stage. However, blatant wrongdoing may have occurred. If so, action must be taken to end the harassment. It is necessary to consider restitution for the victim. This may involve transfer to another department, reconsidering a withheld promotion, or granting other appropriate types of compensation.

Determine the facts

Understanding Office or Shop Politics

How do some people maintain excellent relationships with their bosses and appear to profit therefrom? Why do some workers have more influence than others? Perhaps, these people excel at **office or shop politics**, which involve ways of getting things done that are not formally recognized practices or procedures. Working hard to achieve results is not undesirable. However, many people view deliberate cultivation of a friendly relationship with the boss solely to get a raise or promotion as inappropriate political behavior.

What is office or shop politics?

There are many reasons why people engage in office or shop politics. All promote self-interest. Some desire power and authority; others want to build reputations and gain respect from colleagues, bosses, or workers. Some forms of politics, such as sacrificing company objectives for personal gains, are unethical. Political behaviors exist in all aspects of the workplace. You must recognize and understand them.

Self interest: a key to political behavior

People who have mastered their jobs and are known for their expertise have advantages. Besides respect, they may have professional development opportunities that are not available to others. Bosses value the abilities of such people and often take greater personal interest in them. Consequently, they encounter fewer obstacles and less resistance in the practice of political behaviors.

Some people always seem to say the right thing at the right time. How do they sense what is going on before others do? They probably know the value of communication skills, a critical component in political success. By judging a listener's receptivity, a person can advantageously use communication abilities. For example, a subordinate might take cues from what you say, accept your viewpoint, and gain your favor. By agreeing, the worker might ultimately expect your support on an issue of importance to him or her.

Using Political Strategies

As noted previously, a concern for self-interest is the primary reason to practice office or shop politics. Deceitful behavior is granting favors or giving assistance solely to obligate others. This involves the "he (or she) owes me one" concept. A definite repayment is expected. Taking credit for accomplishments or ideas of others or wrongly blaming them for failures is also deceitful. It is equally inappropriate to make recommendations solely to enhance your personal status and prestige. Worst of all are attempts to destroy the credibility of others to meet self-serving goals. Political behavior should not involve dishonesty. Honorable and successful people do not destroy competitors. It is not necessary, and their support may be needed in the future. Let's examine some commonly practiced political strategies.[31]

Doing Favors.   People remember who does favors for them, especially if they are under pressure and need assistance. Assume your boss delegates a major assignment to you with a very short completion deadline. In addition to the usual workload, it is now necessary to find the time to do this extra work. One of your subordinates learns of the situation and asks, "Is there anything I can do to help?" You likely will be grateful because this person can perform some of your routine duties. Most importantly, you are not likely to forget this person who volunteered assistance.

Making Impressions.   We constantly form judgments about others based on factors such as knowledge, reputation, appearance, and conduct. A record of accomplishments and recognized potential to get things done are valued personal characteristics. Skillful politicians understand the importance of favorable impressions and strive to create positive images of themselves.

Cultivating the Grapevine.   The grapevine, an informal method of communication, is often used to transmit rumors, gossip, and opinions about numerous personal and job-related topics. Generally, communication flows rapidly through the grapevine, which is a source for information before it becomes widely known. Since being in the know is essential to the practice of office or shop politics, politically active persons seek to cultivate relationships with those who possess or have access to desired information. This is accomplished by gaining memberships on committees, making friends, developing informal contacts, and being accessible to others.

Supporting the Boss.   Wise politicians hesitate, even privately, to make negative comments about the boss and never publicly criticize a superior. Many employees fail to understand frustrations managers encounter, especially in making difficult decisions. Subsequently, some attempt to put their boss "on the spot" at meetings or freely express negative opinions to others. Those adept at politics recognize that embarrassing the boss or putting him or her in a difficult position is not an advantageous political strategy.

Avoiding Negativism.   It is easy to focus on negative factors involving your job, employer, or others. Managers constantly listen to complaints, handle disputes, and hear how better decisions might have been reached. Instead of dwelling on such negative topics, capable politicians devote energy to suggesting remedies, not just criticizing. Events do not always work out as anticipated. When it becomes apparent a setback will occur, it is politically wise to explain the circumstances to the boss—before he or she hears comments from others who may not have your best interests in mind.

Giving Praise. People like to be praised, yet many do not extend congratulations to others for their attainments. Adept politicians know compliments are not quickly forgotten, especially by the boss who is often unaccustomed to receiving them from subordinates. Therefore, politically motivated persons seldom miss opportunities to take advantage of praise as a potential strategy, which may encourage others to view them positively.

People like to be praised

Minimizing Undesirable Political Behaviors

Office or shop politics is an inherent part of workplace life. Unfortunately, undesirable behaviors can strain relationships, build resentment, and cause morale to decline. A first step for reducing such behaviors is to define job duties clearly so employees know what they are to do and how they will be evaluated. When responsibilities and appraisal criteria are vague, political maneuvering is a likely consequence. Recognize the importance of worker involvement and job satisfaction. When possible, let subordinates have personal discretion to perform job tasks without "breathing down their necks." "People whose jobs give them little satisfaction, little autonomy, and little hope of promotion are the ones most likely to see the invisible hand of company politics playing a major role in the decisions that affect their personal lives."[32]

Undesirable behaviors do occur

Effective communication reduces the potential of detrimental political actions. Frequently, decisions are based on negotiation, compromise, and misinterpretation—factors not fully understood by those who are affected by them. Employee participation and explanations alleviate possible negative reactions and enhance understanding. Supervisors should create a work atmosphere where subordinates consider themselves to be important. "This means not giving up on people who may gradually be coming to see themselves as marginal members of the work unit. Supervisors who create a greater sense of in-ness among their subordinates can expect to have more effective work units."[33]

Practice effective communication

Examine your managerial practices. If subordinates perceive you as insecure or irresponsible, it is an invitation for political manipulation. Lack of respect, perceptions of incompetence, and failure to enforce standards encourage efforts to discredit you. This may give some persons a built-in excuse to campaign for allegiance of co-workers and develop a power base, which can cause conflict. Therefore, it is necessary for you to think carefully about issues and have sound rationales for actions.

Examine your own behavior

Firms compete with one another, but competition for financial, equipment, and human resources also occurs within organizations. Supervisors must allocate budgeted monies and workloads.

A systematic approach for allocating resources according to justifiable criteria is advantageous and has the potential of reducing excessive political behavior. Firmly established policies and guidelines are mandatory, but managers must be careful to apply them consistently. Otherwise, politics can evolve as a primary competitive approach in which empire building predominates.[34]

Workers are conditioned to "reality." When subordinates observe how requests are actually granted, they adapt their strategies accordingly. Assume, for example, a supervisor habitually approved half of the items requested by his or her workers. Soon, employees will simply double their requests to get the number of items wanted.

Consider This

1. Why has increased attention been focused on the issue of sexual harassment in the workplace?
2. Frequently, political behaviors are viewed negatively. How can a *firm* benefit from the practice of office or shop politics?
3. Why are some persons much more skillful at office or shop politics than others?

Looking Back

In this chapter, you studied several important issues — prejudice and discrimination, ethics, sexual harassment, and office or shop politics. It is necessary to be knowledgeable about these topics, as you will encounter circumstances involving them. Take time now to review the objectives listed at the beginning of the chapter.

☐ **Understand how discrimination affects women, minorities, older workers, and the handicapped.** Greater numbers of females have entered the labor force and also earned a college education, yet few have attained top-management positions. Females average about two thirds of the salary earned by men. Sometimes, women are stereotyped because of misperceptions that they do not make good managers, are too passive, and exert little power.

Although blacks are the largest minority group, they are not proportionately represented in higher-status managerial job categories. Consequently, they have fewer role models to emulate and less opportunity to develop mentor relationships. Employment of Hispanics, America's fastest growing minority group, is concentrated in lower-paying jobs, partially because they lack formal education and encounter language barriers. A failure to understand the culture and traditions of American Indians has contributed to discrimination against them. Asians, especially the Chinese and Japanese, have been more competitive in the labor force than other minorities, largely because of the value their cultures place on education.

America's work force is getting older, and common stereotypes prevail about older workers. These include views that they are less productive, too costly to employ, and prone to frequent absences. In managing workers, supervisors must avoid references to age and not condone age-related comments expressed by subordinates.

Relatively few handicapped persons hold managerial and professional positions. For the handicapped, obstacles include beliefs that employment necessitates costly accommodations, causes greater absenteeism, and leads to more accidents. Supervisors should avoid stereotypes, try to understand the nature of handicaps, and encourage subordinates to accept handicapped colleagues.

☐ **Recognize the importance of ethical behavior.** Ethics refer to standards that govern behavior and dictate choices between appropriate and inappropriate actions. Supervisors who have firm personal convictions, yet remain flexible enough to be realistic, will have the least difficulty with ethical issues. Since supervisors are leaders, the extent to which they uphold ethical principles sets examples for workers.

☐ **Explain the nature of sexual harassment.** Sexual harassment involves unsolicited, coercive, or unwanted suggestive annoyances. In addition to monetary costs, victims suffer from emotional and psychological pressures. Creating awareness, dissemination of information, and a policy of not tolerating such behaviors are integral factors in preventing sexual harassment.

☐ **Discuss the practice of office or shop politics.** Office or shop politics involve informal ways of getting things accomplished that are not formally recognized practices or procedures. Promotion of self-interest is a major reason for engaging in political behavior, which includes doing favors, making impressions, cultivating the grapevine, supporting the boss, avoiding negativism, and giving praise. Undesired political maneuvering can be reduced through effective communication and by defining job duties clearly so employees know what they are to do and how they will be evaluated.

Key Terms

code of ethics	handicapped person
discrimination	office or shop politics
equal employment opportunity legislation	prejudice
ethics	sexual harassment

Review and Discussion Questions

1. What is the difference between prejudice and discrimination?
2. Explain the primary purpose for the following legislative enactments.
   a. Equal Pay Act of 1963
   b. Title VII of the Civil Rights Act of 1964
   c. Age Discrimination in Employment Act of 1967
   d. Rehabilitation Act of 1973
   e. Pregnancy Discrimination Act of 1978
3. Discuss procedures to be followed by a supervisor who becomes aware that a subordinate is possibly being sexually harassed.
4. What actions can a supervisor take to reduce the likelihood of sexual harassment in his or her work unit?
5. Why is there a lack of agreement on criteria for judging ethical behaviors?
6. To what extent do the ethical practices of business differ from those of society?
7. How should supervisors respond to situations in which their ethical principles conflict with the employer's practices?
8. How do communication skills influence the practice of office or shop politics?
9. Discuss the primary reason why people engage in office or shop politics.
10. On their jobs, to what extent do workers engage in office or shop politics?

Action Incident 18.1

We're Losing Money[*]

International Builders is constructing a major missile project for the government. Jim Hansen is the assembly coordinator, and his boss, Robert Clayton, is the project manager. The project is behind schedule; more difficulties than anticipated have been encountered.

Jim: I don't know what's going to happen. Costs are above estimates, and unreliable deliveries are commonplace. Some of the suppliers tell me they are going to demand cash payments before materials are shipped.

Robert: This project is a disaster. We're going to lose a lot of money on it. The inaccurate cost estimates hurt, and we're definitely in a bind.

Jim: How about shifting some costs to one of the other government contracts? Or what do you think about substituting cheaper materials and cutting corners in places that aren't so obvious?

---

[*] Source: Donald S. Miller and Stephen E. Catt, *Human Relations: A Contemporary Approach* (Homewood, Ill.: Richard D. Irwin, 1989), pp. 207–8.

We could save quite a bit, and it's unlikely that anyone will know the difference.

Robert: What you're suggesting is wrong; we can't do it. I'm reluctant to complicate an already messy situation.

Jim: I know other companies transfer costs. Anyway, the substitute materials won't affect performance capability of the missile system. We're already in trouble because things have gotten out of control.

Robert: Life isn't easy. We've already got some challenges. Maybe we should meet with the other managers, explain the problems, and see what they think.

Jim: There's a lot of pressure. Perhaps we need to stall for time and get a better perspective.

Robert: I disagree. Let's face the facts and get started making some progress to get things resolved.

Discussion Questions

1. What ethical dilemmas are apparent in the discussion between Jim and Robert?
2. Why do they have different perspectives about how to handle problems related to the missile project?
3. How could a corporate code of ethics help avoid questionable ethical practices?
4. Is Robert's suggestion to meet with other managers an appropriate course of action? Explain your response.

Action Incident 18.2

I'm the Person

Cecil Bolin is a star performer in a regional office of Valeron Enterprises. Because of Cecil's excellent performance and superb job skills, James Waldron, his supervisor, has taken a special liking to him and often asks Cecil to help prepare reports and special assignments. Waldron often uses Cecil as a sounding board for ideas. James shares confidences and inside information related to the work unit with Cecil.

Cecil uses this close relationship to discredit members of his peer group who appear to be in competition with him. Often, he is the first one to learn about upper-management decisions, and he tries to use the information to his personal advantage. Such knowledge gives him additional time for thinking and preparing polished proposals.

To his co-workers, Cecil's comments indicate how easily he thinks tasks can be accomplished. "I could have completed the job in half the time," or "Look how easily I did it," he says. To spite him, some of his co-workers routinely oppose positions he takes on issues. Cecil is aware of their feelings toward him; on important issues, he persuades friends to present and support his viewpoints.

Recently, James received a promotion to a middle-management position. Cecil wants to further his own career by becoming supervisor of the work group, and he thinks he can handle the job. If Cecil is promoted, several workers who are offended by him or who are jealous of his ability to get things done will be disappointed. Cecil thinks, "I'm the person for the job." But he wonders whether he will get it.

Discussion Questions

1. In his relationship with James, does Cecil effectively use office politics?
2. Why is James willing to share confidences and inside information with Cecil? Is James behaving ethically? Explain your response.
3. In interacting with his co-workers, does Cecil use office politics to his advantage? Explain your response.
4. If he is promoted, is Cecil likely to be an effective supervisor? Explain your response.

Action Incident 18.3

She's Quite a Package*

For the past three months, Darla Grover has worked as an administrative assistant to two married executives, Bob Parks and Gene Howard. She is single and dresses attractively. Darla is a good worker who promptly completes her job duties and aims for an office manager position. She is a dedicated employee who willingly works extra hours to meet deadlines.

The office atmosphere is informal, and the executives tell a lot of jokes, most of which are sexually oriented. Darla's bosses deliberately try to embarrass her. She considers the jokes offensive but has not related her

---

* Source: Donald S. Miller and Stephen E. Catt, *Human Relations: A Contemporary Approach* (Homewood, Ill.: Richard D. Irwin, 1989), pp. 411–12.

feelings to anyone. During a recent telephone conversation, Darla overheard Bob remark to another party that she has a fantastic body and outstanding legs. Previously, she had not thought much about it, but now she realizes that Bob often stands close and glances over her shoulder while discussing work assignments.

Darla's experiences with Gene have been more problematic. After working late one evening, he asked her out for dinner. During the evening, Gene put his arm around Darla and attempted to kiss her. She exclaimed, "Gene, what would your wife say?"

"If you don't tell, I certainly won't," he replied. "I think a lot of you and want to know you better. Besides, you're quite a package." Shortly thereafter, Darla thought of an excuse and left. Since then, Gene remains persistent and has suggested getting together on several occasions. Darla always has a believable excuse, but she is running out of excuses.

Darla contemplates her predicament and thinks to herself, "I do good work and like the salary, but I resent the way my bosses are treating me. I don't want to give up the job. Being 'quite a package' certainly creates problems."

Discussion Questions

1. Is Darla a victim of sexual harassment? Explain your response.
2. How should Darla handle her predicament?
3. Assuming she personally confronts each executive, how should Darla prepare herself?
4. Should Darla give up her job? Explain your response.

Notes

1. Donald S. Miller and Stephen E. Catt, *Human Relations: A Contemporary Approach* (Homewood, Ill.: Richard D. Irwin, 1989), p. 344.
2. "More Women Seek Higher Education," *The Wall Street Journal,* March 27, 1989, p. B1.
3. Carol Hymowitz and Timothy Schellhardt, "The Glass Ceiling," *The Wall Street Journal* March 24, 1986, p. 1D.
4. Stephen J. Rexford and Lisa A. Mainiero, "The 'Right Stuff' of Management: Challenges Confronting Women," *SAM Advanced Management Journal* 51 (Spring 1986), pp. 36–37.
5. "Myths About Women in Management," *Behavioral Sciences Newsletter* 13 (July 14, 1986), pp. 2–3.
6. Helen Reagan, "Top Women Executives Find Path to Power Is Strewn with Hurdles," *The Wall Street Journal,* October 25, 1984, pp. 35, 37.
7. Geraldine Spuell, "Making It, Big Time—Is It Really Tougher for Women?" *Training and Development Journal* 39 (August 1985), p. 33.

8. "Facts and Figures," *Black Enterprise* 16 (August 1986), p. 27.

9. James E. Ellis, "The Black Middle Class," *Business Week* (March 14, 1988), p. 63

10. "A Nation Divided on Black Progress," *Business Week* (March 14, 1988), p. 65.

11. Miller and Catt, *Human Relations: A Contemporary Approach,* p. 347.

12. "Hispanics: Some Basic Facts," *Chronicle of Higher Education* 34 (September 16, 1987), p. A36.

13. Elizabeth Ehrlich and Susan B. Garland, "For American Business, a New World of Workers," *Business Week* (September 19, 1988), p. 118.

14. Jeffrey Trachtenberg, "Aging Base Spurs Effort to Draw Young," *The Wall Street Journal,* March 23, 1989, p. B1.

15. Sidney P. Freedberg, "Forced Exits? Companies Confront Wave of Age-Discrimination Suits," *The Wall Street Journal,* October 13, 1987, p. 33.

16. John J. Coleman III, "Age-Conscious Remarks: What You Say Can Be Used Against You," *Personnel* 62 (September 1985), p. 22.

17. Joseph Weber, "The 'Last Minority' Fights for Its Rights," *Business Week* (June 6, 1988), p. 140.

18. David Bauer and Jeannine Green, "The Disabled Battle Bleak Job Prospects," *Management Review* 77 (April 1988), p. 59.

19. Barbara Solomon and William H. Wagel, "Spreading the Word on New Technologies for People with Disabilities," *Personnel* 65 (July 1988), p. 15.

20. Miller and Catt, *Human Relations: A Contemporary Approach,* p. 353.

21. Rod Willis, "Mainstreaming the Handicapped," *Management Review* 76 (March 1987), pp. 45–46.

22. "Why Wasn't $1 Million a Year Enough?" *Business Week* (August 25, 1986), p. 73.

23. Albert Z. Carr, "Is Business Bluffing Ethical?" *Harvard Business Review* 46 (January–February 1968), p. 143.

24. John L. Hysom and William J. Bolce, *Business and Its Environment* (St. Paul, Minn.: West Publishing, 1983), p. 119.

25. Gary Dessler, *Management Fundamentals: Modern Principles and Practices,* 3d ed. (Reston, Va.: Reston Publishing, 1982), p. 530.

26. Cathy Trost, "Sexual Harassment Persists on Jobs, U.S. Study Finds," *The Wall Street Journal,* June 30, 1986, p. 44.

27. Miller and Catt, *Human Relations: A Contemporary Approach,* p. 400.

28. Paul J. Champagne and R. Bruce McAfee, "Auditing Sexual Harassment," *Personnel Journal* 68 (June 1989), p. 126.

29. "Workshops Aimed at Ending Harassment," *Emporia* (Kansas) *Gazette,* July 24, 1986, p. 2.

30. "Sexual Harassment in the Workplace," *New York Times,* November 9, 1986, p. F13.

31. Miller and Catt, *Human Relations: A Contemporary Approach,* pp. 200–02.

32. Richard D. Terrell, "The Elusive Menace of Office Politics," *Training* 26 (May 1989), p. 52.

33. Robert Vecchio, "Are You In or Out with Your Boss?" *Business Horizons* 29 (November–December 1986), p. 78.

34. Miller and Catt, *Human Relations: A Contemporary Approach,* p. 204.

Suggested Readings

Baron, Alma S. "Working Partners: Career-Committed Mothers and Their Husbands." *Business Horizons* 30, September–October 1987, pp. 45–50.

Davidson, Jeffrey P. "Boosting Your Career with Politics." *Management World* 17, September–October 1988, pp. 11–13.

Dolecheck, Maynard M. "Doing Justice to Ethics." *Supervisory Management* 34, July 1989, pp. 35–39.

Glynn, Kathleen. "Providing for Our Aging Society." *Personnel Administrator* 33, November 1988, pp. 56–59.

Leo, John. "Retreat for Advances?" *Time* 127, April 8, 1986, pp. 62–63.

Murray, Thomas J. "Ethics Programs: Just a Pretty Face?" *Business Month* 130, September 1987, pp. 30–32.

Nelson, Andre. "Can a Woman Gain Acceptance in a Male-Dominated Job Setting?" *Supervision* 48, January 1986, pp. 14, 16–17.

Roane, Susan. "How to Use Office Politics to Your Advantage." *Practical Accountant* 19, June 1986, pp. 86, 88.

Shapiro, Joseph P. "Shortchanging the Disabled." *U.S. News & World Report* 105, July 25, 1988, pp. 50–51.

Willliams, John M. "Technology and the Disabled." *Personnel Administrator* 33, January 1988, pp. 81–83.

Glossary

The number(s) following the definition refer to the chapter(s) where the term is discussed.

Administrative Skills: the skills necessary to operate a department or unit, including recordkeeping, guiding and overseeing operations, budget preparation, and employee appraisal (1).

Agenda: a list of items or issues to be discussed at a meeting (5, 11).

AIDS: acquired immune deficiency syndrome, a disease that attacks the human neurological system and diminishes the body's ability to fight infection (17).

Alcoholism: habitual drinking to the extent that a person ceases to function effectively in social and work situations (17).

Appraisal: the process of evaluating work accomplishments that involves comparing actual performance to standards or expectations (14).

Audio/Video Materials: tapes or cassettes used as teaching aids in presenting or studying subject matter (6).

Authoritarian: a leadership style of leaders who keep power to themselves and insist on making most or all decisions (3).

Avoidance: a strategy for resolving conflicts by doing nothing (15).

Bounded Rationality: acceptance of "good enough" outcomes (4).

Brainstorming: a process in which participants present ideas about a problem or issue regardless of whether they appear logical or sensible (4).

Burnout: emotional and physical exhaustion that brings feelings of chronic frustration and depression (17).

Cafeteria Plan: an approach in which employees allocate a set amount of benefit dollars according to personal choice (14).

Central Tendency Effect: an inclination to rate all employees toward the middle of an evaluation scale (14).

Checklist Technique: a series of statements or questions that can be checked to show representative work-performance characteristics of the person being rated (14).

Civil Inattention: the practice of gazing momentarily at someone for about one second, then switching attention to another person or object (9).

Clearinghouse Question: a question usually asked near the end of an interview to seek any additional relevant information the respondent may have to offer but has not presented (13).

Closed Question: a question that restricts or limits the answer options available to the respondent (13).

Coaching: the job-related guidance and instruction supervisors provide to their employees (10).

Codes of Ethics: formal, written policy statements establishing ethical guidelines for an organization (18).

Collective Bargaining: the process through which representatives of management and the union negotiate an employment contract for workers (15).

Communication: the sharing of meaning between the sender and the receiver of a message (1, 8).

Communication Process: the sending and receiving of messages for the purpose of sharing meaning (8).

Communication Skills: the meaningful transfer of information from various sources and the accurate interpretation of that information (1).

Comparable Worth: involves comparing pay for jobs that are not identical but are of equivalent value (14).

Compensation: includes direct monetary remuneration for employment and a variety of indirect benefits, such as insurance, pensions, education allowances, and paid vacations (14).

Compound Question: a question that includes two or more questions (13).

Comprehensive Listening: listening for the purposes of understanding and remembering the information contained in a verbal message (9).

Compressed Workweek: a schedule whereby employees work 40 hours in fewer than 5 days (7).

Compromise: a strategy for resolving conflicts by selecting a solution that satisfies some needs of both parties to a conflict (15).

Conflict: when one person believes another person is preventing him or her from achieving a goal (15).

Contingency Model of Leadership: a leadership model that views a leader's success in leading a group as contingent upon the degree of task or relationship motivation of the leader and the extent to which the leader has situational control and influence (3).

Controlling: the process for deciding how well actions conform to plans (2).

Counseling: the process of understanding the personal problems of an employee and helping the person deal with them (10).

Creative Objectives: new ideas that can be applied to enhance productivity, profitability, or both (4).

Crisis Management: reacting to situations and making decisions without opportunity for planning (5).

Critical Incidents: an appraisal technique that involves recording especially strong and weak examples of work performance (14).

Culture: the customs of the groups that influence employees (10).

Database: data items stored within a management information system (4).

Decision Making: choosing one among several courses of action and carrying out that choice to reach desired goals (4).

Decision-Oriented Objectives: objectives formed after recognition that solutions to some problems or issues require decisions (4).

Delegating: assigning responsibility for performing tasks and giving authority to accomplish them (2).

Democratic: a leadership style in which leaders involve followers in the decision-making process (3).

Directing: the process of instructing and guiding work activities of subordinates (2).

Directive Interviewing Approach: a technique in which you establish the purpose of the interview and control it through a structured set of questions (13).

Discipline: any action directed toward an employee for failing to follow company rules, standards, or policies (16).

Discrimination: involves initiating either favorable or unfavorable actions (18).

Downward Communication: the flow of messages from superiors to subordinates (9).

Drug Abuse: the improper use of a variety of substances, such as stimulants and depressants, which may include alcohol (17).

Effectiveness: proper selection of the task to be performed (5).

Efficiency: doing a task properly (5).

Electronic Spreadsheets: use computer technology to change numbers in columns and rows of data on worksheets (4).

Empathy: an ability to see situations from another's viewpoint (1, 10).

Employee Assistance Programs (EAPs):   programs designed to help employees cope with alcohol and drug, personal, or emotional problems (17).

Equal Employment Opportunity Legislation: forbids unfair discrimination in the job selection process and performance of job duties (18).

Ergonomics: the study of relationships among people, equipment, and the work environment (17).

Essay Technique: written statements about positive and negative aspects of work performance (14).

Esteem Needs: the fourth level in Maslow's hierarchy of needs, which is satisfied through developing self-respect and respect of others (12).

Ethics: the standards that govern behavior and dictate choices between appropriate and inappropriate action in the workplace (18).

Ethnocentrism: the belief that one's own culture or ethnic group is better than all others (10).

Excess Thought Time: the extra time you have while listening to think about things while the speaker is talking (9).

Exit Interview: used to learn why an employee is leaving a job voluntarily and to collect other information that might be valuable to the company (13).

Expectancy: in Vroom's theory, the likelihood of obtaining rewards (12).

Flextime: gives employees an option to choose starting and quitting times, provided a prescribed number of hours are worked each day (7).

Forced-Choice Appraisal: an evaluator chooses among most and least likely descriptive statements to characterize employee performance (14).

Forcing: a strategy for resolving conflicts in which a person uses his or her position power to force others to accept a solution (15).

Formal Classes: classroom sessions within the company or in outside facilities (6).

Formal Communication: communication between individuals in the organization about formal work-related matters (9).

Formal Roles: expectations specified by descriptions of job duties (1).

Functional Organization: an arrangement in which job tasks are organized according to work duties (2).

Functions: activities that aid in reaching goals (2).

Geographic Organization: an arrangement, usually regional, used by firms having physically separated functions or operations (2).

Grapevine: a firm's informal communication system or the unofficial flow of information about people or events (9).

Graphic Rating Scales: graphs to rate employees on relevant job performance factors (14).

Graphics Programs: enable numerical data to be converted into line graphs, bar charts, or pie charts (4).

Grievance: any formal complaint by an employee, usually written, related to some aspect of a labor agreement or employment policy (16).

Group: two or more people working together and satisfying needs through interaction (11).

Groupthink: occurs when a group avoids critically testing, analyzing, and evaluating ideas in order to minimize conflict and reach a consensus (11).

Halo Effect: giving high or low evaluations based on liking or disliking one aspect of an employee's job performance (4, 14).

Handicapped Person: an individual who has a physical or mental impairment that substantially limits one or more of such person's life activities, has a record of such impairment, or is regarded as having such an impairment (18).

Heterogeneous Groups: have members who differ in traits and characteristics (11).

Homogeneous Groups: have members who are much alike in traits and characteristics (11).

Horizontal Communication: lateral exchange of messages among people on the same level of authority in the organization (9).

Hygiene Factors: according to Herzberg's theory, such job factors as company policies, salary, supervision, interpersonal relations, and working conditions (12).

Inference: the act or process of drawing a conclusion based on facts or indications (8).

Informal Roles: unwritten expectations that arise as a result of a leadership position (1).

Interviewing: a process in which two people with a specific purpose share information through asking and answering questions (13).

Intimate Distance: the distance from actual physical contact to about 18 inches (9).

Job Description: a written statement of job functions, duties, and responsibilities (13).

Job Evaluation: a process used to determine the relative value of jobs (14).

Job Instruction Training: a four-step approach that includes learner preparation, presentation, try out, and follow-up (6).

Job Rotation: a sequence of movement from job to job, providing workers with opportunities to broaden their background and experience in various parts of the firm (6).

Job Satisfaction: the level of enjoyment or contentment individuals feel toward their jobs (7).

Job Skills: abilities to understand the technical aspects of jobs (1).

Job Specification: a written statement of the required knowledge, skills, and attributes needed to do a job (13).

Key Words: words that help the listener recall parts of what the speaker has said (9).

Laissez-Faire: a leadership style in which leaders basically abdicate their responsibility to lead (3).

Leader-Member Relations: the degree to which a leader has the support and loyalty of group members (3).

Leadership: the ability to influence the activities of others, through the process of communication, toward the attainment of a goal (3).

Leading Question: a question that directly or indirectly leads an interviewee to believe a particular answer, which is desired by the interviewer, should be given (13).

Learning: the acquisition of knowledge and skills resulting in a change of behavior (6).

Leniency/Strictness Effect: a tendency to be either too hard or too easy in evaluating workers (14).

Leveling: open, honest, and sincere communication with workers (12).

Line and Staff Organization: combines the line form of oganization with staff departments (2).

Line Organization: direct chain of command from top to bottom of a firm (2).

Listening: paying attention to what is said and giving meaning to what you have heard (9).

Listening Process: paying attention to what you hear in order to give meaning to the verbal message and consider a reaction (9).

Management: achievement of objectives through directing human and equipment resources (1).

Mangement by Objectives (MBO):   involves manager and employee participation to establish formal work-related objectives and includes progress reviews of those objectives (4, 14).

Management Information System (MIS):   a method used to provide managers with information needed to perform their responsibilities (4).

Measurement: the process of determining whether standards are being met (2).

Meeting: a group of people assembled to discuss issues in a structured setting according to an agenda (11).

Monochronic-Time Value: a view that emphasizes completing one task at a time (10).

Motivation: the internal force directing a person toward satisfying needs and desires (12).

Motivators: job-related factors such as the work itself, achievement, additional responsibility, job advancement, and recognition (12).

Nominal Group Technique (NGT): a technique to help members interact in meetings and develop practical yet creative solutions to problems (11).

Nondirective Interviewing Approach: a technique that permits the respondent to control the direction of an interview and what is discussed (13).

Nonverbal Communication: communication other than through spoken words (9).

Objectives: statements of results that people or companies seek to achieve (1, 4).

Occupational Safety and Health Act: passed by Congress in 1970 to ensure safe and healthful working conditions for all employees (17).

Office or Shop Politics: ways of getting things done that are not formally recognized practices or procedures (18).

Ombudsman: a respected, neutral person who investigates an employee's complaint and recommends action to management (16).

Open-Door Grievance Procedure: enables employees to take their grievances to top management (16).

Open Question: a question that allows the respondent a great deal of freedom in responding (13).

Ordinary Group Technique: an informal group decision technique that consists of a viewpoint exchange only (4).

Organization Chart: a structure for managing the firm, the chain of command, and the various levels of authority (2).

Organizing: grouping tasks and assigning authority (2).

Paralanguage: the way something is said can influence how the verbal message is interpreted (9).

Participative Management: solicitation of employee involvement in decisions (2).

Peer-Review Panel: a panel that considers an employee's complaint and renders a decision (16).

People Skills: abilities to lead, direct, motivate, and understand others (1).

Perceptions: how persons view and interpret what goes on around them (8).

Performance: measurement of whether an employee is accomplishing or failing to complete job assignments (14).

Personal-Bias Effect: interference of personal feelings with objectivity in performance appraisals (14).

Personal Distance: ranges from 18 inches to 4 feet (9).

Personal Objectives: objectives people seek to achieve for themselves (4).

Personal Space: the movable space you carry around with you (9).

Planning: setting of goals and forming policies and procedures (2).

Policies: general guidelines (2).

Polychronic-Time Value: a view that interruptions and delays are to be expected because human activities seldom proceed as anticipated (10).

Position Power: the formal authority an organization gives a leader to make decisions and give orders to subordinates (3).

Prejudice: an attitude toward an individual or group that is based on incomplete information (18).

Procedures: steps to be followed to reach a goal (2).

Productivity: measure of output per person-hour worked (1).

Professional Development: the use of educational opportunities and other experiences to further career potential (6).

Programmed Instruction: a method of learning in which content is divided into steps and learners are required to answer questions on what they have just read or observed (6).

Progressive Discipline: a procedure that sets increasingly stiffer penalties for repeated or serious misconduct (16).

Public Distance: the distance from 12 feet to whatever distance the people involved can still hear and see each other (9).

Qualitative Objectives: the presence or absence of acceptable levels of excellence (4).

Quality Circles (QC): workers performing similar job duties who voluntarily meet regularly for the purpose of identifying and solving job-related problems (12).

Quantitative Objectives: determined and measured on the basis of production (4).

Ranking: a number of appraisal techniques that involve comparing employees according to demonstrated performance abilities (14).

Recency Effect: the influence of recent events on performance appraisals (14).

Recency Syndrome: a natural tendency for persons to be aware of more recent events (4).

Recruitment: soliciting potential job applicants for available positions (13).

Reflective Question: a question that seeks clarification by incorporating part of the respondent's answer in a follow-up question (13).

Reinforcement Theory: focuses attention on consequences of behavior (12).

Relationship Behavior: a leader's efforts to develop rapport, trust, friendship, and open communication with workers (3).

Risky-Shift Phenomenon: a tendency for individuals to be greater risk takers when participating in a group than when acting alone (11).

Role Playing: a training method in which participants are assigned roles, given background information, and then act out the roles (6).

Routine Objectives: repetitive tasks related to work duties (4).

Rules: detailed guidelines for performing a job (2).

Rumor: unofficial information without evidence to confirm (9).

Safety: measures taken to protect people from injuries and accidents (17).

Safety Audit: a process to determine if safe workplace behaviors are practiced (17).

Safety Needs: the second level in Maslow's hierarchy of needs, which is fulfilled through protection from physical harm or economic misfortune (12).

Salary: compensation based on a weekly or monthly basis (14).

Self-Actualization: the highest level in Maslow's hierarchy of needs, which is fulfilled through the development to one's full potential (12).

Self-Concept: the relatively stable perceptions people have about themselves (10).

Self-Esteem: the evaluation people make of their self-concept (10).

Seminars and Workshops: provide a concentrated study of topics (6).

Sexual Harassment: generally understood to be suggestive annoyance of the opposite sex in the workplace (18).

Simulation: an artificially structured situation that reflects realities of the job (6).

Situational Leadership Theory: a technique that requires a leader to analyze the maturity of workers to find the right leadership style (3).

Smoothing: a strategy for resolving conflicts by trying to get along with others at all costs (15).

Social Distance: the distance from 4 to 12 feet between people (9).

Social Needs: the third level in Maslow's hierarchy of needs, which is fulfilled through developing individual and group relationships (12).

Span of Control: the number of people that one person can effectively manage (2).

Special Assignment: assigning work on a specific task (6).

Spectrum Approach: a strategy to promote development of creative ideas in groups that encourages group members to focus on strengths of new ideas (11).

Standards: guidelines that set expectations managers and employees are to meet (2).

Statistical Analysis: gathering numerical data and computing results based on averages (4).

Stereotyping: making judgments about persons on the basis of their class or culture (10).

Strategic Objectives: goals for control of costs, profitability, and maximizing markets (4).

Stress: an individual's inability to respond adequately without undue emotional or psychological strain (17).

Study Circle: an employee group that discusses work-related concerns as well as personal, educational, and social needs (6).

Suboptimization: a lesser attainment of some worthy goals to maximize a meaningful objective (4).

Supervisors: first-line managers who have direct contact with employees and facilitate completion of work tasks (1).

Survival Needs: the basic needs for food, clothing, and shelter in Maslow's hierarchy of needs (12).

Tactical Objectives: short-range goals applying to performance of routine job tasks (4).

Task Behavior: the leader's efforts to set well-defined patterns of organization, channels of communication, and work procedures (3).

Task Structure: the degree to which there is a set procedure for completing a job (3).

Team Building: a strategy designed to help group members work together in a spirit of cooperation to improve the efficiency and effectiveness of their performance (11).

Territory: the fixed space and the objects therein to which a person lays claim (9).

Theory X: employees do not like work, prefer to be led, and are essentially unmotivated (12).

Theory Y: employees enjoy work, are ambitious, and willingly assume responsibility (12).

Theory Z: improved productivity and job satisfaction are achieved through involving employees in the decision-making process and giving them a shared responsibility for those decisions (12).

Time Log: a record of how time is spent, showing priorities placed on it and noting who initiates various activities (5).

Time Theft: deliberate waste or abuse of time that should be spent on job-related duties (5).

Time Wages: compensation based on the number of hours worked (14).

Time Wasters: a term that refers to nonproductive uses of time (5).

Training: acquiring job competencies (6).

Trait Approach: an attempt to identify characteristics found in all successful leaders (3).

Unimportant-Person Gaze: a blank or indifferent gaze given to another person as if he or she did not exist (9).

Union: an organization that represents employees to management and tries to protect workers' rights and improve their economic status through collective bargaining (15).

Unity of Command: each worker reports to a single supervisor (2).

Upward Communication: the flow of messages from subordinates to superiors (9).

Valence: in Vroom's theory, the perception of the value attached to the expected reward in relation to the effort put forth (12).

Value: the worth, utility, or merit given to something (10).

Win/Win: a strategy for resolving conflicts that focuses on finding a solution to satisfy the goals of both persons involved in a conflict (15).

Word-Meaning Confusion: the same word given different meanings or different words given the same meaning by the sender and receiver (8).

Word Processing: a system linking electronic hardware and software to produce and process written communication (4).

Index